THE
REGULATION
OF DESIRE

For George W. Smith (1935-1994) from whom I learned so much; for Patrick Barnholden without whose love and support this second edition could never have been completed; and to all those who fight for lesbian and gay liberation everywhere.

THE
REGULATION
OF DESIRE

Homo and Hetero Sexualities

GARY KINSMAN

2nd edition, revised

BLACK ROSE BOOKS

Montréal/New York
London

Black Rose Books No. Z232
Hardcover ISBN: 1-55164-041-4 (bound)
Paperback ISBN: 1-55164-040-6 (pbk.)
Libary of Congress No. 95-79359

Canadian Cataloguing in Publication Data

Kinsman, Gary
The regulation of desire: homo and hetero sexualities

Rev. ed.
First ed. published in 1987 under title: The regulation of desire: sexuality in Canada. Parts of this book initially presented in 1983, as an M.A. thesis, at the Ontario Institute for Studies in Education. Includes bibliographical references and index.
ISBN 1-55164-041-4 (bound) —
ISBN 1-55164-040-6 (pbk.)
1. Homosexuality—Canada. I. Title.
HQ76.3.C3K55 1996   306.76'6'0971   C95-900781-4

Mailing Address

BLACK ROSE BOOKS
C.P. 1258
Succ. Place du Parc
Montréal, Québec
H2W 2R3 Canada

BLACK ROSE BOOKS
340 Nagel Drive
Cheektowaga, New York
14225 USA

To order books: (phone) 1-800-565-9523 (fax) 1-800-221-9985

A publication of the Institute of Policy Alternatives of Montréal (IPAM)
Printed in Canada

CONTENTS

Acknowledgements

This book could never have been written without the love and support of many friends and colleagues. It is very much a product of discussion with others, of practical activities in the gay liberation, AIDS-activist, and socialist movements for twenty-five years, of the sharing of research at the Ontario Institute for Studies in Education (OISE), where parts of this book were born as an M.A. thesis in 1983, and the collective rediscovery of our Canadian lesbian and gay histories. Responsibility for mistakes or errors of interpretation are mine alone. While I cannot individually thank everyone who has assisted me in this project, I am particularly grateful to a number of people.

For first interesting me in the delights and pleasures of gay history, I thank Bruce Russell, Bert Hansen, and the late James Fraser. For support above and beyond the call of duty: Robert Champagne, Ross Higgins, and especially Patrick Barnholden and Brian Conway, without whose love and support this book could never have been written. For inspiration and for teaching me about history: Doug Sanders, Bruce Somers, and Jim Egan. I am indebted to the Canadian Lesbian and Gay Archives for their invaluable assistance.

The following people offered insights and help in various ways: Katherine Arnup, Peter Birt, Deborah Brock, Varda Burstyn, the late Lina Chartrand, Philip Corrigan, Amy Gottlieb, John Greyson, Didi Khayatt, Julie Lee, Ian Lumsden, Steven Maynard, Mary O'Brien, Ruth Pierson, Becki Ross, Dorothy E. Smith, the late George Smith, Mariana Valverde, Lorna Weir, John Wilson, Blye Frank, Barry Adam, Lynne Fernie, Sharon D. Stone, Lisa Steele, Kim Tomczak, Greg Pavelich, Nancy Nicol, Elise Chenier, Maureen FitzGerald, Mary Louise Adams, Jonathan Ned Katz, Eric Mykhalovskiy, Alan Sears, Cynthia Wright, Merv Henwood, Nancy McKinnel, Patrizia Gentile (whom I also thank for producing the index for this book) and Heidi McDonell. Thanks to the students I have taught who have challenged me on these questions at Nipissing University College, Ryerson Polytechnical Institute, Memorial University of Newfoundland in St. John's, Acadia University, the Ontario Institute for Studies in Education, and Laurentian University. Thanks also to my editors Jane Broderick (first edition), John Woolfrey (second edition) and Natalie Klym, Linda Barton, Frances Slingerman and Dimitri Roussopoulos at Black Rose Books.

Thanks also to my mother, for invaluable assistance time after time, and to my brother, for introducing me to the joys and horrors of computers. Thanks to Diva, our cat.

Introductions

Inspirations

Take One. Anger, excitement, and a surging sense of power fuelled our steps as we moved south on Yonge Street, sweeping aside queerbashers and police alike.

It was February 6, 1981. I was among three thousand gay men and lesbians and our supporters taking over Toronto's main street. We were expressing our outrage at the arrest the previous night of close to three hundred men on "bawdy-house" charges following raids on four gay baths. The police had invaded institutions that were central to the gay male community and the social and sexual spaces that we had established for ourselves. The demonstration was an unprecedented show of strength — a real high for me. The cops were disoriented and the city was turned on its ear.[1]

In the weeks that followed the police attack, a widespread sense of resistance, rebellion, pride, and community developed among Toronto's gay men and many of its lesbians. Thousands of gay men now realized that the police were not our friends — if we had any such illusions before — and that the cops, and the social institutions they defended, found something profoundly disturbing and threatening about gay men, gay sex, and a visible gay community. We not only felt the power of the police and the State, but also the power of gay resistance. It was in this energy and excitement that I found the inspiration for the first edition of this book, published in 1987.

Take Two. Fifteen years after the rebellious resistance to the bath raids, the situation has changed dramatically. I can look back rather nostalgically to the rebellious days of 1981, but I also remember the new struggles that gay men, lesbians, bisexuals, people living with AIDS/HIV, and our supporters have engaged in. I have lived through the rebirth of "queer" activism in the late 1980s and the early 1990s as we have fought for our very survival against anti-queer violence and AIDS, and as we have continued to push for our liberation. I use "queer" here to identify with this new activism, and to reclaim a term of abuse so that it can no longer be used against us.[2]

Activism subsided in Toronto following the bath raids by the mid-1980s as the tide of gay resistance receded, but it picked up again in the context of the ravages of the AIDS crisis in our communities. Initially the AIDS crisis decreased the militancy of gay communities as we tended to our sick and dying and were put on the defensive. While police arrests of gay men for having sex continued, the large-scale bath raids ended after 1983. Police raids were no longer seen as necessary to keep us in line as we were once more labelled "sick" and "diseased" by dominant social agencies and the mass media.

By 1988 it had became clear to many people living with AIDS/HIV (PLWA/HIVs) that they were being denied access to promising treatments that could extend their lives. Standing up to this denial by State regulations and pharmaceutical corporations gave birth to a treatment-based activism that came initially from gay activists but extended far beyond them to raise crucial questions about both health care and the social regulation of sexuality.[3] I became involved in this AIDS activism through Toronto's AIDS ACTION NOW! as we recaptured some of the spirit of the resistance to the bath raids in our organizing.

During a demonstration in 1988, we burned an effigy of then Minister of Health Jake Epp in the streets of Toronto to protest against AIDS inaction. Along with AIDS activists from Montréal and New York City, we took over the opening session at the International AIDS Conference in Montréal in 1989 to protest the exclusion of the concerns and needs of PLWA/HIVs. We sat in at the offices of the multinational drug corporation Bristol Myers in 1989 to protest their withholding of an anti-HIV drug that PLWA/HIVs needed to access.[4] We won some victories in gaining more access to badly needed treatments, but governments, the professions, social agencies, and the media continued to organize problems in the lives of PLWA/HIVs. Over the next few years, I continued to be involved in AIDS activism in the rather different settings of St. John's, Newfoundland and the Annapolis Valley in Nova Scotia, lobbying with government officials and doing educational and media work.

Meanwhile, partly inspired by this AIDS activism, a new generation of queer activists formed "Queer Nation" type groups in Toronto, Ottawa, Montréal, and Vancouver to bash back against anti-queer violence and to promote lesbian and gay visibility in militant street actions and "in your face" protests.[5] In the 1990s some lesbians — inspired by the direct-action dimensions of AIDS activism and Queer Nation — would set up chapters of Lesbian Avengers across the U.S. and in a number of centres in Canada.[6] It was out of these new queer and AIDS activisms that I found the initial inspiration to begin work on the revised edition of this book.

Take Three. On June 9, 1994 the Ontario Legislature defeated Bill 167, which would have granted same-sex benefits and family-relationship-recognition rights to lesbians and gays in the province in what would have been the most advanced legislation on these questions in North America. The right-wing moral conservative opposition as well as the opposition of the majority of the Liberal Party and a number of New Democrats focused on the inclusion of adoption rights in Bill 167. While this was largely directed at securing the legal right for the non-biological lesbian/gay co-parents to adopt their partners' children this was focused on by these forces and by much of the media as a threat to young people and to the heterosexual family itself. The vote was fifty-nine for the bill and sixty-eight against. That night close to 8,000 angry lesbians, gays and our supporters gathered at the legislative buildings at Queen's Park to express our outrage. Some chanted "Burn Down the House."

The organizing for Bill 167 by the Coalition for Lesbian and Gay Rights in Ontario and later the Campaign for Equal Families and the protests against its defeat were unprecedented with lesbians and gays coming together for the first time in activism in many smaller centres across the province.[7] And at Lesbian and Gay Pride Day that year in Toronto tens of thousands of lesbians and gay men affirmed that "We Are Family!" This struggle was far more extensive than the resistance to the bath raids.

A year later in 1995 the election of a new Conservative government seems to have closed off possibilities for further provincial legislative action on this front for the foreseeable future. Important discussions have opened up on evaluating the struggle for Bill 167, the relation of lesbians and gays to the legal and social constructs of "family" and "spouse" and on ways forward for lesbian and gay organizing on these questions. I hope this book can contribute to clarifying the terrain of these debates.

Meanwhile, after the passage by the House of Commons of the hate-crimes legislation that included sexual orientation as one ground for hate-crimes sentencing in June 1995,[8] the federal government seems reluctant to proceed on basic sexual-orientation protection at the federal level. This is despite a recent Supreme Court decision affirming that the equality-rights section of the Charter should be read as including sexual orientation. Liberal backbenchers Roseanne Skoke, Tom Wappel and others have been allowed to speak out against lesbians and gay men suggesting that our rights are no priority for the current federal government. Fortunately Skoke's visibility in opposition to our rights has produced some very significant organizing by lesbians, gays, and others against her in Nova Scotia. In 1994 a protest of more than one hundred people outside her constituency office in New Glasgow was organized. Given my years of activism in St. John's, the Annapolis Valley in Nova Scotia, and now in Sudbury, I am much more conscious than when I wrote the first edition of this book about the importance of queer organizing in smaller centres and rural areas.

Sexual Policing and Human Rights

In 1996 the sex police are still very much with us, if not on the same scale as in 1981. The police continue to lay "indecent act" and "bawdy-house" charges against men for engaging in consensual sex. In 1993 men engaging in consensual sex in washrooms were arrested by the police in St. John's, where video surveillance by the Royal Newfoundland Constabulary led to "indecent act" charges being laid against twenty-six men who also got their names published in the local newspaper.[9] Men continue to be arrested in parks and washrooms in the Metro Toronto area.[10] And the police continue to provide little protection against anti-gay and anti-lesbian violence, often joining in the harassment and violence — as we saw in the police attacks on a gay party in Montréal in 1990 and their lack of response until late 1993 to the murders of gay men in Montréal. On February 17, 1994 Montréal police arrested 175 men as "found ins" in a "common bawdy house" at the Katacombes bar. This was the largest mass arrest of gay men since the early 1980s bath raids in Toronto.

At the same time, there has been escalating sexual censorship by the police and especially by Canada Customs against lesbian and gay magazines, books, and videos coming into the country and against lesbian and gay bookstores such as Glad Day in Toronto and Little Sister's in Vancouver and a growing number of women's bookstores. Little Sister's took Canada Customs to court in 1994 to try to put a stop to this discrimination, and in January 1996, they won only a partial legal victory. The 1992 Butler decision of the Supreme Court which altered the test for "obscenity" has been interpreted by the police and Canada Customs so as to extend their seizures of gay and lesbian materials. One of the first seizures using this new interpretation was of the lesbian publication *Bad Attitude* from Glad Day in Toronto in 1992.[11] There has also been the use of new legislation passed in 1993 allegedly designed to deal with "youth pornography" against male hustlers and to collect evidence to re-criminalize consensual male/male sex in southern Ontario, especially in London (see chapter 10).

Sexual policing has been selectively intensified. This has been combined with violence against lesbians and gays; and moral conservative mobilization around AIDS, against lesbian and gay rights, feminism, and progressive sex education in the schools.[12] The mass media and the right have continued to use the AIDS crisis to associate gay sex with sickness and disease. The social response to the AIDS crisis has become a condensation of many social relations including a heterosexist response to gay men and lesbians.[13] Through the 1989-1990 Hughes Commission hearings into the cover-up of "abuse" at Mount Cashel in St. John's in the mid-1970s and associated media coverage, once again homosexuals have been associated with "child sexual abuse." This framing of gay men has been picked up by the media across the country to cover similar events and has also been recycled by the anti-gay right wing.[14]

And we are still denied our basic human rights in many jurisdictions even though we have made remarkable progress on this front on many provincial levels. As of January 1996, Québec, Ontario, Yukon, Manitoba, Nova Scotia, New Brunswick, British Columbia and Saskatchewan have added "sexual orientation" protection to their human rights codes, a number of municipalities have instituted forms of protection and many unions have won such protection in their contracts. At the same time governments, social agencies, businesses, and landlords often continue to deny us our basic civil and human rights.

Some of these positive developments have occurred in the context of the equality-rights section (Section 15) of the Canadian Charter of Rights and Freedoms. This is a partial modification of the strategy of State legal formation, and it opened up some spaces and possibilities for the establishment of formal lesbian and gay legal equality that could be taken advantage of through court challenges. Lesbians, gays, feminists, and human-rights supporters — and the federal government's equality-rights committee and human-rights commission — have been arguing that sexual-orientation protection must be included in all human-rights legislation. In 1986, the federal Conservative government, in response to the equality-rights committee, stated that it believed the courts would interpret Section 15 as including sexual-orientation protection. Almost ten years later in 1995 in the Egan/Nesbitt case the Supreme Court of Canada decided that Section 15 must be read as including sexual-orientation protection.

The Conservatives in office were extremely slow to move on the issue, and there was lots of opposition among Tory backbenchers. Many Tories and the military elite — who in October 1992 in the Michelle Douglas case were finally forced to give up their official policies that discriminated against lesbians and gay men in employment — had been strongly opposed to even these limited steps. On December 10, 1992 — International Human Rights Day — Kim Campbell, federal Minister of Justice, attempted to add sexual orientation to Canada's human-rights act but with an important restriction prohibiting same-gender marital relations, which would have had important repercussions on our struggles for spousal benefits and immigration rights for our partners. In response, on a few hours notice more than twenty-five lesbians, gay men, and bisexuals gathered in the Minister of Justice's office in Halifax in protest against this restriction.[15]

On December 13, 1994 Liberal Allan Rock became the latest Minister of Justice to delay enactment of sexual-orientation protection in federal human-rights legislation. At the time of writing — even though there have been positive court decisions and the new Liberal federal government has promised to move on basic human-rights protection for lesbians and gay men — it has yet to do so. Prime Minister Jean Chrétien has apparently urged delay and faces opposition from within the Liberal caucus from Skoke, Wappel, and others.

The result of the May 25, 1995 Supreme Court decision in the Jim Egan/Jack Nesbitt same-sex spousal benefit case was mixed. They lost the case with four of the judges arguing that there was no discrimination in the denial of the pension benefit to Jack Nesbitt, and one arguing that there was, but that it was a "justified" form of discrimination (four judges argued that there was discrimination and it was not justified). At the same time, the Supreme Court judges clearly decided that the equality-rights section of the Charter should be read as including sexual-orientation protection.[16] This decision embodies the ambiguous and contradictory character of the current legal situation facing lesbians and gays in Canada. On the one hand, on an abstract basis our rights are recognized but not in the context of our actual and substantive relationships and sexualities. The 1995 legal decision in Ontario regarding the adoption rights of non-biological mothers is important but of limited jurisdiction. In the face of a hostile provincial government, its implications are very important but unlikely to be far reaching.[17]

Lesbians and gays have won some important legal and social victories through our own struggles and the allies we have won and coalitions we have forged. There is now a more widespread tolerance and acceptance for us than ever before in Canadian history. At the same time, there is also a more vociferous minority opposition than ever before, which often has important support within State relations, especially within police forces and among right-wing and — as we have seen — Liberal and even Social Democratic politicians. NDPer George Mammoliti made some incredibly vile remarks against gay men and lesbians in the Ontario legislature during the Bill 167 debate.[18] We are closer than ever to winning our abstract formal rights but, at the same time are also still criminalized and face denial of our sexualities and our relationships.

Elites and Differences

Most disturbing for me as an activist, a new gay elite (the lesbian elite is much smaller) of professionals (doctors, lawyers, managers, social workers) has ironically been the main beneficiary of the early 1980s rebellions in Toronto and other large centres, rather than the radicals and grass-roots bar people who led the surges into the streets in the late 1970s and early 1980s, and who formed Queer Nation groups later on. These professionals are now in a position to speak for the "community" as its legitimate representatives, since they speak the same language as those who govern society and are already associated with relations of ruling. This is also often the case in "community-based" AIDS groups that are often dominated by a professional and managerial stratum.[19] These professional groups do have valuable skills that need to be put at the disposal of our movements and communities, but without accountability to grass-roots communities they develop their own interests as "respectable" and "responsible" gays and lesbians.

In smaller centres and rural areas where there is usually less visible activism, there are different dynamics and histories. In these areas, the layer of "out" people is often quite limited and there are few professionals who are "out." This can limit organizing possibilities, but the experiences of the Saskatchewan Gay Coalition in organizing across that province in the late 1970s, the recent organizing against Roseanne Skoke in Pictou County in Nova Scotia, and the success of the first ever Northern Ontario regional lesbian, gay, and bisexual conference held in Sudbury in April 1995 that attracted more than one hundred people all suggest possibilities for organizing in these areas.

Social differences among and between lesbians and gay men have also continued. There are other differences within the lesbian and gay communities as well — differences of class, race, gender, HIV status, age, ability, language, whether living in large urban centres or more rural areas, and sexual practice. Some of these differences have been highlighted by the self-organization of lesbians and gays of colour and the organization of two-spirited people's among the First Nations, as racism within gay and lesbian communities and the construction of lesbian and gay as "white" has been challenged. It is important, to not only recognize and celebrate differences, but also to deal with transforming the underlying social power-relations of discrimination and inequality. There have also been challenges from bisexuals against their perceived exclusion from lesbian and gay establishments and events that have led to the incorporation of bisexual into the names of many gay and lesbian groups; as well as challenges from transgendered people to their exclusion form lesbian/gay community formation.

Tensions, Heterosexual Hegemony, and the Left

This book attempts to account for these various experiences, and in a broader sense, to account for both lesbian and gay oppression and resistance in a historical and sociological perspective.

My experience as a gay man — one that I know is shared by many lesbians and gay men, although it is lived differently on the basis of class, race, and gender — is that there exists a constant tension between, on the one hand, how we live our daily lives and give and receive erotic pleasure, and, on the other, the sexual categories imposed by the social relations of a presumed universal heterosexuality. The mass media, the psychiatric, sexological, and medical professions, government policies, the denial of spousal and family-recognition rights to lesbian and gay couples, and police actions such as the bath raids and washroom arrests, defend and construct heterosexual hegemony. Heterosexuality is socially organized as "natural" and "normal"; we gays and lesbians are outsiders — we cannot see ourselves through mainstream social categories, institutions, and images. The "normality" of heterosexuality is organized in relation to the "deviance" and "abnormality" of homosexuality. The "normality" of heterosexuality rests on lesbian and gay sexualities being constructed as "abnormal" and "deviant."

This disparity between our reality and the categories used to interpret us is fostered not only by the right-wing, State agencies, and the social mainstream; it is also the "tradition" within the progressive movement. Some lesbians and gay men, like myself, have looked to the socialist and Marxist traditions because of their promise of liberation for all the oppressed and exploited. There were a number of tenuous connections between early homosexual-rights reformers and the left from the late nineteenth century to the early 1930s.[20] These ties were severed, however, with the establishment of the hegemony of the Stalinist position that homosexuality was a symptom of capitalist and "fascist degeneration," and with the male-dominated working-class movement's defence of the heterosexual "proletarian" family. The socialist movement thus reinforced the practices of heterosexual hegemony, integrating them into its own organizations. The recent collapse of "communism" (what I would refer to as bureaucratic class societies of a new type that were neither socialist nor communist in a Marxist sense) in the Eastern Bloc has created some new legal opportunities for lesbians and gay men in these formerly Stalinist states, but has also generated attempts to reassert patriarchal relations including the oppression of women and lesbians and gay men. The gains of women in employment and social services in many of these countries are being rapidly eroded.[21]

Leftists have continued to initiate lesbian and gay resistance, but this struggle has often been marginalized by the left-wing mainstream, although there have been some important gains since the first edition of this book was written.[22] Heterosexism — the ideology that proclaims lesbians and gays to be "deviant" and "sick" and heterosexuals to be "normal" — has therefore been integrated into the analysis and traditions of the socialist movement. My experiences in several socialist organizations — as a gay activist influenced by socialism and feminism — is that this norm of heterosexuality is reproduced. In these groups, "class struggle" is often still counterposed to the "peripheral" or "secondary" issue of gay liberation. Much of the organized left has participated in this social marginalization of lesbians and gay men.[23]

Within the current debates on the reasons for the crisis of the federal and some provincial New Democratic parties, some try to suggest that the problems have been caused by too much support for the gay, feminist, or anti-racist movements and not enough for real "working-class concerns" (read the concerns of white working-class heterosexual males). This is one interpretation that has been produced over the defeat of Bill 167 and its implications for the Ontario NDP and the NDP across the country.

A theme that will run through this book is the relationship between our struggles and socialist organizing and the new liberationist possibilities that are opening up for this in remaking a democratic socialist movement informed by various progressive social movements including lesbian and gay liberation. While there have been downturns in other struggles, there have been continuing mobilization around lesbian and gay concerns. There are active movement organizations, and layers of activists who are not only involved in lesbian and gay struggles but also in other social-justice struggles. These are important resources to be built on. This means that lesbian/gay/queer activism is not peripheral to but has a central "role" to play in reconstituting a vibrant socialist movement. This new socialist movement would be informed by the perspectives that queers can bring to it.

The gay liberation movement that followed the Stonewall riots in New York City in 1969 ignited by Puerto Rican drag queens, bar dykes and street people against routine police repression of a gay bar[24] challenged the hegemony of heterosexuality by calling on us to come out of the closet and affirm that lesbian and gay is just as good as straight. The movement focused on "coming out" as a means of proclaiming gay "identity" and community, suggesting in the process that such acts of will could, in and of themselves, cause the walls of heterosexual hegemony to come tumbling down.[25] The many years of struggle since Stonewall have demonstrated that heterosexual hegemony is a far more complex terrain and is far more entrenched than was ever imagined in 1969. Heterosexual hegemony is still very much with us, even though feminists, lesbians, and gay men have certainly helped alter the relations of sexual regulation through our struggles.

Remaking History

These questions create the need for a more historically grounded perspective for gay, lesbian, and bisexual liberation: a view that understands the social forces that have both organized our oppression and made it possible for us to resist. This perspective helps account for the relationship between gay oppression and the regulation of sexuality generally, including the construction of heterosexual hegemony and the relationships between our oppression and the organization of gender, class, race, and State relations. This historical inquiry needs to be combined with more concrete investigations of how our oppression is presently socially organized. This perspective could also help erase the dichotomy between "class struggle," defined in a narrow economic way, and a gay-liberation struggle seen as solely a middle-class or "cultural" issue. Sexual rule[26] and heterosexual hegemony have historically played an important part in class struggle and State formation.

Recent historical explorations of the institutions of sexual rule, the emergence of homosexual and lesbian "identities" and cultures, and our resistance to oppression can account for this dialectical emergence and confrontation of gay resistance and heterosexual hegemony.[27] This work, which can be called the social-constructionist "emergence" thesis, suggests that while same-gender erotic pleasures have always existed, they have been socially organized very differently, and that homosexuality and lesbianism in the contemporary sense of distinct identities and cultures are recent creations. Heterosexuality in the contemporary sense is also a recent creation, developing in response to the emergence of same-gender erotic cultures.[28] This emergence perspective is based on a critique of sexual "naturalism" — the notion that there is an intrinsic, natural gay, lesbian, heterosexual, bisexual, or other form of sexuality.[29] Sexuality is not some natural essence that has been repressed; it is socially made and regulated.[30] It is perhaps more accurate to use words like "sexualities" and "cultures" to express that there is no unitary sexuality, nor culture. Rather than any singular unitary history of sexuality, there are diverse and multiple histories of sexualities and cultures. Pluralizing these words expresses the diversity of these experiences that can often be denied under monolithic categories like a singular "sexuality."

This book is an attempt to develop such a historical perspective for Canada, to develop a gay or sexually "deviant" view of this country's history — one could even say to develop a first glimpse of a "queer history" of what we now call Canada. This history is not just about adding the experiences of queers to the existing canons of Canadian history, it is about rewriting the history of Canada. As Roxana Ng, writing about sexism and racism in Canadian history, argues:

> it is not enough for feminist and ethnic historians to rewrite women's history and ethnic history. In order to understand how Canada came to be a nation with its present configuration, we have to rewrite the history of Canada.[31]

And as feminist historian Karen Dubinsky suggests:

> Historians have started to rewrite the history of Canada as though women and workers mattered. We must now also begin to rethink Canadian history as though sexuality mattered.[32]

This history is not only relevant to queers but it also makes visible major aspects of the social making of heterosexuality as well.

Not for Queers Only

To make this more relevant for the heterosexual reader requires the recognition that heterosexuals in this society have what can be referred to as "heterosexual privilege," and again this is lived differently on the basis of class, race, and gender. This privilege is not a possession or an essence — it is a social practice through which heterosexuals empower themselves through daily participation in the relations of heterosexual hegemony. I ask my heterosexual students to think through the following exercise to help make this visible to them. This is similar to an ethnomethodological breaching experiment within sociology — which requires suspending the "natural" or "common-sense" attitude and the violation of social convention to learn from the social reactions we provoke.[33]

Lesbian feminist Charlotte Bunch once explained to heterosexual women that the best way to find out what "heterosexual privilege" is all about is to go about for a few days as an open lesbian. If you are a heterosexual man, think about going about your life as an openly gay man.

> What makes heterosexuality work is heterosexual privilege — and if you don't have a sense of what privilege is, I suggest that you go home and announce to everybody that you know — a roommate, your family, the people you work with — everywhere that you go — that you're a queer. Try being a queer for a week.[34]

A heterosexual woman or man can easily imagine the discomfort, ridicule, and fear, and even violence that she or he might experience, how his or her "coming out" would disrupt "normal" relations at work and with his or her family. Such experiences are the substance of gay and lesbian oppression in this society and are also the substance of heterosexual privilege and hegemony. Looking at the social world from this place allows one to see aspects of social power and oppression that cannot be seen from other locations. As heterosexual feminist Lynne Segal puts it in her book *Straight Sex*, in which she learns much about the social organization of heterosexual relations from the critiques produced by lesbians and gay men:

> Lesbians and gay people increasingly set the agenda for a reversal in which "the interrogators are interrogated," and compulsory heterosexuality, heterosexism and the roping of sexuality to gender themselves become the problem.[35]

In this sense, doing queer historical and sociological work is not for queers alone,[36] but has many insights for heterosexuals if they are willing to challenge heterosexism in their own lives and practices.

In this book, I sketch in how contradictions between gay and lesbian experiences and practices and heterosexual hegemony have come about in Canadian society, and how our experiences have been organized by a social and historical process that extends outside and beyond our own individual fields of vision. Only when we begin to understand this process can we distinguish between our enemies and our allies. Then we can chart a course toward liberation.

Gay and lesbian liberation politics has not yet been able to adequately account for the historical organization of our oppression, instead often implicitly or explicitly assuming the existence of some sort of natural homogenous lesbian or gay minority outside of history and imprisoning our political perspectives in a naturalist, ahistorical mould. This has shaped even the queer activism that has tried to break away from some of the problems of narrow gay and lesbian "identity" politics.[37] In the 1980s and 1990s, we have begun to realize that while coming out and defending the gay ghetto and lesbian spaces are crucial, this alone will not determine a strategy for liberation. We must move beyond this to a more general understanding of sexual rule and resistance. Historical work helps us evaluate the shifting policies of sexual rule within the Canadian State. It helps us examine the significance of the 1969 Criminal Code reform, for example, which some felt had "legalized" homosexuality, and to look at equality rights and the Canadian Charter of Rights and Freedoms — a charter that is shaping legal decisions even as the sexual policing of lesbians and gay men selectively intensifies — and also to look at spousal and family-recognition rights, and how significant a challenge to heterosexist social and family policies they are. This helps us to account for the gains we have won, but also the continuing violence toward us, the continuing hatred, and the continuing deafening silence about our actual lives in the dominant culture. This history of sexual regulation and resistance is not of theoretical interest only. It has a great deal of relevance both for our present struggles and for future possibilities.

Before outlining the chapters that follow, I must discuss the book's scope and limitations. The terms "gay," "lesbian," "heterosexual," and "bisexual" are used in a historically specific sense. This may make for difficult language at times because it goes against the grain of "common sense" assumptions about the naturalness of sexuality, but I feel it is necessary to be specific. Contemporary social categories and experiences emerge only in specific social and historical settings. There is no lesbian, gay, heterosexual, or bisexual standing outside history, even though "common sense" perspectives project the present hetero/homo polarity back in time. For instance, the essentialist view that posits essences that are outside history finds the "homosexual" of Ancient Greece to be comparable to the "homosexual" in modern times.[38] However, sexual life throughout history has been regulated and made meaningful in very different ways:

> Modern homosexuality and ancient pederasty, for example, share at least one feature: that the participants were of the same sex and that sexual intercourse is often involved — but the significant features are those that are not shared, including the entire range of symbolic, social, economic, and political meanings and functions each group of roles possesses.[39]

And as Jonathan Katz also argues:

> It is only the most one-dimensional, mechanical "behaviourism" that suggests that the act of male with male called "sodomy" in the early [American] colonies was identical to that behaviour called "homosexual" in the 1980s. It is only the most vulgar technological determinism of sexual organs that suggests their "contact" sums up that complex of intimate acts, behaviours, feelings and relationships now called "lesbian" and "gay."[40]

Similarly earlier practices of reproductive and different-gender forms of sexual practice are not the same as contemporary heterosexuality that only emerges in the first parts of this century.[41] I will use the term "heterosexual" to describe the practices and identities of men and women who no longer simply were engaging in reproductive forms of sex or participating in a familial division of labour, but were guided by a "necessary" and "essential" erotic orientation to the "opposite" gender.

Similarly I will use the word "homosexual" to describe the activities, identities, and experiences of homosexual or gay men over the last two centuries. Clearly a number of different terms to be mentioned throughout this book were used, and where appropriate I will use fairy, queer and other terms. I generally prefer the word "gay" to describe homosexual men since the post World War II growth of homosexual cultures and ghettoes. It is less clinical than "homosexual" and was coined by homosexual men ourselves.

"Lesbian" is used here to describe a

> woman who has sexual and erotic-emotional ties primarily with women or who sees herself as centrally involved with a community of self-identified lesbians whose sexual and erotic-emotional ties are primarily with women and who is herself a self-identified lesbian.[42]

These possibilities only emerged over the last 150 years as I will outline later.

Bisexuality arose even later as a term men and women who are erotically interested in both genders began to take up to describe themselves. Even though Freud and others used it in their writings on sexuality much earlier, bisexual networks and "identities" really only emerged after the recent wave of gay liberation and feminism had already emerged.[43] In this sense I would disagree with those who argue it is the most "natural" form of sexuality since bisexuality can only emerge in the context of the hetero/homo polarity which was fully put in place only over the last two centuries. Prior to this it would have had no real basis for existence.

For previous historical periods, I will try to use the words in common usage at the time. For erotic activity among men, for example, "sodomite," "catamite," "Molly," "invert," "faggot," "queer," "cocksucker," "pogue," "fairy," "moffie" (in South Africa), or "queen" might have been used in different periods; for activity among women "tribadist," "sapphist," "man royal,"[44] "bull dagger," or "dyke" have been used. These do not necessarily have equivalent social meanings with "homosexual" or "lesbian" today.

This work cannot address the diversity of same-gender erotic practices in the "Third World" since in these contexts sexuality takes on other features and is rooted in a rather different social and historical process.[45] I will, however, at a number of points disrupt or problematize the construction of a distinct "white" European derived character of the hegemonic construction of lesbian and gay "identities" and cultures in Canada.[46] This is not necessarily the path to liberation for "Third World" lesbians and gays. There are other possible ways put forward, building on other traditions and cultural resources. It is important not to impose the "American" model on the rest of the world.[47] In making this racial/ethnic construction visible my point is not to label previous white lesbians and gays as "racist" thereby dismissing their experiences. My point rather is that we have much to learn from their experiences of resistance to oppression including how the construction of lesbian and gay as "white" and European-derived has also excluded other groups of people from being able to redefine what being lesbian and gay is all about through drawing on other traditions and cultural practices. This is one point I was not very conscious of in the first edition and I hope this edition is a much better effort at challenging some of the historical roots of racism in Canadian society in general but also within sexual regulation and lesbian and gay communities/cultures more specifically.[48]

I look at the lives of lesbians, gay men, and of heterosexuals as well from time to time. Given that I am a gay man, however, I focus more on erotic activity among men and what this tells us about sexual rule in general. I recognize that lesbianism cannot be lumped uncritically together with male homosexuality for purposes of analysis. Given differences in the social organization of gender as it affects our sexual lives, any use of a unitary homosexual category for both male and female experiences necessarily distorts lesbian experience to fit the male category. Lesbians are thereby transformed into female homosexual "men." This is the case even in much current "queer" theorizing where queer is coded most often as male.[49] Differences in the social organization of gender — of forms of masculinity, femininity, and sexuality — tend to become obscured and the effect of patriarchal social organization is overlooked.[50] Gay men may be "queer," but we are still men, and we can even be "masculine" men in this society.[51]

Lesbian feminist theory developed from the diverse experiences of lesbians can at the same time be useful in examining gay male experiences, bringing with it a critique of institutionalized heterosexuality.[52] Lesbian-feminism, in general, has developed a broader social vision than has most gay men's liberation since lesbians are oppressed as "women" and as "lesbians," and this has led to a broader and more diffuse social radicalization among lesbians. Fewer laws have been used to specifically regulate lesbian sexual activities. Gay men have been more directly affected by State regulation of sex and tended to organize around specific laws and police actions,[53] prior to AIDS activism when a series of new questions have been faced. The experiences of lesbians and gay men, along with bisexuals, must be examined in their specificity and their synthesis to give us a fuller picture of the ways in which heterosexual hegemony is organized.[54]

Since the mid 1980s a lot has changed and new questions need to be addressed. At the same time as new queer activisms were emerging, a new theory — "queer theory" — emerged in the U.S and began spilling across the border into Canada. This literary and culturally derived theory began to again put in question the polarity between homo and hetero sexualities.[55] "Queer theory" was refreshing in once again placing on the agenda the contestation of what I call heterosexual hegemony. As Eve Kosofsky Sedgwick, one of the key American architects of "queer theory," puts it:

an understanding of virtually any aspect of western culture must be, not merely incomplete, but damaged in its central substance to the degree that it does not incorporate a critical analysis of modern homo/heterosexual definitions ...[56]

This important challenge is unfortunately limited by the character of "queer theory," which largely only contests heterosexual hegemony on "cultural" and "literary" terrains. The notion of language used in "queer theory" — drawn from poststructuralism and postmodernism[57] — tends to have a rather non-social character to it not clearly seeing how language and discourse are social practices that people accomplish in our daily lives.[58] This can lead "queer theory" to veer off in the direction of a discourse reductionism that reduces the complexities of social processes to the discursive domain alone, and obscures that it is people located in various social places and positions who produce discourse. These critiques will be developed further throughout this book. One of my objectives in this edition is to try to give the insights of "queer theory" a more social and materialist grounding to make them more relevant to critical historical, social, and political investigations, and to social-movement activism.

Part I, "Finding a Place to Begin," surveys the perspectives and methods used in this book. This can be skipped over for those less interested in questions of "theory" and "method" or come back to later after investigating the rest of the book. Chapter 1 covers the crucial notion of shifting standpoints in studies of erotic desires and sexual regulation, and sketches in the key perspectives I have used in looking at sexualities in Canadian social history. This is followed by a chapter on the historical and social conditions necessary for the emergence of lesbian, gay, and heterosexual identities and cultures; it draws primarily on English, European, and American experiences. This then allows us to move on to see how this process took place in Canada.

There follows the main body of the book, which deals with sexual regulation in Canadian history. This sets the stage for the stories of sexual rule and sexual resistance in Canada, focusing on the regulation of same-gender desire and how the social organization of homosexuality and lesbianism has affected the emergence of same-gender and different-gender erotic cultures. These categories have shaped the very terrain upon which our resistance has taken place. This exploration will also bring into focus more general features of social, moral, and gender regulation and the organization of class and State rule. This section covers the period from European colonization and marginalization of the aboriginal peoples to the contemporary moral conservative mobilizations against gay liberation and feminism and the social construction of the AIDS crisis.

I present merely an outline of these histories, focusing on periods of transition. This is intended as a starting point for discussion, debate, and further research. It focuses much more on the historical experience in "English Canada" than that of the distinct national experience in Québec. It is more developed for the 1950s and 1960s in Canada since that is where I have done the most research and more information is available. In this second edition chapters 7 and 8 — largely addressing the 1950s and 1960s

— have been enriched by the addition of some of the analysis I undertook for my Ph.D. thesis on "Official Discourse as Sexual Regulation," completed in late 1988.[59]

The latter sections of the book are not intended to be a history of the lesbian and gay liberation movements in the 1970s and 1980s.[60] This I leave to others, although there are some suggestions here. The book is still far more Toronto and Ontario centric, especially for the 1970s to 1990s, than I would wish. I hope others will take the suggestions here and take them further for other regions of Canada. I have also updated this edition to take account of the explosion of research since the first edition,[61] but it still needs to be developed and taken much further. As it stands, this is still a limited, and partial, history of the regulation of erotic desires in the Canadian State.

The last chapter, "From Resistance to Liberation," ties the book together, drawing a number of conclusions for gay and lesbian liberation, and socialist and feminist change more generally, and it zeroes in on a number of contemporary sexual and social struggles, including struggles for spousal and family-recognition rights and the impact of the AIDS crisis. I argue that current struggles over social benefits, support and family policies, and the need to address the needs of people living with AIDS/HIV begin to put in question some of the fundamental features of the capitalist, patriarchal, and racist society we live in. This holds out the possibility that lesbian and gay liberation could be at the centre of reconstituting a dynamic movement for socialist-feminist transformation.

Notes

1. See Tim McCaskell, "The Bath Raids and Gay Politics" in Frank Cunningham, Sue Findlay, *et al.*, *Social Movements/Social Change: The Politics and Practice of Organizing* (Toronto: Between the Lines/Socialist Studies, 1988), pp. 169-188. Also see George Smith "Policing the Gay Community: An Inquiry into Textually-Mediated Social Relations" in *International Journal of the Sociology of Law*, No. 16, 1988, pp. 163-183.
2. "Queer" can sound very different when uttered by a queerbasher against lesbians and gay men than when used by lesbians and gay men as an affirmation of ourselves in a society that often tries to deny our very existence. I also use queer in this book as a broader term than lesbian or gay to try to include the experiences of people before the emergence of homosexual/lesbian classifications, and to also include people who engaged in same-gender passions who would not identify as lesbian or gay. While I now use it to identify with the new wave of queer activism, I do not use it in the same ways that it is used in "queer nationalism" or in "queer theory."
3. See Gary Kinsman, "Managing AIDS Organizing: 'Consultation,' 'Partnership,' and the National AIDS Strategy" in William K. Carroll, ed., *Organizing Dissent: Contemporary Social Movements in Theory and Practice* (Toronto: Garamond, 1992), pp. 215-231; George Smith, "AIDS Treatment Deficits: An ethnographic study of the management of the AIDS epidemic, the Ontario case" unpublished paper presented at the Fifth International AIDS conference, Montréal, 1989 and his "Political Activist as Ethnographer" in *Social Problems*, V. 37, No. 4, Nov. 1990, pp. 629-648.
4. On the activism of AIDS ACTION NOW!, see John Greyson's videos *The World is Sick (Sic)* (1989) and *The Pink Pimpernel* (1989).
5. On some of the limitations of queer nationalist activism, see Steven Maynard, "When Queer Is Not Enough" in *Fuse*, V. 15, No. 1-2, Fall 1991, pp. 14-18, and my unpublished paper, "Queer

'Nations,' Queer Spaces: Academic Institutionalization and Queer Activism," given at the Canadian Sociology and Anthropology Meetings, Charlottetown, June 1992.

6. On the Lesbian Avengers in the U.S., see Sarah Schulman, *My American History: Lesbian and Gay Life During the Reagan/Bush Years* (New York: Routledge, 1994), especially "Excerpts from the Lesbian Avengers Handbook," pp. 289-319.

7. On the Bill 167 struggle, see David M. Rayside, "Inside the Fringe: Mobilizing for Same-Sex Benefits in Ontario," paper presented at the second annual meeting of the Canadian Lesbian and Gay Studies Association, Montréal, Jun. 3-4, 1995 and Nancy Nicol's two-channel video, *Gay Pride and Prejudice* (1994).

8. See Philip Hannon, "Reason Prevails: Hate Crimes Bill Passes House of Commons" in *Capital Xtra!* No. 22, Jun. 30, 1995, p. 13. In November 1995 the federal government did move to provide some same-sex leave benefits for federal employees (bereavement, family-related responsibilities leave, etc.). This did not cover medical, dental, pension and other benefits.

9. Glen Whiffen, "Sex Case Details Outlined for Court" in *The Evening Telegram* May 21, 1993, p. 1.

10. Eleanor Brown, "Hot Spots: Arrests for Public Sex Are on the Rise, Warns Lawyer" in *Xtra!* No. 228, Jul. 23, 1993, p. 15, and later articles in *Xtra!*.

11. See Clare Barclay and Elaine Carol, "Obscenity Chill: Artists in a Post-Butler Era" in *Fuse* Winter 1992-1993, V. 16, No. 2, pp. 18-28. Also see Janine Fuller and Stuart Blackley, *Restricted Entry, Censorship on Trial*, (Vancouver, Press Gang, 1995).

12. See Linda Gordon and Allen Hunter, *Sex, Family and the New Right*, New England Free Press, reprinted from the Nov. 1977-Feb. 1978 issue of *Radical America*; Rosalind Pollack Petchesky, *Abortion and Woman's Choice* (Boston: Northeastern University Press, 1985); for Canada, see the work of Lorna Erwin including "Neoconservatism and the Canadian Pro-family Movement" in *The Canadian Review of Sociology and Anthropology*, V. 30, No. 3, Aug. 1993, pp. 401-420; and Didi Herman, *Rights of Passage: Struggles for Lesbian and Gay Legal Equality* (Toronto: University of Toronto Press, 1994), especially chapter 5 "'Normalcy on the Defensive': New Christian Right Sexual Politics," and chapter 6, "The Saints Go Litigating," pp. 77-127.

13. See Cindy Patton, *Sex and Germs: The Politics of AIDS* (Montréal: Black Rose Books, 1986) and *Inventing AIDS* (New York and London: Routledge, 1990); Simon Watney, *Policing Desire: Pornography, AIDS and the Media* (London: Comedia, 1987) and his *Practices of Freedom: Selected Writings on HIV/AIDS* (Durham: Duke University Press, 1994); Douglas Crimp, ed., *AIDS: Cultural Analysis, Cultural Activism* (Cambridge, MA: MIT Press, 1988) and Douglas Crimp with Adam Rolston, *AIDSDEMOGRAPHICS* (Seattle: Bay Press, 1990); Gary Kinsman "Their Silence, Our Deaths: What can The Social Sciences Offer to AIDS Research?" in Diane E. Goldstein ed., *Talking AIDS*, Institute for Social and Economic Research (ISER) Policy Papers 12, Memorial University of Newfoundland, 1991); my "Managing AIDS Organizing: 'Consultation,' 'Partnership,' and the National AIDS Strategy" in William Carroll, ed., *Organizing Dissent: Contemporary Social Movements in Theory and Practice* (Toronto: Garamond, 1992), pp. 215-231; and George Smith, "Political Activist as Ethnographer" in *Social Problems* V. 37, No. 4, 1990, pp. 629-648.

14. See Gary Kinsman, "The Hughes Commission: Making Homosexuality the Problem Once Again" in *New Maritimes* V. 11, No. 3, Jan./Feb. 1993, pp. 17-19 article and my unpublished manuscript, "Constructing 'Child Sexual Abuse': Mount Cashel, The Media and the Making of Homosexuality as a Social Problem."

15. See Patrick Barnholden, "A Different Drummer: Lesbians and Gays in the Region: An Activist's Overview" in *New Maritimes*, No. 88, Jan./Feb. 1993, p. 7.

16. See Philip Hannon, "Checkered Victory: No pension for spouse of 47 years, court rules" in *Capital Xtra!*, No. 22, Jun. 30, 1995, p. 11.

17. See Jeff Lindstrom, "Limited adoption rights granted" in *Xtra!*, No. 276, May 26, 1995, p. 12. Although this decision is limited in its impact, it is very useful for lesbian couples and their children.

18. See Nancy Nicol's, *Gay Pride and Prejudice*, 1994.

19. See Kinsman, "Managing AIDS Organizing," *op. cit.*
20. For instance, Edward Carpenter, a homosexual writer and activist in the late nineteenth and early twentieth centuries, had connections with anarchist, socialist, and libertarian circles. His writings helped numerous men and women come to terms with their lesbian and homosexual experiences in the English-speaking world. Magnus Hirschfeld, a leader of the early German homosexual rights movement and the international sex-reform movement, was associated with the German Social Democratic Party. The German homosexual movement drew most of its parliamentary support from the Social Democrats and later the Communist Party. The Bolsheviks in the USSR repealed the Czarist anti-homosexual legislation and participated in the World League for Sexual Reform. In the 1930s, with the emergence of a new bureaucratic ruling class in the USSR, the laws against homosexuality were reinstated. On Carpenter, see Sheila Rowbotham, "Edward Carpenter: Prophet of the New Life" in Rowbotham and Weeks, *Socialism and the New Life: The Personal and Sexual Politics of Edward Carpenter and Havelock Ellis* (London: Pluto, 1977), and Rowbotham, "In Search of Carpenter" in *Dreams and Dilemmas* (London: Virago, 1983), pp. 239-256. Also see *Edward Carpenter, Selected Writings. Vol. 1, Sex,* with an introduction by Noel Greig (London: Gay Men's Press, 1984). On the early German movement, see John Lauritsen and David Thorstad, *The Early Homosexual Rights Movement* (New York: Times Change Press, 1974), and James Steakley, *The Homosexual Emancipation Movement in Germany* (New York: Arno Press, 1975). Also references in Lorna Weir, "Studies in the Medicalization of Sexual Danger: Sexual Rule, Sexual Politics 1830-1930," Ph.D. thesis, 1986, York University, Toronto, Department of Social and Political Thought. Also see Barry D. Adam, *The Rise of a Gay and Lesbian Movement* (Boston: Twayne, 1987), especially "Early Movements and Aspirations," pp. 17-44.
21. On some of this, see Nanette Funk and Magda Mueleer, eds., *Gender Politics and Post-Communism* (New York and London: Routledge, 1993).
22. Leftists have been active in lesbian and gay resistance from the Mattachine Society in the 1950s in the U.S. to the Gay Liberation Fronts to more recent queer and AIDS activism. On Mattachine see John D'Emilio, *Sexual Politics, Sexual Communities* (Chicago: The University of Chicago Press, 1983). pp. 57-74.
23. My own experiences in a series of Canadian Trotskyist groups is documented in Gary, Amy, and Natalie, "We May Not Be Witches But We Sure Have Been Burned," our resignation letter from the Revolutionary Workers' League, March 8, 1980. Other Canadian experiences are included in the Gay/Lesbian Caucus of In Struggle, "Our Resolution for In Struggle's 4th Congress," printed in *In Struggle*, V. 9, No. 25, May 4-18, 1982, pp. 6-7; and in Brian Mossop, "Gay and Socialist, or Some Reflections of a Commie Fag" in *Canadian Dimension,* Jun. 1980, V. 14, No. 7, pp. 49-51. For experiences in England, see Bob Cant, "A Grim Tale: The International Socialist Gay Group, 1972-1979" in *Gay Left*, No. 3, pp. 7-10; Philip Derbyshire, "Sects and Sexuality: Trotskyism and the Politics of Homosexuality" in Gay Left Collective, ed., *Homosexuality, Power and Politics* (London: Allison and Busby, 1980), pp. 104-115; Jamie Gough and Mike Macnair, *Gay Liberation in the Eighties* (London: Pluto, 1985); and Bill Marshall, "Gays and Marxism" in Simon Shepherd and Mick Wallis, ed., *Coming on Strong: Gay Politics and Culture* (London: Unwin Hyman, 1989), pp. 258-274. For the U.S., see Ruth Dubrovsky and Lorna Miles, *Lesbian and Gay Exclusion: The Policy that Dare Not Speak Its Name,* United Labour Press, 1982; A. Rausch, *In Partial Payment: Class Struggle, Sexuality and the Gay Movement,* published by the Sojourner Truth Organization, 1981; Los Angeles Research Group, "Towards a Scientific Analysis of the Gay Question" in Pam Mitchell, ed., *Pink Triangles: Radical Perspectives on Gay Liberation* (Boston: Alyson Publications, 1980), pp. 117-135; David Thorstad, ed., *Gay Liberation and Socialism* (Self-published, New York, 1976); Steve Forgione and Kurt T. Hill, *No Apologies* (Self-published, New York, 1980); and also Robin Podolsky, "Sacrificing Queers and Other 'Proletarian' Artifacts" in *Radical America* V. 25, No. 1, Jan.-Mar. 1991 (Sept. 1993), pp. 53-60.
24. See Martin Duberman, *Stonewall* (New York: Dutton, 1993).
25. A useful critique of the ideology of early gay-liberation groups can be found in Simon Wat-

ney, "The Ideology of GLF" in Gay Left Collective, eds., *Homosexuality, Power and Politics, op. cit.,* pp. 64-76.

26. On "sexual rule," see Lorna Weir, "Studies in the Medicalization of Sexual Danger: Sexual Rule, Sexual Politics, 1830-1930," *op. cit.,* particularly pp. 1-75.

27. For a general survey of some of this historical literature, see Joe Interrante, "From Homosexual to Gay to ?: Recent Work in Gay History" in *Radical America,* V. 15, No. 6, Nov.-Dec. 1981, pp. 79-86; Martha Vicinus, "Sexuality and Power: A Review of Current Work in the History of Sexuality" in *Feminist Studies,* V. 8, No. 1 (Spring 1982), pp. 133-156; Jeffrey Weeks, *Sex, Politics and Society* (London and New York: Longman, 1981); Weeks, *Sexuality and Its Discontents* (London, Melbourne, and Henley: Routledge and Kegan Paul, 1985); Jonathan Ned Katz, *Gay/Lesbian Almanac* (New York: Harper and Row, 1983), especially pp. 1-19; David M. Halperin, *One Hundred Years of Homosexuality* (New York and London: Routledge, 1990) and a number of the chapters in Martin Duberman, Martha Vicinus, and George Chauncey Jr., eds., *Hidden From History: Reclaiming the Gay Past* (New York: Meridian, 1989) although the book as a whole tends to try to straddle the fence between "naturalist" or "essentialist" positions and social constructionist ones. Also see my "'Homosexuality' Historically Reconsidered Challenges Heterosexual Hegemony" in the *Journal of Historical Sociology* V. 4, No. 2, Jun. 1991, pp. 91-111.

28. See Jonathan Ned Katz, "The Invention of Heterosexuality" in *Socialist Review* No. 1, 1990, pp. 7-34 and his *The Invention of Heterosexuality* (New York: Dutton, 1995).

29. For a critique of sexual naturalism see the above sources and Lorna Weir and Leo Casey, "Subverting Power in Sexuality" in *Socialist Review,* No. 75/76 (V. 14, No. 3/4), May-Aug. 1984, pp. 139-157.

30. This critique of the repression thesis of sexuality, a thesis which suggests that during the Victorian period a regime of sexual repression was established from which we are freeing ourselves today and revealing our "natural" sexuality, draws on the work of Michel Foucault; see *History of Sexuality, Volume One: An Introduction* (New York: Vintage, 1980).

31. Roxana Ng, "Sexism, Racism, and Canadian Nationalism" in Himani Bannerji, ed., *Returning the Gaze, Essays on Racism, Feminism and Politics* (Toronto: Sister Vision Press, 1993), pp. 183-184.

32. Karen Dubinsky, *Improper Advances, Rape and Heterosexual Conflict in Ontario, 1880-1929* (Chicago: University of Chicago Press, 1993), p. 167.

33. On "breaching experiments" see Harold Garfinkel, *Studies In Ethnomethodology* (Englewood Cliffs, New Jersey: Prentice-Hall, 1967). Ethnomethodology is the study of the methods people use to produce society.

34. Charlotte Bunch, "Not For Lesbians Only" in *Quest* V. II, No. 2, Fall 1975.

35. Lynne Segal, *Straight Sex, The Politics of Pleasure* (London: Virago, 1994), p. xiv.

36. This borrows from Bunch's "Not For Lesbians Only," *op. cit.*

37. On the problems with identity politics see Mary Louise Adams, "There's No Place Like Home: On the Place of Identity in Feminist Politics" in *Feminist Review* No. 31, Spring 1989, pp. 22-33; Judith Butler, *Gender Trouble: Feminism and the Subversion of Identity* (New York: Routledge, 1990); and also see a number of the articles in Himani Bannerji, *Thinking Through, Essays on Feminism, Marxism and Anti-Racism* (Toronto: Women's Press, 1995). When I use identity in this book (often I prefer identification) I do not use it as a fixed psychological or essential notion but rather as a social practice. Also see Lorna Weir, "Limitations of New Social Movement Analysis" in *Studies in Political Economy* No. 40, Spring 1993.

38. Kenneth Plummer, "Going Gay: Identities, Life Cycles and Lifestyles in the Male Gay World" in John Hart and Diane Richardson, *The Theory and Practice of Homosexuality* (London: Routledge and Kegan Paul, 1981), p. 94.

39. Robert A Padgug, "Sexual Matters: On Conceptualizing Sexuality in History" in *Radical History Review,* No. 20, Spring/Summer 1979, pp. 13-14. On Ancient Greece also see K.J. Dover, *Greek Homosexuality* (New York: Vintage, 1980); Michel Foucault, *History of Sexuality Volume 2:*

The Use of Pleasure (New York: Pantheon, 1985); and David M. Halperin, *One Hundred Years of Homosexuality op. cit.*

40. Jonathan Katz, *Gay/Lesbian Almanac, op. cit.*, pp. 17-18.

41. On this see Jonathan Ned Katz, *The Invention of Heterosexuality, op. cit.*

42. Ann Ferguson, "Patriarchy, Sexual Identity, and the Sexual Revolution" in *Signs*, V. 7, No. 1, p. 166. Also see her *Blood at the Root, Motherhood, Sexuality and Male Dominance* (London: Pandora, 1989), pp. 188-208 and *Sexual Democracy, Women, Oppression and Revolution* (Boulder, San Francisco, Oxford: Westview Press, 1991), pp. 133-158.

43. See Mariana Valverde, "Bisexuality: Coping With Sexual Boundaries" in her *Sex, Power and Pleasure* (Toronto: The Women's Press, 1985), pp. 109-120 and Clare Hemmings, "Locating Bisexual Identities, discourses of bisexuality and contemporary feminist theory" in David Bell and Gill Valentine, *Mapping Desire*, (London and New York: Routledge, 1995), pp. 41-55.

44. This term, along with sodomite, is used to describe lesbians and independent women in Jamaica. See Makeda Silvera, "Man Royals and Sodomites, Some Thoughts on the Invisibility of Afro-Caribbean Lesbians" in Sharon Dale Stone, ed., *Lesbians In Canada* (Toronto: Between the Lines, 1990), pp. 48-60.

45. For some ideas see Peter Drucker, "'In The Tropics There is No Sin': Homosexuality and the Gay/Lesbian Movements in the Third World," Amsterdam, Working Papers of the International Institute for Research and Education, July 1993; Makeda Silvera, "Man Royals and Sodomites: Some Thoughts on the Invisibility of Afro-Caribbean Lesbians" in Sharon Stone, ed., *Lesbians in Canada, op. cit.*, pp. 48-60; Didi Khayatt, "The Place of Desire: The Exclusion of Women in the Third World in Theorizing Sexual Orientation," unpublished paper presented at the Toronto, Queer Sites conference, May 13, 1993; T. Dunbar Moodie (with Vivienne Ndatshe and British Sibuyi), "Migrancy and Male Sexuality on the South African Gold Mines" in Duberman, Vicinus and Chauncey, Jr., eds, *Hidden From History* (New York: Meridian, 1989); Mark Gevisser and Edwin Cameron, *Defiant Desire, Gay and Lesbian Lives in South Africa* (New York, London: Routledge, 1995); Ian Lumsden, *Homosexuality, Society and the State in Mexico* (Mexico City and Toronto: Solediciones, Colectivo Sol, and the Canadian Gay Archives, 1991) and Joao S Trevisan, *Perverts In Paradise* (London: GMP, 1986).

46. See Lisa Gribowski's paper, "Reading Between The Lines: Exposing 'Whiteness' in Lesbian Coming-Out Narratives," presented at the Canadian Sociology and Anthropology Association meetings, Montréal, Jun. 1995.

47. This is outlined in some ways by Dennis Altman in *The Homosexualization of America, the Americanization of the Homosexual*, (New York: St. Martin's Press, 1982).

48. For some useful insights on the social construction of "whiteness" see Vron Ware, *Beyond the Pale, White Women, Racism and History* (London, New York: Verso, 1992); Ruth Frakenburg, *The Social Construction of Whiteness: White Women Race Matters* (Minneapolis: The University of Minnessotta Press, 1993) and David R. Roediger, *The Wages of Whiteness, Race and the Making of the American Working Class* (London and New York: Verso, 1991).

49. See Mary McIntosh, "Queer Theory and the War of the Sexes" in Joseph Bristow and Angelia R. Wilson, eds., *Activating Theory, Lesbian, Gay and Bisexual Politics*, (London: Lawrence and Wishart, 1993), pp. 30-52.

50. On patriarchal social relations and their relation to capitalist relations, see Dorothy E. Smith, "Women, Class and Family" in *Socialist Register* (London: Merlin, 1983), pp. 1-44.

51. This line is taken from Mike Brake, "I may be queer but at least I'm a man" in D.L. Barker and S. Allan, *Sexual Division and Society: Process and Changes* (London: Tavistock, 1976), pp. 174-198.

52. See Adrienne Rich, "Compulsory Heterosexuality and Lesbian Existence" in Stimpson and Persons, eds., *Women, Sex and Sexuality* (Chicago and London: University of Chicago Press, 1980), pp. 62-91; and Charlotte Bunch, "Not For Lesbians Only ..." *Quest*, V. 11, No. 2, Fall 1975.

53. See Lorna Weir and Eve Zaremba, "Boys and Girls Together: Feminism and Gay Liberation" in *Broadside*, V. 4, No. 1, Oct. 1982, pp. 6-7, 9.

54. For work on lesbian history and sociology see Ferguson, *op. cit.*; Adrienne Rich's illuminating but ahistorical "Compulsory Heterosexuality and Lesbian Existence," *op. cit.*; Lillian Faderman, *Surpassing the Love of Men* (New York: William Morrow, 1981) and her *Odd Girls and Twilight Lovers, A History of Lesbian Life in Twentieth-Century America* (New York: Columbia University press, 1991); Elizabeth Lapovsky Kennedy and Madeline D. Davis, *Boots of Leather, Slippers of Gold, The History of a Lesbian Community* (Routledge,New York and London: 1993); Annabel Faraday, "Liberating Lesbian Research" in Kenneth Plummer, ed., *The Making of the Modern Homosexual* (London: Hutchinson, 1981); E.M. Ettore, *Lesbians, Women, and Society* (London: Routledge and Kegan Paul, 1980); Sharon Dale Stone, ed., *Lesbians In Canada* (Toronto: Between The Lines, 1990); Makeda Silvera, "Man Royals and Sodomites, Some Thoughts on the Invisibility of Afro-Caribbean Lesbians" in Sharon Stone, ed., *Lesbians In Canada, op. cit.*, pp. 48-60 and in other collections; Didi Khayatt, "Legalized Invisibility, The Effect of Bill 7 on Lesbian Teachers" in *Women's Studies International Forum* V. 13, No. 3, 1990, pp. 185-193; Madiha Didi Khayatt, *Lesbian Teachers, An Invisible Presence* (Albany: SUNY, 1992); the work of Becki Ross including "Sex, Lives and Archives: Pleasure/Danger Debates in 1970s Lesbian Feminism" in Sandra Kirby, Michele Pujol, Kate McKenna, Michele Valiquette, Danya Daniels, eds., *Women Changing Academe* (Winnipeg: Sororal Publishing, 1991), pp. 74-91 and her book *The House That Jill Built* (Toronto: University of Toronto Press, 1995); Kathleen Martindale, "What Makes Lesbianism Thinkable? Theorizing Lesbianism From Adrienne Rich to Queer Theory" in Nancy Mandell, ed., *Feminist Issues, Race, Class, and Sexuality* (Scarborough: Prentice-Hall, 1995), pp. 67-94; Martha Vicinus, "Lesbian History: All Theory and No Facts or All Facts and No Theory?" in *Radical History Review*, No. 60, Fall 1994, pp. 57-75; and Biddy Martin, "Sexual Practice and Changing Lesbian Identities" in Michelle Barrett and Anne Phillips, eds., *Destabilizing Theory, Contemporary Feminist Debates* (Stanford, California: Stanford University Press, 1992), pp. 93-119. Also Mary McIntosh, "Postscript: The Homosexual Role Revisited" in Kenneth Plummer, ed., *The Making of the Modern Homosexual, op. cit.*, p. 46, and later references in this book.
55. On "queer theory" see Michael Warner, ed., *Fear of A Queer Planet, Queer Politics and Social Theory* (Minneapolis: University of Minnesota Press, 1993); Rosemary Hennessy, "Queer Theory, Left Politics" in *Rethinking Marxism*, V. 7, No. 3, 1994, pp. 85-111; and my "'Queer Theory' Versus Heterosexual Hegemony: Towards A Historical Materialism for Gay Men and Lesbians," unpublished paper given at the "Queer Sites" lesbian and gay studies conference, Toronto, May 14, 1993.
56. Eve Kosofsky Sedgwick, *The Epistemology of the Closet*, (Berkeley and Los Angeles: University of California Press, 1990), p. 1.
57. Poststructuralism is a word describing a theoretical approach that no longer believes in a structuralist form of analysis where the social is constituted and determined through social structures. Rather than focusing on structures, poststructuralism tends to focus on fragmentation, diversity and difference. Poststructuralists often combine a number of different perspectives in their work. I view "postmodernism" as a general space or mood that has a number of common themes. On the social and political terrains, there is a general assumption that we are in a new period and are moving beyond "modernity." There is an emphasis on language and discourse and often a certain emphasis on psychoanalysis. In general, the subject — or subject positions — are seen as being constituted through discourse. For an interesting Marxist — but far too "fundamentalist" critique of postmodernism — see Alex Callinicos, *Against Postmodernism: A Marxist Critique* (Cambridge: Polity Press, 1990). Also see the useful comments of bell hooks, "Postmodern Blackness" in *Yearning: race, gender and cultural politics* (Toronto: Between The Lines, 1990, pp. 23-31); Rosemary Hennessy, *Materialist Feminism and the Politics of Discourse* (New York and London: Routledge, 1993), and Linda Nicholson, ed., *Feminism/Postmodernism* (New York: Routledge, 1990).
58. This insight comes from some of the recent work of Dorothy E. Smith including "Notes on

telling the truth or 'Is there any point to sociological inquiry?'" a draft paper presented to the Stone symposium, University of Illinois, May 1994.

59. See Gary Kinsman, "Official Discourse as Sexual Regulation," Ph.D thesis, Department of Educational Theory, University of Toronto, 1989.
60. There is a need for more of these movement histories, like Becki Ross's *The House that Jill Built: A Lesbian Nation In Formation* (Toronto: University of Toronto Press, 1995).
61. See references in chapter 3 and later.

Part One

Finding a
Place to Begin

1.

The Creation of Homosexuality as a "Social Problem"

Why Historical Materialism?

My method of exploration is a historical materialist one: that is, a perspective that views historical transformation as central to understanding our lives and that sees social relations and practices, rather than ideas or discourse separate from these,[1] as the primary elements in social change. Discourse both organizes and is organized through social relations. I am using "materialism" here in a broad sense, including eroticism and sexualities, as sensuous human practices. I do not view class as separate from other social relations and struggles, or as simply "economic" in character. Rather than displacing class relations and struggles, we need new ways of viewing class — not as a reified concept — but as lived historical, social experience and practice.[2] Sexual relations have been an important part of the formation of class relations and struggles; and class relations have shaped sexual relations and struggles.[3]

We can learn a great deal from the method of historical materialism. But to do this, we cannot read historical materialism — as a critical method of analysis — as a form of economic determinism in which "the economy" determines everything. This is unfortunately the main reading in current postmodernism and queer theory.[4] This is also a major problem with the "political economy" tradition that has been the hegemonic intellectual interpretation of Marxism in Canada until recently and that has not engaged seriously with critical work on gender, and especially with sexual regulation.[5] Unfortunately, it is this very reading of Marxism that has provided part of the basis for the growth of a "queer theory" divorced from and often antagonistic to the insights of historical materialism.

While Marx's and Engels' public and private writings on sex, and same-gender sex in particular, are an instance of "unthinking sex," as Andrew Parker[6] suggests, this was in part because in the context of the times in which they lived and of their own gender and sexual practices they were unable to apply their revolutionary method to this arena. Their critical social method that contested naturalism in other spheres of social life accepted a form of sexual naturalism. The "founding fathers" of Marxism relegated sex and eroticism to a historically insignificant terrain. Marx remained a prisoner of hegemonic social ideologies and practices, taking for granted the hegemonic forms of sexuality (and to some extent gender and race) he lived and found around himself as "natural." At the same time his critical method can be extended to these areas if it is taken up and transformed from the standpoints of women, gays, people of colour and others who face oppression and marginalization.

Marx's critique of capitalist political economy shattered the "natural" and ahistorical character of capitalist social relations and provided a way of moving beyond the appearance of "fair" exchange between capitalist and worker to disclose the underlying relations of exploitation upon which this rested. He was able to go beyond the equal and ahistorical appearance of the exchange between capitalist and worker to reveal the underlying appropriation of surplus value by the capitalist, which defined the exploitation of the worker during the process of production; yet he proved unable to move beyond the "natural" appearance of the existing and developing heterosexual social forms of sexual life to reveal how these, too, were historical and social creations. In the sphere of commodity production, exchange, and circulation, Marx and Engels were able to analyze commodity fetishism as the mystified surface appearance of capitalist social relations in which social relationships appear to be relations between products.[7] They could therefore reveal in the realm of commodities the relation between this phenomenal form, or the ways in which the everyday accepted phenomena of the world present themselves, and the underlying social relations organizing this experience.[8] Marx and Engels could not, however, go beyond the surface appearance of sexual relations to reveal the process of fetishism that obscures the social relations in which our sexuality is made. Insofar as they considered the matter, they were prisoners of a naturalist and essentialist view.

Marx focused on the social character of the processes of production and capitalist relations and did not produce a narrow "economic" theory. He was able to disclose the ideological practices through which bourgeois political economy separated its concepts from the social practices and relations through which they were produced.[9]

In stressing the insights of historical materialism, I am focusing on the revolutionary aspects of Marx's method: the historical character of social processes, the importance of social practices and relations, and his vital critique of ideological practices. People's social worlds are made through the practices and activities of people themselves. I emphasize the need for a central critique of "naturalism," of "surface appearances," and of the phenomenal forms through which social processes often get presented to us. This centrally includes a critique of the ideological practices that produce forms of knowledge separated from the social practices that produce them, resulting in forms of knowledge that are removed from experience and that attend to ruling and managing people's lives.[10] I am also pointing to Marx's crucial critique of reification — his opposition to converting social relations between people into relations between things.[11] Above all, this liberatory approach emphasizes that what is socially made can be socially transformed.

Rather than dismissing the insights of a non-reductionist historical materialism, we need to reclaim and transform them *for* queers in our struggles for liberation. It will be through various subordinated, marginalized and exploited groups taking up critical historical materialist work from their own standpoints that the resources for new transformative socialist theoretical and activist movements will be made.

Historical materialism *for* queers, as I develop it here, shatters the natural and ahistorical character of heterosexual hegemony, discloses the oppressions lying beneath the "natural" appearance of this hegemony, points to the socially and historically made character of sexualities, and puts heterosexual hegemony in question. It directs our attention to the ideological practices through which heterosexual hegemonic relations are constructed. This points toward the possibilities of overturning heterosexual hegemony and transforming erotic relations, and would link this to the transformation of State, class, gender, and race relations. Marx's work and method still have a lot to tell us about the dynamics of capitalist social relations and how these shape the lives of lesbians and gay men as well as others. This approach also sharpens our focus of attention on class relations and struggles within gay, lesbian, and other communities.

History, in this sense, belongs not only to the past. It participates in forming what Jeffrey Weeks calls the "historical present."[12] Examining historical experiences and practices can help us understand from where lesbian and gay oppression and, more generally, oppressive sexual regulation has come, where it may be going, and the possibilities for transformation. The concepts necessary for an understanding of sexual rule and resistance exist only in initial form at present. One way of proceeding is by studying our past to develop the historically rooted categories necessary for this exploration. This approach explores how people's experiences are socially organized and how they change over time.[13] When examining official government documents or police records, we must immediately place them in the context of people's lives. The emergence of "lesbianism" and "homosexuality," and that of lesbian, homosexual, and heterosexual categories in official discourse, were part of broader shifts in class, gender and social organization. Same-gender sex was relegated to a subordinate position through relations of sex and gender regulation that established a particular form of heterosexuality as the social norm.

If analysis can be rooted in the social relations that have organized these experiences, then a much better understanding of how sexuality has been defined, organized, and regulated in capitalist and patriarchal societies will be possible. Capitalism is a dynamic social system that is constantly "transforming the 'ground' on which we stand so that we are always ... experiencing changing historical process."[14] History does not stand still, and it is this very undermining of previous forms of sex and gender regulations that has created the basis for gay liberation and feminist movements.

These needed historical investigations do not replace the need for critical social analysis of the contemporary forms of social organization of our oppression, including studies of policing, AIDS, family and social policies, violence against lesbians and gay men, problems facing lesbian and gay youth, and others.[15] At the same time, this critical historical work can help to develop the concepts needed for critical analysis of the present and future possibilities.

In undertaking these historical materialist journeys, I have drawn on a number of sources. These are the historical and social organization of sexuality perspective; the perspective of taking up the standpoint of the oppressed, and the social organization of knowledge approach of Marxist-feminist Dorothy E. Smith; and various Marxist-inspired approaches to State formation, moral and cultural regulation, historical sociology, and the social organization of hegemony.

Sexuality, History, and Social Organization

Contrary to "common sense," sexuality is not natural nor innate. Cross-cultural and historical studies have unearthed the diverse ways in which eroticism has been organized in various social settings. Sexuality is not simply biologically defined; it is socially created, building on physiological potentialities.

> Biological sexuality is the necessary precondition for human sexuality. But biological sexuality is only a set of potentialities, which is never unmediated by human reality, and which becomes transformed in qualitatively new ways in human society.[16]

The various possible erotic zones of the human body provide the preconditions for the social and cultural forms of activity and meaning that come to compose human sexual practices. It is in this transition from "biological"[17] to historical and social that the definitions and regulations of sexuality have emerged. Physiological capacities are transformed to create sexuality as a social need, and, in turn, to produce new erotic needs.

Our various forms of sexuality and the social identities built around them are organized through the sex and gender relations that have existed in different societies.[18] Sex is fundamentally a social activity. A history of sexuality *is* a history of social relations. Human sexual practice is composed of thoughts (eroticized images, socially learned courses of action, or "sexual scripts"[19]) and physical/sensual activities themselves. The way in which our erotic capacities come together with mental constructs, language, and symbolic systems and images is a social process. For instance, in our everyday lives we are able to differentiate between the touch of a doctor on our genitals as part of a medical examination and the caress of a lover in a more intimate setting. Our lover's touch will be responded to erotically through the enactment of a "sexual script" even though the touch of the doctor could have been the same physical touch as that of a lover. Together, thought and activity form human praxis that provides the basis for a historical materialist view of sexual relations.[20]

In making sense of sexuality as a social practice, a historical materialist method is very useful. At the most general level, erotic activity, in all its diversity and meanings, can be seen as a human universal similar to the way in which Marx saw human production. Sexual activity, like production in general, has existed in all human societies.[21] However, what can be said about sexual practice in this general sense is extremely limited. It provides us with no basis from which to explore sexuality in the historical sense. What organizes and comprises sexual relations in each period is therefore a historical and empirical question — a topic for exploration.[22] We need historically rooted concepts, and we must reject transhistorical categorizations — for instance, the notion that the homosexual, the lesbian, or the heterosexual have been around for all time (or, for some, since Sodom and Gomorrah). Both same-sex and different-sex sexual practices have existed throughout human history, but they have differed radically in their social organization.

But it is even more complex than this when we enter the social construction of gender into the picture since there have also been same-gender and different-gender erotic practices. For instance, in some aboriginal cultures in North America, there were same-sex erotic relations between what might be described as "regular" men and "berdache" (biological males who were members of a "third" gender that combined masculine/feminine characteristics). This would have been seen culturally as different-gender eroticism since there were more than two gender groupings in these societies (see chapter 4).

Contemporary "heterosexuality" and "homosexuality" are historically and socially specific organizations of different-gender and same-gender desires and pleasures. For instance, male same-gender erotic activities have ranged from structured "educational" relationships between men and boys in particular class, family, and State relations, to acts surrounding puberty or masculinity rituals, to cross-dressing and gender activity reversals.[23] These had different social meanings in different social/cultural contexts and were different social practices. Among the Sambia of Papua, for instance, same-gender sex for males between seven and nineteen was mandatory. Boys fellated men on a daily basis, so that they would grow into masculine adults. According to this culture males cannot produce sperm on their own; they can only recycle it from one generation to another. In their adult lives, these males engage in sex with women.[24] Our contemporary notions of the heterosexual/homosexual dichotomy make no sense in a culture like this. It is impossible to hold onto any transhistorical notion of homosexuality or homosexual behaviour — or transhistorical heterosexuality, for that matter — in the face of these diverse practices and social meanings.

Much critical understanding of the social organization of sexuality comes from how we see the social organization of gender. Sexuality, like gender, is a product of social interaction — a continuous social accomplishment.[25] Gender is assigned in our society at birth by doctors and nurses based on apparent genital features. It then takes on many social features that have nothing to do with physiology, even though biological determinist approaches argue that biology determines gender, whether it be through genes or hormones.[26] Tied in with this social organization of gender is an associated sexuality and sexual "identity." Through this social process a "natural" attitude toward sexuality and gender is created.[27]

In patriarchal and capitalist societies, sexuality and sexual identities connect a number of needs — emotional contact, friendship, sensual closeness, bodily pleasure, and genital sex — with notions of biology, gender, and reproductive capacity. This formation of sexuality implants naturalized constructs of masculinity and femininity within our very social and sexual beings, making it very difficult to disentangle our various needs grouped together as sexuality from biology, reproduction, and gender. Sexuality can be seen as a collecting category that groups together diverse needs, capacities, and desires.[28] Our sexuality has come to be defined by naturalist notions to such a degree that the process of social organization is rendered invisible (or unconscious).[29] We tend to "reify sex as a thing-in-itself."[30] We see our sexualities as a personal essence defining who we are rather than as constituted through the social practices that we ourselves have been active in through which our sexualities have been made. To critically investigate sexuality, we must put in question this "natural attitude" to recover the social practices and relations through which sexualities are made.

The human and social praxis involved in the formation of sexualities is obscured by the relations in which this process takes place. In a similar but different fashion to Marx's analysis of commodity fetishism, sexuality has come to be fetishized as something individual, "natural," and essential in which social relations and practices disappear. It should be clear, however, that the social relations organizing commodity fetishism and sexual fetishism are not the same and need their own historical investigation.[31] Ideologies of naturalism and an essential sexual nature are tied to the appearance of sexual fetishism. It must be stressed that powerful State and social policies lie behind the "naturalness" of heterosexuality in this society.

Sexual practice and "identity" is formed through a process of social interaction and encounters with social discourse, significant others, and bodily-based pleasures.[32] There is no "natural" or "unitary" sexuality. No situation is inherently sexual, but many situations are capable of being eroticized. Sexuality is subject to "socio-cultural moulding to a degree surpassed by few other forms of human behaviour."[33] Sexuality is not simply individual or "private," and the individual is only an individual in a social context. Social individuals come to take part in and take up particular sexual practices and identities. "Proper" gender is associated with "normal" sexuality, since gender shapes sexual conduct. Part of this process of normalization "derives from organs being placed in legitimate orifices."[34] "Identities" such as heterosexual, homosexual, lesbian, and bisexual are socially created.

While heterosexuality in contemporary societies is established as "natural," some of us do come to realize that we are erotically "different." Masculinity, femininity, heterosexuality, and family life itself, are contradictory. Subversive readings of dominant erotic images, along with the experiences of bodily pleasures and erotic play, are the initial bases for our queer desires. We may see ourselves as "outsiders" or as "different" as we grow up or at a later stage of development. This is a dialectic of broader social and self-definition. We may eventually encounter homosexual, lesbian, bisexual, or "queer" labelling and discover other lesbian and gay individuals and cultures that have managed to seize social spaces from the dominant order.[35]

Mary Douglas, in her anthropological work, explores one bridge between the individual and broader social worlds; how social and moral notions of purity, pollution, and taboo have been built on the social relations of biological reproduction and sexuality. These symbols play an important role in organizing social boundaries and in providing a sense of social and moral order in a chaotic world.

> Ideas about separating, purifying, demarcating and punishing transgressions have as their main function to impose system on an inherently untidy experience. It is only by exaggerating the difference between within and without, above and below, male and female, that a semblance of order is created.[36]

As Douglas writes, "nothing is more essentially transmitted by a social process of learning than sexual behaviour and this of course is closely related to morality."[37] Reproductive and sexual norms and taboos produce a "natural" order around which life comes to be organized. This natural order depends on boundaries separating the normal from the ambiguous. Any challenge to these boundaries by anomalous behaviour leads to the mobilization of fear and anxiety. This moral order therefore depends on the marginalization of anomalies and firm social boundaries demarcated by "natural" markers that are rigorously policed: heterosexuality, in contemporary Western society, is associated with the natural, the normal, the clean, the healthy, and the pure; homosexuality, with the dangerous, the impure, the unnatural, the sick, and the abnormal.[38]

Frank Pearce used Douglas's perspective in an analysis of the presentation of gay men in the media. Homosexuals are viewed as anomalies since they violate and defy the natural boundaries of sex and gender behaviour. Homosexuals, according to Pearce:

> Fracture the coherence of the core gender identities thought to be necessarily associated with male and female biological equipment. These men finding other men attractive are anomalies, and "anomalies," as Mary Douglas points out, endanger the natural moral order of this society.[39]

We therefore mobilize anxiety, fear, and hatred. Pearce describes four main strategies whereby the threat to heterosexuality is deflected: ignoring or condemning homosexuality; providing easy definitions such as gender "inversion" to explain it away and reduce ambiguity; using homosexuals as a negative reference point; and labelling us as dangerous, even inciting violence against us.[40]

The Social Organization of Sexual Knowledge

This book proposes a shift of focus in the study of same-gender and different-gender desire and pleasure and sexual regulation: a shift away from homosexuality and lesbianism as a "problem" and toward a historical and social account of the emergence of sexual life, including heterosexuality. The "traditions" of religion, psychology, medicine, criminology, sexology, history, sociology, and anthropology have created the "problem," defining us as sick, deviant, abnormal — even criminal — and defining heterosexuality as "normal." These socially organized forms of knowledge have been crucial to the construction of heterosexual hegemony. In these forms of knowledge production that have also been forms of social power (what Foucault describes as "power/knowledge"[41]), lesbians and gay men have been treated as objects of study to be researched. It has always been homosexuality and lesbianism and not heterosexuality that stands in need of explanation. The "problematization" of homosexuality has been a crucial part of the normalization[42] of heterosexuality. Four examples help clarify this social process.

Anthropology in the eighteenth and nineteenth centuries was engaged in setting sexual and social norms. Classification of the races was a main preoccupation,[43] integral to which was the classification of sexual behaviour. "Savages" came to be defined as more primitive with regard to sexual behaviour than "civilized" peoples, although sometimes the savages were romanticized as acting more "naturally." Anthropologists carried their own cultural values with them, displaying an acute ethnocentric and Eurocentric[44] bias but, at the same time supplying much of the data upon which the work of the sex psychologists and sexologists in the metropolitan countries relied.[45] Anthropology as a profession was very much involved in the organization of colonial, class, racial, gender, and sexual relations.

Perhaps this process can best be seen through an examination of Bronislaw Malinowski's classic study of the Trobriand Islanders. The villagers described their villages from ground view as a number of bumps. Malinowski saw them as a series of concentric circles, describing them from above using a mapping representation. This disparity in descriptions was socially rooted. Malinowski came from a vigorously class-divided society, and he was a member of the academic discipline of anthropology. His account was addressed to a specialized intelligentsia in the metropolitan countries. There was no position within Trobriand culture from which their villages could be seen thus, but Malinowski, located as he was outside and "above" their society, could so describe them. Malinowski's anthropological work embodied the developing social relations of imperialism.[46]

Malinowski's work also embodied a developing heterosexual hegemony. Among the Trobriand Islanders, they did not see different-gender sexual intercourse and reproduction as linked. In one book, Malinowski included homosexuality, masturbation, and fellatio in a section entitled "The Censure of Sexual Aberrations."[47] Despite accounts of widespread same-gender sex in Melanesian societies, he argued that homosexuality was not prevalent and that it was treated with contempt and derision.[48] His work embodied the imposition of sexual norms on indigenous populations. Malinowski saw things from the standpoint of the missionaries, the administrators, and a developing heterosexual hegemony. In the next chapter, I again touch on the links between imperialism and heterosexual hegemony.

The work of nineteenth-century forensic psychiatrists and sex psychologists — who classified and categorized sexualities and sexual practices — also reveals the social relations that their work embodied and helped organize. Dr. Richard Von Krafft-Ebing, the foremost forensic psychiatrist of the last century who addressed sexual pathologies (and the "grand-daddy" of sexology), felt that sexual relations outside heterosexual marriage represented not only a degeneration to an earlier, lower stage of evolution, but that they threatened Western civilization itself. For example:

> Every expression of the sex-drive ... which does not comply with the goals of nature, i.e., procreation, must be declared perverse ... Episodes of moral decline in the life of peoples fall regularly together with times of effeminacy, voluptuousness, and luxury ... Rapidly growing nervousness results in an increase in sensuality and by leading to the dissipation among the masses of people, undermines the pillars of society: morality and purity of family life. If this is undermined through dissipation, adultery and luxury, then the fall of the state is inevitable.[49]

Krafft-Ebing's work expresses not only the standpoint of State agencies, but also middle-class assumptions about the class character of sexual morality.

Mainstream psychiatry and psychology in the twentieth century have generally viewed homosexuality as a symptom of "infantile regression" or some other pathological disorder, and have developed various strategies to cure, regulate, or adjust patients to the heterosexual norm.[50] This has included various forms of aversion therapy, as well as partial lobotomies. Psychiatrists and psychologists rarely treated lesbians and gay men as individuals with our own unique biographies and experiences. Instead we are slotted into clinical and abstract categories of "homosexuality" and produced as "cases." We were already cut out of "normal" social interaction by this diagnosis.[51] Before we even enter a psychiatrist's or a psychologist's office, a homosexual or lesbian "typology" has often already defined us as "deviant," laying out a particular course of "treatment."

Homosexual "deviance" is investigated with the aim of our elimination, containment, or control. Knowledge has been produced so that ruling institutions can formulate legal codes, policing policies, and social policies. According to Magnus Hirschfeld, an early sex psychologist and homosexual-rights reformer, most of the thousand or so works on homosexuality that appeared between 1898 and 1908 were addressed to the legal profession.[52] Many early works by medical and legal experts

> were chiefly concerned with whether the disgusting breed of perverts could be physically identified for the courts, and whether they should be held legally responsible for their acts.[53]

The men and women engaged in same-gender love have thus been labelled "deviants," "perverts," "gender inverts," "gender non-conformists," "sexual psychopaths," "dangerous sex offenders," "promiscuous," guilty of committing "gross indecency," engaging in "anonymous" sex, and have been the subjects of the distinction between "public" and "private" sex.

Official knowledge about homosexuals and lesbians came chiefly from studies of imprisoned or "psychologically disturbed" homosexuals.[54] Much of this work relies on data such as the legal codification of offences, court and police records, and sexological, medical and psychological discourse,[55] and often incorporates features of the power relations of the legal and prison systems and the psychiatric and medical professions. A great deal of official knowledge about homosexuality and lesbianism has been produced so that social agencies can "understand," classify, police, and regulate our sexual lives.

This knowledge has in turn shaped popular cultures and "common-sense" notions of how society is organized, through the mass media, the schools, government policies, the Criminal Code, police action, and the social organization of intended "moral panics"[56] on sexual questions.

During the last part of the nineteenth century, homosexuality was often seen by the scientific disciplines as a form of congenital inversion rooted in biological degeneration or anomaly. These approaches reduced homosexuality to a biological cause. More recently, given the challenge presented by lesbian and gay liberation to psychological theories of homosexuality and lesbianism as a mental illness, there has been a certain return to these types of approaches by some researchers. Initial results of some of this research has been magnified and intensified by mass-media coverage. The research usually starts off by assuming the "normality" of heterosexuality and that it is (usually male) homosexuality that stands in need of explanation. It assumes that there are only two rigidly dichotomous sexualities (heterosexuality and homosexuality), and these are based in biological difference. Men and women who are interested in both men and women undermine the basis of this research.

Ignoring the rich work done on the historical and social construction of sexuality, this research is directed at finding the biological cause or causes of homosexuality. This reduces the complex social and cultural process through which sexuality is formed to biological causes, whether they be located in a different structure in the hypothalamus, or genetic or hormonal elements — there is even one theory suggesting that stress for the mother during pregnancy produces homosexuality in the male fetus.[57] Liberal proponents of this more recent research argue that the establishment of homosexual difference as biological in character will lead to greater social acceptance, as homosexuality will now be "natural" for a minority of the population. This does not address how the acceptance of "race" as biological in character has done nothing to eliminate racism against people of colour. Appeals to "nature" do not get rid of discrimination and oppression. And the response of some to reports that there may be a "gay gene" is to try to eliminate this gene in order to eliminate homosexuality. Again the problem to be explained is "homosexuality," while the "naturalness" of heterosexual hegemony is just accepted.[58]

The resurgence of biological determinist explanations of homosexuality is occurring in the context of a new popularity for biological explanations of human behaviours and differences. This is also related to a resurgence of biological explanations of gender and gender inequality and in some circles of race and racial inequality.[59] For instance, some researchers now suggest that women's math and spatial skills really are biologically inferior to men's. Therefore, the social equality that feminism has demanded is seen to go against "nature."[60] This is part of a broader social organization of a "backlash" to feminism, and not the first time biological explanations have been used to buttress social inequality. "Biology" has long been invoked to justify the social subordination of blacks, women and lesbians, and gay men.

Heterosexist ideas about the naturalness of heterosexuality and the sickness of homosexuality are not simply backward individual ideas; they are organized through the social relations and practices of heterosexual hegemony. This points to one of the problems with the use by gay, lesbian, queer, and other activists of the concept of "homophobia" — the "dread of being in close quarters with homosexuals."[61] This term quite accurately describes the panic some heterosexuals feel when confronted by visible lesbians and gays. It has also been used to explain homosexual oppression in general, however, and as such tends to simply reverse existing psychological definitions of homosexuality as mental illness, turning them back onto heterosexuals who have difficulty dealing with "queers." "Homophobia" does not seriously dispute these psychological definitions; it individualizes and privatizes gay and lesbian oppression and obscures the social relations that organize it. It reduces homophobia to a mental illness, detaching it from its social contexts and reproducing all the problems of psychological definitions.[62] Unfortunately, "homophobia" has also been the main way in which other movements and groups of people beyond the feminist movement have taken up our oppression, and this leads them to misunderstand the roots of our oppression.[63]

"Homophobia" also continues to be used as a major way of accounting for our oppression even in the new forms of queer activism that emerged in the late 1980s and early 1990s. "Queer Nation" groups with their "in your face" politics took "anti-homophobic" politics to their most militant expression. At times it seemed as if militant confrontations with individual homophobes would lead to the ending of our oppression, which has not allowed this queer activism to get at the social roots of queer oppression. "Homophobia" is continued as a central concept even in much of the new "queer theory" that emerged in the late 1980s and early 1990s in the U.S. In Eve Kosofsky Sedgwick's influential book *The Epistemology of the Closet*, for instance, her taking up of an antihomophobic position has allowed her to separate sexual oppression from gender oppression, and has allowed her to focus on literary and cultural re-readings of texts to discern homophobic assumptions.[64] Such a focus on homophobia often operates to obscure the social relations and practices that shape lesbian and gay oppression.

I therefore prefer to use the term "heterosexism," relating the practices of heterosexual hegemony to institutional and social settings and to sex and gender relations without reducing gay and lesbian oppression to an "effect" of gender. In this context, homophobia can be seen as a particularly virulent personal response organized by heterosexist discourse and practice.

Until recently, heterosexuals rarely encountered visible gays, lesbians, or bisexuals. Most images were those projected by the mass media and those circulating in popular cultures, which generally came from psychology, sexology, the churches, and the courts and police. Dorothy E. Smith describes the "ideological circle" through which the world is interpreted by the media and other agencies;[65] this is one of the ways heterosexual hegemony operates. The world is interpreted through the schemas of "expert sources" (police, policy analysts, government bureaucrats) and hegemonic cultural narratives to confirm the dominant interpretation of same-gender sexuality. "Scientific" theories of homosexual deviance, criminality, or sickness thereby enter public discussion.

Shifting Standpoints

In suggesting that the basis of sexual inquiry be reoriented, I draw upon what can be called a standpoint approach, which, as formulated by Dorothy E. Smith, calls for a change in vantage point from that of hegemonic ruling relations to that of women and other oppressed groups.[66] Ruling relations and regimes are the agencies involved in the management of contemporary capitalist patriarchal societies. Ruling relations are broader than those of State agencies, and include the mass media, various professional groups, and the forms of bureaucracy that have emerged over the last century.[67]

In "A Sociology for Women," Smith analyzes how ruling relations produce knowledge from the standpoint of a male-dominated ruling class.[68] A sociology *for* women entails a reorientation of inquiry starting from the social experiences of individual women or groups of women. Smith's analysis provides insights into how ruling knowledge is produced and how it rules — bringing into view the social relations through which women are subordinated.

> As we explored the world from this place in it, we became aware that this rupture in experience, and between experience and the social forms of its expression, was located in a relation of power between women and men, in which men dominated over women.[69]

Inquiry, then, begins with questions about everyday experiences and the social practices we engage in on a day-to-day basis. It proceeds to render the everyday world "problematic" by investigating the social relations in which women's experiences (or the experiences of other groups) are located.[70] For this perspective, the notion of social relation is key, being the process by which our own activities participate in but are also shaped, constrained, and regulated by broader social forces. The notion of a social relation links together social practices in different local sites in a combined and inter-linked social process. While we participate in producing these social relations, we also, as individuals and as groups, tend to lose control over them, and they come to stand over and against our everyday lives. While social relations develop historically, in contemporary societies, they render the world in which we live natural and ahistorical. This provides a social basis for the ideologies and discourses of naturalism that we find around us.

The social world is, however, composed of people's own activities articulated through these social relations. We daily engage in practices that produce relations of class, gender, race and sexuality. Social "structures" cannot be seen as separate from human activity; they are organized by, and, at the same time, organize social interaction. Social relations are actual practices, not merely concepts or structures. They are produced by people but they are not constituted by individual actors alone, as they are sequences of actions and relationships that no single individual can complete.

The social relations that organize women's experiences in this society are capitalist, patriarchal, racist, and heterosexist. An example from the work of Marx may help clarify this: a commodity (a product made to be exchanged) as a social object is realized — made socially real as a commodity — only through exchange in a market. If the commodity is not exchanged, its value cannot be realized. If it does not enter into a series of social relationships between different individuals composing a social relation, it cannot be realized as a commodity. As Marx also argued, through this process of exchange the commodity comes to appear as though it has intrinsic value as a thing. Exchange therefore comes to be seen as a relation between different commodities (between things) rather than a social relationship between producers, buyers, and sellers. This is what Marx called the fetishism of commodities,[71] and can also be seen as a form of reification (or "thingification").

Similarly, although differently, women's experiences are organized through a series of social practices that define and regulate sex and gender and in which women are themselves active. This web of relations shapes gender identifications, gender dichotomies, sexualities, and patriarchal social organization.[72]

Making the everyday world problematic moves analysis from "experience" itself to the specific social relations that organize it. This helps to make people's social practices visible. There is no pure unmediated "telling of experience," as this is always affected by social discourse, but starting with the experiences of the oppressed and marginalized and then making it problematic locates our investigation in a very different place, at least partially outside of or in rupture with ruling regimes and discourse. This allows us to see the workings of ruling relations from the standpoint of the oppressed. As Smith notes:

> It is not individual social behaviour which is our interest but the social determinations of our everyday experience. The object of inquiry is the historical processes and development of social relations which organize, shape and determine our directly experienced worlds.[73]

In this book I apply this method of inquiry to the historical and social situations of lesbians and gay men. A history and sociology for lesbians and gay men involves both a critique of official knowledge (which I begin in this chapter) and a reorientation of inquiry to begin from the experiences of those who have engaged in same-gender sex and others who have been oppressed by ruling sexual regulation (which I begin in the historical sections). The purpose is not to interrogate the experiences of lesbians and gay men but instead to learn from their experiences about the social organization of heterosexual hegemony and oppressive sexual regulation so that these ruling practices can be interrogated and transformed.[74]

The contemporary lesbian and gay experience of a rupture between our lives as "deviants" or outsiders and the heterosexual norm serves as the beginning of inquiry. This rupture is lived differently by people on the basis of class, race, and gender. How this tension has come about is one of the key questions to be explored. By making our everyday experiences problematic and locating them in emerging social relations, we can reveal aspects of our oppression and of heterosexual hegemony that are not visible from the vantage point of ruling relations. This process exposes not only the work of the agencies who have labelled us "perverts" and "criminals," but also the activities of those engaged in same-gender sex ourselves. We have been able to construct a certain "naturalness" and "normalness" for ourselves in opposition to heterosexual hegemony. If we start from here — the experiences of lesbians, gays, and others who engage in queer sex of the ruptures we feel between hegemonic heterosexuality and the actualities of our lives — then the problem is no longer homosexuality, but rather heterosexual hegemony and sexual rule more generally.

From this socially and historically grounded standpoint, the absolute distinction between homosexuality and heterosexuality is rooted in the work of the ruling regime and relations. This distinction is not as clearly expressed in our individual erotic lives, however. The actual relationship between social categories, identity construction and formation, and sexual activity is not as clear-cut as official discourse contends.

Sexual preferences and "identities" are not fixed in stone. They develop unevenly, are often contradictory, and are potentially fluid. Kinsey's statistics suggested that a majority of men involved in reported homosexual acts did not see their experiences as defining them as homosexual.[75] Many are able to engage in occasional erotic delights with males while maintaining a heterosexual and masculine gender "identity." Prison inmates and hustlers often managed their identities so that they were not tainted by the stigma of homosexuality. For instance, in prison, the "masculine" man who plays the "active" role in anal intercourse but never plays the "passive" position in anal intercourse and who gets his penis fellated but never sucks another penis, may be able to escape the label of "queer" and preserve his "heterosexual" identity. Some hustlers manage their identities by claiming they have sex only for the money, or that they engage only in acts that don't define them as homosexual. John Rechy in *City of Night* quotes Pete, a hustler:

> Whatever a guy does with other guys, if he does it for money that don't make him queer. You're still straight. It's when you start doing it for free, with other young guys, that you start growing wings.[76]

George Chauncey, in an illuminating historical analysis, shows us that, in the early twentieth century in the U.S. among working class and other cultures, there was often a distinction made between "queer" men who were associated with effeminacy and full-time participation in same-gender sexual activities and those men who occasionally would allow these "queers" to have sex with them. This latter group of men would not be tainted with "queerness."[77] And in the Canadian Navy in the 1950s, some doctors felt that only "effeminate" men were real homosexuals while men who were more "masculine" and only occasionally engaged in sex with other men when women were not available were basically "normal" (see chapter 7). Men who are married and have children may feel that their sexual adventures in tea rooms (washrooms), steam baths, or parks do not define them as homosexual.[78]

Ruling discourse rigorously associates sexual acts with gender and sexual identity (or else views homosexual activity as merely a brief "phase" one is passing through). In real life, however, it is not that neat. A sexual act may not be immediately associated with a particular sexuality or sexual identity. There is also the experience of bisexuality that undermines the dominant sexual dichotomy and that allows some people to combine same and different gender erotic desires. While bisexuality is not the only "natural" sexuality, as some bisexual liberationists argue, given it is as socially constructed as other sexualities, it does destabilize the heterosexual/homosexual polarity in a powerful way.[79]

At the same time, the historical and social accounts presented in this book demonstrate that contemporary lesbian and gay experiences are very real social and experiential realities that cannot be dismissed as simply the imposition of ruling sexual classifications. Lesbians and gay men have participated in the creation of our own cultures and networks.

Ruling concepts cannot simply be stretched to cover our experiences. We must step outside ruling discourses — as we must as women, people of colour, and other oppressed groups — if we are to create knowledge to help us in our struggles.[80]

This perspective starts from our own experiences and practices.[81] We must become the subjects of our work rather than its objects. We must move beyond this starting point, however, to view everyday life as problematic; to see the struggles between ruling institutions and lesbians and gays over the meanings, images, and definitions of sexual regulation. We must move beyond our immediate experiences and the assumed "naturalness" of our existence by uncovering the social relations in which homosexuality and heterosexuality have emerged historically.

Hegemony, State Formation, and Cultural Revolution

My analysis also draws upon a number of recent developments within Marxism and historical materialist approaches.[82] Recent historical and sociological explorations of capitalist or bourgeois State formation have illuminated how crucial to the formation of the contemporary State has been what can be called a "bourgeois cultural revolution."[83]

Building on earlier State forms, the capitalist class made itself the ruling class and forged contemporary State relations by attempting to remake society in its own image. Crucial to this process was the creation of approved or respectable social identities, which necessarily meant the denial of alternatives. State formation is therefore always an active process, always contested and resisted, and riveted with contradictions. Heterosexual hegemony, as a part of this process, was constructed at the expense of other social and sexual possibilities, such as emerging homosexual and lesbian cultures. Heterosexuality was established as "normal." Homosexuality and lesbianism were disadvantaged as perverted, sick, and criminal.[84]

This approach stresses the importance to capitalist and patriarchal rule of the cultural and moral regulation of social identities and practices. The oppressive regulation of social life establishes some forms of activity as acceptable, respectable, responsible, normal and natural; some ways of life are empowered, others are devalued. This approach refuses to reduce capitalism to its economic dimensions alone. State formation is seen as central to capitalist development. Class relations include struggles over cultural norms, social identities and sexualities. Non-economic relations are thereby crucial to class relations.[85] Within historical materialism using these insights, the relationship of class, State formation, and sexual rule can be explored. This perspective on State formation will be particularly useful when we examine the making of the Canadian State and its relation to English and U.S. State formation.

A crucial aspect of this State formation and cultural revolution has been the establishment of social, cultural and political forms of hegemony. "Hegemony," as I use the term, derives from the writings of the Italian Marxist Antonio Gramsci in the 1920s and 1930s.[86] Hegemony unites the process of coercion and consent, viewing the two as often taking place through the same social practices. Hegemony occurs through the normalization or naturalization of existing relations and is achieved when one class can exert social authority and leadership over others. This includes the power to

> frame alternatives and contain communities, to win and shape consent so
> that the granting of legitimacy to the dominant classes appears not only
> "spontaneous" but natural and "normal."[87]

Hegemony is, however, not simply imposed by State agencies and the ruling class. It must be continually reestablished. It is therefore never total or exclusive.

> [Hegemony] is not self-securing, it is constructed, sustained, reconstructed,
> by particular agents and agencies, in part by violence.[88]

When successfully established, hegemony shapes, redefines, and incorporates the needs and concerns of the subordinated groups so that they conform to the interests of ruling groups.[89]

The development, transformation, and struggle over cultural and social definitions, boundaries, acceptable knowledge, identities, and norms is a key terrain for the continuous organization and reorganization of hegemonic relations:

> The dominant culture represents itself as *the* culture. It tries to define and contain all other cultures within its most inclusive range. Its views of the world, unless challenged, will stand as the most natural, all-embracing culture.[90]

Hegemonic approaches therefore allow for a combination in historical explorations of people as active participants in the making of their worlds with the social constraints that limit their activities. Unfortunately, until recently, most attempts to use hegemony to explore the process of ruling have confined it to a rather narrow economic realm, or to narrow, economically defined notions of class relations, and have remained male, white and heterosexually defined.[91]

I use a hegemonic approach to examine Canadian struggles over sexual definitions and regulations. Hegemony must therefore be freed from its narrower meanings and made relevant to sexual and other political movements so that the organization of racial, patriarchal, and heterosexual hegemonies can be explored and challenged. While these forms of hegemony have their own features, they are part of a larger social and historical organization of class and State rule.

Hegemonic approaches can be used to explore lesbian and gay oppression and resistance. Heterosexual hegemony came about with the emergence of distinct heterosexual and homosexual/lesbian identities and cultures over the last two centuries. Its bases are the relations of ruling class morality, sex and gender, the gender division of labour, family and kinship relations, State policies, and sexual policing, and it relies not only on consent, legitimation, and "common sense," but also on moments of denial, silencing, and coercion. Heterosexuality is "freely compelled" for many in this society. Coercive laws, police practices, "queer-bashing," and limited social options all attempt to make heterosexuality compulsory (or compulsive).[92] At the same time, there is an active social construction of "consent" to heterosexual desire through strategies of the naturalization and normalization of heterosexuality and the construction of heterosexual cultures.

Heterosexual hegemony is produced on many fronts — from family relations that often marginalize and sometimes exclude gays and lesbians,[93] to the violence we face on city streets, to State policies, to the medical profession, to sociology, sexology, and psychiatry, to the church, the school system, and the media. These forms of sexual regulation (which do not develop in a linear fashion)[94] interact with the social relations we live to produce heterosexist "common sense." There exist also conflicts between and within various agencies over definitions of homosexuality and jurisdictional disputes over who can best deal with the sexual deviant.

The entry of heterosexual hegemony into public "common-sense" involves many variants of heterosexist discourse, each of which merits its own analysis (which I explore in later chapters). These include homosexuality as a sin (in religious discourse); as unnatural (in both religious and secular discourse); as an illness (in medicine and psychiatry and, in a new sense, with the current AIDS crisis); as a congenital disorder or inversion (in sex psychology and sexology); as deviance (in some sociological theory); homosexuals as child molesters, seducers, and corruptors (in certain sexological studies, the law, and the media); as a symptom of social or national degeneration (in Social Darwinist and eugenic discourse); homosexuals as communists, "pinkos," and a national security risk because of the potential for blackmail (rooted in McCarthyism, military organization, the Cold War and 1950s/1960s security regime practices); as tolerated only when practised between consenting adults in "private" (the Wolfenden strategy of privatization); and as a criminal offence or a social menace (in police campaigns, "moral panics" and the media).

How these various forms of heterosexism interact, and how they are based in social practices and relations, is a question for social and historical investigation. It is sufficient to note here that all these ideas can be found in contemporary discourse. There is a continuing resiliency for anti-gay/anti-lesbian discourses formed in previous historical periods that can still be remobilized against us. In certain periods, some regulatory strategies and discourses achieve a degree of cogency for maintaining and reconstructing heterosexual hegemony.[95] Given the various social processes at play, heterosexual common sense clearly suffers from many internal contradictions.

My historical investigation involves an analysis of the social relations that have organized heterosexual hegemony. Heterosexual hegemony and contemporary lesbian and gay cultures are two sides of the same relational social process. Heterosexual hegemony necessarily involves lesbian and gay subordination. As Rachel Harrison and Frank Mort note:

> The "deviant" subject is not absent from the discourse but she/he is only permitted to speak from a subordinate position: as "patient," as "pervert," etc.[96]

Heterosexual hegemony, and oppressive sexual regulation more generally, are an integral aspect of the organization of class, State, gender, and race relations. Let us now turn to look at how this has historically come about, first in England and the United States, and then in Canada.

Notes

1. This can be a danger in "queer" and much discourse-driven theory.
2. See Dorothy E. Smith, *The Everyday World as Problematic* (Toronto: University of Toronto Press, 1987), pp. 128-135; 223-224.
3. See Michel Foucault, *The History of Sexuality.* V. 1, *An Introduction* (New York: Vintage, 1980), pp. 116-127.
4. See my unpublished paper "'Queer Theory' versus Heterosexual Hegemony: Towards a His-

torical Materialism for Gay Men and Lesbians" presented at the "Queer Sites" lesbian and gay studies conference, Toronto, May 14, 1993.

5. See Dorothy E. Smith, "Feminist Reflections on Political Economy" in *Studies in Political Economy*, No. 30, Autumn 1989, pp. 37-59, and Lorna Weir, "Socialist Feminism and the Politics of Sexuality" in Heather Jon Maroney and Meg Luxton, eds., *Feminism and Political Economy* (Toronto: Methuen, 1987), pp. 69-83.

6. See Andrew Parker, "Unthinking Sex: Marx, Engels and the Scene of Writing" in Michael Warner, ed., *Fear of a Queer Planet: Queer Politics and Social Theory* (Minneapolis: University of Minnesota Press, 1993), pp. 19-41. Unfortunately, Parker does not focus on how lesbians and gay men can use the method of historical materialism, and also seems unable to view sex and sexuality as forms of human practice/production.

7. Fetishism "is a definite social relation between men (sic) that assumes, in their eyes, the fantastic form of a relationship between things." Karl Marx, *Capital: A Critique of Political Economy*, V. 1 (New York: International Publishers, 1967), p. 72.

8. See Sayer, *Marx's Method* (Sussex and New Jersey: Harvester/Humanities, 1983) pp. 8-9.

9. Dorothy E. Smith, *The Conceptual Practices of Power* (Toronto: University of Toronto Press, 1990), pp. 31-57; Dorothy E. Smith, *Texts, Facts and Femininity* (London and New York: Routledge, 1990), pp. 86-119.

10. See D.E. Smith, *The Conceptual Practices of Power, op. cit.*, pp. 31-57; Himani Bannerji, "Writing 'India,' Doing Ideology" in *Left History*, V. 2, No. 2, Fall 1994, pp. 5-17.

11. On this type of approach to Marxist method, see, among others, Derek Sayer in *Marx's Method* (Sussex and New Jersey: Harvester/Humanities, 1983) and his *The Violence of Abstraction* (Oxford and New York: Basil Blackwell, 1987); Roslyn Wallach Bologh, *Dialectical Phenomenology: Marx's Method* (London: Routledge and Kegan Paul, 1979); I.I. Rubin, for his emphasis on social forms and social relations in his *Essays on Marx's Theory of Value* (Montréal: Black Rose Books, 1982); Frigga Haug's comments on Marxism, especially in her *Beyond Female Masochism: Memory-Work and Politics* (London, New York: Verso, 1992); and the work of Dorothy E. Smith.

12. Jeffrey Weeks, *Sexuality and Its Discontents* (London, Melbourne and Henley: Routledge and Kegan Paul, 1985), pp. 5-10, and Roslyn Wallach Bologh, *Dialectical Phenomenology: Marx's Method* (Boston, London and Henley: Routledge and Kegan Paul, 1979), p. 241. My use of "historical present" differs from that of Weeks in that my usage is not that of a history of relatively ungrounded discourses of sexuality, but rather a history of official discourses as actively organizing practices and relations that to some extent still participate in the organizing of the present. My use of historical data is also non-ideological in character in always being grounded in forms of social life. I use the notion of "historical present" to focus on how sexual regulations were socially put in place and not to deny differences in time, place and historical context.

13. This can be seen as an attempt to use Dorothy E. Smith's sociological perspective of starting from people's social experiences to develop a critical and grounded analysis of social organization in a more historical context. See Dorothy E. Smith, *The Everyday World as Problematic: A Feminist Sociology, op. cit.*; *The Conceptual Practices of Power: A Feminist Sociology of Knowledge* (Toronto: University of Toronto Press, 1990); and *Texts, Facts and Femininity: Exploring the Relations of Ruling* (London and New York: Routledge, 1990) and the other references to her work later in this chapter. Also see my Ph.D. thesis, "Official Discourse as Sexual Regulation" and my "The Textual Practices of Sexual Rule: Sexual Policing and Gay Men" in Marie Campbell and Ann Manicom, eds., *Knowledge, Experience and Ruling Relations: Studies in the Social Organization of Knowledge* (Toronto: University of Toronto Press, 1995), pp. 80-95.

14. Dorothy E. Smith, "Women, Class and Family" in *Socialist Register 1983* (London: The Merlin Press, 1983), p. 7.

15. There has been some important progress on these fronts. See: George Smith, "Policing the Gay Community: An Inquiry Into Textually-Mediated Social Relations" in *International Journal of the Sociology of Law*, V. 16, 1988, pp. 163-183, and his "Political Activist as Ethnographer" in

Social Problems, V. 37, No. 4, pp. 629-648; Madiha Didi Khayatt, *Lesbian Teachers, an Invisible Presence* (Albany: State University of New York Press, 1992) and her "Compulsory Heterosexuality: Schools and Lesbian Students" in Marie Campbell and Ann Manicom, eds., *Knowledge, Experience and Ruling Relations: Studies in the Social Organization of Knowledge* (Toronto: University of Toronto Press, 1995); Carol-Anne O'Brien and Lorna Weir, "Lesbians and Gay Men Inside and Outside Families" in Nancy Mandell and Anne Duffy, eds., *Canadian Families: Diversity, Conflict and Change* (Toronto: Harcourt Brace Canada, 1995); Carol-Anne O'Brien, "The Social Organization of the Treatment of Lesbian, Gay and Bisexual Youth in Group Homes and Youth Shelters" in *Canadian Review of Social Policies*, No. 34, Winter 1994, pp. 37-57; and Carol-Anne O'Brien, Robb Travers and Laurie Bell, "No Safe Bed: Lesbian, Gay and Bisexual Youth in Residential Services" (Toronto: Central Toronto Youth Services, 1993).

16. Robert A. Padgug, "Sexual Matters: On Conceptualizing Sexuality in History" in *Radical History Review*, No. 20, Spring/Summer, 1979, p. 9. Also in other collections including *Passion and Power* and *Hidden from History*.

17. It is also to be remembered that all biological knowledge, like all other forms of knowledge, is socially constructed. See Suzanne J. Kessler and Wendy McKenna, *Gender: An Ethnomethodological Approach* (Chicago and London: The University of Chicago Press, 1978), especially pp.42-80 and Donna Haraway, *Simians, Cyborgs, and Women* (New York: Routledge, 1991), especially pp. 7-68, among others.

18. This perspective draws some of its insights from Gayle Rubin's "The Traffic in Women" in Rayna R. Reiter, ed., *Toward an Anthropology of Women* (New York: Monthly Review Press, 1975), and her notion of a "sex/gender" system. I do not use sex/gender system because it tends to conflate questions of sexuality, and gender and also because it suggests that sex/gender relations are some sort of system separate from other social relations rather than an integral aspect of them. It also suggests that this system has been static throughout history rather than historically transformed. In my view, sex and gender relations vary historically and always exist in articulation with class, race, and other social relations. They are therefore part of class relations in a broad sense. Rubin herself has now rejected her earlier approach. In "Thinking Sex: Notes for a Radical Theory of the Politics of Sexuality" in Vance. ed., *Pleasure and Danger: Exploring Female Sexuality* (Boston and London: Routledge and Kegan Paul, 1984), pp. 307-309, she rejects this category, but in a pre-feminist regression asserts that sex and gender are two completely autonomous and separate systems. This later position of Rubin's continues to shape recent "queer theory," including the influential work of Eve Kosofsky Sedgwick who, in her *The Epistemology of the Closet* (Berkeley and Los Angeles: University of California Press, 1990), uses Rubin's later work to argue for the need to separate gender and sexual analysis

19. On "sexual scripts," see the work of symbolic interactionists, such as J.H. Gagnon and William Simon, *Sexual Conduct* (Chicago: Aldine, 1973) and Kenneth Plummer, *Sexual Stigma* (London: Routledge and Kegan Paul, 1975).

20. Padgug, *op. cit.*

21. As Marx states: "all epochs of production have certain common traits, common characteristics. Production in general is an abstraction, but a rational abstraction insofar as it really brings out and fixes the common element ... Still this general category, this common element sifted out by comparison, is itself segmented many times over and splits into different determinations. Some determinations belong to all epochs, some only to a few." Karl Marx, *Grundrisse* (Harmondsworth: Penguin, 1973), p.85.

22. See Derek Sayer, *op. cit.*, for this type of view in relation to production. Also see Roslyn Wallach Bologh, *Dialectical Phenomenology: Marx's Method, op. cit.*

23. See K.J. Dover, *Greek Homosexuality* (New York: Vintage, 1980); Michel Foucault, *The Use of Pleasure*. V. 2, *History of Sexuality* (New York: Pantheon, 1985); David Halperin, *One Hundred Years of Homosexuality* (New York and London: Routledge, 1990); Ford and Beach, *Patterns of Sexual Behavior* (New York: Harper Colophon, 1972), p. 132; Vern Bullough, *Sexual Variance in Society and History* (Chicago and London: The University of Chicago Press, 1976), pp. 32-34.

24. On the Sambia see sources cited in Joseph Harry, *Gay Children Grown Up: Gender Culture and Gender Deviance* (New York: Praeger, 1982), p. 3.

25. See S.J. Kessler and W. McKenna, *Gender: An Ethnomethodological Approach, op. cit.* Despite its date of publication, this is still one of the best books on the social making of gender. In many ways, it provides a much better socially grounded account of gender than that which is common in poststructuralist or postmodernist theory, including within queer theory. Judith Butler's *Gender Trouble, Feminism and the Subversion of Identity* (New York and London: Routledge, 1990) is often cited within queer theory regarding gender. Despite Butler's use of the term "performativity," she does not focus on gender as actual social performance or accomplishment, but instead on the performative effects of discourse. I would argue quite strongly that gender is not simply a discursive effect.

26. For a critique of these biological reductionist approaches, see Nelly Oudshoorn, *Beyond the Natural Body: An Archeology of Sex Hormones* (London and New York: Routledge, 1994), and Gail Vines, *Raging Hormones: Do They Rule Our Lives?* (Berkeley and Los Angeles: University of California Press, 1994).

27. On the "natural attitude" toward gender, see Harold Garfinkel, *Studies in Ethnomethodology* (Englewood Cliffs, NJ: Prentice-Hall, 1967) and Kessler and McKenna, *Gender: An Ethnomethodological Approach, op. cit.*

28. On collecting categories and devices that bring together a range of different activities, practices, or groups under common administrative classifications so they can be dealt with by ruling agencies, see Philip Corrigan, "On Moral Regulation" in *Sociological Review,* V. 29, 1981, pp. 313-316.

29. See the very interesting account developed by the Red Collective, who describe the "givenness" of our sexuality and feelings that prevents analysis and change. *The Politics of Sexuality in Capitalism* (London: Red Collective and Publications Distributors Cooperative, 1978).

30. Ellen Ross and Rayna Rapp, "Sex and Society: A Research Note from Social History and Anthropology" in *Comparative Studies in Society and History, V. 23* (1981), p. 71; also in Snitow, *et al., Powers of Desire* (New York: Monthly Review, 1983).

31. On commodity fetishism see Marx, *Capital, V. 1* (New York: International, 1975), pp. 71-83.

32. J.H. Gagnon and William Simon, *Sexual Conduct* (Chicago: Aldine, 1973).

33. *Ibid.*, p. 26.

34. *Ibid.*, p. 5.

35. See Kenneth Plummer, *Sexual Stigma* (London: Routledge and Kegan Paul, 1975). Plummer applies a social interactionist perspective to gay men. However, his perspective is severely limited because it is based on an isolated individual abstracted from social relations. He thereby neglects the questions of cultural and historical investigation that are necessary to explore these relations. To further clarify these points, a historically grounded social interactionist account that is able to investigate how sexuality is organized through broader social relations would be necessary.

36. Mary Douglas, *Purity and Danger* (London: Routledge and Kegan Paul, 1979), p. 4.

37. Mary Douglas, *Natural Symbols* (New York: Penguin, 1973), p.93.

38. For some similar analysis, see Gayle Rubin's "Thinking Sex: Notes for Radical Theory of the Politics of Sexuality" in Carole S. Vance, ed., *Pleasure and Danger: Exploring Female Sexuality* (Boston, London: Routledge and Kegan Paul, 1984), pp. 280-283.

39. Frank Pearce, "How To Be Immoral and Ill, Pathetic and Dangerous, All at the Same Time: Mass Media and the Homosexual" in Cohen and Young, eds., *The Manufacture of News: Deviance, Social Problems and the Mass Media* (London: Constable, 1973), pp. 284-301.

40. *Ibid.*, pp. 287-288.

41. Unfortunately, valuable insights in Foucault's work, such as "power/knowledge," are limited by his lack of attention to social standpoint and the deletion of active subjects from his discourse analysis. Foucaultian-derived notions of "power/knowledge" often tend to be relatively ungrounded from the social practices that produce them. Sometimes "power/

knowledge" almost seems to be self-generating and not produced through social practices. For some useful critical analysis of this, see Dorothy E. Smith, "The Social Organization of Textual Reality" in *The Conceptual Practices of Power, op. cit.,* pp. 70, 79-80.

42. On normalization as a strategy of power, see Michel Foucault, *Discipline and Punish* (New York: Vintage, 1995).

43. George L. Mosse, *Toward the Final Solution: A History of European Racism* (New York: Harper Colophen, 1978), pp. 16-17 and his *Nationalism and Sexuality* (New York: Howard Fertig, 1985).

44. On Eurocentrism see Samir Amin, *Eurocentrism* (New York: Monthly Review Press, 1989) and Edward W. Said, *Orientalism* (New York: Vintage, 1979).

45. Jeffrey Weeks, "Discourse, Desire and Sexual Deviance" in Plummer, ed., *The Making of the Modern Homosexual* (London, Hutchinson, 1981), p. 77.

46. This point comes from a lecture by Dorothy E. Smith in the Social Organization of Knowledge course, Sociology Dept., Ontario Institute for Studies in Education, Fall 1980.

47. Bronislaw Malinowski, *The Sexual Life of Savages in North-Western Melanesia: An Ethnographic Account of Courtship, Marriage, and Family Life Among the Natives of the Trobriand Islands, British New Guinea* (London: Routledge and Kegan Paul, 1968), pp. 395-402.

48. See Randolph Trumbach, "London's Sodomites: Homosexual Behaviour and Western Culture in the Eighteenth Century" in *Journal of Social History*, V. 2, No. 1 Fall 1977, note 11, p. 26.

49. Isabel J. Hull, "The Bourgeoisie and Its Discontents: Reflections on Nationalism and Respectability" in *Journal of Contemporary History*, V. 17, No. 2, April 1982, p. 258. Also see Krafft-Ebing, *Psychopathia Sexualis* (New York: C.P. Putnam's Sons, 1965), and Lorna Weir, "Studies in the Medicalization of Sexual Danger," Ph.D. thesis, Dept. of Social and Political Thought, York University, Toronto, 1986, chapter on sex psychology.

50. Freud's psychoanalytical work was simultaneously a recognition of how sexual desire was organized in a particular class, patriarchal, racial and historical setting, and a universalization of this experience, which made it ahistorical, thereby articulating new oppressive regulations of erotic life. Freud's work has been transformed and integrated into the strategies of heterosexual hegemony and sexual rule. While there is much to be learned from Freud's work, Freudian psychoanalysis has been incorporated into the present practices that define sex and normalize only a particular form of male-dominated heterosexuality. Also see Jennifer Terry's "Theorizing Deviant Historiography" in *differences*, V. 3, No. 2, Summer 1991, pp. 55-74. For one lesbian's struggle with the psychiatric system, see Persimmon Blackbridge and Sheila Gilhooly, *Still Sane* (Vancouver: Press Gang, 1985). Also see "Mad, Angry, Gay and Proud: A Lesbian and Gay Supplement" in *Phoenix Rising*, V. 8, No. 3/4, July 1990.

51. On "cutting out" operations, see Dorothy E. Smith's "K Is Mentally Ill" in her *Texts, Facts, and Femininity: Exploring the Relations of Ruling* (London and New York: Routledge, 1990), pp. 12-51.

52. Lon G. Nungessar, *Homosexual Acts, Actors and Identities* (New York: Praegar, 1983), p. 55.

53. Arno Karlen, *Sexuality and Homosexuality* (New York: W.W. Norton, 1971), p. 185.

54. Diane Richardson, "Theoretical Perspectives on Homosexuality" in John Hart and Diane Richardson, eds., *The Theory and Practice of Homosexuality* (London: Routledge and Kegan Paul, 1981), p. 34. The major exceptions were the Kinsey Studies and the psychological work of Evelyn Hooker, which was directed at uprooting the construct that gay men were mentally ill.

55. See George Smith's "Overturning State's Evidence: From Social Constructionism to Historical Materialism," unpublished paper given at the "Sex and the State Lesbian/Gay History Conference" in Toronto, July 1985; "Policing the Gay Community: An Inquiry into Textually-Mediated Social Relations" in *International Journal of the Sociology of Law*, 1988, 16, pp. 163-183; and his "Political Activist as Ethnographer" in *Social Problems*, V. 37, No. 4, Nov. 1990, pp. 629-648.

56. "Moral Panics" are defined by Stan Cohen:

A condition, episode, person or group of persons emerges to become defined as a threat to societal values and interests; its nature is presented in a stylized and stereotyped fashion by the mass media; the moral barricades are manned by editors, bishops, and politicians and other right-thinking people; socially accredited experts pronounce their diagnoses and solutions; ways of coping are evolved, or (more often) resorted to; the condition then disappears, submerges or deteriorates ... Sometimes the panic is passed over and forgotten, but at other times it has more serious and long-term repercussions and it might produce changes in legal and social policy or even in the way in which societies conceive themselves.

Stan Cohen, *Folk Devils and Moral Panics* (London: MacGibbon and Kee, 1972), p. 9. Unfortunately, "moral panic" tends to get so overused in the literature that it almost seems to be self-generating. I try to specifically locate and ground the notion of moral panic in social and institutional relations and practices actively constructed between the media, the police, the courts, "citizen's groups," professional experts, and State agencies. These relations combine in different ways in different "panics." They are an active process of social organization. I do not see "moral panics" as an explanation of a social process, rather as pointing toward an investigation of social relations.

57. The theory that stress during pregnancy can lead to homosexuality is put forward in "Brain Sex," which was shown on *Witness*, CBC TV, 1992. Also see Simon LeVay, *The Sexual Brain* (Cambridge, Massachusetts: The MIT Press, 1994). For more critical commentary, see Kay Diaz, "Are Gay Men Born That Way?" in *Z Magazine*, V. 5, No. 12, Dec. 1992, pp. 42-46; Gail Vines, *Raging Hormones: Do They Rule Our Lives?* (Berkeley, Los Angeles: University of California Press, 1993), especially pp. 85-123; Sarah Schulman, "Biological Determinism, Uncontrollable Instincts — 'He's gotta have it'" in *Rouge*, No. 20, 1995, pp. 20-21; and also see Gary Kinsman, "Not in Our Genes: Against Biological and Genetic Determinism, *"Sociologists' Lesbian and Gay Caucus Newsletter*, Issue No. 76, Fall 1993 Newsletter, pp. 4-6.
58. Also see Gary Kinsman, "Queerness Is Not in Our Genes: Against Biological Determinism - For Social Liberation," *Border/Lines*, No. 33, 1994, pp. 27-30.
59. See Richard J. Herrnstein and Charles Murray, *The Bell Curve: Intelligence and Class Structure in American Life* (New York: Free Press, 1994) and the controversies surrounding it. See Steven Fraser, *The Bell Curve Wars* (New York: Basic Books, 1995).
60. See "Brain Sex," *op.cit.*
61. George Weinberg, *Society and the Healthy Homosexual* (New York: Anchor Books, 1973).
62. See Kenneth Plummer, "Homosexual Problems: Some Research Problems in the Labelling Perspective of Homosexuality" in Plummer, ed., *The Making of the Modern Homosexual* (London: Hutchinson, 1981), pp. 53-75.
63. See Gary Kinsman, "'Inverts,' 'Psychopaths,' and 'Normal' Men: Historical Sociological Perspectives on Gay and Heterosexual Masculinities" in Tony Haddad, ed., *Men and Masculinities: A Critical Anthology* (Toronto: Canadian Scholars' Press, 1993), pp. 7-8.
64. Sedgwick, *Epistemology of the Closet, op. cit.*
65. See Dorothy E. Smith, "No One Commits Suicide: Textual Analysis of Ideological Practices" (particularly the diagram on p. 14), unpublished paper, Feb. 1980. Also see Smith's "The Social Construction of Documentary Reality" in *Sociological Inquiry*, 44:4, 1974, pp. 257-268. Revised versions of these articles appear in *The Conceptual Practices of Power, op. cit.*
66. This is not the same as what is referred to as feminist-standpoint theory, which implies that women have a common standpoint and perspective. Instead, Dorothy E. Smith's work argues for a shift in where we begin our inquiry to take up a particular social standpoint in exploring social relations. Standpoint is then a place from which to explore social relations and practice. The standpoints of oppressed groups allow us to see aspects of ruling relations not visible from within ruling institutions.

67. Dorothy E. Smith, "Women, Class and Family," *op. cit.*, p. 12.

68. Dorothy E. Smith, "A Sociology for Women" in Sherman and Back, eds., *The Prism of Sex: Essays in the Sociology of Knowledge* (Madison: University of Wisconsin Press, 1979), p. 135-187. A revised version of this article appears in *The Everyday World as Problematic, op. cit.*

69. *Ibid.*, p. 137 in *The Everyday World as Problematic*, p. 51.

70. Dorothy E. Smith, "The Experienced World as Problematic: A Feminist Method," The Twelfth Annual Soroken Lecture, University of Saskatchewan, Saskatoon, Jan. 28, 1981, p. 23. A revised version of this article appears in *The Everyday World as Problematic, op. cit.*

71. Karl Marx, *Capital* V. 1 (New York: Vintage, 1977), pp. 163-177.

72. Also see Dorothy E. Smith, "Femininity As Discourse" in her *Texts, Facts and Femininity, Exploring the Relations of Ruling, op. cit.*, pp. 159-208 and her "Women, Class and Family" in *The Socialist Register* (London: Merlin Press, 1983), pp. 1-44.

73. Dorothy E. Smith, "The Experienced World as Problematic," *op. cit.*, p. 17, also in *The Everyday World as Problematic*.

74. For important contributions, see: George Smith's "Policing the Gay Community: An Inquiry Into Textually-Mediated Social Relations" in *International Journal of the Sociology of Law, op. cit.*; his "Political Activist as Ethnographer" in *Social Problems, op. cit.* and his "The Ideology of 'Fag': The School Experience of Gay Students," unpublished paper, Ontario Institute for Studies in Education; and Madiha Didi Khayatt, *Lesbian Teachers, an Invisible Presence, op. cit.* and her "Compulsory Heterosexuality: Schools and Lesbian Students," *op. cit.*

75. See Mary McIntosh, "The Homosexual Role," originally in *Social Problems*, V. 16, No. 2 (Fall 1968), reprinted with a postscript in Plummer, ed., *The Making of the Modern Homosexual, op. cit.*, pp. 38-43; and Kinsey, Gebhard, Pomeroy, and Martin, *Sexual Behavior in the Human Male* (Philadelphia: W.B. Saunders, 1953).

76. John Rechy, *City of Night* (New York: Grove Press, 1963), p. 40. This expression is also used by the character played by Keanu Reeves in the film *My Own Private Idaho.*

77. George Chauncey, Jr., "Christian Brotherhood or Sexual Perversion? Homosexual Identities and the Construction of Sexual Boundaries in the World War I Era" in *Journal of Social History* (1985), pp. 189-212, and in Duberman, Vicinus and Chauncey, eds., *Hidden from History* (New York: Meridian, 1990), pp. 294-317; also see his *Gay New York* (New York: Basic Books, 1994).

78. See Laud Humphreys, *Tea Room Trade* (Chicago: Aldine, 1975).

79. On bisexuality see Mariana Valverde, *Sex, Power and Pleasure* (Toronto: Women's Press, 1985), especially "Bisexuality: Coping with Sexual Boundaries," pp. 109-120; L. Kaahumanu and L. Hutchins, *Bi Any Other Name: Bisexual People Speak Out* (Boston: Alyson, 1991); Clare Hemmings, "Resituating the Bisexual Body: From Identity to Difference" in J. Bristow and A. Wilson, eds., *Activating Theory: Lesbian, Gay and Bisexual Politics* (London: Lawrence and Wishart, 1993); and Clare Hemmings, "Locating Bisexual Identities: Discourses of Bisexuality and Contemporary Feminist Theory" in David Bell and Gill Valentine, eds., *Mapping Desire: Geographies of Sexualities* (London and New York: Routledge, 1995), pp. 41-55.

80. See Dorothy E. Smith, "A Sociology for Women," *op. cit.*

81. Some inkling of this shifting in vantage point from "outsider" to "insider" can be seen in Joseph Styles, "Outside/Insider Researching Gay Baths" in *Urban Life*, V. 8, No. 2, July 1979, pp. 135-152. Styles describes how an insider vantage point let him see things in a way that the outsider perspective obscured. On an insider's sociology, also see the work of Dorothy E. Smith, especially *The Everyday World as Problematic*.

82. Also offering important insights is recent work on governmentality influenced by the work of Michel Foucault. Among others, see Graham Burchell, Colin Gordon, and Peter Miller, eds., *The Foucault Effect, Studies in Governmentality* (Chicago: The University of Chicago Press, 1991) and Mike Gane and Terry Johnson, eds., *Foucault's New Domains* (London and New York: Routledge, 1993).

83. In particular, see Philip Corrigan and Derek Sayer, *The Great Arch: English State Formation as Cultural Revolution* (Oxford: Basil Blackwell, 1985).

84. See Philip Corrigan, "Towards a Celebration of Difference(s): Notes for a Sociology of a Possible Everyday Future" in D. Robbins, ed., *Rethinking Social Inequality* (London: Gower, 1982).
85. See the work of the late E.P. Thompson, particularly *The Making of the English Working Class* (Harmondsworth: Penguin, 1968), and Dorothy E. Smith, "Women, Class and Family," *op. cit.*, for an account of women's activity in the organization of this broader notion of class relations.
86. See Antonio Gramsci, *Selections from the Prison Notebooks* (New York: International Publishers, 1971); Carl Boggs, *Gramsci's Marxism* (London: Pluto Press, 1976); Perry Anderson, "The Antimonies of Antonio Gramsci" in *New Left Review*, No. 100, Nov. 1976-Jan. 1977, pp. 5-78; Chantal Mouffe, ed., *Gramsci and Marxist Theory* (London: Routledge and Kegan Paul, 1979); and Ernesto Laclau and Chantal Mouffe, *Hegemony and Socialist Strategy: Towards a Radical Democratic Politics* (London: Verso, 1985). Unfortunately, while Laclau and Mouffe trace some of the genealogy of the concept of hegemony, they treat hegemony as only a discursive concept, separating it from social practices and severing it from its historical, social, and organizational contexts. They also completely sever hegemony from class relations and class struggles in their latest work. There are difficulties with notions of "hegemony," especially if hegemony is construed as an explanatory category in and of itself. But it points us toward the relational and social character of social regulation in a clearer fashion than do terms like dominant culture or notions of domination. Unlike social or ideological reproduction, it suggests that social regulation is actively accomplished by individuals in diverse institutional sites and is always "problematic." It points us toward the social organization of ruling relations while including within it the activities and resistances of the subordinated. It is never total, never exclusive, and there is always the possibility of subversion and transformation. It is these opportunities we have to seize.
87. John Clarke, Stuart Hall, Tony Jefferson, and Brian Roberts, "Subcultures, Cultures and Class: A Theoretical Overview" in Hall and Jefferson, eds., *Resistance Through Rituals* (London: Hutchinson, 1976), p. 38.
88. Corrigan and Sayer, *The Great Arch, op. cit.*, p. 142.
89. See Gary Kinsman, "Managing AIDS Organizing: 'Consultation,' 'Partnership,' and the National AIDS Strategy" in William K. Carrol, ed., *Organizing Dissent: Contemporary Social Movements in Theory and Practice* (Toronto: Garamond, 1992), pp. 215-231.
90. Clarke, *et al., op. cit.*, p. 12.
91. See Mary O'Brien, "The Comatization of Women: Patriarchal Fetishism in the Sociology of Education," paper presented to the British Sociological Association Conference, Manchester, 1982.
92. See Adrienne Rich, "Compulsory Heterosexuality and Lesbian Existence" in *Signs*, V.5, No. 4 (Summer 1980), pp. 631-660. Despite the many insights of this article, her suggestion that heterosexuality is simply "compulsory" for women is rather one-sided. It does not adequately take into account that "consent" to heterosexuality is also actively constructed through practices of normalization and naturalization. This is why I prefer heterosexual hegemony to compulsory heterosexuality since it includes these moments of coercion *and* consent.
93. See Carol-Anne O'Brien and Lorna Weir, "Lesbians and Gay Men Inside and Outside Families" in Nancy Mandell and Anne Duffy, eds., *Canadian Families: Diversity, Conflict and Change, op. cit.*
94. See Frank Mort, "Sexuality: Regulation and Contestation" in Gay Left, ed., *Homosexuality: Power and Politics, op. cit.*, pp. 41-42.
95. See Gary Kinsman, "The Textual Practices of Sexual Rule: Sexual Policing and Gay Men" in Marie Campbell and Ann Manicom, eds., *Knowledge, Experience and Ruling Relations: Studies in the Social Organization of Knowledge* (Toronto: University of Toronto Press, 1995), pp. 80-95.
96. Rachel Harrison and Frank Mort, "Patriarchal Aspects of Nineteenth-Century State Formation: Property Relations, Marriage and Divorce and Sexuality" in Philip Corrigan, ed., *Capitalism, State Formation and Marxist Theory* (London: Quartet, 1980), p. 106.

2.

The Historical Emergence of Homosexualities and Heterosexualities: Social Relations, Sexual Rule, and Sexual Resistance

I now look at the English, and, to a lesser extent, the American and German social emergence of homosexuality, lesbianism, and heterosexuality. This examination includes an outline of how the present regime of sexual rule was formed. Each country's history is unique; however any understanding of Canadian State and sexual formation must take into account the experiences of other countries. For Canada, this especially includes those of England and the U.S., given the generally referenced (although at times autonomous) character of Canadian State formation to these two powers during different periods of Canadian history.

Sex, Class, and Capitalism

The formation of hetero and homosexual experiences and categories is based in the transformation of the social relations of production, reproduction, and sexuality that have occurred over the last few centuries. It would be a major mistake, however, to see this transformation as simply reflecting the development of the capitalist mode of production, particularly if this definition of capitalism is reduced to the economic domain.[1]

I try to avoid the dangers of economism — the view that there is a direct cause-and-effect relationship between capitalist economic relations and non-economic relations. Capitalist relations are based on the private ownership of the means of production (offices, factories) and the exploitation of the working class. These relations are not simply "economic" in character, they are profoundly social, cultural, and political. Sexuality as a social practice cannot be reduced to an "effect" of the economy or to narrow notions of class. I attempt to develop a more historically specific approach and a wider notion of class — as embodying all social life, including sexual relations. As I argue in this broader historical materialist sense, struggles over sexual relations have been important parts of class struggles.

The transformation of sexual experience and regulation is part of a process that has integrated previous forms of sexual organization and struggle over sexual and gender definitions into new capitalist settings. These new relations "are actively constructed through the transformation of pre-existing social forms."[2] Capitalism was built on already existing social forms, while these have at the same time been redefined to conform to the dynamics of capitalist development, class hegemony, and State organization and even to the resistance of the exploited and oppressed in these contexts. This dialectic of State and social construction, constrained by existing social forms,[3] recognizes both continuity in sexual regulation from pre-capitalist to capitalist societies and the ruptures brought about by new sexual definitions, categories, and experiences.

Until the mid-sixteenth century in England, men who engaged in anal intercourse or fellatio with other men were dealt with by Church courts. After the Reformation and abolition of the Church courts, Parliament passed a statute in 1533 making "sodomy" between men a felony that the criminal courts could punish by death.[4] Sodomy was generally seen as a sinful act that grouped together all non-reproductive sex — whether different or same gender — it was not a distinctly "homosexual" offense. These attitudes to non-procreative sex were retained and transformed in emerging capitalist societies.

The contemporary oppression of lesbians and gays in Western societies comes from a centuries-long "tradition" in Western Christian cultures of prohibiting non-reproductive sexual activity. Once this tradition had been embedded in social, moral, class and State relations, it came to be viewed by ruling groups as necessary to the maintenance of class, gender, and State power. This suggests that notions of a "proper" or "respectable" sexuality came to play an important part in class and State organization. Harrison and Mort note some of the different tendencies at work in their study of State formation in the nineteenth century:

> Nineteenth-century state legislation addressing homo-sexuality is as much determined by pre-existing legal structures governing forms of sexual "deviancy" as it is by particular social and cultural developments during the period. We have come to define the significance of the legislation in this area by locating the beginnings of a shift in the modality of state control of particular sexualities, which is more generally related to the way in which sexual meanings are constructed within specific practices and institutions.[5]

The homosexual, however, is not simply a "sodomite" who has accidentally stumbled into new capitalist conditions. His very being comes to be defined by "deviant" sex and gender characteristics. There is an important difference between the "sodomite" and what we now call a homosexual.

Three major processes were involved in the emergence of the "homosexual" and the "lesbian," which in turn set the stage for the "heterosexual." These social processes developed unevenly over several centuries. They can be summarized as, first, the emergence and development of capitalist social relations that opened up some social spaces for same-gender erotic networks and cultures[6] — these capitalist relations were in many ways established by legal and State relations; second, the resistance, and the accommodation, of those engaged in same-gender sex as an integral feature of the formation of lesbian and gay cultures since lesbians and gays participated in making themselves and seizing these social spaces; and third, the regime of sexual regulation itself, which policed these social spaces defining "normal" and "deviant" sexualities.[7] None of these social processes alone would have led to the emergence of lesbian, gay or heterosexual experiences; what is important here is their intersection. These developments were internally related and not separate; I am distinguishing them here for analytical purposes.

The protracted transition from feudalism to capitalism removed the labouring population from ownership and control over the means of production, increasingly separating "productive" labour from the household "economy" and reproductive realms. This occurred much more quickly and more smoothly for some people than for others. The working class made itself, and was a creation of these new social relations: including commercialization, industrialization, and urbanization. This social transformation integrated and shifted previous gender and labour divisions and forms of sexual regulation.[8] As Dorothy E. Smith has explained:

> It is only in capitalism that we find an economic process constituted independently of the daily and generational production of the lives of particular individuals and in which therefore we can think economy apart from gender.[9]

Social Relations, Social Space and Family/Household Relations

Part of this process was a transformation of family/household and sex/gender relations. Market processes developed unevenly, but began to provide for meeting some daily needs outside the household economy. Previously these needs for most people would only have been able to be met within familial relations. The separation of "work" from the household economy and the process of proletarianization meant that men in cities could now live outside or on the margins of the family/household system, earning wages and living in boarding-houses.

They would later eat in taverns and restaurants and rent rooms in inns, hostels, and hotels.[10] Only the wealthy could afford rooms at first, but these later became available to working-class men with pay in their pockets. Much later, working-class women could also rent rooms. Some people were beginning to be able to live in non-conformity with social and family norms.

Several kinds of social space now opened up outside the family/household network. These included a distinct "work" space as wage-labour became separated from household labour; a "recreational" space of bars or clubs where men with a discretionary income could go after work (recreational spaces for women would come much later); and what may be too modern a category, "private" space — usually rooms where men (and later women) could have intimate liaisons. This private space for same-gender sex existed more precariously than did other social spaces.[11] Men who were married and lived at home, younger men who did not have their own rooms, and other men whose situations did not permit them to bring home the men they met had to develop creative ways to meet and have sex. Women searching for same-gender liaisons may have had similar difficulties, although, ironically, the domestic middle-class realm may have allowed women's erotic friendships to flourish in the nineteenth century.[12]

Male erotic same-gender networks emerged within the limits of these social spaces. Some men, given the constraints placed on "private" space, found ways to meet and have sex in socially defined "public" spaces like parks, and later washrooms, movie-houses, and other cruising spots. These men handled the problem of their lack of "private" space in an innovative fashion that would help form homosexual erotic cultures. These early sexual/cultural networks can be seen as struggling to redefine social space and claim areas for themselves.

Sexual activities had previously been organized through the household, where marriage, family, and procreation were major productive institutions. This family/household, through an uneven and protracted historical process, was now separated from ownership of the means of production (particularly land ownership), leading to a profound transformation of generational, gender, and sexual relations.

The domestic and "productive" aspects of the household economy were being ripped apart. The prerogative of patrilineal land inheritance (from father to son) began to break down as the system of production/inheritance played less of a role in marriage. This led to a loosening of inter-generational social regulations. Youths began to leave the family in order to find work, which in the long run increased the potential for autonomy among young people, particularly young men. These processes decreased the chances of a smooth transition from family of origin to family of procreation.[13] The undermining of several institutions contributed to this weakening of social regulation: domestic service, arranged marriage, dowries, closely supervised courtship, and apprenticeship. Young people (especially boys and young men) could now more easily break free of family relations. This facilitated some men's entry into erotic male networks.[14]

These social changes affected men and women differently, generally increasing men's autonomy and women's dependence. Women's subordination in the increasingly privatized "domestic" sphere, which was now separated from "production," was intensified. Middle-class women came to be imprisoned in the private sphere, playing a crucial role in moulding the social life and morality of their class. The first stages of entrepreneurial capitalism depended on a particular form of bourgeois family and property organization in which the wife as a civil person was subsumed under the person of her husband, allowing him to appropriate her earnings, children, and property.[15] Working-class women continued to be responsible for domestic and reproductive labour and also took on paid work, including casual and occasional forms of prostitution, to ensure the survival of their families.

Only much later — at the end of the nineteenth century and in the early twentieth century with the rise of feminism and increased opportunities for their economic independence — would it be possible for women to create their own erotic networks apart from men. This points once again to the need for separate, although overlapping, social histories of homosexuality and lesbianism in order to see how differences in the social organization of gender help shape differences in erotic practices.

Previously, it would have been impossible for men to live as homosexuals in the modern sense. In monasteries, within the aristocracy, among theatre performers, and in the army and navy, same-gender sex certainly went on, but it was not a basis for the generation of a distinct erotic culture and social identity.

With these transformations of social, sex/gender, and familial relations, however, there were increased possibilities for men to live at least partly outside family networks. The existence of these new social spaces did not spontaneously create the homosexual, however. This would require, as well, a relational process of struggle between the developing agencies of sexual rule and those who would later be called homosexuals and lesbians. This process would include the seizing of these social spaces by "deviant" cultural networks. A historical relation exists between the emergence of the outcast status of the homosexual and lesbian and that of the "normality" of heterosexuality.

Mollies and Sodomites

The men engaged in same-gender sex were beginning to congregate by the late seventeenth century in both London and Paris, and were developing their own sub-language. These emerging networks provided a place in which men could meet others for sex, but also in which they could develop a self-consciousness that social institutions denied them. In England, they gathered in "Molly houses" and were called "Mollies."[16] Many of these cultural networks were associated with cross-dressing. If we are to judge from the court records, most of the Mollies, or "sodomites," were working class and lower middle class. Many of them used as their defence in court that they were married and had children, and for many this was true. Bray argues that these men claimed to be married with children simply as a good defence in court; however, many of them were probably married or lived with women, often with children, and only occasionally participated in the Molly networks.[17] Bray reports that these court records suggest that there were few aristocrats in the Molly networks. This contrasts with the social image of "sodomites" as effete and decadent aristocrats.

The arrest of sodomites was correlated with campaigns by the Society for the Reformation of Manners, in London and in the provinces, against sodomy and debauchery. The Society's arguments against sodomy were based on its "sinfulness" and "unnaturalness," and they played a key role in prosecuting the perpetrators of various "immoral" acts. Records show that in 1709 the Society closed down a number of Molly clubs, and in 1726 it broke up more than twenty of these. It helped prosecute not only sodomites, but also violators of the Sabbath, profane swearers, prostitutes, keepers of bawdy houses, and actors in "indecent" plays.

The Society's activities came in the period after the old ecclesiastical jurisdiction had broken down and before State authorities could fill the breach. It received the encouragement of State officials in the royal court for its efforts in moral regulation, which was particularly valued given the weak police forces of the day.

The Society for the Reformation of Manners was part of a religious revival that also included the rise of Methodism. The common people, however, seem to have been more tolerant of the Molly houses in their midst.

The classification of sodomy was no longer a sinful potential that existed in everyone, but a characteristic of the particular type of man who inhabited the Molly houses. Certain sexual and cultural attributes separated the sodomite from other men. By the nineteenth century, sodomite had become the typical epithet for the sexually deviant, usually male.[18] The Molly was a historically transitional "type" between the isolated sodomite and the homosexual. He provided one of the cultural sources for later homosexual networks. Molly culture was created not only through the suppression of the Molly houses, but also by the solidarity that grew among the Mollies. Alan Bray reports that when "a molly house in Covent Garden was broken up in 1725, the crowded household, many of them in drag, met the raid with determined and violent resistance."[19] In 1726, William Brown, who had been entrapped by constables, defended himself in the following way:

> I did it because I thought I knew him ... and I think that there is no crime
> in making what use I please of my own body ...[20]

A supportive cultural network and a certain group social consciousness must have existed to make possible such a statement of defiance.

Buggery and the Royal Navy

In the military, particularly in the navy, where men were segregated on ships, there existed both possibilities for erotic friendships between men but also severe prohibitions against "buggery" (generally but not always referring to anal intercourse). From the seventeenth century onwards, "the unnatural and detestable sin of buggery ... with man or beast" was mentioned in the British Articles of War as punishable "with death by sentence of a Court Martial."[21] The navy was concerned not so much with religious or political heresy, or social and sexual identities, but with maintaining proper military discipline. While there was some dispute as to exactly what constituted buggery, and whether proof of emission was necessary for conviction, it was nonetheless a capital crime on a par with desertion, mutiny, and murder. Records show that sailors were more likely to be hanged for buggery than for desertion or mutiny. The number of buggery trials increased in wartime when men were thrown together in crowded conditions. More than eighty were executed for sodomy under English criminal and naval law between 1800 and 1835.[22]

The military regime operated through an extremely rigorous code of conduct. Buggery, or sodomy, was seen as challenging the navy's hierarchical order and its clear boundaries between proper and improper behaviour. Men engaging in sex with other men created ambiguity and challenged military ideals of masculinity.[23] The military

> believed themselves to have special problems of order and discipline: sexual
> contact between men, and especially across ranks, threatened to tear asunder the carefully maintained hierarchy.[24]

The extension and development of hierarchical and bureaucratic institutional relations within the military and other State and professional agencies led to a clamping down on passionate relationships between men. Sex between men within hierarchical and bureaucratic forms of organization complicates relationships between subordinates and superiors and denies the "impartiality" and "objectivity" of the bureaucratic order.[25] This is also part of the construction of a hegemonic form of masculinity that was defined in opposition to those who engaged in buggery and sodomy.

Individuality and Sexual Identifications

With the development of capitalist social relations and State formation there emerged the discourse of individualism:

> In this society of free competition, the individual appears detached from the natural bonds, etc., which in earlier historical periods make him the accessory of a definite and limited human conglomerate.[26]

Marx viewed individualism as a social construction in the context of capitalist social relations. The individual (usually seen as a male) emerged as a social actor entering into social and economic relations with other individuals. The historical practices producing this individual identity included the competitive character of the capitalist marketplace, the conversion of labour into an individually owned commodity to be bought and sold in the marketplace, the transformation of the existing divisions of labour, the creation of the individual as a unit of administration and governance for the State (in the census, as voter or citizen, as a social statistic) that depended on the development of particular forms of documentation, administration and organization,[27] and the emergence of legal conceptions of the individual and the assertion of the body as one's personal property over which one had the fundamental right of control. This latter process has yet to be fully extended to women.[28] These experiences made it possible to conceive of an individual social and sexual identity. Individuality in the bourgeois epoch is based not only on property ownership (the isolated male property owner of liberal theory) but also on experiences of gender and sexuality as decisive components of the "respectable" and "civilized" individual.

Lust Acquires a Gender

In previous epochs, a form of social identification as man or woman had been organized on the basis of the division of labour in the household and in relation to the social relations of biological reproduction. However, this "identity" was not defined in an explicitly erotic or sexual sense. As Jonathan Katz states when referring to the early American colonies, "the early colonists did not distinguish between lust in terms of its 'same-sex' or 'different-sex' objects."[29]

In the capitalist epoch, with the partial separation of gender divisions from the division of labour in the household economy, and the emergence of the regime of sexuality, gender categorizations became more intensely polarized as they were combined with notions of a distinct sexuality. Sexuality emerged as an autonomous personal terrain of identity formation by the late nineteenth century. There now existed a diversity of sexual practices and their simultaneous categorization by the emerging sexual sciences. Erotic practices under this regime of sexual categorization became the basis for the articulation of specific sexual identities. The sodomite as a sinful, perverse, and deviant sexual being provided the basis for the initial articulation of a "deviant" sexual identity and culture in many Western societies.

Men could now begin to live outside the household system — which had previously united production, reproduction, and sex.[30] The existence of same-gender erotic networks and cultures (even in their tentative beginnings) presented a challenge to the developing norms and practices of respectable sexuality. In previous periods, a necessary participation in the interdependent household economy and the necessity of procreative sexual relations, along with religious and legal prohibitions against sodomy and buggery, had been enough to enforce reproductive sexual norms. Heterosexuality as a distinct and defined sexuality did not exist.[31]

With sexuality now being experienced as a distinct and important realm of experience, sexual cultures and identities needed their own justification. Reproductive sexuality, and eventually heterosexuality (although not specifically named as such), came to be defended by the bourgeoisie and its agencies through a historical and social process integrating and transforming previous forms of sexual organization and regulation. The new capitalist and middle-class elite associated "heterosexuality" and respectable family life with social and moral order itself — with the maintenance of its own class unity and hegemony. The blood and kinship ties of feudalism were transformed into the norms of "heterosexual" love and attraction, shifting the emphasis in the regulation of sexuality from marriage and kinship networks to sexuality and sexual identity themselves. The blood ties of the aristocracy that marked the antiquity of its ancestry and marriage alliances were replaced by the sexuality and gender practices of the new ruling class. This was specified through biological, medical, and eugenic concepts that sought to avoid the menaces of heredity and to produce "healthy" children who would improve the ruling class.[32] The class body of the bourgeoisie was differentiated from the body of the "lower" orders, and central to this sense of class embodiment were sexuality and sexual practices. The categories of sexuality were first applied to the body of the bourgeoisie, which served to draw a boundary between it and other social classes. People's "truth" came to be found in their sexuality. The bourgeoisie as a class thus came to regard "heterosexuality" as necessary to its own class reproduction, hegemony, and social ways of life.

These notions of personal sexual identity were articulated first in the bourgeoisie and the middle classes because of the earlier emergence of a distinct "personal" life within these classes, and that this was the initial site of the deployment of sexual classifi-

cations and "norms." Notions of sexual culture and identity came about through an uneven social process, making it necessary to discuss the formation of class, race, and gender sexualities rather than any sexuality in general.

The respectable sexual identity of the ruling class served in the first instance to
erect a boundary between the ruling class and the working class. In the face of potential
challengers like the Mollies and sodomites, tribadists and later fairies, queers,[33] bull dag-
gers and dykes, reproductive different-gender sexuality needed to be defended as the
only approved way of life. Any challenge to the "natural" moral order of reproductive
sexuality mobilized a response from right-wing religious groups, the police, and various
State agencies. Heterosexuality emerged as the "universal" order, requiring new forms
of social, cultural, and political defence. This new hegemony was established through
secular, legal, sexological, and medical practices forged through State formation and social struggles. "Sexual respectability" has been used to defend this institutionalized form
of heterosexuality from queer sexualities that can potentially claim equal status for
themselves.

It is in this social process that the emergence of polarized gender and sexual classifications can be located. Too often, studies of homosexual/lesbian or queer cultures
and practices have been limited or distorted by their failure to look at the other side of
this process — the emergence of the heterosexual man and woman. The contemporary
male heterosexual, for instance, is no longer simply engaged in sexual activity that leads
to reproduction. He has become a particular "type" of being with a particular erotic orientation tied to a heightened sense of masculine gender identification. Lust now had a
gender.[34] If your lust and your gender did not match up properly, you were an "invert,"
a "pervert," a "queer," or, later, a "homosexual." You were excluded from emerging social norms.

This emerging heterosexuality is tied to the shifting social organization of gender
and patriarchal relations. Male heterosexual practice is bound up with the institutionalization of a particular form of masculinity and is associated with the daily practices of
men in the gender division of labour: a class organization of masculinity that contains
common features across class boundaries, shifting forms of family organization, the
struggle for a family wage paid to the male breadwinner, male responsibility for "his"
wife and children, and male control over women's bodies and sexuality.[35] Add to this
the redefinition of "public" and "private" that associated masculinity with the public
spheres of the economy and politics, and trapped women (middle-class white women especially) in an increasingly privatized domestic sphere shorn of its previously "productive" dimensions. Patriarchal hegemony organizes an apparent unity of interests
between men in different classes, as "real men" in opposition to the women of their
classes whose subordination it actively organizes and also in opposition to "queers" and
"fags." Heterosexual hegemony thus organizes and is organized through capitalist patriarchal relations.

Class and Race Sexualities

We can now see the historical intersection of sexual experience with the relations of class, gender, age, and race. In the symbolic world views articulated by and for the Victorian male ruling class, middle-class white men came to be seen as the "head" of the household and the social system, middle-class women as the guardians of emotions and respectability — the "heart" of society, yet lacking in sexual/erotic drives. Middle-class women themselves helped construct this image of passionlessness in an attempt to defend themselves from unwanted male sexual advances and sexual violence, in a context where women were denied access to birth control, abortion and information about their own bodies.[36]

The "lower orders" were defined as the "hands" of society, the unthinking but physical "doers" associated with menial work and "nature." Working-class and black women were seen as more "sexual" than middle-class women, and there emerged double standards separating male from female and middle-class "ladies" from working-class women. This symbolic system affected the social organization of prostitution, and eroticism more generally.

This middle-class male-defined view of sexuality also affected the organization of same-gender desires among some white middle-class and elite homosexual men in the late nineteenth and early twentieth centuries. Many of these men perceived young working-class men as not only erotically more interesting but as not hostile to engaging in sex with men. The working class was viewed as less infected with social hostility toward same-gender erotic pleasure. This pattern has been described as a form of "sexual colonialism" that coincided with an idealization of the reconciling effects of cross-class liaisons.[37] The "lower orders" came to be sexualized from this middle-class vantage point, suggesting that social power relations and the deployment of sexuality were linked through the eroticization of social differences of class, race, age, and gender. At the same time, working-class men and women and black women did not necessarily experience their sexualities in this way at all.

The "lower orders" were also seen by the respectable middle class as a threat, as having the potential to pollute the rising ruling class. Chauncey describes part of this process as it occurred in the U.S.:

> The medical profession grew out of the white middle class and reflected its values and concerns in an extremely class conscious manner: it perceived not only non-Europeans but also America's own lower classes as immoral. Doctors assumed that sexual license and sensuality characterized the poor and working classes, and that only the middle and upper classes had "achieved" a sense of sexual propriety.[38]

Doctors accused servants of introducing perversion into the middle-class household, of showing children how to masturbate — thus causing some of them to engage in same-gender sexual activities.[39] This formation of class morality and sexuality was the setting for Victorian debates over prostitution and social purity. These debates had an important influence on the regulation of same-gender sexual activities and sex generally — in Canada as well.[40]

The Sexual Sciences and Sexual Rule

It was in these social conditions that sexuality became an object of study and an arena for the production of "scientific" knowledge. Sexuality became a terrain for medicalization by professional groups: the new medical, psychiatric, and scientific professions became the legitimizers and definers of sexual identities and norms. A specific sexual instinct was demarcated by Heinrich Kaan in 1846 and became an object to be classified, categorized, and managed.[41] Various "irregular" forms of sexual behaviour were studied and classified. The forms of behaviour and identity that were produced and classified in medical and psychiatric discourse included the "hysterical" woman, the simultaneously "innocent" and masturbating child, and the perverse adult. There emerged the sexual sciences, a regime of sexual categories and definitions including parts of forensic psychiatry, sex psychology, and later sexology.[42]

> It was the work of medical, psychological, educational, and eugenic practices — articulated in a new sub-discipline of sexology — which defined the unity of these strategies around a new concept of sex as expressive of basic instincts.[43]

This regime of sexual sciences and disciplines was two-sided in its implications for sexual experience. On the one side, a number of the early sex psychologists were also sex reformers of one persuasion or another. In naming the various sexual categories, they also created the possibilities for these categories, like homosexual or lesbian, to be taken up as a basis for opposition to sexual rule. On the other side, these disciplines participated in the construction of oppressive sexual regulations that were used to police sexual life. The development of these sexual sciences was uneven, contradictory, and never monolithic.[44] As Weeks describes:

> The paradox was that the early sexologists, who by and large were also conscious sex reformers, were simultaneously powerful agents in the organization, and ... control, of the sexual behaviours they sought to describe.[45]

The work of sexual scientists was and is a key part of the contemporary relations of sexual rule.[46] Regardless of the individual intentions of these early sex researchers, their work was entered into the social relations and practices of sexual policing. Sex-scientific knowledge was used to mandate police action, to assist Parliaments, judges, and courts in the formation of criminal-code offences, and to help organize psychiatric, medical, media, and social policies for dealing with sexual and social "problems." The categorization of different sexual "types," "deviations," "perversions," and "norms" were entered into an administrative and policing apparatus of sexual regulation, mandating action for the containment of sex deviants and perverts.

The sex sciences first labelled the perversions — the "deviant" masturbating child or the homosexual — and separated them from acceptable behaviour, before returning to outline in more detail the norm of heterosexuality itself. The term "heterosexual" does not seem to have been used in its present sense until the 1890s in medical discourse in the U.S. and later in Canada.[47]

These sexual practices were both forced on and taken up by the working class and the poor in what Foucault described as the "moralization of the poorer classes."[48] This was a major part of the bourgeois cultural revolution. Class struggles were fought not only at the point of production; they also included struggles over gender, sexual, and moral relations. Sexuality came to play an important role in State policies and as a locus for social surveillance and intervention, providing access to the life of the species and the life of the individual: it became a crucial arena for the surveillance of the body politic. The emergence of the "problem" of sexuality was grounded in that of the politics of population, which was centrally concerned with sexual and reproductive life.[49] This export of sexual norms was resisted, negotiated, shifted and accepted by the male-dominated organizations of the working class. Within the working class itself, a struggle also took place — women and the least "skilled" male workers including black, Asian and other non-whites being the losers.[50] The white male "skilled" working class tended to defend its own interests in the conditions of exploitation it faced, and built on existing traditions and divisions of labour to fight for the formation and defence of a male-dominated working-class family form. Working-class people often had their own reasons to fight for their versions of "respectable" and "proper" sexuality.

These social transitions, had a dramatic effect on same-gender intimacy and friendship, whether this took openly erotic forms or not. While this process has been explored regarding women at the end of the nineteenth century, particularly concerning the destruction of white female support networks and passionate friendships,[51] a similar, but perhaps earlier, process occurred among men. Foucault has suggested that in Europe, male same-gender passionate friendships were first prohibited in the sixteenth and seventeenth centuries. Institutions like the army, schools, and bureaucratic administration could not handle intense friendships among men because of the need for hierarchical relations and "proper" discipline. Passionate friendships between men were seen to violate the new norms of bureaucratic rationality. When passionate friendships were prohibited between men, all close relationships became suspect. Foucault speculated that the "disappearance of friendship as a social relation, and the declaration of homosexuality as a social/political/medical problem, are the same social process."[52]

Respectability and Masculinities

It was during the late nineteenth century that notions of respectability and distinctions between proper and deviant forms of life became generalized among the skilled working class. The skilled "respectable" sections of the working class adopted their own version of middle-class family and sexual norms. This can perhaps best be seen in the social-purity campaigns of the late nineteenth and early twentieth centuries:

> Sexual respectability became a hallmark of the labour aristocrat, anxious to distance himself from the "bestiality" of the casual labouring poor, as increased pressure was placed on the respectable working class to break their ties with "outcast" groups ... Changing employment patterns seem to have reinforced patriarchal tendencies among skilled sectors of the working class by the end of the century, as the proportion of married women working outside the home declined and the family wage for male workers became a demand of trade unions. Seen in this context, social purity, which called on men to protect and control their women, served as the ideological corollary of the family wage, morally legitimating the prerogatives of patriarchy inside and outside the family. Thus social purity served to undermine working-class solidarity, while tightening definitions of gender among respectable working men and working women.[53]

Social-purity agitation, which I examine in more detail in the Canadian context, was directed against schoolboy masturbation, sexual perversion, and prostitution.[54] Notions of social purity and respectability played an important role in organizing working-class heterosexism, and also united the middle class and the respectable working class against aristocratic decadence, lust, and selfishness, and at the same time against the pariah sexual practices of the outcast poor.[55] Similarly, working-class social-purity campaigns often had a different character than those initiated by the middle class. They were more often directed against the elite. In these ways some working-class forces tried to shift social-purity discourse and practice away from bourgeois hegemony.[56] These efforts were not usually very successful since bourgeois forces usually came to hegemonize these campaigns. Social-purity campaigns often had a clear white racial character and were often directed against "sexually depraved" images of people of colour.[57]

"Respectability," then, was used to articulate and establish a broad social bloc of different class, gender, and social groups under the hegemony of moral conservative political and religious forces. This historic social bloc played an important role in shaping State policy and the present relations of sexual rule.

The struggles for a "family wage" and for "protective" legislation to keep children and women out of competition with the male worker — thus establishing the male "role" as breadwinner — along with the call for sexual protection and control over women, organized a particular form of family life in the working class. The formation of gender within the working class included the affirmation of working-class forms of masculinity and patriarchal relations. Male workers have resisted the devaluing of manual labour by associating real masculinity with "hard" manual work, and effeminacy and physical weakness with mental labour. The working class has therefore tended to generate its own forms of heterosexism through its debasement of male "effeminacy" and the assignment of women to primary responsibility in domestic life. Working-class masculinity contains both patriarchal and heterosexist practices, formed in interaction with, and in resistance to, capitalist exploitation. Forms of cultural production, or the resistance of subordinate groups, can, ironically, act to reinforce the social hegemony of the ruling class, gender, race, and sexuality.[58] Patriarchal hegemony within the working class is the other side of the construction of heterosexual hegemony. Through the organization of these forms of hegemony, not only were women and homosexuals oppressed, but working-class organizations positioned themselves on the same side as the ruling regime on these questions.

Enter the Homosexual

The specification of "homosexuality" in forensic psychiatry, sex psychology and later in sexological discourse was used to explain the "deviants" encountered by the police, courts, doctors, and moral reformers in the larger urban centres. The emergence of the "homosexual" is a complex historical interaction between social conditions, social discourse and cultural developments and the resistance of same-gender lovers ourselves.

Some distinction was being made between homosexuality and other sex "perversions" by the late nineteenth century[59] — in official sexual and medical discourse in the 1890s but largely not until after the turn of the century in Canada. This category developed in an uneven process, with same-gender sex being classified in various ways before "homosexual" became firmly established. In early sexual psychiatric discourse it was seen as a form of gender inversion: male homosexuality was associated with effeminacy and female "masculinity" with lesbianism. Within the gender categories of the day, masculinity began to be defined as inherently heterosexual.

Some men were able, however, to continue to engage in same-gender sex without fear of being labelled a fairy or queer by asserting a "masculine" position in the sexual activities they engaged in with other men. This was before the social generalization of the concepts of a sharply dichotomized heterosexuality and homosexuality that took place unevenly over the first half of the twentieth century.[60] Homosexuality began to mean not only that there was something crucially significant about one's sexuality, but also about one's gender.[61] It would only be after 1900 that the distinctly sexual aspects of homosexuality would be classified in the works of Havelock Ellis and Freud.[62]

The origin of the term "homosexual" itself illustrates the struggle between those who experienced same-gender desires and heterosexual hegemony. It first appeared in 1869 in the writings of the Hungarian Karoly Maria Benkert, although it did not enter into the English language until the 1890s in the work of Havelock Ellis and in U.S. medical literature.[63] Benkert, who himself engaged in sexual affairs with men, appealed to the government to keep out of people's sexual lives in response to German legislation against male same-gender sex.[64] The word "homosexual" was elaborated by white professional men who engaged in same-gender sex in order both to name what they experienced as their "inborn" difference and to protect themselves from the law. This category, then, arose in the context of a lived reality of same-gender sexual networks and in the context of a social explosion of sexual classifications.[65]

Homosexuality was defined in relation to a discourse then emerging in the medical, psychiatric, and legal professions initially as a form of "reverse discourse"[66] in an attempt to oppose sexual rule — by asserting that homosexuals were "congenital inverts" and not a social threat. However, this formulation was trapped within the confines of the ruling regime of sexual definition and regulation. This category was, then, removed from the context of experiences of people like Benkert and became part of the official discourse of the legal system, the police, the medical profession, the media, and, later, social work.

The "homosexual" thus became a component in the campaign against the moral standards of the poor, represented by the male prostitutes involved in the scandals of the period, and the image of the decadent upper-class man preying on working-class youth developed in the Oscar Wilde scandal.[67] Childhood and adolescence were defined as years of sexual innocence, and masturbation, or "self-abuse," among young boys, particularly in the middle class, became a focus of fear. "Self-abuse" was said to cause sexual inversion.[68]

The social-purity campaigns focused on the image of upper-class men corrupting working-class and poor youth. When these concerns were taken up by the ruling regime, however, hardest hit were the poor male prostitutes and working-class men engaged in same-gender sex. It was the same in relation to female prostitution. Poor and working-class women always got hit the hardest.

Imperialism and Sexuality

The rise of imperialism, with its military efficiency and industrial competition, and the shifting character of capitalism had an important effect on sex and gender relations:

> The old system of capitalist production (which itself had nourished imperial expansion) with its mobile super-abundant workforce of people who were underpaid, underfed, untrained, and infinitely replaceable, was passing. In its place, with the introduction of capital-intensive methods, was needed a stable workforce of people trained to stay in them, neither moving on, nor losing too much time through ill health.[69]

This led to the

> recognition that under the need for growing productivity and efficiency labour was not simply a commodity that could be used up and discarded: that

capitalism had both an immediate interest in its healthy maintenance and reproduction.[70]

The growth of a "managed" capitalism led to changes in family and gender relations. The new labour force had to be physically healthy, familiar with factory discipline, and generally more highly "skilled." This led to the reinforcement of reproductive sex along with institutionalized training for motherhood among working-class women and girls and the expansion of universal, compulsory schooling.

Imperialist wars such as the Boer War, in the meantime, led to concerns over the malnutrition and ill health of the working-class "cannon fodder" of the imperial armies, and a "surge of concern about the bearing and rearing of children — the next generation of soldiers and workers, the Imperial race."[71] The liberation of women for work in the home became an objective of the ruling class: to rear healthy babies and thus replenish the male labour force and the armies. Women were denied access to contraception and abortion information. Although they met with resistance, male professionals increasingly gained control over women's bodies.[72] For women, sex was officially defined as a racial instinct for the perpetuation of the species. The spread of venereal disease and illegitimacy was blamed on the "unnatural promiscuity" of deviant women.[73] All this occurred in a climate of white middle-class fear of not only moral and national decay, but also race and class suicide due to the low white middle-class birth rate. This reinforced stringent standards of proper femininity, masculinity, and reproductive sexuality. Said President Theodore Roosevelt: "The woman who flinches from childbirth stands on a par with the soldier who drops his rifle and runs in battle."[74]

Para-military youth organizations drilled young boys in the spirit of nationalism and imperialism. An association was established between imperialism, nationalism, militarism, masculinity, and sexual respectability.[75] Sexual perversion became a symptom of national and moral decline.

The State built on previous public/private distinctions to allow "private" economic enterprise to flourish, while also creating a "private" form of regulation of women's domestic lives and sexuality. The public sphere was therefore built in distinction from at least two "private" spheres, the private economic sphere of "free enterprise," and the private domestic realm.[76]

The regulation of sexual pleasure moved from the local community and the Church to a bureaucratic State, with its criminal code, police, professional groups, official knowledge, and social policies. This increasingly extra-local organization of sexual rule was part of a broader shift in social power and decision making away from local settings.[77] Religious discourse against same-gender sexuality did not disappear, of course. Churches have continued to influence moral campaigns against homosexuality. Earlier notions of immorality and sinfulness helped shape "scientific" theories, which, in turn, moulded the moral climate in which psychiatric, medical, and sexological work on "queers" took place. Sexuality became a matter to be regulated, managed, administered, and policed.

Degeneracy and Legal Codifications

New psychiatric and medical theories of degeneracy associated with homosexuality were accepted by the institutions of sexual rule. The creation of the homosexual as outcast was part of the same process that cast prostitutes outside "respectable" sexuality. As Isabel Hull argues, "For the state to punish sexual acts, it had to define them first."[78]

Cesare Lombroso's criminal anthropology operated in this general field to specify anatomical differences between criminal "types," that he related to evolutionary theory. For Lombroso, degeneracy was a sign of inherent criminality, and he saw "homosexuals, like criminals, as throwbacks to earlier stages of civilization."[79] Lombroso's criminal anthropology "provided a powerful argument for racism and imperialism at the height of European colonial expansion."[80]

The work of early forensic and sex psychologists like Krafft-Ebing and Havelock Ellis was influenced by degeneration theory.[81] Marx and Engels, in their few written references to male same-gender passion, were influenced by these fears of "degeneracy."[82] Eugenic theory grew out of this intersection of degeneration theory and fear of ruling-class suicide, resulting in proposals for the castration or sterilization of sex "perverts," including sodomites.[83]

These categories of homosexuality in official discourse mandated police campaigns against the emerging cultures and networks of men who had sex with men just as those of "decadence" and "degeneration" organized media interpretation of the Oscar Wilde trial. "Inverts" and homosexuals emerged as particular categories of criminal suspects as the police played an important role in holding dominant gender, class, and sexual relations in place.[84]

Legal offences such as "gross indecency" marked a transition from the broad term "sodomy" to more specific charges. "Gross indecency" brought various male same-sex acts under a common legal category, beginning to create the legal personality of the "homosexual" (although the word homosexual was never used in the text of the law).[85] These legal changes were part of a broad social process in which the various components of homosexual practice and culture were brought together to define not only particular offences but a particular sexual being.

Homosexual Cultures and Resistance

Not only did the law and sexual science play a crucial part in the organization and transformation of sex/gender relations,[86] same-gender lovers also played a very active part in the articulation of homosexual experience. As with the making of the working class, homosexuals were present at and very involved in our own making. To paraphrase Marx, we make our own history, but we do not make it just as we please; we make it under circumstances given us by the past and the constraints these present for our own activities.[87]

In the context of sexual categorization, certain homosexuals (like K.M. Benkert,

Karl Heinrich Ulrichs, Magnus Hirschfeld, and Edward Carpenter) participated in naming and defining their experiences through the categories available to them.[88] These men were the middle-class or professional expression of broader cultural networks. Wrote G. Frank Lydston of the U.S. in 1889: "... in every community of any size [there exists] a colony of male sex perverts; they are usually known to each other and are likely to congregate together."[89]

The lives of homosexuals were never completely defined by the State and the medical professionals; there was always resistance and subversion. This resistance seems to have taken on visible collective and political forms only in Germany during this period, however.[90] Some homosexuals used the category of "homosexual" to articulate a separate identity and culture, shifting it in a more progressive direction. Their cultural resources included earlier cultural forms such as the Mollies and ongoing same-gender erotic networks; Walt Whitman's important notion of the "adhesiveness of comrades" (which played an important transitional role in the making of a homosexual consciousness among both men and women); Edward Carpenter's writings on the "intermediate sex"; and the more "liberal" sex psychological and sexological literature of the day like that of Ellis and Hirschfeld. The appropriation of the literature and art of classical Greece with an emphasis on "homosexuality" as a valid way of life may have played a role in the formation of homosexual cultures among middle-class and upper-class intellectual men.[91]

In the years prior to the creation of "the lesbian" as a specific category, some lesbians shared these cultural sources as well. I will come back to this when we look at Elsa Gidlow's experiences in the early twentieth century in Montréal (chapter 6). This construction of homosexual culture had a generally white and European-derived character, especially through the use of the example of ancient Greece to justify contemporary homosexuality and the references to European sexological work. This associated homosexual identities with a Eurocentric perspective on the world, making it more difficult for those coming from different cultural and sexual traditions to identify with this process of identity formation.

Homosexual and lesbian cultures formed differently in relation to class and race.[92] I have already suggested that hegemonic patterns of class eroticization affected the formation of middle-class and elite homosexual practices. For a number of historical and social reasons, individual homosexual identifications appear to have emerged first among some men in the bourgeoisie and middle class. This was also the case with heterosexual identifications that developed somewhat later. This is by no means to suggest that the middle class was more sexually "advanced" or that the working class suffered from a process of "cultural lag." It must be stressed that working-class men played a crucial and very active part in seizing and creating social spaces for same-gender sex and in resisting sexual policing during these years. We must also be very wary of drawing conclusions from personal texts since working-class men who engaged in sex with other men were less likely to have left behind written diaries or records of their erotic experiences.

In the working-class, indigenous practices of same-gender sex that were not understood as possessing a distinct homosexual identity or as homosexuality already existed. In the early twentieth century in some working-class communities, a distinction may have been made between "fairies" or "queer" men who organized their lives around sex with other men and may have been associated with "effeminacy," and those men who allowed these fairies and queers to have sex with them. These men would not have been seen as queer and would have been able to construct themselves as masculine in character.[93] It took a few more decades, it appears, for networks of working-class men (as compared to networks of middle-class men) to begin to take up homosexual classifications as the "truth" of their beings.[94] Homosexuality emerged in a different way among working-class men than for middle-class men. This process of identity formation was organized partly through psychiatry and medicine: doctors would describe homosexuality as an inversion or a disease "afflicting" middle-class patients, but as an immoral form of behaviour wilfully chosen by the poor and working class.[95] This attitude blended in with middle-class notions of sexual excess in the "lower" classes.

Part of this process was also the uneven and protracted "colonization" of working-class practices of same-gender sex by middle-class, sex-psychological and sexual-policing classifications of "homosexuality" that were understood by working-class men in rather different terms. This process of "colonization," resistance, and accommodation needs to be explored much more fully. George Chauncey begins to raise some of these questions:

> We need to be paying more attention to *other* social forms of homosexuality — other ways in which homosexual relations have been organized and understood, differentiated, named and left deliberately unnamed. We need to specify the *particularity* of various modes of homosexual behaviour and the relationships between these modes and particular configurations of sexual identity.[96]

A bit later in the same article, he adds that there are problems in using contemporary sexual classifications in grasping how people, even in the early parts of this century, would have made sense of their own erotic experiences and lives.

> To classify their behaviour and character using the simple polarities of "homosexual" and "heterosexual" would be to misunderstand the complexity of their sexual system. Indeed the very terms "homosexual behaviour" and "identity," because of their tendency to conflate phenomena that other cultures may have regarded as quite distinct, appear to be insufficiently precise to denote the variety of social forms of sexuality we wish to analyze.[97]

This social process was also tied into the emergence of "heterosexuality" within the working class coming to eclipse indigenous forms of different-gender sexuality and social-support relations. A similar but also different process of sexual "colonization" has gone on in relation to indigenous practices of same-gender and different-gender sexualities in many "Third World" countries where indigenous practices through an uneven process have been hegemonized by Western notions of heterosexuality and homosexuality.[98]

In North America and Europe, it was in response to indigenous same-gender erotic practices that the stigmatized classification of the "homosexual" was put in place as were the social relations of "the closet." This reverses the "common-sense" historical narrative that has been accepted by many lesbians and gays. It has been assumed that the relations of the closet have been in place for a long time and that we are only now slowly freeing ourselves from them as we come out. Instead, historical work by Chauncey[99] and others points out that the relations of the closet are recent in their formation and were constructed as a way of decreasing the visibility and acceptance of same-gender sexualities. In this sense, the closet was actively constructed through the relations of heterosexual hegemony in response to challenges from fairies, queers, and dykes. We were forced into the relations of the closet. This in turn had a profound impact on how heterosexuality was lived and defined.

Middle-class homosexual-identified men in the late nineteenth century and early part of this century may have had a sense of a private, personal life that most working-class men did not share. They may have therefore adopted a homosexual identification earlier; they had more mobility, they could live outside or on the fringes of family networks that were still necessary for the survival of most working-class men, and they were more likely to encounter the medical and sex-scientific literature categorizing homosexuality as different. Given the middle-class identification of respectability with "proper" family life, these middle-and upper-class men may have found themselves excluded from their class mores at an earlier date.[100] Working-class cultures, particularly their more "outcast" or "rough" sections, were much more resistant to linking occasional same-gender sexual acts with an exclusive homosexual identity, and had their own practices of same-gender sex that did not revolve around homosexual identities. Many working-class men did engage in same-gender sex and were involved in the emerging homosexual cultures and networks,[101] but they often participated in them differently than middle-class men and did not seem to feel as compelled to adopt a particular overall homosexual "identity."

George Merrill lived for a number of years with the early homosexual socialist writer Edward Carpenter. Merrill had grown up in the slums of Sheffield, England. Early on, he became involved in the late Victorian male/male sexual "underground" and developed a particular erotic interest in middle-and upper-class men. He certainly loved Carpenter very much and had no reservations about openly living with him. Experiences such as Merrill's must be examined more closely in order to give us more insights into working-class homosexual life in this period.[102] Nonetheless, it seems to have taken several decades for working-class homosexual cultures to emerge. The reasons for this include not only the later development of a "respectable" heterosexual culture in the working class, but also that a popular culture and mass communications industry carrying the values of heterosexual hegemony into the heart of the working class did not come about until the early to mid-twentieth century.

Some of these late nineteenth-century emerging homosexual networks were organized around male prostitution. Some working-class boys and men took advantage of middle-class and elite men's erotic interests in them for their own financial advantage as well as for erotic pleasures. Many of the slang words still common in gay cultures, such as "trick" and "trade," can be traced back to this period and also to interaction with female prostitutes. Male prostitutes, or hustlers, often did not identify themselves in terms of their sexuality, but rather by the acts in which they engaged for money. Identities were produced through complex sexual, gender, and class interactions. According to Weeks, there were few professional "Mary Annes" (male prostitutes for men) in nineteenth-century England; however, those male prostitutes who stayed involved in the emerging homosexual cultures, participating in its interactions, were more likely to take up homosexual identifications.[103]

The homosexual was someone whose very existence was defined by his sexuality according to the definitions of sexual science. The articulation of this "identity" was both imprisoned within the "scientific" categorization of sex as truth, and also potentially capable of subverting and challenging this regime of classification. There has been debate and struggle for at least the last century and a half over the meanings and definitions of homosexuality and lesbianism engaged in by sexologists, psychiatrists, the police, the legal system, politicians, and gays and lesbians. The development of new sexual definitions was an attempt to establish heterosexuality as the norm and exclude the deviations. Unwittingly, however, these categorizations also provided a basis for the dialectical emergence of homosexual and lesbian experiences, pleasures and desires — for a consciousness developed in resistance and affirmation. A historic bloc of social forces was constructed of the medical profession, sex scientists, the legal apparatus, the police, middle-class moral reformers, and the "respectable" working class. This informal alliance helped shape the main contours of the regime of sexual regulation that is in many ways still with us today.

The implicit alliance between State agencies and the dominant union organizations created the conditions for the subordination of women, for the suppression of female sexuality other than male-dominated heterosexuality, and for the subordination of homosexuality and lesbianism. It also narrowed the terrain of working-class struggle to a trade-unionist economic and workplace realm, and associated unions and working-class struggles with a particular construction of heterosexual masculinity and manhood.[104] Homosexuals and women were subordinated — in different ways — in the organization of heterosexual hegemony and capitalist patriarchal "civilization."

The emergence of corporate or managed capitalism has had an important impact on sexual and moral regulation. As Dorothy E. Smith points out, "Economic organization became increasingly separated from the local organization of the household"[105] as social power shifted from the local community and the household to State bodies and national and eventually international corporate bodies, and as administrative and managerial positions in the new corporations have shifted gender and household organization. In the working class, women's labour has been increasingly appropriated in the waged workforce, and in the middle-class into the professional, bureaucratic, and managerial levels. These areas have continued to be male-dominated. Corporate ownership has been accompanied by increased bureaucratic management that increasingly relies on abstract and universal forms of categorization and textual/documentary communication.[106]

The Heterosexual Counter-Revolution

It is in this context that practices of masculinity, femininity, and sexuality were re-organized. During the 1920s, media, advertising, and the beginnings of a mass consumer culture created a setting in which heterosexual images were amplified and commercialized in the Western countries — selling both products and social norms at the same time. Says Jonathan Katz:

> The word and concept "heterosexual" was produced and distributed in late nineteenth- and early twentieth-century America to express and to idealize qualitatively new relationships between men and women in which eroticism was defined as central and legitimate.[107]

In this context, "personal" life emerged as a distinct realm, for managerial and professional employees (and later for growing sectors of the working class), for the accumulation of goods, personal and family investment, life insurance, and leisure "capital." Heterosexuality as an erotic relation was "naturalized" through advertising, the mass media, and the developing entertainment industry.[108] Household and family relations shifted, and the nuclear family began to be isolated from relatives and support networks in the expanding urban centres.

In the first decades of the twentieth century, women were re-sexualized in mainstream sexual ideology. Sexual-advice literature placed an important new emphasis on "companionate" marriage, defined by heterosexual friendship and erotic attraction and satisfaction. This literature was written largely by male "educators, social workers, psychologists, physicians, and others in a rising class of trained professional people."[109] Male professionals began to play an important role in the restructuring and taming of female desires. Taking account of, and at the same time organizing aspects of, female heterosexuality in the organization of companionate marriage "meant the extension of assembly-line techniques into the bedroom."[110] Experts were called upon to intervene in the realm of the body, pleasure, and desire through prescribed sexual techniques.

This construction of heterosexuality did not only come from above, however. It also arose in part out of various forms of resistance to previous forms of the regulation of reproductive and male dominated male/female sexuality and family relations. Paradoxically, forms of resistance to earlier forms of different-gender familial and sexual regulation played a part in the construction of heterosexual hegemony. This led to the articulation of the "ideal" of companionate marriage and notions of an "active" female heterosexual desire that was based on a necessary or essential erotic attraction between men and women. While some women were able to expand their possibilities for pleasure in relations with men, the longer-term implications of this shift would not be so positive for women, and certainly not for women who loved other women. This process developed unevenly over several decades.

This period has been described as one of veritable "heterosexual counter-revolution" against feminism, whereby forms of female same-gender friendship, intimacy, and support networks were transformed into the perversions of "lesbianism."[111] Early studies of sapphism, or lesbianism, had investigated the "masculine" partner in female same-gender relationships for her supposed physiological peculiarities in menstruation and for her allegedly large clitoris. Attention was now extended to all women — even those deemed "feminine" — involved in same-gender sex.[112]

Distinct lesbian experiences and cultures came about through a different social process than did male homosexuality, and it did not reach fruition until a few decades later. This process involved a degree of economic independence and social spaces apart from men, the seizure of these spaces and the cultural resistance of women involved in same-gender sex, and the articulation of "lesbian" in scientific and medical discourse — which was used to police women's sexuality in general. In the late nineteenth and early twentieth centuries, it became possible for more women to live alone or to share boardinghouse rooms with other women.[113] The rise of feminism facilitated the emergence of female autonomy and support networks for some women. Companionate marriage and heterosexual culture were partly a response to feminism and same-gender eroticism among women.

Lesbian experience in the U.S. had roots in the tradition of working-class women who passed as men — sometimes living with other women — and the tradition of passionate romantic friendships between white middle-class women. Among black and working-class women, this cultural formation took place in the 1920s American jazz scene, in early networks of apartment parties, and in the few bars and clubs in which women could gather.[114]

Among the middle-class and intellectuals, there emerged a number of lesbian literary circles. In the 1920s, a community of middle-class lesbians, most of them financially independent, was formed in Paris. The case of Radclyffe Hall's *The Well of Loneliness* in 1928 was the lesbian equivalent of the Oscar Wilde trial. The book was banned because Hall "had not stigmatized [lesbianism] as in any way blameworthy."[115] The resulting suppression of lesbian literature generated enormous publicity for lesbianism. Thousands of women wrote to Hall, and this helped give lesbianism a name and an image.[116]

The development of the Welfare State meant the entrenchment of women's subordination and sexual regulation into the centre of State social policy.[117] State policy now embodies defence of the "traditional" family, institutionalized motherhood, and women's dependence on men — or, in their absence, on hand-outs and policing by welfare agencies. State intervention established as normative the two-parent heterosexual family and as deviant all other forms of family and social life. These same social policies helped organize institutionalized heterosexuality.[118]

Lesbian and homosexual cultures have taken on different features according to gender and patriarchal social organization and according to class and race. Heterosexual hegemony emerged in response to these "deviant" forms of sexuality. Homosexual and lesbian cultures and heterosexual hegemony, then, are two sides of the same relational process that is part of a series of gender, class, and social struggles in the formation of a capitalist and patriarchal society. In the next chapter, I will explore how this historical process took place in Canada. Many of the same influences I have explored in this chapter are also present in Canadian history, but they are combined in a specific fashion.

Notes

1. Rachel Harrison and Frank Mort argue that "the structure of specific apparatuses or institutions outside the sphere of economic relations cannot be 'read off' from any general concept of the mode of production or its abstract conditions of existence." From "Patriarchal Aspects of Nineteenth Century State Formation: Property Relations, Marriage and Divorce, and Sexuality" in Philip Corrigan, ed., *Capitalism, State Formation and Marxist Theory* (London, Melbourne, New York: Quartet, 1980) p. 108.
2. Philip Corrigan and Derek Sayer, *The Great Arch* (Oxford: Basil Blackwell, 1985) p. 189.
3. *Ibid.*, p. 140.
4. Paul Crane, *Gays and the Law* (London: Pluto, 1982), p. 11. For a broader historical context during this period, see Corrigan and Sayer, *The Great Arch*, *op. cit.*, pp. 45-46.
5. Harrison and Mort, *op. cit.*, p. 100.
6. On this, see John D'Emilio's "Capitalism and Gay Identity" in Snitow, Stansell and Thompson, eds., *Powers of Desire: The Politics of Sexuality* (New York: Monthly Review Press, 1983), pp. 100-113, and in John D'Emilio, *Making Trouble* (New York and London: Routledge, 1992), pp. 3-16.
7. My use of the term "sexual regime," that has been influenced by the work of Foucault (particularly Volume 1 of *The History of Sexuality*), differs from his perspective in several major respects. Foucault's perspective, despite its insights, has several major limitations. His introductory volume on sexuality is not about the social organization of sexual life, but about the social construction of sexual categories and discourses. The relation between these discourses and lived historical experience is rarely investigated. As a result, his work tends toward idealism: he suggests that the reality of "sexuality" lies in official discourses rather than in erotic life and the practices of sexual rule. Clearly, the historical implementation of official discourse in institutional settings has played an important role in shaping sexual identities and practices, but this cannot in and of itself account for historical developments. For example, contrary to Foucault's suggestion, the homosexual did not spring forth fully formed simply from medical, sexological, legal, or psychological discourse. We also have to investigate the formation of cultures and resistance among men engaged in same-gender sex along with the social spaces opened up for these cultures through capitalist social relations and the moral and sexual policies of State regulation. Foucault's perspective is remarkably androcentric — he virtually ignores the social relations of biological reproduction, the gender division of labour, and patriarchal social organization, except as they enter directly into the official discourse about sexuality he examines. As a result, Foucault is unable to name the patriarchal character of the ruling agencies from which this regime of sexuality was, and continues to be,

deployed. This disconnection of official discourse from its groundings in historically emerging social relations seriously limits the usefulness of his work. In his rush to avoid any narrow legal concept of power, Foucault also fragments any conception of State formation as an articulation of social relations into many diverse micro-centres of power with no social or historical unity. He is therefore unable to analyze how the process of sexual regulation has been integrally tied up with capitalist and patriarchal State formation. Foucault's critique of the repression thesis, mentioned earlier, while very insightful, also tends to be one-sided. In relation to homosexuality, he focuses on the sexological and medical definitions and does not deal with the important role of the criminal justice system in regulating sexual life. He generally views power based in law as simply coercive, ignoring its important role in constructing definitions and norms. Regarding homosexuality, the law operates, not simply as a coercive instrument, but legal discourse helps construct a specific homosexual subject as a criminal type. The law and the police, as well as medical, psychological, sexological, and other discourse are all crucial aspects of this sexual regime. For similar critiques of Foucault, see: Harrison and Mort, "Patriarchal Aspects of Nineteenth Century State Formation," *op. cit.*, pp. 107-108; Nicos Poulantzas, *State, Power, Socialism* (London: Verso, 1980), pp. 148-151; Lorna Weir, "Studies in the Medicalization of Sexual Danger," Ph.D. thesis, 1986, York University, Toronto, Dept. of Social and Political Thought; and Dorothy E. Smith, "The Social Organization of Textual Reality" in *The Conceptual Practices of Power* (Toronto: University of Toronto Press, 1990), pp. 70, 79. Some of the limitations of Foucault's relatively ungrounded discourse perspective continue to inform innovative queer historical work. For instance, Jennifer Terry, in her very insightful essay "Theorizing Deviant Historiography," in *differences*, V. 5, No. 2, pp. 55-74, only notes in an endnote that the resistance that she was able to detect in medical discourse by women "deviants" was not "entirely dependent on the medical discourse for its enunciation." (p. 72). Throughout most of the essay, it seems that even the resistance detected in these texts is constituted through official discourse.

8. See Heidi Hartmann, "Capitalism, Patriarchy and Job Segregation by Sex" in Eisenstein, ed., *Capitalist Patriarchy and the Case for Socialist Feminism* (New York and London: Monthly Review Press, 1979), pp. 204-247.

9. Dorothy E. Smith, "Women, Class and Family" *The Socialist Register* (London: Merlin Press, 1983) p. 2.

10. This point is developed in the work of John D'Emilio. See his *Sexual Politics, Sexual Communities* (Chicago: The University of Chicago Press, 1983), pp. 10-13, and his "Capitalism and Gay identity," in Snitow, *et al., Powers of Desire, op. cit.* and in *Making Trouble, op. cit.* D'Emilio can be criticized, at times, for his relatively one-sided emphasis on the seemingly spontaneous effects of the social relations of capitalism, particularly its "free labour" system in bringing about homosexual or gay identity, and his neglect in his general theoretical framework (although, interestingly, enough not in his actual historical work) of the regime of sexual rule and resistance to it in the formation of homosexual and gay cultures.

11. The analysis of these different kinds of social space comes from Wally Seccombe in a class on family formation at OISE. See his books *A Millennium of Family Change, Feudalism to Capitalism in Western Europe* (London: Verso, 1992) and *Weathering the Storm: Working Class Families from the Industrial Revolution to the Fertility Decline* (London: Verso, 1993).

12. See Lillian Faderman, *Surpassing the Love of Men: Romantic Friendship and Love Between Women from the Renaissance to the Present* (New York: William Morrow, 1981) and Carroll Smith-Rosenberg, "The Female World of Love and Ritual: Relations between Women in Nineteenth-Century America" in her *Disorderly Conduct: Visions of Gender in Victorian America* (New York: Knopf, 1985).

13. This notion of the transition from family of origin to family of procreation also comes from Wally Seccombe.

14. Later, there emerged other forms of social regulation of the transition from family of origin

to family of adulthood, including compulsory schooling, mass culture, and new ways of legally regulating young people's sex lives.

15. Dorothy E. Smith, "Women, Class and Family," *op. cit.*, p. 11.

16. See: Alan Bray, *Homosexuality in Renaissance England* (London: Gay Men's Press, 1982), particularly ch. 4: "Molly," pp. 81-114; Randolph Trumbach, "London's Sodomites: Homosexual Behaviour and Western Culture in the 18th Century" in *Journal of Social History*, V. 11, No. 1, pp. 1-33 (Fall 1977-1978); and Jeffrey Weeks, *Coming Out* (London, Melbourne, New York: Quartet Books, 1977), pp. 33-44. Bray criticizes Weeks for focusing, in his earlier work (like *Coming Out*), on the psychological, medical, and legal definitions of homosexuality in the late nineteenth century, while neglecting earlier cultural developments. See Bray, *op. cit.*, pp. 134-137, note 18. "Molly" seems to have been developed in the Molly culture itself, as a taking over of Molly, a form of the name Mary. See Bray, p. 133, note 5. Also see Trumbach, "Gender and the Homosexual Role in Modern Western Culture: The 18th and 19th Centuries Compared," in Dennis Altman *et al.*, *Which Homosexuality?* (London: GMP Publishers, 1989), pp. 149-169, and Trumbach, "The Birth of the Queen: Sodomy and the Emergence of Gender Equality in Modern Culture, 1660-1750" in Duberman *et al.*, eds., *Hidden From History: Reclaiming The Gay Past* (New York: Meridian, 1990), pp. 129-140.

17. Court records are not always reliable sources, and we must be careful not to simply accept them as "factual" accounts; rather, we must use them critically and try to understand their social context and social construction. See Bray, pp. 85-86, and p. 138, note 26.

18. According to Makeda Silvera, "Sodomite" and "Man Royal" were used in Jamaica to describe women who had sex with other women, and sometimes just for strong independent women. This use of sodomite seems peculiar to Jamaica and is rooted in interpretations of the Old Testament. See Makeda Silvera, "Man Royals and Sodomites: Some thoughts on the Invisibility of Afro-Caribbean Lesbians," in Sharon Dale Stone, *Lesbians in Canada* (Toronto: Between the Lines, 1990), pp. 49-50.

19. Bray, *op. cit.*, p. 97.

20. *Ibid.*, p. 114.

21. Arthur N. Gilbert, "Buggery and the British Navy: 1700-1861," in *Journal of Social History*, Fall 1976, V. 10, No.1. p. 79.

22. Crane, *Gays and the Law, op. cit.*, p. 12.

23. This paragraph is based on Gilbert, *op. cit.*, and Weeks, *Coming Out, op. cit.* Also see David Greenberg, *The Construction of Homosexuality* (Chicago and London: The University of Chicago Press, 1988), especially "Bureaucracy and Homosexuality," pp. 434-454, and L.J. Moran, "The Uses of Homosexuality: Homosexuality for National Security" in *International Journal of the Sociology of Law*, 1991, Vol. 19, pp. 150-153.

24. Weeks, *Coming Out, op. cit.*, p. 13.

25. See David F. Greenberg, *The Construction of Homosexuality, op. cit.*, pp. 434-454. Also see my review of Greenberg's book in *The Canadian Journal of Sociology*, V. 15, No. 1, Winter 1990, pp. 112-115.

26. Karl Marx, *Grundrisse* (Harmondsworth: Penguin, 1973), p. 83.

27. See: Philip Corrigan, "On Moral Regulation: Some Preliminary Remarks" in *Sociological Review*, V. 29, No. 2, 1981, p. 329; Derek Sayer and Philip Corrigan, *The Great Arch, op. cit.*,; Michel Foucault's Introduction to *Herculine Barbin* (New York: Pantheon, 1980) p. viii; Ian Hacking, "How Should We Do the History of Statistics?" and other articles in Graham Burchell, Colin Gordon and Peter Miller, eds., *The Foucault Effect: Studies in Governmentality* (Chicago: The University of Chicago Press, 1991); and Mike Gane and Terry Johnson, eds., *Foucault's New Domains* (London and New York, 1993).

28. And even this is contested, as feminists have asserted women's rights to control their own bodies. See Rosalind Petchesky, "Reproductive Freedom: Beyond a Woman's Right to Choose" in Stimpson and Person, eds., *Women, Sex and Sexuality* (Chicago and London: The University of

Chicago Press, 1980), pp. 94-96; and Petchesky, *Abortion and Women's Choice: The State, Sexuality and Reproductive Freedom* (New York and London: Longman, 1984), pp. 1-21.

29. Jonathan Ned Katz, *Gay/Lesbian Almanac* (New York: Harper and Row, 1983), p. 13. Also see Jonathan Ned Katz's, "The Political Economy of Pleasure: Toward a Theory of the Socio-Historical Structure of Erotic Activity, with Special Reference to Heterosexuality," unpublished paper, 1994, and his *The Invention of Heterosexuality*, (New York: Dutton, 1995).

30. See Katz's "The Political Economy of Pleasure," *op. cit.*

31. Again, see Katz's, *The Invention of Heterosexuality, op. cit.*

32. This section draws on Foucault's *History of Sexuality*, V. 1. At the same times as Katz points out in *The Invention of Heterosexuality, op. cit.*, Foucault does not specifically problematize heterosexuality (see pp. 170-181). This is a significant limitation in his theorizing about sexuality.

33. On fairies and queers, see George Chauncey, *Gay New York: Gender, Urban Culture, and the Making of the Gay Male World*, (New York: Basic Books, 1994), especially pp. 47-63. Also see the review of Chauncey's book by Ann Holder, "Fairies and Normals and Queers, Oh My! Gay New York Before the Rise of the Closet," *Radical America*, V. 25, No. 3, pp. 53-64.

34. Katz, *Gay/Lesbian Almanac, op. cit.*, p. 145. Also see Katz, *The Invention of Heterosexuality, op. cit.*

35. The process of the emergence and development of the contemporary heterosexual male needs more investigation and study. For some useful explorations, see: Andrew Tolson, *The Limits of Masculinity* (London: Tavistock, 1977); Joe Interrante, "The History of Masculinity" in *Gay Community News* (Boston), April 26, 1980, pp. 4 and 6; R.W. Connell, *Which Way is Up?* (Sydney, London, Boston: George Allen and Unwin, 1983), Connell, *Gender and Power* (Stanford, CA: Stanford University Press, 1987); Connell, *Masculinities* (Berkeley and Los Angeles: University of California Press, 1995); Lynne Segal, *Slow Motion: Changing Masculinities, Changing Men* (London: Virago, 1990); Kobena Mercer and Isaac Julien, "Race, Sexual Politics and Black Masculinity: A Dossier," in Rowena Chapman and Jonathan Rutherford, eds., *Male Order, Unwrapping Masculinity* (London: Lawrence and Wishart, 1988), pp. 97-164; David H.J. Morgan, *Discovering Men* (London and New York: Routledge, 1992); Victor J. Seidler, *Recreating Sexual Politics: Men, Feminism and Politics* (London and New York: Routledge, 1991); Steven Maynard, "Rough Work and Rugged Men: The Social Construction of Masculinity in Working-Class History," *Labour/Le Travail*, V. 23, 1989, pp. 159-169; Blye Frank, "Hegemonic Heterosexual Masculinity," in *Studies in Political Economy*, V. 24, 1987; Frank, "Hegemonic Heterosexual Masculinity: Sports, Looks and a Woman, That's What Every Guy Needs To Be Masculine," in *Violence and Social Control in the Home, Workplace, Community and Institutions*, ISER Conference Papers, No. 3, St. John's, NF, Institute for Social and Economic Research, 1992, pp. 273-303; Frank, "Queer Selves/Queer in Schools: Young Men and Sexualities" in Susan Prentice, ed., *Sex in Schools, Canadian Education and Sexual Regulation* (Toronto: Our Schools/Our Selves, 1994), pp. 44-59; and Gary Kinsman, "'Inverts', 'Psychopaths', and 'Normal' Men: Historical Sociological Perspectives on Gay and Heterosexual Masculinities," in Tony Haddad, ed., *Men and Masculinities: A Critical Anthology* (Toronto: Canadian Scholars' Press, 1993), pp. 3-35.

36. See: Leonore Davidoff, "Class and Gender in Victorian England: The Diaries of Arthur J. Munby and Hannah Cullwick," *Feminist Studies*, No. 5 (Spring 1979), pp. 88-91; Nancy F. Cott, "Passionlessness: An Interpretation of Victorian Sexual Ideology, 1750-1850" in Cott and Pleck, eds., *A Heritage of Her Own* (New York: Simon and Shuster, 1979), pp. 162-181; Linda Gordon, *Women's Body, Women's Right* (New York: Penguin, 1977); and Ellen Dubois and Linda Gordon "Seeking Ecstasy in the Battlefield: Danger and Pleasure in Nineteenth Century Feminist Sexual Thought" in Carol S. Vance, ed., *Pleasure and Danger: Exploring Female Sexuality* (Boston, London, Melbourne and Henley: Routledge and Kegan Paul, 1984), pp. 31-49.

37. See Weeks, "Discourse, Desire and Sexual Deviance" in Plummer, ed., *The Making of the Modern Homosexual* (London: Hutchinson, 1981), p. 105; Weeks, *Sex, Politics and Society* (London and New York: Longman, 1981), pp. 112-113; and Weeks, *Coming Out, op. cit.*, pp. 40-41.

38. George Chauncey Jr., "From Sexual Inversion to Homosexuality: Medicine and the Changing Conceptualization of Female Deviance," in *Salmagundi* (Fall 1982/Winter 1983), p. 135.
39. *Ibid.*, p. 135.
40. Judith Walkowitz, *Prostitution and Victorian Society*, (Cambridge: Cambridge University Press, 1980) and Weeks, *Coming Out, op. cit.*, pp. 16-17. On Canada, also see Mariana Valverde, *The Age of Light, Soap and Water: Moral Reform in English Canada, 1885-1925* (Toronto: McClelland and Stewart, 1991) on social purity and moral reform.
41. See: Martha Vicinus, "Sexuality and Power: A Review of Current Work in the History of Sexuality," *Feminist Studies*, V. 8, No. 1 (Spring 1982), p. 135; Foucault, *History of Sexuality*, V. 1 (New York; Vintage, 1980), pp. 117-118; and Lorna Weir, "Studies in the Medicalization of Sexual Danger: Sexual Rule, Sexual Politics, 1830-1930," *op. cit.*, particularly Chapter Four, "Sex Psychology."
42. For a critique of an overly expansive and ungrounded notion of sexology that is not located in specific organizational and institutional settings and practices, see Weir, "Studies in the Medicalization of Sexual Danger," *op. cit.*, particularly pp. 240-246.
43. Jeffrey Weeks, "Foucault for Historians," *History Workshop*, No. 14, p. 114. Also see Weeks, "Uses and abuses of Michel Foucault" in Weeks, *Against Nature* (London: Rivers Oram Press, 1991), pp. 157-169.
44. See Weeks, *Sexuality and Its Discontents, op. cit.*, pp. 61-95, and Lorna Weir, *op. cit.*
45. Weeks, *Sex, Politics and Society* (London: Longman, 1981), p. 145.
46. See Lorna Weir, *op. cit.*, pp. 1-70.
47. See: Isabel J. Hull, "The Bourgeoisie and Its Discontents: Reflections on Nationalism and Respectability" in *Journal of Contemporary History*, V. 17, No. 2, April 1982, p. 258; Katz, *Gay/Lesbian Almanac, op. cit.*, pp. 148-149; and Katz's *The Invention of Heterosexuality* (New York: Dutton/Penguin, 1995).
48. Foucault, *History of Sexuality*, V. 1, *op. cit.*, p. 122. On these questions, also see Lynette Finch, *The Classing Gaze: Sexuality, Class and Surveillance* (St. Leonards, New South Wales: Allen and Unwin, 1993).
49. Foucault, *History of Sexuality, op.cit.*, pp. 25-26, 146.
50. See: Heidi Hartmann, "Capitalism, Patriarchy and Job Segregation by Sex" in Eisenstein, ed. *Capitalist Patriarchy and the Case for Socialist Feminism, op. cit.*, and her "The Unhappy Marriage of Marxism and Feminism" in Lydia Sargent, ed., *Women and Revolution* (Montréal: Black Rose Books, 1981), pp. 1-41; Philips and Taylor, "Sex and Skill: Notes Toward a Feminist Economics" in *Feminist Review*, No. 6, 1980, pp. 79-88; Barbara Taylor, *Eve and the New Jerusalem* (London: Virago, 1983); and Dorothy E. Smith, "Women, Class and Family," *op. cit.*
51. See: Carroll Smith-Rosenberg, "The Female World of Love and Ritual: Relations Between Women in Nineteenth-Century America" in her *Disorderly Conduct: Visions of Gender in Victorian America, op. cit.*; Lillian Faderman, *Surpassing the Love of Men* (New York: William Morris, 1981); and Sheila Jeffreys, *The Spinster and Her Enemies: Feminism and Sexuality, 1880-1930* (London: Pandora, 1985). Also see Jeffreys, *Anticlimax: A Feminist Perspective on the Sexual Revolution* (London: The Women's Press, 1990).
52. Bob Gallagher and Alexander Wilson, interview with Michel Foucault, "Sex, Power and the Politics of Identity" in *The Advocate*, No. 400, Aug. 7, 1984, p. 30. This question of the transformation of male same-gender friendships deserves more detailed historical investigation. On some of this, also see David Greenberg, *The Construction of Homosexuality, op. cit.*
53. Walkowitz, "The Politics of Prostitution" in *Signs*, V. 6, No. 1, 1980, p. 130. Also see her *Prostitution and Victorian Society: Women, Class and State* (New York: Cambridge University Press, 1980) and her later *City of Dreadful Delight: Narratives of Sexual Danger in Late-Victorian London* (Chicago: The University of Chicago Press, 1992).
54. Weeks, *Coming Out, op. cit.*, pp. 16-17. Also see Mariana Valverde, *The Age of Light, Soap and Water: Moral Reform in English Canada, 1885-1925, op. cit.*

55. On the outcast poor, see Gareth Stedman Jones, *Outcast London* (Harmondsworth: Penguin, 1984).
56. On this, see A.M. Givertz, "Considering Race and Class in the Regulation of Sexuality and the Prosecution of Sexual Assault in Hamilton, 1880-1929," unpublished paper given at the Canadian Historical Association meetings, Carleton University, June 7, 1993.
57. On racism in Canadian social purity, also see Mariana Valverde, *The Age of Light, Soap and Water: Moral Reform in English Canada, 1885-1925, op. cit.*
58. Paul Willis, "Cultural Production is Different from Cultural Reproduction is Different from Social Reproduction is Different from Reproduction" in *Interchange*, V. 12, Nos. 2 and 3, 1981, pp. 48-67. Also see Paul Willis, *Learning to Labour* (London: Saxon House, 1977).
59. Chauncey, "From Sexual Inversion to Homosexuality ...." *op. cit.*, p. 122.
60. On this, see Chauncey *Gay New York, op. cit.*
61. See John Marshall, "Pansies, Perverts and Macho Men: Changing Conceptions of Male Homosexuality" in Plummer, ed., *The Making of the Modern Homosexual, op. cit.*, pp. 133-154.
62. Chauncey, "From Sexual Inversion to Homosexuality," *op. cit.*, p. 130.
63. Katz, *Gay/Lesbian Almanac, op. cit.*, p. 16.
64. See John Lauritsen and David Thorstad, *The Early Homosexual Rights Movement* (New York: Times Change Press, 1974), pp. 6-9 and James D. Steakley, *The Homosexual Emancipation Movement in Germany* (New York: Arno Press, 1975), pp. 10-13.
65. For instance, Westphal had "discovered" cases of "contrary sexual feeling," which he saw as a form of congenital psychopathology, also in 1869. See James D. Steakley, *The Homosexual Emancipation Movement in Germany, op. cit.*, p. 9.
66. On "reverse discourse," see Foucault: "There is no question that the appearance in nineteenth-century psychiatry, jurisprudence, and literature of a whole series of discourses on the species and subspecies of homosexuality, inversion, pederasty and 'psychic hermaphrodism' made possible a strong advance of social controls into this area of 'perversity'; but it also made possible the formation of a 'reverse' discourse: homosexuality began to speak on its own behalf, to demand that its legitimacy or 'naturality' be acknowledged, often in the same vocabulary, using the same categories by which it was medically disqualified." *The History of Sexuality*, V. 1, *op. cit.*, p. 101. Unfortunately, Foucault does not specify the extra-discursive basis for this resistance. This limitation is continued in much queer-theory influenced work.
67. See Weeks, *Coming Out, op. cit.*, pp. 16-22, and Weeks, "Inverts, Perverts, and Mary Annes: Male Prostitution and the Regulation of Homosexuality in England in the 19th and Early 20th Centuries," Licata and Peterson, eds., *Historical Perspectives on Homosexuality* (New York: Haworth/Stein and Day, 1981), p. 124. On Wilde, also see Neil Bartlett, *Who Was That Man? A Present for Mr. Oscar Wilde* (London: Serpent's Tail, 1988).
68. Chauncey, *"From Sexual Inversion to Homosexuality" op. cit.*, p. 130.
69. Anna Davin, "Imperialism and Motherhood" in *History Workshop*, Issue 5, 1978, pp. 9-65.
70. Chris Jones and Tony Novack, "The State and Social Policy" in Philip Corrigan, ed., *Capitalism, State Formation and Marxist Theory, op. cit.*, p. 147.
71. Davin, *op. cit.*, p. 12.
72. See Rosalind Petchesky, *Abortion and Women's Choice* (Boston: Northeastern University Press, 1985).
73. See: Lucy Bland, "Guardians of the Race, or Vampires upon the Nation's Health? Female Sexuality and Its Regulation in Early Twentieth Century Britain" in Elizabeth Whiteleg, *et al.*, eds., *The Changing Experience of Women* (Oxford: Martin Robertson, 1982), pp. 373-388; Lucy Bland and Frank Mort, "Look Out for the 'Good Time' Girl: Dangerous Sexualities as a Threat to National Health" in *Formations of Nation and People* (London, Boston, Melbourne and Henley: Routledge and Kegan Paul, 1984), pp. 131-151; and also the related article by Lucy Bland, "Marriage Laid Bare: Middle Class Women and Marital Sex 1880s-1940" in Jane Lewis, ed., *Labour and Love* (Oxford: Basil Blackwell, 1986), pp. 123-146. Also see Allen M. Brandt, *No Magic Bullet: A Social History of Venereal Disease in the United States Since 1880* (New

York and Oxford: Oxford University Press, 1985) and Frank Mort, *Dangerous Sexualities, Medico-Moral Politics in England Since 1830* (London: Routledge and Kegan Paul, 1987).

74. Quoted in Angus McLaren, "Birth Control and Abortion in Canada, 1870-1920" in *Canadian Historical Review*, Sept. 1978, p. 319. Also see Angus McLaren and Arlene Tigar McLaren, *The Bedroom and the State: The Changing Practices and Politics of Contraception and Abortion in Canada, 1880-1980* (Toronto: McClelland and Stewart, 1986) and Angus McLaren's *Our Own Master Race, Eugenics in Canada, 1885-1945* (Toronto: McClelland and Stewart, 1990).

75. See Michael Blanch, "Imperialism, Nationalism and Organized Youth" in Clarke, Critcher and Johnson, eds., *Working Class Culture* (London: Hutchinson, 1979), pp. 103-120; and George L. Mosse, *Nationalism and Sexuality, Respectability and Abnormal Sexuality in Modern Europe* (New York: Howard Fertig, 1985). Also see some of the articles in Andrew Parker, Mary Russ, Doris Sommer and Patricia Yaeger, eds., *Nationalisms and Sexualities* (New York and London: Routledge, 1992).

76. This point comes from Philip Corrigan. Also see Jacques Donzelot, *The Policing of Families* (New York: Pantheon, 1979). Donzelot's insightful analysis is unfortunately limited by anti-Marxist and anti-feminist tendencies. On this see Barrett and McIntosh, *The Anti-Social Family* (London: Verso, 1982), pp. 95-105, 116-118.

77. On this also see Ellen Ross and Rayna Rapp, "Sex and Society: A Research Note from Social History and Anthropology" in Snitow *et al.*, eds., *Powers of Desire* (New York: Monthly Review Press, 1983), pp. 61-69.

78. Isabel J.Hull, "The Bourgeoisie and Its Discontents ..." *op. cit.*, p. 258.

79. Weeks, *Coming Out, op. cit.*, p. 27. Also see: Mosse, *Toward the Final Solution* (New York: Harper Colophon, 1978); Mosse, "Nationalism and Respectability ..." *op. cit.*; Stephen Jay Gould, *The Mismeasure of Man* (New York: W.W. Norton, 1981), pp. 123-142; for later developments see Nikolas Rose, "The Psychological Complex: Mental Measurement and Social Administration" in *Ideology and Consciousness*, Spring 1979, No. 5, pp. 5-68 and Rose, *The Psychological Complex: Psychology, Politics and Society in England, 1869-1939* (London: Routledge and Kegan Paul, 1985). Degeneration was apparently first formulated as a concept by Benedict Augustin Morel in 1857. The theory of degeneration was popularized by Max Nordau in his book *Degeneration*.

80. Stephen Jay Gould, *Ever Since Darwin* (London: Burnett, 1978), p. 226.

81. Weeks, *Coming Out, op. cit.*, pp. 27, 58-59.

82. In reference to same-gender sexuality between men, Marx and Engels were bothered by the then current fears of "degeneracy." In his historical work, Engels makes specific derogatory mention of male same-gender sexuality. Engels wrote about Ancient Greece: "... this degeneration of women was avenged on the men and degraded them also, till they fell into the abominable practice of sodomy and degraded alike their gods and themselves with the myth of Ganymede." Engels, *The Origin of the Family, Private Property and the State* (New York: International, p. 128). In their personal correspondence, Marx and Engels were very clear in their attitudes. They were not unaware of the beginnings of "homosexual" emancipation efforts in Germany. In 1868 there was an interchange between Marx and Engels over a book by Dr. Karl Boruttau. Engels is translated as referring to Boruttau as the "cock queer." In 1869 Marx sent Engels the latest book on "Uranians" by Ulrichs. Uranians for Ulrichs were basically a "third sex" defined by a congenital anomaly, among men a woman's soul trapped in a man's body. Engels replied: "This is a very strange 'Uranian' that you have sent me. Here are really unnatural disclosures. The pederasts are beginning to count themselves and find that they form a power in the state ... it is only by luck that we are personally too old to have to fear that at this victory we will have to pay bodily tribute." See Hubert Kennedy, "J.B. Schweitzer: The Faggot Marx Loved to Hate," *Fag Rag*, No. 19, Spring 1977, p. 6, which quotes in translation from *Marx Engels Werke*, V. 32, pp. 324-325. Notice that Marx and Engels used such terms as "unnatural disclosures" and "pederasts" (they do not use the category of "homosexual," which was invented only in 1869). On Ulrichs and his concept of Uranian, see: Steakley, *The Homosexual Emancipation Movement in Germany, op. cit.*, pp. 3-9; Hubert C. Kennedy, "The Third Sex

Theory of Karl Heinrich Ulrichs" in Licata and Peterson, eds., *Historical Perspectives on Homosexuality, op. cit.*, pp. 103-111; and Hubert Kennedy, *Ulrichs* (Boston: Alyson, 1988). When J.B. Schweitzer, an early leader of the Lasallean wing of the German Social Democratic movement, was accused of same-gender sex in a park, he was defended by Lasalle, but not by Marx and Engels. Marx and Engels apparently saw the Uranians, the sodomites, and the pederasts as symptoms of degeneration and unnatural behaviour. They evidently felt that "proper," "normal" sexuality would take the exclusive form of what we now call heterosexual genital intercourse. Also see Andrew Parker, "Unthinking Sex: Marx, Engels, and the Scene of Writing," in Michael Warner, ed., *Fear of a Queer Planet* (Minneapolis: University of Minnesota Press, 1993), pp. 19-41.

83. Katz, *Gay American History, op. cit.*, pp. 135-137, 143-144. Also see Weir, *op. cit.*, sections on "Sex Psychology" and "Sex Reform."

84. See Gary Kinsman, "The Metro Toronto Police Department and the Gay Community" in the "Sexuality and the State" issue of *Atkinson Review of Canadian Studies*, V. 1, No. 2 (Spring 1984).

85. This is in contrast to the perspective advanced by Foucault in *The History of Sexuality*, V. 1, in which he basically views the creation of the homosexual as the result of sexological and medical discourses themselves that are not seen as directly linked to this apparatus of sexual policing.

86. Although, as I suggested earlier, this effect of sexual science is overemphasized in a one-sided manner in Foucault, *History of Sexuality, V.1, op. cit.*

87. "Men (sic) make their own history but they do not make it just as they please; they do not make it under circumstances chosen by themselves, but under circumstances directly encountered, given and transmitted by the past." Marx, *The Eighteenth Brumaire of Louis Bonaparte* (New York: International, 1973), p. 15.

88. See previously mentioned sources. Also see Barry Adam, *The Rise of a Lesbian and Gay Movement* (Boston: Twayne Publishers, 1987), pp. 17-25. On Hirschfeld, also see *The Writings of Dr. Magnus Hirschfeld*, a bibliography compiled and introduced by James D. Steakley (Toronto: Canadian Gay Archives Publication Series, No. 11, 1985).

89. Chauncey, "From Sexual Inversion to Homosexuality," *op. cit.*, p. 142.

90. See Steakley, *The Homosexual Emancipation Movement in Germany, op. cit,* and also Lauritsen and Thorstad, *The Early Homosexual Rights Movement, op. cit.*

91. On Whitman, see: Geoffrey Egan "These Things May Lead to the Tragedy of Our Species: Notes Toward a History of Homosexuality in Canada, 1890-1930," unpublished paper, Concordia University, April 1980, p. 26; Michael Lynch, "The Lover of His Fellows and the Hot Little Prophets: Walt Whitman in Ontario," *The Body Politic*, No. 67, Oct. 1980, pp. 29-31; Lynch's "Walt Whitman in Ontario," in Robert K. Martin, ed., *The Continuing Presence of Walt Whitman: The Life after the Life* (Iowa City: University of Iowa Press, 1992), pp. 141-151; and Robert K. Martin, *The Homosexual Tradition in American Poetry* (Austin, University of Texas Press, 1979). On Carpenter, see previously cited references, and Katz, *Gay/Lesbian Almanac, op. cit.*, pp. 160, 165, 250-254, 364-365, 395-397, 414; Ruth F. Claws, "Confronting Homosexuality: A Letter from Frances Wilder," *Signs*, V. 2, No. 4, 1977. John Addington Symonds in England drew upon the writings of Ancient Greece, stating that "… here alone in history do we have the example of a great and highly developed race not only tolerating homosexual passions, but deeming them of spiritual value and attempting to utilize them for the benefit of society." Symonds, "A Problem in Greek Ethics: Being an Inquiry into the Phenomenon of Sexual Inversion Addressed Especially to Medical Psychologists and Jurists" in John Lauritsen, ed., *John Addington Symonds: Male Love* (New York: Pagan Press, 1983), p. 1. As Weeks argues, "His aim was to establish, by using the Greek analogy, that homosexuality could be accepted as part of the social mores." Weeks, *Coming Out, op. cit.*, p. 52. Using the example of Classical Greece in this way was part of a long Eurocentric tradition that traced the origins of "civilization" back to Ancient Greece which was then claimed as a European culture.

92. The class, racial, and ethnic dimensions of the formation of homosexual and lesbian identi-

ties and cultures need to be explored much more fully. For some exploratory work on sex between men, see: Kobena Mercer and Isaac Julien, "Race, Sexual Politics and Black Masculinity: A Dossier," in Rowena Chapman and Jonathan Rutherford, eds., *Male Order: Unwrapping Masculinity* (London: Lawrence and Wishart, 1988), pp. 97-164; Kobena Mercer, "Skin Head Sex Thing: Racial Differences and the Homoerotic Imaginary" in Bad Object Choices, eds., *How Do I Look? Queer Film and Video* (Seattle: Bay Press, 1991), pp. 169-210; Richard Fung, "Looking for My Penis: The Eroticized Asian in Gay Video Porn" in Bad Object Choices, eds., *op. cit.*, pp. 145-160; Eric Garber's "T'aint Nobody's Business: Homosexuality in Harlem in the 1920s," *The Advocate*, No. 342, pp. 39-43, and his slideshow by the same name, and his "A Spectacle in Color: The Lesbian and Gay Subculture of Jazz Age Harlem," in Martin Duberman, *et al.*, *Hidden from History* (New York: Meridian, 1990), pp. 318-331; George Chauncey, Jr., "Christian Brotherhood or Sexual Perversion? Homosexual Identities and the Construction of Sexual Boundaries in the World War I Era" in *Journal of Social History*, V. 19 (Winter 1985), pp. 189-211, and also in Duberman *et al.*, eds., *Hidden From History*, *op. cit.*, and his *Gay New York*, *op. cit.*; and the work of Steven Maynard on working-class men, masculinity and homosexuality in late 19th and early 20th century Ontario, "Rough Work and Rugged Men: The Social Construction of Masculinity in Working-Class History," *Labour/Le Travail*, *op. cit.*; and "Through a Hole in the Lavatory Wall: Homosexual Subcultures, Police Surveillance, and the Dialectics of Discovery, Toronto, 1890-1930" in *Journal of the History of Sexuality*, V. 5, No. 2, October 1994, pp. 207-242. Analysis of the formation of lesbian cultures had largely remained confined to white and middle-class women until recently. For example, see Faderman, *Surpassing the Love of Men*, *op. cit.* Faderman's later book, *Odd Girls and Twilight Lovers: A History of Lesbian Life in Twentieth-Century America* (New York: Columbia University Press, 1991) makes a better attempt to deal with class and race differences. However, there has now been some very important work done on the formation of black and working-class lesbian networks. See the work of the Buffalo Women's Oral History project. For instance, Madeline Davis and Elizabeth Lapovsky Kennedy, "Oral History and the Study of Sexuality in the Lesbian Community: Buffalo, New York, 1940-1960" in *Feminist Studies*, V. 12, No. 1, Spring 1986, pp. 7-26, and their pathbreaking book, *Boots of Leather, Slippers of Gold: The History of a Lesbian Community* (New York and London: Routledge, 1993). Also see Martha Vicinus, "Sexuality and Power," *op cit.*, pp. 147-151, for some of the earlier controversies in lesbian history and her later "'They Wonder to Which Sex I Belong': The Historical Roots of the Modern Lesbian Identity," in Dennis Altman, *et al.*, *Which Homosexuality? op. cit.*, pp. 171-198. On black women's experiences, see Audre Lorde, *Zami: A New Spelling of My Name* (New York: Crossing Press, 1982) and *Sister/Outsider: Essays and Speeches* (New York: Crossing Press, 1984); Hazel V. Carby, "It Jus Be's Dat Way Sometime: The Sexual Politics of Women's Blues" in *Radical America*, V. 20, No. 4, pp. 9-22; Erua Omosupe, "Black/Lesbian/Bulldagger," *differences*, V. 3, No. 2; Queer Theory, Lesbian and Gay Sexualities Issue, Summer 1991, pp. 101-111; and Helen (charles), "'Queer Nigger': Theorizing 'White' Activism" in Joseph Bristow, and Angelia R. Wilson, *Activating Theory: Lesbian, Gay and Bisexual Politics* (London: Lawrence and Wishart, 1993), pp. 97-106.

93. See George Chauncey, Jr., "Christian Brotherhood or Sexual Perversion? Homosexual Identities and the Construction of Sexual Boundaries in the World War I Era" in *Journal of Social History*, Vol. 19 (1985), pp. 189-212, and in Duberman, Vicinus, and Chauncey, eds., *Hidden From History* (New York: Meridian, 1990), pp. 294-317 and his book *Gay New York*, *op. cit.* In his book, Chauncey distinguishes between fairies and queers in a much sharper fashion. Fairies were largely working-class men who engaged in some of the practices of "gender inversion," while "queer men" first emerged in middle-class cultures and did not necessarily adopt "effeminate" behaviours. They did, however, identify their primary sexual interest as being in other men. See *Gay New York*, especially "The Fairy as an Intermediate Sex," pp. 47-63 and "The Forging of Queer Identities and the Emergence of Heterosexuality in Middle Class Culture," pp. 99-127. Also see Ann Holder, "Fairies and Normals and Queers, Oh My! Gay New York before the Rise of the Closet," *Radical America*, *op. cit.*

94. Weeks, *Sex, Politics and Society, op. cit.*, pp. 111-114.

95. Chauncey, "From Sexual Inversion to Homosexuality ..." *op. cit.*, p. 135.

96. George Chauncey, Jr., "Christian Brotherhood or Sexual Perversion? Homosexual Identities and the Construction of Sexual Boundaries in the World War 1 Era," in Duberman, Vicinus, and Chauncey, eds., *Hidden From History, op. cit.*, p. 315. He unfortunately tends to use homosexuality in a transhistorical fashion in this quote.

97. *Ibid.*, pp. 315-316.

98. For some thoughts beginning to move in this direction, see Peter Drucker, "'In The Tropics There is No Sin,' Homosexuality and Gay/Lesbian Movements in the Third World," Working Paper No. 31, Working Papers of the International Institute for Research and Education, July 1993.

99. See Chauncey, *Gay New York, op. cit.*, especially pp. 331-361.

100. Chauncey's description in *Gay New York, op. cit.*, especially pp. 99-127, moves in this direction.

101. We continue to suffer from the lack of historical recovery of working-class men's voices describing their own experiences. However, there are some important leads and new developments. See, for example, Earl Lind's accounts of his contacts with young working-class men in the late nineteenth and early twentieth centuries. Earl Lind, *Autobiography of an Androgyne* (New York: Arno Reprint, 1975) and his *The Female Impersonators* (New York: Arno Reprint, 1975). Also see Steven Maynard's groundbreaking work looking at court records to try to recover working-class men's experiences of same-gender sex and policing. On working-class men's encounters with sexual policing, see "Through a Hole in the Lavatory Wall: Homosexual Subcultures, Police Surveillance, and the Dialectics of Discovery, Toronto, 1890-1930" in *Journal of the History of Sexuality*, V. 5, No. 2, October 1994, pp. 207-242. I will examine this article in more detail in chapter 6.

102. See previous references to Carpenter in the introduction. Also see Noel Greig, "The Dear Love of Comrades" in Greig and Griffiths, *Two Gay Sweatshop Plays* (London: Gay Men's Press, 1981), pp. 71-142.

103. For this section, see Weeks, "Inverts, Perverts and Mary Annes," *op. cit.*, pp. 115-130.

104. See D.E. Smith and G. Malnairch, "Where Are the Women? A Critique of Communist and Socialist Political Organization," paper presented at the Conference on Marxism: The Next Two Decades, University of Manitoba, 1983.

105. Dorothy E. Smith, "Women, Class and Family," *op. cit.*, p. 13.

106. See Dorothy E. Smith, *The Conceptual Practices of Power* (Toronto: University of Toronto Press, 1990) and her *Texts, Facts and Femininity* (London and New York: Routledge, 1990).

107. Katz, *Gay/Lesbian Almanac, op. cit.*, p. 661.107. Also see his *The Invention of Heterosexuality, op. cit.*

108. For explorations of how the ideologies of naturalism work, see Roland Barthes, *Mythologies* (London: Granada, 1982). For the development of U.S. consumer markets and cultures, see Stuart Ewen, *Captains of Consciousness* (New York: McGraw Hill, 1976); and Stuart and Elizabeth Ewen, *Channels of Desire: Mass Images and the Shaping of American Consciousness* (New York: McGraw Hill, 1982).

109. Christina Simmons, "Companionate Marriage and the Lesbian Threat" in *Frontiers: A Journal of Women's Studies*, Lesbian History Issue, V. 1, No. 3, Fall 1979, p. 54. Also see Jeffries, *The Spinster and Her Enemies, op. cit.*, although I strongly disagree with her one-sided critique of sex-scientific discourses and the sex-reform movements, which does not recognize their contradictory character. Some feminists like Stella Browne and Dora Russell were able to use aspects of sexual scientific work to push forward their campaigns for greater access by working-class women to birth control and abortion so they could have greater control over their reproductive and (hetero)sexual lives. On this, also see Mariana Valverde's review of *The Spinster and Her Enemies* in "Sex Versus Purity: Conflicts in the First Wave of Feminism" in *Rites*, V. 3, No. 2, June 1986, pp. 10-11 and Margaret Hunt, "The De-Eroticization of Women's Liberation: Social Purity Movements and the Revolutionary Feminism of Sheila Jeffreys," *Feminist Re-*

view No. 34, Spring 1990. On women's resistance to conventional norms, which ironically participated in the construction of the new social norm of companionate marriage, see Ellen Kay Trimberger, "Feminism, Men, and Modern Love: Greenwich Village, 1900-1925" in Snitow, *et al.*, eds., *Powers of Desire, op. cit.*, pp. 131-152. Also see Carroll Smith-Rosenberg, "The New Woman as Androgyne: Social Disorder and Gender Crisis" in her *Disorderly Conduct* (New York, Oxford: Oxford University Press, 1985), pp. 245-29 and Kathy Peiss, *Cheap Amusements: Working Women and Leisure in Turn-of-the-Century New York* (Philadelphia: Temple University Press, 1986) and her "'Charity Girls' and City Pleasures: Historical Notes on Working Class Sexuality, 1880-1920," in Kathy Peiss and Christina Simmons, eds., *Passion and Power, Sexuality in History* (Philadelphia: Temple University Press, 1989), pp. 57-69 and earlier in *Powers of Desire, op. cit.* Also see Christine Stansell, *City of Women: Sex and Class in New York, 1789-1869* (New York: 1986) and Carolyn Strange, *Toronto's Girl Problem, The Perils and Pleasures of the City, 1880-1930* (Toronto: University of Toronto Press, 1995).

110. Atina Grossmann, "The New Woman and the Rationalization of Sexuality in Weimar Germany" in Snitow, *et al.*, *Powers of Desire, op. cit.*, pp. 163-164. Also see Katz, *The Invention of Heterosexuality, op. cit.*

111. The reference to "heterosexual counter-revolution" is from George Chauncey, Jr., "From Sexual Inversion ..." *op. cit.*, pp. 144-145. Also see Simmons, *op. cit.*; Estelle Freeman, "Separatism as Strategy: Female Institution Building and American Feminism, 1870-1930," *Feminist Studies*, V. 5, No. 3, Fall 1979, pp. 512-529. Also Jeffreys, *op. cit.*, with the above-noted limitations.

112. Chauncey, "From Sexual Inversion ..." *op. cit.*, p. 132. Also see Lisa Duggan, "The Trials of Alice Mitchell: Sensationalism, Sexology, and the Lesbian Subject in Turn-of-the-Century America," *Signs*, Summer 1993, V. 18, No. 4, pp. 791-814.

113. Ann Ferguson, "Patriarchy, Sexual Identity, and the Sexual Revolution" in *Signs*, V. 7, No. 1, p. 167-169, and her *Blood at the Root, Motherhood, Sexuality and Male Dominance* (London: Pandora, 1989), pp. 188-208 and *Sexual Democracy: Women, Oppression and Revolution* (Boulder: Westview Press, 1991), pp. 52-65, 133-158.

114. See Madeline Davis and Liz Kennedy, *Boots of Leather, Slippers of Gold, op. cit.*, and other references to their work; for an exploration of some of the diverse literary sources of lesbian identity formation, see Cy Thea Sand, "Lesbian Writing: Adventure into Autonomy" in *Fireweed*, special "Lesbiantics" issue, No. 13, pp. 24-38; Joan Nestle, "Excerpts from the Oral History of Mabel Hampton" in *Signs*, Summer 1993, V. 18, No. 4, pp. 925-935; Eric Garber, "A Spectacle in Color: The Lesbian and Gay Subculture of Jazz Age Harlem" in Duberman *et al.*, *Hidden from History*, pp. 318-331; "Gladys Bentley: The Bulldagger Who Sang the Blues" in *Outlook*, 1(1), pp. 52-61, and Hazel V. Carby, "It Jus Be's Dat Way Sometime: The Sexual Politics of Women's Blues" in *Radical America*, June/July, 1986, V. 20, No. 4, pp. 9-24.

115. Weeks, *Sex, Politics and Society, op. cit*, p. 117.

116. *Ibid.*; Sonja Ruehl, "Inverts and Experts: Radclyffe Hall and the Lesbian Identity" in Rosalind Brunt and Caroline Rowan, eds., *Feminism, Culture and Politics* (London: Lawrence and Wishart, 1982), pp. 15-36; and Esther Newton, "The Mythic Mannish Lesbian: Radclyffe Hall and the New Woman" in *Signs*, No. 9, 1984, pp. 557-575.

117. See Elizabeth Wilson, *Women and the Welfare State* (London: Tavistock, 1980); Mary McIntosh, "The State and the Oppression of Women" in Kuhn and Wolpe, eds., *Feminism and Materialism* (London: Routledge Kegan and Paul, 1978), pp. 254-289; and Michelle Barrett, ch. 7, "Feminism and the Politics of the State" in *Women's Oppression Today* (London: Verso, 1980).

118. See Charlotte Bunch, "Not for Lesbians Only" in *Quest*, V. 11, No. 2, Fall 1975.

Part Two

TOWARD A
QUEER VIEW
OF CANADIAN
HISTORY

3.

Sexualities in Canadian History: Problems of Sources and Interpretation

"Canadian historians have been particularly reticent to discuss the historical phenomena of homosexuality," wrote Geoffrey Egan in 1980.[1] This has only begun to change in 1995 as I write this.[2] The other side of this reticence has been an assumption that everyone has been heterosexual throughout the history of the Canadian State. This, of course, has not led to any critical problematization of the construction of heterosexuality. History, like other "disciplines," has been dominated by heterosexism. My approach is rooted in a critique of the dominant Canadian historical "traditions" — that of the orthodox history of the "great white men who founded the country" and of the "fathers" of Confederation, but also of most left-wing and political economy oriented approaches.

There has been little historical investigation until recently of same-gender sexual experiences, the emergence of heterosexuality, and the development of heterosexual hegemony in Canada. This excursion toward a queer history of Canada, draws on some important early efforts. Even though I celebrate and have learned much from the important contributions from feminist, gay, and lesbian historians in developing critical histories and analyses of sexual regulation in Canada since the first edition, this is still a largely pioneering work.[3] My purpose, given that the scope of this book is so broad, is to present these various historical narratives often in a rather fragmented and partial form; the work of more adequately interpreting them and constructing a more comprehensive

history still needs to follow. It is work I hope to inspire others to do. My historical research has been more detailed for the period from the 1950s on and includes interviews
with those involved in queer activities during these years. My analysis is therefore more
developed and grounded for these years.

The first question in this exploration of sexuality in what is now called Canada is
one of scope, sources and interpretation. I cannot analyze the specific national developments in Québec given its distinct national, cultural, linguistic, and religious history.
However, much of what I outline will be applicable to Québec society given the common
State and criminal-law framework since the English conquest.[4]

There has been no constant gay or lesbian minority or heterosexual majority in Canadian history. When looking for evidence of same-gender sexual activity, we must not
read back into the past our own modern-day categories. What we are looking for, then,
is not a continuous history of homosexuality, lesbianism, or heterosexuality, but a history
of the shifting social organization of sex and erotic pleasures.

Various social meanings have been attached to sex and gender activity in the languages and literatures of the past. The actual names for same-gender sex (and same-sex
sex when these do not coincide) have ranged from many different terms in the cultures
of the indigenous peoples, to the legal terms of "sodomy," "buggery," and "crime
against nature" in the French and English periods, to terms like an "Oscar Wilde type,"
a member of the "third sex," to "queer" and "dyke," and to more contemporary terms
like "homosexuality" and "lesbianism" after the formation of the Canadian State and
the rise of the medical and sexual sciences at the turn of this century. Furthermore, the
use and meaning of the words themselves have varied markedly according to period and
social context.

In the period between the establishment of British North America and the formation of an urban capitalist society and an autonomous Canadian State, sexual regulation
and understanding were radically transformed. In the nineteenth century, terms used to
describe same-gender sex in various official discourses ranged from "crime against nature," to "sodomy" and "buggery," to the "secret sin," "sex perversion," "sexual immorality," and the "social evil." As we will see, others toward the end of the century began to
use expressions like a man of the "Oscar Wilde type" and a member of the "third sex."
In Western Canada from 1880 to 1920, says Terry Chapman, "sodomy" generally referred to anal intercourse with a human (either male or female), while bestiality referred to anal intercourse with an animal. The term "buggery," however, officially
included both sodomy and bestiality.[5]

Vern Bullough and Martha Voght have pointed to what they call the confusion of
homosexuality and masturbation, which were both called the "secret sin" in nineteenth
century U.S. medical and popular discussions.[6] In the context of nineteenth-century
North American social life, however, the two were not yet necessarily distinguished as socially different types of activity. Bullough and Voght are therefore projecting back a distinction that did not yet exist.[7]

All non-reproductive sex was thought to lead to degeneration in the theory of the "spermatic economy," since "precious bodily fluids" were considered wasted.[8] Such notions established the context for much official and indeed popular discussion of sexuality in the nineteenth and early twentieth centuries. In *Our Sons* (1914), for instance, William Lund Clark refers to the "secret vice" and "self-abuse" that cause the body's secretions to be wasted, and he laments a boy's not becoming "the splendid young man he might have been." He refers to boys who were "taught that act by an older companion," "even in the presence of their friends," and quotes one boy: "I was taught that habit three years ago ... by a man in my home town. He took six of us to his house and taught us that evil."[9] In this text, there is no notion whatsoever of the homosexual or the contemporary homo/hetero polarity, and there is no distinction between the "secret vice" of solitary masturbation and joint sessions, or indeed being introduced to the practice along with five other boys by an older man. The "homosexual" in this Protestant and social-purity-oriented discourse had not yet emerged as a distinct sexual type. It is important to remember the unevenness of the development of sexual discourses. In some more medicalized discourses, the homosexual would already have emerged while in other more religiously based discourses the homosexual did not yet exist. Sexual discourse is never monolithic and different discursive frameworks are in use in different sites at the same time.

Throughout the nineteenth and early twentieth centuries in Canada, a number of words may have been used to describe same-gender desire by those in positions of power and influence. Most, building on earlier social definitions, grouped same-gender pleasures with other prohibited sexual or social activities. For instance, the Canadian Social Purity movement grouped prostitution, masturbation, and same-gender sex under "social evil," "sexual perversion," and "sexual immorality." Only in the 1890s would emerge "homosexual" and "lesbian," and later "heterosexual." The important work of tracing the specific emergence of "the heterosexual" in Canada, as Jonathan Katz has done for the U.S., remains to be carried out.[10]

Because of the socially organized "private" or "personal" character of intimate sexual relations, there has been little public record of same-gender sex aside from the "deviant" or "criminal" behaviour found in police records, government reports, newspaper articles, medical and psychiatric discourse, and sex-advice literature. Since same-gender eroticism was stigmatized, historically valuable diaries and letters have not been preserved. Gay and lesbian oppression has led to the destruction of many first-hand accounts, or to their never having been recorded or written down because they would provide evidence of "homosexuality" with possible damaging consequences for those individuals. Or these records have been destroyed by those who came later to preserve (or more accurately to produce) the heterosexual "purity" of the individual's public record. The voices of those people engaged in same-gender sex have thereby been silenced. This has been a feature of the social organization of heterosexual hegemony.

While we must use police records, legal and court reports, social-purity tracts, social-service reports, and newspaper stories, we must be wary of relying uncritically on them. All of these sources stand in an administrative relation to the actual experiences of the men and women engaged in same-gender sex and are part of constructing them as a social problem. We can critically examine accounts from these ruling agencies, however. I try to analyze them to expose their process of social construction and the work of the ruling regime in sexual categorization. These official accounts are therefore not treated as "objective" or "factual." Instead, I attempt to interrogate them from the vantage point of those who engaged in same-gender eroticism. This becomes easier and clearer when we have first-hand accounts from these people themselves.[11]

The resources necessary for a historical account of the emergence of lesbian and gay life in Canada and of heterosexuality remain widely dispersed, waiting to be recovered from the mists of the past by innovative activists and historians. Lesbian and gay history has been one of the most exciting frontiers to emerge out of the lesbian and gay liberation movements. Lesbian and gay historians are not necessarily professionally trained historians, which has often given the lesbian and gay history movement a grass-roots character. Much of the early innovative work was done by community-based groups. Lesbian and gay history, along with feminist history, have been the major inspirations behind the development of more general critical sexual histories and has made it possible for some people to begin to investigate the history of heterosexuality.

Historical investigation is also hampered by a general lack of critical analysis of Canadian social and State formation, especially as it relates to moral, gender, sexual, and racial regulations. While the Canadian political-economy tradition has undertaken some useful historical examinations, there has been little critical work on social organization and social policies until recently. Political-economy approaches have tended to reduce class relations to a narrow economic realm that marginalizes sexual and gender relations.[12]

A major pre-condition of the Canadian State was the colonization and marginalization of the indigenous peoples; a continuing problem is their containment, regulation, and management as we saw in Kanehsatake in 1990.[13] The management of French-speaking people and the Québécois and the Acadians has also been a key aspect of Canadian State formation. From the days of the fur trade and the colonization of the Native peoples, Canadian State formation has been bound up with French, British, and then American social, and political developments.

British interest in a territory in opposition to the U.S. led to alliances among the regional elites and a division between the central State and the provinces as laid out in the British North America Act in 1867. During the period 1850 to 1930, Canada was transformed from a series of rural trading colonies tied to England to a consolidated State apparatus divided between Ottawa and the provinces. Canada was at this point a tributary territory in a subordinate alliance with British imperialism.

> In Canada the indigenous development of class arising in relation to indigenous economic organization is given a distinctive character by the intersection of the leading section of the Canadian ruling class with that of Britain.[14]

The United States would later, in an uneven fashion, replace Britain as the chief influence. Within the context of referenced and semi-autonomous development in relation to Britain and then the U.S., there has been an active and somewhat autonomous State-making strategy within the Canadian territories.

This history has resulted in the adoption of British and American forms of sexual organization. Sexual discourses and practices from England and the United States have entered into Canada subordinating or ruling out other possible ways of sexual life. Any examination of Canadian sexual history must therefore be prefaced by a brief overview of English and U.S. developments (as I provided in chapter 2).

Before Confederation, the statutes of the Imperial British Parliament applied to the colonies, and after Confederation legal statutes and procedures were borrowed from England.[15] The medical and sexological literature was either English or American, or was derived from such works, and many doctors received their training outside Canada.[16] At a popular level, the sexual-advice literature circulating in English Canada was often American or English.[17] Finally, the social-purity organizations had ties with similar groups in the U.S. and England, and their speakers regularly crossed the Canadian/American border.[18]

Specifically, Canadian sources in a number of areas are therefore often difficult to come by for the early years. An examination of Canadian history reveals processes of sexual formation and regulation similar to those of its colonizers, although perhaps in a more truncated form and within a more compressed time frame.

The specific features of this process have to do with the particular features of Canadian State and social formation more generally. In the following chapters, I outline how Canadian history from a queer perspective might look.

These narratives focus on major transformations in sexual regulation, the emergence of lesbian and gay experiences, the emergence of heterosexuality, and their relation to other social changes. For the earlier years, the analysis is still quite skeletal, needing to be elaborated and fleshed out by others.

Notes

1. Geoffrey Egan, "These things may lead to a tragedy of our species: Notes towards a history of homosexuality in Canada, 1890-1930," unpublished paper, April 1980, p. 30. On the ignoring of the history of sexual morality and sexual offences in Canada, see Terry L. Chapman, "Sex Crimes in Western Canada, 1890-1920," unpublished Ph.D. dissertation, University of Alberta, 1984, pp. 1-2, 20-21. For more recent work on critical sexual history in Canada, see: Angus McLaren, "Sex Radicalism in the Canadian Pacific Northwest, 1890-1920," *Journal of the History of Sexuality*, V. 2, No. 4, April, 1992, pp. 527-546; Mariana Valverde, "'When the Mother of the Race is Free': Race, Reproduction, and Sexuality in First-Wave Feminism," and Karen Dubinsky, "'Maidenly Girls' or 'Designing Women'? The Crime of Seduction in Turn-of-the-Century Ontario," in *Gender Conflicts, New Essays in Women's History* (Toronto: University of

Toronto Press, 1992), pp. 3-66; Valverde's, *The Age of Light, Soap and Water: Moral Reform in English Canada, 1885-1925* (McClelland and Stewart: Toronto, 1991); and Dubinsky's *Improper Advances, Rape and Heterosexual Conflict in Ontario, 1880-1929* (Chicago and London: The University of Chicago Press, 1993).

2. There are now positive signs of change. A conference on lesbian, gay and bisexual history called "Out of the Archives" was organized through the York University History Department, January 13-15, 1994, and a book edited by Sara Stratton and David Kimmel bringing together some of the papers delivered is to be published. There are now more courses on sexuality in history departments across the country and groupings of lesbian and gay students doing research on queer histories on a number of campuses. Also see Paul Deslandes and Dan Healey, compilers, *Queer Lives, Queer Cultures: A Selected Bibliography of Lesbian and Gay History* (Toronto: The Lesbian and Gay History Discussion Group, University of Toronto History Department and the Toronto Centre for Lesbian and Gay Studies, 1995).

3. Some of the useful early work that I draw on here are: G. Egan's work, *op. cit.*; Terry L. Chapman, *op. cit.*, and her "Sexual Deviation in Western Canada, 1890-1920," unpublished paper presented at the Northern Great Plains Conference, Winnipeg, 1979, her "'An Oscar Wilde Type': 'The Abominable Crime of Buggery' in Western Canada, 1890-1920," *Criminal Justice History* 4, 1983, pp. 97-118, and "Male Homosexuality: Legal Restraints and Social Attitudes in Western Canada, 1890-1920" in Louis Knafla, ed., *Law and Justice in a New Land: Essays in Western Canadian Legal History* (Toronto: Carswell, 1986); the work of the Canadian Gay and Lesbian Archives in Toronto; Ross Higgins' work on gay history in Montréal, in *Sortie, Pink Ink*, and *Rites*; and the pioneering work of Indiana Matters, "Unfit for Publication: Notes Towards a Lavender History of British Columbia," paper presented at the "Sex and the State: Their Laws, Our Lives" conference, Toronto, 1985; Lyle Dick, "Heterohegemonic Discourse and Homosexual Acts: The Case of Saskatchewan in the Settlement Era," paper presented at the "Sex and the State" conference; and John Grube, "Queens and Flaming Virgins: Towards a Sense of Gay Community" in *Rites*, V. 2, No. 9, pp. 14-17, pp. 14-17. The Canadian Lesbian and Gay History Network was an important resource in developing this research. For a more comprehensive listing of sources, see Gary Kinsman, "Towards a Source List for Doing English-Canadian Lesbian/Gay Histories," in *Canadian Lesbian and Gay History Newsletter*, No. 1, Dec. 1985, Toronto, pp. 8-19; also see: No. 2, Sept. 1986; No. 3, Dec. 1987; and the final issue, No. 4, Nov. 1990. Also see: Steven Maynard "In Search of 'Sodom North': The Writing of Lesbian and Gay History in English Canada, 1970-1990" in *Canadian Review of Comparative Literature*, V. 21, Nos. 1-2, Mar.-Jun. 1994, pp. 117-132. Some of the work of the history newsletter is now carried on by the Toronto Centre for Lesbian and Gay Studies and its publication *Centre/fold*, which carries "Pages from the Past" in every issue. Since the first edition of this book, there has also been very exciting work done by Lesbians Making History in Toronto, including their "People Think This Didn't Happen in Canada" in *Fireweed: A Feminist Quarterly*, 28, Spring 1989, pp. 81-86, 142; Elise Chenier, "Tough Ladies and Troublemakers: Toronto's Public Lesbian Community, 1955-1965," MA thesis, History, Queen's University, 1995; Makeda Silvera, "Man Royals and Sodomites: Some Thoughts on the Invisibility of Afro-Caribbean Lesbians," in Sharon Dale Stone, ed., *Lesbians in Canada* (Toronto: Between the Lines, 1990) and in a number of other anthologies; Mary Louise Adams, including "The Trouble with Normal: Post-War Teenagers and the Construction of Heterosexuality," Ph.D. thesis, Department of Educational Theory, University of Toronto (OISE), 1994, and her "Precedent-Setting Pulp: Women's Barracks Was Deemed 'Exceedingly Frank'" in *Xtra!*, No. 231 (Sept. 3, 1993), p. 21; Steven Maynard, "Through a Hole in the Lavatory Wall: Homosexual Subcultures, Police Surveillance, and the Dialectics of Discovery, Toronto, 1890-1930," *Journal of the History of Sexuality*, 1994, V. 5, No. 2, pp. 207-242; Ross Higgins, Line Chamberland and Robert Champagne, "Mixed Messages: Lesbians, Gay Men, and the Yellow Press in Québec and Ontario During the 1950s-1960s," in Ian McKay, ed., *The Challenge of Modernity: A Reader on Post-Confederation Canada* (Toronto: McGraw-Hill Ryerson, 1992), pp. 421-438; Line Chamberland, "Social Class

and Integration in Lesbian Culture" in Sandra Kirby, Dayna Daniels, Kate McKenna and Michelle Pujol, eds., *Women Changing Academe* (Winnipeg: Sororal Publishing, 1991), pp. 75-88, and her "Remembering Lesbian Bars, 1955-1975" in *Journal of Homosexuality*, V. 25, No. 3, 1993, pp. 231-269; David Churchill, "Coming Out in a Cold Climate: A History of Gay Men in Toronto during the 1950s," MA thesis, University of Toronto, 1993; and Becki Ross, "The House That Jill Built: Lesbian Feminist Organizing in Toronto, 1976-1980," *Feminist Review*, 35, Summer 1990, pp. 75-91, and her book *The House That Jill Built: A Lesbian Nation in Formation* (Toronto: University of Toronto Press, 1995) among others. Also see the exciting and witty film *Forbidden Love: The Unashamed Stories of Lesbian Lives* by Aerlyn Weissman and Lynne Fernie (National Film Board, 1992), which is, in part, based on interviews with Canadian lesbians who were out in the 1950s and 1960s, and Lisa Steele's and Kim Tomczak's *Legal Memory*, 1992, which addresses the Leo Mantha case I refer to in chapter 7.

4. On developments in Québec, also see the work of Line Chamberland and Ross Higgins cited above. A number of important lesbian and gay studies conferences with important historical dimensions have been organized in Montréal over the last few years. "La Ville en Rose: Lesbians and Gays in Montreal: Histories, Cultures, Societies," took place Nov. 12-14 1992; and the Groupe interdisciplinaire de recherches et d'études: homosexualité et société (GIREHS) held conferences on the "History of Gay and Lesbian Militancy in Quebec" on March 31, 1995, and a conference on "The National Question and Gays and Lesbians: Distinctions or Exclusions?" on June 2, 1995.

5. It is therefore difficult to easily or immediately determine from the court and police records the character of a particular legal case given they were all classified as "buggery." Chapman, "Sexual Deviation in Western Canada, 1890-1920," *op. cit.*, p. 11. Also her thesis, *op. cit.*, pp. 17-18. Also see Chapman, "Male Homosexuality: Legal Restraints and Social Attitudes in Western Canada, 1890-1920," in Louis Knafla, ed., *Law and Justice in a New Land: Essays in Western Canadian Legal History, op. cit.*

6. Vern L. Bullough and Martha Voght, "Homosexuality and its Confusion with the 'Secret Sin' in Pre-Freudian America" in *Journal of the History of Medicine*, V. 27, No. 2, 1973.

7. See Katz, *Gay/Lesbian Almanac* (New York: Harper and Row, 1983), pp. 2-3.

8. See Michael Bliss, "Pure Books on Avoided Subjects: Pre-Freudian Sexual Ideas in Canada," published in Canadian Historical Association, Historical Papers 1970 Communications historiques, pp. 80-108. On the relation of this to the construction of individual character and self-regulation, see Mariana Valverde, *The Age of Light, Soap and Water: Moral Reform in English Canada, 1885-1925, op. cit.*, especially pp. 27-28. Also see Angus Mclaren, "Sex, Science and Race Betterment," in *Our Own Master Race* (Toronto: McClelland and Stewart, 1990), pp. 68-88.

9. William Lund Clark, *Our Sons* (Ontario: W.L. Clark, 1914) pp. 96-106. Clark toured Canada under the auspices of the Young Men's Christian Association and did sex hygiene education for the Methodist Department of Temperance and Moral Reform. On W.L. Clark, also see Valverde, *The Age of Light, Soap and Water, op. cit.*, pp. 27, 46, 70-72, and 93.

10. See Jonathan Ned Katz, *The Invention of Heterosexuality* (New York: Dutton, 1995). For some very useful initial explorations of the construction of heterosexuality in Canada, see: Karen Dubinsky, *Improper Advances: Rape and Heterosexual Conflict in Ontario, 1880-1929, op. cit.*; Carolyn Strange, *Toronto's Girl Problem: The Perils and Pleasures of the City, 1880-1930* (Toronto: University of Toronto Press, 1995); and for a later period, Mary Louise Adams, "The Trouble with Normal: Post-War Teenagers and the Construction of Heterosexuality," *op. cit.*

11. On reading official discourse such as medical and court reports "against the grain," see Jennifer Terry, "Theorizing Deviant Historiography" in *differences*, V. 3, No. 2, Summer 1991, pp. 55-74. She reads the medical texts she is examining for "effects" of the violence of dominant discourses. At the same time, she is unable to specify the basis for the "extra-discursive." Also see Steven Maynard's "Through a Hole in the Lavatory Wall ..." *op. cit.*, for a critical way of reading and using court records. For later historical periods, particularly post-World War II,

oral histories or other first-hand accounts, which will not be used systematically in this book until the 1950s, are vital. Also see Gary Kinsman, "Official Discourse as Sexual Regulation," Ph.D. thesis, Department of Educational Theory, University of Toronto, 1989.

12. On the limitations of political economy, see Dorothy E. Smith, "Feminist Reflections on Political Economy" in M. Patricia Connelly and Pat Armstrong, eds., *Feminism in Action: Studies in Political Economy* (Toronto: Canadian Scholars' Press, 1992), pp. 1-21, and previously in *Studies in Political Economy*, No. 30, Autumn 1989, pp. 37-59. An important break with this political-economy tradition is the innovative work of Bruce Curtis, in particular his "Preconditions of the Canadian State: Educational Reforms and the Construction of a Public in Upper Canada, 1837-1846" in *Studies in Political Economy*, No. 10, Winter 1983. He develops an analysis of early Upper Canadian State formation where he points out that educational reforms in the late 1830s and 1840s were directed at the construction of political subjects in the wake of the 1837-1838 rebellions. While this approach encompasses broader, political, cultural, and moral dimensions than the political economy tradition, it still has not dealt adequately with sex/gender relations as central to State formation and nation-building. Also see Curtis's *Building the Educational State: Canada West, 1836-1871* (London: Althouse Press, 1988) and "'Illicit' Sexuality and Public Education, 1840-1907," in Susan Prentice, ed., *Sex in Schools: Canadian Education and Sexual Regulation* (Toronto: Our Schools/Our Selves, 1994), pp. 101-130. This kind of work is continued and extended in many of the articles in Allan Greer and Ian Radforth, eds., *Colonial Leviathan: State Formation in Mid-Nineteenth Century Canada* (Toronto: University of Toronto Press, 1992). On examining sexism and racism as constituent features of Canadian nation building see, Roxana Ng, "Sexism, Racism and Canadian Nationalism" in Himani Bannerji, ed., *Returning the Gaze: Essays on Racism, Feminism and Politics* (Toronto: Sister Vision, 1993), pp. 182-196.

13. See Donna Kahenrakwas Goodleaf, "'Under Military Occupation': Indigenous Women, State Violence and Community Resistance," in Linda Carty, ed., *And Still We Rise: Feminist Political Mobilizing in Contemporary Canada* (Toronto: Women's Press, 1993), pp. 225-242, and Alanis Obomsawin, director, *Kanehsatake: 270 Years of Resistance* (National Film Board, 1993).

14. Dorothy E. Smith, "Women, Class and Family" in *The Socialist Register* (London: Merlin Press, 1983) p. 19.

15. See Alex K. Gigeroff, *Sexual Deviations in the Criminal Law: Homosexual, Exhibitionistic, and Pedophilac Offences in Canada* (Toronto: published for the Clarke Institute of Psychiatry by University of Toronto Press, 1968), p. vii. In 1869, Canada required uniform criminal law and borrowed wholesale from England. In 1890, Canada used the Stephens Draft Code that had been prepared for Britain but had not been accepted there and had been made "available for export to the colonies that were in those days without the resources or the manpower to develop to any great extent their own criminal law." Gigeroff, p. 36. There will be more on this in chapter 6.

16. See: Egan, *op. cit.*, pp. 5-6; Bliss, "Pure Books on Avoided Subjects," *op. cit.*; and Wendy Mitchinson, "Historical Attitudes toward Women and Childbirth" in *Atlantis*, V. 4, No. 2, Part II, Spring 1979, p. 16. Also see Wendy Mitchinson, *The Nature of Their Bodies: Women and Their Doctors in Victorian Canada* (Toronto: University of Toronto Press, 1991).

17. Bliss, *op. cit.*

18. The connections between social-purity organizations can be seen in J.S. Shearer's guest introduction to the American Clifford G. Roe's *The Great War on White Slavery* (Clifford G. Roe and B.G. Steadwell, 1911). Shearer was secretary of the Moral and Social Reform Council of Canada and is referred to as "the leader of the fight against white slavery in Canada," p. 144. (Also as a Coles reprint under the title *War on the White Slave Trade* (Toronto: Coles, 1980). Also see A. Bell, ed., *Fighting the Traffic in Young Girls* (Ernest A. Bell, 1910), which contains a section by Shearer called "The Canadian Crusade," and an article by William Alexander Coote, Secretary of the National Vigilance Association, London, England. Also see Rev. C.W. Watch, "Social Purity Work in Canada," and D.A. Watt, "The Canadian Law for

the Protection of Women and Girls, with Suggestions for Its Amendment and for a General Code," in Aaron M. Powell, ed., *The National Purity Congress: Its Papers, Addresses, Portraits* (New York: Arno Press reprint, 1976), pp. 272-279, 437-451. This was the first Social Purity conference held under the auspices of the American Purity Alliance, in Baltimore, Oct. 14-16, 1895. It was originally published in New York by the American Purity Alliance in 1896. Also see Linda Kealey, "Introduction" to *A Not Unreasonable Claim: Women and Reform in Canada 1880s-1920s* (Toronto: The Women's Press, 1979), p. 3; and Valverde, *The Age of Light, Soap and Water, op. cit.*

4.

Sexual Colonization of the Indigenous Peoples

The colonization of what would later be called Canada led to major conflicts between European social, moral, and sexual life and that of the indigenous peoples. A crucial part of the subjugation of the Native peoples in most of the regions of what would come to be called Canada was the marginalization and destruction of their diverse forms of erotic, gender and social life and their subordination to white, European-derived social and sexual organization.

There were a number of different processes of colonization that occurred across North America. One of these was experienced in the northwest, which I will focus on here. As Ron Bourgeault points out in a study of Native peoples and the fur trade, "Class, racial and sexist divisions came to be imposed upon the indigenous Indian population through colonial relations based upon a particular form of exploitation."[1]

While there existed a vast panorama of erotic and gender relations among North American aboriginal peoples, with wide-ranging regional and "national" variations, aboriginal women generally enjoyed more social equality and more decision-making power than European women. There was also social acceptance for men and women who cross-dressed and cross-worked as the other gender or as a mixed or third gender, and there was acceptance of some forms of same-sex and same-gender erotic pleasure within and outside these relationships.[2] At the same time, as Jonathan Goldberg points out in a critique of European accounts of "sodomy" among aboriginal people:

> Cross-dressing does not mean the same thing from one native situation to another, or even within the same tribe; to believe otherwise is to homogenize all natives into the figure of the Indian, and to once more give in to the ethnocentricity that has invented the category of people without history.[3]

In some aboriginal groups, women had a degree of erotic freedom that seemed scandalous to the fur traders. Pre-marital sex was common, and many Native groups did not view the marriage tie as indissoluble.[4] Early white explorers, missionaries, and military men brought back stories of men who dressed and worked as women and engaged in "sodomy."[5] Early anthropologists expressed shock and horror at this eroticism between men. According to one English-language text, North American Indians were inclined to "practical homosexualism."[6] An early Jesuit missionary writing in the years 1711-1717 tells of "men who dress as women" and "special friendships among men."[7] Others reported encounters with male and female "berdache" (derived from the French word for male prostitute).[8] These berdache were cross-dressing, cross-working people who constituted a third gender or fourth gender in some of these indigenous cultures. Other European observers interpreted them as "hermaphrodites," a term gaining currency in Europe to describe people with physiological features of both biological sexes. Unfortunately, we have mostly European accounts on which to rely,[9] and these are imbued with a white, Christian, "civilizing," missionary attitude. Stories based on Native peoples' accounts of their own experiences would be quite different.[10]

These cross-dressing/cross working or alternate-gender people who were called berdache cannot simply be interpreted as a form of institutionalized homosexuality. These Native cultures were not divided up between heterosexuals and homosexuals as in contemporary "Western" societies. It was believed in some indigenous cultures that cross-working and cross-dressing men and women[11] actually belonged to the other gender or to a third gender that either combined male and female features or that was "not man, not woman."[12] Changing one's clothes, one's work, and one's social interests in the prevailing division of labour was enough in some groups to transfer or to constitute one's gender.[13] In some of these cultures, these alternate-gendered people were seen as combining the spirits of the other two genders. In many of these groups, gender was seen as a cultural construction that had to do with the passage through social rituals and engagement in social activities. In some cultures these alternate gender people were known as "two-spirited" and this term has now been reclaimed by Native lesbian, gay, bisexual, queer, and two-spirited activists.

This was a very different social organization of gender then in Europe at that time or in dominant white North American culture today. It is clear that gender was not primarily defined by physiology, but rather through the types of work done and other social activities, and there was not always a direct link between "biological" sex, gender, and sexual activity. In some cultures there were not just two gender groups, but three and perhaps four gender groups, when there was an alternate gender group for "biological" females.

Within and between these gender groupings there were forms of regulation of erotic relations. For a biological male berdache, sex could take place with a "biological" and "social" man. In the context of some of these cultures this would have been considered to be different-gender sex since berdache and "men" were socially different genders. Sex might also take place among biological and social men as well. Same-sex and sometimes same-gender sexual activity did not threaten the boundaries of gender or sexual life.

Furthermore, cross-dressing and cross-working did not always signify same-sex sexual activity — charges of "sodomy" often represented the interpretation of Native activities through European religious and legal categories.[14] What was going on here was a clash between radically different forms of social, gender, and erotic life. Aboriginal cultures did not always distinguish between sex with males and sex with females or with a berdache, and contemporary "deviant" sexual or gender categories did not exist.

Analysis of Native erotic practices before the coming of white "civilization" must take into account their forms of social life and not simply read them through white European eyes. I can only begin to do this and still have much to learn from "two-spirited" peoples. I am not suggesting in this book a return to these earlier forms of gender and erotic life, although contemporary "two-spirited" peoples have found much affirmation and much to reclaim in these practices and traditions as they have developed a different construction of same-gender sex from "white" gay and lesbian identifications. Rather, on seeing how different sex and gender relations have been in the past, this points out how different they could be in the future. Questions that are raised include: Why do there have to be only two genders? And perhaps, and more radically, why does there have to be gender at all?

Returning to the story of the colonization of the indigenous people in the north-west, the communal and relatively egalitarian division of labour in Native society was transformed so that aboriginal peoples would produce the desired commodities for the fur trade.[15] The North West Company and the Hudson's Bay Company developed highly structured organizations tied into mercantile capitalism. Native social equality was slowly undermined,[16] and inequalities between Indian men and women intensified as their labour was appropriated. Trading was organized through Indian men only, creating a dependency of women on men and imposing on Native people a patriarchal division of labour. Part of this transformation was a gradual process of sedenterization of people who previously moved and migrated over larger territories.

As individual commodity production developed, the communal organization of Indian cultures ripped apart. Merchant capitalism was compelled to destroy Native women's previous decision-making powers, making them into dependent support workers. Some Native women began to realize it would be in their interests to take advantage of relationships with European men.[17] The male colonizers, meanwhile, saw that these women could be of use in penetrating the communal societies and establishing trading relations. "Indian women became a valuable commodity," says Bourgeault, "and were exploited both politically and sexually in the conquest of Indian society."[18] White women were prohibited from the fur-trade territories so that traders were permitted to take "country wives" (*mariage à la façon du pays*). They could thus take advantage of not only Native women's skills and their bodies, but their all-important kinship networks as well. Through such marriages, the women were linked to both particular Indian-kinship networks and specific trading posts. The children of mixed marriages were raised as Indians, creating the basis for a new labour market of mixed-blood people who would later be called Metis. Indian women's dependency on men increased as they became support workers within the individual family and reproducers of labour. These social changes, along with Church and State practices, transformed Native sex and gender life.[19] By the 1820s, however, white women were being admitted to the fur-trade territories and many of the traders repudiated their Native wives for white wives.

There were many regional variations in this process of colonization, and there were various instances of Native resistance depending on differences in involvement in productive labour and mode of production, gender relations, the official policies of French and English authorities, and the role of the Church and the missionaries. Karen Anderson stresses, in her somewhat contrasting account to that of Bourgeault, the key part of

State and Church agencies in the subordination of Native peoples. Her account of the effect of the Europeans on two different Native groups finds that women among the Montagnais-Naskapi were denied access to productive activity and made dependent on male relatives, while among the Hurons, kin-based social relations of production contin- ued to guarantee women, as well as men, access to the necessities of life. As a result, it was not until later that gender relations were radically transformed among the Hurons.[20] Anderson's analysis points to the need to examine the specific effects of the European incursion into the economic, social, sexual and gender life of different Native groups. There is a diverse range of Native resistance and accommodation that must be examined in much more detail than can be done here.

Christianity played a fundamental role in "civilizing" aboriginal peoples and in cre- ating one of the central preconditions for the Canadian State. Formation of this State was constructed in opposition to, and was based on the partial destruction and margi- nalization of, the indigenous ways of life of the Native peoples. Says Bourgeault, "It was with Christianity that the ideological conquering of the Indian finally took place."[21] Mis- sionaries, fur traders, and colonial agencies attempted to firmly link gender with mascu- linity and femininity and with reproductive forms of sex and Christian marriage. In the 1880s, for instance, as part of this mission, Canadian police forced a berdache to wear men's clothes and cut his hair.[22] As Katz explains for the American experience:

> It seems reasonable to speculate that the elimination of native sodomy, cross-dressing and cross-working was early a common part of the Europe- ans' conversion mission, that genocidal enterprise by which white men in the employ of the church and state systematically forced their own "civiliza- tion" upon the original inhabitants in America, exterminating them in the name of Christian morality and rights of Empire.[23]

With the centralization of British North American possessions into the Canadian State, the Anglo bourgeoisie shifted its interests to the West, the preserve of the fur-trading companies. This brought State agencies and white settlers into conflict with the remain- ing Indian and Metis populations, which existed at least partially outside their rule. With the crushing of the Riel rebellions in 1885, "the subjugation of the Metis was completed with the formation of Canada as a Nation-State."[24]

Also key to this subjugation was the official State strategy of assimilation and the residential school system through which young Native people were taken away from their parents and communities and were denied the right to speak their own language and to engage in the cultural practices of their communities. The treaties imposed on the Native peoples and the conditions that they laid down for life on reserves also played a major part in the subordination and transformation of Native life.

Native erotic and gender relations were subordinated to those of the Europeans. This story of extreme cultural, social, and physical violence lies at the root of Canadian State formation. It is to this white European-imposed history that I now turn, but it must be remembered that resistance to this colonization continues in the struggles for Native liberation, as at Kanehsatake in 1990, and that are continuing today.[25] We also see this in the self-organization of two-spirited people across the Canadian State.[26]

Notes

1. Ron G. Bourgeault, "The Indians, the Metis and the Fur Trade: Class, Sexism and Racism in the Transition from 'Communism' to Capitalism" in *Studies in Political Economy*, No. 12, Fall 1983, p. 45.
2. See Jonathan Katz, *Gay American History* (New York: Thomas Y. Crowall, 1976), pp. 281-334, and his *Gay/Lesbian Almanac* (New York: Harper and Row, 1983), pp. 23-28; Martin Bauml Duberman, Fred Eggan, and Richard Clemmers, eds., "Documents in Hopi Indian Sexuality: Imperialism, Culture and Resistance" in *Radical History Review*, No. 20, Spring/Summer 1979, pp. 99-130; Evelyn Blackwood, "Sexuality and Gender in Certain Native American Tribes: The Case of Cross-Gender Females" in *Signs*, 1984, V. 10, No. 1, pp. 27-42; Harriet Whitehead, "The Bow and the Burden Strap: A New Look at Institutionalized Homosexuality in Native North America" in Ortner and Whitehead, eds., *Sexual Meanings: The Cultural Construction of Gender and Sexuality* (Cambridge: Cambridge University Press, 1981), pp. 80-115; Walter L. Williams, *The Spirit and the Flesh: Sexual Diversity in American Indian Culture* (Boston: Beacon, 1986) is quite a useful contribution although see my review in *Rites*, V. 4, No. 8, February, 1988, p. 15 on some of its limitations. Also see Gay American Indians and Will Roscoe, eds., *Living the Spirit: A Gay American Indian Anthology* (New York: St. Martin's Press, 1988) especially Midnight Sun, "Sex/Gender Systems in Native North America," pp. 32-42; and the first section on "Artists, Healers, and Providers: The Berdache Heritage," and the work of Will Roscoe who in his later work has moved away from viewing berdache as a "traditional gay role" to seeing them as a third gender group. See Will Roscoe, "The Zuni Man-Woman" in *Out/Look* V. 1, No. 2, Summer 1988, pp. 56-67; my interview with him, "Berdache: Alternative Genders and Gays" in *Rites*, V. 4, No. 8, February 1988, pp. 11-12; and his *The Zuni Man-Woman* (Albuquerque: University of New Mexico Press, 1991). As should be clear from my remarks in this section, I reject the notion of the berdache and cross-dressing/cross-working men and women as representing some form of "institutionalized homosexuality." I find myself closest to the perspectives outlined by Blackwood, Midnight Sun and the later Roscoe, and I view berdache as members of a third or even fourth gender group. Also see the discussion between Jeffrey Weeks and Mary McIntosh recorded in "Postcript: 'The Homosexual Role' Revisited" in Plummer, ed., *The Making of the Modern Homosexual* (London: Hutchinson, 1981), pp. 47-49. For excellent commentary on problems of data and interpretation regarding berdache, see Kessler and McKenna, *Gender: An Ethnomethodological Approach* (New York: University of Chicago, 1978), pp. 24-36. Also see Jonathan Goldberg, "Sodomy in the New World: Anthropologies Old and New" in Michael Warner, ed., *Fear of a Queer Planet: Queer Politics and Social Theory* (Minneapolis: University of Minnesota Press, 1993), pp. 3-18.
3. Jonathan Goldberg, "Sodomy in the New World: Anthropologies Old and New" in Michael Warner, ed., *Fear of a Queer Planet: Queer Politics and Social Theory, op. cit.*, p. 12. The use of "tribe" here is quite debateable, especially when read in the Canadian context.
4. See: Sylvia Van Kirk, *Many Tender Ties: Women in Fur Trade Society, 1670-1870* (Winnipeg: Watson and Dwyer, 1980), pp. 23-24, and Karen Anderson, "Commodity Exchange and Subordination: Montagnais-Naskapi and Huron Women, 1600-1650" in *Signs*, Autumn 1985, V. 11,

No. 1, pp. 48-62; her "A Gendered World: Women, Men and the Political Economy of the Seventeenth Century Huron" in Heather Jon Maroney and Meg Luxton, eds., *Feminism and Political Economy* (Toronto: Methuen, 1987) pp. 121-165; her "As Gentle as Little Lambs: Images of Huron and Montagnais-Naskapi women in the writings of the 17th Century Jesuits" in *The Canadian Review of Sociology and Anthropology*, V. 25, No. 4, Nov. 1988, pp. 560-576, and her book *Chain Her by One Foot: The Subjugation of Native Women in Seventeenth-Century New France* (New York: Routledge, 1993).

5. Katz, *Gay/Lesbian Almanac, op. cit.*, p. 23.

6. Edward Stevenson (pseud. Xavier Mayne), *The Intersexes: A History of Simisexualism as a Problem in Social Life* (Rome: privately printed, preface dated 1908; reprinted New York: Arno Press, 1975), pp. 7-8.

7. Katz, *Gay/American History, op. cit.*, pp. 288-290.

8. On the derivation of berdache, see Whitehead, *op. cit.*, p. 86; and Blackwood, *op. cit.*, p. 27, note 1. Also see Katz, *Gay American History, op. cit.*, pp. 293-298, and Paul-François Sylvestre, *Bougrerie en Nouvelle-France* (Hull: Editions Asticou, 1983), pp. 27-34.

9. Kessler and McKenna, *op. cit.*, pp. 30-32.

10. On this, see Gay American Indians and Will Roscoe, eds., *Living the Spirit: A Gay American Indian Anthology* (New York: St. Martin's Press, 1988), especially Midnight Sun, "Sex/Gender Systems in Native North America," pp. 32-42, and the first section on "Artists, Healers, and Providers: The Berdache Heritage."

11. See Blackwood, *op. cit.*, who emphasizes cross-dressing/cross-working women in the face of a literature that has focused largely on cross-dressing men.

12. See Will Roscoe, "The Zuni Man-Woman" in *Out/Look* V. 1, No. 2, Summer 1988, pp. 56-67, and my interview with him, "Berdache: Alternative Genders and Gays" in *Rites*, V. 4, No. 8, Feb. 1988, pp. 11-12. Also see Will Roscoe, *The Zuni Man-Woman, op. cit.*

13. Katz, *Gay/American History, op. cit.*, p. 24.

14. *Ibid.*, p. 26.

15. Bourgeault, *op. cit.* The next paragraph is based on my reading of Bourgeault's argument.

16. *Ibid.*, p. 55.

17. *Ibid.*, p. 56.

18. *Ibid.*, pp. 60-61.

19. See Anderson, "Commodity Exchange and Subordination ..." *op. cit.*, particularly p. 62.

20. Anderson, "Commodity Exchange and Subordination ..., " and "A Gendered World ..., " *op. cit.*

21. Bourgeault, *op. cit.*, p. 86.

22. Trumbach, "London's Sodomites" in *Journal of Social History*, V. 22. No. 1, p. 8. Also see the reference in C.S. Ford, *Smoke from Their Fires: The Life of a Kwakiute Chief*, c. 1941, pp. 129-130. For other references to berdache, see Canadian Gay Archives, *Homosexuality in Canada: A Bibliography, second edition*, compiled by William Crawford (Toronto: Canadian Gay Archives, 1984), Archives publication No. 9, pp. 2-5.

23. Katz, *Gay/Lesbian Almanac, op. cit.*, p. 28.

24. Bourgeault, *op. cit.*, p. 73.

25. See Donna Kahenrakwas Goodleaf, "'Under Military Occupation': Indigenous Women, State Violence and Community Resistance" in Linda Carty ed., *And Still We Rise: Feminist Political Mobilizing in Contemporary Canada* (Toronto Women's Press, 1993), pp. 225-242, and the film *Kanehsatake: 270 Years of Resistance*, directed by Alanis Obomsawin (NFB, 1993).

26. Groups such as Two-Spirited Peoples of the First Nations (Toronto) now exist across Canada.

5.

Buggery and Sodomy in New France, Upper Canada, and the West

The North American colonies imported forms of social and sexual regulation from Europe. In the largely rural French and British colonies, despite their differing social organization, the interdependent household economy became the main form of social life. In rural Upper and Lower Canada, women and men laboured together in an interdependent family division of labour working on the land. "Men without wives and families laboured under severe handicaps,"[1] and both men and women married out of economic and social necessity. While same-gender sex took place, there was no social place for lesbian and gay networks or for contemporary heterosexuality.

Buggery in New France

In New France a number of cases of male same-gender "sodomy" have been uncovered. The first reported case, in which the governor sentenced to death a young drummer convicted of a "crime against nature," dates from 1648 and is reported in the *Journal des Jesuites*:

> About this time, there was Convictus criminal pessimo [convicted of the worst crime], whose death our fathers who were at Montreal opposed sed occulte; he was then sent hither and put in the prison. It was proposed to him, so that he might at least escape the galleys, to accept the office of executioner of Justice; he accepted it, but his trial was first disposed of, and then his sentence commuted.[2]

The Montréal Jesuits opposed the initial death sentence and managed to get the convicted man transferred to Québec City.[3] This suggests a conflict between the Church and the colonial adminstration over the regulation of sexual activity — part of a more general conflict between Church and secular State authorities.

A second case is recorded in a judgement of the Supreme Council, the colony's court of final appeal, in 1691. The court accused three soldiers of sodomy — one lieutenant in a company of marines, and two soldiers of the same detachment. The lieutenant was pronounced guilty of "corrupting the morals" of several men, and was banished from the colony on pain of death. The other two were reprimanded before the court for having stooped to such "shameful affections and actions."[4] The central focus of the legal proceedings seemed to be proof of insertion of penis into the anus. Robert-Lionel Séguin, in his book on libertine life in New France, reports that brutal punishments —

including the death sentence — for crimes against nature were reserved for the ordinary farmer-soldier as opposed to members of the establishment.[5] This story also suggests the emergence of networks in the military where, for men who had been separated from their families, comradeship could grow into same-gender sex.[6]

Same-gender sex took place throughout the history of the colonies, from the days of the *coureurs de bois*. Regulation of such activity was most severe, as it was in England, in the armed forces and in the new settlements. Military forms of organization brought together groups of men in a same-gender context that created possibilities for male/male friendships and eroticism. These networks of same-gender eroticism among military members produced some of the resources and experiences for the later expansion of same-gender erotic networks. At the same time, the existence of these erotic friendships between men also led to heightened forms of policing of same-gender sex in military contexts.[7]

Buggery in Upper Canada

There were also instances of prosecution for same-gender sex in Upper Canada. In 1838, just months after the 1837 rebellion for democracy and independence had been crushed, George Herchmer Markland, the Inspector-General of Upper Canada, was forced to resign after charges that he took young men, often soldiers, into his office for sex. He was accused before the Executive Council of behaviour "derogatory to his character as a public officer."[8] Markland's troubles started when a housekeeper alleged that she heard noises and movements coming from his office that led her to believe "there was a female in the room with whom some person was in connection." When she learned that it was not women, but young men, she exclaimed, "Well, sir, these are queer things from the bottom to the top." An inquiry was launched and Markland was forced to resign. During the course of the inquiry, a number of young men remarked on Markland's "criminal intentions" and "uninvited advances." The exact reason for his resignation is unclear. He may have been used to show that the Family Compact (the Upper Canadian ruling clique) could clean up its act following the rebellions. It may have been that his activities became public, or that he crossed class lines in his erotic tastes. It was fortunate for Markland that the full force of the law was not used against him. Under the Imperial statutes then in force, the penalty for sodomy and buggery was death. As Ed Jackson suggests, the inquiry gives us some idea of the terminology for male same-gender sexual acts in official circles in nineteenth-century Canada:

> The references by witnesses are consistently in terms of the "crime" or "criminal conduct" or else distasteful circumlocution ("an ugly look about it"). The concepts of sickness and perversion were to come later.[9]

In 1840 and 1841, Toronto newspapers carried a story about Richard Yeo, a dancing master who was "arraigned on an abominable charge" for committing an "unnatural crime" against a private. The papers referred to him as "resembling less a man than a monkey." Yeo was sentenced to one year in the new Kingston penitentiary.[10]

In 1842, Samuel Moore, Lance Corporal, and Patrick Kelly, Private, of the 89th Regiment of Foot were convicted of sodomy. Another private, in sworn testimony before Her Majesty's Justice of the Peace in Canada West, Eastern District, stated that he had found the two men together in bed. Kelly

> was lying on his belly, the bed clothes were on the floor — both men were naked. I saw Moore on the top of Kelly working away as if it was a woman. When the Alarm was given Moore rose up and I saw his private parts come out of Kelly's body.[11]

They were found guilty and sentenced to hang, but this sentence was later commuted to life imprisonment. Both served about a decade in the Kingston penitentiary.[12]

These incidents suggest the beginnings of networks for male sex among soldiers and guards and, in some cases, involving members of the elite and middle class. Some of these elite men may have been in positions to help working-class youth, in Markland's case by getting a young man out of the army and into another occupation. Working-class young men in the military may have been able to negotiate relations with elite men that not only led to erotic pleasure but also economic benefits for themselves as well. Prostitution may also have been involved. These networks seem to be have some similarities to those involving guards and regiments in England.[13]

Community Social Regulation and the Charivari

In the small towns and rural communities where there was no extensive form of State policing, social regulation was based on community pressure and exclusion combined with religious and church prohibition and, less prominently, the law.

Beth Light and Alison Prentice describe the regulation of women's lives:

> Community pressure and the forces of public opinion operate in myriad ways. Exclusion, a typical response to deviance in traditional societies, was one method of controlling women. Thus, bad women were chased out of town, white women denied access to fur trade country, and "respectable" women discouraged from walking the city streets at night.[14]

Based on traditions of European popular justice, community rituals like the charivari, or rough justice, sometimes regulated social behaviours.[15] Charivari, which were common in early Canada, were used to punish wife-beaters, adulterers, and violators of ethnic, racial or religious values. It was a way of enforcing gender and sexual norms before the centralized State and police forces had developed. The charivari often took on the character of a community celebration, although violence and riots sometimes broke out. Some forms of the ritual involved cross-dressing since it granted a license to defy social conventions. While the charivari enforced traditional social practices, it also had a potentially subversive side: it was used, for instance, during the Patriote agitations in Lower Canada preceding the popular democratic rebellions of 1837-38.

> Charivari, here was a world turned upside down, a carnival atmosphere of disguise producing the possibility of overturning the social relations of a paternalistic order.[16]

The magistrates and the police therefore vigorously opposed this form of popular justice — it was not the kind of social life required by a "civilized" capitalist State. In Newfoundland the cultural practice of mummering — when people would get dressed up in disguises (including cross-dressing) — was also used as part of popular protests and class struggles in the 1840s and 1850s against the power and exploitation of the merchant elite. The colonial government of Newfoundland in 1861 in "The Act to Make Further Provision for the Prevention of Nuisances" criminalized anyone "dressed as a Mummer, masked or otherwise disguised."[17]

Following Confederation in 1867, in most of the Canadian territories the administration of justice was gradually and unevenly taken out of the hands of the local community and moved into the mandates of State institutions. In the immediate post-Confederation years, the federal and provincial supreme courts were established.[18]

The Uneven and Combined Development of Sexual Regulation Across the Canadian State

The processes of community sexual regulation followed various patterns. Community and legal regulation did not develop uniformly across the country, and often combined and interacted differently in different regions.

Terry Chapman says that in the West during the late nineteenth and early twentieth centuries sex among males was a "socially tolerated and accepted fact of life"[19] in largely male logging and mining communities and threshing and railroad gangs.[20] In Northern Ontario, in late nineteenth- and early twentieth-centuries bush camps, men not only danced with each other, but some engaged in sex with other men. Gérard Fortin, a Québec Communist Party member and union organizer who spent his early years as a bushworker, gives us a glimpse into his experience:

> We all lived together in the big cabins, mostly on stretchers with springs and a mattress, though there were still a few of the old bunks with straw mattresses, on which two men slept side by side under one blanket. I slept with a quiet, decent fellow who was going to get married in the spring. Unfortunately, I guess in anticipation of the event, he lost control of himself during one night. Imagine! I woke up with this fellow busy giving me the works.

Not my ring (my ring is intact to this day, in spite of my many misadven-
tures) but he was massaging both of us. We were in the top bunk. I couldn't
move too much or everyone would know something was going on. I felt like
a stupid ass trying to get rid of him without embarrassing him. He was so shy
with me after that![21]

Beth Light and Joy Parr point out that "single men had long lived away from kin in Canadian bunkhouse communities. Domestic forms did not so govern males."[22] In these
communities, says Chapman, residents might have "deemed it unnecessary to press
charges [for participation in same-gender sex] as the act was not considered either deviant or criminal."[23]

> [These groups] had their own form of law and methods of punishment ...
> the culprit could have been subjected to the communities or an unofficial
> system of law, rather than the official, criminal law ... the person could have
> been ostracized or banished from the area.[24]

In the West, therefore, and possibly in parts of eastern Canada as well, community
forms of justice may have continued to exist in concert with and in conflict with developing legal forms of regulation.

Legal records show that buggery (both sodomy and bestiality) was not an unknown
"offence." There are recorded cases for the years 1890-1920 in the West in places ranging from Vancouver, Victoria, Calgary, Edmonton, Winnipeg, and Moosimin and Hum-
bolt in Saskatchewan.[25] In Victoria in 1891, two men were sentenced to fifteen years
imprisonment for sodomy; their sentences were commuted to seven years in 1895. The
ultimate penalty for buggery (including sodomy) was life imprisonment.

> Even though buggery was viewed by a large segment of society as an unnatu-
> ral act, a crime against nature, more of a sin than a crime, the western
> judges and juries once again displayed a reluctance to convict and pass the
> full sentence.[26]

The penalty in the West for buggery ranged from the option of a fine to one year in
prison, to sentences of two to fifteen years.[27] The punishment for "gross indecency,"
which was entered into the Canadian Criminal Code in 1890, was usually a short prison
term and flogging.[28] In the West, sentences for flogging or whipping were partially or totally remitted.[29] In 1894, two Vancouver men were convicted of "gross indecency" and
sentenced to two years plus twenty-five lashes, but two years later twelve lashes each were
remitted.

In Regina in 1895, three men were charged with the "most revolting offence" of
"gross indecency of an unnatural character."[30] One of the men was Frank Hoskins, the
"leading member of the largest dry goods, grocery and wholesale liquor firm in town."

Witnesses reported that through the windows of the dry goods store they saw the three men go into the cellar, where they observed two of the men with pants down around their knees in an apparent act of anal intercourse. One of the participants was apparently overheard saying that they needed some lard; they got some butter but it was rejected because it was too salty. Later, all three men, with pants around their knees, were apparently observed in acts of mutual masturbation.

Before judgement was delivered in this case, a petition for leniency was admitted to court. The petition, which was signed by fifty-one people "personally acquainted" with Hoskins, argued for "as much leniency as possible, even to discharge him under suspended sentence," and asked that Hoskins be "taken from the Territories." Hoskins was convicted and fined $200. He was also ordered to give security of $500 to keep the peace for one year — certainly a lenient sentence under the circumstances. The petitioners' request that Hoskins be removed from the territories had the desired result: he left the firm and apparently disappeared from the community, continuing a Prairie tradition of banishment in dealing with sex "offenders."[31]

Petitions for leniency may also have been used even in central Canada when the man charged was a member of an ethnic minority group. Steven Maynard reports that, after a Jewish man was charged in 1917 in Toronto for rubbing the penis of another man, the judge was presented with a petition. In the context of widespread anti-semitism that often associated Jews with sexual "immorality" and "perversion," it testified to the Jewish man's good character and was signed by dozens of Jewish women and men, including presidents of garment-manufacturing firms. The petition did not save this man from six months in the jail farm, but as Maynard suggests "it is evidence that for some men, a tightly knit immigrant community, capable of organizing a collective response, was an important source of support."[32]

In the late 1900s, and particularly by the last few years of the century, Western Canada was being transformed from a "frontier" to a more settled white-dominated society (although it was already populated by Native peoples and Metis), based upon State-supported immigration.[33] White settlement was one of the themes of Macdonald's National Policy of 1878.[34] The West was intended as an agricultural hinterland for central Canadian business, particularly in the transportation, financial, and manufacturing sectors.[35] By placing Native groups on reserves and by suppressing Metis resistance in 1870 and 1885, the Dominion opened up millions of acres of land to white settlers. The land survey system, centring on the "free" homestead, was intended to place agricultural settlers on individual tracts of land best suited to family production. The creation of the family farm and interdependent farm economy was a conscious objective of State policy. Legislative and judicial institutions were established, and in 1873, the government set up the North West Mounted Police as a quasi-military force.

As these plans developed, "bachelors" were increasingly defined as a "social problem." Young, single male settlers were associated with drinking, card playing, and sexual license, thereby threatening Christianity and the image of the holy family.[36] As "respectable" middle-class family life was imposed on the West, as part of this State-building strategy, campaigns of moralization and Canadianization were organized. Immigrants from southern Europe, and particularly those from Asia, were seen as "morally" inferior.[37]

In seems that the race or ethnic background of a man charged with a sex-related offence influenced the punishment and sentence he would receive. Steven Maynard reports that in Halifax in 1777 a black man named Prince was charged with committing "sodomy on the body of John Smith," a white soldier. Prince was found guilty and his sentence was to be "carried through the streets of the town and receive 39 lashes in different places and be imprisoned for 1 month." In contrast, Smith was found not guilty. Maynard points out that the court seemed not only concerned with the act of sodomy itself but was also "concerned by the subversion of racial hierarchies that the sex seemed to represent."[38]

Racism against people of Asian descent also influenced the application of the Criminal Code, including the laying of sexual charges. The work of Indiana Matters suggests that the laws concerning homosexual acts were used particularly strenuously against South Asians in turn-of-the-century Vancouver including the use of police entrapment.[39]

As settlement and institution building proceeded, regulations of sexual behaviour became more rigid. Says Chapman, "... as the West became settled [by Europeans] and more [white] women arrived, ... the rise in conviction rates reflected a shift in social tolerance."[40]

Regarding developments in Ontario, Karen Dubinsky, in her study of rape and heterosexual conflict in the late nineteenth and early twentieth centuries, describes how, in an uneven process, earlier community-based forms of social and sexual regulation were often combined with newer legal forms of regulation shaping how these legal processes were implemented. Eventually, these community forms of regulation were supplanted by legal hegemony.

> I have documented the slow and uneven pace of development of legal hegemony. Sexual crimes provide a distinctive forum for studying the development of legal authority, for in this period, in these regions, legal structures were often rudimentary and communities continued to play an active role in moral regulation and punishment. The change in moral regulation from community scrutiny to community participation in the legal system to the final 'triumph' of legal hegemony did not occur in a straightforward or linear manner, for all three were evident for this period.[41]

I now turn to the formation of the Canadian State and the shift to an increasingly urban capitalist society. These social transformations had an important impact on the emergence of homosexuality, lesbianism, and heterosexuality.

Notes

1. Leo Johnson, "The Political Economy of Ontario Women in the Nineteenth Century" in Acton, Goldsmith, Sheperd, eds., *Women at Work: Ontario 1850-1930* (Toronto: Canadian Women's Educational Press, 1974), p. 17.

2. *Journal des Jesuites,* 1647-48; also see Paul-François Sylvestre, *Bougrerie en Nouvelle-France* (Hull: Éditions Asticou, 1983), pp. 31-34.

3. Jacques Briand, "Sodomy in New France" in *The Body Politic,* No. 42, Apr. 1978, p. 27.

4. *Ibid.,* p. 27, and Sylvestre, "Trois Soldats Accusés des Sodomie" in *Bougrerie En Nouvelle-France, op. cit.,* pp. 37-43.

5. Briand, *op. cit.,* p. 27, and Robert-Lionel Séguin, *La Vie libertine en Nouvelle-France au dix-septième siècle* (Montréal: Lemeau, 1972), pp. 343-344. Also see Jay Cassel's paper "Love in the Time of War: Same-Sex Activity in New France" presented at the "Out of the Archives" conference on the history of bisexuals, lesbians and gay men in Canada at York University, January 14, 1994.

6. See Jay Cassel's paper, *op. cit.*

7. These thoughts were inspired by hearing Jay Cassel's paper "Love in the Time of War: Same-Sex Activity in New France" *op. cit.*

8. Robert Burns, "'Queer Doings': Attitudes Towards Homosexuality in 19th Century Canada" in *The Body Politic,* Dec.-Jan., 1976-1977, "Our Image" section, pp. 5-7. The rest of this paragraph is based on Burns's account.

9. Ed Jackson, "Some Further Comments" in *The Body Politic,* Dec.-Jan., 1976-77, "Our Image" section, p. 7.

10. Paul Romney, "… Horrible Indecent Liberties: The Trial of a Dancing Master, Toronto, 1840" in *The Body Politic,* No. 30, Feb. 1977, p. 24. And see remarks by Philip McLeod, *Canadian Lesbian and Gay History Newsletter,* No. 1, Dec. 1985, p. 5.

11. From records of sworn evidence of John Cooper before Robert Reynolds, Esq., Her Majesty's Justice of the Peace in Canada West, Western District, April 5, 1842, in relation to the charge of sodomy against Samuel Moore and Patrick Kelly. In holdings of Canadian Lesbian and Gay Archives. Reported in *The Body Politic,* No. 108, Nov. 1984, p. 35.

12. McLeod, *op. cit.,* p. 5.

13. Weeks, "Inverts, Perverts and Mary Annes …" in Licata and Peterson, ed., *Historical Perspectives on Homosexuality* (New York: Haworth and Stein and Day, 1981).

14. Beth Light and Alison Prentice, eds., *Pioneer and Gentlewomen of British North America, 1713-1867* (Toronto: New Hogtown Press, 1980), p. 204.

15. Weeks, *Sex, Politics and Society* (London and New York: Longman, 1981) pp. 13-14; Bryan D. Palmer, "Discordant Music: Charivaris and Whitecapping in Nineteenth Century British North America" in *Labour/Le Travailleur,* 1978, pp. 5-62; and Palmer's *Working Class Experience* (Toronto and Vancouver: Butterworth, 1983), pp. 42-44. Most of the Canadian information here is based on Palmer. The word "charivari" originates in European shaming festivals.

16. Palmer, *Working Class Experience, op. cit.,* p. 44.

17. Quoted in Chris Brookes, *A Public Nuisance: A History of the Mummers Troupe* (St. John's: Institute of Social and Economic Research, 1988), p. 29. Also see pp. 23-30 more generally.

18. Chapman, "Sex Crimes in Western Canada, 1890-1920" in Ph.D. dissertation, University of Alberta, 1984, pp. 10-11.

19. Chapman, "Sexual Deviation in Western Canada, 1890-1920" in an unpublished conference paper given at the Northern Great Plains Conference, Winnipeg, 1979, pp. 15-16.

20. Also see Steven Maynard, "Rough Work and Rugged Men: The Social Construction of Masculinity in Working Class History" in *Labour/Le Travail,* No. 23, 1989, pp. 159-169.

21. Gérard Fortin and Boyce Richardson, *Life of the Party* (Montréal, 1984) p. 38. Cited in Steven Maynard, "Rough Work and Rugged Men: The Social Construction of Masculinity in Working Class History" in *Labour/Le Travail,* No. 23 (Spring 1989), p. 167.

22. Beth Light and Joy Parr, eds., *Canadian Women on the Move, 1867-1920* (Toronto: New Hogtown Press and OISE, 1983), p. 49.
23. Chapman conference paper, *op. cit.*, p. 15.
24. *Ibid.*, p. 16.
25. *Ibid.*, p. 12. On an earlier case from Atlantic Canada, see Lorna Hutchinson, "Buggery Trials in Saint John, 1806: The Case of John M. Smith" in *University of New Brunswick Law Journal*, No. 40 (1991), pp. 130-148.
26. *Ibid.*, p. 13.
27. *Ibid.*
28. *Ibid.*, p. 14.
29. *Ibid.*; and Lyle Dick, "Heterohegemonic Discourse and Homosexual Acts: The Case of Saskatchewan in the Settlement Era" in a paper presented to the "Sex and the State" Lesbian/Gay History conference, Toronto, July 1985, p. 10.
30. Quote from the headline of the *Medicine Hat Times* in Dick, "Heterohegemonic Discourse ..." *op. cit.*, p. 12. The following account is based on Dick, pp. 11-15.
31. Dick, op. cit., p. 14.
32. Steven Maynard, "Through a Hole in the Lavatory Wall: Homosexual Subcultures, Police Surveillance, and the Dialectics of Discovery, Toronto, 1890-1930" in *Journal of the History of Sexuality*, V. 5, No. 2, 1994, p. 219.
33. Chapman, conference paper, *op. cit.*, p. 2.
34. Chapman, thesis, *op. cit.*, p. 31.
35. Dick, *op. cit.*, p. 3.
36. *Ibid.*, pp. 4-6.
37. Chapman thesis, *op. cit.*, pp. 31-33. More on this next chapter. Also see Mariana Valverde, *The Age of Light, Soap and Water* (Toronto: McClelland and Stewart, 1991) especially "Racial Purity, Sexual Purity, and Immigration Policy," pp. 104-128.
38. Steven Maynard, "In Search of 'Sodom North': The Writing of Lesbian and Gay History in English Canada, 1970-1990" in *Canadian Review of Comparative Literature*, V. 21, 1-2, Mar.-June 1994, p. 128. The records of the trial are housed at the Provincial Archives of Nova Scotia.
39. Indiana Matters, "Unfit for Publication: Notes Towards a Lavender History of British Columbia" in paper presented at the "Sex and the State" Lesbian/Gay History conference, Toronto, July 1985.
40. Chapman, conference paper, *op. cit.*, p. 18.
41. Karen Dubinsky, *Improper Advances, Rape and Heterosexual Conflict in Ontario, 1880-1929* (Chicago: The University of Chicago Press, 1993), p. 166.

6.

"These Things May Lead to the Tragedy of Our Species": The Emergence of Homosexuality, Lesbianism, and Heterosexuality in Canada

Foundations of Canadian State Formation

From the mid-1800s to the early twentieth century, Canada was becoming increasingly industrialized and urbanized, with its own State and ruling relations. Some of these changes were pre-figured in developments concerning the Upper Canadian school system. Bruce Curtis points out that educational reforms in the late 1830s and 1840s were made with a view to the construction of political subjects and at "proper" political socialization in the wake of the 1837-1838 popular democratic rebellions. The school system played an ever more important role as it was extended to more and more young people in making "citizens" and a Canadian "public."[1] Central to the concerns of the school promoters, says Alison Prentice, were questions of gender, sex, and the body: "How to deal with the growing gap between childhood and manhood was greatly complicated, if not entirely governed, by the whole question of sex."[2]

A more specific concern with relations of sex and gender emerged in the context of this political "socialization" and construction of "character" through various practices of moral regulation and governance.[3] In the first half of the nineteenth century in both Upper and Lower Canada, the conditions for industrial development were being laid with the formation of internal markets and the intentional creation of an urban working class. By the 1840s, access to the land was restricted, forcing many farm families onto smaller plots and new immigrants into wage-labour.[4]

A number of new concerns were generated through these social changes: the decline of the older Family Compact or Chateau Clique-type colonial elites; the emergence of a clearly defined capitalist class and middle class; increasing urbanization (although Canada would only become more than fifty percent urban in 1926[5]); and the formation of an urban working class. Previous paternalist forms of social authority were gradually replaced by more centralized State and ruling relations. The old colonial elite gave way to a new capitalist class that developed an alliance with male middle-class professionals in managing and regulating society. Canadian State formation facilitated the formation of these professional groups. The Canadian Medical Association was founded in 1867, the same year that Confederation took place.[6] This was all part of a shift from community regulation to "national" and increasingly centralized forms of bureaucratic and professional organization.

Confederation came about through the conjunction of British and developing

Anglo-Canadian bourgeois interests to block integration with the U.S. giant to the south. There emerged a particular Canadian system in which there was a division of jurisdiction and tasks between the central federal State and the provinces. Canadian State- and nation-building strategies in the late nineteenth and early twentieth centuries combined railway expansion in the West — and the development of a wheat commodity on which it could depend for freight — with land settlement through extensive white immigration.[7] In Canada, perhaps more integrally than elsewhere, the development of capitalist relations and State formation went hand-in-hand.[8] In the late nineteenth century, "frontiers" were being settled (after the indigenous people had been expropriated), new agricultural communities were opening up along the railways, towns were emerging, immigration was increasing, and an East-West transportation and communications system was dramatically altering the landscape, the social fabric, and the lives of Canadians.

New Forms of Social Regulation

The new elite and their ruling agencies, along with middle-class moral reformers, searched for ways to regulate and administer the social organism in the new urban setting.[9] Older means of moral and social regulation were no longer working. "Traditional" social boundaries were rapidly eclipsed with the emergence of new social spaces and sites and the development of class relations. A fundamental feature of this process was the reorganization of sex and gender relations:

> The market economy, the capitalization and mechanization of production,
> the partition of home and workplace, of producer and consumer, were
> transforming life in farm and city, separating and increasingly differentiating the material and social circumstances of men and women.[10]

The middle class increasingly became interested in the life of the "lower orders." As early as 1816 (and probably earlier), in Upper Canada, concern had been generated over the living arrangements of mechanics in Kingston. Bryan Palmer reports that "it was suggested that the establishment of a church and individual homes for workmen" would solve this problem.[11] Craftsmen were encouraged to marry local women as a way of promoting social stability.[12]

By the late nineteenth century, urban poverty came to be defined by State agencies and middle-class moral reformers as a perplexing problem. The poor were now to be classified and administered as the professionals sought to comprehend and contain them. The "poor," as a social category, were a creation of these early philanthropic and welfare agencies.[13] Middle-class women played an important role in organizing class relations through their volunteer welfare work, in the process classifying the surplus labour pool in the cities and further defining the boundary between the middle class and the "lower orders." In Toronto, "increasingly the 'poor' lived apart from and unconnected to 'respectable' society in a way unprecedented in the city's history."[14] The poor were considered either reformable or beyond redemption — as worthy or unworthy — categories that would later become integral features of the policies of the Welfare State.

By the 1890s, social order seemed to be in crisis as the "underside of industrial capitalism" — poverty, unregulated homeless children and young people, prostitution, non-Anglo-Saxon and non-Christian immigration, and crime — was the subject of numerous studies and reports.[15] The legal term "juvenile delinquent" was used to classify the "waifs and strays" appearing on city streets. The increasing visibility of ill-clad, undisciplined, and unschooled working-class youth symbolized for middle class-reformers a breakdown of the family contract and a threat to moral order itself.[16] This street culture was seen as a breeding ground for immorality, vice, and crime. Control of the streets meant control of the city as "public" social space emerged. Emerging social agencies policed the "surplus" population, intervening directly in working-class social life. Young people who did not belong to a "proper" family were considered a social problem. Unsupervised youths were shepherded into schools or reformatories. The school system became a crucial agent of discipline and "socialization."[17]

These agencies began to fear that the "foreign" culture of the working class and the poor would "pollute" and "corrupt" society as class cleavages deepened and as working-class struggles emerged. Some of these concerns were focused on the morality of working-class women.[18] Female workers were seen as suffering from both poverty and lack of morals. This anxiety informed the work of the 1886 Royal Commission on the Relations of Labour and Capital:

> The commissioners searched diligently for immorality, assuming it to be a necessary consequence of the mingling of the sexes in the factories .... Their questions indicated an overwhelming concern about whether overhearing "immoral" language in the factories would cause them to become immoral.[19]

In different ways, both pro-capitalist members of the Commission and the worker representatives constructed women workers as raising troubling "moral" questions. While working-class representatives (largely male) defended the virtue of women working outside the home, they also constructed them as at risk for moral dangers. Male workers testified that women working in large mills would be exposed to "immoral words which could lead them to become immoral." The Commissioners agreed: "... morally corruptible women [have] to be protected from the ill effects of words."[20] Female workers were considered both physically and morally weak. Dr. T.A. Morre, Secretary of the Temperance and Reform Department of the Methodist Church, carried out an investigation of women's wages. He was far more interested, however, in maintaining the "innocence" and "purity" of working women than in their low wages.[21] Alice Klein and Wayne Roberts explain: "Their often compulsive concern for the working women's purity was rooted in profound anxiety about the changing roles and endangered status of women."[22]

State agencies, religious leaders, and many male workers all played a role in creating the image of the immoral woman who worked outside the home. This provided justification for "protective" legislation — keeping women from competing with males in certain job categories, usually in the skilled and better-paid areas.

> Protective legislation placed the parameters of reform well within their traditional notions of womanliness and femininity. Through factory inspection, the state acted as watchdog … over the morality and cleanliness of the environment of women workers.[23]

Within the working class, patriarchal family relations were organized by class pressures and the pressures of industrial capitalism and State moralization. The Canadian Trades and Labour Congress had an avowed aim, early in this century, of eliminating women — particularly married women — from the wage-labour force.[24] Working-class social and political life came to be dominated by men. The emergence of the skilled trades was intrinsically tied to notions of social respectability, which, in turn, was equated with economic independence and the family wage paid to the male worker. Working-class men could thereby avoid the stigma associated with charity. Further, this sense of social respectability linked skilled workers with the middle class, establishing a cross-class alliance around certain social and moral "norms."[25] The division of the working class into "respectable" and "rough" was just one more distinction dividing workplace and society: skilled/non-skilled now joined masculine/feminine and adult/child.

Concerns were also generated about the morality of middle-class women. Women who rode bicycles clad in pant-like bloomers were likened to prostitutes.

> The essential costume for women cyclists, pant-like "bloomers," scandalized education trustees who charged that women teachers thus attired resembled prostitutes. Unchaperoned riders were "exposed at the road houses to the most dangerous temptations," warned evangelist Methodists. Fantasies of blazing saddles flashed before the editor of the *Dominion Medical Monthly*, who condemned [bicycle riding] as the latest outlet of carnal passion. "Bicycle riding produces in the female a distinct orgasm," he wrote. Already, he continued, "Toronto's scorching thoroughfares make the streets of Sodom and Gomorrah appear as pure as Salvation Army shelters."[26]

There was also official concern about "race suicide" as the birth rate among Anglo-Saxons in Ontario dramatically declined; it was feared that Anglo-Saxon stock was being submerged by "inferior" races through immigration and a higher birth rate among Irish-Canadian and French-Canadian Catholics. During much of this time, Catholics were almost seen as a separate race by many Protestants.[27] English Protestant social character was considered necessary to the ruling class. Yet, more middle-class Anglo-Saxon women were staying single.[28] There was a particularly low marriage and birth rate among college-educated women. Furthermore, Canada had a high infant and maternal mortality rate, and this was seen as indicative of "race degeneration."[29] Immigrants from China, Japan, and southern Europe were considered a particular threat to the "physical and mental superiority of the native white Anglo-Saxon-Canadian."[30]

In the West, alcohol and opium were associated with immigrants while "proper" religion, morality and good character were associated with Anglos. Native and mixed-blood women and their families found themselves outside the "newly forming respectability."[31] Opium use was prohibited except for medicinal purposes. The image of young white women being "seduced" by Chinese men helped to instigate riots against the Chinese.[32] The Criminal Code sex legislation was used to discriminate against Asians. Black males were considered by official white society to be long on sex drive and short on mental ability.[33] All this demonstrates connections between sexuality, sexism, and racism, and Canada's roots as a class, gender, and race-divided society.

Thus were fuelled the campaigns for the regulation of immigration and for the "Canadianization" of immigrants. People were denied entry if they were of "bad character" or if they were physical or moral "degenerates." The churches and the Women's Christian Temperance Union tried to teach immigrants to be good Christians, and to assimilate them to middle-class Anglo-Protestant respectability. This was all part of broader attempts to establish social rule over a stable, efficient, disciplined work force made up increasingly of non-English immigrants. A key aspect of this project of moral regulation and reformation was to create a particular kind of Canadian "citizen."[34] Campaigns against alcohol and opium consumption were linked to campaigns against the "secret vice," the "social evil" and promiscuity.[35]

The emergence of eugenics, the study of improving the "quality" of the "race" through selective breeding, led to proposals for the segregation and sterilization of "inferior" immigrants so that "Canada would forever remain white, Anglo-Saxon and Protestant."[36] In 1928, the Alberta government enacted Canada's first legislation for the sterilization of the "mental defective," which lasted until 1972. Under the terms of this Act thousands were sterilized. Similar legislation in British Columbia was also repealed in 1972.[37]

Defending Marriage and Family

There were campaigns to defend and shore up patriarchal family and gender organization. Initiatives were launched against birth control and to get women out of the paid work force and into the home and institutionalized motherhood. The feminist and suffrage movements were blamed for the decreasing birth rate among middle-class women, the growing divorce rate, the growing numbers of middle-class women who were not marrying, women's economic independence, and for involving women — horrors of horrors — in the "public" world of production. These campaigns, in a number of ways, were a response to feminism — an attempt to shore up the institutions of marriage and motherhood. In 1908 Rev. C. Sharp told his Toronto congregation:

God abhors the spirit so prevalent nowadays which condemns motherhood. How it must grieve Him when He sees what we call race suicide;
when He sees the problems of married life approached lightly and wan-
tonly; based on nothing higher and nobler than mere luxury, and gratification of passion.[38]

Concerns over motherhood had been developing throughout the late nineteenth century.[39] By the early twentieth century, the surveillance of motherhood had led to the
generation of the concept of the "inadequate mother" — usually immigrant or working-
class women without enough time to spend with their kids according to middle-class
standards. The anxiety over race suicide and infant mortality was exacerbated by losses
in World War I. The war heightened the emphasis on patriotism and maternity and the
interdependence of cradle and sword. These national and "racial" concerns led to the
introduction of domestic-science training for girls.[40] By the "early twentieth century,
motherhood, now a burden of State, a sacred office and a scientific practice could be
none other than a full-time occupation."[41] And as Beth Light and Joy Parr also point
out:

The ideological sanctity of motherhood as the fount of and essence of female nature grew stronger as the need to bear many children decreased
and the choice to raise large families became less common.[42]

These social trends led to concerns over sexual morality, particularly sex outside marriage. There had already been considerable middle-class and "respectable" working-
class concern over family instability in the years before World War I due to the social
strains of industrialization and urbanization. Divorce had been difficult to obtain: in Ontario and Québec, there was no provincial divorce law, which meant divorce had to be
granted through a private-member's bill passed by federal Parliament — a process which
took a year and cost at least $1,000, and was thus not available to the working class.[43]
The divorce rate, however, seemed to be doubling every decade. Desertion, meanwhile,
"the poor man's divorce," was defined by moral reformers as a serious problem.

Marriage and the family were perceived to be weakening, undermined by
general causes such as urbanization, but also by increasing immorality as
demonstrated by such "sins of the flesh" as prostitution, adultery and co-
habitation outside marriage and by a diminishing sense of responsibility on
the part of individuals as shown by non-support, desertion and divorce.[44]

Marriage, home, and the family were considered by ruling social agencies as the essence of a "healthy" community. In the words of Ontario Conservative Member of Parliament E.A. Lancaster, if divorces were granted freely, "the whole social fabric of the
country would go to pieces."[45] Moral reformers, the social-purity movement, and poli-

ticians pushed the State to play a stronger role in defending marriage and discouraging sex outside its confines. Prostitution, the "social evil," symbolized all forms of sexual immorality and perversion, and all women's sexual activity outside marriage was thus identified.[46]

> Marriage breakdown operated as a similar, negative symbol. Marriage represented a code of moral and sexual behaviour which was felt to have long ordered society: marriage breakdown, on the other hand, symbolized a wide variety of conduct that was considered immoral, anti-social and unacceptable.[47]

The link between marriage breakdown and sexual conduct was only reinforced by adultery being the main grounds for divorce. Marriage was the only State-sanctioned terrain for sex. Laws were passed to "protect" marriage, to inhibit the social process of marriage breakdown. With the formulation of the Criminal Code in 1892, it became clear that Parliament, and not the courts, would be the main agent of legal change.

The Society for the Protection of Women and Children, under the leadership of D.A. Watt, made use of social-purity literature from England and the United States. Young girls and women must be protected from seduction, they said, and the brothels and the "white slave trade" must be crushed. Use of the term "white slave trade" had clear racial connotations informed by social purity's symbolic emphasis on whiteness, cleanliness and purity.[48] They attempted to make an analogy between the black slave trade and white female prostitution. Social-purity agitation ignored the plight of Native women and women of colour and focused on an image of the virginal white girl being led astray by moral perverts.[49]

Watt wrote lengthy tracts on "morals legislation" between 1889 and 1892.[50] As a result, the 1892 Criminal Code included a comprehensive system of offences designed to "protect" young women and girls.[51] The Criminal Code also included "gross indecency," referring to all sexual acts between men not already covered under "buggery." These sex offences were codified as part of an attempt to establish the patriarchal family as an unshakeable institution.

Within the House of Commons social-purity activists like Watt often supported the campaigns of Norfolk County MP, John Charlton, for morals legislation to censor "obscene" literature, to criminalize sexual acts outside marriage and to oppose abortion and birth control. For Charlton there was a close relationship "between a strong morality and a strong state."[52]

Charlton became especially associated with new legislation against "seduction," which he argued was necessary to protect women, especially young women, from moral danger. He first introduced such legislation in 1882, and by 1886 a version of it became law. This criminalized "seduction" as opposed to coercive or forcible sexual attack. In these cases, consent was not an issue since the law proclaimed that in certain situations consent to sexual relations could not exist. The law applied only to younger women who

were "of previously chaste character" and were between the ages of fourteen and sixteen, or were under twenty-one when sex was tied to a promise of marriage, or were
twenty-one and their employer or guardian had "seduced" them.[53] Throughout the
1880s and 1890s, Charlton attempted to raise the age limits for the protection of women
from "seduction." In her study of the use of these laws in the late nineteenth and early
twentieth centuries in Ontario, Dubinsky found that criminal "seduction" laws were
often used by parents to regulate consensual different-gender relationships.[54]

Social-purity activists continued their campaigns in the succeeding decades in the
belief that "the state had a clear right and duty to intrude into the bedrooms of the nation."[55] Their work, however, was only one aspect of a broader effort to coerce working-
class men into accepting their responsibilities as "proper" husbands and breadwinners
and to force women to be "proper" wives and mothers. The imposition of these middle-
class standards onto the working class was, in turn, only one part of the establishment of
the family wage system and patriarchal family relations within the working class.[56] One
way in which this was established was through an intensification of the regulation of
non-matrimonial different-gender sex and same-gender sex.

Social-purity arguments influenced both "public" opinion and State policy. This
public discussion, meanwhile, also produced a form of secular and popular consciousness of sexuality and sex "education."

Social Purity

The Canadian social-purity movement was a main force behind the increasing regulation of sexuality, including same-gender sexualities. In social-purity discourse, the "social evil," and sex itself, were a metaphor for concerns about sexual violence, gender,
and racial and class morality.[57] The social evil became a symbol for national and social
degeneration. In England, the social-purity movement emerged partly out of feminist
protests against the sexual double standard and the "victimization" of female prostitutes. However, given that feminists did not control the institutions and discourses which
were coming to define and regulate erotic life, and given the prevailing notions of male
sexual lust and female lack of sexual passion, the movement took a morally conservative
direction, led by organizations which not only tried to control male lust and violence,
but also tried to stigmatize and criminalize such female sex-linked activities as prostitution. The movement which had initially rejected aspects of women's subordination and
attempted to challenge male sexual violence, now moved in a repressive and anti-feminist direction, arguing for much of the sexual legislation that continued to shape the policing of sexuality until recently: higher age-of-consent-laws for engaging in sexual
activities, the criminalization of prostitutes, and "gross indecency."[58] Jeffrey Weeks describes the movement's views on homosexuality:

> In their minds, homosexuality was barely differentiated from prostitution.
> For the morality crusaders ... both were part of the continuum of undiffer-

entiated lust, products of man's selfishness. Let one crack appear in the moral order and floods of lustfulness would sweep society away. In their minds the syndromes of schoolboy masturbation, public school "immorality" (meaning homosexuality) and prostitution were closely intertwined.[59]

The weakness of a progressive radical or socialist feminism in the Canadian women's and suffrage movements rendered them less resistant to the social-purity trend. Feminism based on equal rights for women was often subordinated to a maternal feminism that advocated women's rights as a way of protecting and extending the institution of motherhood in the home and in society.[60] Canadian women, unlike their U.S. sisters, did not have the same radicalizing experiences of the anti-slavery movement, and only a "small minority suggested that women be freed from familial ties to allow them to pursue careers of their choice."[61] Canadian feminists like Flora MacDonald Denison, Agnes Deans Cameron, and Carrie Derick were exceptions to this trend.[62] Indeed, several of the women's movement and suffrage leaders belonged to social-purity groups.[63] At that time, mainstream feminism in Canada had a white, largely Christian character, and was very concerned about non-white and non-Christian immigrants.

> In order to understand the suffragists' social attitudes we have to understand the values of the group with which they identified. As Anglo-Saxon, Protestant, middle-class, such women shared the anxieties and expectations of this group. They saw women's problems through glasses tinted with values shaped by this allegiance.[64]

At the same time, African-Canadian women were beginning to organize, but these women were excluded and marginalized from the mainstream of Canadian feminism.[65]

The social-purity movement was led for a number of years by Reverend J.G. Shearer, the secretary of the Toronto-based Social and Moral Reform Council of Canada — "a federation of the social and reform departments of all the leading churches and temperance and reform organizations of Canada" and the "strongest force in the Dominion for the advancement" of social purity. The Social and Moral Reform Council was affiliated with social-purity organizations in the U.S. and England. *The Light* — the official organ of the International American Purity Federation — reached a reported 75,000 readers in the U.S., Canada, Mexico, and elsewhere.[66] The Canadian Purity Education Association, staffed by medical doctors, existed in Toronto from 1906-1915.[67] The previously mentioned Society for the Protection of Women and Girls, led by D.A. Watt, which played a crucial role in law reform, was an important part of this movement.

The purity movement — moral reformers, clergymen, doctors, and members of the National Council of Women — focused their campaigns on the "social evil," usually referring to female prostitution but often referring to sexual immorality in general — masturbation, possibly same-gender sex, sex outside marriage, as well as male sexual violence against women. Their definitions could include "self-abuse," or masturbation, and same-gender sex with "perverse" practices. For example, *Jack Canuck*, the Canadian equivalent of the *Police Gazette* in its sensationalizing of the underworld, once warned in an article of the white slave trade "of boys being led astray by moral perverts."[68] It is not clear who the "moral perverts" are here, but there is a suggested linkage between female prostitution and boys engaging in masturbation or same-gender sex. In 1912 the social-purity-inspired Vigilance Committee listed in a pamphlet as one of its objectives to support "efforts to aid in preventing boys being led astray by moral perverts."[69] Here the mobilization of this expression against male same-gender sex was part of a broader social-purity campaign against prostitution, immoral plays, and indecent pictures.

Many women engaged in casual forms of prostitution as a means of survival.[70] The social-purity campaigns, in alliance with business interests and the police, took advantage of middle-class fears about the character of "public" space to stigmatize and criminalize prostitutes. Yet at the same time they created an image of the prostitute as a "victim" in the white slave trade.

> Belief in the essential vulnerability of women precluded recognition of the fact that a woman may not have been duped at all, but may have acted on her own evaluation of her position and alternatives.[71]

The social-purity perspective ignored women's financial reasons for involvement in the trade, simply calling for State "protection" rather than looking at women's social, economic, and sexual situations. They also ignored many young working-class women's desires to actively explore and experience the pleasures of city life.[72]

Social purity helped establish a number of commissions to investigate and survey the "social evil." In 1913 a Social Survey Commission was set up in Toronto at the request of the Toronto Local Council of Women.[73] The Commission was made up of members of the Young Men's Christian Association, the Toronto Local Council of Women, the Roman Catholic Archbishop, the Salvation Army, the city's medical health officer, other religious figures, and academics. Their report, released in 1915, relied on various other vice commission reports, including the report of the Chicago Vice Commission. While noting that they found little evidence of the white slave trade in Canada, they criticized police indifference to prostitution and recommended the "total suppression" of prostitution. They also generated a new concept of the "occasional prostitute," referring to women who went out on dates with men to parks and ice cream parlours and may have had sex with their male companions.[74] Among the causes of the "social disease," they listed poverty, overcrowding, boarders — "which necessarily lead towards immorality" — and the great tide of immigration which brought with it "foreigners" with different standards of sexual morality and the growth of "feeblemindedness." There were 5,000 unmarried men in Toronto with no living quarters except a bedroom, said the report.

At the same time, their major focus was on young, white, unregulated working women who were tempted by the amusements of the city to engage in occasional prostitution. Poverty itself was not seen to be the cause of this since some working women survived on low wages and managed to protect "their virtue," but was seen instead as a moral failing. The report associated feeblemindedness with "sexual immorality" and pronounced that prostitution was caused by "abnormal sensual propensities and lack of moral perception." "feebleminded" women (often including unwed mothers) were linked with low morals. The report also linked the increase in infant mortality and sexual diseases like syphilis with prostitution and "promiscuous sex relations." A sexual appetite was natural in men, it said, but in women "... the desire for motherhood [was] the primary factor ... The abnormal development of sex desire when it does occur, is, however, more pronounced in women than in men."[75] The report recommended social-purity education to deal with the "perversion of natural instincts by bad social environment" and also suggested raising the age of consent for sexual acts to sixteen.

While "social evil" generally meant female prostitution, there were also references to sexual immorality and perversion. "Perversion" in social-purity discourse usually referred to non-reproductive sex but was sometimes used in a broader sense. In the Chicago Vice Commission report, a section entitled "Sexual Perversion" noted an increase in same-gender sex and referred to "colonies of these men who are sex perverts," but who did not often come into contact with the police or physicians.[76] These men adopted the "carriage, mannerisms and speech of women," were "often people of a good deal of talent," and had a "vocabulary and signs of recognition of their own." The report also referred to "female impersonators" and men who dressed as women and solicited other men for "perverse practices." It recommended the "practical ideal of a straight and pure sexual life both before and after marriage" and tougher legislation. Another section of the Chicago report discussed "pervert methods" in the higher-priced prostitution houses, apparently referring to oral sex. The Toronto study included no such exploration of pervert practices.

Social-purity rhetoric combined notions of "feeblemindedness," moral degeneration, and race degeneration, from the language of Social Darwinism, with the Christian terms of "immorality," "vice" and "evil."[77] The social purists advocated the prohibition of all non-matrimonial and non-reproductive sex, but they also proposed and indeed instituted a particular form of sex "education."[78] J.S. Shearer called for educating boys and girls

in the purpose and problems and perils of sex, including information as to the awful penalty nature imposes in the forms of social diseases, such as syphilis and gonorrhoea, well designated the Black Plague upon those who violate her laws of sex.[79]

Sexual Advice: Sex Education for Purity

During the late nineteenth and early twentieth centuries, social-purity-advice literature was widely available, and lectures were heard by thousands. In the early 1890s Reverend W.J. Hunter was reportedly lecturing to as many as 1,500 men a night at St.James
Methodist Church in Montréal. He addressed such topics as prostitution, masturbation
— the "solitary vice" — and puberty. He defended sexual purity as necessary to the vig-
our of the race, since "loss of semen is the loss of blood."[80]

According to the Methodist Church, the best-selling sex-advice literature in Canada
between 1900 and 1915 were the eight volumes of the *Self and Sex* series.[81] These books
were based on the "spermatic economy" theory of a limited-energy model of sex and development. "Self-abuse" was equated with waste and with moral and physical degeneration. Two Canadian doctors had in their respective 1865 and 1877 reports supported
this "self-abuse" scare. *The Dominion Medical Monthly* and the *Ontario Medical Journal* had
both concluded that in single men, masturbation led to insanity. The *Self and Sex* series
was favourably reviewed in the *Canadian Journal of Medicine and Surgery*, and leading Canadian doctors supported this sexual discourse. Dr. Maurice Bucke, who we will meet
again in another context, not only linked masturbation with insanity, but operated on
the "insane" to correct the "problem."[82]

There also began to develop a sense that something was wrong with close same-gender intimacies. This affected friendships and emotional support networks among both
men and women. "Proper" non-erotic friendships were promoted, in contrast to the
horrors of same-gender perversion. In *What a Young Woman Ought to Know*, part of the
Self and Sex series, Dr. Wood Allen warned:

> I believe in reserve even in girl friendships. Girls are apt at certain periods in
> their lives to be rather gushing creatures. They form the most sentimental at-
> tachments for each other. They go about with their arms around each other,
> they loll against each other, and sit with clasped hands by the hour. They fon-
> dle and kiss until beholders are fairly nauseated, and in a few weeks, perhaps
> they do not speak as they pass each other, and their caresses are lavished on
> others. They are a weakening of moral fibre, a waste of mawkish sentimental-
> ity. They may be even worse. Such friendship may degenerate even into a spe-
> cies of self-abuse that is most deplorable.
>
> When girls are so sentimentally fond of each other that they are like silly
> lovers when together, and weep over each other's absence in uncontrollable
> agony, the conditions are serious enough for the consultation of a physician.
> It is an abnormal state of affairs, and if probed thoroughly might be found to
> be a sort of perversion, a sex mania, needing immediate and perhaps severe
> measures.
>
> I wish the friendships of girls were less sentimental, more manly. Two
> young men who are friends do not lop on each other, and kiss and gush. They

trust each other, they talk freely together, they would stand by each other in any trouble or emergency, but their expressions of endearment are not more than the cordial handgrasp and the unsentimental appellation, "Dear old chap."

I admire these friendships in young men. They seem to mean so much, and yet to exact so little.[83]

Josephine E. Young, M.D., warned that the affection of a girl for an older woman "is abnormal and unwholesome and should be positively dealt with as a manifestation of sex perversion."[84] Social purity was now applying the notion of perversion more specifically to same-gender erotic activities, although here it seemed tied to age distinctions as well.

The Women's Christian Temperance Union (WCTU) and evangelical churches hired purity reformers such as Beatrice Brigden, William Lund Clark, and Arthur W. Beall to tour the schools warning young people against self-abuse and promiscuity and educating them for a "pure" life and character. It was felt that a proper Christian upbringing required proper sex education, not an ignorance of sex. Ignorance, it was thought, left young people without the fortitude to resist temptation. Brigden and Clark were hired by the Canadian Methodist Church.[85] Brigden spoke to girls and women from 1913 to 1920. After being hired in 1913, she was sent to the home of American purity leader B.S. Steadwell for three weeks of intensive training and reading on sex. She specialized in "The Girl and Her Problems" and argued for pure living and citizenship.[86] Brigden was also influenced by currents within feminism and later became involved in supporting working-class activism.[87]

Clark, as we have seen, had already been busy giving lectures to boys and it was apparently he who urged Brigden to "take on a similar task among girls, to lecture and counsel on sex hygiene and social problems."[88] He was much more influenced by masculinist and patriarchal writings on sex then Brigden.[89] A Methodist report commended Clark for having "given careful and long study to the life problems of boys and young men."[90] He urged boys to avoid degrading influences, wrong thoughts and wrong pictures, and the company of "immorally clothed young women." He recommended that they drink neither tea nor coffee and refrain from dancing, and that they seek improved ventilation and take frequent baths.[91] Through these means they could produce a strong character and a pure self. Clark toured Canada and the United States with this message.

Beall lectured between 1905 and 1911 to a reported 13,463 schoolboys on behalf of the Ontario WCTU.[92] Lesson Nine of Mr. Beall's classes in sex education instructed the boys to repeat after him, "The more you use the penis muscle the weaker it becomes; but the less you use the penis muscle the stronger it becomes."[93] This would likely have been the boys' first introduction to this naming of their genitals and would surely have led to erotic experimentation and play as well as the intended self-repression. Beall stressed the national importance of sex hygiene and its importance in producing the "character" needed for Canada. Beall was hired by the Ontario Department of Education in 1911 and he worked there until the 1930s.[94] Rather than social purity opposing sex education, it actively promoted its own form of sex education and, at least in Ontario, had some success in introducing it into the schools.

Venereal Disease: "Polluting the Race"

In the years preceding World War I, the social-purity movement made much of the reported increase in venereal disease. VD was seen as a challenge to the health of the Anglo-Saxon "race."[95] As Lucy Bland explains when discussing the mood in England, VD stood as a metaphor,

> condensing and "carrying" many of the fears of the period — the concern
> with the falling birth rate ... concern with national efficiency and physical
> deterioration of troops and civilians.[96]

By 1912 the Canadian Methodist Church was demanding that all cases of VD be reported to medical health officials. Its association with "feeblemindedness" was made perfectly clear with the naming, in 1918, of the Ontario Government's Royal Commission on Venereal Disease and Feeblemindedness.[97] World War I and a push by public-health agitation around venereal disease provided the basis for the establishment of a Canadian Department of Health in 1919. State regulation now took the form of "public health" legislation and management of sexual disease, prostitution, sexual "promiscuity," and "deviance."[98] Laws were directed against prostitutes and "loose women."

In Canada, in the late nineteenth and early twentieth centuries, there were a whole series of measures, often social-purity inspired, to try to wipe out the "social evil." In 1918 the Canadian government moved to further regulate prostitutes. It stipulated that "no woman who is suffering from Venereal Disease in a communicable form shall have sexual intercourse with any member of His Majesty's forces or solicit or invite any member of the said forces to have sexual intercourse with her."[99] Notice that in this discourse there was no responsibility placed on the men involved. Government educational pamphlets during these years included such statements as — "Practically all prostitutes and loose women are diseased," and "Prostitution cannot be made safe."[100] Prostitutes and "loose" women were constructed as the "problem" in the spread of VD. Clearly embedded in this official and professional discourse were sexist or patriarchal double standards. The regulatory focus was on the women and not the men, as women's "sexual deviance" came increasingly to be defined as "promiscuity" and prostitution. The precedent was set for more State intervention into the realm of bodies, desires, and pleasures.

The Emergence of Sex Psychology

It is within this social context that the psychiatric and medical professions began to import the sex-scientific knowledge being developed in Europe and the U.S. As Xavier

Mayne put it, "The topic of simisexuality is taboo in the United States and in Canada except through observation by and for medical students and physicians."[101] An article entitled "Perversion," for instance, by Ezra Hurlburt Stafford, M.B., First Assistant Physician at the Asylum for the Insane in Toronto, was published in 1898 and read before the Toronto Medical Society.[102] The article discusses the degree to which perversions are a disease and the degree to which they are a product of evolution, explaining that long-suppressed characteristics may appear and take hold of isolated members of the species. "Many cases of sexual perversion," Stafford argues, "may be set down as a reversion or a miscarriage in the chain of evolution."

Stafford uses most of his article, however, to deal, with two different types of perversion:

> These cases of perversions form not a distortion of a natural instinct, but an excrescence apparently completely foreign, and not so often of the nature of a physical defect as of a mental aberration, and therefore a form of insanity.

These perversions referred to prostitution and sex between men (he never uses the word "homosexual"). He refers to the work of Krafft-Ebing, in naming and describing the sex perversions, but he also calls Krafft-Ebing's work the "bible of the bawdy house." Here Stafford exhibits an understanding of the potentially two-sided dynamic of sex-scientific theories. On the one hand, the perversions are named so that they can be identified and contained. On the other hand, the very naming of the perversions provides the opportunity for people to identify with them and to develop resistance to sexual rule. Stafford explains that there exist forms of perversion other than prostitution "which occupy a place of their own in the lives of nations — forms of perversions long familiar to readers of the late classical writers." After an examination of the writings of Ancient Greece and Rome, he tells us that "even in Corinth, a thoughtful man would surely have been forced to admit that these usages constituted a wilful and mischievous trifling with the laws of nature."

He associates this perversion with "periods of racial degeneration." He uses the work of Cesare Lombroso to justify his position that the sexual overuse or misuse of an organ leads to an imbalance of the nervous system and degeneration. Society exists in a rather artificial situation of highly structured relations between the sexes, Stafford contends, of intense religious sentiments and the repression of "natural" physiological inclinations, and this has led the race into "an abnormal condition" whereby perversions are acquired. "These things [prostitution and sex between men] may lead to the tragedy of our species." He links these perversions to an "insidious process of degeneration which is taking place in the inmost structure of modern civilization."

Stafford's analysis is rabidly anti-Catholic: he even suggests that the Roman Catholic Church itself led to abnormal lust, associating perversion with conversion to the Catholic faith — all this in the context of middle-class Anglo-Saxon anxieties over in-

creasing birth rates among Irish and French-Canadian Catholics. While there was always a tendency in sex-scientific literature to blame "foreign" cultures for perversions,
Stafford's analysis takes on a particular Anglo-Canadian character with its anti-Catholic
fervour.

Stafford's work is rooted in the popularization among Canadian doctors of the works
of Lombroso and Krafft-Ebing. The main themes of European sex-scientific debates are reproduced in his article, such as the debate over whether same-gender sex practices are innate or acquired, whether congenital or representative of moral degeneracy.[103]

Resources for Queer Cultures

The literature of forensic psychiatry regarding sex perversion and later sex psychology began to be taken up in professional circles in Canada as networks of men who engaged in sex with each other became more visible in the larger urban centres. Some of
these networks grew out of earlier urban networks of men who had sex with men within
the military and the interactions between younger men and boys and elite men. Sex-scientific classifications of "perversion" and "inversion" began to be used against these
men.

Some of these networks were associated with cross-dressing. In Montréal it was reported in *La Presse* in 1886 that she-men (*hommes-femmes*), would gather in the evening
behind the Court House. There they were reported to "hold their filthy revels" and
to treat "passers-by to the spectacle of their vile pastimes." Police constables apparently entrapped some of the men but *La Presse* complained that light sentences allowed them "to slip quickly back to the pleasures of their kind." Here we get a sense
of these gathering places, organized through the cultural practices of "gender inversion" and cross-dressing. There was also a certain awareness of these networks as a
"social threat" generated through the media and police action.[104]

Steven Maynard reports on the 1894 arrest of Mary Cullen in Halifax, Nova Scotia:

> Mary, a tailoress, was arrested at her home when several of the men she had
> been dating discovered that — as the newspaper put it — "Mary was not all
> she pretended to be." When Mary, who was in fact Thomas Cullen, was
> asked why he dressed as a woman, he replied he could fool the "chappies"
> and "nearly every evening" he could "stroll down Hollis Street and be sure
> to make a pick up."[105]

These examples suggest the development of networks that had some similar characteristics to the "fairies" that George Chauncey describes in New York City from the
1890s into the early twentieth century. These working-class fairy cultures were defined
by taking up certain aspects of "effeminacy" and sometimes cross-dressing.[106] Maynard
suggests that, in Toronto, by 1912, some of the men were being referred to as "sissies"

and "fairies."[107] This may have been one of the ways in which a distinct group of men who had sex with other men were referred.

In the nineteenth century, there were also many reports of passing or cross-dressing white women in Canada.[108] They cross-dressed to gain access to the economic and social privileges enjoyed by men, and perhaps also to establish intimate and erotic relationships with other women.[109] A woman who dressed in men's clothes was described in 1872 as follows: "... her demeanour was so masculine as to put in doubt her sex. Was she man or woman or hermaphrodite?"[110] Before the emergence of specific homosexual or lesbian categories, these women were seen as odd for challenging gender practices but were not necessarily considered sexually suspect. By the 1880s, there were already, in some professional circles, "two distinct types of womanhood." On the one hand, there was the "timid, confiding, trusting woman" who "comes to realize that her mission in this world is a domestic one." On the other, there were "the self-confident, self-asserting, self-reliant, fearless, masculine women" for whom "domestic duties have but a secondary attraction."[111] With the emergence of the "homosexual" and the "lesbian," same-gender passionate friendships became suspect. Cross-dressing now became associated with sexual inversion; the history of gender-crossing women formed one of the foundations for lesbian cultures.[112]

A number of men who were influential in the formation of homosexual "identities" visited Canada in the late nineteenth centuries. Oscar Wilde visited English Canada in the 1880s, prior to the homosexual scandals in which he was involved in England in the 1890s.[113] Newspaper coverage of Wilde's trip reflects an ambiguous and hostile response to a (pre-homo) English dandy.[114] Walt Whitman visited Canada in the summer of 1880 and kept in close contact with Dr. Maurice Bucke, who he met earlier as superintendent of the Mental Hospital in London. Whitman influenced not only Dr. Bucke and Edward Carpenter (who himself visited Canada in 1884), but also Upper Canadian intellectuals such as the feminist-activist Flora MacDonald Denison.[115]

Denison, one of the few Canadian suffragists to call herself a feminist, was profoundly influenced by Whitman, as well as by the American feminist Charlotte Perkins Gilman, Victoria Woodhul, August Bebel, Olive Schreiner, and Edward Carpenter.[116] Denison was involved in the Canadian Theosophical Society, whose early publications included many poems by Whitman. She held quite progressive views for her day on questions of divorce, prostitution, and sexuality, although she certainly mobilized racism against immigrants.[117] She believed that prostitution was fundamentally an economic rather than a moral issue. She was opposed to violent punishment and flogging.

> Denison's ideas about sexuality itself were influenced by her Whitmanite spiritualism. In her view "sex was not only necessary for both men and women, it was an exalted function."[118]

In 1910, Denison bought a cottage at Bon Echo in southern Ontario as a combination summer hostel and avant-garde spiritual community dedicated to Whitman. In 1916 a Walt Whitman Club was formed at Bon Echo. The club published a magazine, *The Sunset at Bon Echo*, from 1916 to 1920, a consistent theme of which was male friendship.[119]

> It seems likely that this group would have attracted gays and provided a supportive community as they tried to come to terms with coping with the hostile world outside.[120]

This development also suggests possible overlaps between early progressive feminist, socialist, sex-radical, lesbian and male homosexual networks, especially among the white intellectual middle class. On Denison's death, *The Canadian Theosophist* concluded that "… no one in the present generation of Canadians has done more for the 'institution of the dear love of Comrades' than Flora MacDonald Denison."[121] Her funeral service was sponsored by the Whitmanite Fellowship of Toronto.

The Greek "ideal" may also have played an important role in the making of homosexual identifications among middle- and upper-class and intellectual white men,[122] although the effect of classical literature on the identity formation of white middle-class homosexuals in Canada has yet to be explored. It was apparently feared by some that classical literature might inspire "self-abuse." Reverend James Carmichael, writing in 1877, refers to Socrates:

> He faced the most disgusting and abhorrent lusts, thank god, almost unknown by name to western civilization, with a joking nod of recognition … Fancy our handsome boys listening to the great Athenian. Our girls would be safe but for the sake of pure boy life we would raise and fling the teacher from our ruddy hearthstone.[123]

Elsa Gidlow's account of the formation of her lesbian identification in the years 1914-1919 in Montréal gives us a rare and precious glimpse into the formation of the lesbian and male homosexual worlds in the early twentieth century.[124] In those days, before the demarcation of a specific lesbian identity, male and female homosexual identity formation had shared features. Gidlow tells us of her early sense of being an "outsider" as she struggled to survive as an independent woman. By now, many young women were challenging convention by getting jobs and taking rooms in boardinghouses, which became possible as some women gained more economic independence. Gidlow heard another woman labelled a "mofredite" (slang for "hermaphrodite," a word that could then be used for people involved in same-gender sex). This gave Gidlow an introduction to the naming of another sexuality.[125] Through a writer's group she met a young homosexual man, Roswell George Mills, whom she describes as follows:

> He was beautiful. About nineteen, exquisitely made up, slightly perfumed, dressed in ordinary men's clothing but a little on the chi-chi side. And he

swayed about, you know. We became friends almost instantly because we were both interested in poetry and the arts.[126]

Through Roswell, she was able to begin exploring and naming her sense of difference. He introduced her to the writings of Sappho and Wilde. Together they read Havelock Ellis, Edward Carpenter, and the works of Krafft-Ebing, Lombroso, and Freud.[127] She describes how the "trial and jailing of Oscar Wilde were not far in our past and very real."[128] Gidlow and Mills delved "into the mores of Ancient Greece" and the writings of "homosexuals" throughout history, which gave them "reasons for loving ourselves and each other."[129] Here we see a process through which Gidlow and Mills were able to name their difference through the sex-scientific category of homosexuality, and were able to transform it into an affirmation of their desires against social denial. The various influences in this identity making included the sex-scientific literature itself, media portrayals of the Wilde trial, a clear homosexual cultural influence on Roswell, as well as a certain reading of the classical Greek tradition.

Mills was given a "Four-F — physically, mentally, emotionally and morally incompetent" rating, and hence was not drafted into the armed forces during the war,[130] perhaps because of his "gender invert" characteristics. Such military labelling may have helped to create early homosexual networks, by cutting some homosexual men out of "normal" social interaction, as it did on a more extended scale during and after World War II.

These experiences of Gidlow and Mills offer valuable insights into the formation of white lesbian and homosexual identities among intellectuals and artists during the World War I era. The white, European-derived character of much of this construction of "homosexuality" (and perhaps "lesbianism") is important to stress. The reading they produced of sexuality in Ancient Greece, the sex-scientific literature they read, and the references to Oscar Wilde all referenced them to "traditions" within white, European "civilization." Carpenter was a limited (and only partial) exception. Men and women with different cultural, intellectual, and social experiences may not have been able to identify their experiences and desires with this image of homosexuality. For them other "traditions," literatures and experiences may have been drawn upon to define their experiences of sexual and gender differences.

Men of the "Oscar Wilde Type"

References to same-gender sex began to appear in Canadian literature during these years. Toronto journalist C.S. Clark's *Of Toronto the Good*, published in 1897, makes a number of references to sex among "boys" (adolescent males it seems) and men.[131] Clark's major purpose in his book was to demonstrate that Toronto was not "the good" but rather was one immense house of ill-fame. He charged that "loose" women could be found everywhere. Clark was also concerned about the lives of unregulated, often homeless poor boys. This was part of a broader social construction of concern over street youth and urban space that was then being generated. Clark argues that the repression of male/female prostitution through bawdy-house raids has led to cases like that of Oscar Wilde in England, and to the blackmailing of these types, many of whom, he says, are of "wealth and high standing."

> If saintly Canadians run away with the idea that there are no sinners of Oscar Wilde's type in Canada, my regard for the truth impels me to undeceive them. Consult some of the bellboys of the large hotels in Canada's leading cities ... and find out what they can tell from their own experiences. A youth of eighteen once informed me that he had blackmailed one of Canada's esteemed judiciary out of a modest sum of money by catching him in the act of indecently assaulting one of the bellboys connected with a hotel in that city. This is one case only, but they are countless. Some of Canada's leading citizens could be implicated just as Oscar Wilde was implicated, if some of these bellboys chose to make public what they knew. I know two different merchants in the city of Toronto who have a similar reputation ... Both these men are so well known in Toronto that there is scarcely a boy who does not know of their reputation. I have no doubt that, notwithstanding the positions they occupy, both would be punished to the full extent of the law, could the police catch them. But this fact serves to demonstrate how little is actually known to the police of what is taking place ... while these very men and their acts of indecency are the talk of boys all over the city. Where under heaven people ever learned such appalling things God only knows and humanity can only conjecture that the people in the places I mention appeal to the degraded tastes of their patrons simply because they are paid for it ... Houses of ill-fame are blots on the morality of a country ... because everyone knows of them, and the fact of their being public is what constitutes the sin ... These other places [sites of same-gender sex] are not usually known to the public, and consequently they thrive, and no effort is made to suppress them, as far as I am aware.[132]

The "Oscar Wilde type," given meaning by coverage of the Wilde trials, was of the wealthier classes and seems to pay for sex with bellboys and working-class street youths. The emergence of this "type" is an important part of the transition to a more defined homosexual category, but it also constructs this "type" with a particular class character. References to the Oscar Wilde type were common around the turn of the century in Canada.[133]

Clark's highly ideological account suggests the existence in Toronto of subterranean networks, involving elite and middle-class men and working-class boys and young men. Although less developed, shared a number of features with emerging homosexual networks in England — the importance of male prostitution, for example, and the existence of sexual relations between middle-class men and working-class youths. While some of these youths took advantage of the social and legal prohibitions to blackmail the men, most never went to the police, which suggests that they participated for either pleasure or money, or both. This suggests that, within the constraints of the class and social relations in which these young men found themselves, they acted to try to get benefits from their erotic relations with this "type" of man. And even though Clark dismisses this possibility, reading against the grain, we can see that many of these working-class young men and boys did get erotic pleasures from these encounters. What Clark does not tell us is whether these boys and young men also had sex among themselves.[134]

These activities were not very visible to the police, says Clark, and therefore could not be suppressed. He may be lamenting the lack of a major public scandal which would direct police activity against these networks; police surveillance of city streets and hotels was not yet very extensive, but it was growing, and Criminal Code classifications were beginning to direct the police against men who had sex with other males.

Working-Class Men and Queer Sex

Maynard's pioneering research, which has been critically examining court, police and reformatory records from 1880-1930 in Ontario — especially Toronto — is very useful here. He reports that his research has turned up clerks, barbers, shoemakers, porters, painters, carpenters, peddlers, machinists, plasterers, and numerous labourers who were charged with offences relating to sex between males.[135] The majority of the men charged were working class, both "skilled" and "unskilled." Among skilled workers there were tailors, butchers, printers, and illustrators, reflecting the significance of the clothing, food, and printing industries in Toronto. Among the unskilled, labourers were the most numerous. There were also clerks, bookkeepers, sales workers, and other office employees.[136] Most of these men were white Anglo-Saxons but there were also Italian, Jewish and eastern European men involved.[137] The middle-class men involved in these activities often travelled from the suburbs into the more working-class areas of the city core for sex.[138] Many working-class men also had sex with other working-class men.[139]

As new and more social spaces opened up with urbanization and industrial capitalism in Toronto, more men began to seize some of these spaces to meet other men for sex, and this in turn provoked a response from moral reformers, social-purity advocates, the law, and the police. These men met for sex not only in commercial establishments, homes, and the rooms they rented or boarded in, but also in parks, laneways, and lavatories. Many of these working-class men, even if they did live apart from their families would have been residing in boarding houses or in other working-class households.[140] This would have restricted these men's access to any sort of "private" or intimate space, leading some of them to search for sexual contacts in more "public" spaces.

Men who had sex with other men seized certain urban spaces for their activities. Parks that were frequented during these years included Memorial Square (at the corner of Portland and Wellington Streets), Allan Gardens and Queen's Park, and parks associated with amusement areas such as Sunnyside Beach and the Exhibition Grounds.[141]

Men took advantage of the city's maze of laneways to seek out other men for sex.[142] Men also used the lavatories of Queen's Park, Allan Gardens, Union Station, Sunnyside Amusement Park, certain hotels, and the YMCA.[143] In some of these lavatories, men used "gloryholes" (holes in the partitions between cubicles) to facilitate their erotic encounters.[144]

According to Maynard, "it was the park that figured most prominently in the sexual struggle over urban space."[145] City authorities attempted to regulate the use of parks by working-class youth, as well as the young women and men who sometimes resorted to parks to have sex.[146] More lighting and policing was proposed as ways of tightening regulation.

New spaces were also being opened up in this period. Toronto, according to Maynard, "embarked upon something of a lavatory building boom" in the early 1900s.[147] The opening of these spaces unintentionally increased the number of places men could meet other men for sex. Maynard points out:

> Aspects of the city-building process, along with the spread of wage labour, established some of the material conditions for the emergence of a subculture, while class and ethnic differences structured sexual relations between men and shaped their journey to sex.[148]

Public-health campaigns were mobilized to regulate outhouses and lavatories. These campaigns raised both health and moral questions.[149] Park attendants were urged to report any holes made in the partitions between cubicles in the lavatories. In response to sexual activity, some of these were covered over.[150]

Many of the men who participated in these activities may have begun to see themselves as homosexual, while others rejected this labelling. Others may have seen themselves more as fairies or queers.[151] This was during a period before "homosexual" had secured its uncontested hegemony as a definition for men who had sex with other men.

Partly in response to the emergence of these networks, and given legal developments in England, there was an intensification of the regulation of same-gender sexual activities between men.

Legal Categories: Gross Indecency, Sexual Surveillance, and the Making of Criminal Perverts

It is in the context of these changing social relations and the initial emergence of same-gender erotic networks in Canada that a homosexual "type" began to emerge, partially shaped by the development of legal discourse, judicial institutions, and police organization and activity. Legal and police administration in Canada followed the English model in the nineteenth century.[152] In the Consolidated Statutes of Canada, drawn up in 1859, "buggery" with man or beast was punishable by death.[153]

The need for a new Criminal Code after Confederation was met "principally through the wholesale borrowing, with minor adaptations, of English statutes."[154] Stephen's draft code, which had not been accepted in England but had been made available for export to the colonies, was used in proposals for Canada's first Criminal Code in 1890.[155] Alex Gigeroff wrote:

> One can trace back the sex offences in the present Criminal Code of Canada to our earliest criminal legislation in 1869 only to find that most sections had been borrowed almost word for word from the earlier English statutes.[156]

The social relations in which English legal history and practice had developed were thereby integrated into the foundations of the Canadian State. Confederation also divided responsibility between Parliament, which enacted criminal law, and the provinces, which administered it. The Canadian statute governing buggery varied very little from the English until the early 1950s.[157] In the 1869 Act respecting offences against the person, buggery was classified as an "Unnatural Offence"; in 1892, it was placed under "Offences Against Morality," where it stayed until the 1950s. In 1886, the legal category of "indecent assault" was restricted to males, thus creating the "first distinct male homosexual offence" in Canada — only one year after the Labouchere Amendment in England had defined "gross indecency" between men.

Gross indecency was introduced into Canadian statute law in 1890 and entered into the first Criminal Code when it was adopted in 1892. It covered all sexual acts between males not already covered by buggery and applied to anyone

> who in public or private is a party of the commission of or procures or attempts to procure the commission by any male person of any act of gross indecency with another male person.[158]

Punishment was set at a maximum of five years with provisions for whipping.

The introduction of gross indecency as an offence occurred in the midst of agitation for social and sexual purity. D.A. Watt, the driving force behind the Society for the Protection of Women and Young Girls, had responsibility for some of the fundamental changes in the first draft of the bill. Watt was strongly influenced by W.J. Stead's social-purity campaign in England.[159] Stead's campaign had culminated in the passage of the Criminal Law Amendment Act of 1885, which raised the age of consent for sexual acts from twelve to fourteen years, and in the Labouchere Amendment, which included the offence of gross indecency. Sir John Thompson, the originator of the Canadian code, supported the inclusion of gross indecency. In 1890, while moving second reading, he said:

> The third section of the Bill contains a penalty for acts of gross indecency committed in reference to a male person. We have upon that subject very

little law, and we have no remedy for offences which are now notorious in
another country, and which have made their appearance in this country. It
will, therefore, be necessary, I think, that a clause of that kind, which is in
the English Act, shall be adopted here. I propose, however, in committee to
enlarge the maximum term of imprisonment from two years. In this class of
offences which, as I said, have obtained notoriety in the mother country,
and which have made their appearance here in one or two places, the maximum of two years imprisonment, I think, is entirely inadequate.[160]

Thompson suggested that a five-year sentence be substituted for the original proposal of
two years. Sir Richard Cartwright asked whether

the words he has used, "gross indecency," are not sufficiently precise, and
might lead to consequences he does not intend? ... I am quite aware that
the particular crime which he has in mind is one which, I very much fear,
has been on the increase in certain sections of society, and can hardly be
punished too severely. In my opinion the words are not legal words, and it
strikes me that consequences might flow from the phraseology which the
honourable gentlemen does not contemplate.

Thompson responded:

I think it is impossible to define the offences any better. The provision is the
same as the English provision ... It is impossible to define them any better,
for the reason that the offences aimed at are so various. The notorious cases
I mentioned a few moments ago are not the same in their characteristics
and the description which would cover them would not apply to these cases
which have been brought to my attention as occurring in Canada within the
last few months. I think it is better to leave it in this form. It is no more
vague than the English Act.

Mr. Blake, who doubted "very much whether there is any other class of cases in which
there is more danger of brutalizing people than in the class of cases dealt with in this
clause," argued that the penalty of whipping be added to the clause. Mr. Charlton, who
we met earlier, and Mr. Mitchell argued that gross indecency be specifically defined so
that, in Mr. Mitchell's words, "there may be no mistake about it."

During final reading in 1892, after discussion of the vagueness of what constituted
an "indecent act," the following exchange took place in the House of Commons:

Mr. Laurier: What makes the objection stronger is that in the next section
you make a gross act of indecency an indictable offence. It is difficult to
know what is a gross act of indecency and what is not.

Sir John Thompson: You get the higher judge for an indictable offence.

Mr. Mills (Bothwell): All these offences against morality have crept into the common law from the earlier ecclesiastical law, and they were rather sins than crimes, not being attacks upon property or life, or upon any other members of the community. The offences are wholly subjective and altogether different in that respect from the other crimes embraced in the Statute book; and it is a question whether crimes of this sort should be punished by long terms of service in the penitentiary. I do not think they should. I think that flogging, or something of that sort, and the discharge of the prisoners is preferable, and a far better deterrent than anything else.

Sir John Thompson: There is a distinction, I think. We only punish them as crimes when they are offensive to people, or set a bad example. As to Section 178, relating to acts of gross indecency, I have no objection to reducing the term of imprisonment, considering that whipping accompanies it. It is impossible to define these cases by any form of words.[161]

While Thompson argued that this new legal category was necessary because certain offences notorious in England were now becoming common in Canada, he did not cite any specific Canadian cases.[162] The English Act, and the scandals surrounding it, were enough to justify adoption of the new offence.

Through this process legal categories relating to sexual offences became more specific, defining specifically homosexual offences and helping to define the "homosexual" as a criminal suspect and subject. The new legal definitions moved beyond "sodomy" and "buggery," which were retained as well, grouping together various kinds of non-reproductive sex and instructing the police to clamp down on emerging homosexual networks. Not only were medical and psychiatric definitions important in the emergence of knowledge about "the homosexual," but so were the police and the courts.[163] The offence of "gross indecency" encouraged the police to direct their attention against sex between men.

Between 1880-1930 in Ontario, Maynard reports that there were 313 reported cases of sexual "offences" between men. Of these, 113 were from the City of Toronto.[164] Both Carolyn Strange and Steven Maynard report that the numbers arrested for "buggery" and "gross indecency" were low until 1900 and began to increase in the 1910s and 1920s.[165]

In order to detect these activities, new means of surveillance were required. Some men having sex with other men were discovered by constables on the beat in working-class and poor neighbourhoods. Others were captured by park caretakers who patrolled the parks. The police also conducted surveillance operations in and around the men's lavatories in Queen's Park and Allan Gardens from 1918 to 1922.[166] The police used a hole in the wall in the back of the lavatory, ladders, light, and photography (to establish the scene of the sexual crime) to survey men and to construct the "facts" or "particulars" of the case against the men who were charged. This defined the reported activities as sexual-offences as they were classified in the criminal law; in this case, as "gross indecency."[167] This evidence could then be used against the men in court.[168]

The policing of sex was under the jurisdiction of the Morality Department. As Maynard reports:

> In 1886, Toronto mayor and moral reformer William Howland appointed David Archibald to the position of staff inspector of the new Morality Department. Variously described by historians as "an ardent moral reformer" and the "city's moral watchdog," Archibald is a key figure in the history of homosexuality in Toronto ... Archibald made it clear from the beginning that police action against men having sex with other men would be one priority of his department. In his first report in 1886 Archibald made reference to "several cases" involving sex between men.[169]

Maynard reports that police concerns with public lavatories began by the 1880s. In 1887 a committee of Toronto City Council recommended that the police inspect the various urinals two to three times a day "to prevent persons from using them for any other purpose than that for which they are intended."[170] The powers of the Morality Department to police same-gender sex between men was greatly expanded with the enactment of "gross indecency," which led to an increase in the charges laid. However, this increase was gradual and uneven until an intensification of policing of same-gender sex between men beginning in 1913 and reaching its peak in 1917 and the two years following the end of the war. The intensification of sexual policing led to the collection and production of statistics that moral reformers and social-purity activists could use in their campaigns against sex between men and also produced the basis for print-media reports of same-gender sex offences between men. These were both new and more extensive forms of social surveillance and new forms of power/knowledge relations.

Maynard reports that this escalation of sexual policing was shaped by the social-purity agitation focusing on "white slavery" and the "social evil" that also seemed to produce an intensification of police surveillance of same-gender sex in "public" places and by the wartime conditions that motivated increased police action between 1917-1922.[171] In the first period, this concern was generated by social-purity groups, the Toronto Social Survey Commission (mentioned earlier in this chapter) and local clergy, the Toronto Vigilance Committee, and Morality Department campaigns against "sexual immorality." These campaigns were largely directed against "public" activities on city streets, in parks, in lavatories, and in commercial establishments and theatres. They were not largely directed to what went on in "private" households. The Vigilance Committee tended to single out sissies, fairies and "moral perverts" as part of its broader purity campaign.[172] This suggests an important linkage between social-purity agitation, the municipal State response, a heightened media focus, and stepped-up police activity.

The second period of escalation was shaped by wartime conditions and mobilization. The large number of soldiers in training in the city led to a focus of concern on female prostitutes. But soldiers were also involved in sex with civilian men and with other men in the military. This included soldiers propositioning men for sex on the street. The large numbers of military men in the city increased some of the possibilities for erotic interaction between men, and sexual policing also focused on these interactions.[173] Heightened policing of sex between men was related to concerns over prostitution and sexual purity.

Some men attempted to resist arrest by running away; others made up explanations for their activities even though many of these attempts failed.[174] Even in these circumstances men tried to resist suggesting the growth of networks that made these forms of non-cooperation possible.

Sexual policing, organized through the categories of the Criminal Code,[175] develops in response to the visibility of networks of men having sex with other men as well as social-purity agitation, concerns by municipal authorities, and through concerns generated regarding wartime mobilization. As Maynard suggests, this social process brings together concerns over social spaces that could be used for queer sex, the activities of men who had sex with men, as well as the response of the legal system and the police. This brings together analysis of ruling sexual discourse and the emerging regime of sexual regulation and the emergence of cultures and networks constructed by men who had sex with other men. Maynard refers to the interaction between these men who had sex with men and policing as a reciprocal process — "the dialectics of discovery." In this dialectic, the men were surveyed by the police, but it was also through this policing that a certain popular consciousness regarding the existence of "homosexuality" was created, which played a part in the emergence of a distinct homosexual consciousness and identification.[176]

There were also concerns generated over "unnatural practices" in prisons. An official from the Central Prison for Ontario wrote in 1885 that:

> Owing to the crowded state of the Prison, scores of cells have two convicts in each. On moral grounds this is most undesirable; the practice of Sodom's sins did not die with the fiery destruction of that city.[177]

And from a number of years later:

> Another common belief of that period ... is that inmates of prisons were particularly prone to homosexual behaviour. On March 23, 1912, the newspaper [Jack Canuck] complained that "unnatural practices" were common among the inmates of the city's gaol, with the facility's greenhouses providing the requisite "shelter and opportunity" and with the result that a great deal of disease was being transmitted among the inmates.

While there is no reason to believe that such practices became more common throughout the period in question, the authorities became more
sensitive to the idea. While the rules of the prison system in Ontario in
1903 had forbidden only "indecent behaviour and language," by 1922
"unnatural" intercourse between prisoners had been specifically added to
the list of impermissible activities.[178]

During these years of transition in sex/gender relations, the same general features
discerned for England and the U.S. can also be uncovered for Canada. The emergence
of capitalist social relations led to increasing urbanization and created the opportunity
for men, and later women, to live at least partly outside family relations or on its margins. A new regime of sexual classification and policing took shape, rooted in legal and
policing changes, medical and scientific discourse, and State formation. Networks of
homosexuals and later, lesbians adopted the category of "homosexual" to identify their
own needs. The specific character of the Canadian experience lies in the derived nature of Canadian legal and professional developments in relation to England and to a
lesser extent the U.S. The major missing dimension in this work of historical recovery
are the voices of those who themselves engaged in same-gender pleasures, especially
those who were not middle-class and not white. With the formation of many of the contemporary institutions of the Canadian State and with the generation of social and family policies, the assumption of heterosexuality would now become institutionalized in
State policy.

Heterosexual Hegemony and the Welfare State

World War I left Canada with an ever-increasing corporate concentration of capital
and with a hierarchy of finance, business, Parliament, the judiciary, the civil service, and
various professional groups and agencies forming ruling institutions and relations that
were constructed in opposition to working-class and other social struggles.[179] The war
brought with it increasing State intervention in the realms of social and economic life
and introduced "scientific management" techniques.

American companies were now doing more and more business in Canada, bringing
with them the social relations found south of the border. Agriculture, however, did not
lose its leading economic role until the 1930s, and because of its dependence on other
powers, Canada did not develop a strong industrial base. The 1920s and 1930s were the
years of monopoly capital's boom and bust. It was only in this environment of corporate
capitalism and the initial creation of the Welfare State that heterosexual hegemony became fully established in Canadian social formation.

Beginning with the federal Department of Health and the Division of Child Welfare
in 1919, the institutions of State social regulation were put firmly in place. Dr. Helen
MacMurchy, first chief of the Division of Child Welfare, who had earlier been Ontario's

Superintendent of the Feebleminded, felt that "the decent wish for a true woman is to be a mother"[180] and used her position to "educate" women in the areas of reproduction and motherhood. Her widely circulated "Little Blue Books" signalled motherhood as the highest form of patriotism, for if "No Baby — No Nation."[181]

In the 1930s and 1940s, the foundations of the Welfare State were laid after protracted social and political struggles for family allowances and unemployment insurance.[182] But the form these benefits took was not always that which the social and union activists had been demanding. For instance, the original struggles for unemployment insurance saw it as a fund that only the employers should pay into. The provision of services in many cases also served to justify extended State and professional surveillance and regulation of working-class and poor people's lives.

Women's social, economic, and sexual dependence and institutionalized heterosexuality were cornerstones of these State social policies, so that the heterosexual family unit became the only legally and socially sanctioned way of life.[183] The State enacted legislation

> constitutive of a family in which dependence of women and children ... became legally enforceable and ... progressively incorporated into the administrative policies of welfare agencies, education, health care, etc. ... The man as breadwinner and the woman as dependent become the legally enforceable and administratively constituted relation.[184]

At the same time, the corporatist perspective of the Mackenzie King government attempted to integrate the unions into the workings of the State with government management of negotiations and collective bargaining.

All this transpired in concert with the emergence of mass heterosexual culture and the 1920s' "companionate marriage." This cultural revolution had a dramatic effect on the lives of ordinary people. Sexual intercourse between women and men was defined as "normal" and "natural," and women who were not erotically turned on by men, whether they were labelled "spinsters" or "lesbians," were considered a "social problem." The mass media, with its advertising, the entertainment and amusement industries, and the opening up of new consumer markets all led to the proliferation and eroticization of heterosexual images. The new heterosexual culture was also produced socially in dance halls, movie theatres, ice cream parlours, and among young women and men in factories and schools. Some young men and women developed relationships including erotic ones that broke away from the previous conventions of different-gender sex that had been regulated by families and reproduction.[185]

Mass consumer culture helped bring about the fragmentation of working-class cultures. Associational life outside the factory was increasingly replaced by privatized family activities and by commercialized leisure activities.[186] The family, ever more separated from community and kinship networks as it became an even smaller consumer unit, was no longer at the centre of production for the household.[187] By the 1920s, it was actually possible for a minority of male workers in the manufacturing sector to live up to the ideal of the family wage and earn enough income to support an economically dependent wife and children.[188] Later there was the construction of national consumer markets and the development of department stores, especially for middle-class women.[189]

The English-Canadian media was influenced, if not dominated, by U.S. economic interests and advertising. This brought to Canada social relations in which American gender and sexual images were being reproduced. The nascent Canadian film industry was eclipsed by the development of the U.S. industry. Homosexuality was generally denied by its exclusion from films. However, Vito Russo describes the "sissy" as a presentation of male homosexuality according to the model of gender inversion — an image of improper masculinity. As such it was a humorous presentation of what a man should not be. At the same time, some queer-influenced images did enter into films and plays during these years. Homosexuality and lesbianism in films was banned from the screen under the U.S. film industry's Motion Picture Production Code in 1934.[190] This was part of what George Chauncey describes as the exclusion of homosexuality from the public sphere in the 1930s in response to the previous visibility of queer networks and was part of constructing the relations of "the closet."[191] This had an important impact in Canada as well.

More than three hundred American mass-circulation magazines entered the Canadian market in the 1920s, led by *Ladies Home Journal, Saturday Evening Post,* and *McCalls.*[192] This was a period of both change and continuity in white middle-class women's magazines.[193] More women were being schooled and entering into the wage-labour force. By the 1920s it was assumed that a woman would work outside the home for a few years before marriage, while a husband's social status continued to be measured by his ability to keep a wife at home. The magazines clearly opted for marriage as opposed to a career, but they also expressed the tensions which women felt in having to choose. On the subject of child-rearing, biology was no longer enough: women had to be trained for motherhood.

> [It was] no longer assumed that natural instinct, trial and error, or practice
> with young siblings taught a woman to be a mother. Now a professional ap-
> proach must be taken: women must be trained for the task.[194]

Not only was the middle-class housewife expected to be "educated," the modern woman was also expected to have some business experience before marriage in order to be socially competent and to properly oversee the "socialization" and schooling of her children. The magazines attempted to maintain patriarchal sex/gender relations while also endorsing contemporary ideas of capitalist rationality and efficiency.

By the late 1920s, neo-Freudian ideas, including the notions of "proper" and "deviant" mother/child relations and heterosexuality as the norm, began to enter into popular discussion.[195] These ideas would later be propagated through the marriage, sex-advice, and child-rearing manuals that would reach their heyday in the post-World War II period.[196]

The household was further reorganized by State-provided compulsory schooling and everything that went with it. This led to the lengthening of the socially organized period of adolescence. Schooling led to a reorganization of working-class women's labour so as to prepare children for school. This set new standards for children's health, cleanliness, and "character."[197] In the middle-class family, the mother provided the communicative skills which would help the child do well in school, and, if it was a boy, to advance into a professional career (doctor, lawyer, manager, executive). The work of the housewife/mother was organized, in part, by the imperatives of the school system.

Adolescent peer-based cultures now emerged often seizing or moving into the new social spaces opened up by consumer-capitalist relations. These were not simply a reflection of dominant trends; indeed, they often faced stiff opposition from parents and other authorities. But although teenagers did rebel against adult restrictions, their cultural forms were generally heterosexual and male-defined. Sexuality was central to teenage social interaction and culture but in a patriarchal and heterosexual context, including sexual coercion and violence against women. Adolescent forms of rebellion and resistance against rigid forms of reproductive marriage relations ironically helped create some of the basis for the new heterosexual "norm."

Despite the construction of heterosexual hegemony and the enforcement of institutionalized heterosexuality, there were those who resisted. They sought out others of the same gender for pleasure and companionship, establishing some of the resources for the subsequent formation of gay and lesbian communities. For instance, in Toronto in the 1920s, homosexually-inclined men picked up soldiers in Queen's Park and in the 1930s cruised the Bay Theatre at Bay and Queen.[198] Many Canadian women who loved or had sex with other women were profoundly affected by Radclyffe Hall's *The Well of Loneliness*, published in 1928. This book and the controversy surrounding it provided a naming for their sexual desires and also provided the media with an image of "the lesbian. " In a review written by journalist S.H. Hooke in *The Canadian Forum* in 1929, the censorship of the *Well of Loneliness* was criticized, and Hooke, despite using the language of "abnormality" in relation to lesbians, took up a relatively tolerant view. He ended the review with the following insight:

> But by the irony of life, society's blind reaction in the censorship to certain facts of life defeats itself. As a result of the ban upon *The Well of Loneliness,* thousands upon thousands of people have read the book and become aware of the facts of inversion who would ordinarily never have seen the book, nor become cognizant of the facts which it deals with.[199]

Women inspired by Hall's novel and men who picked up sailors and cruised theatres would open up some of the spaces for the expansion of queer networks in the 1940s and 1950s. It is to these stories and the conservative social responses to them that I now turn.

Notes

1. Bruce Curtis, "Preconditions of the Canadian State ..." in *Studies in Political Economy*, No. 10, Winter 1983, pp. 103-107; Bruce Curtis, "The speller expelled: Disciplining the common reader in Canada West" in *Canadian Review of Sociology and Anthropology* V. 22, No. 3, 1985, pp. 346-368; his *Building the Educational State: Canada West, 1836-1871*, (London: Althouse Press, 1988); and his "'Illicit' Sexuality and Public Education, 1840-1907" in Susan Prentice, ed., *Sex in Schools, Canadian Education and Sexual Regulation* (Toronto: Our Schools/Our Selves, 1994), pp. 101-130.

2. Alison Prentice, *The School Promoters* (Toronto: McClelland and Stewart, 1977), p. 40.

3. See Mariana Valverde, *The Age of Light, Soap and Water: Moral Reform in English Canada, 1885-1925* (Toronto: McClelland and Stewart, 1991); Bruce Curtis's work already cited; and the new Foucault-derived literature on governance including Graham Burchell, *et al.*, *The Foucault Effect, Studies in Governmentality* (Chicago: The University of Chicago Press, 1991) and Mike Gane and Terry Johnson, *Foucault's New Domains* (London and New York: Routledge, 1993).

4. Bryan D. Palmer, *Working Class Experience* (Toronto and Vancouver: Butterworth, 1983), pp. 9-10.

5. Angus McLaren, "Birth Control and Abortion in Canada, 1870-1920" in *Canadian Historical Review*, Sept. 1978, p. 320; also see Angus McLaren and Arlene Tigar McLaren, *The Bedroom and the State: Changing Practices and Politics of Contraception and Abortion in Canada, 1880-1980* (Toronto: McClelland and Stewart, 1986); and Angus McLaren, *Our Own Master Race: Eugenics in Canada, 1885-1945* (Toronto: McClelland and Stewart, 1990).

6. Heather MacDougall, "Public Health in Toronto's Municipal Politics: The Cardiff Years, 1833-1890" in *Bulletin of the History of Medicine*, V. 55, 1981, pp. 186-202.

7. Dorothy E. Smith, "Women's Inequality and the Family" in Allan Moscovitch and Glen Drover, eds., *Inequality: Essays on the Political Economy of Social Welfare* (Toronto, Buffalo, London: University of Toronto Press, 1981), p. 163.

8. Palmer, *Working Class Experience, op. cit.*, p. 61.

9. See Joey Noble, "Classifying the Poor: Toronto's Charities, 1850-1880" in *Studies in Political Economy*, No. 2, Fall 1979, pp. 109-128; and Susan E. Houston, "The 'Waifs and Strays' of a Late Victorian City: Juvenile Delinquents in Toronto" in Joy Parr, ed., *Childhood and Family in Canadian History* (Toronto: McClelland and Stewart, 1982), pp. 129-142; and Mariana Valverde, *The Age of Light, Soap and Water, op. cit.*

10. Beth Light and Joy Parr, eds., *Canadian Women on the Move* (Toronto: New Hogtown Press and OISE, 1983), p. 2.

11. Palmer, *Working Class Experience, op. cit.*, p. 55.

12. *Ibid.*, p. 14.

13. On the social construction of poverty, see Mitchell Dean, *The Constitution of Poverty: Toward a Genealogy of Liberal Governance* (London and New York: Routledge, 1991). Also see his "'A Social Structure of Many Souls': Moral Regulation, Government, and Self-Rule" in *Canadian Journal of Sociology*, V. 19, No. 2, 1994, pp. 145-168.

14. Noble, "Classifying The Poor," *op. cit.*, p. 113. This paragraph is based on information in Noble's article. For later years, see Margaret Hillyard Little, "'Manhunts and Bingo Blabs': The Moral Regulation of Single Mothers" in *Canadian Journal of Sociology*, V. 19, No. 2, 1994, pp. 233-247.

15. Wayne Roberts, "Rocking the Cradle for the World: The New Woman and Maternal Feminism, Toronto, 1877-1914" in Linda Kealey, ed., *A Not Unreasonable Claim: Women and Reform in Canada, 1880s-1920s* (Toronto: Women's Educational Press, 1979), p. 30.

16. T.R. Morrison, "Their Proper Sphere: Feminism, the Family and Child-Centred Social Reform in Ontario, 1875-1900," Part II, *Ontario History*, June 1976, p. 73.

17. See Houston, *op. cit.*, p. 136; and Livy Visano, "Tramps, Tricks and Troubles: Street Transients

and Their Controls" in Tom Fleming and Livy Visano, eds., *Deviant Designations* (Toronto: Butterworth, 1983), p. 21. Also see the previously cited work of Bruce Curtis.

18. See Carolyn Strange, *Toronto's Girl Problem, The Perils and Pleasures of the City, 1880-1930* (Toronto: University of Toronto Press, 1995), pp. 27-37.

19. Constance Backhouse and Leah Cohen, *The Secret Oppression: Sexual Harassment of Working Women* (Toronto: Macmillan, 1978), p. 57. Also see G. Kealey, ed., *Canada Investigates Industrialism* (Toronto: University of Toronto Press, 1973).

20. Susan Trofimenkoff, "One Hundred and Two Muffled Voices: Canada's Industrial Women in the 1880s" in Cross and Kealey, eds., *Canada's Age of Industry, 1849-1896* (Toronto: McClelland and Stewart, 1982), p. 220.

21. Alice Klein and Wayne Roberts, "Besieged Innocence: The 'Problem' and Problems of Working Women — Toronto, 1896-1914" in Acton, *et al.*, eds., *Women at Work* (Toronto: Canadian Women's Educational Press, 1974), p. 216.

22. *Ibid.*, p. 218. Also see Jane Ursel, *Private Lives, Public Policy: 100 Years of State Intervention in the Family* (Toronto: Women's Press, 1992), especially pp. 83-99.

23. Klein and Roberts, *ibid.*, p. 222.

24. Smith, "Women's Inequality ..." *op. cit.*, p. 182.

25. Palmer, *Working Class Experience, op. cit.*, pp. 31-33 and 80.

26. Roberts, "Rocking the Cradle," *op. cit.*, p. 16. This reference to Sodom and Gomorrah seems to refer to a notion of masturbation leading to a life of prostitution and immorality and not to the legal offence of sodomy or same-gender sex between women. In the United States, Pivar reports, some people "imagined the bicycle as a social vehicle for transporting girls into prostitution. Alarmists even feared bicycle seats might cause women's moral downfall." David J. Pivar, *Purity Crusade: Sexual Morality and Social Control, 1868-1900* (Westport, Conn., and London: Greenwood Press, 1973), p. 176.

27. On the shifting historical and social character of constructs of race and ethnicity, see Roxana Ng, "Sexism, Racism and Canadian Nationalism" in Himani Bannerji, ed., *Returning the Gaze: Essays on Racism, Feminism and Politics* (Toronto: Sister Vision Press, 1993), pp. 184-185.

28. Angus MacLaren, "Birth Control and Abortion in Canada," *op. cit.*, pp. 321-322; and Linda Kealey, "Introduction" in *A Not Unreasonable Claim, op. cit.*, pp. 1, 4.

29. Between 1891 and 1901, the number of Canadians born of British stock declined while the number of Europeans and Asians born in Canada almost doubled. Non-British immigrants were considered by State officials and moral reformers as being mentally and physically inferior to Anglo-Canadians and of a lower sexual morality. They were associated with "feeble-mindedness" and "mental deficiency." See Carol Lee Bacchi, *Liberation Deferred? The Ideas of the English-Canadian Suffragists, 1877-1918* (Toronto: University of Toronto Press, 1983), pp. 89, 97, 109; Suzann Buckley, "Ladies or Midwives? Efforts to Reduce Infant and Maternal Mortality" in Kealey, ed., *A Not Unreasonable Claim, op. cit.*, pp. 131-134; Light and Parr, eds., *Canadian Women on the Move, op. cit.*, p. 5; Suzann Buckley and Janice Dicken McGinnis, "Venereal Disease and Public Health Reform in Canada" in *Canadian Historical Review*, V. 63, 3, 1982, p. 346; and Chapman, "Sexual Deviation in Western Canada, 1890-1920," unpublished conference paper given at the Northern Great Plains Conference, Winnipeg, 1979, p. 9.

30. Terry Chapman, "The Anti-Drug Crusade in Western Canada, 1885-1925" in Bercuson and Knalfa, *Law and Society in Canada, Studies in History*, University of Calgary, No. 2, 1979, pp. 89-90.

31. Light and Parr, *op. cit.*, p. 2.

32. Chapman, "The Anti-Drug Crusade," *op. cit.*, pp. 90-94; and Marie Campbell, "Sexism in British Columbia Trade Unions, 1900-1920" in Latham and Kess, eds., *In Her Own Right* (Victoria: Camosun, 1980), p. 174. It is interesting that there was no focus on same-gender sex among Chinese men who were denied access to Chinese women. This comment comes from a conversation with Richard Fung.

33. Terry Chapman, "Early Eugenics Movement in Western Canada" in *Alberta History*, V. 25,

1977, p. 12; and Indiana Matters, "Unfit For Publication: Notes Towards a Lavender History of British Columbia," paper presented at the Sex and the State Lesbian/Gay History conference, Toronto, July 1985, for some suggestions on the racial character of sex-offence legislation. Also see Karen Dubinsky, *Improper Advances, op, cit.*, on how race/ethnicity entered into sex offence legal proceedings.

34. See the work of Bruce Curtis, *op. cit.*, and Mariana Valverde, *op. cit.*

35. See Nancy M. Sheehan, "Women Helping Women: The WCTU and the Foreign Population in the West, 1905-1930" in *International Journal of Women's Studies*, V. 6, No. 5, Nov./Dec. 1983, pp. 395-411; Wendy Mitchinson, "The WCTU: For God, Home and the Native Land" in Kealey, ed., *A Not Unreasonable Claim, op. cit.*, p. 163. Also see Barbara Roberts, "Ladies, Women and the State: Managing Female Immigration, 1880-1920" in Roxana Ng, Gillian Walker, and Jacob Muller, eds., *Community Organization and the Canadian State* (Toronto: Garamond, 1990), pp. 108-130.

36. Chapman, "Early Eugenics Movement in Western Canada," *op. cit.*, pp. 9-10. Also see Angus McLaren, *Our Own Master Race, Eugenics in Canada, 1885-1945* (Toronto: McClelland and Stewart, 1990), especially pp. 99, 159, and 169.

37. Chapman *op. cit.*, p. 9. Also see McLaren, *op. cit.*

38. Angus McLaren, "Birth Control and Abortion in Canada," *op. cit.*, p. 319.

39. Constance C. Backhouse, "Shifting Patterns in Nineteenth- Century Canadian Custody Law" in David H. Flaherty, ed., *Essays in the History of Canadian Law*, V. 1 (Toronto: Published for the Osgoode Society by the University of Toronto Press, 1981), p. 228; also see other Backhouse articles on Canadian legal history: "Nineteenth Century Canadian Rape Law" in Flaherty, ed., *Essays in the History of Canadian Law*, V. 2, 1983, pp. 200-247; and her "Nineteenth-Century Canadian Prostitution Law: Reflection of a Discriminatory Society," unpublished paper, Oct. 1982. Also see her *Petticoats and Prejudice: Women and Law in Nineteenth Century Canada* (Toronto: Women's Press, 1991).

40. See Suzann Buckley, "Ladies or Midwives?" *op. cit.*, p. 131; Light and Parr, *op. cit.*, pp. 5-6, 154, 112; and Bacchi, *Liberation Deferred? op. cit.*, pp. 89-94.

41. Light and Parr, *op. cit.*, p. 112.

42. *Ibid.*, p. 5. Also see Joy Parr, *The Gender of Breadwinners: Women, Men and Change in Two Industrial Towns, 1880-1950* (Toronto: University of TorontoPress, 1990).

43. This section is based on James G. Snell, "The White Life for Two: The Defence of Marriage and Sexual Morality in Canada, 1890-1914" in *Histoire sociale-Social History*, V. 16, No. 31, May 1983, pp. 111-129. Reprinted in Bettina Bradbury, ed., *Canadian Family History: Selected Readings*, (Toronto, 1992). Also see Snell, *In the Shadow of the Law: Divorce in Canada, 1900-1939*, (Toronto 1991), and with Cynthia Comacchio Abeele, "Regulating Nuptiality: Restricting Access to Marriage in Early Twentieth-Century English-Speaking Canada" in *Historical Perspectives on Law and Society in Canada*, Toronto 1994. Thanks to Chris Burr for these references.

44. "The White Life for Two," *op. cit.*, p. 113.

45. E.A. Lancaster quoted in Snell, "The White Life for Two," *op. cit.*, p. 115.

46. Chapman, "Sex Crimes in Western Canada, 1880-1920," *op. cit.*, p. 41.

47. Snell, "The White Life For Two," *op. cit.*, p. 112.

48. On this see Mariana Valverde, *The Age of Light, Soap and Water, op. cit.*, especially pp. 77-128.

49. See Deborah Brock, "'Unwholesome Truths': Reforming Turn of the Century Urban Ontario," unpublished paper, April 1986, p. 12-13. Also see Mariana Valverde, *The Age of Light, Soap and Water, Moral Reform in English Canada, 1885-1925, op. cit.*, especially pp. 77-103.

50. See Brock, *op. cit.*, p. 12-13, and Snell, "The White Life for Two," *op. cit.*, pp. 117-118, 122. Also see D.A. Watt, "The Canadian Law for the Protection of Women and Girls, with Suggestions for its Amendment and for a General Code" in Aaron M. Powell, *The National Purity Congress* (New York: Arno Reprint, 1976), pp. 437-451.

51. Historical investigation reveals that "protective" legislation usually constructs certain legal or

social incapacities in the "protected" group, and all too often comes to be used against the very groups it was designed to protect, whether it be women or young people.

52. Dubinsky, *Improper Advances, Rape and Heterosexual Conflict in Ontario, 1880-1929* (Chicago and London: The University of Chicago Press, 1993) p. 66.

53. *Ibid.*, pp. 68.

54. *Ibid.*, especially pp. 66-71.

55. Snell, "The White Life for Two," *op. cit.*, p. 119.

56. On the family-wage system, see Michelle Barrett and Mary McIntosh, "The 'Family Wage': Some Problems for Socialists and Feminists" in *Capital and Class*, V. 2, Summer 1980, pp. 51-72. As a result of this defence of marriage, the possibilities for conviction on sex-related offences increased as arrest rates increased. See Snell, "The White Life for Two" *op. cit.*, p. 127. Only in 1926 would the first major divorce legislation be passed in Canada, and only in 1968 would a general liberalizing divorce law be passed. Snell, "The White Life for Two," *op. cit.*, p. 115.

57. See Valverde, *The Age of Light, Soap, and Water, op. cit.*

58. See Judith Walkowitz, *Prostitution and Victorian Society* (Cambridge: Cambridge University Press, 1980); and Mariana Valverde, "Sex versus Purity: Conflicts in the First Wave of Feminism" in *Rites*, V. 3, No. 2, June 1986, pp. 10-11.

59. Weeks, *Coming Out* (London, Melbourne, New York: Quartet Books, 1977), pp. 16-17.

60. Linda Kealey, "Introduction" in Kealey, ed., *A Not Unreasonable Claim, op. cit.*, p. 9.

61. Bacchi, *Liberation Deferred? op. cit.*, p. ix.

62. See Bacchi, "Race Regeneration and Social Purity: A Study of the Social Attitudes of Canada's English-Speaking Suffragists" in *Histoire sociale-Social History*, V. 11, No. 22, Nov. 1978, p. 467; Deborah Gorham, "Flora MacDonald Denison: Canadian Feminist" in Kealey, ed., *A Not Unreasonable Claim, op. cit.*, pp. 47-70; and Roberta J. Pazdro, "Agnes Deans Cameron" in Latham and Kess, eds., *In Her Own Right, op. cit.*, pp. 101-123.

63. Bacchi, *Liberation Deferred?, op. cit.*, p. ix.

64. Bacchi, "Race Regeneration ..." *op. cit.*, p. 474.

65. For African-Canadian women's experiences, see Peggy Bristow, *et al.*, *We're Rooted Here and They Can't Pull Us Up: Essays in African Canadian Women's History* (Toronto: University of Toronto Press, 1994); Dionne Brand, "A Working Paper on Black Women in Toronto: Gender, Race and Class" in Himani Bannerji, ed., *Returning the Gaze* (Toronto: Sister Vision Press, 1993), pp. 220-242 and Dionne Brand, *No Burden to Carry: Narratives of Black Women in Ontario, 1920s to 1950s* (Toronto: Women's Press, 1991).

66. G. Roe, *The Great War on White Slavery* (Clifford G. Roe and B.G. Steadwell, 1911), p. 446.

67. Bacchi, *Liberation Deferred? op. cit.*, p. 112; and Roe, *op. cit.*, p. 445.

68. Geoffrey Egan, "These Things May Lead to the Tragedy of Our Species: Notes towards a History of Homosexuality in Canada, 1890-1930," unpublished paper, April 1980, p. 7, quoting from an article in *Jack Canuck*, Nov. 25, 1911.

69. Quoted in Steven Maynard, "Through a Hole in the Lavatory Wall: Homosexual Subcultures, Police Surveillance, and the Dialectics of Discovery" in *Journal of the History of Sexuality*, V. 5, No. 2, 1994 p. 234.

70. See Walkowitz, *op. cit.*, for England. For Canada, see Judy Bedford, "Prostitution in Calgary, 1905-1914" in *Alberta History*, V. 29, No. 2, Spring 1981, pp. 1-9; Deborah Nilson, "The Social Evil: Prostitution in Vancouver, 1900-1920" in Latham and Kess, eds., *In Her Own Right, op. cit.*, pp. 205-228; and Lori Rotenberg, "The Wayward Worker: Toronto's Prostitutes at the Turn of the Century" in Acton, *et al.*, eds., *Women at Work, 1850-1930* (Toronto: Canadian Women's Educational Press, 1974), pp. 33-69.

71. Nilson, "The 'Social Evil' ..." *op. cit.*, p. 207.

72. See Carolyn Strange, *Toronto's Girl Problem, op. cit.*, especially pp. 116-143.

73. Social Survey Commission Report (Toronto: Carswell Company, 1915). References in the next two paragraphs are to this text, unless otherwise mentioned. On the Social Survey Commis-

sion, also see Carolyn Strange, "From Modern Babylon to a City upon a Hill: The Toronto Survey Commission of 1915 and the Search for Sexual Order in the City" in Roger Hall *et al.*, eds., *Patterns of the Past: Interpreting Ontario's History* (Toronto, 1988), 225-278 and also *Toronto's Girl Problem, op cit.*, especially pp. 102-115.

74. See Valverde, *The Age of Light, Soap, and Water, op. cit.*, p. 83.
75. Social Survey Commission Report, *op. cit.*, p. 136.
76. The Vice Commission of Chicago, *The Social Evil in Chicago: A Study of Existing Conditions*, Chicago 1911, p. 296. The following references are from pp. 73, 297, 73.
77. On this, also see Valverde and Strange, *op. cit.*
78. Again see Mariana Valverde, *op. cit.*
79. J.S. Shearer, "Introduction" to Roe, *op. cit.*, p. 23.
80. W.J. Hunter, *Manhood Wrecked and Rescued* (Toronto: William Briggs, 1894), p. 71; and Bacchi, "Race Regeneration and Social Purity," *op. cit.*, pp. 469 and 471.
81. The Methodist Church is not necessarily the most "objective" of sources. See Bliss, "Pure Books on Avoided Subjects" in *Historical Papers 1970* (Ottawa: Canadian Historical Association, 1970), pp. 89-108; Dick in his paper "Heterohegemonic Discourse and Homosexual Acts: The Case of Saskatchewan in the Settlement Era," presented at the "Sex and the State" history conference, also lists a number of other Canadian sex-advice titles, including J.E. Hett, *The Sexual Organs: Their Use and Abuse — The Subject Upon Which Men and Women Know the Least* (Berlin: Ontario, 1899); B.G. Jeffries, *Search Lights on Health: Light on Dark Corners — A Complete Sexual Science and a Guide to Purity and Physical Manhood, Advice to Maiden, Wife, Mother Love, Courtship and Marriage* (Toronto: J.L. Nichols, 1899); and Reta Gray, *Queer Questions Quaintly Answered, or Creative Mysteries Made Plain to Children* (Toronto: J.L. Nichols, 1899).
82. Bliss mentions the reports of Drs. Joseph Workman and Daniel Clarke, *op. cit.*; on Bucke, see Wendy Mitchinson, "Gynecological Operations on Insane Women, London, Ontario, 1895-1901," Dept. of History, University of Windsor, unpublished paper, 1980, pp. 6, 13. Also see her *The Nature of Their Bodies: Women and Their Doctors in Victorian Canada* (Toronto: University of Toronto Press, 1991).
83. Dr. Wood Allen, *What a Young Woman Ought to Know* (Philadelphia: VIR Publishing, 1894), pp. 173-174.
84. Josephine E. Young in Roe, ed., *The Great War on White Slavery, op. cit.*, p. 433.
85. Valverde, op. cit., p. 46
86. Strange, *Toronto's Girl Problems, op. cit.*, p. 126.
87. Valverde, *op. cit.*, pp. 72-74.
88. Bacchi, *Liberation Deferred? op. cit.*, pp. 113,171; Chapman, "Sexual Deviation in Western Canada, 1890-1920," *op. cit.*, p. 11; and Gigeroff, *Sexual Deviations in the Criminal Law* (Toronto: Published for the Clarke Institute by University of Toronto Press, 1968), p. 39. Also Beatrice Brigden, in Light and Parr, *op. cit.*, p. 210.
89. Valverde, *op. cit.*, pp. 69-70.
90. Dept. of Evangelism and Social Service, Dept. of Temperance and Moral Reform, Sixth Annual Report, p. 131.
91. Clark, *Our Sons* (Ontario: W.L. Clark, 1914), pp. 153, 155.
92. Bliss, *op. cit.*; and Bacchi, *Liberation Deferred? op. cit.*, p. 171.
93. Bliss, *op. cit.*
94. Deborah Brock, "Unwholesome Truths," *op. cit.*, p. 36. Also see Arthur W. Beall, *The Living Temple: A Manual on Eugenics for Parents and Teachers* (Whitby, Ont.: The A.B. Penhale Publishing Company, 1933) and Valverde, *op. cit.*, 70-71.
95. VD was linked with feeblemindedness and fear of non-Anglo immigrants, and with concerns over military efficiency given its rate of incidence among troops and recruits. It was feared that VD threatened national defence by "incapacitating Canadian manpower." Buckley and McGinnis, "Venereal Disease and Public Health Reform in Canada," *op. cit.*, p. 338. Also see

Jay Cassel, *The Secret Plague: Venereal Disease in Canada, 1838-1939* (Toronto: University of Toronto Press, 1987), especially pp. 122-144.

96. Bland, "Guardians of the Race ..." in Elizabeth Whiteleg *et al.*, eds., *The Changing Experience of Women* (Oxford: Martin Robertson, 1982), p. 381.

97. Buckley and McGinnis, *op. cit.*, p. 343.

98. *Ibid.* This points to the ambiguous and contradictory character of "public health" legislation. While it has brought about real gains, it has also extended state and medical surveillance of sexual life and has been used to brand certain sexual activities as deviant or "sick." On this, see my review article, "Which Public, Whose Health?" in *Rites*, V. 3, No. 1, May 1986, pp. 16-17; "Their Silence, Our Deaths: What Can the Social Sciences Offer to AIDS Research?" in Diane E. Goldstein, ed., *Talking AIDS: Interdisciplinary Perspectives on Acquired Immune Deficiency Syndrome* (St. John's: Institute for Social and Economic Research, 1991); and "Managing AIDS Organizing" in William K. Carroll, ed., *Organizing Dissent* (Toronto: Garamond, 1992), pp. 215-231. Also Lucy Bland and Frank Mort, "Look Out for the 'Good Time' Girl: Dangerous Sexualities as a Threat to National Health" in *Formations of Nation and People* (London: Routledge and Kegan Paul, 1984), pp. 131-151 and Frank Mort, *Dangerous Sexualities* (London: Routledge, 1987). On the U.S. experience, see Alan M. Brandt, *No Magic Bullet: A Social History of Venereal Disease in the United States Since 1880* (New York, Oxford: Oxford University Press, 1985).

99. Quoted in Jay Cassell, *The Secret Plague: Venereal Disease in Canada, 1838-1939* (Toronto: University of Toronto Press, 1987), p. 141.

100. *Ibid.*, p. 216.

101. Edward Stevenson (real name Xavier Mayne), *The Intersexes* (Rome: privately printed, preface dated 1908; reprinted New York: Arno Press, 1975), p. 638.

102. Ezra Hurlburt Stafford, "Perversion" in Canadian Journal of Medicine and Surgery, Toronto, V. 3, No. 4, April 1898, pp. 179-185. The following references and quotes are all drawn from this article.

103. Ebing himself moved from his 1887 position — that homosexuality is a disease with a biological basis — to his 1901 position, that some varieties of homosexuality are congenital anomalies. The emerging Canadian medical and psychological discourse regarding sex must be studied in much more detail: it affected State policy, newspaper reports, popular culture, and homosexual consciousness.

104. See Ross Higgins, "L'Association Nocturne: A Montreal Cruising Story from 1886" in *Canadian Lesbian and Gay History Network Newsletter*, No. 3, December 1987, pp. 5-7. The article was from *La Presse*, June 30, 1886, p. 4. The article was rediscovered by Cyrille Felteau, a journalist at *La Presse*. It was reprinted in that newspaper, April 19, 1982, and later in Felteau's *Histoire de la Presse*, (Éditions La Presse, Montréal) 1983, Vol. 1, p. 170.

105. Steven Maynard, "In Search of 'Sodom North': The Writing of Lesbian and Gay History in English Canada, 1970-1990," pp. 127-128.

106. See Chauncey, *Gay New York, op. cit.*

107. Maynard, "Through a Hole in the Lavatory Wall," *op. cit.*, p. 234.

108. Light and Prentice, *Pioneer and Gentlewomen of British North America, op. cit.*, pp. 1-204, 214-215.

109. See Katz, *Gay American History* (New York: Thomas Y. Crowall, 1976) and *Gay/Lesbian Almanac* (New York: Harper and Row, 1983).

110. Light and Parr, *Canadian Women on the Move, op. cit.*, p. 24. For use of the term "hermaphrodite" in a later period, see the section on Elsa Gidlow's experiences later in this chapter. At least one cross-dressing woman fought in the American Civil War. Katz, *Gay/Lesbian Almanac, op. cit.*, p. 191-194. Also see Steven Maynard's critical review of Don Akenson, *At Face Value: The Life and Times of Eliza McCormack/John White* (Kingston and Montréal: McGill-Queen's University Press, 1990) in *Rites* V. 8, No. 4, Sept./Oct., 1991, p. 13.

111. See "The Higher Education of Women" Medical and Surgical Reporter, in the *Canadian Lan-*

cet, May 1893, p. 285. The relationship between this initial distinction and the later emergence of the "lesbian" remains to be explored more fully.

112. Other early experiences of female friendships that may have influenced the emergence of lesbian networks are explored by Frances Rooney in "Edith G. Watson, Photographer, and Victoria Hayward, Writer" in *Fireweed*, Lesbiantics issue, No. 13; and in Frances Rooney, "Loring and Wyle, Sculptors" in *Pink Ink*, V. 1, No. 1, July 1983, pp. 18-20.

113. The scandals involving Wilde were to have an important effect on Canadian debates. Dick, for instance, refers to an 1895 editorial in the *Regina Leader*. Referring to Wilde's activities as "effeminating, debilitating and immoral," it describes his "vile companionships," "scandalous associations," "spiritual corrosion," and "moral leprosy" and calls for Wilde to be jailed for life. See Dick, *op. cit.*, p. 8, quoting from "Oscar Wilde in Jail" in *The Leader* (Regina), Apr. 11, 1895, p. 4.

114. On Wilde, see Kevin O'Brien, *Oscar Wilde in Canada: An Apostle for the Arts* (Toronto: Personal Library, 1982).

115. On Whitman, see Michael Lynch, "The Lovers of His Friends and Hot Little Prophets: Walt Whitman in Ontario" in *The Body Politic*, No. 67, Oct. 1980, pp. 29-31 and "Walt Whitman in Ontario" in Robert K. Martin, ed., *The Continuing Presence of Walt Whitman: The Life After the Life* (Iowa City: University of Iowa Press, 1992), pp. 141-151; and Robert K. Martin, *The Homosexual Tradition in American Poetry* (Austin, University of Texas Press, 1979). For Carpenter, see Canadian Gay Archives Publication No. 5, "Lesbian and Gay Heritage of Toronto" in Toronto, 1982.

116. Deborah Gorham, "Flora MacDonald Denison: Canadian Feminist" *op. cit.*, p. 55, 62, 67.

117. See Dubinsky, *Improper Advances*, *op. cit.*, p. 140.

118. Gorham, *op. cit.*, p. 66.

119. Gorham, *op. cit.*; Lynch, *op. cit.*; and Egan, *op. cit.*, p. 16.

120. Egan, *op. cit.*, p. 16.

121. "A Comrade Passes" in *The Canadian Theosophist*, V. 11, No. 4, Toronto, June 15, 1921.

122. Weeks, *Coming Out*, *op. cit.*, p. 52, and *Sex, Politics and Society* (London and New York: Longman, 1981), p. 111.

123. Rev. James Carmichael, in *Balford's Monthly Magazine*, Toronto, 1877. Reference from the *Gay Archivist*, published by the Canadian Gay Archives, No. 4, Sept. 1981.

124. Elsa Gidlow, "Casting a Net: Excerpts from an Autobiography," in *The Body Politic*, No. 83, May 1982, pp. 27-30, and "Elsa Gidlow: Memoirs," introduced by Rayna Rapp, *Feminist Studies*, V. 6, No. 1, Spring 1980, pp. 103-127. Also see Elsa Gidlow, *Elsa: I Come with My Songs, The Autobiography of Elsa Gidlow* (San Francisco: Bootlegger Press, 1986). Elsa Gidlow died on June 8, 1986.

125. "Elsa Gidlow: Memoirs," *op. cit.*, p. 115.

126. "Elsa" in Adair and Adair, *Word is Out: Stories of Some of Our Lives* (New York: New Glide/Delta, 1978), p. 17.

127. Gidlow, "Casting a Net," *op. cit.*, p. 30. This included Ellis's *Psychology of Sex* and Carpenter's *The Intermediate Sex* and *Towards Democracy*.

128. *Ibid.*

129. *Ibid.*

130. Gidlow, "Casting A Net," *op. cit.*, p. 30. A 4-F classification was also used to stigmatize homosexual draftees in World War II in the U.S. See Allan Berube, "Coming Out Under Fire" in *Mother Jones*, Feb./Mar. 1983, p. 24 and Berube, *Coming Out Under Fire* (New York: The Free Press, 1990).

131. C.S. Clark, *Of Toronto the Good: A Social Study, the Queen City of Canada as It Is* (Montreal: The Toronto Publishing Company, 1898). Toronto as a social study was brought before the world by the remarks of Canadian delegates to the Social Purity Conference in Baltimore and the World's Convention of the Women's Christian Temperance Union held in Toronto in 1897. The following is based on my reading of this book, particularly pp. 89-90.

132. *Ibid.*, pp. 89-90.

133. For instance, a Swift Current, Saskatchewan, doctor refers to another doctor as "an Oscar Wilde type" in a 1913 letter to the province's Attorney-General. This reference comes from Terry Chapman's research reported in the *Lesbian/Gay History Researchers Network Newsletter*, No. 5, Dec. 1981, p. 14. Also see Terry Chapman, "'An Oscar Wilde Type': 'The Abominable Crime of Buggery' in Western Canada, 1890-1920" in *Criminal Justice History*, No. 4, 1983, pp. 97-118. Another term then used was "third sex." In 1913 an article entitled "Toronto Skating Club Carnival" refers to a "third-sex" costume at a costume party. From *Toronto Saturday Night*, Mar. 8, 1913, p. 38, quoted in Egan, *op. cit.*, p. 10.

134. On this, see Steven Maynard's work examining court and police records, as well as training-school and reformatory records for his Ph.D. thesis, especially his chapter called "Boys and Their Men: The Homosexual World of Working-Class Youth in Urban Ontario," given in a preliminary fashion at the "Out of the Archives" conference, York University, 1994.

135. Steven Maynard, "In Search of 'Sodom North,'" *op. cit.*, p. 127.

136. Maynard, "Through a Hole in the Lavatory Wall," *op. cit.*, p. 216.

137. *Ibid.*, p. 219.

138. *Ibid.*, pp. 217-219.

139. *Ibid.*, p. 220.

140. *Ibid.*, p. 217.

141. *Ibid.*, pp. 211-212.

142. *Ibid.*, p. 212.

143. *Ibid.*, p. 213.

144. *Ibid.*, p. 213.

145. *Ibid.*, p. 235.

146. On this, also see Carolyn Strange, *Toronto's Girl Problem*, *op. cit.*.

147. Maynard, "Through a Hole in the Lavatory Wall," *op. cit.*, p. 214.

148. *Ibid.*, p. 240.

149. *Ibid.*, p. 215.

150. *Ibid.*, p. 237.

151. See Chauncey, *Gay New York*, *op. cit.*

152. Philip C. Stenning, *Legal Status of Police*, Criminal Law Series Study Paper (Law Reform Commission of Canada, July 1981), p. 7.

153. Referred to in James Edward Jones, *Pioneer Crimes and Punishment in Toronto and the Home District* (Toronto, 1924), p. 7.

154. Gigeroff, *op. cit.*, p. viii.

155. *Ibid.*, p. 36; also see remarks quoted in Gigeroff by Thompson on the importance of this new Criminal Code, pp. 69-70.

156. *Ibid.*, p. 3.

157. *Ibid.*, p. 39. The following section is based on Gigeroff's account, particularly pp. 39-46, unless otherwise cited. Also see Graham Parker, "The Origins of the Canadian Criminal Code" in Flaherty, ed., *Essays in the History of Canadian Law*, V. 1, pp. 249-277; and R.C. Macleod, "The Shaping of Canadian Criminal Law, 1892-1982," Canadian Historical Association Paper, 1978.

158. Chapman, "Sexual Deviation in Western Canada," *op. cit.*, p. 13.

159. On Stead's campaign, also see Judith R. Walkowitz, *City of Dreadful Delight* (Chicago: The University of Chicago Press, 1992), pp. 81-134.

160. Debates, House of Commons, Canada, April 10, 1890, V. 2, pp. 3161-3162. Other references in this session quoted below are from pp. 3170-3171

161. These exchanges reveal the imprecise character of the official language of the day and the heterogeneous offences apparently included under the heading of "gross indecency." Debates, House of Commons, Canada, May 25, 1892, pp. 2968-2969.

162. See Gigeroff, *op. cit.*, p. 46-47; the following case may have influenced this law reform process. This story was reported in the *San Francisco Call*, Jan. 29, 1890, under the headline "Canadian Scandal."

Government has been acquainted with the facts of a most revolting story in which a young clergyman in the Province of Ontario figures conspicuously. Sir John Thompson admitted that the charges have been made, and says that it will, in his opinion, ensure the passage of the purity bill, which provides for the flogging of persons found guilty of such crimes.

It is unclear whether the "offence" is same or different gender in character. From Toronto Lesbian and Gay History Project, "Proposed History Projects," No. 10, 1981.

163. Maynard, "Through a Hole in the Lavatory Wall," *op. cit.*, p. 210.

164. *Ibid.*, pp. 207-208.

165. Toronto's Girl Problem, *op. cit.*, p. 224, and Maynard, "Through a Hole in the Lavatory Wall," *op. cit.*, p. 230.

166. Maynard, "Through a Hole in the Lavatory Wall," *op. cit.*, p. 222.

167. See George Smith, "Policing the Gay Community: An Inquiry into Textually-Mediated Social Relations" in *International Journal of the Sociology of the Law*, V. 16, 1988, pp. 163-183.

168. Maynard, "Through a Hole in the Lavatory Wall," *op. cit.*, pp. 224-229.

169. *Ibid.*, p. 222-223.

170. *Ibid.*, p. 223, Quoting from Toronto City Council, Minutes, 1887, app., item 1061, p. 1030.

171. *Ibid.*, pp. 232-236

172. *Ibid.*, p. 234.

173. *Ibid.*, pp. 234-235.

174. *Ibid.*, p. 237-238.

175. See George Smith, "Policing the Gay Community" *op. cit.*, and Gary Kinsman, "Official Discourse as Sexual Regulation," Ph.D thesis, Department of Educational Theory, University of Toronto, 1989.

176. Maynard, "Through a Hole in the Lavatory Wall," *op. cit.*, pp. 238-242.

177. Cited in Steven Maynard, "Saturday night in the bunkhouse: Prospects for gay history" in *Rites*, Mar. 1990, p. 12.

178. Egan, *op. cit.*, p. 8.

179. Dorothy E. Smith, "Women's Inequality" in Allan Moscovitch and Glen Drover, eds., *Inequality: Essays on the Political Economy of Social Welfare* (Toronto, Buffalo, London: University of Toronto Press, 1981), p. 168; and Palmer, *Working Class Experience* (Toronto and Vancouver: Butterworth, 1983), p. 137.

180. Veronica Strong-Boag, "Canada's Women Doctors: Feminism Constrained" in Kealey, ed., *A Not Unreasonable Claim* (Toronto: Women's Educational Press, 1979), p. 124; and Katherine Arnup, "Education for Motherhood: Government Health Publications, Mothers and the State," unpublished paper delivered at the Canadian Sociology and Anthropology Association annual meeting in Winnipeg, June 1986. Also see Mariana Valverde, *The Age of Light, Soap and Water: Moral Reform in English Canada, 1885-1925* (Toronto: McClelland and Stewart, 1991), p. 53.

181. Also see Katherine Arnup, *Education for Motherhood: Advice for Mothers in Twentieth-Century Canada* (Toronto: University of Toronto Press, 1994).

182. Palmer, *Working Class Experience, op. cit.*, p. 234. Also see Jane Ursel, *Private Lives, Public Policy: 100 Years of State Intervention in the Family* (Toronto: Women's Press, 1992).

183. See Smith, "Women's Inequality," *op. cit.*; and Brigitte Kitchen, "Women's Dependence" in the Sexuality and the State issue of *Atkinson Review of Canadian Studies*, V. 1, No. 2, Spring 1984, pp. 11-16.

184. Dorothy E. Smith, "Women, Class and Family" in *Socialist Register*, 1983, pp. 31-32.

185. Also see Strange, *Toronto's Girl Problem, op. cit.*, especially pp. 116-174.

186. Palmer, *Working Class Experience, op. cit.*, pp. 189, 195.

187. Beth Light and Joy Parr, eds., *Canadian Women on the Move* (Toronto: New Hogtown Press and OISE, 1983), p. 49.

188. Palmer, *Working Class Experience, op. cit.*, p. 192.

189. See Cynthia Wright, "'Feminine Trifles of Vast Importance': Writing Gender into the History of Consumption" in Franca Iacovetta and Mariana Valverde, *Gender Conflicts: New Essays in Women's History* (Toronto: University of Toronto Press, 1992), pp. 229-260.

190. Palmer, *Working Class Experience, op. cit.*, p. 194. For a fun and intriguing exploration of American films, many of which would have been seen in Canada, see Vito Russo, *The Celluloid Closet: Homosexuality in the Movies* (New York: Harper and Row, 1981). Also Chauncey, *Gay New York, op. cit.*, p. 353.

191. See Chauncey, *Gay New York*, pp. 331-354.

192. Palmer, *Working Class Experience, op. cit.*, p. 94.

193. This is from Mary Vipond's "The Image of Women in Mass Circulation Magazines in the 1920s" in Susan Trofimenkoff and Alison Prentice, eds., *The Neglected Majority* (Toronto: McClelland and Stewart, 1977), pp. 117-122. Much of the next two paragraphs draws on this article.

194. *Ibid.*, p. 121.

195. Strong-Boag, "Canadian Women's Doctors: Feminism Constrained," *op. cit.*, p. 129.

196 See Katherine Arnup, *Education for Motherhood, op. cit.*

197. See Dorothy E. Smith, "Women, Class and Family" in *The Socialist Register-1983* (London: Merlin, 1983), p. 31.

198. See John Grube, "Queens and Flaming Virgins: Towards a Sense of Gay Community" in *Rites*, V. 2, No. 9, p. 16.

199. Quoted in Steven Maynard, "Radclyffe Hall in Canada" in *Centre/Fold*, No. 6, Spring 1994, p. 9. This is quoted from S.H. Hooke, *The Canadian Forum*, Apr., 1929.

7.

World War II, Coming Out and Constructing Homosexuality as a National, Social, and Sexual Danger

War Mobilization and "Psychopathic Personalities with Abnormal Sexuality"

World War II has been described as "a nationwide coming out experience" for the United States.[1] Mobilization uprooted millions of Americans, weakening the hold of the heterosexual family and separating women and men from each other in the armed forces, in war production, and in industry. A new setting for same-gender erotic liaisons was thus created.

Homosexuals were officially excluded from military service. Disciplinary State organizations like the military and the police had come to embody heterosexual masculinity as a central organizing ideology, and prohibitions against lesbianism were directed at regulating the lives of all women in the military as they started to enter its ranks.[2] On the one hand, the military through its bringing together of men and women in gender-segregated contexts facilitated same-gender erotic friendships and activities; on the other, it developed disciplinary regulations against these very same-gender erotic practices. This set up a contradictory situation for the military, which it attempted to handle through new administrative policies and regulations.

Even though, at the height of the World War II mobilization in the United States prohibitions against homosexuality were relaxed in the interests of the war effort, homosexuals could still be routinely discharged.[3]

> The military assigned the task of identifying homosexuals to draft-board members and military doctors ... Standardized psychiatric testing, developed after World War I, made their job easier. Millions of men were asked at induction physicals if they ever had homosexual feelings or experiences. For many, this was the first time they had to think of their lives in homosexual terms. This mass sexual questioning was just one of the ways that homosexuality became an issue during the war.[4]

This was part of the entry of the psychiatric and later the psychological professions much more centrally into the work of social administration, including the areas of gender and sexual regulation, at first in the military, and then in other areas.[5] People determined to be homosexual could be given "blue discharges," which disqualified them from military pensions and other benefits and decreased their chances of finding civilian employment. Thousands of these men and women who carried the stigma of homosexuality after being discharged during and after the war joined the developing lesbian and gay networks in such cities as New York, San Francisco, and Los Angeles.

War mobilization also affected sex/gender relations in Canada when thousands of women entered industry for the first time. At first, only single women were hired; then came married women without children. This situation was portrayed as only a temporary sacrifice: women's "proper place" was still in the home.[6] This shift, however, had a major effect on the social fabric of Canadian life.

The *18th Annual Report of the United Church of Canada, Division of Evangelism and Social Services*, published in 1943, expressed moral conservative concern. "War-time conditions are having a serious effect upon family life," said the chairman, warning of child neglect and an increase in both "illegitimate" births and "juvenile delinquency."[7]

> It is evident that wartime conditions are resulting in a serious disintegration of the family. That is not surprising when hundreds of thousands of men are absent from their homes on active service in H.M. Forces, and when the demands of war-time industry have necessitated the greatest migration in Canadian history. Sometimes both parents and all the older members of the family are working and younger children are often left without adequate supervision ... many families have migrated to new communities, where they find unfamiliar conditions and new excitements and temptations, and where the old restraints no longer obtain. Many young people receiving war-time wages have larger amounts of money to spend at a premature age ... This problem is aggravated further by the prevalence of pernicious theories of sex relationships derived from the so-called "new psychology" and the unjustified currency which has been given the doctrines of "self-expression" in certain circles.

Sexual indulgence was denounced:

> Evidence points to widespread laxity and promiscuity in sex relations and to a dangerously indulgent attitude on the part of large numbers. The use of contraceptive devices, the prevalence of sexual intercourse outside marriage, the frequent lack of shame or condemnation for sexual license, the tendency to regard the moral standards of the past as out-moded "taboos" are very disturbing.[8]

The Department of National Defence was criticized by the Church for its policies on venereal disease.[9] VD once again became a symbol for moral anxiety over shifting sex and gender relations. Under the rubric of fears of VD and sexual activity came issues ranging from children being left without supervision, to industrial upheaval, to the separation of thousands of men and women because of active service.

Fears of "sexual promiscuity" and VD were compounded with concerns by ruling social agencies when thousands of women joined the military and were deemed to have lost their sexual respectability.[10] A look at the VD-control programme in the Canadian Women's Army Corps offers a valuable glimpse into the military attitudes of the time. The army's concern reached a fever pitch in 1943. The campaign was primarily directed against prostitutes and "loose women," who were considered "carriers." This sexist policy was based on a flagrant double standard. There was no focus, for instance, on men who transmitted disease to their wives or female partners. There was no equivalent "loose man" to that of "loose woman." Women who violated the code of sexual propriety were labelled "promiscuous." Women were the scapegoats in the VD scare. The impact of VD policies on sex between men during these years remains to be explored.

While there was an attempt to escalate the sexist regulation of women's sexual lives during the war, its effectiveness was limited by the very upheavals of war. People did not necessarily obey or believe the official proclamations. While the war mobilization clearly made possible same-gender liaisons in the military and among women in industry, there is still less evidence that World War II fostered coming out and the formation of lesbian and gay networks in Canada than for the experience in the U.S. However, there are some wonderful first-hand accounts I mention in the next section.

One of the main differences between Canadian and U.S. military regulation of sexuality was in the classification of "sex deviates." From 1943 on, American military recruits were actually asked upon induction whether they were homosexual or whether they had ever been in love with someone of the same sex; in Canada, however, the military placed homosexuals and lesbians under the heading "psychiatric disorders" (which included psychoneurosis and psychosis) and more specifically as "anti-social psychopaths" and "psychopathic personalities" with "abnormal sexuality."[11] While thousands of Canadian men and women were discharged as such, many of them for same-gender sex, there was less specific labelling of homosexuals than in the U.S. They would have been classified as sub-groups of these broad psychological collecting categories and not as a specifically demarcated homosexual type. Clearly, this association was an important feature of military categorization but at the same time it was an inscription into a highly psychiatrically defined concept that privileged "psychopathic" personality and not same-gender sexuality.[12]

At the same time, as one American study conducted in 1943-1944 concluded, "The problem of sexual psychopathy in the military service is essentially that of homosexuality."[13] In 1921 the American army had established its first written regulations excluding men who were sexual "perverts" or "psychopaths," and during World War II both the army and navy were diagnosing homosexual men and women as "sexual psychopaths."[14]

This also raises the question of whether during these years as Freedman suggests, "*psychopath* served in part as a code for *homosexual* ..."[15] One of the concepts psychiatrists brought with them into military administration was "psychopath," which originated in the nineteenth century within forensic psychiatry as a "collecting category" to classify habitual criminals who exhibited "abnormal" social behaviour. It was used by Heinrich Kaan and Krafft-Ebing in regards to "abnormal" sexual activities.[16] Forensic psychiatrists were called upon to testify in court as to a person's mental soundness at the time of committing an offence. An important and lasting interconnection was established between these psychiatric knowledges and criminal proceedings. At first those categorized as psychopaths were "hypersexual" women and unemployed or transient men who lived beyond the boundaries of familial and social regulation. By the 1930s, the category was used more to classify male sex deviants and criminals.

The sexualization of the male psychopath took place in the U.S. in the 1930s. This decade saw psychiatrists and psychologists investigating gender and sexual "deviance." In the process, they were creating a sharper definition of heterosexual masculinity. Those who were deviant in their "masculinity" increasingly became targets for psychiatric and psychological investigation. In the 1930s in the U.S., the male sex deviant began to be seen as a danger to children and it was during this decade that homosexuals began to emerge as an important part of this psychopathic category.[17]

There was an unevenness of conceptualizations used in different discourses and institutional sites. In some, *homosexual* — taken from sexological and psychological discourse was used — and in others, *sexual psychopath* — taken from psychiatric discourse — had more currency. This was part of the unevenness of developments in official and popular discourses where, in some, "homosexuality" per se, was being used; in others, "homosexuality" was part of broader administrative collecting categories. In some discourses, homosexuality was not clearly distinguished from other sexual deviances or had been re-conflated with broader psychiatric categories as part of larger diagnostic units. The social conceptualization of "homosexuality" was still only in the process of being generalized within official and more popular discourses.

At the same time, there were other popular and professional discourses in which homosexual "labelling" was more directly taking place. Even though official military language might use psychiatric terms, a person discharged from the military could still be identified as "queer" by other unit members. Sidney Katz writes in a *Maclean's Magazine* article that "Every Canadian serviceman can recall at least a few instances where one of the fellows in his outfit was suddenly sent home for discharge because he was a 'queer.'"[18] Even if one was disposed of as a "psychopathic personality" — if word got round that it was because of same-gender sex — because of other available discourses and popular cultures, he or she could still be labelled as "homosexual" or "queer."

Military mobilizations before and during the war created a series of problems that psychiatric personnel, among others, were called upon to manage. As people with "abnormal sexuality" were identified as a "danger" or a "disruptive influence" in the military, an official course of action was put in place to deal with this "problem." This involved bringing together the work of military classification and discipline with medical and psychiatric discourse and professionals.

Medical records and statistics were kept throughout the war as part of a documentary form of administration in the military. A documentary reality of files and records came to define the recruits' relation to the military. This was organized by, and provided an opening for, psychiatric and psychological classifications as part of these administrative regulations. The military came to be increasingly organized through forms of textually mediated discourse that mandated courses of action in military procedure and discipline. These administrative policies were designed to make the war effort more "efficient" and to get rid of "unfit men" so that they "are not permitted to impede the fighting forces."[19]

On induction, each man had to undergo an Order Medical Examination. Physicians classified recruits according to the categories laid out in the *Physical Standards and Instructions for the Examination of Recruits* (1938), which considered recruits with "nervous or mental disorders" to be "unfit for service." In 1942, this manual was criticized by medical and personnel officers because it did not allow them to match recruits with military positions. That same year, military psychiatrists introduced the Psychiatric Questionnaire, which was designed to test the emotional stability of recruits and was used in conjunction with the standard medical classifications.

Originally in the war effort, there was no specific psychiatric screening although some was initiated in the summer of 1941. The original manuals and regulations that were designed for a smaller professional army were found wanting in the context of a rapidly expanding draft army. New procedures and classifications were required to manage the new problems that were emerging for military administration. These were in part to be provided by psychiatry and psychology and by training military personnel in these disciplines. As the Feasby official military history reports "the psychiatrist in the Second World War developed a new relationship to administrative authority."[20] Psychiatric practices thus became integrated with military rule. Military practices after enlistment were focused on those who showed "unusual" behaviour or who were "emotionally unstable."[21] These were considered problems within military organization.

However, "homosexual" was used in the *Physical Standards and Instructions for the Medical Examination of Recruits* (1943) where it was mentioned under "psychopathic personality."[22] In military psychiatric practice the Feasby text reports that, "a group of cases was met for which the name psychopathic personality" became defined (only in professional discourse do people become "cases").[23] In the official account of the Canadian Medical Service it is reported that "opportunities to study this group of cases are particularly plentiful in times of war."[24] The people who were claimed by this category were various individuals and groups who could not adapt or conform to institutionalized military life.

In the 1943 instructions under "Stability (S)," the following is stated as instructions to assist doctors and psychiatrists in diagnosing "psychopathic personality" (section 195):

> The chief characteristic of this disorder is inability of the individual to profit by experience. Men with this disorder are unable to meet the usual adult social standards of truthfulness, decency, responsibility and consideration for their fellow associates. They are emotionally unstable and absolutely not to be depended on. They are impulsive, show poor judgement and in the army

they are continually at odds with those who are trying to train and discipline them ... Among this group are many homosexuals, chronic delinquents, chronic alcoholics and drug addicts. All such men should be regarded as medically unfit for service anywhere in any capacity.[25]

This reference to "many homosexuals" would have provided a guide for detection and diagnosis for military doctors.

This category of "psychopathic personality" contained a diverse range of behaviour and problems, even "psychopathic personality with abnormal sexuality." In 1942 a committee on the nomenclature of mental disorders concluded that these "cases" — and the Feasby text quotes positively from it — "exert a bad influence on their fellow soldiers and are therefore unwanted in any unit."[26] "Psychopathic personality with abnormal sexuality" was the "diagnosis used when abnormal sexuality is the basic feature of the case, and is not apparently based on mental deficiency, psychoses or psychoneurosis."[27] The job of military psychiatrists was to "facilitate the disposal of [these] cases."[28]

If a "problem" was detected among military personnel, a doctor or psychiatrist would be called in to make a diagnosis. Some of those examined would be diagnosed as "psychopathic personalities" with "abnormal sexuality." If military doctors and psychiatrists could successfully fit or "inscribe" those they were examining into this classification, they would be given an S-5 rating (S for suitability) as laid out in the *Physical Standards and Instructions for the Medical Examination of Recruits,* which meant they were "Unsuitable for service anywhere in any capacity because of instability." This would then mandate discharge from the military bringing into action the administrative discharge proceedings of the military.

From 1939 to 1945, the navy rejected a reported 10,734 males and 775 females for medical reasons.[29] This group included a reported 387 men and 49 women in the period May 1941 to September 1945 because of nervous and mental disorders.[30] Under category E, "unfit for service," 5,535 men and 159 women were rejected from 1st September 1939 to 30th of September, 1945.[31] As for the army, 1,127 recruits were rejected because of "psychopathic personality" in 1944 alone.[32] Unfortunately, the statistics do not differentiate between "psychopathic personality" and other "disorders," let alone between various "problems" and "psychopathic personality with abnormal sexuality." We are therefore left with no recorded "pervert" count. It is clear, nevertheless, that thousands of men and women were labelled "psychopathic personalities," many of them for suspected same-gender erotic interests. How they reacted to this classification has yet to be investigated.

Significant for our purposes is that the classification "psychopathic personality" did not have the same impact as the more explicit homosexual labelling in the U.S. Not only was it a more psychologically and technically defined term, it also grouped together various "problems," some of them having little or nothing to do with sex. As an ideological classification it had very little to do with the actual lives of men and women engaging in same-gender eroticism. Many women and men engaging in same-gender sex would not have exhibited the characteristics associated with "psychopathic personality" allowing for many of them to be overlooked. In many ways it would have been an ineffective means of policing and excluding same-gender eroticism.[33] At the same time, this "psychopathic" classification would be built upon in the policing and regulation of same-gender sex in the post-war years in Canada in the military and within State relations more generally.

Coming Out and Queer Doings

There were those, however, who managed to slip through the apparatus of military sexual policing to explore their same-gender desires and to participate in homosexual and lesbian networks in large cities and naval ports. Official military and psychiatric classification of their sexuality as "psychopathic" didn't stop them from having same-gender erotic pleasures. The following little gems culled from a few sources give us a sense of these very "unofficial" stories, which also make visible a line of fault between these lived experiences and the official categories used to police sexual life. These accounts have a very different character than official military/psychiatric accounts. In them we can begin to see how the experiences of men engaging in sex with other men were socially organized and how they would help to lay the basis for post-war expansion of gay networks. They also begin to reveal very practical aspects of the social organization of male same-gender sex and begin to pose and answer such questions as "where to go to meet men for sex?" or "how to tell if another man is interested in sex with men?"[34]

Bert Sutcliffe describes his experiences:

> I joined the army when I was twenty-three, in 1940. I was completely unaware — I had never heard the expression gay, homosexual, lesbian or faggot. Not even negatively … When I was a young teenager I was aware of the fact that men appealed to me. But I had no idea about anything until myself and a sergeant were sent to England in 1941 …. We went to the dance on New Year's Eve and then went back to our quarters … We had a few drinks and he said, "Well, c'mon, let's sleep in my quarters," and of course one thing led to the other. He was the one who began my education. He took me into the first gay bar I'd ever been into, London during the war time was heaven, really — people on leave, and all kinds of gay clubs. I made sure before I came home to ask the men I knew overseas who were gay: okay, where do you go in Toronto? They told me of two or three places. None of these places was exclusively gay and you had to be cautious. You had to feel your way and make sure the guy you were working on was in fact gay.[35]

Sutcliffe writes in his autobiography that

> it should be understood that many young men who were to enter the Community of gays during the war were able to do so because they were

free from family control ... A few of these young men may have returned to the "so-called straight and narrow path" on returning to Canada, but to use an old adage, "How can you keep them down on the farm after they have seen Paris?"[36]

Sutcliffe learned a lot from his encounter with English same-gender erotic male cultures and military sex experiences and was able to use some of this practical knowledge when he got back.

> I came home with a number of facts. One, there were a number of steam baths where one could meet ... I never did use this outlet. Two, that certain pubs and bars in Toronto were popularized by members of Toronto's gay Community: The King Edward Hotel, the Ford Hotel (to a lesser extent).[37]

His companion Ralph Wormleighton remembers that during the war "In my outfit, it was generally known certain men were gay. Nothing was ever done about it."[38]

Several of Maurice Leznoff's gay male "informants" in his 1954 thesis on homosexuals in Montréal refer to their wartime or military experiences as pivotal to their "coming out" — to themselves and to friends:

> At about the age of 19 I met up with my first genuinely homosexual experience in the army. I met this one particular chap at the training camp ... we became fast friends ... This attachment existed for a long time until we eventually drifted into bed ... Neither of us had the courage to suggest such a thing, nor the knowledge of homosexuality. I think it was more than a physical attraction. It occurred in London on a weekend leave. We were both a little high and had come home from a dance ... without asking any questions I simply got into his bed. It was a question of instinct rather than technique. Neither of us felt any regrets. It was certainly primitive but genuinely homosexual and the first that either of us had experienced. After this we often had sex together and advanced all along the way in a completely parallel course of development. At one point we danced together in the privacy of our room and afterwards kissed. That had been the first time that either of us had kissed another man ... Another curious thing about the whole affair was that neither of us considered ourselves homosexual ... We both went back to university, too. I remember that I had keen sexual powers. Then we began a new practice ... We used to take out the girls on a double date, get ourselves worked up, take the girls home, and then go home together, and have sex ... The separation from him was perfectly ghastly. Even now when I think about it I am a little saddened. It was at this point that we both realized that we were homosexual.[39]

Canadian men cruised abroad during the war:

> I remember once in London during the war. Capital Square was as gay as
> hell. And the blackout made it a cruising paradise. Every night you could go
> out and just bump into hundreds of gay people. Americans, Canadians,
> British, Australians, everything. I picked up this Australian fellow and we
> went back to my room to have sex.

The effect of such experiences on life back in Canada is a subject worthy of further exploration. One man discusses his own experiences:

> Nothing really happened until I got to London during the war. I was a secretary in the air force. I lived all through the war in London. I knew that I was
> gay all this time, but I wasn't doing anything about it ... London was very
> gay. Then one night at the theatre one of the comedians made a joke about
> the blackout being as thick as the queers in P.C. That's how I knew where to
> go and I made a b-line for P.C. ... I had my first gay experience there and I
> went back very often afterwards ... I was getting a special living-out allowance so that I had my own quarters ... My closest friend all this time had a
> room in the same house ... we used to go out cruising together and we
> would have a hell of a lot of fun just talking to each other and telling each
> other what we picked up ... I don't know what I would have done without
> Charley ... I felt miserable and well ... just perverted by what I was doing
> but the fascination of it kept me going back for more. Charley knew what I
> was going through because he went through the same thing himself. I owe
> him a hell of a lot. He convinced me that it wasn't my fault I was gay and the
> only thing to do was accept it and make your life as happy as you can in
> spite of it ... By the time I got back to Canada, gay life was just about natural
> to me. I went to university ... I found out that universities could have their
> gay people too, and I made a lot of contacts there.

Another gay man explains the difference between the wartime and peacetime moods:

> During the war people were scattered all over the place and morals were
> very loose. At the same time facilities became numerous. I mean places
> where homosexuals could go and also the number of practising homosexuals. This was because of the close association of people in the services. After the war there was this period of unsettlement. On the other
> hand, I think that in a period of peacetime and the necessity of settling
> in a job, people became more sedate ... It was no longer as easy to lose
> oneself as long as people were permanently established in one particular
> place and with a steady job.

Wartime circumstances led to the expansion of gay and lesbian networks. A post-war tightening up of sex and gender regulations would have left these networks stranded outside the social mainstream, which in turn would have facilitated further networking and community formation for group support.

Reconstructing Patriarchal and Heterosexual Hegemonies: Contending Strategies of Regulation

The end of the war brought with it reconstruction of the gender division of labour in Canada. Women were removed from industry and day-care centres were closed. Heterosexual hegemony was reconstructed after the war in response to social changes, at the same time, building on, and transforming, previous forms of heterosexism. Sexual organization, however, was also shifted over the post-war decades. The 1940s and 1950s reinforcement of the family and reproductive heterosexuality gave way, by the 1960s and 1970s, to new forms of class and family organization. By the late 1960s membership in a "proper" heterosexual family unit was no longer always essential for advancement in the corporate and professional worlds, especially the lower rungs. While women's labour was still needed in the rearing of children, corporate capital's commitment to the "proper" heterosexual family, was not what it had previously been.[40]

There were now new struggles over homosexual and lesbian definitions. A "liberalizing" or rationalizing tendency emerged with the Kinsey studies, the expansion of sex research, and new psychological knowledge. This was partly shaped by the expansion of gay and lesbian networks. A more conservative trend also surfaced, one that focused on the homosexual as a national, social and criminal sexual danger. This image built on the previous association of homosexuality with national degeneration and decay and the homosexual as "child molester," which, in turn, was derived from the earlier image of homosexual men "preying" on adolescent boys.

During the 1950s and 1960s, two contending strategies of sexual regulation were struggled over as part of the transformation of a range of relations in post-war capitalism, including class, gender, sexual and State relations. The main strategy to be explored in this chapter is that of the extending criminalization strategy that constructed homosexuality as a social and sexual danger. This includes the U.S.-influenced criminal-sexual-psychopath and later dangerous-sexual-offender sections of the Criminal Code, but also the "national-security" campaigns. Put in place in the 1950s, this regulatory framework was shifted over the next two decades to a second strategy, the public/private partial decriminalization frame of regulation identified with the 1957 Wolfenden Report, which will be explored in chapter 8. This shift in focus included active contention and struggle and the subordination of one strategy to the other in the social construction of hegemony. This had an important impact on both professional and popular discussions.

The Kinsey Earthquake and New Psychological Knowledges

The 1948 publication of Alfred Kinsey's *Sexual Behavior in the Human Male* and *Sexual Behavior in the Human Female* in 1953 challenged some of the common sense notions of heterosexism formed in the pre-World War II and immediate post-war years.[41] Kinsey's studies demonstrated that the number of men and women engaged in same-gender sex was much larger than previously imagined. The study on men also showed that masturbation among boys and men was regular and widespread. The Kinsey reports were widely circulated and publicized and generated numerous reviews in professional journals and popular magazines.

Using a research method derived from the natural sciences, Kinsey asserted that he was producing "value-free" facts. He was not interested in questions of sexual meaning, identity, consciousness, or how sexual experiences were socially organized, but only with what he saw as the development of a "scientific" classification of sexual behaviour. His approach focused on orgasm/ejaculation. Central to the Kinsey Institute's work was "sexual outlet," which measured the number of genital sexual contacts. Since Kinsey's methods were not concerned with social meaning, they ripped apart people's actual experiences, separating "outlet" from social context and practice.

Kinsey was not interested in notions of homosexual (or heterosexual) identity. Indeed, he questioned whether there was any such thing as homosexuality beyond what he called "homosexual sexual outlets." These limitations mean that the Kinsey data is not very illuminating on the subject of the formation of homosexual cultures and identities. His work is, however, very important to an examination of the social organization of sexual knowledge and the social and political struggles over the meanings and consequences of this knowledge.

While the Kinsey studies revealed some shocking information for some about the extent of same-gender sex, it generally championed heterosexual and male-defined forms of intercourse. In a sense, these reports expanded the existing definitions of heterosexual normality — to include, for example, limited homosexual fooling around at points in people's lives.

Kinsey classified people according to their sexual outlets. His famous continuum of sexual behaviour placed people along a scale from exclusive heterosexual acts (0) through to exclusive homosexual acts (6). Kinsey challenged the stereotype of homosexuality as a form of gender inversion. He defined the capacity to participate in homosexual acts as a relatively common "inherent physiologic capacity" that should not be punished.[42]

The Kinsey findings highlighted the significant number of male homosexual acts but established that only a small proportion of males were involved in exclusively or predominantly homosexual activity. As Chauncey suggests, these statistics may be capturing traces of a somewhat earlier form of organization of male same-gender sex before the full hegemony of institutionalized heterosexuality. This may have allowed for more of a combining of same-and different-gender erotic activities.[43] For instance, fifty percent of the white males interviewed admitted erotic response to other males, and thirty-seven percent of men in all occupational groups admitted at least one homosexual experience to the point of orgasm between adolescence and old age. Only four percent, however, were found to be exclusively involved in homosexual activity throughout their lives: thirteen percent reported more involvement in homosexual than heterosexual activity for at least three years of their lives.

The Kinsey researchers asserted that female sexual responses were not that dissimilar to those of men and argued that male and female orgasms were equivalent physiological phenomena. They reported that twenty-eight percent of women said that they responded erotically to their own gender, that thirteen percent had experienced orgasms with other women, and that the number of women exclusively or primarily involved in activity with other women were from one-third to one-half of the equivalent figures for men. The Kinsey study thereby perpetuated hegemonic social assumptions about women's general lack of sexual autonomy.

The release of these findings was met with moral outrage in the context of the initiation of the Cold War and the "national-security" scares that also targeted homosexuals. Sexual conservatives simply refused to believe these statistics. The most vehement attacks were levelled at the volume of female sexual behaviour.[44] Some U.S. conservatives used the findings to magnify the danger of homosexuality, arguing that it was an epidemic sweeping the nation.[45] The findings were used in the context of the McCarthyite witch hunts to whip up hatred and fear against lesbians and gay men. However, the relatively small percentage of those reported to be engaged in exclusively homosexual acts was used to visualize homosexuality as "deviant" behaviour practised by only a small minority of the population, thus buttressing notions of heterosexual normality for the vast majority.[46]

The Kinsey Institute research and publications were a primary reference point for sexual policy and discussion throughout the post-war years. The reports legitimized the discussion of sexuality in newspapers, magazines, and on radio and television. The Kinsey findings were taken up by the agencies and institutions that administer and regulate our erotic lives. They were also used by the new homophile and gay movements in the 1950s and 1960s as a way to legitimize our existence. It provided the basis for the claim that gays and lesbians are ten percent of the population, even though Kinsey himself never argued this. In the 1950s, Kinsey himself urged the officers of the Mattachine Society, an American homophile group, to avoid "special pleas for a minority group" and to restrict themselves to aiding "qualified research experts," in the process reinforcing tendencies toward caution, accommodation, and reliance on professionals.[47]

The Kinsey perspective on homosexuality served to inform Canadian medical, psychological, and popular literature in the 1950s and 1960s. Early 1950s medical and psychological articles often combined use of the Kinsey statistics with Freudian-derived psychological theories.[48] These articles used psychological theories to explain homosexuality, such as the familiar argument that homosexuality is caused by "mothers who blocked their [sons'] masculine tendencies, encouraged their feminine interests, and tied their sons to themselves emotionally."[49] There was an uneven and gradual shift away, nevertheless, from the theory of gender inversion and toward the idea of homosexuality as a sexual-object choice.

The Kinsey statistics were used to show that the number of exclusive homosexuals was quite small, and that those who only occasionally participated in same-gender erotic activities should not be labelled as such but encouraged to take up a heterosexual life through therapy and adjustment. These articles were often clearly intended as instructions for doctors and health professionals. Their advice to those who could not change was to live "as normal a life as may be possible" — to live in the closet and pretend to be heterosexual. This professional advice was an active part of the social construction of the relations of the closet. This literature also called for "further scientific and objective treatment of the problem"[50] — coincidentally, this research would be undertaken by these very same medical doctors, psychiatrists, and psychologists. This knowledge would play an important role in professional practice and eventually in popular discussion. It would be used to diagnose and "treat" homosexuals in the 1950s, 1960s, and 1970s.

Freud Rules OK?

The 1950s saw neo-Freudian ideas enter popular discourse in a major way. Psychiatric and psychological definitions of sex deviation and homosexuality became more firmly established, displacing older categories of "perversion" and "criminality." Models of "treatment" were now developed, including aversion therapy and other forms of psychological and physical terrorism. Aversion therapy was directed at creating an aversive response, including physical pain and vomiting, to homosexual images as part of attempts to "cure" homosexual men and lesbians. Johann Mohr and R.E. Turner of the Toronto Forensic Clinic reported that

> in sporadic homosexual behaviour, where the major question is one of control of impulsive acting out, aversion may be induced by showing homosexual stimuli in conjunction with mild electric shocks or emetic drugs.[51]

Psychological testing had been developed on the basis of surveys of American soldiers in wartime and became more generalized in personnel and social administration in the 1950s and 1960s.[52] In the 1950s, the U.S. Employment Service developed many standardized tests that were used by private vocational-guidance agencies, mental hospitals, employment agencies, and school counsellors and psychologists. They were used in personal assessments, for determining aptitude, and in rehabilitation programmes in Canada as well as the U.S. in the 1950s and 1960s. It was not until the early 1970s that their use was widely challenged within the professions.

These tests were also based on the development of MF (masculine/feminine) scales and psychological testing based on them. These tests embedded concerns over "proper" gender attributes in the practices of social administration in a number of different sites. "Homosexuality" came to be central to the articulation of these gender tests, as notions of gender inversion were crucial to the assumptions upon which they were constructed.[53]

A number of the tests used in Canada classified homosexuality as a "disorder."[54] One of these defined heterosexuality as an expressed need "to go out with or be in love with one of the opposite sex" and "to tell or listen to sex jokes." More men than women responded positively to the questions regarding "heterosexuality." Forty-two percent of the women responded to five questions or less. Scoring low on the heterosexuality scale could have serious consequences, however. One could be identified as sexually deviant or homosexual, and then subjected to more testing.[55] Another test defined the homosexual as highly anxious, neurotic, tender-minded, depressive, and submissive. Male homosexuality was associated with other deviant behaviour. Male homosexuals supposedly suffered from "guilt-proneness," "frustration-tension," and "emotional immaturity." If preliminary testing confirmed the diagnosis, then various forms of therapy, including the use of certain drugs, were recommended.[56]

Nonetheless, the 1950s also saw the establishment of gay and lesbian networks in major centres across the Canadian State. The rule of "homosexuality as mental illness" or "deviance" was neither monolithic nor total.

Gay Life in 1950s Montréal

In May 1954, a remarkable thesis was accepted by McGill University in Montréal. "The Homosexual in Urban Society" by Maurice Leznoff,[57] particularly through its many excerpts from interviews with gay men, offers important glimpses into gay male life in Montréal (which Leznoff tries to disguise by calling it "Easton"). Because hiding the location was important to Leznoff, the language question and tensions between the English and French were not focused on. This is unfortunate for learning about the intersection of language, nation, class, and gay-network formation during these years. While the study of homosexuality had been virtually ignored by sociologists, Leznoff argued, "the most relevant theoretical statements that may be applied in analyzing homosexual society are to be found in the sociological theory."[58] Here he was drawing on the ethnographic approach of the Chicago School of Sociology that had some influence at McGill.[59]

This work marked a shift from a preoccupation with the origins of homosexuality and the various psychiatric, medical, and legal means of regulation to a recognition of a developing homosexual culture and an attempt to understand its "deviant" features as a response to a hostile society. Leznoff examined how gays, through association and participation in a subcultural system, sought satisfaction of needs not legitimately sanctioned in society. He was interested in how homosexual men survived, how they built their own social groups and avoided the social controls of heterosexual culture, and "how homosexual society is functionally integrated on a sexual basis."[60] He refers to the works of Krafft-Ebing, Havelock Ellis, Freud, the Kinsey study on male sexual behaviour, and Donald Webster Cory's *The Homosexual in America,* quoting a long passage from Cory on cruising and gay slang.[61]

Using cross-cultural and historical examples, Leznoff argued that homosexuality is universal. He held the ahistorical view that homosexuals have remained basically unchanged throughout history while levels of social tolerance for homosexuality have varied, becoming more hostile in recent centuries. Leznoff was also influenced by the notion of sexual orientation as the distinct feature separating homosexuals from heterosexuals, which was in some discourses beginning to replace the theory of homosexuals as gender inverts: "It is the object of his sexual drive that distinguishes the homosexual from other men."[62]

Leznoff made contact with a group of thirteen or fourteen Montréal homosexuals (his "informants") through a client at a social-welfare agency. This man was part of a homosexual group whose "queen" name was Robert.[63] The "queen" played a central role in the organization of gay male networks at that time, providing a place for meetings and sexual affairs. He helped finance members in distress, made sexual contacts for them, controlled membership in the network, warned of potential problems like dangerous "tricks" who might prey upon them, and even negotiated with the police. Often the queen was an older homosexual who had wide experience in the gay world.[64]

Leznoff labels Robert and his group the "overts" because they lived almost exclusively within the homosexual culture, as opposed to the "coverts" who lived outside these networks. This distinction between overt and covert homosexual groups, which was so central to Leznoff's work, continued to be a mainstay in sociological writings on gays in the 1960s, and even entered into Evelyn Hooker's psychological work on the emotional stability of gay men.

Leznoff accompanied these men to house parties, restaurants, and bars for about eight months. His thesis relies on observations made during these outings as well as interviews with forty homosexual men (both overts and coverts), surveys of twenty others, and an examination of letters from one gay man to another. The letters were written by a travelling salesman who described gay life in various Canadian cities. Leznoff had difficulty meeting and talking to professional and middle-class men — the "coverts," while the overts, who were usually working-class were more accommodating.[65]

The awarding of a Canadian Social Science Research Council grant for his thesis project was made public just as a park used for cruising came under heavy police surveillance, resulting in a number of arrests. Many of Leznoff's contacts blamed the press coverage for the police activity and held him personally responsible.[66] There were also fears that Leznoff's data, including the interviews, would be turned over to the Research Council. He therefore found it increasingly difficult to get cooperation from his "informants" and his research came to an end.[67]

The crucial distinction for Leznoff was that of overts and coverts. "Overts" lived mostly within homosexual networks and were not overly concerned with concealing their homosexuality, while "coverts" were likely to live most of their lives in the heterosexual world and were very fearful of being discovered. Occupation and social status played a central role in Leznoff's distinction between the two, which he relates to the different strategies of concealment necessary to evade occupational controls.[68] The need to hide one's homosexuality was greater in some occupations than in others. Professionals could not afford to be identified with homosexuality, so they "adapt themselves to society through concealment and secret participation in homosexual activity." The overt group, on the other hand, tended to work in areas where homosexuality was more tolerated. Of the forty men interviewed, most identity-concealing were professionals, students, managers, businessmen, and upper-level clerks and salesmen. Among the non-concealing men, most were clerks and salesmen, artists, waiters, and hairdressers. Clearly Leznoff was discovering an aspect of the social relations of class as they related to gay network formation.

Remarks one of Leznoff's informants:

> I know a few people who don't care [that it is known they are homosexuals]. Those who don't care are really pitiful. They are either people who are very insignificant in position or they are in good positions but are independent … I have to care a lot.[69]

A manager of a small appliance shop states:

> My promotions have made me more conscious of the gang I hang around with. You see for the first time in my life I have a job that I would really like to keep and where I can have a pretty nice future … if word were to get around town that I am gay I would probably lose my job … I don't want to hang around with Robert [the queen of the "overt" group] any more or any of the people who are like Robert.[70]

The threat of discovery also influenced the selection of occupation or career. Says a student:

> I wouldn't like to end up with a job that requires mixing with normal people too much … I would never think of going into law. I would like to go into the type of job where you can be more or less your own boss.[71]

Leznoff's coverts formed a number of overlapping social groups with no queen figure playing a central role.[72] They were also involved in groups associated with their work; indeed, their social lives were often organized through the heterosexual worlds of the professions and business. They therefore tended to regard the overts "as a threat to their social position [because the coverts] think of themselves as different from that category of homosexuals who are not similarly motivated towards concealment."[73] They even saw overts as "riff-raff" — as "low-class people with low-class manners."[74] Yet, since in both groups there was a taboo on sex with friends because this caused tensions within the group, coverts and overts developed erotic relations and coverts were forced to frequent homosexual spots to meet sexual partners.

Ross Higgins, in his important account of Leznoff's thesis, describes the overts:

> These took little or no pains to conceal their homosexuality, though some did at work. Some had jobs where it was possible to be out, as artists, waiters, hairdressers, or low-level clerical and sales staff. At their head was the "queen" Robert/Roberta. He was an older man with a wide experience of gay life (his address book contained three thousand names). He sponsored younger men in the "life," provided a place where they could gather to "let their hair down" (sometimes a place they could bring someone for the night) and mediated their fights.[75]

The coverts stayed away from "the gay world" as much as possible, but the overts developed "effeminacy" and swish behaviour as an affirmation of their gayness. For them, the homosexual group was a vital support. "Effeminacy" in this context should not be understood as simply acting stereotypically feminine, but rather as a particular cultural form produced among gay men based on the taking up and exaggeration of certain attributes associated with femininity. It was both a deconstruction and reconstruction of gender. This was a crucial component of gay male cultures until the last decade or so, and continues today in some important forms.

While the coverts feared public exposure by an overt, the overts often disliked the coverts: one who referred to the coverts as the "intelligentsia" said:

> Sometimes they stoop down and have an affair with somebody from our gang. They even come to a party over at Robert's sometimes but they never hang around for very long … I think you could say they mix sexually but not socially.[76]

What was at the root of this tension and resentment between the two groups? The social organization of class has an important effect on our erotic lives and on homosexual cultures. Advancement in the business and professional worlds of the 1950s required that social life be tied to the corporation or the professional group — ideally, it required a middle-class nuclear family. It would have been next to impossible to be openly gay, so the "coverts" had to live a double life in the extreme: passing for straight and maintaining a secret homosexual life on the side. This was an important part of the construction of the relations of the closet. We also begin to see how the social relations of the closet are articulated unevenly to the social organization of class. The social pressures of "the closet" and living a "double-life" were much stronger in the lives of these middle-class and professional men.

At the same time, capitalism continued to open up social spaces in which people could more fully live beyond heterosexual family networks, and also created low-status jobs around which there was relative indifference towards homosexuality, or even a possible grudging acceptance, and which gays came to occupy. Indeed some occupations came to be stereotyped as gay preserves such as hairdressing and interior decorating. In these often dead-end jobs and job ghettoes one was not as required to organize one's social life through work or through heterosexuality. Men in such jobs, as well as artists and self-employed people, were able to create their own networks and their own cultures. Some of the earlier roots of these "overt" networks may also lie in the fairy networks that George Chauncey writes about in New York City earlier in the century.[77] Concealment was not a major constraint on their lives. It was these men who would create and fight for visible gay space in the 1950s and 1960s.[78]

It is this social organization of class that created the tension between Leznoff's coverts and overts. These distinct social groups were shaped by the social relations organizing class relations outside gay networks and their effect on class formation within emerging gay community formation.

Leznoff's thesis pointed to other aspects of gay life in the 1950s. Increasing urbanization, for instance, meant that homosexual men could escape familial and religious regulations that were often still stronger in rural areas. Big cities often offered greater opportunities for sexual and social contacts.

On the subject of the police, Leznoff reported that none of those interviewed said they had ever been the target of police action.[79] He suggested that legal and police action was effective only against the most flagrant displays of homosexuality. The response of his "informants" to the arrests in the park, however, indicates a very real fear of the police.

Leznoff's work includes valuable information on cruising and contact techniques, on cruising areas, homosexual slang, and the bars, restaurants, and street corners frequented by gays in Montréal. He produced a remarkable, if sometimes flawed, window into the past. For instance, the following wonderful tale:

> I know a guy who gets dressed up in tight slacks to cruise the harbour area. He likes sailors. He'll get dressed up in these slacks and go to the taverns around the harbour. You can pick up a sailor that way pretty easy.[80]

Seizing Queer Spaces: Butch/Femme Cultures, Bar Dykes and Queer Sites

Just as the "overts" Leznoff wrote about struggled for social space in the 1950s, so did working-class lesbian butch/femme cultures struggle for lesbian space and to affirm dyke identities.[81] Butch lesbians were not attempting to be "male" but were developing a specifically lesbian cultural and erotic style in concert with the femmes that appropriated certain cultural forms from hegemonic masculinity and femininity but put them together in a new lesbian context. Many lesbians, given the gendered division of labour where women were segregated into lower-paying forms of wage-labour and the need for these women to support themselves, their partners and sometimes their children, needed relatively higher-paying jobs. This is why many may have

entered or tried to enter into "non-traditional" jobs that were generally done by men
at this point. In these jobs they would also have been able to get away with being
more "butch" and not face as much pressure to conform to the standard codes of
"femininity." Line Chamberland, in her pioneering study of lesbian bars in Montréal
stresses the important part played by working-class lesbians in establishing lesbian
public space and also points to the class-related divisions among women and the class
and job-related constraints on lesbian expression during these years.[82]

In Toronto in the 1950s, white women came together at the Continental, a hotel
bar located in the middle of Chinatown. Straight men, prostitutes, and "gay women"
who were mostly working class gathered at this bar. For some lesbians, this became the
centre of their lives except when they were working to survive. For women who worked
in factories or in low-paid service jobs, the Continental was the place to socialize. According to Elise Chenier who has done oral histories with fourteen women who went to
the Continental, an "uptowner" was a woman who passed as straight during the work
week and spent the weekends at the Continental. The working-class women who hung
out at the Continental used "uptowners" to describe gay women who lived in greater
secrecy and material comfort. A "downtowner" was a woman who spent much more of
their time at the bar, usually every day and who did not regularly attempt to pass as
straight. Mostly these "downtowners" were out and butch. Prostitution, occasional or
full-time, was common among these "downtowners" as a way of surviving.[83] Women
who frequented the Continental in the 1950s and 1960s faced considerable police harassment including for some, being taken by the cops to Cherry Beach and then being
beaten up. At the same time, there were also more suburban networks of lesbians who
had little contact with the women at the Continental, and women's baseball teams in
various centres provided a basis for lesbian networking.

In the 1960s, downtown Toronto's Street Haven, a shelter for poor street women,
many of whom were prostitutes, tried to "rehabilitate" lesbians. Becki Ross tells us that
crucial to their efforts were attempts to make butch lesbians into more "feminine"
women by removing their tattoos and getting them to dress more "femininely." "Butch"
lesbians were clearly seen as the major problem since more "feminine" appearance was
praised and rewarded.[84]

Other women read the lesbian-themed pulp novels that were produced during these
years, trying to read past the death or punishment of the lesbian character(s) at the end of
the novel to find some reinforcement for their erotic desires for women. Some read the
more lesbian-positive lesbian pulps, often written by lesbians like Ann Bannon.[85] One of
these lesbian pulp novels was The Women's Barracks. In 1952 the National News in Ottawa
was charged with "obscenity" for carrying The Women's Barracks. Even though the defence
argued that the book actually warned against lesbianism, it was decided that the presentation of lesbianism was too frank. National News was convicted.[86]

Men in Toronto and other cities in the 1950s were able to create what David Churchill
calls "gay sites" in parts of cities also used for other purposes. This included parks, washrooms, bars and the back rows of old movie theatres in downtown Toronto.[87] In the Ottawa

area gay men began to congregate in a section of the Chez Henri bar in Hull, in the old rail yards, in the Honeydew near the Chateau Laurier, in the parks and train station near the Chateau and in the tavern at the Lord Elgin. It was during World War II, that the Lord Elgin — built to house itinerant military officers — began to become a gay meeting place. Officers would even pick up enlisted personnel there.[88]

Jim Egan: Canada's First Gay Activist

As gay gathering places expanded in the large cities, gays and lesbians began organizing on social and political levels. A few Canadian lesbians and gays subscribed to U.S. homophile publications like the *Ladder*, put out by the lesbian organization the Daughters of Bilitis, *The Mattachine Review*, published by the Mattachine Society, and *One*, a homophile magazine. Homophile was generally used in early gay/lesbian groups to describe a relatively moderate orientation that expressed concerns about homosexual issues but was not necessarily defined as gay or lesbian.

In its March 1957 issue, *One* reprinted a letter from Canada Customs and Excise stating that one of its associated publications, *Homosexuals Today — 1956*, had been stopped at the border because of its "immoral and indecent" character.[89] A letter in the October 1959 issue from a Mr. E. in Toronto again mentioned the problems *One* was having with Canadian Customs. The same letter told of police raids on Toronto theatres frequented by gays. In one raid, a reported fifty men were arrested.[90]

Jim Egan, a gay small businessman who lived in the Toronto area until 1964, began writing letters and articles for various publications in 1949 with great persistence, commitment, and energy. Egan criticized anti-homosexual articles and defended the humanity of homosexuals, inspired by extensive readings of the literature on homosexuality — the writings of Walt Whitman, John Addington Symonds, and Edward Carpenter. He also read the U.S. homophile publications, attended a conference organized by *One* magazine, and was part of the original sample of "well-adjusted" gay men that Evelyn Hooker used in her psychological study.

In the 1950s Egan also wrote to various government committees on sex-related matters.[91] In 1955 he wrote to the Parliamentary Legislative Committee arguing for law reform. His letter included:

> The Negro "problem" was created by the white majority; the Jewish "problem" by the Gentile majority, and the homosexual "problem" by the heterosexual majority — who alone can take the necessary steps to bring this problem to a speedy end.[92]

Egan submitted material to "respectable" publications, like the *Toronto Star* and the *Telegram*, as well as to the scandal sheets or "yellow journals," whose lurid and homophobic accounts of the arrests and trials of gay men, says Egan, were just about the only news on gay issues.

> The only place you could get published information about homosexuality
> was in the scandal sheets. I would read those things and I would be abso-
> lutely outraged. If you didn't read those then there was very little opportu-
> nity to be exposed to it ... The large newspapers like the *Star* and the
> *Telegram* did not give very much publicity to this sort of thing. Of course,
> there was absolutely nothing even mentioned on a news broadcast.[93]

The "yellow journals" responded to pressure from Egan for more positive coverage of
homosexuality. *Justice Weekly* ran two series of his pioneering columns on homosexuality under the initials "J.L.E." The first series, "Homosexual Concepts," run in 1953-54,
recounted developments in England and discussed the Kinsey Report, the Mattachine
Society, *One*, and many other topics. The second series included a discussion of the
ways in which legislation criminalized homosexuality, the "national-security" campaigns against gays in the U.S. government, a defence of the term "gay," and an argument against the notion of gays as "corruptors" of youth.[94] Egan was the primary gay
activist in 1950s Toronto.

Egan also convinced *Justice Weekly* to reprint articles from the U.S. magazines *Mattachine Review*, *One*, and *The Ladder*, and for a number of years, it regularly published excerpts from these publications. *Justice Weekly* may have doubled as an important source
of information for gays and lesbians. Egan's columns, the reprints, and some advertisements provided a homophile or gay subtext. A regular advertiser in the mid-1950s, for
instance, was the St. Charles Tavern. The working-class gays who frequented the tavern
may have glanced at *Justice Weekly* and thus been introduced to the existence of a homophile movement for the first time, or a reader of *Justice Weekly* may have been able to figure out that the St. Charles was a gay hangout and had the information to find his first
"gay site." One woman that the Lesbians Making History collective interviewed reported
that she read some of these "scandal sheets":

> And of course there was a magazine, called, little crummy magazines —
> something like the National Enquirer, but in these magazines there were ad-
> vertisements, and they would be for gay women or gay men.[95]

This is how this woman found out about the Toronto lesbian and gay scene and
through reading this publication found her way to the Continental. These articles and
advertisements may have had double meanings that were capable of being read in a subversive fashion by gay and lesbian readers. Yellow journals also existed during these years
in Montréal.[96]

Egan, an important link in the piecing together of Toronto's and Canada's gay histories and who has remained involved in an important legal challenge in the 1990s, will
turn up again later in this chapter and in chapter 8. In a column published in the
Toronto Star in 1963 — prefiguring later campaigns in Ontario for sexual orientation
protection in the 1970s and 1980s, when the "respectable" media finally began to print
his submissions — Egan argued that:

The Ontario Human Rights Code must be amended so as to provide the same protection for the homosexual now accorded every other minority group in Ontario.[97]

Cleaning Up the Law?

Legal discourse surrounding the regulation of homosexuality began to shift in the post-war period, and in 1949 a federal commission was appointed to deal with inconsistencies in the Criminal Code.[98] When the Commission was instructed to prepare a draft bill in 1951, its terms of reference directed it to "revise ambiguous and unclear provisions," "adopt uniform language," "eliminate inconsistencies, legal anomalies, or defects," and propose "procedural amendments for the enforcement of the criminal law." As a result, in 1953-54 the Criminal Code was revamped, and while most of the changes simply represented a rationalization of the existing law, there were some substantive revisions regarding sex-related legislation. Sexual offences were shifted from "offences against morality" to a new section called "Sexual Offences."[99]

The revised code applied buggery only to acts between humans, separating it from bestiality, although they remained part of the same section. Most significantly, "gross indecency" was broadened from a male homosexual offence to cover "everyone who commits an act of gross indecency with another person." It remained undefined and even though by and large it continued to be used against gay men largely for oral sex, it now covered heterosexual and lesbian acts. This represented a significant departure from the development of "gross indecency" in England, where it has continued to apply only to male homosexual acts. "Criminal sexual psychopath" legislation was also expanded to include "buggery" and "gross indecency" as "triggering" offences, and this would have very serious consequences in the future as we will see later in this chapter.[100]

In the early 1950s, a select committee was appointed by the Ontario government to look into the problem of "delinquent" individuals in "reform" institutions.[101] Their report included a section on "sex deviates," defined as a threat to decency and morality, especially to children and women. The committee's major concern was whether these sex deviates were physically or psychologically sick and whether they could be cured. They were worried about releasing people who could not be "cured" in custody because they were removed from "normal sexual outlets." "Sex deviates," to the committee, included homosexuals as well as people who engaged in other types of sexual "offences." They also made a distinction between passive sexual deviates — who had accidentally developed "abnormalities" — and what they described as "sex perverts" or "psychopaths," who needed special treatment. The report relied on information provided by doctors, psychiatrists, scientists, and institutional personnel.

While the select committee reported relatively low conviction rates for buggery and gross indecency, they were disturbed by what they perceived as the widespread incidence of homosexuality, which they felt was not captured in these statistics.

> Relatively few inmates are incarcerated for the crime of homosexuality be-
> cause of apprehension. It is a generally disturbing fact ... that homosexual-
> ity exists in our society to a disturbing degree ... Homosexuality is a
> perplexing problem which custodial institutions attempt to handle with in-
> adequate facilities and inadequate staffs.[102]

The report expressed fears that the custodial system, with its gender segregation,
only facilitated homosexuality. It recommended outlawing the dormitory system, and it
also expressed the need for psychologists, doctors, and other trained personnel. Calling
for indefinite sentences for sex offenders so that they could be treated and kept out of
circulation, the report also argued for more scientific study into these matters.

Keeping Queers Out: Homosexualism and Immigration

An early component of Canada's participation in the U.S.-inspired national-security
campaigns against homosexuals was an amendment to the Immigration Act to keep homosexuals out.[103] Now, for the first time, an act of Parliament explicitly referred to the homosexual as "a status or a type of person." Previously, only the acts — "buggery" and "gross
indecency" — were officially discussed. The new 1952 Canadian Immigration Act treated
homosexuals as "subversives." The previous act had contained a clause denying admission
to people who had been convicted of "moral turpitude," and this was used to bar people
with a record of gross indecency and buggery.[104] People with "constitutional psychopathic
personality" were denied entry as well, and this terminology could very well have been used
to keep out lesbians and gay men.

The decision to revise the Immigration Act had been made in the fall of 1948
and an interdepartmental committee was struck to draw up the proposals. The first
draft called for the exclusion of "prostitutes, homosexuals, lesbians and persons coming to Canada for an immoral purpose." Later, in 1951, the proposal to include "lesbians" was dropped, and a clause that included "living on the avails of prostitution or
homosexualism" was added.[105] While there was some controversy over barring homosexuals, the RCMP was strongly in favour.[106] It should be kept in mind that this same
year the anti-gay and anti-lesbian security hunts were reaching a fever pitch south of
the border.

When the bill came up in the House of Commons in June 1952, there was no debate on the section relating to homosexuality, and it was quickly passed. The status of
homosexuals in the Immigration Act was not changed until 1977 after a series of commissions had heard protests regarding this policy from many lesbian and gay groups.[107]
While the effect of this legislation on prospective immigrants is not entirely clear, it is
known that many lesbians and gays did enter Canada in that period. It was, however, another weapon that could be used against lesbians and gay men. The inclusion of homosexuals and "homosexualism" in the Immigration Act, however, was symbolic of the
Cold War hostility to homosexuality that extends into the 1970s.

Queers, Commies, and "National Security"

The dominant political themes in the Western world of the late 1940s, the 1950s and into the 1960s were those of the Cold War. This climate helped set the stage for McCarthyism and anti-communist and anti-homosexual purge campaigns, and for increased police activity against homosexuals. Many gay men and lesbians were purged from the U.S. civil service and military. But these campaigns also sparked forms of lesbian and gay organization, such as the Mattachine Society and the Daughters of Bilitis in the U.S.[108] and limited forms of non-cooperation or "resistance" in Canada as well.

In right-wing, conservative, and often liberal discourse, homosexuals were either associated directly with communism and spying for the USSR or seen as an easy target for blackmail and therefore a risk to "national security" — whose security? we might ask. These campaigns in Canada were directed not only at communists and homosexuals but also at socialists, peace activists, trade unionists, immigrants, and the black community in Halifax, Nova Scotia in the late 1960s for suspected connections with the U.S. Black Panther Party.[109] Once someone was defined as a "national-security risk" they were cut out of regular social interaction, surveillance was mandated, and denial of basic human, civil and citizenship rights was justified.

Homosexuals were seen not only as violators of sexual and gender boundaries, but also as violators of class and political boundaries as well.

> Homosexual officials are a peril for us in the present struggle between West and East: members of one conspiracy are prone to join another ... many homosexuals from being enemies of society in general become enemies of capitalism in particular. Without being necessarily Marxist they serve the ends of the Communist International in the name of their rebellion against the prejudices, standards, ideals of the "bourgeois" world. Another reason for the homosexual-Communist alliance is the instability and passion for intrigue for intrigue's sake, which is inherent in the homosexual personality. A third reason is the social promiscuity within the homosexual minority and the fusion of its effects between upperclass and proletarian corruption.[110]

A series of trials and scandals in England meant that "homosexuality came to be associated with spying and treason."[111]

> Both in the United States and in Britain homosexuality came to be associated with moral unreliability and, like Communism, with treason. Guy Burgess represented the archetype of the unreliable pervert, in whom one proof of his sinister nature was his sexuality, another his Communism.[112]

In Canada, the anti-communist witch hunts were less extensive, although they were partially inspired by the U.S. investigations as well as pressure from American military and security officials.[113] Initial security screening focused on the Canadian Broadcasting Corporation and the National Film Board.[114]

A security panel established in 1946 as a small, secret committee of top civil servants and Mounties had formulated a policy of transferring to less sensitive posts civil servants about whom there were doubts. Then in 1948, the departments of national defence and external affairs were designated as "vulnerable" to subversion. In Canada, within the security regime, at first homosexuals were associated directly with communism. Later they were seen as vulnerable to "blackmail" since they suffered from a "character weakness" and had something to hide. In contrast, gay men and lesbians located the problems of blackmail that they faced in their lives in the practices criminalizing homosexual activities and the "security" campaign itself.

In the following decades, homosexuals in the civil service feared discovery and dismissal as scores of people were fired. Hundreds lost their jobs for "security" reasons in the late 1950s and 1960s. Within the security regime, a focus on homosexuals as the major "character weakness" making people vulnerable to compromise developed in 1958-1959.

The External Affairs department in Ottawa and its embassies around the world were seen by right-wingers as "a notorious cess-pool of homosexuals and perverts" in the 1950s.[115] No department, with the possible exception of the navy, was perceived to harbour more "queers." In 1960, therefore, all known homosexuals were arbitrarily fired from the department and surveillance was intensified.[116]

To get a taste of how this campaign was organized in Canada I begin with an excerpt from the official construction of homosexuality as a security problem in a national-security text: "Sexual abnormalities appear to be the favourite target of hostile intelligence agencies, and of these homosexuality is most often used ..." stated a 1959 Security Panel memorandum. The document goes on:

> The nature of homosexuality appears to adapt itself to this kind of exploitation. By exercising fairly simple precautions, homosexuals are usually able to keep their habits hidden from those who are not specifically seeking them out. Further, homosexuals often appear to believe that the accepted ethical code which governs normal human relationships does not apply to them. Their propensity is often accompanied by other specific weaknesses such as excessive drinking with its resultant instabilities, a defiant attitude towards the rest of society, and a concurrent urge to seek out the company of persons with similar characteristics, often in disreputable bars, night clubs or restaurants ... The case of the homosexual is particularly difficult for a number of reasons. From the small amount of information we have been able to obtain about homosexual behaviour generally, certain characteristics appear to stand out — instability, willing self-deceit, defiance towards society, a tendency to surround oneself with persons of similar propensities, regardless of other consideration — none

of which inspire the confidence one would hope to have in persons required to fill positions of trust and responsibility.[117]

The preceding quote comes from the previously secret government documents on
the anti-gay/anti-lesbian purge campaign in the Canadian civil service that Canadian
Press secured the release of through the Access to Information Act in 1992.[118]

The firings and transfers were carried out at the urging of the security panel, and
were based on confidential reports. These were mandated by the ideological constructions of "national security" and "character weaknesses." First, a series of groups were defined as risks to "national security," and second, some of these were seen as risks to
national security because they suffered from a "character weakness." This character-
weakness conceptualization was increasingly homosexualized in Canada.[119]

One question that I am interested in is how it was that the major focus in the Canadian national-security State against homosexuals took place from 1958-1959 on while
in the U.S. it began much earlier in the 1950s. I am not suggesting that there were no
anti-gay security investigations prior to 1958 in Canada since there clearly were many,
but that it seems that it was in 1958-1959 that a more specific focus on homosexuality as
a "security threat" developed in the Canadian State and the concept of "character
weakness" basically became homosexuality. There seems to have been an event in the
late 1950s that focused RCMP and Security Panel attention on "the homosexual" as a
"national-security threat."

There may have been a tie-in of the investigations following Leo Mantha's murder
of his estranged boyfriend Aaron Jenkins on September 6, 1958 on the Naden naval
base, at Esquimalt, B.C. and the initiation of a more central focus on homosexuals as a
security threat. In 1959 Mantha was the last person to be hanged in British Columbia.
He had earlier been discharged from the navy in 1956 partly for his homosexuality.
While discussions on clarifying the security panel's policies regarding "character weaknesses" had been initiated prior to Jenkins being murdered, the report that initiated the
more specific focus on homosexuals as a security threat, and from which I just quoted,
was presented on May 12, 1959.[120]

As part of the investigation of the murder of Jenkins by Mantha, RCMP officers were
sent to Victoria from Ottawa to assist in the investigation. They found a diary as part of the
evidence in the case that belonged to Jenkins and included the names of a number of gay
men in the military, merchant marine, and civilian gay networks on the west coast. We
know that a number of men in the military and outside it were interrogated as part of this
investigation and that a number of men presumed to be gay were either purged or transferred.[121] Bruce Somers, who at that time lived in Victoria, comments that prior to the
murder the gay networks that linked together men in the navy with civilians through a network of bars, washrooms, house parties, and even beach parties were relatively open and
not highly policed. Following the murder and the subsequent investigation, this all
stopped as many feared they would be called in for questioning.[122]

This investigation may have alerted the RCMP and the security panel to the ex-

tent of the possible homosexual "national-security threat" and sharpened the focus
on homosexuality in these discussions on the security panel and within the RCMP.
The Mantha investigation may also have alerted the RCMP and Naval Intelligence
that the conceptualization of homosexuality as "gender inversion" was not adequate
for detecting homosexuals.

The Mantha case gives us some insight into the gender assumptions of the anti-
homosexual practices in the military. Bud (Aaron) Jenkins, who Mantha would later
kill, went to get help from a navy neuropsychiatrist Dr. Douglas Alcorn after he was
stationed at H.M.C.S. Naden in 1957. Alcorn diagnosed Jenkins as a "Homosexual of
the feminine type," but in the same report concluded that the other sailors with
whom he had been intimate were "simply individuals who have fairly normal tastes,
but who wish to experiment in other ways."[123]

This suggests that at this time there was still a certain distinction being made in the
military between men who engaged in sex with others who had some of the marks of
"gender inversion" — who were in some ways the real "homosexuals" — and men who
might occasionally have sex with other men but in all other ways were "normal" and
"masculine." These men were not "real" homosexuals. This distinction was still largely
oriented around the gender-inversion conceptualization of homosexuality. George
Chauncey has found similar examples from the U.S. navy earlier in the century.[124]

With the emergence of homosexuality as a sexual-object choice, as a sexual orientation, and as a "character weakness," both these groups of men would now become suspect. Even the man who occasionally engaged in sex with other men but was otherwise
"masculine" could be blackmailed because he suffered from a "character weakness"
and had something to hide. To a certain extent the homosexualization of "character
weakness" and the identification of homosexuality as a major "national-security risk"
were also part of renegotiating the boundaries between homosexuality and heterosexual
masculinity that conflicted with other social trends I previously mentioned. Occasional
participation in same-gender sex now could place one beyond the boundaries of heterosexual masculinity. Now all men who had sex with other men — not just those who were
"effeminate" — could be targeted within the military and through the security campaigns. By expanding homosexuality to cover not only those men who were "effeminate," the number of men who could be homosexuals was expanded and the borders of
proper heterosexual masculinity were narrowed. However, this process took place unevenly within the practices of the military and the RCMP with many of the assumptions
of gender inversion continuing to inform their practices into the 1960s.

Of the more than 150 civil servants fired between 1956 and 1963, two-thirds lost
their jobs because of a "character weakness" such as homosexuality, which supposedly
left them open to subversion.[125] In 1952, at the height of anti-communism in the
U.S., a homosexual working in the Communications Branch, which intercepted radio
signals from the Soviet Union, was asked to resign. Others were "discovered" at the
Communications Branch in the late 1950s, and in 1963 a "ring" of homosexual code
clerks was uncovered. Some were transferred, others were fired. Philip Girard argues

that the homosexual witch hunt in Canada was much stronger than any campaign against leftists, socialists, or communists.[126]

RCMP policy, meanwhile, was to fire all known homosexuals even if they had no access to security information.[127] RCMP policy was also informed by the criminalization of homosexuality and, like the military, by a policy that prohibited the membership of lesbians and gay men in its own ranks. The RCMP set up an investigative unit within the force, called A-3, to hunt down, identify, locate, and purge homosexuals within its own ranks and in government generally. Informants watched bars and parks frequented by gays. They took photos of men going into bars and even inside bars that gay men frequented. Ottawa-area parks were swept to ensnare gay men and to try to collect the names of homosexuals.[128] Male homosexuals were known to inform on others, but lesbians apparently resisted, and their circles were not very accessible to male RCMP officers. The RCMP developed interrogation techniques to unearth homosexuals, who were then either forced to resign or were transferred. By 1963 the A-3 unit produced a map of Ottawa using red dots to designate homosexual activity. The map was soon so covered with red dots as to be practically useless.

By the mid-1960s, the security mood in the civil service mellowed somewhat and there were fewer firings;[129] however, the RCMP fought the security panel's new, more restricted policy and won at least tacit support for its broader ranging campaign. It initially maintained that all homosexuals were a security risk, then that they should be fired because homosexuality was illegal and the government should not be condoning it. It held to its view that all homosexuality was a criminal offence and a character weakness. Meanwhile, the RCMP discovered a "ring" of homosexuals in its own central-records section, and created its own internal homo-hunt unit; it developed a series of indicators of homosexuality, ranging from driving white cars, to wearing rings on pinkie fingers, to wearing effeminate clothing. The RCMP's internal investigations reportedly reached their peak just about when, in 1967, Justice Minister Pierre Trudeau introduced the proposal to decriminalize homosexual acts in private between two consenting adults. They collected close to 9,000 names of "suspected" and "confirmed" homosexuals by 1968 mostly, but not entirely, in the Ottawa area.[130] At the height of the security scares, the Security Service investigations extended to the universities and the community at large. By the 1980s, the Mounties had compiled files on 800,000 Canadians, including thousands of lesbians and gays.[131]

Many people's lives were affected by these security investigations including lesbians and gay men who may have been investigated for "communist" or "socialist" connections. Lesbians Making History collected the following story from one lesbian they interviewed. She is describing her sexual and personal relationship with another woman who was from the U.S.:

> We got together every weekend we could. We used to camp for the summers, and that was great. We had four kids together and everything was fine until this McCarthy thing came up. We both espoused left-wing causes, she

more than I. She was left-wing and her husband was a communist ... She and I ran some camps, international, interracial, and left-wing — it was advertised in the left-wing newspapers, you know, the *Tribune* ... My husband was working for the Department of National Defence at this point, in the early 1950s — it was the wrong time, and we got caught up in the Rosenberg murders — you know they were murdered, of course — and we were really working to try to prevent them from being murdered. ... But when all this happened to us, W. [her husband] was told he had to resign. And it was even mentioned, you know, the Rosenberg thing. ... So he lost his job and I was told I might lose mine. ... Somebody in the Department told W. they'd been following us; we'd been under twenty-four-hour surveillance because she had come up to Canada to live with us. And this is what the guy told W.: "The reason that this has happened is that friend of your wife's. Get rid of her." And so he came home and the whole world just collapsed again. They threatened me with losing my kids as well as losing my job. In fact they suggested that I give up teaching. It was "too sensitive a job" to work at![132]

There were also, however, signs of obstruction and resistance within security discourse itself based on the expansion of gay and lesbian community formation in the 1960s. The RCMP faced problems in its investigations with non-cooperation from homosexual "informants." In 1962-1963 they reported that:

During the past fiscal year the homosexual screening program ... was hindered by the lack of cooperation on the part of homosexuals approached as sources. Persons of this type, who had hitherto been our most consistent and productive informers, have exhibited an increasing reluctance to identify their homosexual friends and associates ...[133]

For 1963-64 the RCMP reported that given a "growing reluctance on the part of homosexuals to identify their associates, additional emphasis is being placed on establishing close liaison with the morality branches of police forces, particularly in the larger centres ..."[134] The "resistance," or non-cooperation of homosexuals in the face of this security campaign forced the RCMP to devise a new strategy to secure the cooperation of homosexual informants.[135]

The RCMP responded by developing working relationships with the morality branches of various police forces and enlisting local police support to procure homosexual informants. Given the criminalization of all homosexual activity, this meant that the police could "lean on" those who had committed "offences" and on street informants in order to get them to provide information to the RCMP. This extended RCMP powers of surveillance through local police forces and once again gives us a sense of the "power/knowledge" relations actively constructed through this security campaign. Later RCMP reports suggest that the situation improved in terms of getting homosexual informants to provide information after this relation with morality branches was put in place. More research is clearly needed on these forms of resistance and regulatory responses.

In September 1968, the Royal Commission on Security released its report. While the findings were never officially acted upon, we can see that the Commission condoned the generally anti-gay, anti-lesbian employment practices in the higher echelons of the civil service, particularly in those areas relating to security and defence.

> In general we do not think that past homosexual acts or even current stable homosexual relationships should always be a bar to employment with the public service or even to low levels of clearance. We feel ... that in the interest of the individuals themselves as well as the interest of the state, homosexuals should not be recruited if there is a possibility that they may require such clearance in the course of their careers and should certainly not be posted to sensitive positions overseas.[136]

Although the scale of the RCMP homosexual hunt decreased in the 1970s, it continued until recently at a lower level of intensity.[137]

Attempting to Develop a "Fruit Machine"

During the 1960s there was an attempt to develop a more efficient and "scientific" way of detecting lesbians and gay men which came to be known as the "fruit machine." This was both a continuation of and a shifting of earlier psychiatric and psychological practices for "detecting" homosexuals or "sex deviates" which had been institutionalized in the military in detection and disposal strategies for "psychopathic personalities with abnormal sexualities." Now homosexual was differentiated much more fully from these broader collecting categories, and increasingly from notions of gender inversion, for purposes of this security campaign. As in most other research, the "normality" of heterosexuality was assumed and homosexuality was defined as the problem.

Following up on the approval for such a study in the security-panel memo to cabinet in early 1961, Professor Wake of the Carleton University psychology department was funded to go to the U.S. by National Health and Welfare to research and study detection tests and technologies regarding homosexuality. He produced a report in 1962 which got the "fruit machine" research going.[138] This research continued to be funded by National Health and Welfare. A critical analysis of Wake's special-project proposal gives us insight into the social character of this research and its interrelation with the social-power relations mobilized through the security campaign. This is why I spend a bit of time here analyzing this research attempt.

This "fruit machine" research arises both from an interest by Wake in doing research on homosexuality (disguised as an interest in "suitability" for employment) and

also to establish a more effective, efficient and cheaper mode of surveillance and investigation than that of RCMP field investigations.

The name "fruit machine" was given to this project, according to John Sawatsky, by
members of the RCMP who did not want to be recruited to be the "normals" who were
to be tested on it.[139] The technique used included the measurement of pupils while
showing the subject pictures including those of naked men and women. The "fruit machine" project involved psychiatrists, psychologists, and the departments of national defence and national health and welfare for a period of four years, but it never worked
and the Defence Research Board eventually cut its funding. The research suffered from
major technical problems as well as problems with getting the numbers of "research
subjects" that were needed for the research; there were problems getting gay men, and
especially lesbians, to participate in the "fruit machine" detection research.

Dr. F.R. Wake, in his 1962 "Report on Special Project," stressed from his review of
the research — especially in the U.S. — that there was no single method of tests that can
detect homosexuality and that instead a battery of tests is necessary. Wake's report and
research are based on a review of the professional literature and his investigations of detection research while he was in the U.S. He takes up a general standpoint that there is
something wrong with homosexuals which makes them unsuitable for certain positions,
that they can be identified, and their behaviour controlled.

Wake was quite aware of the "liberal" psychological and sexological work then going on in the U.S. including the work of Evelyn Hooker critiquing the notion of male
homosexuals as "unstable" and the Kinsey reports. He is even aware of the distinction
being made between overt and covert homosexuals used by Hooker that was developed
in the work of Maurice Leznoff on male homosexuals in Montréal.[140] Although Wake
knew about and used this more "liberal" work, he linked it to a more investigative and
control-oriented perspective. Later he stated that "The general run of opinion ... is that
homosexuals almost always are maladjusted" even though he referred to Hooker as
holding a contrasting opinion.

As a result of his research, he argued that there is no distinct homosexual personality type. This is a shift away from notions of homosexuals as gender inverts and
away from notions of homosexuals as psychopathic personalities. Since Wake argued
there was no single, distinct homosexual personality type there could be no single
test. Under "Methods of Detecting Homosexuality," he surveyed the various detection
tests and procedures that had been used to try to identify homosexuals. These ranged
from psychiatric interviews, to medical examinations, to various tests for changes in
emotional conditions.[141]

In his commentary, Wake suggested that the Palmer Sweat test would be best used
in conjunction with a "word association" test. Words with definite homosexual meaning
according to the appended list include queen, circus, gay, bagpipe, bell, whole, blind,
bull, camp, coo, cruise, drag, dike (dyke), fish, flute, fruit, mother, punk, queer, rim,
sew, swing, trade, velvet, wolf, blackmail, prowl, bar, house, club, restaurant, tea room,
and top men.[142]

Wake found the Pupillary Response test to be quite "productive" in looking for homosexuals. It measured different interest patterns by means of a machine which simultaneously projected a visual stimulus and photographed the pupil of the eye. This procedure was supposed to produce an involuntary "response that cannot be controlled by the subject." Wake discovered this procedure and technology through his research in the U.S. E.H. Hess and J.M. Polt, researchers at the University of Chicago, had developed this test and apparatus. Professional- and academic-knowledge relations are directly tapped into in this security-based research.

Wake's report refers to a study done using the Hess-Polt apparatus by Hess's graduate student Allan Seltzer. In Seltzer's study the "stimuli were slides made of pictures from physical culture magazines (some of which were near pornographic) plus neutral pictures of good paintings and at least one modified picture of Christ on the cross." This use of physique magazines, which often had a large gay male readership,[143] seems to have become common in the U.S. by this point; they were also being used in aversion therapy. It also suggested some awareness of the formation of gay men's cultures during these years. Wake argued that the

> results clearly permitted Seltzer to distinguish the homosexual subject when the results of *all* pictures were compared. No single picture would determine who was homosexual and who heterosexual. Not only was the change in size of pupil indicative of the direction of sex interest but the pattern followed by the eyes (and recorded on film) was very important (e.g., the homosexual who could not take his eyes away from the genital area of the vaguely-seen Christ on the Cross) ... Perhaps the most important incidental finding in this experiment was the confession of a homosexual subject who reported that he had done his best to defeat the machine but knew he had failed. ... Here, then, is a most promising instrument for detection, not only of homosexuals but of homosexual potentiality.

Wake proposed the following research experiment that would combine

> the Hess-Polt pupillary test with suitable visual stimuli; a measure of skin perspiration ...; the plethysmograph with a modification to measure pulse rate. Subjects: Fifteen normal males; fifteen normal females; fifteen homosexual males; fifteen homosexual females. As the experiment progresses, additional normal and homosexual subjects in unspecified numbers. All subjects to be supplied by the RCMP...[144]

The RCMP, which was the chief investigative arm of the security campaign, was also to provide the "research subjects." Here we have another side of the construction of power/knowledge relations in this research context. Also notice the language through which heterosexuality is constructed as "normal." At the same time, heterosexuality is also not specifically named as such since this was prior to "heterosexuality" more fully emerging as a popular term which historically follows the rise of gay liberation and lesbian feminism in the 1970s and 1980s. Also notice the equal emphasis placed on "homosexual females" in the research design.

Then Wake outlined the procedure to be used:

> The experimental stimuli will be pictures designed to elicit the subject's interest in males and females ... The first sixty subjects will be processed to determine the reaction patterns of normals and homosexuals. Then, using these patterns as criteria, the experimenter will attempt to distinguish homosexual's presented by the RCMP, where nothing of the subject is known to the research team. Those methods proving successful will be retained for continuing research.

This research is more psychologically oriented than earlier studies that sometimes focused on biological anomalies (like marks of gender inversion on the body for instance).[145] It is directed at finding a "scientific" means to test "involuntary" responses that demonstrate sexual orientation. This is based on a series of assumptions about the relation between stimulus and response, about the power of visual images as stimulators, about common responses of homosexuals as viewers, and an assumption of there being two, and only two, dichotomous and essential sexualities (men or women who were sexually interested in both men and women would have undermined their assumptions).

Predictably there were many problems in trying to get this experiment to work. In a 1963 memo to the secretary of the security panel, J.R.M. Bordeleau, RCMP Assistant Commissioner, and Director of Security and Intelligence, wrote:

> While we are most anxious to assist Dr. Wake in his research programme we feel that we cannot meet his request in its entirety. We are in the process of contacting known male homosexuals in this area [Ottawa] and soliciting their co-operation in the proposed tests, however we are not yet in a position to determine how many will volunteer for the project ... We have no contacts within the female homosexual community in this area and no safe ground upon which an approach might be made to these persons. In this respect, we would suggest that other government departments, who will benefit directly from the results of the tests, might be requested through your office, to solicit the co-operation of female homosexuals known to them ... We have some doubts also as to the propriety of our soliciting normal females to participate in the tests. We believe that this should be undertaken by some government department or departments which have a large pool of female employees under their control. ... Similarly we believe that the required number of normal males should be drawn from the government service at large ...[146]

The RCMP had very little contact with lesbian networks during these years and were quite apprehensive about approaching "normal" women for this research. This account also suggests that there was resistance to participation in this research from RCMP members themselves. As Sawatsky suggests RCMP members did not want to be determined to be "fruits" through participating as "normals" in this experiment.[147]

The 1965-66 DSI Annual Report reported that "to date the tests have been inconclusive, the main obstacle to the Program being a lack of suitable subjects for testing purposes." In the same report of 1966-67 they stated that, "although the research group has made some progress, the objective has not, as yet been achieved." A major problem in the operationalizing of the experiment was with perfecting the technology itself, which had to be adapted to deal with people of different heights, with different-sized pupils and different distances between eyeballs.[148] The assumption was that there would be some sort of discernible difference in the responses of homosexuals and "normals." They were never able to demonstrate this and their underlying assumption of a difference in response in relation to homosexuality/heterosexuality was destabilized. The "fruit machine" never worked and it was abandoned in 1967.

The Armed Forces and "Sex Deviates"

During these years and tied into the "national-security" campaigns, the armed forces routinely discharged lesbians and gays upon "discovery." Earlier prohibitions of sodomy and buggery, and the classification of "psychopathic personality with abnormal sexuality," were carried over into contemporary military organization.

Women in the military were routinely purged as suspected lesbians during these years under military regulations. For instance, a Franco-Ontarian woman was discharged from the Royal Canadian Air Force in the mid-1950s for being a lesbian. She was given an honourable discharge for medical reasons and was deemed to be unsuitable for further service. There was also mention of the danger of blackmail because she was a lesbian.[149] Over the last two decades women have been the most visible of those purged from the military. While the military is male dominated, it also provides for economic and social survival for women who wish to survive outside marriage and family. Anti-lesbian policies, however, have worked to keep all women in line as part of the military's sexist organization.

In 1966, the Toronto gay magazine *Two* printed an interview with George Marshall, who had been involved in *Gay*, another mid-1960s Toronto publication. Marshall reports that discharge for homosexuality during the Korean war would have prevented him from receiving a pension. He had been in the army for twelve years and says that the buddy system worked as a cover for his gay affairs. His "army marriages" were long-lasting — one surviving as long as five years. Homosexuals were automatically given a special rating, says Marshall, since "according to government authorities (all) homosexuals are emotionally unstable — unable to accept authority, unable to tell the difference between right and wrong."[150] While it was possible for privates or corporals to be

closeted homosexuals since they needed only a Confidential Clearance, officers required a Secret Clearance, which meant a security check involving an RCMP investigation. Marshall repeatedly got drunk in order to avoid promotion, since "promotion
would mean exposure."[151] When he was finally being processed for promotion, the
RCMP investigated his life for a full ten years prior to his joining the army. He describes them as "pretty ruthless" when it comes to this sort of thing. He was subjected
to various tests which showed him to be "extremely masculine" and to a questionnaire
of 350 multiple-choice questions from one of the masculinity/femininity tests. But the
RCMP discovered him to be homosexual: "They even claimed I'd been a homosexual
prostitute. The bastards even knew I'd been buying pornographic physique photos
from a firm in Sweden."[152] Marshall had to fight for an "honourable discharge" and
was successful only because of a conflict between the psychiatrists and the medical doctors over his case because of his "masculine" appearance. Some of them apparently still
accepted that only "gender inverts" were "true" homosexuals.

Bert Sutcliffe, whom we met earlier, was purged from the military for his homosexuality in 1962. Just prior to his being posted to the Pentagon as an integrated Canadian
officer in G-2 (intelligence), the director of military intelligence told him, "The RCMP
has confirmed that you are a Homosexual." Within three days, Sutcliffe's career was
over. He was honourably discharged.[153]

The 1969 reform which de-criminalized adult homosexual acts in "private" was not
extended to the armed services. Men and women could no longer be expelled for engaging in "private" acts with one other adult under article 103.61 ("Offences Against
Other Canadian Law") of the military's Queen's Regulations and Orders, which is
based on the National Defence Act.[154] There existed, however, a number of other provisions under which they could be discharged. These included: article 103.25, "Scandalous Conduct by Officers"; 103.26, "Cruel or Disgraceful Conduct"; and 103.60,
"Conduct to the Prejudice of Good Order and Discipline." People accused of engaging
in same-gender sex have also been dismissed under Release Section S.D. of the Queen's
Regulations, "Not Advantageously Employable." A 1967 version of the Canadian Forces
Administrative Order (CFAO 19-20, 1967) calls for the removal of homosexuals and
others displaying a sexual abnormality. The order, "Sexual Deviation — Investigation,
Medical Examination and Disposal," clearly lays out the procedure for dealing with sex
deviates.[155] The deviant behaviour is to be reported to the commanding officer, who
will then investigate the case with the help of a medical officer, the military police, and
other means "at his disposal." If the investigation substantiates the allegation, the commanding officer will call in the Special Investigative Department (SID, later SIU), who
will carry out interrogation and surveillance of personal correspondence. All this in a
situation wherein the suspect has few rights under military law — in other words, anyone suspected of lesbianism or homosexuality is subject to unrestricted surveillance and
harassment.[156] If necessary, a psychiatric examination can be ordered. A copy of the investigation report, the SID report, and the medical report are then forwarded to the
Canadian Forces Headquarters along with the base commander's recommendations. If

the behaviour has "scandalized" other service members, or "brought discredit" to the forces, disciplinary action will be taken. If not, they will simply be "disposed" of — to use the military's own language.

Criminal Sexual Psychopaths and Dangerous Sexual Offenders

A central aspect of the strategy to regulate homosexuality by extending criminalization was criminal-sexual-psychopath legislation. This legislation participated in constructing homosexuality as criminal sexual danger.

In 1948, a section on "criminal sexual psychopaths" was added to the Canadian Criminal Code. It was tied into the same part of the Criminal Code as the "habitual offenders" section. A criminal sexual psychopath was defined as

> a person who by a course of misconduct in sexual matters has evidenced a lack of power to control his sexual impulses and who as a result is likely to attack or otherwise inflict injury, loss, pain or other evil on any person.[157]

The legislation mandated a course of action linking several State and professional sites together — the Criminal Code, the police, the office of the attorney general, psychiatry, and the prison system. The course of action first required a police arrest and conviction on certain specified "triggering" sex offences. These "triggering" offences were largely offences that could only be committed in the "public" realm. They did not include incest and, given prevailing legal and police practices, they ignored most sexual violence and harassment in the household or domestic realm. Also, given the legal impossibility during these years of a husband raping his wife, they were focused on men who committed sexual offences coming from outside the domestic/familial realm.

When dealing with these certain named sexual offences (not including in 1948 buggery or gross indecency but including "indecent assault" on a male), a court could now hear evidence as to whether the offender was a "criminal sexual psychopath." Following conviction on a triggering offence or offences, a sentencing procedure to declare a person a criminal sexual psychopath could be initiated with the approval of the attorney general. If the defendant was thus sentenced (in part based on psychiatric testimony) as to whether he fit the definition of criminal sexual psychopath, he could be sentenced for an "indefinite period." This legislation was passed after criminal-sexual-psychopath laws had been enacted in more than half the U.S. states following Michigan's example in 1938 (which, incidentally, was later ruled unconstitutional).[158] The language used in the Canadian legislation was taken from a 1947 Massachusetts statute.[159] These Canadian and American criminal-sexual-psychopath laws were the result of a media focus on violent sex crimes, particularly against children and organizing efforts by psychiatrists, other professionals and some politicians. There was the construction of an attempted moral panic on these questions. In this context, U.S. legislatures turned to psychiatrists for answers, and it was at their urgings that many of the new laws were passed. These laws and the discussions surrounding them generally recognized homo-sexuality as a socially-threatening disease.

In Canada, "buggery" and "gross indecency" were added to the list of offences that could trigger criminal-sexual-psychopath legislation in 1953. All homosexual-related of-fences then became triggering offences. Homosexual sexual activity discovered or re-ported by the police and resulting in conviction could then make one subject to the criminal-sexual-psychopath procedure. This further blurred the distinction between various sexual activities, lumping together violent and non-violent and consensual and non-consensual acts. It also further intensified the focus on sexual danger being in the public realm. As part of this procedure, psychiatric evidence was crucial. In establishing whether the person fit the criminal-sexual-psychopath definition, this procedure was or-ganized at two different levels of "inscription": first through the "triggering" sex of-fence of the Criminal Code, and second, through the definition of criminal sexual psychopath at sentencing.

The criminal-sexual-psychopath process of "inscription" is therefore more complex than just the transformation of people's activities (which might have been experienced as sexual pleasure) into sex-offence categories. The procedure is coordinated and or-ganized at a number of sites. Through this procedure, psychiatric and criminal practices intersected to regulate the lives of some gay men.

Philip Girard points out that this law has generally been most severe when used against homosexual "offenders," even when no violence is involved and when the rela-tionships have a consensual character.[160] In a situation where all gay sex was technically illegal, when these became "triggering offences," this section could be used in a more severe fashion against men having sex with other men and with adolescent boys than against people engaging in heterosexual acts that may in contrast have involved vio-lence and force. In official and police circles, the rape of a woman by a man was seen as more of a "normal" crime and therefore much less likely to be captured within crimi-nal-sexual-psychopath definitions than if one committed a homosexual act or an activity with a young person, even if less or even no violence or coercion were involved. As Freedman states referring to the U.S. situation:

> As long as he did not mutilate or murder his victim, the rapist might be con-sidered almost normal and certainly more "natural" than men who commit-ted less violent, and even consensual, sexual acts such as sodomy and pedophilia. Accordingly, men diagnosed as psychopaths were more likely to be accused of pedophilia and homosexuality than of rape or murder.[161]

"Psychopaths" were visualized as a small group of men that suffered from a lack of power to control their sexual impulses. The ideological framing of homosexuals as sex crazed melded easily with this sexual psychopath frame.

The criminal-sexual-psychopath definition and procedure focused on "deviant" males outside local, familial forms of regulation as the sexual danger. Criminal sexual psychopaths were not usually family members of those they were convicted of committing offences in relation to (in particular the fathers or husbands) when we know that much sexual violence against women and young people was taking place in these contexts.[162]

Public and political controversy surrounding the inadequacy of this legislation led to the appointment of a Royal Commission in 1954 (known as the McRuer Commission, after its chair) to study the criminal-sexual-psychopath sentencing procedure. The major problem for the government and the mass media was that there did not seem to be enough sentences under these provisions. This set up a contradictory situation with media coverage producing a sense of fear and anxiety which was out of proportion to the numbers actually sentenced as criminal sexual psychopaths. This allowed the legislation to be criticized for not being effective enough, for letting sex criminals slip through its grasp, and to be released where they could again be a "threat." There were even criticisms that these men were being released without any "treatment."

Royal Commissions are textually mediated processes.[163] The terms of reference given to a Royal Commission by the government are central to guiding how it accomplishes its work.[164] The mandate given to the McRuer Commission did not question the "triggering" sex offences in the Criminal Code or the indefinite detention provision. The commission was not asked to study sexuality or sexual danger as it was experienced in all its diversities. Rather, its mandate focused on sexual danger in the "public" realm to which the triggering offences referred.

The work and terms of reference of the commission thus presupposed the basic features of the criminal-sexual-psychopath section and related triggering offences; it presupposed the criminalization of homosexuality. Its terms of reference allowed for the holding in place while shifting — from a limited administrative standpoint — of this sentencing procedure and this section of the Criminal Code. This served to remove the focus of the commission's work from the heterosexual family and household as a terrain of sexual danger. The terms of reference therefore provided for a patriarchal and heterosexist account of sex and gender troubles since they ignored the social and historical grounds of the organization of violence against women and young people. In the work of the commission in trying to determine who was a criminal sexual psychopath, or their preferred conceptualization of dangerous sexual offender, "homosexuality" was often the main example used. Homosexuality thereby became central to the work of the commission. These terms of reference also provide the basis for excluding the accounts and experiences of gay men, as we will see, and also for the exclusion of the Wolfenden law-reform perspective.

The McRuer Commission was composed of the Chief Justice of the High Court of Ontario, an assistant medical superintendent, and a County Court Judge. One of the researchers was Professor Wake of Carleton University whom we have already met. It held hearings in thirteen cities providing an opportunity for the media to construct "public opinion" on these questions across the Canadian State. It heard the testimony of many "experts" — psychiatrists, psychologists, lawyers, doctors, professors, social workers, police officers, and government bureaucrats, and relied on RCMP records as well as studies of "sex offenders" in England, California, and Michigan.[165] The work of the commission was embedded in networks of ruling State and professional relations.

It also received several letters and at least one private-session submission from gay men. Much of the proceedings were taken up with a debate over whether "sexual psychopath" was an adequate classification and whether the prison system or psychiatrists and doctors should have jurisdiction over these offenders. This was part of a conflict then going on within and between the psychiatric and legal profession and criminal-justice system over the definitions of sex offences and who should treat and confine the offenders. Many of the psychiatrists, as well as the commission itself, suggested substituting "dangerous sexual offender" for "criminal sexual psychopath" to emphasize that the person so designated is likely to inflict injury or pain on others. The conceptual framework of the commission report was defined by an argument for changing the definition in this sentencing section. It argued that dangerous sexual offender would be less psychiatrically defined, and therefore would be an easier category under which people could be sentenced.

The report of the McRuer Commission grouped together homosexual offenders and "dangerous sexual offenders." While some of the deputations that the committee heard argued that all homosexuals should be imprisoned as such, others suggested that only those engaged in "public" acts or those involved with boys should be dealt with harshly.[166] There were a range of submissions, including some that had a more "liberal" character that were influenced by the emerging Wolfenden reform approach, and that even mentioned the problems of "blackmail" that the legal situation created for homosexuals.

Rev. Francis Howard Kelly Greer of St. Mark's Rectory in Halifax, referring to a young person involved in sex with an older man, said:

> The thing that happens in a certain number of these cases is that a quite young person, quite an inexperienced person, is faced with the full majesty of the law, which is a more terrifying experience in some ways ... than the actual sexual encounter itself may have been. One of the things that we would like to see a change made in is possibly the legal process by which some of these cases are handled ... I can give you an example of that kind of thing that happened when I was doing seaman's welfare work. There was a boy of, I think he was over sixteen, who came to Halifax looking for a job and was picked up by a rather older man with whom he lived in a homosexual relationship for some time. The reason that that happened was the boy was here all alone and the older man was decent to him in one way or another. For some reason this came to the attention of the police, and they were hauled into court and the boy was sent to serve a sentence at Rockhead, which of course was very unsatisfactory also, because all that happened there was that he learned rather more about what he already had begun to do.[167]

Greer also stated:

> In some of the sexual offences the way that the law reads now there is a ter-
> rible danger of a kind of blackmail which does go on ... This man, who is an
> overt homosexual, was robbed and quite badly beaten by somebody he
> knew, but he was unable to do anything about it because he would have
> been charged ... with an offence that would have gotten him fourteen years,
> or five years and lashes ...

Greer also suggested the commission look to the work currently going on in England
pointing to the discussion in some church circles and the initiation of the Wolfenden
committee. In response, McRuer interrupted and responded to this local "liberal"
social-work account telling Greer that this did not come "within the scope of this
Commission" and he basically narrowed the mandate of the commission to the definition clause of the criminal-sexual-psychopath section. Greer also suggested that the
situation might be improved if this activity was not always dealt with as criminal and
that this would decrease the possibility of blackmail. In response to Greer's concerns
McRuer asserts:

> I do not think it comes within the purview of our Commission, within our
> terms of reference, to decide what changes ought to be made in the crimi-
> nal law with respect to these various offences. I think we are restricted to
> this classification of the so-called psychopathic sexual offender as defined in
> the Code.

The terms of reference were used here to exclude interest in the Wolfenden reform
process which had just been launched and also to exclude the concerns of blackmail regarding gay men. This gives us a glimpse into the work process of the commission.

The final report of the commission was released in 1958, a year after the Wolfenden
Report came out in England, and argued that mere conviction for a homosexual act
should not be grounds for an indeterminate sentence but that the matter should be left
up to the courts.[168] The relationship between "dangerous sexual offender" and homosexual "offenders" would become an important terrain of legal and political struggle in
the 1960s.

Axel Otto Olson: "I don't believe the sex deviate ... is the main problem"

There was, however, one gay voice raised in protest to the commission itself. At one
of the commission's private sessions, Axel Otto Olson, then living in Toronto, raised several objections. He was one of the few "non-expert" witnesses to give testimony before
the commission. He is, in part, the "other" (the "sex deviate" speaking for himself) that
the McRuer Commission totally denies in its final report. There is not a trace left of his

submission for those reading the final report; it has been completely obliterated as part of the construction of a consensus on the criminal "problem" of homosexuality.[169]

Olson, speaking in a very different first-hand voice than that of the authoritative commissioners and their counsel, detailed in his testimony, blackmail attempts against himself and other men which followed accusations of homosexuality and which were carried out by "certain police officers, court officials, and members of religious youth organizations." Like other gay men during these years, he located the very real problems of blackmail that they faced in the laws criminalizing homosexuality, in police actions, in the "security" campaigns, and in heterosexist social practices. He described being falsely charged with having sex with boys and being dragged to the police station and through the courts in Montréal where he was kept in jail for several weeks. He was denied the right to make a phone call and spent a week at the Bordeaux jail without seeing anyone. His experiences led him to a somewhat speculative and conspiratorial account of the organization of police activity since he could not fully grasp from his local situation the broader social organization of police activity. At the same time, he does make visible how the anti-gay campaigns of the 1950s had powerful support in sections of the State apparatus.

Olson went on to argue that there were not "any more sex offenders to-day than there was twenty-five or fifty years ago" and that the current furore was largely a media scare. The government, he said, was investigating and blackmailing men in the civil service. It was "almost impossible to teach school," said Olson, "because if you are friendly with the pupils you run the risk of being accused of being homosexual or a sex deviate." In his opinion, the blackmailers were the "most serious problem." This was an important reversal or inversion of hegemonic discourse. He went on:

> There are a minority of people, who from no fault of their own, most of them from birth probably, have never been able to love a woman or have any sexual relations with a woman. Apparently such persons were meant to be female, but by some freak of nature had the outward appearance of being a male person, but inwardly they had all the characteristics, all the feelings and desires, of a woman. The doctors and psychiatrists, I have talked to some of them, and they claim there is no cure whatsoever for these people; so what are they going to do?

In this reverse or counter discourse, Olson used the congenital-invert theory[170] to argue against legal persecution. Later in his testimony, after referring to André Gide's *Corydon*, he stated:

> This author claims that by nature it is natural for any person, regardless of sex, to fall in love with another person of the same sex, and it is only by convention and by enforcing laws trying to put men and women together and so on that it has been possible. I believe that about fifty percent of the male

population at some time or other during their lives have had sexual relations with another person of the same sex.

Olson also offered this view:

> I believe as far as the state and the police are concerned, sexual relationships between persons of the same sex — or a different sex; it doesn't matter — in private, if the person is over sixteen years old, should not be considered an offence as far as the state is concerned.

In taking this position, Olson was influenced by some of the European experiences of sexual-law reform, particularly law reform in his homeland of Denmark. He was also influenced by homophile organizing in Europe and possibly in the U.S. and the emerging Wolfenden perspective.

An account based on the experience of a gay men was clearly what the commission did not want to hear. Throughout his presentation, Olson was interrupted by the examiner for the commission. At one point Chairman McRuer stated:

> I cannot see that what you are saying is relevant to our terms of reference. If you have something to contribute about our specific law and what amendments ought to be made to it, then we want to hear you, but this record is not for the purpose of reviewing complaints about the administration of justice ...

When Olson stated that: "I believe that blackmailing should be a very serious offence" Justice McRuer responded that blackmail was "not one of the things within the compass of our terms of reference."[171] This was the active mobilization of the terms of reference as an exclusion device typical in official commission-work processes. Olson had more to say but the commissioners were eager to put an end to his testimony. The Chair concluded: "Well, I think probably what you have stated will be quite sufficient for us."[172]

Olson's remarkable story of resistance, albeit couched in the available psychiatric, sexological and homophile languages of the day, as well as the commission's treatment of him, says much about the clash between the world of official legal discourse and the experiences of gay men. The prevailing heterosexist social relations and the commission's restricted mandate precluded its hearing what Olson had to say. What he was telling them was outside their interpretation of their mandate since they were attending to quite different concerns and were unable to take up the standpoints of gay men. The evidence, knowledge, and data that the work of the commission and its report relies on and embodies, which is largely of a police or psychiatric character, has an administrative relation to the lives of gay men. Again the terms of reference given to the commission play a crucial part in this organizing "out" of the experiences of gay men. A rupture or line of fault exists between the official discourse of the commission and the experience and narrative provided by Olson. As Robert Champagne comments regarding Olson's testimony:

> The Royal Commission provides us with a means to explore the tendency of officially mandated commissions of inquiry to ignore, subvert and reinterpret the actual lived experiences of gays and lesbians and to construct accounts of our lives as problematic and in need of regulation.[173]

"Homosexuality is a constant problem for the Police ..."

The commission believed, in contrast, that there were "profound problems raised by homosexuality."[174] On this matter they relied heavily on police data and deputations. A submission by Chief Constable John Chisholm of the Toronto Police Force was quoted extensively in the final report:

> Homosexuality is a constant problem for the Police of large cities, and if the Police adopt a laissez-faire attitude ... city parks, intended for the relaxation of women and children and youth recreation purposes, will become rendezvous for homosexuals. In addition to his immoral conduct, the homosexual requires Police attention, as he is often the victim of gang beatings, or robbery with violence, and is easy prey for the extortionist and blackmailers. Homosexuals have been stabbed and wounded and in a few cases have been murdered. The saddest feature of all, however, is that homosexuals corrupt others and are constantly recruiting youths into their fraternity.[175]

Chief Chisholm was later reported as saying that "marital status of suspects is no guide to the Police in sex investigations, as both married and single men are found in the ranks of homosexuals and other sex offenders."[176]

Jim Egan would later brilliantly contest and deconstruct Chisholm's account, and it is worth quoting extensively from it as a critique of Chisholm's remarks and of the standpoint the commission adopted. After reading the final report of the commission, which included Chisholm's comments, Egan wrote the following:

> The Report under discussion lists 81 organizations and 100 individuals who either submitted briefs or personally appeared before the Commission. Need it be said that no reference appears to any representation on behalf of the homosexual minority? Is it any wonder, then, that the Commission findings as regards homosexuality were much less than fair or favorable. Since it is largely upon the briefs and evidence that the Commission bases its findings, it is hard to see how they could have arrived at conclusions other than those set out in their Report ... On the other hand, apparently deemed of such value as to warrant inclusion in the Report itself, we have excerpts from the

evidence of Chief of Police (Toronto) Chisholm relating to homosexuality ... His evidence which follows, with comments, is a typical masterpiece of libel, distortion, innuendo and gross misrepresentation.

"Homosexuality is a constant problem for the Police in larger centres": note the word "constant." It insinuates that every day and night the police are dealing with homosexual offenders or "problems" — obviously untrue. Not even "some of the police" but "the police" — every one of them ... When do they have the time to arrest bankrobbers or put parking tickets on cars? ...

"And if the Police adopt a laissez-faire attitude toward such individuals, City Parks, intended for the relaxation of women and children and youth recreation purposes will become rendezvous for homosexuals": certainly no one will accuse the Chief's uniformed bully-boys of a "laissez-faire attitude" — but despite this lack there are a number of Toronto parks that are, and have been for years, homosexual rendezvous without interfering in the slightest with the "relaxation of women and children etc."

The reason for this, which the Chief just forgot to mention (an honest slip, no doubt) is that the homosexual who "cruises" the park invariably does so long after dark and long after the women and children are so relaxed as to be sound asleep at home ...

"In addition to his immoral conduct, the homosexual requires further Police protection, as he is often the victim of gang beatings, or robbery with violence, and is easy prey for the extortionist and blackmailer": note the skill with which the phrase "his immoral conduct" is used. Not "some homosexual immoral conduct" but his — implying that all homosexuals are per se: immoral. And just imagine! Not only are all homosexuals immoral, but they (deliberately?) get beaten up and murdered just to make more work for the long-suffering Police — who, one might think, if properly attending to the "constant problem," should be able to prevent the "robberies with violence and gang beatings" — or do they really care? No doubt it escaped the Chief's attention that only the unjust anti-homosexual laws make it possible to beat, rob, murder and blackmail the homosexual with virtual impunity. And by the vindictive manner of the laws' enforcement by both police and courts, the criminals are actually encouraged to victimize the homosexual.[177]

Unfortunately the voices of Olson and Egan were not listened to in the work process of the McRuer Commission. Instead the commission took up the standpoint of the police against gay men. Invoking its terms of reference in this way enabled the commission to exclude the experiences of gay men, to rule that blackmail and violence against gays was not relevant to its task.

In the conclusion of its report, the commission argued for the establishment of a new category, "dangerous sexual offender," to replace "criminal sexual psychopath."

The report formalized the official intersection and interaction between psychiatrists and the police, courts, and penal system. In order to label someone a "dangerous sexual offender," the court would have to hear the testimony of at least two psychiatrists.[178] The report also called for the extension of out-patient services to released offenders, for the education of parents, teachers, and those who care for the young, on the topic of sexual deviation, and for intensive "research in all aspects of sexual deviation, with a view to the development of means of correction and punishment."[179]

Parliament did not deal with the McRuer proposals until 1961, when the recommendations regarding "dangerous sexual offender" were adopted. Meanwhile, the legislation drafters at the department of justice added a new clause: "Or who is likely to commit another sexual offence,"[180] apparently to give an alternative definition so that the sentencing rate would increase. As we will see, this added clause would come to mean that someone convicted of "gross indecency" with consenting men or adolescent boys could be classified as a dangerous sex offender. The legislation was passed in 1961. The strategy of extending the criminalization of homosexuality, while shifting it in a limited way from criminal sexual psychopath to dangerous sexual offender, was fundamentally held in place.

This helped set up a dynamic tension to be explored in the next chapter between the extending criminalization of homosexuality strategy being enacted in Canadian law versus the "liberalization" or Wolfenden approach which began to be used to organize support for homosexual-law reform. This was also a tension between U.S. versus English legal influences in the Canadian context.

The deliberations of the McRuer Commission were also affected by the organizing on "sex deviates" that took place outside its State-mandated confines that I now explore. People influenced by emerging more "liberal" approaches to sexual regulation argued for the expansion of psychiatric clinics, for the extension of more State resources to such facilities whether they were within State jurisdictions or organized more "privately," and for more funding for sex research.

Child Molesters, Shrinks, and Clinics

The 1950s were the years in Canada in which the notion of child molestation as a social problem became more generalized through the work of the professions, the police, and mass-media coverage. Molestation was identified as coming from strangers in the "public" realm who were often visualized as homosexuals.

This was partly a social response to the "disruptions" of the World War II mobilizations on Canadian social life and part of an attempt to reconstruct "proper" family, gender, and sexual relations after the war. While women had entered into more "public" defined areas of waged work and social life during the war mobilizations, they were now being pushed back into the realm of the family, the household, institutionalized motherhood and heterosexuality. As part of this, sexual danger came to be identified with the "public" realms of social life. "Public" in this context covered the social worlds outside the domestic familial realm, especially city streets and downtown areas. Part of this was also the social construction of homosexuality as a national, social, and sexual danger during these years through a series of regulatory practices I have already sketched in and the identification of homosexual danger with these "public" spaces.

The post-World War II years were a period of rapid urbanization and suburbanization transforming working-class and middle-class life. Workers now travelled further to get to and from work, which, in turn, meant increased separation of the sites of waged work and leisure for male workers. Pre-World War II communities were broken down in favour of subdivisions and urban developments. In the suburbs, housing was spread out so that family, kinship, and community networks were fragmented and dispersed. This could give rise to a sense of insecurity that could be quickly mobilized against "strangers."

In this social environment when sexual violence and assaults on young people occurred, it was easier to organize "child molester" scares, and with it an association of homosexuality and child molestation.[181] The image of the "child molester" was created from a number of social constructions. The media and professionals established childhood and youth as a particular area of concern, building on earlier concerns over masturbation and sexuality. The idea of "innocence" — the asexual and vulnerable nature of children — was itself a product of the historical separation of childhood and adolescence from adulthood, which the compulsory school system and the lengthening of the period of childhood and youth dependence served to strengthen.[182]

By the later 1950s and early 1960s there emerged concerns about youth cultures, youth "crime waves," and the effects of rock' n' roll. There was a gendered construction of sexual delinquency with sexual "promiscuity" often being seen as the major form of delinquency among girls and young women. These "social problems" were often blamed on the mother who worked outside the home and therefore supposedly neglected her children.[183] This played on the moral regulatory power of being a "good" mother by defining some mothers as "deficient" or as "bad" mothers who produced the problems of "juvenile delinquency" and "sexual deviance."

It was in the context of these anxieties and fears that the mythology of homosexual "seduction" and "corruption" of young people was organized and took root. There emerged the image of the child molester as an anonymous stranger, often an older, homosexual man. The media played an active part in constructing this image,[184] feeding on the very real fears of city parents, especially mothers given the prevailing gender division of labour regarding parenting and childrearing. Mothers were warned to keep an eye on their children and to alert their children to the dangers of talking to strangers. Very real fears of sexual danger were focused against an image of the sex deviate as a stranger who was often homosexual. This operated to displace sexual danger from the realm of the "private" and from "normal" family men to the realm of the "public" and the "deviant." This not only participated in the normalization of matrimonial heterosexuality but also constructed it as safe in contrast to the dangers of homosexuality. There was a relational character to this process with the private realm being constructed as safe while the public realm and the homosexual were constructed as sexually dangerous. Actual danger, however, was often much closer to home. The vast majority of sexual assaults on children concern heterosexual-identified men attacking and harassing girls, very often within the heterosexual family.[185]

This hegemonic social narrative of sexual danger[186] led to looking in the wrong places for those responsible for most sexual violence and harassment. It helped to construct the heterosexual family as safe — and the realm outside it as dangerous — even though heterosexual familial relations were often very dangerous for women and children. The organizing of this social consciousness in Canada during these years has to do with media coverage on this topic, professional work during these years, the mobilization of "concerned citizen's groups" like the Parents' Action League that I will mention in a moment, and the development of the criminal law relating to sexual offences I have just examined.

In late 1955 and early 1956, there were reports of a series of violent sex crimes in southern Ontario. There were reports of several cases of violent rape and sexual assault in Hamilton, and a number of young girls were murdered in London and Toronto. These crimes became a major media event and led to demands for both tougher laws and more stringent enforcement of the existing law.[187] Sexual assaults and murders were often presented in the media through the frames already articulated in relation to sex deviates and criminal sexual psychopaths. The mood was heightened when a series of sex-related child murders and assaults occurred in Toronto. This media produced outcry influenced the proceedings of the Royal Commission. The media response was in part organized in relation to the commission hearings and the social spaces they provided for public organizing. The Parents' Action League and the *Toronto Star* Forum — which I will mention shortly — interacted with and helped to shape the context of the work of the commission.

The media was not monolithic in its approach; parts were associated with more liberal reform approaches, while others amplified more "law and order" and moral conservative approaches. "Popular" organizations like the Parents' Action League were organized through media coverage and the interventions of psychiatric professionals. This organizing also had a direct relation to the campaign for the establishment of a forensic clinic, and the expansion of the psychiatric domain to capture more funding and resources.

The Parents' Action League (PAL) was founded by four middle-class Toronto housewives in 1954-1955 who were rather well-connected with the political and social elite. They were concerned about assaults on women and children and felt that something needed to be done. They were not particularly concerned about homosexuals at first. As an organization of parents, they could claim to have a special interest in this matter. The objectives of the original group were shifted through their reliance on male psychiatric experts and the crucial tie-in of PAL with mass-media coverage.

With psychiatric and media influence and involvement, PAL campaigned to disseminate information about sex deviation to encourage research into the causes, treatment, and prevention of sex deviation, to encourage the establishment of "treatment" clinics for sex deviates, and to influence government with respect to legislation, control, and treatment of sex deviates.[188] While PAL was generally associated with the more liberal treatment-oriented regulatory strategy for sex deviates they were not opposed to incarceration and confinement. PAL did, however, earn the opposition of those who wanted a widespread clampdown on all sex deviates and from those opposed to the sickness and treatment framings of sex deviates.[189]

It was through the local press that PAL's initial contacts were made. Following a series of attacks on women and girls, one of the founders of PAL had a letter published in the *Telegram*. PAL members called lawyers, medical officials, and politicians to get assistance. Some of the connections were made through the relatives of the founding women's group. The print media played a central role in putting some of these people in touch with each other and in organizing consciousness of this "problem."

After "Lotta Dempsey, of the Toronto *Globe and Mail* wrote a column about us ... our phone never seemed to stop" PAL members said.[190] Evelyn Dorfman, a PAL member, visited the editors of the *Telegram*. They published articles on their activities and "the paper also let us use its staff writers to help cope with inquiries."[191] "Almost overnight," they go on "it seemed, we had a big-league organization."[192]

While PAL began at the middle-class family and community level, it soon gained establishment support. At the same time, its ability to portray itself as speaking for parents and mothers was crucial to its success. The PAL executive included Allan Grossman, Conservative MPP, as its vice-president, and psychologists, psychiatrists, and lawyers sat on its Scientific Advisory Committee. While this was an attempt by the original organizers to achieve legitimacy and respectability that their middle-class social and family networks allowed them to draw upon, it also profoundly shaped the character of the organization. These professional connections were part of the middle-class reliance on experts that was quite prevalent (and was being extended) during these years. This professional reliance was being intensified in relation to the regulation of familial relations, especially in relation to middle-class families.

Dr. Gray, the chair of PAL's Scientific Advisory Committee, stated at the "Star Forum on Sex Deviates" that early in its development PAL had set up this advisory committee with the object of bringing to PAL, its directors, and members whatever information was available on the subject.[193] PAL founders were quoted as stating that "As housewives, we've discovered many things from the experts" particularly that the most pressing need now is for more research.[194] Here we can begin to see how PAL began to become defined organizationally by the social interests of these professional experts. As Rose suggests, in the twentieth century, campaigns for family reform have often been influenced by professionals and experts, and while family members have participated in reforming campaigns, they have called upon scientific expertise to back up their proposals with claims to authority based in science.[195] In this realm, it added to the work of mothering, especially for middle-class women reading this professional literature as well as the more "popular" versions of it directed at women and mothers, but also as a standard for all mothers: it was their responsibility to raise their children not only to avoid molesters but also so that they don't become molesters. Since it was suggested that many sex deviates were "bred in the home,"[196] mothers were in part blamed for producing sex deviates. To prevent this, they needed to rely on expert male advice. This was an uneven intensification of the professional regulation of mothering work and family relations establishing relations of "dependency" of mothers in the home on professional power and knowledge.

PAL lobbied the provincial government to establish a system for collecting information on sex deviates and to open a "treatment" clinic.[197] These proposals, which met with some major success, were themselves part of constructing the relations of psychiatric research on sex offenders and the establishment of forensic clinics, which in turn would be important institutional sites for the production of psychiatric knowledge, the linking together of psychiatric testimony to courtroom decisions, and psychiatric probationary treatment in sex-related cases.

The *Star* Forum

The Toronto *Daily Star* editorialized in October 1955 after the sexual assault and murder of a nine-year-old Toronto boy:

> What must be faced is the unpalatable fact that Toronto has become a "big city" in the worst as well as the best sense of the term. The hazards of living in a great city are many. Generally speaking, the downtown section of any large metropolis is no place for children to be. The unsupervised child is in the greatest danger. That is something every parent should remember — though, it is true, no mother or father can keep an eye on a child all of the time ... it is up to all of us to guard our children as best we can.[198]

On January 26, 1956 the *Star* sponsored a Citizens' Forum on Sex Deviates at Massey Hall, which was attended by more than 2,000 people. As James Fraser put it, "The partial list of guests at the Forum reads like a Who's Who in government, law enforcement and social services."[199] The platform was packed with members of the social welfare, medical, legal, and religious establishment, and several MPPs. Among them was the mayor of Toronto, Nathan Philips.

The *Star's* own motivation for the forum is provided in a letter dated January 20, 1956 inviting the mayor to attend.

> You are likely aware of the increasing public concern in recent weeks over the problem of sex offenders ... *The Star*, in a effort to channel this interest in a constructive path, has arranged a panel discussion — a "Citizen's" Forum on Sex Crimes.[200]

"Unconstructive" responses would be based on ignorance that this educational forum was meant to remedy by relying on professional experts. The *Star* specifically organized this forum to get distinguished officials and the elite of society there and to tie-in with the hearings of the Royal Commission to be held in Toronto in the following weeks. It was part of organizing a perspective that relied on psychiatric experts and was a crucial part of the campaign for a forensic clinic. The introduction to the meeting explicitly referred to the criminal-sexual-psychopath legislation.

Four experts spoke on the subject of sex deviation: Dr. Kenneth Gray of the Toronto Psychiatric Hospital and chief consultant to PAL; Dr. Fred Van Nostrand, chief of neurological services of Ontario's department of reform institutions; Dr. Guttmacher, chief medical officer of the supreme court bench in Baltimore, Maryland; and Dr. Ralph Brancale, director of New Jersey's diagnostic centre for sex offenders.

Dr. Gray defined sex deviation as "an act performed for sexual gratification other than sexual intercourse with an adult of the opposite sex." Notions of sex perversion were now replaced with those of sexual deviation. In distinguishing between various sex deviates, Gray described only two types as dangerous: sadists and pedophiles. He defined pedophiles as engaging in the "sexual molesting of young children," and he spoke on behalf of PAL calling for facilities to categorize and treat sex offenders.

Taken together, the "experts" presented somewhat contradictory views. Guttmacher, for instance, said that "homosexuals are usually the result of a bad child-parent relationship." Again the focus seems to be on "defective" mother/child relations. Yet he argued that homosexuality "should be considered a private matter unless it involves force or is an affront to the public."

Van Nostrand focused on "problem families," arguing that "time after time comes the pathetic story of a family of six, seven, or eight living in one or two rooms, and the actual sleeping together of children up to teenage, and following through with incest and some perversions." This resonates with earlier claims going back to the nineteenth century that incest was produced by poverty and crowded living conditions. The relations carried in this statement are part of organizing "respectable" ways of life as "ideals" for the working class, despite the financial situations of working-class and poor households including the lack of affordable and suitable housing, which often precluded more spacious sleeping accommodations. While the focus was put on the "public" character of sexual danger, the roots of this danger were traced back to bad mothering practices, especially in poor and working-class homes.

Guttmacher and Van Nostrand both warned parents against their children being friendly with people much older than themselves. Gray, however, reported that more than seventy-five percent of the men involved in molestation knew the child beforehand. This did begin to challenge the "stranger" myth of the child molester. Brancale discussed the now familiar image of the homosexual teacher as child molester: "It has been found that children have often been molested — not only by men they knew — but men who are in constructive positions such as teachers or counsellors at boys' clubs." This shifts attention to "public" institutions like schools and boys' clubs and away from families, households and relatives.

These "experts" stressed more reliance on professional experts and treatment than on penalties and punishment. They were arguing that not all sex deviates were dangerous and that only the psychiatrist could tell for sure. They wished to preserve and extend psychiatric and psychological hegemonies over the regulation of sexual deviations. The *Star* basically took up the perspective produced by PAL and Dr. Gray in its editorial on the Forum.[201]

The citizen's forum and PAL[202] were expressions of the organization of "public opinion" on this issue. This also highlights how these concerns were organized and mobilized through the media and the involvement of psychiatric and medical experts. The motivation for the psychiatric and medical involvement would appear to be to expand the psychiatric domain and the opportunity it provided to capture more resources (including government research grants and clinic facilities). This organizing was important to the establishment of the eventual hegemony of the mental-illness conceptualization of homosexuality and lesbianism. It expanded the power of medical and psychiatric discourses and practices within sexual regulation more generally, including in relation to parents, families and young people.

PAL, Dr. Gray and the *Star* achieved success in their clinic campaign. In 1956, under the provisions of the Ontario Mental Hospitals Act, a forensic clinic was established as a division of the Toronto Psychiatric Hospital in affiliation with the department of psychiatry at the University of Toronto.[203] This later became the Forensic Service of the Clarke Institute of Psychiatry in 1966. Here the interlocking character of the relations established between lobbying by a "parents" group, the media, and the State agreeing to set up an institutional site, its connections with a professional academic discipline and institution, and the expansion of psychiatric jurisdiction is visible.

New Sexual Types: Pedophiles, Transvestites, Transsexuals

The forensic clinic at the Toronto Psychiatric Hospital had as its mandate to undertake research into the nature of sexual deviation. The clinic was created under the leadership of Dr. Peter Thomson, who had already done work on the subject. He argued that about forty percent of all homosexuals suffer from some form of neurotic or psychotic mental disorder and that those at the lower end of the Kinsey scale (those not exclusively homosexual) could attain complete heterosexuality through psychotherapy.[204] There was an argument generated for extending the jurisdiction of the forensic clinic into "education" in relation to parents, the school system, and other institutions in attempts to prevent young people from becoming sex deviates. In the 1960s doctors and researchers from the clinic regularly advised magistrates and the police on methods of identifying and treating sex deviates.[205]

Johann Mohr and R.E. Turner reported that forty to sixty percent of the people they studied at the clinic were referrals from the legal system and about one-third were from what they called "community sources," including hospitals, clinics, and doctors in private practice. They reported that eighty percent of "adult-oriented" homosexuals were referred from these "community" agencies and twenty percent from the legal apparatus.[206] These statistics are an indication of how doctors and psychiatrists regulated the lives of gay men, and indeed how at least some gays came to accept the theory of homosexuality as an illness.[207] In 1963 only about fifteen percent of the people seen at the clinic were classified as homosexual. Lesbians were apparently harder to deal with and few came to them or were referred. Still, Mohr and Turner argued that homosexuality could be treated in individual cases, sometimes by the use of aversion therapy. "Treatment is possible for most cases if not in terms of a cure at least in terms of an amelioration of problem situations."[208]

There were also attempts to break up or break down broad collecting categories like "sex deviates" or "criminal sexual psychopaths" and even the "homosexual" in the 1950s and this expanded in the 1960s. Emerging psychiatric and psychological approaches also suggested, as we have seen, that while some sexual activities were "dangerous," heterosexual activities that were not geared to reproduction and not between a wife and her husband might be anomalous or immoral but not criminal. Some of this work began to differentiate between "dangerous" sexual acts and more acceptable acts such as masturbation, premarital petting, and heterosexual oral and anal sex if done in "private."[209] The boundaries of heterosexual normality were being expanded.

Mohr and Turner conducted some of the work creating pedophilia as a separate and distinct concept.[210] The creation of the "pedophile" was part of the mobilization of concerns over children and youth during these years as well as being part of the creation of new sexual types. Pedophilia was defined as "the expressed desire for immature sexual gratification with a prepubertal child."[211] There was a limited attempt at that time to distinguish between homosexuality and pedophilia in much psychological and sexological work. A *new sexual being* thus emerged — the person defined by sexual interests in children.[212] Mohr also made a distinction between heterosexual and homosexual pedophilia,[213] however "homosexual pedophilia" continues to be associated with homosexuality in general and most often continues to be used in standard media coverage. There has also been a process both within media and popular discourses — but also professional ones — of the homosexualization of the pedophile. While psychological and sexological discourse defines pedophilia technically as a sexual interest in the pre-pubertal child, the media often uses the term when covering homosexual acts involving postpubescent adolescents as well.

Again this construction of "pedophilia" leads to a focus on "deviant" men as the sexual danger. It focuses on sexual assaults and harassment of young people as being carried out by "mentally ill" and "deviant" individual men and not to a broader focus on the social relations of power and the practices leading to violence and harassment against young people. Both homosexuals and pedophiles are defined as being found outside families and households[214] and are identified with the "public" realm. These processes constructed sexual danger as being in the "public" realm from "sex deviates" and not from "normal" men in "normal" families.[215] This also participated in shifting social attention away from the major social sources and sites of sexual danger.

The different "liberal" and more "conservative" currents in professional discourse all agreed on one thing, however: heterosexuality was the undisputed social norm. In this period, however, there developed

> the gradual emergence of a newer and quite different conception based not upon gender ideas but upon the notion of "sexual object choice" or "sexual orientation" which came to be defined independently of gender identity.[216]

This uneven and partial separation of the concept of homosexuality from notions of gender inversion that had earlier hegemonized this concept allowed for the articulation of new sexual and gender types. At the same time, earlier conceptualizations associating "queers" with gender inversion were still very much alive and could still be re-mobilized.

The classifications of transvestism and transsexualism, as distinct from homosexuality, were made in this period.[217] "Effeminacy" was now less identified with male homosexuality in general.[218] In the 1950s and 1960s, with a number of publicized transsexual operations beginning with the celebrated case of Christine Jorgensen, the transsexual was the centre of attention for sexologists and psychologists interested in gender and sexual "disorientation." The State, for a number of administrative, economic, and social reasons, laid down the criteria for determining gender assignment on the basis of genital features at birth.[219] Those who did not easily fit into these rigid classifications therefore provoked anxiety, concern, interest, and study. Gender-identity clinics were established, one of which was set up in the 1960s at the Clarke Institute in Toronto. Work centred on the development of procedures to allow for the firm maintenance of male/female gender dichotomies by establishing an early "core gender identity" that could, in a tiny minority, actually conflict with biological sex at birth.[220] This would then be used to justify operations to bring the individual's anatomy into line with their "core gender." At the same time, pre-operative transsexuals living and being taken as the gender they wish to be seen as, also challenge the rules of the "natural attitude" to gender and show how gender is a continuous social accomplishment.[221]

These new sexual and gender categories were created in the context of broad post-war shifts in gender and sexual organization. Part of this process was a shift in the practices of some professional and social agencies, especially those that adopted a more "liberal" approach. They now became less interested in homosexuals and lesbians in general and more concerned with what they saw as specific anomalies — transvestism, transsexuality, and pedophilia. This helped to set the stage in the 1960s for the expansion of gay and lesbian cultures, for the emergence of a small but important homophile movement in Canada, and for homosexual-law reform.

Notes

1. John D'Emilio, "Gay Politics, Gay Community: San Francisco's Experience" in *Socialist Review*, No, 55, Jan./Feb. 1981, pp. 80-81.
2. See Leisa D. Meyer, "Creating G.I. Jane: The Regulation of Sexuality and Sexual Behaviour in the Women's Army Corps During World War II" in *Feminist Studies*, V. 18, No. 3 (Fall 1992), pp. 581-601.
3. See Allan Berube, "Marching to a Different Drummer: Lesbian and Gay G.I.s in World War II" in *The Advocate*, No. 328, Oct. 15, 1981; "Coming Out Under Fire" in *Mother Jones*, Feb./Mar. 1983, pp. 22-29; and "Marching to a Different Drummer: Lesbian and Gay GIs in World War II" in Snitow *et al.*, eds., *Powers of Desire* (New York: Monthly Review Press, 1983), pp. 88-99; and Berube, *Coming Out Under Fire: The History of Gay Men and Women in World War Two* (New York: The Free Press, 1990).
4. Berube, "Marching to a Different Drummer" in *The Advocate, op. cit.*, p. 21; Snitow, et al., *op. cit.*, p. 92.
5. See Nikolas Rose, *The Psychological Complex: Psychology, Politics, and Society in England, 1869-1939* (London: Routledge and Kegan Paul, 1985).
6. See Ruth Pierson, "Women's Emancipation and the Recruitment of Women into the Labour Force in World War II" in Trofimenkoff and Prentice, eds., *The Neglected Majority* (Toronto: McClelland and Stewart, 1977), pp. 144-145; "Canadian Women and the Second World War" published by the Canadian Historical Association, Historical Booklet No. 37, Ottawa, 1983; and *"They're Still Women after All": The Second World War and Canadian Womanhood* (Toronto: McClelland and Stewart, 1986).
7. 18th Annual Report, United Church of Canada, Division of Evangelism and Social Services, 1943, p. 68. The following quotes are from the Chair's Address to the Board.
8. 19th Annual Report, United Church of Canada, Division of Evangelism and Social Services, 1944, p. 43.
9. *Ibid.*, p. 42.
10. See Ruth Roach Pierson, "Ladies or Loose Women: The Canadian Women's Army Corps in World War II" in *Atlantis: A Women's Studies Journal*, V. 4, No. 2 (Spring 1979), pp. 235-266; Ruth Pierson, "The Double Bind of the Double Standard: VD Control and the CWAC in World War II" in *The Canadian Historical Review*, V. 62, No. 1 (Mar. 1981), pp. 31-58; and *"They're Still Women after All" op. cit.*
11. W.R. Feasby, ed., *Official History of the Canadian Medical Services, 1939-1945*, V. 2, "Clinical Subjects," published by the authority of the Ministry of National Defence (Edmund Cloutier, Queen's Printer, 1953), pp. 85-86. The following references are based on this text as well as on V. 1, "Organization and Campaigns." Also see Gary Kinsman "Official Discourse as Sexual Regulation," Ph.D. thesis, Department of Educational Theory, University of Toronto, 1989.
12. This may help to account for the Canadian war mobilization seeming to play less of a role in forming and expanding homosexual and lesbian networks than that in the U.S. At the same time, more research is needed.
13. Lewis H. Loeser, "The Sexual Psychopath in the Military Service: A Study of 270 cases" in *The American Journal of Psychiatry* V. 102, Jul. 1945, p. 99.
14. Berube, *Coming Out under Fire, op. cit.*, p. 14.
15. Freedman, "'Uncontrolled Desires': The Response to the Sexual Psychopath, 1920-1960" in *The Journal of American History* (V. 74, No. 1) and also in Kathy Peiss and Christina Simmons, eds., *Passion and Power, Sexuality in History* (Philadelphia: Temple University Press, 1989), p. 213.
16. On these points, see Lorna Weir, "Studies in the Medicalization of Sexual Danger: Sexual Rule, Sexual Politics," Ph.D. thesis, 1986, York University, Toronto, Department of Social and Political Thought, pp. 256-274; also see Gary Kinsman, "Official Discourse as Sexual Regulation," *op. cit.*, pp. 79-84, for more elaboration.

17. See Gary Kinsman, "Official Discourse as Sexual Regulation," and Estelle Freedman, *op. cit.*

18. Sidney Katz, "The Truth about Sex Criminals" in *Maclean's Magazine*, Jul. 1, 1947, p. 12.

19. Feasby, V. 1, *op. cit.*, pp. 3-4.

20. Feasby, V. 2, *op. cit.*, pp. 100-101.

21. Feasby, V. 2, p. 59.

22. *Physical Standards and Instructions for the Medical Examination of Recruits*, 1943, p. 62.

23. Feasby, V. 2, *op. cit.*, p. 83.

24. *Ibid.*

25. *Physical Standards and Instructions for the Medical Examination of Recruits*, 1943, p. 62.

26. Feasby, V. 2, *op. cit.*, p. 84

27. *Ibid.*, p. 85.

28. *Ibid.*, p. 86.

29. *Ibid.*, p. 95.

30. *Ibid.*, p. 401.

31. Feasby, V. 2, p. 405.

32. *Ibid.*, p. 405, p. 417.

33. See Gary Kinsman, "Official Discourse as Sexual Regulation," *op. cit.*, for more elaboration, pp. 86-89.

34. No doubt there were similar experiences for women, and these will be uncovered by lesbian and other historians.

35. Bert Sutcliffe interviewed by Rick Archbold in "Growing Old, Staying Gay" in *The Body Politic*, No. 89, Dec. 1982, p. 28; also see H.F. Sutcliffe, *Herbert Frederick Sutcliffe, MBE, CD: An Autobiography* (Toronto, 1981, unpublished autobiography), particularly the addendum, "Will the Real Herbert Frederick Sutcliffe, MBE, CD, Please Stand Up (Or Come Out of the Closet and Be Frank)," pp. 151-165, especially p. 153. My current research into the security regime campaign against lesbians and gay men is allowing me to uncover more first-hand accounts of men and women who were affected by these policies in the military.

36. H.F. Sutcliffe, *Herbert Frederick Sutcliffe, MBE, CD: An Autobiography* (Toronto, 1981, unpublished autobiography), addendum, "Will the Real Herbert Frederick Sutcliffe, MBE, CD, Please Stand Up (Or Come Out of the Closet and Be Frank)," p. 155.

37. *Ibid.*

38. Quoted in Dana Flavelle, "Homosexuality Destroyed Decorated Soldier's Career" in *The Toronto Star*, Mar. 15, 1986, p. A15.

39. Maurice Leznoff, "The Homosexual in Urban Society," M.A. thesis, McGill University, Montréal, 1954, pp. 81-83. The following quotes are from pp. 176, 196, 207-208.

40. For some suggestive analysis that moves in this direction, see Barbara Ehrenreich, *The Hearts of Men: American Dreams and the Flight from Commitment* (Garden City: Anchor Press/Doubleday, 1984); and Dorothy E. Smith, "Women, Class and Family" in *The Socialist Register-1983* (London: Merlin, 1983).

41. Alfred C. Kinsey, *et al.*, *Sexual Behavior in the Human Male* (Philadelphia and London: W.B. Saunders, 1948); and *Sexual Behavior in the Human Female* (Philadelphia: W. B. Saunders, 1953). The volumes are based on interviews with more than 10,000 white American and Canadian men and women. See also Paul Robinson, *The Modernization of Sex* (New York: Harper and Colophon, 1976), p. 53; and D'Emilio, *Sexual Politics ...* (Chicago: The University of Chicago Press, 1983), p. 34. Also see George Chauncey, *Gay New York (New York: Basic, 1994)*, pp. 70-74.

42. D'Emilio, *Sexual Politics, op. cit.*, p. 36.

43. Chauncey, *Gay New York, op. cit.*, pp. 70-72.

44. D'Emilio, *Sexual Politics, op. cit.* , p. 36.

45. *Ibid.*, pp. 37, 42.

46. The four-percent figure of those involved in exclusive homosexual behaviour has been used by right-wing groups like Renaissance and "Positive Parents" in Canada in the 1980s to dem-

onstrate that gays are a very small minority, and by Citizens United for Responsible Education (CURE) in the 1990s. The right wing has often attempted to portray homosexuals as a tiny minority of men having nothing to do with the vast majority of men. More on these groups later. There are continuing "scientific" and political battles over the number of gay men and lesbians. Many of the surveys that have been conducted have major methodological flaws given the current social organization of sexuality and continuing heterosexism. Critiques can also be made of the percentage of the population claimed as "heterosexual."

47. D'Emilio, *Sexual Politics, op. cit.*, pp. 83-84.

48. Two early articles may demonstrate how this took place in Canada. In the Sept. 1950 issue of the *Canadian Medical Association Journal,* S.R. Laycock, Dean of Education and Professor of Educational Psychology at the University of Saskatchewan and Director of the Division of Education and Mental Health of the Canadian Mental Hygiene Association, published "Homosexuality — A Mental Hygiene Problem" (V. 63, Sept. 1950, pp. 245-250). An article by John K. McCreary entitled "Psychopathia Homosexualis" in a play on Krafft-Ebing's "classic" Psychopathia Sexualis was published in the *Canadian Journal of Psychology*, No. 4 (June 1950), p. 63. For later years, see Kenneth G. Gray, "Sexual Deviation: Problem and Treatment," originally published in *Saturday Night*, Nov. 26, 1955, and reprinted in Laskin, *Social Problems: A Canadian Profile* (Toronto: McGraw Hill, 1964), pp. 408-411; and P.G. Thomson, "Sexual Deviation" in *Canadian Medical Association Journal,* No. 80, Mar. 1959. Also see Patricia E. Stevens and Joanne M. Hall, "A Critical Historical Analysis of the Medical Construction of Lesbianism" in *International Journal of Health Services,* V. 21, No. 2, 1991, pp. 291-307.

49. Laycock, *op. cit.*, p. 247.

50. McCreary, *op. cit.*, p. 74.

51. Johann Mohr and R.E. Turner, "Sex Deviations," Part I: "Introduction" and Part II: "Homosexuality" in *Applied Therapeutics,* Jan. and Feb., 1967, V. 9, Nos. 2, 3, reprinted in W.E. Mann, ed., *Social Deviance in Canada* (Toronto: Copp Clark, 1971), p. 363. For very different accounts, see Martin Duberman, *Cures: A Gay Man's Odyssey* (New York: Dutton, 1991); Michael Riordon, "Blessed are the deviates: a post-therapy check-up on my ex-psychiatrist" in Ed Jackson and Stan Persky, eds., *Flaunting It!* (Vancouver, Toronto: New Star/Pink Triangle, 1982), pp. 14-20; and Persimmon Blackbridge and Sheila Gilhooly, *Still Sane* (Vancouver: Press Gang, 1985).

52. See Gould, *The Mismeasure of Man* (New York: W.W. Norton, 1981), pp. 192-233. Also see Henriques, Hollway, *et al., Changing the Subject* (London and New York: Methuen, 1984).

53. See Joseph H. Pleck, "The Theory of Male Sex Role Identity: Its Rise and Fall, 1936 to the Present" and Miriam Lewin, "Psychology Measures Femininity and Masculinity" in Miriam Lewin ed., *In The Shadows of the Past: Psychology Portrays the Sexes* (New York: Columbia University Press, 1984).

54. For instance, see Allen L. Edwards, *Edwards Personal Preference Schedule* (New York: The Psychological Corporation, 1953); and Ivan Scheirs and Raymond Cartell, *Handbook for the Neuroticism Scale Questionnaire (NSQ)* (Chicago: Institute for Personality and Ability Testing, 1961).

55. This refers to the Edwards Schedule.

56. This is an account of the Neuroticism Scale Questionnaire.

57. Leznoff, "The Homosexual in Urban Society," *op. cit.* Also see Ross Higgins, "Montreal 1953" in *Pink Ink*, V. 1, No. 5, Dec./Jan. 1984, pp. 31-32. I am very much indebted to Ross Higgins for bringing this important work to my attention. This thesis was only hinted at in the joint work by Leznoff and his professor, William Westley, in "The Homosexual Community" in *Social Problems*, No. 3 (Apr. 1956), pp. 257-263, which was reprinted in a number of anthologies on deviancy and homosexuality in the 1960s. Also see Leznoff's "Interviewing Homosexuals" in *American Journal of Sociology*, No. 62 (Sept. 1956), pp. 202-204. On Leznoff's work, also see Higgins' forthcoming Ph.D. dissertation, Anthropology Department, McGill University. Also see Ross Higgins, "Murder Will Out: Discourse and Gay Identity Processes in Montreal," unpublished paper, 1993.

58. Leznoff, "The Homosexual in Urban Society," *op. cit.*, p. 12.
59. On the connection between the Chicago School and the Sociology Department at McGill, see Robert J. Brym with Bonnie J. Fox, *From Culture to Power: The Sociology of English Canada* (Toronto: Oxford University Press, 1989), pp. 16-17.
60. *Ibid.*, p. 14.
61. *Ibid.*, pp. 10-11, 166-167. Cory's book was first published in 1951, and argued for the new perspective that homosexuals were a minority group similar to national, religious, or ethnic minorities in the denial of civil rights and exclusion from the mainstream. See Donald Webster Cory, *The Homosexual in America: A Subjective Approach* (New York: Greenberg, 1951), pp. 13-14.
62. Leznoff, *op. cit.*, p. 1.
63. Leznoff and Westley, "The Homosexual Community" in *Social Problems*, *op. cit.*, note 2.
64. On the "role" of the queen, see Leznoff, *op. cit.*, pp. 97-106; Leznoff and Westley, *op. cit.*; and John Grube, "Queens and Flaming Virgins: Towards a Sense of Gay Community" in *Rites*, V. 2, No. 9, pp. 14-15, although it should be pointed out that at times Grube's very useful account is marred by a structural-functionalist perspective.
65. Leznoff, "Interviewing Homosexuals," *op. cit.*, p. 203; and Leznoff, "The Homosexual in Urban Society," *op. cit.*
66. The grant was reported in the Montréal *Gazette*, June 11, 1953, p. 26. The police arrests are mentioned in "Interviewing Homosexuals," *op. cit.*, p. 204. On the response of the gays he was interviewing, see "The Homosexual in Urban Society," *op. cit.*, p. 19.
67. Leznoff, "The Homosexual in Urban Society," *op. cit.*, p. 19.
68. *Ibid.*, p. 41. The following section is based on the Leznoff thesis, pp. 32-41.
69. *Ibid.*
70. *Ibid.*, p. 34.
71. *Ibid.*, p. 36.
72. This differs from Grube's account that describes Peter as the queen of a middle-class group. See Grube, *op. cit.*, pp. 14-15.
73. Leznoff, "The Homosexual in Urban Society," *op. cit.*, p. 69.
74. *Ibid.*, p. 75.
75. Higgins, "Montreal 1953," *op. cit.*, p. 31.
76. Quoted in Higgins, *op. cit.*, p. 31. This can be compared with Grube's accounts of class conflict within gay community formation in Toronto; with reference to a middle-class "cultured gay group," see the comment "but if you were ignorant or a stable boy you weren't part of that society ..." and the reference to class differences in clientele between the St. Charles and The Parkside (generally working class) and Letros (generally middle class) in 1950s Toronto. See "Oh my dear, carriage trade is ... they're coming uptown tonight," and "oh ... the piss elegant crowd are here tonight!" Grube, *op. cit.*, p. 15.
77. See Chauncey, *Gay New York*, *op. cit.*
78. On this notion of gay space, see Grube, *op. cit.*, p. 16. On queer space, also see David Bell and Gill Valentine, eds., *Mapping Desire: Geographies of Desire* (London and New York: Routledge, 1995).
79. *Ibid.*, p. 28-29. This should be compared with Grube's account that suggests that a significant number of the men his oral history project interviewed had been arrested but that even more effective was the climate of fear and intimidation instilled by the police. Grube, *op. cit.*, p. 17.
80. Leznoff, "The Homosexual in Urban Society," *op. cit.*, p. 165.
81. See Joan Nestle, "Butch-Femme Relationships: Sexual Courage in the 1950s" in *Heresies*, No. 12, 1981, pp. 21-24 and also in her *A Restricted Country* (Ithaca, New York: Firebrand, 1987), pp. 100-109; Elizabeth Lapovsky Kennedy and Madeline D. Davis, *Boots of Leather, Slippers of Gold, The History of a Lesbian Community* (New York and London: Routledge, 1993); Aerlyn Weissman and Lynne Fernie, directors, *"Forbidden Love"* NFB, 1993; and Becki Ross's edited collection *Forbidden Love: The Unashamed Lives of Post-War Canadian Lesbians*, forthcoming.

82. Line Chamberland, "Remembering Lesbian Bars, 1955-1975" in *Journal of Homosexuality* V. 25, No. 3, 1993, pp. 231-269.
83. See Elise Chenier, "Risks, Roles and Rounders: Lesbian Bar Culture in Toronto, 1950-65," paper presented at the "Out of the Archives" conference on bisexual, lesbian and gay history in Canada, York University, January 1994 and her M.A. thesis, "Tough Ladies and Trouble-makers: Toronto's Public Lesbian Community, 1955-1965," History, Queen's University, Kingston, 1995. Chenier's work builds on and extends earlier work by the Lesbians Making History collective. See their "People Think This Didn't Happen in Canada — But it Did" in *Fireweed*, "Lesbiantics 2," Issue 28, Spring 1989, especially p. 86. Also see comments in Becki Ross, "The House That Jill Built: Reconstructing The Lesbian Organization of Toronto, 1976-1980," Ph.D. thesis, University of Toronto, 1992, pp. 86-87, p. 99.
84. Becki Ross, "'Destaining the Delinquent Body' Moral Regulatory Practices at Street Haven, 1965-1969" in Ross, ed., *Forbidden Love: The Unashamed Lives of Post-War Canadian Lesbians*, forthcoming.
85. See Aerlyn Weissman and Lynne Fernie, directors, *"Forbidden Love"* NFB, 1993.
86. See Mary Louise Adams, "Precedent-Setting Pulp: Women's Barracks was Deemed 'Exceedingly Frank'" in *Xtra!* 231 (3 September 1993), p. 21
87. David Churchill, "Gay Sites and Public Space: Toronto in the 1950s," paper presented at the "Out of the Archives" conference, January 1994, York University. Also see David Stewart Churchill, "Coming Out In A Cold Climate: A History of Gay Men in Toronto During the 1950s," M.A. thesis, History, OISE, University of Toronto, 1993.
88. This information comes in part from research on the security campaigns in the Ottawa area and will be elaborated on in this research. Also see Philip Hannan, "Homosexual Ottawa" in *Ottawa Citizen*, May 8, 1995, p. A9.
89. See *One*, V. 5, No. 3, March 1957, p. 22.
90. See *One*, Oct. 1959; reprinted in *Xtra* (Toronto) Nov. 1985.
91. Information from interview conducted by RobertChampagne with Jim Egan in June 1986. The important work of Jim Egan was brought to my attention by Philip McLeod and RobertChampagne. See RobertChampagne, "An Interview With Jim Egan," and Alfred Taylor, "A Perfect Beginner: Jim Egan and the Tabloids" in *Canadian Lesbian and Gay History Newsletter* No. 2, Sept. 1986, pp. 11-18. Also see "Canada's Pioneer Gay Activist: Jim Egan," Interview and Introduction by Robert Champagne, *Rites*, V. 3, No. 7,Dec. 1986/Jan. 1987, pp. 12-14; Robert Champagne, compiler, *Jim Egan: Canada's Pioneer Gay Activist* (Toronto: Canadian Lesbian and Gay History Network, 1987).
92. James Egan, "Parliamentary Legislative Committee Ignored this Letter from Homosexual Suggesting Changes in Criminal Code" in *Justice Weekly* March 19, 1955, p. 5, 14.
93. From Robert Champagne interview with Jim Egan, in *Jim Egan, Canada's Pioneer Gay Activist*, *op. cit.*, p. 4.
94. See *Justice Weekly* (Toronto), 1953-1954.
95. The Lesbians Making History Collective, "People Think This Didn't Happen in Canada - But It Did" in *Fireweed*, "Lesbiantics 2," Issue 28, Spring 1989, p. 86.
96. More historical work is needed on the role of *Justice Weekly* and other scandal-sheets in lesbian and gay community formation. Ross Higgins has shown me copies of several Montréal tabloids that contained material on lesbian and gay-related issues. These include *Ici Montréal* (which contains the wonderful headline "Fifis versus Homos" in its June 30, 1962, issue), *Jour Nuit*, and *Sentimental*. See Ross Higgins, "Montreal Gays and Lesbians in the Yellow Press of the 50s" in *Canadian Lesbian and Gay History Newsletter No. 2*, Sept. 1986, pp. 9-11 and Ross Higgins and Line Chamberland, "Mixed Messages: Gays and Lesbians in Montreal Yellow Papers in the 1950s" in Ian McKay, ed., *The Challenge of Modernity: A Reader on Post Confederation Canada*, Toronto: McGraw-Hill Ryerson Limited, 1992, pp. 422-431. Also see Eric Setliff, "Sex Fiends or Swish Kids, Gay Men in the Toronto Tabloids, 1946-1956," M.A. thesis, His-

tory, University of Toronto, 1994 and his "Between the Scandal Sheets (1949)" in *Centre/fold* No. 8, Spring 1995, pp. 30-31.

97. James Egan, "Civil Liberties and the Homosexual" in *Toronto Star,* 23 October, 1963, p. 7.

98. See Gigeroff, *Sexual Deviations in the Criminal Law* (Toronto: published for the Clarke Institute of Psychiatry by University of Toronto Press, 1968), pp. 69-82. Unless otherwise cited, the references in this section are from Gigeroff.

99. *Ibid.,* p. 39. This represented a certain separation within the law of sexual offences from offences against morality. See Gigeroff, *op. cit.,* pp. 40, 46, 49-50.

100. See Girard, "Gays, Lesbians and the Legal Process Since 1945," unpublished paper, 1985, p. 84. Also see Girard, "From Subversion to Liberation: Homosexuals and the Immigration Act, 1952-1977," unpublished paper, 1985.

101. Report of the Select Committee Appointed by the Legislative Assembly of the Province of Ontario, to Study and Report Upon Problems of Delinquent Individuals and Custodial Questions and the Place of Reform Institutions Therein, March 8, 1954, Toronto. See particularly pp. 309-315.

102. *Ibid.,* p. 312.

103. See Girard's two unpublished papers already cited on which this account is based and Philip Girard, "From Subversion to Liberation: Homosexuals and the Immigration Act, 1952-1977" in *Canadian Journal of Law and Society,* 2 (1987), pp. 1-27.

104. See Girard, "From Subversion to Liberation," unpublished version, *op. cit.,* p. 10.

105. I wish I knew what "living on the avails of homosexualism" meant! *Ibid.,* p. 11.

106. *Ibid.,* pp. 15-16.

107. Despite victories on the immigration front there are also continuing problems regarding the immigration of lesbian/gay partners and spouses into Canada.

108. See Katz, *Gay American History* (New York: Thomas Y. Crowell, 1976), pp. 91-90; and D'Emilio, *Sexual Politics, op. cit.,* pp. 40-53.

109. On this see Len Scher, *The Un-Canadians* (Toronto: Lester, 1992).

110. R.G. Waldeck, "The International Homosexual Conspiracy," reprinted from *Human Events,* Sept. 29, 1960, in *New York Native,* Sept. 21/Oct. 4, 1981, p. 13. Also in Martin Bauml Duberman, *About Time, Exploring the Gay Past* (New York: Gay Presses of New York, 1986), pp. 199-202.

111. Elizabeth Wilson, *Women and the Welfare State* (London: Tavistock, 1980), p. 67.

112. Elizabeth Wilson, *Only Halfway to Paradise,* (London: Tavistock, 1980) p. 101. Also see Frank Pearce, "How to be immoral...." in Cohen and Young, eds., *The Manufacture of News* (London: Constable, 1973) for analysis of media coverage during these years.

113. Much of this section is based on the important work of Philip Girard, to whom I am grateful. See Girard, "From Subversion to Liberation: Homosexuals and the Immigration Act, 1952-1977," June 1985, unpublished and the published version in *Canadian Journal of Law and Society,* V. 2, 1987, pp. 1-27; and "Gays, Lesbians and the Legal Process Since 1945," unpublished paper, 1985.

114. See John Sawatsky, *Men in the Shadows* (Toronto: Totem, 1980), pp. 111-118. The following section is partially based on the account in this book, pp. 111-134. And see his *For Services Rendered* (Markham, Ont., Penguin, 1983). For the broader social and political context see Reginald Whitaker, "Origins of the Canadian Government's Internal Security System, 1946-52" in *Canadian Historical Review* LXV 2 (1984), 154-187, and *Double Standard, The Secret History of Canadian Immigration* (Lester and Orpen Dennys, Toronto 1987); Reg Whitaker and Gary Marcuse, *Cold War Canada: The Making of a National Insecurity State, 1945-1957* (Toronto: University of Toronto Press, 1994); Dean Beeby and William Kaplan, eds. *Moscow Dispatches, Inside Cold War Russia, John Watkins* (Toronto: James Lorimer, 1987); and Philip Girard, "From Subversion to Liberation: Homosexuals and the Immigration Act, 1952-1977" in *Canadian Journal of Law and Society* V. 2, 1987, 1-27 and his "Gays, Lesbians and the Legal Process Since 1945," unpublished paper, 1985. Also see my article, "'Character Weaknesses' and 'Fruit Machines': Towards an Analysis of the Anti-Homosexual Security Campaigns in the

Canadian Civil Service" in *Labour/Le Travail* No. 35, Spring 1995, pp. 133-161; and Daniel J. Robinson and David Kimmel, "The Queer Career of Homosexual Security Vetting in Cold War Canada" in *Canadian Historical Review*, V. LXXV, No. 3, September 1994, pp. 319-345. And see my ongoing Social Sciences and Humanities Research Council (SSHRC) funded research into the social organization of the anti-homosexual "national-security" campaigns.

115. Pat Walsh in *Speak Up* (Toronto), Aug./Sept. 1981, V. 9, No. 8/9. Walsh was an executive member of the far-right World Anti-Communist League. *Speak Up* was a far-right newspaper.

116. See John Sawatsky, *For Services Rendered* (Markham, Ont.: Penguin, 1983), p. 173.

117. D. F. Wall, Memorandum to the Security Panel, "Security Cases Involving Character Weaknesses, with Special Reference to the Problem of Homosexuality," 12 May 1959, 12-13. In the language that is used in this excerpt we can see how the author is building on earlier notions of homosexuals as psychopathic personalities. See Gary Kinsman, "Official Discourse as Sexual Regulation," *op. cit.*, pp. 71-89.

118. See the Canadian Press stories by Dean Beeby, which were based on these documents. They were printed in *The Globe and Mail* 24 April, 1992, 1-2 as "Mounties staged massive hunt for gay men in civil service" and "RCMP hoped 'fruit machine' would identify homosexuals." I will refer to the individual documents that the Canadian Press secured the release of throughout this section. I am very indebted to the work of Dean Beeby in making these initial Access to Information requests.

119. See my article "'Character Weaknesses' and 'Fruit Machines': Towards an Analysis of the Anti-Homosexual Security Campaigns in the Canadian Civil Service" in *Labour/Le Travail*, *op. cit.*

120. D. F. Wall, Memorandum to the Security Panel, "Security Cases Involving Character Weaknesses, with Special Reference to the Problem of Homosexuality," 12 May 1959, p. 12-13.

121. Thanks to Lisa Steele and Kim Tomczak for sharing their pioneering research on the Leo Mantha investigation with me. See their video *"Legal Memory"* (1992). Also see Neil Boyd, "All May Love, Leo" in *Angles*, July 1987, p. 9.

122. Interview with Bruce Somers, June 10, 1994.

123. Alan Hustack, *They Were Hanged* (Toronto: Lorimer, 1987), p. 101.

124. See George Chauncey, "Christian Brotherhood or Sexual Perversion? Homosexual Identities and the Construction of Sexual Boundaries in the World War 1 Era" in Martin Duberman, Martha Vicinus and George Chauncey, eds., *Hidden From History, Reclaiming the Gay and Lesbian Past* (New York; Meridian, 1989), pp. 294-317.

125. See "Homo Purges Confirmed" in *Rites*, V. 1, No. 10, April 1985, p. 7.

126. See Girard, "From Subversion to Liberation," unpublished version, *op. cit.*, p. 9; published version, *op. cit.*, p. 5. Further research is needed to see if Girard's assertion is accurate.

127. Sawatsky, *Men in the Shadows*, *op. cit.*, p. 125.

128. From my ongoing research into the social organization of the security campaign.

129. The legacy of these practices continue informally today as the military and the RCMP grapple with the ending of their official discriminatory practices. This, despite the 1992 Michelle Douglas case that led to the overturning of the military's anti-lesbian and anti-gay policy practices of discrimination.

130. Directorate of Security and Intelligence Report, 1967-1968.

131. In 1984 it was reported that the RCMP had destroyed all of its files kept solely on the basis of sexual orientation. See John Duggan, "RCMP Destroys Files...Maybe" in *Rites*, No. 5, Oct. 1984, p. 7. Reprinted from *Go Info* (Ottawa).

132. The Lesbians Making History Collective, "People Think This Didn't Happen In Canada" in *Fireweed* No. 28, Spring 1989, p. 84.

133. Directorate of Security and Intelligence Annual Report, 1962-1963, p. 19.

134. Directorate of Security and Intelligence Report, 1963-1964, p. 30.

135. I am tracing this out in my continuing research on the anti-homosexual security campaigns.

136. Quoted in the National Gay Rights Coalition, "The Homosexual Minority and the Canadian

Human Rights Act: A Brief Concerning Bill C-72 Prepared for Presentation to Members of Parliament," (mid-1970s), p. 15.

137. For more on "resistance" based on interviews with those directly affected see my chapter in Sara Stratton and David Kimmel, eds., *Not Going Away: Essays on the History of Bisexuals, Lesbians and Gay Men in Canada*, forthcoming.

138. Wake who died in November 1993 had previously been a researcher for the Royal Commission on the Criminal Law Relating to Criminal Sexual Psychopaths, which is examined later in this chapter. Dr. F. R. Wake, "Report on Special Project," 19 Dec. 1962. The following quotes are also from this text.

139. Sawatsky, *Men in the Shadows*, p. 133.

140. See Maurice Leznoff, "The Homosexual in Urban Society," M.A. thesis, McGill University, Sociology Department, Montréal, 1954.

141. These included the Polygraph (lie-detector) test that, Wake argued, had too many problems to be useful; the Plethysmograph, which measures blood volume in the finger by electronic or pneumatic means; the Palmer Sweat test, which responds to perspiration; the Projective Tests; Word Association Tests; the Pupillary Response Test; the Span of Attention Test, based on the time spent in attending to various images (which Zamansky of Northeastern University had constructed as an apparatus to test for homosexuality in 1956); and Masculinity/Femininity Tests with all their gender and sexuality assumptions.

142. Dr. F. R. Wake, "Report on Special Project," Appendix A, Word Association List, pp. 1-3.

143. See Tom Waugh, "A Heritage of Photography" in *The Body Politic* No. 90, Jan. 1983, 29-33, his "Photography, Passion and Power" in *The Body Politic*, No. 101, March 1984, 29-33 and his "Gay Male Visual Culture in North America During the Fifties: Emerging from the Underground" in *Parellelograme*, V. 12, No. 1, Fall 1986; Alan Miller, "Beefcake With No Labels Attached" in *The Body Politic*, No. 90, Jan. 1983, 33; and Michael Bronski, *Culture Clash, The Making of a Gay Sensibility* (Boston: South End Press, 1984), pp. 160-174.

144. Wake, "Report on Special Project," *op. cit.*, p. 17.

145. This can be contrasted with the research technologies and strategies examined in Jennifer Terry's, "Theorizing Deviant Historiography" in *differences V. 3, No. 2, Summer 1991*, p. 60.

146. A memo to D.F. Wall, Secretary of the Security Panel, 25 Jan. 1963, from J. R. M. Bordeleau, Assistant Commissioner, Director, Security and Intelligence, RCMP, p. 1.

147. See Sawatsky, *Men in the Shadows*, pp. 133-136.

148. *Ibid.*, 135-137

149. This reference comes from Lynn Fernie.

150. *Two*, July/Aug., 1966 (Toronto), p. 12.

151. *Ibid.*

152. *Ibid.*, p. 13.

153. See the Sutcliffe autobiography, *op. cit.*, pp. 157-158; and Dana Flavelle, "Homosexuality Destroyed Decorated Soldier's Career" in *Toronto Star*, March 15, 1986, p. A15.

154. See Queen's Regulations and Orders, Military Code.

155. See Canadian Forces Administrative Order (CFAO-19-20). "Sexual Deviation-Investigation, Medical Examination, and Disposal," issued May 12, 1967.

156. See Glenn Wheeler, "Unfit For Service" in *The Body Politic*, March 1983, No. 91, p. 29.

157. Quoted in Report of the Royal Commission on the Criminal Law Relating to Criminal Sexual Psychopaths (Ottawa: The Queen's Printer, 1958), p. 8. This definition included the notion of "evil" that was taken over from religious and moral discourses. Criminal Sexual Psychopaths were not only criminal and dangerous but also "evil" men. This was sexual but also moral regulation.

158. *Ibid.*, p. ix; Edwin H. Sutherland, "The Diffusion of Sexual Psychopath Laws" in *American Journal of Sociology*, 1950, No. 56, pp. 142-148; Yvonne Chi-Ying Ng, "Ideology, Media and Moral Panics: An Analysis of the Jacques Murder" in M.A. thesis, Centre of Criminology, University of Toronto, Nov. 1981, pp. 59-60; D'Emilio, *Sexual Politics, op. cit.*, p. 17; and George Chauncey,

Jr., "The National Panic Over Child Abuse After World War II and the Emergence of Cold War Anti-Homosexual Politics," paper given at the Sex and the State conference, Toronto, July 1985. Also see Robert Champagne, "Psychopaths and Perverts: The Canadian Royal Commission on the Criminal Law Relating to Criminal Sexual Psychopaths, 1954-58" in *Canadian Lesbian and Gay History Newsletter* No. 2, Sept. 1986, pp. 7-9.

159. Girard, "Gays, Lesbians and the Legal Process Since 1945," *op. cit.*, p. 83.

160. *Ibid.*, pp. 86-88, 96-98.

161. Estelle Freedman, "'Uncontrolled Desires': The Response to the Sexual Psychopath, 1920-1960" in *The Journal of American History* (V. 74, No. 1) and also in Kathy Peiss and Christina Simmons, eds., *Passion and Power, Sexuality in History* (Philadelphia: Temple University Press, 1989), p. 213.

162. None of the 23 men sentenced as criminal sexual psychopaths from 1948-1955 were fathers of, or related to those assaulted or harassed. See report of the Royal Commission, *op. cit.*

163. On textually-mediated social organization see the work of Dorothy E. Smith, *The Conceptual Practices of Power* (Toronto: University of Toronto Press, 1990) and *Texts, Facts and Femininity* (London: Routledge, 1990). On this in relation to the Royal Commission on Criminal Sexual Psychopaths see Gary Kinsman, "Official Discourse as Sexual Regulation," *op. cit.*

164. See my *Constructing "Child Sexual Abuse": Mount Cashel, the Mass Media and Making Homosexuality a Social Problem*, forthcoming.

165. The commission heard testimony from thirty-five psychiatrists, twenty-one members of the legal profession, eleven medical doctors, twenty-one professors, six police officers, eleven representatives of Attorneys-General, twelve representatives of various departments of health. The Report of the Royal Commission, *op. cit.*, p. 2. For a breakdown, see the report, pp. 131-135. Two members of the commission attended the Diagnostic Centre at Menlo Park, New Jersey, p. 2. The Wolfenden Report and the Kinsey studies were also cited. On the use of RCMP records, see the report, p. 61.

166. On this see the submission by Rev. Francis Howard Kelly Greer in the records of the Public Hearings of the Royal Commission on Criminal Sexual Psychopaths, June 14-28, 1954, pp. 318, 320-321 reported on below; and the submission by Axel Otto Olson, referred to below at a private session of the commission in 1956. My thanks to Robert Champagne for bringing these to my attention. See Axel Otto Olson, "1956: The Royal Commission on the Criminal Law Relating to Criminal Sexual Psychopaths," edited and introduced by Robert Champagne in *Rites*, V. 3, No. 6, Nov. 1986, pp. 8-9.

167. Greer also endorsed the briefs submitted by the Welfare Council and the John Howard Society. Public hearings June 14-18, 1954, New Brunswick, PEI, Nova Scotia and Newfoundland, pp. 315-323. The following quotes from Greer and McRuer come from these pages.

168. Report of the Royal Commission on Criminal Sexual Psychopaths, *op. cit.*, p. 28.

169. As we will see Jim Egan was unaware of it since it was not reported or referenced in the commission report.

170. "Congenital inversion" was also the hegemonic perspective in early homosexual rights organizing in Germany and Europe.

171. Hearings of the Royal Commission, 1956, p. 146.

172. See "Report of Private Sessions, Royal Commission on Criminal Sexual Psychopaths, Montreal and Toronto," commencing Feb. 6, 1956, pp. 137-147. Also see the edited version introduced by Robert Champagne in *Rites, op. cit.*

173. Robert Champagne, "Psychopaths and Perverts: The Canadian Royal Commission on the Criminal Law Relating to Criminal Sexual Psychopaths, 1954-1958" in *Canadian Lesbian and Gay History Newsletter*, No. 2, Sept. 1986, pp. 8-9.

174. Report of the Royal Commission, *op. cit.*, p. 27.

175. *Ibid.*

176. *Ibid.*

177. Jim Egan, "'Toronto Fairy-Go-Round,' So the Chief of Police Said To The Royal Commission …" *Justice Weekly*, Nov. 7, 1959, p. 5, No. 15, reprinted from *One* magazine.
178. David N. Weisstaub, ed., *Law and Psychiatry in the Canadian Context* (Toronto: Pergamon Press, 1980), p. 693.
179. Report of the Royal Commission, *op. cit.*, pp. 121-124.
180. Girard, "Gays, Lesbians and the Legal Process Since 1945," *op. cit.*, p. 94.
181. On the continuing resiliency of this narrative, see my *Constructing "Child Sexual Abuse": Mount Cashel, the Mass Media and Making Homosexuality a Social Problem*, forthcoming.
182. See Philippe Aries, *Centuries of Childhood* (New York: Vintage, 1962); and Gay Left Collective, "Happy Families? Pedophilia Examined" in Daniel Tsang, *The Age Taboo: Gay Male Sexuality, Power and Consent* (Boston, London: Alyson/Gay Men's Press, 1981), pp. 53-64; John Fritz, "The Child as Legal Subject" in Dale, *et al.*, eds., *Education and the State. V. 2, Politics, Patriarchy and Practice* (Sussex: Falmer Press, 1981), pp. 285-302; Michel Foucault, *History of Sexuality. V. 1, An Introduction* (New York: Vintage. 1980); and Nikolas Rose, "Beyond the Public/Private Division: Law, Power and the Family" in P. Fitzpatrick and Alan Hunt, eds., *Critical Legal Studies* (Oxford: Blackwell, 1987).
183. See, for instance, "Barnyard Morals and Crimes of Youth" in United Church of Canada Annual Report, No. 32, 1957, p. 46. Also see Mary Louise Adams, "Almost anything can happen: A search for sexual discourse in the urban spaces of 1940s Toronto" in *The Canadian Journal of Sociology*, V. 19, No. 2, 1994, pp. 224-225. Also see her "The Trouble With Normal: Post-War Teenagers and the Construction of Heterosexuality," Ph.D. thesis, Department of Educational Theory, OISE, Toronto, 1994.
184. See Pearce, *op. cit.*, pp. 296-299.
185. Most studies indicate that ninety percent or more of sexual harassment and coercion of children is inflicted by heterosexual men against girls, and that most occurs within the family. Brienes and Gordon say "…approximately 92 percent of the victims are female and 97 percent of the assailants are males." See Wini Breines and Linda Gordon, "The New Scholarship on Family Violence" in *Signs*, V. 8, No. 3, Spring 1983, p. 522. Also see Elizabeth Wilson, *What is to Be Done About Violence against Women?* (London: Penguin, 1983), particularly pp. 117-134. Ms. Spector, in a presentation to the World Congress on Violence and Human Existence in 1992, stated that only ten percent of assaulters are strangers, and 80 percent of those assaulted are girls. "Warnings about sex abuse may miss the mark, experts say" in *The Globe and Mail*, Jul. 14, 1992, p. A7. Statistics Canada reports that the assaulter is a stranger in only eight percent of sexual assault cases involving children, and in 48 percent of the reported cases, is a family member. The Vanier Institute of the Family reports that the young person knows the assaulter in 90 percent of reported cases. The "victims" are 70 to 80 percent girls and those accused are 94 percent men. This is reported in *The Globe and Mail*, Jul. 22, 1994, p. A10. The Jul. 1994 issue of *Pediatrics* reports that of 269 cases of child sexual abuse studied, only two offenders were identifiable as gay or lesbian. A young person's risk of being molested by a heterosexual partner of a relative is more than 100 times greater than by an identifiable gay man, lesbian or bisexual. This is reported in "Homosexuals no threat" in *The Globe and Mail*, Jul. 7, 1994, p. A7. This study is an impressive challenge to right-wing arguments that gays are "child molesters." Also see, *Pediatrics*, July 1994, pp. 41-44.
186. On narratives of sexual danger, see Judith R. Walkowitz, *City of Dreadful Delight: Narratives of Sexual Danger in Late-Victorian London* (Chicago: The University of Chicago Press, 1992).
187. Girard, "Gays, Lesbians and the Legal Process," *op. cit.*, p. 91.
188. From the Parents' Action League: Scientific Advisory Committee statement of April 25, 1955. Also see Hubert Pascoe, "Deviant Sexual Behaviour and the Sex Criminal" in *Canadian Medical Association Journal*, V. 84, Jan. 28, 1962, reprinted in Laskin, ed., *Social Problems: A Canadian Profile* (Toronto: McGraw-Hill, 1964), pp. 413-414.
189. See *Justice Weekly*, Oct. 8, 1958, p. 4.
190. See Ron Kenyon, "You Can Curb Canada's Sex Crimes" in *Liberty* (Toronto), Aug. 1955, p. 68.

191. *Ibid.*, p. 68.

192. *Ibid.*

193. Verbatim transcript of the *Star* "Forum." The quotes below from the "experts" who spoke at this forum are from this text.

194. Kenyon, *op. cit.*, p. 68.

195. Nikolas Rose, "Beyond the Public/Private Division: Law, Power and the Family" in P. Fitzpatrick and Alan Hunt, eds., *Critical Legal Studies, op. cit.*, p. 71.

196. Kenyon, *op. cit.*, p. 69.

197. See interview with Dr. R.E. Turner in the *ASK Newsletter* (Vancouver), Apr. 1965, V. 2, No. 4.

198. "A Murdered Child" in *Toronto Daily Star*, Oct. 11, 1955.

199. James Fraser, "Piecing It Together: The 1950s" in *Lesbian/Gay History Researchers Network Newsletter*, Issue 5, Dec. 1981, p. 13; and "2,000 Hear Experts on Sex Deviates at Star Forum Meeting" and "All Sex Deviates Not Criminals, Must Use Caution — Doctor" in *Toronto Daily Star*, Jan. 28, 1956. The following quotes from the meeting are from the *Toronto Daily Star*.

200. Page one of this letter, which is in the holdings of the Canadian Lesbian and Gay Archives.

201. "Star," Jan. 1956 (Toronto), reprinted in *One* magazine.

202. PAL apparently branched out to also concern itself with "juvenile delinquency," sexually-arousing literature, and campaigns for warnings in the schools against accepting rides from strangers. Chapters were organized across Ontario, elsewhere in Canada, and even in the U.S. See Pascoe, *op. cit.*, pp. 413-414.

203. Report of the Royal Commission, *op. cit.*, p. 117.

204. Peter Thomson, "Sexual Deviation" in *Canadian Medical Association Journal*, Mar. 1, 1959, V. 80, p. 387.

205. Franklin Russell, "Clinic to Curb Sex Crimes before They Happen" in *Maclean's*, Sept. 1961, reprinted in W.E. Mann, ed., *Social Deviance in Canada* (Toronto: Copp Clark, 1971). Russell reports that Dr. Turner had lectured to an annual meeting of Ontario magistrates on how to recognize deviates. A colleague of his, Dr. Stokes, addressed cadets at the Ontario Police College, see p. 423.

206. Mohr and Turner, "Sexual Deviation," *op. cit.*, p. 353.

207. On this see Martin Duberman, *Cures: A Gay Man's Odyssey* (New York: Dutton, 1991). For a later period when more lesbian and gays have rejected this psychiatric terrorism, see "Mad, angry, gay and proud: A Lesbian and Gay Supplement" in *Phoenix Rising*, V. 8, No. 3/4, July 1990.

208. Turner in the *ASK Newsletter*, V. 2, No. 4, Apr. 1985.

209. Freedman, *op. cit.*, p. 103.

210. See Mohr, Turner and Jerry, *Pedophilia and Exhibitionism: A Handbook* (Toronto: University of Toronto Press, 1964); Mohr and Turner, "Sexual Deviations," Part IV: "Paedophilia" in *Applied Therapeutics*, V. 9, No. 4, Apr. 1967, pp. 362-365; and Mohr, "The Pedophilias: Their Clinical, Social and Legal Implications" in *Canadian Psychiatric Association Journal*, V. 7, No. 5 (Oct. 1962), reprinted in Benjamin Schlesinger, ed., *Sexual Behaviour in Canada* (Toronto: University of Toronto Press, 1977), pp. 201-210. Krafft-Ebing had earlier coined the term "pedophilia erotica" as part of his typology of sexual diseases. See Tom O'Carroll, *Paedophilia: The Radical Case* (Boston: Alyson, 1982), pp. 59-60.

211. Gigeroff, *op. cit.*, p. 59.

212. Forms of "pedophile" resistance to oppression, taking up this category, reshaping it or rejecting it (as among those who have defined themselves instead as "boy-lovers") had emerged by the 1970s. See Gay Left Collective, "Happy Families," *op. cit.*, p. 59, and O'Carroll, *op. cit.* Those homosexuals who tried to gain respectability by suggesting it was only those "deviants" interested in sex with young people who caused trouble also helped create this separate category of pedophilia. This position argues that it is not homosexuals but pedophiles who are the "real" deviants. In 1994 debates within the International Lesbian and Gay Association (ILGA), under pressure from the right wing in the U.S. and the U.S. government who were

opposing ILGA's membership in an international UN body because of the alleged presence of "pedophiles" in ILGA's membership, led to the purging of the North American Man Boy Love Association (NAMBLA) and other "pedophile" groups from membership. This set a dangerous precedent of allowing the U.S. right wing to determine the membership of the international lesbian and gay organization. At the same time, NAMBLA has a sexual-libertarian position and does neglect problems of sexual violence and harassment young people face.

213. Mohr, "The Pedophilias," *op. cit.*, p. 205-206.
214. Of course many gay men and lesbians exist within familial relations, see Carole-Anne O'Brien and Lorna Weir, "Lesbians and Gay Men inside and outside Families" in Nancy Mandell and Anne Duffy, ed., *Canadian Families: Diversity, Conflict and Change* (Toronto: Harcourt Bruce Canada, 1995), pp. 111-139.
215. Also see Gary Kinsman, *Constructing "Child Sexual Abuse,"* forthcoming.
216. John Marshall, "Pansies, Perverts and Macho Men" in Plummer, ed., *The Making of the Modern Homosexual, op. cit.*, pp. 133-134.
217. The term "transvestism" was originated by Hirshfeld in 1910. See Dave King, "Gender Confusions: Psychological and Psychiatric Conceptions of Transvestism and Trans-Sexualism" in Plummer, ed., *The Making of the Modern Homosexual, op. cit.*, p. 159.
218. Although this new perspective was not yet hegemonic; for instance, Pascoe still thought that at the core of homosexuality was an inability to appreciate oneself as fully "masculine." Pascoe, *op. cit.*
219. Crane, *Gays and the Law* (London: Pluto, 1982), p. 189.
220. See John Money and Patricia Tucker, *Sexual Signatures* (Boston: Little, Brown and Company, 1975); Janice G. Raymond, *The Transsexual Empire* (Boston: Beacon Press, 1979).
221. See Suzanne J. Kessler and Wendy McKenna, *Gender: An Ethnomethodological Approach* (Chicago and London; The University of Chicago Press, 1978) and Harold Garfinkel, *Studies in Ethnomethodology* (Englewood Cliffs, NJ: Prentice-Hall, 1967).

8.

The Struggle for Law Reform

Wolfenden: A New Strategy of Sexual Regulation

A government report clearly expressing the shifting character of sexual regulation, particularly concerning homosexuality, was produced in England in the 1950s. This text had a major impact in the organizing of law-reform discussions of Criminal Code sex offences in Canada in the 1960s. The way it was read and used played a major part in opening up further space for tendencies toward law reform that began in the 1950s and in bringing them together for more coherent and successful law-reform efforts in the 1960s. This was a very different strategy of sexual regulation from that articulated in the extending criminalization of homosexuality approach that informed the criminal-sexual-psychopath and dangerous-sexual-offender strategy with which it comes into contention in Canada in the 1960s.

The Wolfenden committee was formed by the Home Secretary in response to media-amplified moral outrage and an attempted "moral panic" over sexual vice and prostitution. The media in England portrayed a rapid escalation of homosexuality and prostitution in the early 1950s. The committee was formed in the immediate aftermath of the Montagu-Wildeblood trial for homosexual "offences" in 1954 and in the context of the Cold War spy scandals, which sharpened the dividing line between the "normal" and the "deviant." It therefore had similar roots to the context in which the extension of criminalization of homosexuality had taken place in Canada in the 1950s. An interdepartmental committee under the chairmanship of Sir John Wolfenden was established in 1954 to investigate the "nauseating subject" of male homosexuality and prostitution, the connections between the two having been established historically in the last century through the notion that both were signs of "moral decline."[1] This belief was part of the post-war reassertion of "traditional" heterosexual family relations. Female prostitutes along with male homosexuals were seen to be a threat to heterosexual companionate marriage.[2]

Pressure from the Public Morality Council, the National Vigilance Association, and the Church of England Moral Welfare Council helped to lead up to the formation of the Wolfenden committee. Although most pressure for a commission focused on homosexuality, prostitution was included in the terms of reference of the Wolfenden committee in the context of an attempted "moral panic" over the visibility of prostitutes on city streets, particularly in London.[3] The question raised for the Wolfenden committee was how to manage large-scale deviations from what was defined as "normative" sexual relations — to search for a more effective means of regulating "sexual deviance."[4]

The Wolfenden committee heard testimony from police chiefs, medical associations, and government departments, doctors, and psychologists.[5] Its work and the report it produced were lodged firmly in the social relations of ruling, managing, and administering sexual life. It heard only one individual deputation from a gay man — Peter Wildeblood himself.[6]

The terms of reference given to the committee directed it to consider:

> (a) the law and practice relating to homosexual offences and the treatment of persons convicted of such offences by the courts; and
>
> (b) the law and practices relating to offences against the criminal law in connection with prostitution and solicitation for immoral purposes, and to report what changes, if any, are in our opinion desirable.[7]

These terms of reference clearly assume homosexuality and prostitution to be social problems, but, aside from this underlying assumption, the terms are fairly open. Regarding homosexual offences they direct the attention of the committee to the criminal law and the treatment of people convicted under the criminal law. The terms of reference for prostitution are more restricted and there is no mention of treatment.

Within this framework the committee is given a wide latitude to work over and propose shifts to these sexual regulations. This opens up some space for innovation. The terms of reference allow both for the holding in place and also the shifting of proposed regulations. The space for possible shifting is much wider than that allowed for in the terms of reference given to the Royal Commission on Criminal Sexual Psychopaths. This allows the Wolfenden committee to develop concepts for the reform of the law regarding sexual regulation more generally. The regulatory strategy it articulates must be able to cover both male homosexuality and female prostitution. Public/private categories allowed for this innovative conceptual handling of the diversities of the regulation of both homosexuality and prostitution.

Public/Private Regulation

The overall framework for the *Wolfenden Report* and the regulatory strategy it outlines is the distinction between "public" and "private": "There must be a realm of private morality and immorality that is in brief and crude terms not the law's business."[8] At a general abstract level it argues that the purpose of criminal law should be to preserve public decency, not to enforce private morality:

> Its function ... is to preserve public order and decency to protect the citizen from what is offensive and injurious and to provide sufficient safeguards against exploitation and corruption of others, particularly those who are especially vulnerable because they are young, weak in body or mind, inexperienced, or in a state of specific, official, or economic dependence ... it is not in our view the function of the law to intervene in the private lives of citizens, or to seek to enforce any particular patterns of behaviour.[9]

The committee is not arguing for the abandonment of sexual regulation but rather for the mobilizing of sexual and moral regulation through the broad "public" conceptualization of regulation developed in the Report. Throughout the Report the committee attempts to translate this conceptual distinction between public/private into ideological and policy terms that are then made available to ruling agencies to be taken up as part of the practical activities of regulation and policing. This public/private conceptual distinction allowed for the holding together of the Report's more restrictive proposals regarding "public" prostitution and its less restrictive proposals regarding "private" homosexuality.

The public/private distinction created the basis for a series of public and private classifications within official discourse and practice as a strategy of policing and regulation. The *Wolfenden Report* stresses the distinction already established in English law between crime and sin.[10] It therefore applies to the sexual realm the distinction between "public" and "private" domains that were themselves organized through State and professional practices.

Public/private was a legal distinction that emerged within the framework of capitalist society, for instance, in the writings of Jeremy Bentham and John Stuart Mill. These "classical" texts continued in some ways to actively inform the conceptual framework of the *Wolfenden Report* and the ensuing debates. These categories only seemed to really become legally cogent in this sex-related terrain in this social and historical context. In these views, State intervention in "private" was seen to be justified only to prevent "harm" to others.[11] An "offence" to "public decency" is however much broader than Mill intended when he referred to direct harm to others. Moral discourse in the sexual realm was not abandoned in this strategy but instead moral arguments were tied to a mobilization against public indecency and nuisance that in general disapproved of homosexuality.

Actual experiences of the delights and dangers of erotic life were transformed or inscribed in this language into categories of public and private sex. In the ideological world view articulated by the *Wolfenden Report*, there exists a private moral realm, which it argues, should be free of direct legal intervention. This "private" realm seems to have an almost natural rather than a social character to it.

Judging homosexuality to be a "state or condition" that cannot come under the purview of criminal law, the committee reported that the number of homosexual offences had increased considerably and that this was a "serious problem," particularly when the men involved were in positions of trust and responsibility.[12] They argued against any simple notion of homosexuality as an illness that they felt would undermine the responsibility of these men for their acts and also because there was no clear "cause" or "cure" for homosexuality.[13] At the same time they did accept the importance of psychological approaches in addressing homosexuality. In the section of the report focusing on homosexuality they tended to rely on and integrate "liberal" sex-scientific work on homosexuality. The report was also shaped by the growing presence and visibility of gay networks in England.

The report clearly embodies fears over homosexuality among teachers and other

people in contact with the young, arguing that men found guilty of homosexual offences should not be allowed to continue teaching or as youth leaders. It relates this apparent increase in homosexual activity to the wartime conditions that had loosened
family ties and separated the genders for prolonged periods. It suggested:

> it is likely that the emotional insecurity, community instability and weaken-
> ing of the family inherent in the social changes of our civilization have been
> factors contributing to an increase in homosexual behaviour.[14]

The discursive organization of such statements ties the report to the regulation of gender and age relations. As Bland, McCabe, and Mort point out in their critical analysis of
the report:

> For "emotional insecurity" read problem families and depraved children,
> for "community instability" read the breakdown of the Old pre-War pat-
> terns of community, for "the weakening of the family" read the contradic-
> tions thrown up by the increase in waged work among married women, the
> concern over the growth of antagonistic youth cultures, and the faint begin-
> nings of sexual permissiveness ...[15]

The *Wolfenden Report* suggests in a number of places that a "happy family life" can curtail
a homosexual "propensity." The report clearly embodies the standpoint of heterosexual
hegemony, even if it does suggest a new form for this hegemony. Heterosexuality, in the
shape of heterosexual matrimonial monogamy is constructed as the undisputable social
norm. In its historical context, however, the report had certain progressive consequences and presented new opportunities for gays, lesbians, and others.

The report recommends that the police deal with homosexual acts in public places.
It articulates a new classification for "private" homosexual activity between two adults,
arguing that it be decriminalized and regulated through non-judicial agencies such as
psychiatric, psychological, therapeutic, and medical agencies and the disciplines of social work and sociology. These recommendations played an important part in establishing adult male homosexuality as a "condition," reflecting the bid by psychiatrists and
medical doctors to increase their regulatory terrains. At the same time there was no simple professional "conspiracy" pushing in this direction.

The committee stopped short of including navy and armed forces personnel in its
recommendations. Within services with a disciplinary regime, says the report:

> it may be necessary, for the sake of good management and the preservation
> of discipline and for the protection of those of subordinate rank or posi-
> tion, to regard homosexual behaviour even by consenting adults in private
> as an offence ... The service authorities may ... consider it necessary to re-
> tain Section 66 of the Act [the Army Act, 1955] (which provides for the pun-

ishment of, inter alia, disgraceful conduct of an indecent or unnatural kind) on the ground that it is essential, in the services, to treat as offences certain types of conduct which may not amount to offences under the civil code.[16]

Here again the military was viewed as a particular form of organization that made it a "special case" so that even the limited forms of decriminalization being proposed would not apply to it. Similar arguments would get mobilized regarding the military and the police in the Canadian context following the initiation of law-reform discussions.

The *Wolfenden Report* deals with three major arguments against the decriminalization of homosexual behaviour in "private." These arguments were the main strains of heterosexism formed earlier in the century: that homosexuality threatens the health of society; that it has a damaging effect on family life; and that homosexuals may turn their interest to boys.

The Cold War homosexual-security scares were very intense when the report was commissioned but had died down somewhat by the time of its release. While they agreed that homosexuality may exclude gays from certain types of State employment, they did not feel that this was a sufficient reason for making private homosexual acts with one other consenting adult a crime. They took the issue of the possible danger to family life very seriously, admitting that homosexual behaviour may very well hurt the family that the report regards as the basic unit of society. The committee argued, however, that it had no reason to believe that male homosexuality is any more damaging to the family than "adultery, fornication, or lesbian behaviour ..."[17] They felt that the law can do little to prevent homosexuality in "private," and other means of regulation must be found, says the report, but it also warns that society should not condone or approve male homosexual behaviour.

> It is important that the limited modification of the law which we propose should not be interpreted as an indication that the law can be indifferent to other forms of homosexual behaviour, or as a general license to adult homosexuals to behave as they please.[18]

The committee also took very seriously the possible "menace to boys." Homosexuality is seen not as a single entity but as comprising both men who seek other adult males as partners and "men who seek as partners boys who have not reached puberty." The homosexual "pedophile" was thus created (although here the term tends to be applied to any man interested in males under the age of twenty-one). They added to their public/private strategy of regulating homosexual sex an important, and more extensive, prohibition against any homosexual act involving anyone under the age of twenty-one.

In the public realm, which is broadly defined as any situation wherein more than two people are present, homosexual sex should be dealt with rather severely. The police should vigilantly patrol "public" spaces, says the report, such as public lavatories.

The committee was particularly concerned with the young and the "immature," and the possibility of a young man being led astray from a "normal" adult life. It argued that

> we should not wish to see legalized any forms of behaviour which would swing towards a permanent habit of homosexual behaviour a young man who without such encouragement would still be capable of developing a normal habit of heterosexual adult life.[19]

Here the committee argued for a distinct form of protection for "normal" heterosexuality with the demarcation of homosexuality as "abnormal." The myth of youth seduction by older homosexuals was used to argue that the special characteristics of male homosexuality justified more intense treatment in the criminal law. It was implied that male homosexuals presented a higher "social danger" to youths than heterosexuals.[20] In this area, the *Wolfenden Report* overlapped with aspects of the more right-wing anti-gay criminalization strategy I detailed last chapter in the Canadian context.

The committee relied on State and legal definitions of "juvenile" and on notions of the supposed special vulnerability of adolescent males. The committee therefore chose twenty-one as the age of consent for buggery and gross indecency, in spite of the much lower age of consent for heterosexual sexual acts. The report accordingly recommends severe penalties for adult/youth homosexual sex. This perspective has continued to inform Canadian sexual legislation until the present.

It also called for harsher penalties for male prostitution. The committee was particularly horrified by homosexual buggery since it "involves coitus and this simulates more nearly than any other homosexual act the normal act of sexual intercourse."[21] It toyed with the idea of retaining buggery as an offence, and this would apply to all same-gender acts of anal intercourse, both public and private.

A psychiatric report would be ordered for convicted offenders under twenty-one so that a proper course of "treatment" could be formulated. The report claims that while homosexuality cannot be cured it can be treated. The report outlines various forms of medical and psychiatric therapy: "... there is a place for the clergyman, the psychiatric social worker, the probation officer and, it may be added, the adjusted homosexual, as well as the doctor."[22] This "adjusted homosexual" is a reference to the self-regulated, "respectable," closeted or semi-closeted homosexual.

Probation would be accompanied by medical treatment in some cases so that informal social regulation would be extended. The report also recommends the use of estrogen (a hormone) in certain cases in order to diminish sexual desire. It also advocates more inter-disciplinary research into the causes of homosexuality and of course not into the "causes" of heterosexuality. This research would, of course, be based on prison populations of homosexual offenders and those already undergoing "treatment." A number of factors, according to the report, would discourage homosexuality in the long run. These include the desirability of a healthy home background; moral guidance of parents and children; sensible sex education in matters of sex, not only for children but for teachers, youth leaders and those who advise students. Particularly, it is urged that medical students should be given more information about homosexuality in their classes, and that clergy and probation officers should be better equipped to deal with the problems about which they are often consulted.[23]

Again the standpoint of heterosexual hegemony that the report takes up is clear. This was also a suggestion for an extension of the professional guidance of parents among others.

When applied to female prostitutes, this public/private distinction carries somewhat different results. The report takes the visibility of street-walkers to be an affront to public order and decency.[24] It was the prostitutes — not the customers, they argue — who did the parading; "the simple fact is that the prostitute's do parade themselves more habitually and openly than their prospective clients."[25] They also argued:

> We feel that the right of the normal decent citizen to go about the streets without affront to his or her sense of decency should be the prime consideration and should take precedence over the interests of the prostitute and her customers.[26]

The standpoint constructed and adopted here is that of the "normal decent citizen" and not that of the women working as a prostitute. Integral to this public/private distinction is the social organization of gender, patriarchal relations, and a number of sexist assumptions. The woman is assigned to the "private," and when she transgresses the boundaries into the "public" realm, legal regulation, is called for.[27] The report calls for clearing the streets of "public prostitutes." The report and the resulting legislation did not stop the police from also arresting prostitutes working in more "private" areas. In its broader applications to gender and sexual regulation, this strategy focused on regulation in the socially defined "public" realm and not on sexual violence and harassment in the "private" realm. Sexual dangers and troubles were identified with terrains outside families and households.

The main Wolfenden recommendations on prostitution were quickly implemented in the Street Offences Act of 1959. Here, the report is much more conducive to the hegemonic moral and political climate of the day. Its controversial proposals on homosexuality were opposed on the basis of a heterosexism formed in interaction with nationalism and imperialism. National decline and loss of Empire were associated with the spread of "perverse" and "degenerate" sexual practices.[28] The government argued, therefore, that it did not have enough support to implement the proposals. The report's value, it said, would lie in its educational effects. The recommendations would be adopted only after a series of homophile inspired law-reform campaigns and debates within the legal profession, in church circles, and elsewhere. They would not be passed in England and Wales until 1967, with the Sexual Offences Act, and were not extended to Scotland and Northern Ireland until the 1980s.

These reforms would be adopted in a rather different political and social conjuncture from that in which the committee was set up and in which the report was released. This would be within the context of other reform and "liberal" legislation in the 1960s. By the later 1960s, after years of debate and organizing, the report's proposals were increasingly seen in official circles as a more effective way to regulate homosexuality. In this sense, the *Wolfenden Report* strategy does not simply passively reflect social changes but is actively used by homophile reformers, the media, liberal churches and eventually by liberal and social democratic politicians in the reorganizing of social and moral regulation. Reform efforts regarding the criminal law relating to homosexuality and many other sex-related matters came to be organized through its conceptual strategy in England, Canada, and many other countries.

The *Wolfenden Report* is part of a transformation in sex/gender, State, and class relations. Since World War II, sexuality and sexual discussions had assumed a previously unthinkable social centrality in many people's lives. The post-war years saw a shift in family organization, particularly the integration of married women into the wage-labour force, the development of new birth-control technologies, and the generation of new sexological knowledges. The expansion of consumer capitalism led to increasing commercialization of social life, including sexuality, with women's bodies being used to sell commodities and social values through advertising and the communications and entertainment industries.

As sexuality became more visible in these forms, there emerged the voices of those who wanted it to be less public. Reverend W.G. Berry of Toronto expresses the moral conservative view in a 1959 United Church Report: "Sex today is not only out in the open; it stalks nakedly down the city street, and the village lane. It stares nudely at us from almost every magazine and weekend newspaper."[29]

It is in this context that the new strategy of sexual and moral regulation outlined in the *Wolfenden Report* was developed. The distinction between public and private was an attempt to relax aspects of moral, sexual, and gender regulation in some areas. Sexuality, particularly its "deviant" forms, was being kept in the socially organized private realm. These public/private categories of sex administration defined the work of social agencies in managing sexual "problems." These classifications were able to write a certain coherence into sexual and social regulation in a number of different terrains. This was especially the case given that social changes and the expansion and visibility of gay networks had begun to undermine the effectiveness of previous regulatory strategies that focused on extending the criminalization of homosexual sex. The cogency of these earlier strategies began to be undermined and they began to be seen as generating growing problems. The abstract character of the public/private distinction meant that this classification system could be taken up more easily in widely different State contexts as an administrative classification. This is one of the reasons why the Wolfenden approach has had such extensive influence. The same general social changes in sex/gender relations had also taken place by the late 1960s across the "advanced" capitalist countries making the Wolfenden strategy a possible and often cogent response to pressures for law reform.

The Wolfenden strategy, then, which was one both of sex reform and sexual rule, was part of a shift in social organization.[30] It shaped sexual legislation and discussion for decades to come. "We continue to occupy a space that was very much formed in the aftermath of Wolfenden."[31] Preparing the social field for subsequent legislation and discussions, it identified public/private categories as central elements of sexual regulation that could then be applied to debates on a series of sex, gender, and moral questions. These distinctions have continued to influence British legislation and they are still central to debates over sexual questions in Canada today given the continuing use of public/private and adult/youth regulatory frameworks.[32]

The Wolfenden perspective prepared the ground for what has been called "permissive," but what might be better termed "liberal" legislation, in England and Canada. As Stuart Hall argues, "... descriptively, we may agree that the tendency of the legislation was to shift things in the general direction of a less rigid, looser, more 'permissive' moral order."[33]

This legislation can, however, be described as permissive or "liberalizing" only within narrow boundaries, since it also outlined a certain tightening up of sexual regulation.

> [Wolfenden] is "permissive" in that it opens up an area of private, individual "consent" while maintaining if not tightening its control of the public manifestations of "irregular" sexual conduct.[34]

The report facilitated the "decriminalization" of the adult male homosexual in the limited private realm; it also attempted to remove homosexuality from the "public" sphere. It therefore affected gay-community formation both "positively" and "negatively." Public discussions of homosexuality and recommendations for the decriminalization of adult male homosexual sex opened up social spaces for the expansion of gay networks and cultures. At the same time, this strategy of regulation directs this cultural formation in a privatized direction — toward ghettoization and a strategy of containment. As Mort writes, the 1967 Act that implemented the Wolfenden homosexual reforms

> constructs a new homosexual subject, understood as operating in the private sphere; a subject who in matters of sexuality and morality is defined as consenting, private and person-focused. In fact what the reformed version of the law does is to continue to reproduce the structures through which the gay male subculture had developed over the previous hundred years, while now decriminalizing it. One can speculate ... that the structuring of

the law across this public/private divide may have had much to do with the particular ways in which the gay subculture, and latterly the commercial gay scene, has developed from the late nineteenth century onwards.[35]

The *Wolfenden Report* drew upon a number of definitions of public and private, developed in different discourses and institutional locations. "Private" included the individual moral realm that was not the law's business — a private dwelling space — and not being visible to public view. This conflated the realm of moral choice with the realm of the private home, while the public became the broader social world. The idea of privacy was associated with private property and ownership.[36] There was no focus on the social practices people engage in to actively construct and accomplish privacy and intimacy. These public/private classifications were instead deployed as administrative regulations.

When it came to homosexual offences, "public" was defined rather broadly and "private" much more narrowly. The committee was very clear that a "public" washroom is indeed a public place and therefore that homosexual acts that occurred there would be illegal. The police were to be mobilized against public homosexual sex and against all homosexual sex involving males under the age of twenty-one. In the four years after the 1967 reform was passed in England, the conviction rate for homosexual offences shot up by 160 percent.[37] After the Wolfenden perspective was extended to Northern Ireland in 1982, there was also increased police activity against gay cruising and all forms of homosexual "public display." One observer expressed the police position as "now that you are legal, this should be done in your homes."[38] The implementation of the Wolfenden perspective actually led to an increase in police activity directed against gays. We will see how this played itself out in the Canadian context.

The Hart/Devlin Debates: Law and Morals

The *Wolfenden Report* gave rise to one of the liveliest debates in contemporary legal philosophy in the West and especially in the English language: that between H.L.A. Hart and Lord Patrick Devlin.[39] This debate affected discussions in Canada as well and became a standard part of law school curriculum.

Devlin gave evidence before the Wolfenden committee and was basically in favour of its proposals. It was the duty of society, he felt, to prevent youths from being led astray, and that the law against buggery should be retained for private acts as a deterrent to the corruption of youth and the social acceptance of homosexuality. Devlin disputed the committee's distinction between public and private morality, however, on the grounds that it could not be applied to other issues and that there should be uniformity of the law. There could be no such thing, in his view, as a private realm impenetrable to the law. Furthermore, society would fall apart without conformity and a shared public morality. Devlin saw immorality as what every "right-thinking man" thinks is immoral and he felt that law must be based on Christian morals. The error in Wolfenden, he said, was their attempt to find a general principle to explain the distinction between sin and crime.

Hart, on the other hand, was interested in individual freedom. He observed that the underlying principles of Wolfenden were close to the views expressed by John Stuart Mill in *On Liberty*. He related the public/private distinction to Mill's theories of opposition to government intervention against the individual for beliefs or acts that adversely affect no one. A reading of Mill's work played an active part in forming Hart's position. In Hart's view, homosexuality in private that caused no "harm" to anyone was not a form of treason, sedition, or crime.[40]

Hart accepted Wolfenden's ideological distinction between "public" and "private," obscuring that this was a social rather than a natural distinction, and postulating an individual private sphere somehow outside social organization. Devlin saw this distinction as arbitrary since no truly individualized private realm can exist. From his moral conservative standpoint, Devlin was able to see some of the contradictions that would plague the Wolfenden approach in the years to come. In the end, Devlin supported the criminal-law reform that took place in 1967.

In Canada, the Wolfenden perspective was challenged by moral conservatives. An early 1957 review from *The Church Times*, reprinted in the 1958 *Annual Report of the United Church of Canada's Board of Evangelism and Social Services*, welcomes the report's recommendations on prostitution but parts company with the committee on the matter "that homosexual behaviour between consenting adults in private be no more a criminal offence." The State has an obligation to maintain standards of sexual behaviour, argues the review, to keep the nation "healthy and sound." They were particularly concerned about the effects of these recommendations on the young.

> It is all very well to put heavy penalties upon the adult man who tries to pervert adolescents; but they are not going to be protected if sodomy is accepted by society as an odd, but permissible habit of some grown ups.[41]

Others, meanwhile, including homophile law reformers in England and in Canada, saw the *Wolfenden Report* as a progressive document and adopted its perspectives as their own. The public/private regulatory strategy provided a certain opening for gay and lesbian activists that the extending criminalization strategy actively denied them. Unlike the Royal Commission on Criminal Sexual Psychopaths report, the *Wolfenden Report* could be useful for gay reformers. It was not yet clearly seen, however, that the report was not only a "liberalizing" document, but that it also set the stage for a new set of oppressive regulatory practices. Psychiatrists, doctors, and lawyers also debated and often adopted the perspectives taken up in the report. These various groups produced different readings of the report — and uses for it — but it remained a reference point facilitating and helping to shape law-reform efforts.

In North America, the reception of the *Wolfenden Report* tended to place more weight on the sickness or mental-illness concept of homosexuality than there was in the ambiguous formulations in the original report. In the introduction to the "authorized American edition" of the *Wolfenden Report*, Karl Menninger, M.D., writes

> From the standpoint of the psychiatrist, both homosexuality and prostitu-
> tion ... constitute evidence of immature sexuality and either arrested psy-
> chological development or repression ... there is no question in the minds
> of psychiatrists regarding the abnormality of such behaviour. Not all such
> abnormalities can be cured, but some homosexuals ... can be and are bene-
> fited by treatment.[42]

This introduction provided instructions for reading this text for the North American
audience providing a way for accomplishing a "sickness" frame reading of the report.
This reading of the report would play an important role in how this reform perspective
would get taken up in official circles in Canada. It was argued that if homosexuals were
"sick" or "ill" they should be in a doctor's or therapist's care and should not be simply
addressed as a criminal problem. This reading of this partial de-criminalization strategy
rearticulated the medicalization of homosexuality away from the extending criminalization strategy and toward this new approach. The conceptualization of homosexuality as
an illness was maintained while its deployment was shifted.

At the heart of the Wolfenden reform process was a central contradiction: it did
provide a limited but important basis for the expansion of gay, and in a different way,
lesbian community formation. This community growth, however, would soon move beyond the boundaries of the private sphere (in the sense of clearly defined private places
like bedrooms), since gay cultures involved men meeting other men and erotic and social interaction in bars, clubs, cruising areas, and eventually gay districts of cities. The
police would try to contain this visibility. A struggle would then ensue over what constitutes public and private space as gays tried to extend the boundaries of the areas free of
direct State and police intervention. The gay-liberation movements of the 1970s would
eventually recognize that the Wolfenden strategy of "privatization" was not enough to
bring about gay and lesbian freedom, since it also established new ways to keep us in
subordinate positions.

This exploration of the *Wolfenden Report* has been included as necessary background
to the Canadian Criminal Code reform of 1969. I will now turn to an examination of the
law-reform process in Canada, with particular emphasis on the emerging gay and lesbian
cultures and the organization of a small but significant homophile movement. This is
what set the stage for movement in media, professional, and eventually official political
circles.

Gay/Lesbian Cultural and Community Formation

During the 1950s and 1960s, lesbian and gay networks were expanding and seizing
more social space for themselves and for those of us who would come onto the scene
later. Central to gay-male networks were meeting places such as bars and steam baths,
and cruising areas like parks and washrooms. Lesbians met in bars that women could
frequent, at house parties, within butch/femme cultures, in some workplace networks,

on women's baseball teams, and in more suburban networks. I will look at Toronto, and to a lesser extent Vancouver and Montréal, in this brief exploration of the emergence of gay-male cultures and lesbian community formation in Canada, some key features of which were already sketched in the last chapter.

For both lesbians and gay men, the emergence of bar space they can occupy is especially important. As Esther Newton explains, "bars are central social institutions in the gay community."[43] They are places where we can congregate, socialize, make sexual contacts and meet lovers away from the hostile pressures of the heterosexual world. Before exclusively gay or lesbian bars were established, lesbians and gay men would frequent those that catered to a mixed gay and straight clientele. In the late 1940s in Toronto, for instance, Bert Sutcliffe went to bars at the King Edward and Ford Hotels.[44] In Montréal, in the 1930s and 1940s, gays went to the Lincoln and Monarch Taverns. Michel Tremblay offers a portrait of a *poulailler* (hen house), the gay section of a 1940s bar, in *La duchesse et le roturier*. PJ's was Montréal's main downtown gathering place in the 1950s, and the only place where men could dance together — on Sunday afternoons only, of course. There were also the *tapette* (pansy; literally, "flyswatter") sections of a number of taverns.[45] In Vancouver, women went to the Vanport in the 1960s.

In Toronto, bars at an area called "the corners" at Bay and Queen were frequented by men interested in sex with men from the late 1930s on.[46] By the 1950s, the Municipal Tavern, Malloney's Studio Tavern, the Hotel Metropole, the Red Lion Bar of the Westbury Hotel, Letro's, the St. Charles Tavern, and the Parkside were being frequented by gay men.[47] These establishments were owned and managed by heterosexuals, however, and this sometimes created a negative and alienating atmosphere for gays and lesbians, even though we ourselves established them as part of queer space. As mentioned previously, lesbians in Toronto frequented the Continental but also the King Edward Hotel, Letro's, the Candlelight Lounge, the Juke Box club, the St. Charles, and the front of the Parkside.[48]

In the early 1960s, gay men and lesbians also frequented the gay-owned Regency Club and the Melody Room. The Maison de Lys/Music Room was opened by Sara Ellen Dunlop and Richard Kerr in 1962 as a late night unlicensed club, which meant that it could be patronized by younger gays.[49] Social and politically oriented discussions continued to take place at the club on a regular basis according to Jim Egan.[50] Richard Kerr was also involved with the gay magazine *Two* in the mid-1960s.

Sara Ellen Dunlop, an important figure in Toronto's lesbian history, continued to be active in lesbian and gay organizing into the 1970s, and gained a considerable reputation as a lesbian singer and musician. In the later 1960s, she was part of an all-women band that toured southern Ontario, and was later the founder of Mama Quilla I. I remember her powerful piano and singing performance at the Canadian lesbian and gay conference held in Toronto in 1976. She died of cancer in 1977.[51]

It is likely that men interested in sex with men first used steam baths to meet other men for sex early this century, if not before. A homosexual-oriented steam bath, the Oak Leaf, opened in Toronto in 1941.[52] In the 1950s, gay men went to the Sanitary Baths.

They also frequented several theatres, including the Bay Theatre at Bay and Queen (which was torn down to make way for the Simpson's Tower) to meet men and have sex.[53] Other favourite cruising spots included Philosopher's Walk at the University of Toronto, Allan Gardens, David Balfour Park, Queen's Park, High Park, Hanlan's Point on Toronto Island, and Winston Churchill Park.[54]

Gay men and lesbians lived with their parents, in boardinghouses, or in marginal apartments. Zoning regulations in Toronto suburbs prohibited unrelated persons from living together in houses classified as family dwellings. Central Mortgage and Housing Corporation issued mortgages only to people conforming to the heterosexual nuclear family form. Some gays spent the summer in Centre Island cottages. When Queen's Park and Hanlan's Point became known by the authorities as gay cruising spots, the bushes were cut down to make this more difficult. When it was discovered that gay men cruised Philosopher's Walk, morality lights were installed. Liquor laws also restricted the development of gay and lesbian bars.[55]

Gay- and lesbian-oriented commercial activity was limited by capital investment in what were generally small businesses, and was shaped by the profitability of the bars and baths, as well as State licensing and policing practices. These were part of the regulation of queer social space. At the same time, lesbians and gays fought for, and opened up, social spaces for our communities, establishing many of the places that we take for granted today. Our very right to go to and frequent gay and lesbian establishments rests on the struggles of those in the past.

Gay-male cultures were being created, some of the defining features of which were drag, camp, and physique photography and magazines.[56] At the Music Room in Toronto, there were drag shows every Friday and Saturday night from 1962 to 1966.[57] It is only through a process of cultural support and approval that "the drag queen creates himself."[58] Newton also refers to "street fairies" in the U.S. during the 1960s, whom she describes as often jobless homosexual men who built their lives around the gay cultures. They often lived at least partially outside the law and they played an important role in fighting for gay turf.[59]

Camp sensibility, which has been the subject of some controversy since the rise of gay liberation, played a formative role in the making of distinct gay cultures.[60] Camp plays with elements of incongruity, theatricality, and humour.[61] As well as glorifying certain female stars, it borrows images from Hollywood and transforms them into a distinct cultural context. Camp helps manage the contradictions between our particular experiences of the world as gays and the institutionalized heterosexuality that hegemonizes society. It provides a creative way of dealing with social stigma — a way of fully embracing it, thereby neutralizing it and making it laughable. This form of cultural production embodies both opposition to oppression and acceptance of it. On the one hand, it "denaturalizes normality" and makes fun of heterosexuality. It helps gays survive our oppression and provides us with a good deal of humour. At the same time, the camp homosexual can also agree "with the oppressor's definition of who he is." While the camp may put on a good show, he also can accommodate himself to his oppression and thus undercuts rage and rebellion. As Esther Newton expresses it, "camp is a pre- or proto-political phenomenon."[62]

In the U.S., especially in New York City, there is also a history for some black and Latino gays of drag in the drag balls of Harlem and elsewhere that is captured in the film *Paris Is Burning*.[63] This drag is an attempt to deal not only with heterosexism but also with racism and class inequality. This form of drag includes the performance of, and the taking over and transformation of white cultural symbols. Through these performances, these non-white gay men are able to assume positions of glamour and social status unobtainable in real life given the racist, heterosexist, and class-divided character of this society. Whether this form of drag culture — which provided important support against racism as well as forms of accommodation with a white-dominated society[64] — was practised in Canada during these years, remains to be explored.

Another important component of gay men's culture was the large number of physique magazines produced in the post-World War II period. Building on a history of gay erotic photography and films in the U.S. prior to the war, and the explosion of gay culture following the war, a physique-magazine trade developed in the 1950s. While these magazines often insisted they were produced for artists, nudists, and other people interested in the non-erotic beauties of the male body or in body-building, many of them were a source of erotic inspiration for gay men and helped lay the basis for the gay porn of the 1970s and 1980s. Mark One Studio in Lachine, Québec, began publishing its own photographs in a magazine called *Face and Physique*, and by 1962 this little magazine was beginning to cut into the U.S. market. To get around Canadian obscenity laws, it was printed in the U.S.[65] Physique photos were also published in Toronto's gay magazines *Two* and *Gay* in the mid-1960s.

Historically, there is a key importance of battles against State censorship in the opening up of erotic spaces for gay men and lesbians. This included repercussions in Canada from the U.S. like that of the important *One* magazine Supreme Court case in 1958, which allowed for the distribution of at least some types of information on homosexuality through the U.S. mail.[66]

As mentioned last chapter, lesbian cultures were also developing during these years, with some focused around the affirmation of butch/femme codes and the claiming of lesbian erotic space. As Joan Nestle puts it:

> Butch-femme relationships, as I experienced them, were very complex erotic statements, not phoney heterosexual replicas. They were filled with a deeply Lesbian language of stance, dress, gesture, living, courage, and autonomy.[67]

Lesbians established spaces for themselves in bars and also organized socially through house parties and participation on women's sports teams. Lesbian cultural interactions varied in relation to class and race, but it was butch/femme lesbian cultures that were the most visible during these years.[68] Some lesbian networks also overlapped with women involved in prostitution.[69]

These forms of cultural production were integral to the formation of lesbian and gay cultures. Without these sources of identification and affirmation, little collective political practice would have been possible.[70]

The bars, clubs, and other gathering places were not simply "private" places; they were community gathering places, and as they became more visible they came under police surveillance. Police surveillance and activity developed in relation to the expansion of the gay and lesbian commercial scenes as well as gay and lesbian visibility. In Toronto, police targeting of gay establishments in the 1950s may have been signalled by such statements as that made by Police Chief Chisholm before the Royal Commission on Criminal Sexual Psychopaths that I quoted last chapter. There were police-generated concerns over the "sex perverts" infesting parks, particularly the public lavatories in High Park and Union Station.[71] The opening of gay-frequented and gay-owned establishments in the early 1960s only led to the escalation of police interest.

> The early 1960s marked a new phase in police/gay relations. Undoubtedly the police were aware of such places as Malloney's ... But they were clearly straight places where gays hung out. It was not until The Music Room opened on Yonge Street north of Wellesley in late 1962 that the police were able to perceive an organized community.[72]

After the Music Room opened, Inspector Herbert Thurston of the Morality Squad warned that "sexual perversion is spreading. These people are no longer ashamed to admit what they are."[73] It should be remembered that the Music Room was an unlicensed non-alcoholic after-hours club that meant that the police could not use liquor laws and their age restrictions against this establishment. Sidney Katz wrote in 1964 that the police believed the clubs would cause young people to become homosexuals. Said Michael Hanlon of *The Globe and Mail:*

> Metro Police are reported worried by the growing popularity of clubs for homosexuality ... And police wish they could take action against them. What worries the police ... is the fact that they are gathering places for homosexuals and as such offer a chance for homosexuality to spread by introduction.[74]

A Detective Belcher arrested two dancers at the Melody Room in 1965 and charged them with "gross indecency." The charges were later thrown out of court, but Belcher returned to the club to try to provoke an incident.[75] There were also some "bawdy-house" related charges reported during these years, including at the International steam bath in Toronto, following which the names of those charged as "found-ins" were printed in the papers. Such charges were also laid at a steam bath in Windsor.[76] Lesbians in Toronto were harassed in and around the Continental, and sometimes this was tied up with harassment and violence against the prostitutes and drug dealers who also hung out at the bar and sometimes overlapped with the lesbian clientele. As previously mentioned, some were also taken to Cherry Beach to be beaten up by the cops.[77] There were many complaints of police harassment and brutality throughout these years without any independent means of redress given the police department's own internal investigative procedures.

In Montréal, there were a series of police actions against homosexual institutions in the years 1960-1963, ranging from the arrest of more than a dozen men on "gross indecency" charges at the Colonial Baths, to the arrest of thirty men at the Tapis Rouge Bar and fifteen at the Puccini Restaurant. Accusations by the police had not the slightest connection with what the men arrested had actually done. Arbitrarily choosing pairs of accused, the police would tell them: "You have committed indecent acts together."[78] The police could basically invent accounts of their surveillance work (that is, actually witnessing "indecent acts" — masturbation, or "gross indecency" — oral/genital sex) to lay charges and to contextualize the "facts" of the case in their reports and for any testimony required in court. This testimony and the reports must conform to the proper mandated course of action for these offences. They must report having seen the masturbation that they describe as an "indecent act" or the cocksucking that they describe as "gross indecency." This then allows for the arrest, a charge, and a court case.[79] There was often a police assumption that the men would plead guilty in order not to be exposed, and this was often quite accurate during these years. A name being published in the paper relating to gay sex could have severe consequences.

Police surveillance of a washroom at Vancouver's Stanley Park in 1963 resulted in eight men being charged with "gross indecency." Their names were published in the newspapers and at least one man hanged himself in jail as a result.[80] Police claimed to be acting on "complaints." "Complaints" activate the mandated course of action for police surveillance[81] — leading to the allocation of police personnel for surveillance work that led to the observance of sexual acts followed by arrest on "gross indecency" charges. In 1964, the Vancouver police reported that "there had been more prosecutions involving gross indecency in the past six months than in the previous two years."[82] There were also police raids for "obscene" literature on the Fraser Book Bin in the early 1960s for gay-related titles.

Bruce Somers, a gay man who was the first president of the Association for Social Knowledge in Vancouver, says in 1964 that "if you were a homosexual you were harassed," and describes the ever-present fear of police action. Doug Sanders, however, the second president of the Association and still straight-identified in 1964, says that in the 1960s the police were neither a persistent nor consistent problem for Vancouver gays.[83] This may in part be related to their different social standpoints at this time and their different relations to the gay scene. Sanders also reports that in Vancouver there was little press coverage of these police arrests both in the Stanley Park washroom arrests and later in February 1967 when the vice-president of a federal Crown corporation was arrested for sexual activity with a twenty-one-year-old female impersonator.[84] This points to the unevenness of the intensity of sexual policing across the country organized through police operational policies and the discretionary powers granted to the police in the enforcement of the Criminal Code.

Homophile Groups and Gay/Lesbian Organizing

The expansion of these cultures in the 1950s and early 1960s laid the basis for gay and lesbian self-organization in Canada. While the Mattachine Society in early 1950s California had radical origins, under the pressure of the McCarthyite anti-communist and anti-homosexual witch hunts, it moved in a more conservative direction, deposing its early leaders.[85] Leftists and progressives of various persuasions were also involved in gay and lesbian organizing in Canada.[86] After such radical beginnings, the homophile groups of the 1950s and early 1960s were generally identified with a reliance on medical, psychiatric, and sexological experts to educate the public and legitimize homosexuality. This began to shift in the 1960s again with the influence of the black civil rights and Black Power movements, the student movement, the anti-Vietnam war movement, and the new left. The 1960s were the years when some of the social changes of the post-war years were coming to fruition with the opening up of public discussions on sexuality in a more critical context and with sexuality becoming a more focused topic of political mobilization.

Some limited but important homophile organizations emerged in Canada as well. In the early 1960s, Jim Egan suggested during discussions at Toronto's Music Room that a chapter of the U.S. group and publication *One* be formed in Toronto.[87] The most significant Canadian organization, however, was to be founded on the West coast.

The Association for Social Knowledge

The Association for Social Knowledge (ASK) was officially formed in Vancouver in April 1964. John MacKinnon, one of its founders and the first treasurer, says the group had been proposed a couple of years earlier.[88] In early 1964 a group of gay men met at the home of Bruce Somers. Somers and Gerrald Turnbull, a library student at the University of British Columbia and a member of the collective household that Somers also lived in, provided the strong combination to get ASK rolling. Somers had been inspired by a visit to the Mattachine Society in San Francisco, where he had met Hal Call. There was an important U.S. homophile influence on the founding of the group. Somers was to become ASK's first president.

> [None of the founders] had really suffered any particular injustices but we were very conscious and we certainly knew people who had been beaten up cruising. It was always there in the back of your mind that society was ready to kick you in the crotch.

According to Somers, only men attended the first meeting — although this account is contested by at least one lesbian ex-ASK member. But according to Somers the men's lesbian friends soon got involved in the group and played an important role. Through Gerrald Turnbull the group gained the support of a number of local Quakers, including a then straight-identified articling lawyer by the name of Doug Sanders and a heterosexual woman, Dorothy Sheppard. Sanders, who became ASK's legal advisor when he was brought in to help the group incorporate, was also spokesperson for the Committee to Aid American War Objectors. Over seventy-five people attended the first organizational meeting. When Bruce Somers moved to Ottawa in late August 1964, Sanders became president of ASK. He describes these early experiences: "We had tremendous apprehension about what we were doing ... There was a feeling that we were taking risks the nature of which were not clear."[89]

"The problem in Canada," says Sanders expressing the view he developed during these years, "was not persecution but the pervasive view that gays didn't exist." Police entrapment was not as widely practised in Canada as it was in the United States, he felt, although there seems to have been more consistent police activity in the 1960s against gays in Toronto, Montréal, and Ottawa[90] than in Vancouver.

ASK was generally a fairly balanced gay-male/lesbian group, which was unique for homophile organizations of the period. The founders wanted ASK to be a serious and respectable organization dedicated to educating the "sex variant" and the public on questions of sexual variation. The initial "objectives" of the group were:

> (a) To sponsor projects of education of the general public so as to give them a better knowledge concerning sexual variation and correct general misconceptions, bigotries and prejudices resulting from lack of accurate information concerning sexual variation.
>
> (b) To sponsor projects of education of sexual variants so that they may better know not only the possible causes and conditions of variation, but formulate an adjustment and pattern of behaviour leading to positive and responsible citizenship.
>
> (c) To aid in the adjustment to society of such persons as may vary from the normal moral and social standards of society and to aid in the development of a highly ethical, social and moral responsibility in all such persons.
>
> (d) To sponsor and finance medical, social, social-hygiene, pathological and therapeutic research of every kind and description and publish and disseminate the results of such research as widely as possible.
>
> (e) To propose and support reform of the laws dealing with sex variants to the end that the laws protect the integrity of the individual and the community and be in harmony with the findings of leading psychiatrists and scientific research organizations.[91]

This embodied the homophile orientation of the group, including its reliance on experts and the "adjustment" of homosexuals to society, but also its commitment to law reform. It brought into the organization of ASK and the relations established among its members and supporters similar organizational features that had developed in the 1950s and early 1960s in U.S. homophile groups. Reflecting the early basic homophile orientation of the group, but at the same time almost questioning it, Sanders wrote in the June 1965 issue of the *ASK Newsletter:*

> Lectures by heterosexual experts reinforce to some degree the image of the
> homosexual as someone who needs to be dealt with in some special way. But
> at this stage of the struggle for understanding we have few alternatives to
> the intellectual appeal to reason.[92]

ASK initially included heterosexuals like Sanders (although he would soon come out) and Dorothy Sheppard. They also tried to involve social workers: clergy (only the Unitarians responded, along with a few individual Catholics, Anglicans, and members of the United Church); psychiatrists (whom Sanders describes as basically ghastly in their responses — one psychiatrist said that "homosexuality was a pathology" and that therefore there was a "problem of biological fit"); and lawyers. When the articles of incorporation were drawn up, Lionel Tiger, then a professor at the University of British Columbia, was one of the signatories. Like Mattachine, ASK in its first period was influenced by liberal psychologists and sexologists like the American Dr. Evelyn Hooker, whose work attempted to dispute the hegemonic psychological theory that gays were sick.[93]

While ASK was affiliated with neither the Mattachine Society nor the Daughters of Bilitis (DOB), a U.S. lesbian group, it was clearly inspired and influenced by homophile organizing south of the border. Mattachine was its initial model. The influence was not only one way, however. When a female member of the first executive moved to San Francisco she, along with a woman friend, made the Society for Individual Rights (SIR) into a mixed organization using the ASK model. The *ASK Newsletter* reprinted material from Mattachine, DOB, which published *The Ladder*, and *One*, bringing U.S. news to Canada. Doug Sanders helped found the North American Conference of Homophile Organizations (NACHO) and served as its secretary. NACHO's members included ASK, Mattachine, SIR, DOB, and the U.S. Council on Religion and the Homosexual.[94]

Membership in ASK was open to anyone over twenty-one (which meant that when it was founded, Gerrald Turnbull, one of the most active people involved, was too young to be a formal member), and, according to Sanders, membership for heterosexuals was "a defensive measure of the times."[95] ASK stated that its membership included lesbians, homosexual men, and male and female heterosexuals, although after its initial stages it became largely a lesbian and gay group. In the early years when members were asked their sexual orientation, they would often say that this was nobody's concern. The term "homophile," which can refer to a person interested in homosexual issues but who is not necessarily gay or lesbian, provided a shield against exposure. For Sanders, it actually delayed his coming out for a number of years because he didn't have to be out, or to deal with his homosexual tendencies, to belong to ASK. At the same time, Somers and Turnbull were quite sure he was gay from a much earlier point. But since Sanders did not identify, as gay, his reaction

> to the issue of cure or conversion would be different than others. I saw it as an open question in a technical sense ... I'm not sure whether anybody else saw it the same way as I did.

While Sanders still did not see himself as gay, he could view the question of whether gays were ill as an academic or technical one. After he came out and his experience and social standpoint shifted, he found this position less and less tenable.

ASK applied for registration as a provincial non-profit organization, but the application was not taken seriously on the grounds that its objects did not fall within those specified in the B.C. Societies Act. Given that ASK defined itself as an educational society, and this was one of the specified objects in the Act, heterosexism was at work here. ASK appealed the decision but the matter was not pursued further since Sanders, as legal adviser, did not feel that non-profit status was necessary at the time. As he puts it, "it was an example of discrimination but it wasn't anything that really disadvantaged the organization and we never did anything about it." Later, when ASK was running a community centre, it incorporated without any hassle as a commercial corporation — "The ASK Community Centre" — with no mention of homosexuality.

The *ASK Newsletter* was published from April 1964 to April 1965, with a lapse of eighteen months before it published again from December 1966. Its initial circulation was more than 250 copies. The last issue appears to have been put out in May of 1968.[96] In 1968 Sanders wrote to a correspondent in Montréal that "We are currently not publishing a newsletter, but may begin again fairly soon. It is a very time consuming job and right now we have other things to do."[97]

The newsletter was a valuable means of communication between ASK members and other lesbians and gay men in Vancouver and across Canada. It played an important part in organizing ASK and developing connections between homophile activists across the country. It provided an oppositional discursive focus for gay and lesbian activists. The newsletter discussed the *Wolfenden Report*, the Kinsey studies, the Royal Commission on Criminal Sexual Psychopaths, and homosexual-law-reform efforts in Canada. It carried news of the homophile movement south of the border, including the Mattachine pickets and the COC (a homophile group in the Netherlands) and its community centre, an interview with R.E. Turner from the Toronto Forensic Clinic, and mention of a novel by lesbian writer Jane Rule,[98] books by Donald Webster Cory, and John Rechy's *City of Night*. The newsletter also contained information on gay and lesbian life in Toronto, Montréal, and smaller communities. ASK had some contact with the Toronto gay publications *Two* and *Gay* that started publishing in 1964, shortly before *ASK Newsletter* came on the scene.

In its first year, ASK focused on education. "Gab'n'Java" informal discussions were held in people's homes as a way of attracting new members. A series of public meetings featured speakers: Don Lucas of the Mattachine Society on "The Homosexual Cause: The Aims and Activities of the Mattachine Society"; Rev. J.M. Taylor of East Burnaby United Church spoke to sixty people on "The Church and the Homosexual"; and Doug Sanders spoke on "Legal Reform and Homosexuality." Finding a public hall for these meetings was not easy, however. The first forum was held in *The Sun* building, but when it was learned what the meeting had been about the space was denied for future use. ASK was also refused meeting space by the YMCA. The Unitarian Church eventually offered its hall. According to Sanders, however, interest began to wane after the initial enthusiasm, because the lecture format had limited appeal.

As Sanders put it, "The obvious need in the community at that point was ... a decent social centre,"[99] since there existed few decent bars and clubs in the city. Also, there were tensions within the group between those interested in group and public education and those more interested in social activities. While fund-raising events like "dollar parties" were a regular part of ASK life, the priority for the first year was clearly education, which reflects the group's initial fear of being seen as actually promoting homosexuality by providing a place for lesbians and gays to meet. A social centre feasibility committee, nonetheless, was struck at ASK's general meeting in March 1965. The idea was influenced by the COC clubs in Holland that were funding that group's counselling and lobbying efforts and the commercial clubs that were being established in Toronto. ASK therefore decided to "support but not participate in the formation of a centre,"[100] an autonomous group — "The Circle" — was to establish the centre by getting one hundred people to donate twenty dollars each. But just as the group was beginning to gear up to meet this need, in the summer of 1965 it disbanded, bringing the first phase of ASK's history to a close.[101]

ASK resumed activity in 1966 and opened its community centre at 1929 Kingsway with a New Year's Eve Ball.[102] This was the first such centre in Canada, and it was quite successful in attracting lesbians and gay men. They were forced to move to a larger and more expensive location a year later, however, when their landlord discovered the purpose of the centre. For a period it was Canada's largest gay and lesbian club. Membership in ASK stood at 150 in November 1967, says Sanders, but at its height there could be as many as 200 people at the centre for its regular Saturday night dances.[103] The ASK centre was also used for business and executive meetings, a lending library, facilities for the production of the *ASK Newsletter*, and some counselling and referral services. They provided speakers on such topics as the homosexual subculture and the homosexual rights movement. ASK members went on radio talk shows to provide public education for anyone who would listen.

By 1966-1967, ASK had drawn up a more comprehensive statement of purpose that was significantly different from their first one reflecting the transformations within homophile organizing as the group shifted more clearly to a gay and lesbian identification:

1. To seriously confront Canadian society with the fact of its homosexual minority and challenge Canadians to treat homosexuals with justice and respect.

2. To maintain a community centre ...

3. To facilitate and encourage research into homosexual and minority rights.

4. To work for the reform of the criminal laws relating to sexual activity.

5. To co-operate with other homophile organizations in other parts of the world.

It is important to note the transformation in the character of the organization suggested in this new statement of purpose. There was an important shift in the language that was used. There was more affirmation and assertion and less reliance on professional experts. This both embodied and helped to bring about a transformation of the organization.

Girls and Boys Together?

There were some tensions and debates among and between the men and women in ASK over drag and over butch/femme "roles." As a mixed organization of women and men, ASK encompassed gender differences that in the U.S. led to the formation of separate lesbian groups, like the Daughters of Bilitis. While the *ASK Newsletter* gives the impression of a pre-feminist, male-dominated organization, this was not entirely the case. Almost from the beginning there were a number of strong and dynamic women involved in the group. While none of the women would have identified as feminists at this time there were a number of articles on specifically lesbian concerns, the problems of men and women working together, and an appeal for more women to work on the newsletter entitled "Come on Girls, We need You": "... become a member and join the paper; with only one girl and all those males, it's lovely but lonely! So join us and help us make an even better paper of interest to both sexes." The author goes on:

> Have you ever worried what might happen if your families or your employer were to find out that you were a lesbian? Then help us to educate the public so that, if not in our time, in the generations to come they can hold their heads high, tell their families, tell their bosses and friends without fear of being disowned or losing their jobs or a friendship; so they can take their proper place in society.[104]

In the fall of 1967, Norma Mitchell became president of ASK, a position she held until the organization disbanded. When ASK decided to reduce the size of the newsletter, she wrote, "For the girls there is the DOB magazine." In the April 1967 issue she outlined her perspective on "transvestism" and generally put down the working-class "dyke."[105]

Mitchell also wrote an article in the September 1967 issue on female homosexuality and was interviewed in the *Georgia Straight* (a Vancouver counter-cultural paper) series, "The Lesbians," in 1968.[106] Mitchell is quoted as saying that:

> We have the finances, the backing, and the resources to stand up and say we are homosexuals and that we are here and society is going to have to deal with us ... If they don't accept us peacefully then we are going to have to go for stronger action. We'll go to court and we'll fight if necessary.[107]

Says Doug Sanders:

> You would get people griping every once in a while. Some of the guys would gripe now and then that the organization was being taken over by the women. Some of the women would occasionally gripe that there weren't very many women in the organization. There was always a consciousness of the relationship and if you looked around the city you found that generally speaking you did not have much mixing ... You never had a situation after the group got going in which the leadership [of ASK] was all male.

Rumblings in the Churches

Homophile activities influenced religious discussion and church support for more liberalized attitudes to homosexuality and for law reform. ASK gained some very important early support from the Quakers and the Unitarians. "Towards a Quaker View of Sex" published in 1963 was quite progressive for its day, suggesting that homosexual affection could be as worthy as heterosexual affection.[108] The local Friends group was very supportive of the founding of ASK and in 1967 wrote a letter to the federal government protesting the Supreme Court decision in the Klippert case. Sanders also presented a paper on homosexuality to the Pacific Northwest Quarterly Meeting of the Religious Society of Friends. It was not able to be adopted, even though it got widespread support, because of a consensus decision-making requirement.

When J.M. Taylor of the United Church spoke to ASK in April 1964, he was not new to the topic. He had previously had an article published in the *Mattachine Review* on the need for prevention of homosexuality rather than punishment. In his address to ASK, Taylor stated that the United Church had gone on record as deploring imprisonment for homosexuality and that many United Church people supported the Wolfenden reforms. He outlined four moral problems that homosexual conduct presented for Christians: that it was an offence against the proper expression of sex in monogamous marriage; that it was a misuse of natural functions; that it led to the destruction of "neighbour love" through the involvement of someone of the same sex; and that it undermined a stable society based on heterosexual marriage and family responsibility. He strongly advocated the establishment of medical centres for the treatment of homosexuals and more effective sex education programmes for the young.[109]

In the letters pages of *ASK Newsletter*, two ASK members criticized Taylor's attitude and questioned the sickness theory of homosexuality.

> One statement he made with regard to setting up a clinic for the "cure" of voluntary homosexuals seemed rather incongruous when he went on to say he knew of no such "cure"! What about those of us who don't want to be cured of a way of life that is all we have known? ... I was also annoyed at his inference that homosexuals should not live together as partners ... I would urge Rev. Taylor to come out into "gay" life as an observer, see it from our side, and then report on it factually and fearlessly.[110]

Says Bruce Somers of Taylor's talk:

> He was not really sympathetic. He wasn't as down on us as a lot of others but we were trying to be objective in holding public meetings but we found very little in the way of sympathetic support.

On members' attitudes to the sickness theory of homosexuality in the early days, Somers says "there was quite a division among the various people who attended the [Gab'n'Java] meetings as to whether or not being a homosexual was a sickness that should be treated."

Sickness and mental-illness models of homosexuality were still quite strong in "liberal" church circles during the 1960s. The United Church of Canada report on Christian Marriage and Divorce, published in 1960, includes a section on homosexuality.[111] The report gives credence to psychological and conditioning theories, and also argues that homosexuals are not usually dangerous and do not necessarily engage in sex crimes. It makes an untenable distinction between homosexual feelings and conduct, and suggests that while it is difficult for a homosexual to establish a good (heterosexual) marriage, this is not impossible. The report calls for Christian sympathy, charity, help, and understanding.

There were battles over homosexuality within the various churches. The United Church's Evangelism and Social Services 1964 Annual Report reprinted an article that interestingly enough is partly a polemic against the self-organization of homosexuals and all attempts to "glamorize" homosexuality.[112] It argues that the Mattachine Society, *One*, and *Ladder* "do homosexuals more harm than good." Vulgar Freudian-derived theories of the acquisition of homosexuality are accepted, as well as the idea that it is curable through hypnosis, hormone treatment, electro-shock "therapy," psychotherapy, and psychoanalysis, while imprisonment would merely spread the "disease" among the inmates. Christians should neither condemn nor condone homosexuality, says the report, but the reforms suggested by the American Law Institute and the Wolfenden committee could provide needed legal changes. In the meantime, the church could engage in redemptive and counselling work, and homosexual marriages should be banned.

The North American Conference on Church and the Family, held in Hamilton in 1966, became the centre of debate when Rev. Johnston, principal of the United Theological College of Montreal, expressed the view that the church should never approve nor condone homosexuality, that it was impossible to be a practising homosexual and a practising Christian. The Canadian church would not object to the implementation of a Wolfenden-type reform, said Rev. Johnston, but this would be an act of society, not of the church. Christians should instead encourage people to get more enjoyment out of heterosexual relations within marriage, he said. Johnston was responding to charges that church attitudes on homosexuality were out of date and that homosexuality was "natural" for some people.[113] By this time, after some early law-reform efforts, the Wolfenden reform strategy was beginning to shape discussions in the churches and the mainstream media.

The Canadian Council on Religion and the Homosexual

The Canadian Council on Religion and the Homosexual (CCRH) was formed in Ottawa in 1965 on the initiative of Gary Nichols, who had earlier founded the Committee on Social Hygiene in Stitsville. This organization was, according to Bruce Somers, "in fact pretty well just him." Nichols was a gay federal civil servant who worked on a series of contracts for the government and was an "aspirant to the clergy" of the Anglican Church.[114] He was involved in a series of homophile and law-reform efforts in the 1960s in Ontario, particularly in Ottawa. He worked very hard, often full-time, and often it seems behind the scenes in these efforts.

The Council also involved Bruce Somers, who had moved to Ottawa from Vancouver in 1964, several official representatives from the Anglican Church and unofficial ones from the Roman Catholic Church, a number of gay male federal civil servants, MP Arnold Peters, and several doctors and psychiatrists. Perhaps three dozen people were involved in the Council's activities. Most of the church representatives, especially those from the Anglican church, were heterosexual. In a rather exaggerated statement, the February 1967 ASK Newsletter reported Bruce Somers' connection with the Council:

> The founding of the Canadian Council on Religion and the Homosexual
> was largely the work of the first president of ASK, who moved to Ottawa
> about eight months after ASK's formation.

Arnold Peters, a New Democratic Party MP, described his feelings about the Council during the 1969 Criminal Code reform debate in the House of Commons:

> We believed that homosexuality was abnormal and that it was something in
> respect of which they could use help. I was joined by many people of the re-

ligious community who were aware that many people in the community faced this problem.[115]

According to Somers, even though the Council sent information to the United Church there was never any support; the Anglicans provided the main support. The Council, the first of its kind in Canada, held its first general meeting at St. George's Anglican Church in Ottawa on June 16, 1965 and was open to anyone over twenty-one years of age, regardless of sexual orientation. Philip Rowswell, an Anglican minister, was elected chairman.

One of the group's beliefs was that sexual acts in private by consenting adults as laid out in the *Wolfenden Report* should be of no concern to the law. The Council made plans for discussion groups with psychiatrists, lawyers, and the families and friends of homosexuals. The Council also submitted a brief to the Ontario Select Committee on Youth, which quoted from the *Wolfenden Report* in arguing for law reform as well as making proposals for sex education in the schools.[116]

According to Bruce Somers, in 1966 Professor Wake of Carleton University's Psychology Department — whom we met last chapter as the designer of the "fruit machine" research — approached the CCRH to have its homosexual members fill out a questionnaire. It was apparently between six and twelve pages in length, and was to be filled out anonymously and returned in brown manila envelopes to Wake. Wake presented himself as doing psychological research on homosexuality, but these questionnaires may very well have been used to provide the "fruit machine" research with some homosexual responses to their questionnaire for comparative purposes.[117]

Gary Nichols, the central figure in holding CCRH together, suffered from periodic periods of depression, according to Somers. The September 1967 *ASK Newsletter* reported that the Council had disbanded "but there are several clergy still interested in the group ... ASK sincerely hopes that CCRH will once again become active, and urges all our members and friends to give support to this fine organization." The group did fall apart, however, says Somers, because of Nichols' periods of depression, lack of cohesion, and tensions among its members, with some gay members using it as a place to meet other gay men while others wanted a more "serious" organization, and because it was making little headway with the churches beyond the Anglicans. Somers told me that the gay civil servants who were members of the group were quite fearful of disclosure of their identities. They were opposed to receiving any CCRH information through the mail. This was in the context of the security campaigns against homosexuals in the civil service in Ottawa during these years.

These changing attitudes toward homosexuality and support for law reform within some of the churches — in interaction with homophile organizing — paralleled developments in the United States and England.[118] Limited as they were, these shifts represented a general change in social institutions and helped lay the basis for law reform. This was especially significant because of the relation of churches to issues, like this one, that were constructed as moral ones.

Penal Reform and Forensic Clinics

In its early years, ASK agitated for penal reform and for treatment of sex offenders rather than imprisonment and punishment, although this was never a major focus for the organization.

In June 1964, the executive director of the John Howard Society addressed a meeting of twenty-five members of ASK. The previous month, the Canadian minister of justice had called for clearer policies in the federal correctional field, including the parole system, which was a hint that the federal government might be interested in penal and criminal-law reform. ASK responded positively to a brief by the John Howard Society of British Columbia, which argued the case for penal reform and which basically made the demand for a forensic clinic in the province a public issue. Doug Sanders was the ASK liaison person with the Society. In a radio interview in 1964, he expressed the hope that a hospital would be established in B.C. along the lines of the Forensic Clinic in Toronto, which was the institutional site that had come out of campaigning by PAL and the *Toronto Star*.

An issue of *ASK Newsletter* carried a special report on a 1965 meeting between the John Howard Society and Dr. R.E. Turner of the Toronto Forensic Clinic as well as excerpts from an interview with Turner.[119] Sanders had hoped that the John Howard Society would use this interview to push for a clinic in B.C., but he discovered that "they weren't all that enthusiastic about flogging our newsletter in their cause."

ASK and Law Reform

ASK was always concerned with law-reform issues, although its priority at first was education and later the social centre. It was often suggested that, with growing public education about homosexuality, law reform would naturally follow. The *ASK Newsletter* referred frequently to the *Wolfenden Report* as an indication that similar reform was possible in Canada, and it devoted an entire issue to the topic of law reform. As Sanders expressed it, "Wolfenden had legitimated the arguments for homosexual-law reform in England so the issue was discussable." Although the major influence on Canadian homophile organizing was from the U.S. during these years, there was also some awareness of the Homosexual Law Reform Society and homophile-influenced lobbying efforts in England.[120]

Yet in 1964 law reform appeared as a rather distant goal, and Ottawa, the focus for criminal-law reform, very far away. There was also more generally a tension between the local character of the politics and everyday lives of members of ASK and the extra local and "national" character of the Criminal Code, and the official politics relating to the Criminal Code and its possible reform.

At an ASK forum in October 1964, Sanders, who as a law student and then lawyer was able to articulate ASK to legal discourse, spoke on the history of legal reform. This included the *Wolfenden Report* and recent proposals for reform in the U.S., from the revision of the penal code in the state of Illinois in 1961 to the model penal code developed by the American Law Institute in 1962. He argued:

> the enforcement agencies are making no attempt to enforce the law relating to homosexual offences ... the law in practice is not as it stands on the statute books. To this extent, we have a type of implementation of the *Wolfenden Report* in Canada. Public opinion is not yet ready to make express what is already the legal reality.[121]

Here he is observing that the police were not arresting large numbers of homosexuals for acts in "private" because of their limited resources and powers of surveillance.

A special issue of the newsletter roots the laws against male homosexuality in the Judeo-Christian tradition and contrasts these prohibitions with the widespread homosexual and lesbian activity reported in the Kinsey studies. Says *ASK Newsletter:*

> Moral and legal condemnations of homosexual activity do not apply equally to men and women, being uncommonly severe with male homosexuality and generally ignoring like behaviour in the female.

This position ignores the specific character of lesbian oppression that has not been so specifically focused around sex offences in the Criminal Code and the oppression that all women face, including a general denial of any autonomous female sexuality.

The article concluded by calling for special psychiatric treatment for sex offenders and for law reform. This takes up the "treatment" as opposed to the criminalization frame in relation to homosexuality.

> It would seem to this writer that today's legislators, judges, police officials, and other assorted defenders of public virtue no longer have the excuse of ignorance to justify their intemperate and inhumane attempts at sex suppression.[122]

This position suggests that lesbian and gay oppression was simply a product of ignorance and lack of accurate information and that with further public education law reform would be automatic. This had a lot to do with the character of homophile politics and organizing, which was unable to centrally address the social relations organizing gay and lesbian oppression and their transformation. Instead, while homophile reformers broached the crucial question of criminal-law reform, they often viewed gay oppression as simply the result of unenlightened or backward ideas. Historically, this was crucially important politically, but it also had limitations.

ASK and its members were involved not just in educational work and discussions, however. They also pushed for Wolfenden-type reforms in Canada. In the spring of 1964, Arnold Peters, NDP MP for Temiskaming, Ontario, announced that he would present a private-member's bill to modify the Criminal Code such that homosexuality would be a crime only in the case of an adult assaulting a young person, and would allow for two adults to participate in consenting homosexual acts in private. Apparently, Gary Nichols supported Peters on this — as Somers puts it, "pushing him on." Peters was a controversial New Democrat who also formulated a private-member's bill for legalized abortion in the case of pregnancy as the result of rape or when a woman's health was in danger. ASK wrote to Peters informing him of their existence and requesting a copy of the private-member's bill. They also informed their members about it:

> It is our intention to study it, to circulate it widely and initiate a letter campaign to all members of parliament ... the Board of Directors must request the co-operation of each and every one of you. It is most imperative that your MP be written immediately urging serious consideration of Mr. Peters' bill.[123]

Unfortunately, Peters never replied. "I remember a sense of frustration in ASK," says Sanders, "that Arnold Peters would not answer letters." The bill never reached the floor of the House of Commons, but it did give ASK its first real encounter with law-reform activity and generated publicity for homosexual-law reform. In July of the same year, Peters participated in an attempt to form a homophile reform society and became involved with the Canadian Council on Religion and the Homosexual.[124] In 1969, during the Criminal Code reform debates, he reminded the House that

> individual members of parliament should be given a great deal of credit for introducing legislation which has not been popular and sometimes dangerous. When I presented the bill ... I showed it to members of the press in order to get some comment ... I suggest this was the forerunner of the amendments which later related to the homosexual sections we are now considering ... There was considerable comment about this amendment.[125]

In August 1964, Sidney Katz, then associate editor of *Maclean's* magazine, whom we met previously, announced the formation of the Homophile Reform Society based in Ontario. Again, it appears that Nichols was the moving force behind the scenes. It often seems that if you scratch the surface of early homophile organizing efforts you find an early gay activist. The group, to be chaired by Katz, would have a six-member planning committee. Their first objective was amendment of the gross-indecency section of the Criminal Code. The group apparently had the support of Arnold Peters and certain civil servants, journalists, and broadcasters.[126] *Two* reported, however, that "all attempts to contact the group had been conspicuously unsuccessful." It went on: "We regret the apparent grounding of this operation and urgently request anyone interested in the formation of a similar group to contact the editors of *Two*."[127]

Doug Sanders, ASK's legal advisor and president for much of its existence, played an important role himself in initiating law-reform discussions. In 1966, along with Sidney Simons, another Vancouver lawyer, he proposed changes based on the Wolfenden perspective to the Criminal Law Subsection of the B.C. Division of the Canadian Bar Association.[128] Unlike what Wolfenden recommended, they proposed the age of consent of eighteen for private consensual homosexual sex and suggested decriminalizing such acts in private between participants over the age of fourteen provided that the difference in their ages was not more than two years. They supported Wolfenden's public/private regulation but went beyond it on the age question. Sanders describes the meeting where their proposal was discussed:

> I remember it being buried at the last session it came up at ... People weren't happy with the issue but they didn't have good responses to it. What we were seeking was a resolution from the group supporting homosexual-law reform. ... I remember it being killed by a groan of disgust ... I gave a statement in which I made simply a passing reference to sodomy and a man who is now a judge ... said something like "UNNNNNGH!" and that won the day and the vote was lost. It was a guttural reaction of disgust at the word and it was game over at that time.

In 1967 Sanders also prepared and circulated an ASK paper, "Sentencing of Homosexual Offenders," which was also printed in the *Criminal Law Quarterly*.[129] Originally prepared as part of a sentencing plea in the Boisvert case in Vancouver, which I examine later, it sets out to demonstrate that the sentences in "gross indecency" cases were relatively light. Half of these sentences were for acts in "public" places, according to Sanders (eight in public washrooms in Stanley Park and four others in parked cars). Only one was judged by Sanders to be in "private." Most arrests for homosexual offences were made in public washrooms, parked cars, or public parks, writes Sanders, and the great majority of "gross indecency" cases were heard before a magistrate. Since these cases were rarely discussed in legal reports, writes Sanders, "it is difficult for lawyers to locate precedents for sentences." He reports on twelve unreported cases (they had not been recorded and reported in the law reports) between 1961-1967 involving twenty-four male persons and, in particular, on the sentencing of these offenders. This was explicitly undertaken as assistance for other defence lawyers and for judges making sentencing decisions in these cases. He summarizes the cases he knew of, a number for which the sentence included treatment at a mental-health clinic or "treatment" by a medical doctor or psychiatrist, as well as prohibitions against loitering, or simply being in any public park as part of the sentence. In this latter restriction, we can continue to see how the homosexual threat was constructed as a particular kind of "public" problem in parks. The sentences requiring psychiatric and medical "treatment" displayed the continuing connections between medical and psychiatric practices and the criminal justice system.

In some of the cases reported, we can see the construction of legal/psychiatric relations. In one case where the defence argued that a private, homosexual act (fellatio) between the consenting parties did not constitute an act of gross indecency, the magistrate ruled that even though society's moral standards were changing on this question his job was

> to interpret it [the gross indecency section] as I think society would want it interpreted and as I think the legislature intended it to be interpreted. So that this perhaps has been my conflict, in knowing what I would perhaps like to do as opposed to what I feel I must do in properly interpreting the law.[130]

Here he is suggesting that the law is the law and as a judge he can only enforce it but at the same time he is suggesting that morality is changing and law reform might be called for. This suggests that some pressure for clarification of the law, and even law reform, was beginning to emerge from the strategies of defence lawyers and in the remarks of judges.

In the cases he reported, Sanders found that almost all accused persons got a fine or a suspended sentence — the courts generally treated the homosexual charges as a relatively trivial matter. Sander's article also reports that in three of these cases, a male person was dressed as a woman and that in two of these cases, the "unsuspecting" party was not charged. This points to police discretion in the enforcement of the law — "and it may well be that the police decided not to prosecute the 'innocent' male in return for testimony against the impersonator at trial." The "true" homosexual may still have been seen by some of the police and the Crown as the "gender invert." The range in sentences was wide — fines from $100-$750; sentences reduced to two year's probation; suspended sentences; and sentences of one day, one month, three months, and three years on three counts of the same offence. Sanders attempted to show that the law as it stood is effective only for cases of "public" acts, and basically used the Wolfenden regulation approach. He made very active use of "public/private" classifications. Sanders also mentioned the infamous Klippert case (which will be dealt with later in this chapter), then still before the courts. He attempted to show that the law as it stood was effective only for cases of "public" acts.

Sanders further reports on the very interesting Boisvert/Lupien case that he acted in. It involved two French Canadians, Lupien, who was a top civil servant with Central Mortgage and Housing Corporation, and Boisvert, a young hustler who wore women's clothing.[131] Lupien claimed in his defence that he thought he had picked up a woman. He brought in psychiatric testimony that claimed he had a psychological aversion to homosexuality and therefore must have thought Boisvert was a woman or else he was suffering from lack of sleep, or the consumption of alcohol had impaired his judgement. This became a much-cited legal case over the admissibility of psychiatric evidence.

Sanders interviewed Boisvert in jail because he did not have the money for bail, and he ended up defending him. Here we get a sense of the class dimensions of the criminal-justice system and how this could impact in the lives of working-class hustlers. Sanders remembers:

> The young guy simply wanted to get back home to work in Montréal and so he just pleaded guilty and I submitted an article that was eventually printed in the *Criminal Law Quarterly* ... which results from my sentencing plea in this case ...

Boisvert ended up getting a modest fine, which was his objective. The police, for their part, apparently initially thought this was a case of female prostitution and followed Boisvert and Lupien to a hotel, after they spotted them together in a taxi.

After following them to a hotel the officers went to the room the men had gone to. One officer testified "I remained outside the door of this room and by placing my ear to the door I could hear voices coming from inside the room. They were speaking in a language I did not understand[French]." The officer then got the key and opened the door.

> As I entered I noticed the light in the room was on. I observed a bed in the northwest corner of the room and I observed two male persons on the bed, both completely nude at this time. ... At this time Boisvert was wearing a female's blond wig. He was lying on the south side of the bed and he was lying on his right side. His head was propped up on his right arm ...[132]

This complicated description of body placement on the bed is to establish that the officer could have seen what he describes. He continued, describing Lupien's body placement:

> He was lying with his head on his right side and it was immediately adjacent to Boisvert's privates, and at this time I noticed a white towel on the bed, and was immediately under Boisvert's head ... As I entered the room Mr. Lupien immediately rolled away from Boisvert and turned himself around on the bed so as to be the right way on the bed, and covered himself up and at this point his privates were not exposed to my view. Boisvert then sat up on the bed and stated, "What is the matter? He is an old friend of mine from Montréal and we came up here to make love. What is the matter?"

Boisvert was informed they were going to be charged with "gross indecency." Boisvert was reported as getting dressed in female clothes and they associated his cross-dressing with his homosexuality.

The Crown Attorney asked the officer "When you first went into the room, could you see the state of erection or otherwise of Boisvert's penis?" he answered "Yes, Your

Worship; ... when Boisvert sat up on the edge of the bed and made a statement, I noted at this time that his penis was erect."[133] This was to construct the particulars for the inscription of what the police reported they saw into "gross indecency." It seems here that a police report of an erect penis and a head adjacent to "privates" was enough to constitute "gross indecency" for the police and Crown Attorney in this case.

On January 10, 1968, in reference to the proposed sexual-reform legislation by Justice Minister Trudeau, a letter from ASK to its members stated we: "hope [the bill] will improve our position, and we feel that our club, through the efforts of our lawyer, has had a small part in what we feel is progress."[134] In a letter to Paul Bédard of Montréal in 1968 Sanders wrote:

> As far as I can tell the homosexual reform bill will probably be debated in October. We want to ensure that there is public debate and discussion at that time. We intend to have posters printed up urging people to write to their member of parliament in support of the bill. We plan to have people going door to door with a petition supporting the bill. We want some publicity on armed forces policies in relation to homosexuals. We would like to co-ordinate this to some extent with Montréal and Toronto.[135]

Unfortunately, it appears that there was little response from the east to this attempt at cross-country organizing.

Sanders describes his analysis of the 1960s situation:

> I had developed this kind of analysis in the period and suggested within the organization that the strategy for dealing with the law-reform proposal should be an attempt to make gays more visible. The issue was not getting the reform because the reform was guaranteed .... It was going to come through without any kind of change in public attitudes and that was a problem ... So I proposed to the association that the strategy should be to make the issue more visible and we should go door to door with petitions and this was accepted very reluctantly at one meeting and then killed at the next one.

This bold petition-campaign proposal was vetoed by members who thought that the chances of reform could be hurt if they rocked the boat or if gays and lesbians were too visible.

In the February 1968 issue of the newsletter, Sanders reports on the proposed legal change and on his interview with Everett George Klippert in the Prince Albert Penitentiary. Sanders got to see Klippert, he says, by just demanding as a lawyer to see him. The editorial in the same issue calls for quick action from the House of Commons on law reform.

In 1968, Sanders made a submission to the Royal Commission on Security,[136] focusing on debunking the two main arguments used to deny homosexuals government employment and security clearance put in place during the Cold War security "scares": that homosexuals are not emotionally stable and are more subject to blackmail. Referring to the Kinsey studies and the work of Dr. Evelyn Hooker, Sanders argued that there are no distinct homosexual personality traits and "the idea that homosexuals, as a group, are less stable than heterosexuals is not supportable." On the subject of blackmail, he argued that homosexuals have no character defects and that the potential for blackmail had been overrated in Canada. "There had been no homosexual 'witch hunts' in Canada," he argued, creating the impression that homosexuality had never been the concern in this country that it had been south of the border. This may be partly accounted for by the secret character of the security campaigns but also by Sander's position as a civilian on the west coast who had nothing to do with government employment. This was despite the policies of the RCMP which was brought in for "security" screenings in many State agencies and that of the military that was still to purge homosexuals and deny them "security" clearances.

Regarding employment, Sanders sent letters to government departments, and in their responses they claimed they had no general policy of excluding homosexuals. This included the Department of National Defence. One ASK member challenged this military assertion at a meeting raising memories of purges of homosexuals in the military on the west coast.[137]

Sanders again pointed out that most arrests for homosexual offences concerned acts committed in public. He referred to the work of Gigeroff in cooperation with the Forensic Clinic of the Clarke Institute of Psychiatry, who also suggested this same pattern of arrests making visible the inter-textual character of law-reform discourse. Sanders concluded by supporting Trudeau's Criminal Code reforms and asking the federal government and the Department of National Defense to make clear their employment policies and their position on the granting of security clearances to homosexuals.

ASK collapsed a few months before the Stonewall riots. The social centre, which had become a major financial and administrative burden, was taken on by Norma Mitchell as a commercial venture. It later failed. Toward the end, ASK was doing little educational work. Throughout its history, it had encompassed a number of divergent tendencies and needs, ranging from educational, social-service, and counselling work to social activities and more traditional political and legal lobbying. As well, the group managed to involve both women and men throughout its history. These diverse pressures pulled the group in several directions, yet ASK was able to span most of the period 1964-1969 while other homophile and lesbian/gay groups across the country collapsed after a couple of years at most. Sanders provided much of this continuity.

The social centre, which filled a real need in the city, also helped keep the organization afloat for a number of years, even if in the end it was its downfall. The relative absence of police harassment during this period in Vancouver may have contributed to both ASK's survival and its collapse. "One of the clear factors is that nobody was beating us up," says Sanders. "There was no local police harassment to organize against. Nobody's back was up against the wall ..."

Protest was never a priority for ASK, he says: ASK played a role in the period which was positive. The limitations of it I think were the limitations of the period. It helped some individual people ... It broke ground in a sense for gay liberation. We passed on a gay consciousness. It seems to me it had to precede gay liberation.[138]

And:

The organization could not have had much impact on general public opinion because there was simply not the media coverage. The media was not willing to publicize the existence of the organization ... it could [have had an impact] in limited circles like the John Howard Society and the Unitarians and the Quakers and some people at UBC [University of British Columbia] ... Some people would have been exposed to the issue ... In a sense I have felt that the existence of the homophile organizations, in general, was sort of a necessary prelude to the gay liberation groups. We proved that something modest was possible and so something more adventurous was more possible ... What it comes down to is that the major impact would have been on the individuals who were connected with it. It increased understanding and self-confidence considerably ... Oh, we had a lot of fun.

Gay and Two

While ASK was the most significant pre-1969 gay/lesbian organization, two gay magazines started publishing in Toronto in 1964, *Gay* and *Two*.

Gay, later called *Gay International*, was put out by the Gay Publishing Company "to present the homosexual viewpoint." The first issue appeared in March 1964. Claiming a circulation of more than 6,000 in the Toronto and Montréal areas, *Gay* included a news section, a few lengthier articles, and classifieds. It later printed physique photos from Can-Art Studios of Toronto. It also produced two information pamphlets: "What To Do in Case of Arrest" and "How to Handle a Federal Investigation."[139] *Gay* carried news of the New York Mattachine Society; a story from *One*; news of homosexual pickets of the White House in 1965; an essay by Dr. Franklin E. Kameny, who led the new east-coast homophile militancy influenced by the black civil rights movement,[140] an address to the East Coast Homosexual Conference in Washington, D.C., in 1964; news of local police busts; an analysis of the Kinsey Report; and critiques of media articles. The publication also argued for legal reform. An article entitled "The Philosophy of Law" by Don Philip stated "one major change in the law is most urgently demanded: that acts occurring in private between consenting adults be legal."[141] The two main references in this article were to the *Wolfenden Report* and the American Bar Association model law code.

Two was published first by Gayboy and then by Kamp Publishing, which was located at 457 Church Street, the address of the Melody Room. A letter in the *ASK*

Newsletter referred to *Two* as the "official mouth-piece" of the gay-owned Music Room and the Melody Room, and both regularly advertised themselves as "Toronto's original after-hours gay clubs." *Two* modelled itself after the journal *One* in the U.S.[142] Its first issue declared:

> Our purpose is to promote knowledge and understanding of the homosexual viewpoint among the general public and to educate homosexuals as to their responsibilities as variants from the moral and social standards. It is hoped to find others who will agree with us and join us in our effort to establish these rights and responsibilities ... The much maligned homosexual community has long been in dire need of a "voice" to speak for itself and offer some rebuttal to the irresponsible attacks periodically made upon it.[143]

Most issues included book reviews, news items, and physique photos, some of them taken by Rick Kerr of the Music Room. In accordance with obscenity legislation, none of these photos showed sexual activity or frontal nudity, but this did not stop the police morality bureau, in 1966, from raiding the Kamp Publishing bookstore — which contained a large number of titles of interest to gays[144] — charging them with possession of "obscene" literature for the purposes of distribution. This contributed to the publication's demise, a result that once again demonstrates the significance of censorship and obscenity legislation in regulating gay materials and gay organizing.

The first issue discussed the current wave of publicity about homosexuality — articles in *Maclean's* and the Toronto *Telegram*. It also refers to female impersonators who were an important part of the emergence of gay cultures.

The second issue, while endorsing police activity against sexual acts in public, argued that the recent arrest of two men dancing together at the Melody Room "gives rise to doubts as to police integrity and has focused attention on the meaning of the charge of 'gross indecency'." Here we get a sense of conflict over varying interpretations of "public" and "gross indecency." The police (or at least one officer) were attempting to define men dancing together as "gross indecency." "Gross indecency" would then include any sort of homosexual activity, expanding this offence to include not just overt sexual/genital activity, but any male/male intimacy in a gay club. In contrast, *Two* asserted that gay clubs were not public places and that men dancing together did not constitute "gross indecency." According to the everyday local experience of gay men, gay men in a gay club were in a private gay space, not an area that could be defined as "in public," and men dancing together was not "gross indecency." *Two* attempted to actively use and shift the emerging public/private frame to defend gays and gay clubs.

Another issue printed a guest editorial by Jim Egan in response to a series of articles by Ron Fulton on "Society and the Homosexual" in the Toronto *Telegram*.[145] Egan had sent his point-by-point rebuttal to the *Telegram* but they had refused to publish it. He concludes:

> Homosexuality is a problem in modern society only because of the igno-
> rance and prejudice that surrounds it. The solution to the problem just as
> in the case of the Negro or Jewish problems, lies in the abolition of preju-
> dice and ignorance.[146]

Other issues reported on Sidney Katz's address to the Humanist and Unitarian Society in which, paraphrasing the *Wolfenden Report*, he stated that adult private homosexuality is "in the field of morals, not the field of law"; also included were: a profile of Tracy Roberts, "the only coloured boy working as a female impersonator" in Toronto; a reprint of Freud's famous letter to an American mother about homosexuality; news of ASK; and mention that *Gay* had stopped publishing, but that it was seeking refinancing and would reappear soon. Issue nine reported on Citizen's Alert, a group formed by the Council on Religion and the Homosexual in San Francisco to provide lawyers, photographers, and other assistance to gays, lesbians, blacks, Chicanos, and hippies experiencing police brutality.[147] "It appears that one will soon be needed right here in Toronto," it added.

At the same time, there was only one explicitly lesbian article in *Two* titled "What is a Downtown Butch?" As mentioned last chapter downtown butches referred to those working-class lesbians who worked and lived downtown as opposed to "uptowners," who were often more middle class and lived in the suburbs.[148]

The pages of both *Two* and *Gay* give a sense of the police activity directed against Toronto's expanding gay world. The *ASK Newsletter* reported that since the death of *Two*, which had likely been caused by the legal charges against Kamp Publishing, there had been no gay publication in Toronto.[149]

A short-lived and rather mysterious homophile organization also existed in Montréal in the late 1960s. Paul Bédard, who previously had been involved in the Mattachine Society in the U.S., set up International Sex Equality Anonymous (ISEA) in August 1967, affiliated with the North American Conference of Homophile Organizations (NACHO). He was in correspondence with ASK and Doug Sanders during this period.[150] ISEA aimed to be both educational and social. Bédard, its founder, president, and main member, also opened a small private night club in the east end of Montréal. The police arrested a club member and several youths, and charged Bédard with committing "immoral" acts and "contributing to the delinquency of minors." They claimed that he was running a male prostitution ring. Bédard was tried and acquitted in 1968 while the other club member was sentenced to two years.

In April 1969 Bédard opened a new club, Gemini I, which apparently kept out men dressed as women and vice versa and did not allow touching on the dance floor. A portrait of Pierre Trudeau on the club's wall was referred to by Réal Caouette in the Commons debates on the 1969 reform.[151] The club folded after only a month, partly as a result of police harassment according to Bédard,[152] and Bédard disappeared for a number of months. The Gemini reopened at another location later in the year but Bédard had left the scene by the early 1970s. Bédard was featured in a *Weekend Magazine* story entitled — with characteristic media-hype — "Canada's Leading Homosexual Speaks Out" on Sept. 13, 1969.[153] Bédard is a rather ambiguous figure. He made some significant efforts on behalf of organizing gays and publicizing the need for law reform. At the same time he was also interested in profit and advantage for himself.[154]

This gay/homophile organizing led to increasing church, media, and professional discussions of homosexuality, laying some of the preconditions for law reform. At the same time, the concerns of grass-roots gay and lesbian activists were transformed as they entered into the worlds of official discourse.

Homosexuality as a "Public" Issue

During the 1960s, as gay and lesbian networks expanded and as law-reform discussions began, the mass media started to investigate and survey homosexuality and the gay community. The reports usually centred around some media framework of the "social problems" presented by homosexuality. They focused on gay men to the exclusion of lesbians, with journalist Sidney Katz even arguing that "Lesbians are less obtrusive, less discriminated against and raise fewer social problems."[155] There was a movement away from the earlier official silence on homosexuality and past frames of "perversion" and "criminality" toward various versions of the sickness model of homosexuality that was often combined with the Wolfenden law-reform framework.

An early series of articles by Sidney Katz appeared in *Maclean's* in 1964. Here, if we scratch the surface, a gay homophile activist can be found as a motivating force. Katz had sought out Jim Egan before taking on the work because he had seen some of Egan's writing. According to Egan, Katz knew nothing about homosexuality when this all started, although Katz had written one of the early articles that contributed to the establishment of the criminal-sexual-psychopath section.[156] There is an important shift away from Katz's earlier acceptance of the criminalization of homosexuality strategy in these articles. Working on these articles also led to Katz's connections with homophile reform efforts.

Egan brought Katz to the bars and clubs, and appeared under the pseudonym Verne Baldwin in the first of Katz's two-part series, "The Homosexual Next Door: A Sober Appraisal of a New Social Phenomenon." Interestingly, Egan met with some opposition from within the gay community for his cooperation with Katz and for publicizing gay issues generally. He was told that a number of middle-class gay men were upset because this publicity violated the code of secrecy they felt protected them from exposure. Perhaps he was encountering opposition from a network of "covert" homosexuals. They felt that making more people aware of homosexuality would only make it worse for gays. Egan was urged to break off his collaboration with Katz, but he refused on the grounds that publicity was needed and that the articles could only improve with his help.[157]

The first of Katz's articles was relatively liberal for its time and was based on various discussions with gay men. Although he argued within the framework of "the homosexual problem," he also argued that "the average homosexual is a much-maligned individual, unfairly discriminated against by our laws and society" as he emphasized the "respectability" of most homosexuals.[158] In this construction of public images of the homosexual, Egan participated behind the scenes but did not control the media image that was produced.

The second instalment, "The Harsh Facts of Life in the 'Gay' World," was a less sympathetic account of the problems of the homosexual world and relied more on interviews with psychiatrists, doctors and other "experts." Aspects of the sickness approach to homosexuality were discussed, although it was clearly admitted that homosexuals cannot be cured. Katz cited the *Wolfenden Report* on this point.[159]

A CBC Television show in November 1964 produced a generally tolerant view of gays. In July 1965, an article was published in the *Vancouver Sun* by William Nichols, an Anglican priest who was the head of the Department of Religious Studies at the University of British Columbia. He had spoken at an ASK forum in 1964 calling for law reform along Wolfenden lines. He viewed homosexuality as a condition the homosexual could do little about.[160] The discussion of the Criminal Code reform sparked further media investigations, a number of which supported reform.[161] An editorial in *The Vancouver Sun* in 1966 supported law reform along Wolfenden lines, and also mentioned the attempt by Simmons and Sanders to get the criminal-justice committee of the B.C. Branch of the Canadian Bar Association to support homosexual-law reform.[162] This was all part of the media organization of "public opinion" and how homophile-inspired efforts influenced, and were entered into, public discourse.

By the mid to late 1960s, there were also some media explorations that focused specifically on lesbians. In 1966 Renate Wilson wrote "What Turns Women to Lesbianism," in *Chatelaine*, where she quoted from some middle-class Vancouver lesbians. Wilson portrayed lesbians as "abnormal."[163] In the professional publication *Canadian Nurse* in 1967, lesbianism was defined as a "deviation," as "an addiction," and as "retarded psychosexual development."[164]

Developing a Professional and Legal Consensus for Reform

Debate also took place in professional circles, which in turn provided "expert" opinions that could enter into the media coverage. *The Canadian Medical Association Journal* carried a number of articles on sex deviation and homosexuality encompassing a broad range of opinions.[165] By the 1960s, these articles were generally accepting different variants of the sickness or mental-illness approach. A curious piece by an "anonymous homosexual" was published in 1962, in which the author says he is "handicapped by homosexuality," believing it to be a psychological disorder. He supports the general premise of the *Wolfenden Report* and appeals for liberal tolerance. It is interesting that this layman's account was published in a medical journal. Clearly, someone wanted the psychological disorder and Wolfenden approaches put forward by a homosexual himself.[166]

Groups within the medical, psychiatric, and legal professions supported reform for their own reasons, many having to do with the internal dynamics within these groups, but also because it could extend the jurisdiction of medicine and psychiatry in the regulation of social life. The reasons the Wolfenden perspective was taken up by doctors, psychiatrists, and lawyers differed markedly from those of the grass-roots homophile and gay and lesbian activists. These activists attempted to use it as an opening for popular education while professional and State bodies read the *Wolfenden Report* in an administrative fashion — as a document of sexual rule.

In the field of criminal law, there developed a general consensus that law reform was necessary. Law professor Alan Mewett, who would be consulted during the 1969 parliamentary discussions on law reform, early on accepted the arguments of Wolfenden, but went somewhat beyond them regarding adult/youth regulation:

> Homosexuality is unquestionably undesirable even though this does not mean that it should be legislated against ... All homosexual activities — male or female — should be criminal activities where the accused is over 21 and the partner under 21, but otherwise where both parties are over 21, or both parties under 21, be removed from the Criminal Code. This differs somewhat ... from the recommendations of the Wolfenden Committee.[167]

A legal pocketbook by Raymond Spencer Rodgers written with the assistance of Mewett entitled *Sex and the Law in Canada*, featuring a foreword by Kenneth Gray — whom we met last chapter as the legal advisor to PAL — was published in 1962. It argues that penalties for "deviant" behaviour not dangerous to others were excessive or unnecessary.[168] This text was intended to open up discussion for law reform and to call on the government to "appoint a Royal Commission on the Law as its relates to Sexual Behaviour."[169]

The Wolfenden and law-reform frameworks were beginning to enter into courtroom discussions, trials, and sentencing hearings in Canada by the mid-1960s. They were also entering into appeals and producing some pressure from the courts for clarification of the law. This may have led to difficulties in getting convictions, or getting the sentences that may have been possible previously. The relatively light sentences often handed out in these cases was used, as we have already seen, in the Sanders' article to argue for law reform since the full penalties were rarely being enforced.

Alex K. Gigeroff based his argument for legal reform on research carried out at the Forensic Clinic in conjunction with the University of Toronto.[170] Most of the research was undertaken in the early and mid-1960s, and his main work, based on his thesis, was published in 1968. His *Sexual Deviation in the Criminal Law* was twice referred to in the 1969 parliamentary debate on Criminal Code reform. In his foreword to the book, Kenneth Gray explains that Gigeroff has amassed a great deal of empirical data that allow him to build a bridge between psychiatry, the social sciences, and the law, "clearing the ground ... so that the normative judgements that the law represents can be seen in terms of actualities of human behaviour."[171]

Gigeroff saw his work as preparing the way for legal reform. He was basically supportive of Trudeau's 1967 proposal for Criminal Code reform but criticized its vagueness on the definitions of "gross indecency" and "in public." His studies had financial assistance from the Ontario Mental Health Foundation and help from the Ontario Provincial Probation Service and the Metro Toronto Police Department. Viewing this type of research as the proper basis for reform, he criticized the last round of Criminal Code reforms in the early 1950s, which were limited, he argued, to "simplification" of the code and correction of outstanding errors — amounting merely to neater packaging of a nineteenth-century product. He pointed to the need for input from various professional disciplines. Contrasting the Canadian experience with the reform process in England, he explained that the government there had based its work on expert studies and analysis of sexual offenders. He called for a similar process in Canada. Gigeroff reflected the concerns of those psychiatrists and doctors who advocated placing adult-oriented homosexuals under their jurisdiction, rather than under the direct legal, judicial, and penal apparatus of the State. In his view, public acceptance of such reforms could be won through the media, the churches, and professional organizations.

Gigeroff quotes in his book extensively from the transcript of a Toronto "gross indecency" court case that took place in 1965 as part of his argument for reform and for the more precise definition of legal categories. This gives us both a sense of the legal pressures mobilized in court cases for reform as well as a glimpse into the social organization of the sexual policing of gay men during these years. The transcript reports that two men were charged with committing "gross indecency." One man pleaded guilty and the other not guilty. At first there was a dispute over what evidence would be admissible. During this dispute the Crown Attorney stated:

> The Crown's evidence will be and it is my submission from the observation
> with reference to the accused C.D., it would appear he was standing in the
> rain and every time a lone male driver would come up Yonge Street he
> would rub himself in the area of his privates. The [police] officers felt,
> "Here we have something," and finally parked further along Yonge Street
> and he lured the accused A.B. into his clutches and they went in the car and
> committed an act of gross indecency ...[172]

This reference to "committed an act of gross indecency" — is not an actual description of the sexual encounter that took place but is already inscribed into an "offence" category in the Criminal Code. This is dependent on the police report on which the Crown Attorney's remarks are based. When the police survey this man rubbing his "privates" they see the possibility of an arrest. These two men then become the targets of police surveillance until the police felt they had enough "evidence" to make an arrest.

In introducing his case, the Crown Attorney stated that one of the officers went over to the car in which the two men were "and found the accused before the Court with the other gentleman's penis in his mouth, doing something ... This is gross indecency."[173] An observed sexual act is inscribed into the legal category of "gross indecency." The Crown Attorney then called his first witness who was one of the arresting detectives. The officer stated (his testimony was no doubt based upon his notes on this arrest and the report he and his partner wrote up following the arrest):

> Then I approached the car in question on the passenger's side and upon looking in the window I saw the accused man bent over and had the passenger's penis in his mouth. The passenger had an erection and the accused man was moving his head up and down sucking the passenger's penis.

This is the necessary construction of official police evidence — the "particulars" or "facts" are established through this testimony to intend a "gross indecency" inscription and conviction. Sucking another man's penis only becomes "gross indecency" when it is inscribed as part of police evidence and intends this categorization as part of a court case. If the police had not been present this activity would not have been able to be constructed as a "crime" or as "gross indecency." This then is an instance of an ideological circle where the possible sex acts these men were engaged in is read as the criminal offence of "gross indecency."

"Gross indecency" is hardly what these two men in the car were thinking about prior to their intimacy being intruded upon by the police. This is again a rupture in experience — the experienced pleasures of cocksucking versus "gross indecency." The men had taken steps to remove themselves from public view and to establish a degree of privacy and intimacy for themselves.

In this legal case, an erection and the sucking of it by another man become the "facts" of "gross indecency" in the Crown's case. The legal concept of "gross indecency" lays out the procedures that allow for the organizing and concerting of the work of the police and the Crown Attorney. These become the "facts" of the case because of what the police report states, not because they are necessarily "what actually happened." Only the men charged could tell us what was going on for them and this is no longer recoverable and is irrelevant under the law. The Crown Attorneys case, then, comes to be based on these police "facts." It is upon these "facts" that he argues his case. The detective continued:

> I then opened the door, turned my flashlight on the accused man and the passenger, told them I was a police officer and immediately the accused man remarked, "Please leave us alone. It will cause trouble. Just leave us alone. We will go away." I informed the accused man he and the other party were both under arrest and would have to accompany me to the police station.

On the basis of this evidence, the prosecution rested its case feeling this was sufficient to establish "gross indecency." The Crown Attorney relied entirely on police testimony and called no "expert" witnesses.

In contrast, the defence argued that the prosecution had not proven its case since it had not brought in any scientific evidence as to the definition of "gross indecency."[174] He stated that "the only fact before your Honour is a physical act. There is nothing more. There is nothing to say it is indecent."[175] He argued that the prosecution did not link this evidence with case law, precedent, contemporary "community standards" or psychiatric evidence. This allowed an opening for his defence argument. He argued:

> In view of the recent findings in the *Wolfenden Report* and the Kinsey Report
> I do not think evidence of this kind is indecent, that the Court can take judi-
> cial notice that it is indecent behaviour or homosexual behaviour is inde-
> cent. The *Wolfenden Report* indicates 37 percent of all males have some form
> of homosexual behaviour and that report says this [is the] kind of conduct
> the criminal law should not associate itself with.[176]

This was an instance of pressure for law reform being raised at lower levels in the courts and coming to influence courtroom strategies and proceedings. The defence argued that the prosecution had not proven its case. It was becoming more difficult to accomplish gross indecency convictions. What the police/Crown attorney presented as evidence in this case would have been sufficient previously to secure a conviction. Now a man charged with this sex offence and his lawyer were challenging this way of proceeding.

In response to a question from the judge, the defence lawyer stated:

> My view is it [the activity the men were charged with engaging in] should
> not be criminal. The Criminal Code says it is gross indecency. Indecency is a
> matter of custom and the Crown should have to show the normal range of
> behaviour before it can term this conduct "gross."[177]

Later the defence lawyer again referred to the *Wolfenden Report*, stating that "it is not the function of the criminal law to enter into the private lives of some citizens under certain conditions."[178] Here he raised and used the public/private regulatory distinction as part of his legal argument. And he said "My friend has not brought before this court a grain of law to say because you are a homosexual you are a criminal." Here he disputes the course of action put in place through the extension of criminalization strategy that I investigated in the last chapter that a homosexual is per se criminal. The Wolfenden law-reform framework shapes his defence at the courtroom level. But he also goes further.

The defence also raised the important question of what constitutes privacy. He says that where these men were arrested "There were no pedestrians, no other people. This was not on the street. This was not on the City Hall steps."[179] And surely "grossness or monstrous must be something that extends beyond a private act between two consenting male adults."

The active presence of the Wolfenden Reform perspective and the debates over it that were not yet legally valid or established in the Canadian context opened up a space for this kind of defence argument. Again referring to Wolfenden the defence lawyer argued:

> The *Wolfenden Report* has said in England that this act in private is not even gross indecency.[180] ... they have recommended that act not be considered gross indecency and be removed from the Criminal Code because the Code should not bring the private lives of citizens within its sphere.[181]

To a certain extent, the arguments of the defence lawyer against the Crown and to some extent the judge can be seen as a dramatisation of the contention between the Wolfenden framework and more "old style" criminalization arguments. The judge is even forced to adapt a bit to the public/private regulatory framework that then had no actual legal jurisdiction in Canadian law.[182] The jury in this case has to accomplish the inscription and conviction of "gross indecency" following the judge's instructions, and it has some difficulties in this project. The jury returned to ask whether there was any definition in the law of "gross indecency" and to ask if there were any legal precedents that could help them. Eventually they find the defendant guilty but they strongly recommend "leniency and treatment."[183] The defence lawyer stated during the sentencing hearing that he had spoken to a doctor at the Forensic Clinic and his client was prepared to go there for treatment. The accused got a suspended sentence and probation with the condition that he attend the clinic for treatment. He was entered into legally mandated psychiatric relations. During these years, accepting the need for "treatment" or "therapy" may have also been a strategy used by gays and defence lawyers to try to get light sentences.[184]

By the mid-1960s, a trend toward a consensus for criminal-law reform was becoming evident. The most significant single influence on professional and official debate was the *Wolfenden Report* and the resulting legislation in England and Wales in 1967, demonstrating once again the referencing of Canadian history to English legal tradition. Other significant influences were the emergence of visible gay and lesbian cultures in a number of cities and the growth of a small homophile movement that organized limited popular education and law-reform initiatives. Some church circles, partially influenced by this homophile movement, also began building a certain consensus for reform.

The Klippert Case: Facilitator of Reform

The controversial Everett George Klippert case played a central role in speeding up this process of reform, especially in getting the Wolfenden reform strategy taken up by government. As Doug Sanders expresses it, "it wiped out any middle ground in the debate" since the "most sophisticated argument for retaining the anti-homosexual laws was that changing the law was some form of approval" of homosexuality and that those opposed to changing the laws were "happy with not enforcing the laws but in leaving them on the books." This position became quite untenable with the Klippert decision, suggesting that continuing engagement in gay sex could lead to life imprisonment. This was the continuing legal resiliency of the extending criminalization of homosexuality strategy put in place in previous years that now came sharply into conflict with the partial decriminalization reform strategy.

In the course of an RCMP investigation into a case of arson in 1965 at Pine Point, Northwest Territories, Klippert, a mechanic's helper, told the police that he had been a homosexual for twenty-four years and admitted to certain sexual acts with males. He was charged with four counts of "gross indecency." All acts were consensual and were not "public." There was no suggestion of violence or that children were involved. While some of the "offences" involved adolescents, this was not legally relevant at the time since all homosexual acts were illegal under the letter of the law.

Klippert pleaded guilty and was sentenced on August 24, 1965 to three years for each of the charges, to be served concurrently. He was convicted solely on the basis of his own testimony. While in jail in Saskatchewan, Klippert was visited by two psychiatrists on behalf of the Crown. He had not been given any warning about these interviews and was not aware that the government was attempting to have him declared a "dangerous sexual offender." Sanders, after talking to Klippert in the Prince Albert Penitentiary, wrote that three months following his imprisonment,

> an RCMP officer visited Klippert in the Penitentiary. He handed Klippert official notice that the Crown was proceeding with a hearing to have him declared a "dangerous sexual offender." Klippert was stunned.[185]

Klippert's experience of being stunned can be accounted for since he had no idea until he received the official notice that outside his immediate world in the Penitentiary, in his cell and daily routine, his "case" had been entered into the relations establishing someone as a "dangerous sexual offender." Klippert's life had been entered into an official course of action of which he had no knowledge and which would allow him to be held in indefinite detention. He was entered into a web of legal and psychiatric relations shaped through a procedure laid out in the Criminal Code.

Klippert's problems had begun a number of years earlier in 1960 when a complaint had been laid against him by the father of one of his sexual partners in Calgary. It was often standard police procedure to grill gay men about their sexual contacts. When interrogated by the police, Klippert mentioned sexual activities he had engaged in with eighteen males. As far as Klippert knew the police never investigated these incidents any further. In the hope of avoiding publicity, he pleaded guilty without ever consulting a lawyer. Given the character of the police-judge relation, gay men like Klippert generally knew that the judges would go with the police testimony in court proceedings regarding homosexual sex. Klippert served four years in prison on these "gross indecency" convictions.

He then moved to Pine Point where the police informed him that they knew of his record. Clearly, his record followed him, contributing to this police warning and perhaps continued surveillance. In 1965, when he was questioned by the police, Klippert recounts that he was told that unless he pleaded guilty to "gross indecency" he would be charged with "arson," although there was no evidence for this charge. This displayed the arbitrary powers of the RCMP granted to them through the criminalization of homosexual activity. Again Klippert pleaded guilty without any legal advice and was sentenced to three years on four counts of "gross indecency." His experiences of consensual sex were again transformed into "gross indecency." Police and courtroom work transforming his sexual adventures into "gross indecency" then allowed his case to be entered into the dangerous-sexual-offender sentencing procedure since "gross indecency" was one of the "triggering" offences.

While Klippert knew from his own experience the punitive consequences of his convictions for "gross indecency," he had no idea that the Crown prosecutor and the police were applying to have him sentenced as a dangerous sexual offender. The police reports from Calgary mentioning his previous "gross indecency" convictions were an important "fact" enabling them to proceed with this application. In the application to have him sentenced as a dangerous sexual offender, the Crown counsel pointed out that as well as the four recent convictions, Klippert had also pleaded guilty to eighteen other such "offences" in Calgary. Prior to this sentencing hearing, Klippert was visited by the two psychiatrists and was successfully transformed into a dangerous sexual offender in sentencing.

It was the RCMP who laid the charges against him, who had a record of his previous convictions, and who clearly intended to apply through the Crown prosecutor for dangerous-sexual-offender status. The RCMP has a particular character as the police force of the federal State with law-enforcement powers over much of Canadian territory.

The application for sentencing as a dangerous-sexual-offender status was heard before Justice Sissons. Sissons was very impressed with the psychiatric evidence, says Sanders.[186] He wanted to get treatment for Klippert started as soon as possible given that one of the psychiatrists had made rather vague references to possibilities for treatment. Sissons believed sentencing Klippert as a dangerous sexual offender could allow him to be released quickly on parole where he could receive treatment outside the penitentiary. As Sanders put it:

> No one seemed to be aware that paroles are extremely rare for dangerous sexual offenders. No one seemed aware of the futility of treatment for a man whose exclusive pattern for 25 years has been homosexual. No one seemed to be aware that any parole would have to be terminated if Klippert became involved once more in consensual homosexual activity.[187]

It was the very hegemony of the sickness and treatment frameworks that allowed for the judge's indeterminate sentencing in the first place, even though there was a major contradiction in his approach. There was very little actual "treatment" available.

On March 9, 1966, Klippert was indeed pronounced a dangerous sexual offender and was given a sentence of indefinite preventive detention as mandated by this legislation in lieu of the sentence previously imposed. The psychiatric evidence was key to this decision and future appeals, since an appeal would rest on the original court transcript, his previous criminal record, and the psychiatric testimony. On October 26 of that year, an appeal of this decision was dismissed without written reason.

In 1967, Brian Crane, Klippert's counsel, appealed to the Supreme Court of Canada. Argument centred on the definition of "dangerous sexual offender." This appeal took place over a dispute regarding the proper mandated course of action, particularly over the definition section. This dispute focused on the interpretation of the clause, "or is likely to commit a further sexual offence," that had been added to the legislation in 1961. Crane contended that the evidence of the two psychiatrists did not prove that Klippert had shown "a failure to control his sexual impulses," which was the other central clause in the dangerous-sexual-offender definition. He referred to the statement in the Royal Commission on Criminal Sexual Psychopaths Report that mere conviction for a homosexual offence should not itself warrant an indeterminate sentence. Here he attempted to read the report as establishing a legal precedent — but the report itself left this up to the discretion of the courts. Crane also quoted the original judge as stating that he was motivated by "how soon could we get this man [Klippert] out of the penitentiary and his treatment started."

Klippert's behaviour had always been non-violent, argued Crane, and "if the language of the statute applies to the conduct of Klippert it must apply to any homosexual."[188] The defence view was shared by the decision of two dissenting judges who supported the appeal. Justice Cartwright wrote that the majority of judges were sentencing anyone

> who appears likely, if at liberty, to continue such misconduct to "preventative detention," that is incarceration for life. However loathsome conduct of the sort mentioned may be to all normal persons, I think it improbable that parliament should have intended such a verdict.[189]

While still taking up the standpoint of heterosexual hegemony, these judges adopted a more "liberal" view that could be used to facilitate the reform process. They argued that there had to be an element of danger to another person in any future offences for an offender to be classified as a dangerous sexual offender. They found that the Criminal Code's reference to further sexual offences must be read as relating to others, otherwise it would imply that a person who was not dangerous must nevertheless be dealt with as if he were. Although Klippert would likely engage in further homosexual acts with consenting males, they argued, there was no danger he would use violence or coercion. Their argument was that this did not establish Klippert as a dangerous sexual offender and that he therefore should fall outside the course of action set out in this section.

The majority of the court found in contrast to the minority that this case did fall within the mandated course of action set out in the dangerous-sexual-offender section.[190] The majority also made use of the earlier psychiatric and medical testimony. One of the doctors who had given "expert" testimony testified that Klippert would have the same drive toward homosexual relations in the future as he had in the past. This allowed Klippert to be inscribed into the "commit a further sexual offence" part of the definition since at this point all gay sex was technically illegal. Another medical "expert" contended that Klippert could not stop his homosexual activities for long periods of time on his own, which constituted a "failure to control" his sexual impulses — which was the other crucial part of the dangerous-sexual-offender definition. In the argument before the Supreme Court, the Crown contended that Klippert would continue to commit acts of "gross indecency." This evidence allowed for the successful inscription of Klippert into this category and established a history of gay sex per se as a social danger and threat.

It was only with the case going to the Supreme Court that it generated media publicity. Until then it would only have been known to those directly involved. For Sanders it just "came out of the blue." *ASK Newsletter* commented on the case in June 1967:

> The Klippert case was argued before the Supreme Court of Canada in the last week of May ... If the conviction is upheld it means that any practicing homosexual in Canada can be convicted of being a "dangerous sexual offender" and sentenced to an indefinite sentence. It would not matter that the sexual activity was private, with consent and with adult persons.[191]

Doug Sanders had done the previously mentioned survey of sentencing for "gross indecency" and found that it was generally fairly light. As he put it: "The system with Klippert became widely schizophrenic. What was considered a minor offence, suddenly if you repeated it branded you for life as a dangerous sexual offender."[192] An offence that he argued was treated as minor, now suddenly became one of the most serious offences under Canadian law.

The final decision in the case, handed down on November 7, 1967, was based on a literal interpretation of the dangerous-sexual-offender category by the majority of the judges (three to two). The majority argued that while the provision was aimed at those who are a danger to others, references to "buggery" and "gross indecency," by those who had previously been convicted of these charges, provided an "alternative element" to that of danger to others. This embodied a notion of homosexuality as *socially dangerous*. Since "gross indecency" was one of the triggering offences, it was not necessary to show that a future offence would be a source of danger or injury to specific other persons. Their decision rested on the phrase "further sexual offences."

Since "gross indecency" was one of the triggering offences, it operated as an abstract category obscuring the actual features of the activities Klippert was charged with. For instance, it obscured the age of his sexual partners, whether these acts were in "private" or not, that they were consensual and not abusive. At this time it was not legally relevant whether the sex engaged in was with youths, whether it was in "private," or whether it was consensual. However, once these activities had been inscribed into "gross indecency" and then "dangerous sexual offender," the actual local contexts of these sexual activities can no longer be recovered since they had already been transformed into ruling, ideological, legally-mandated categories. As Gigeroff notes, referring to the Supreme Court majority, "it is not without significance that none of them considered the real situations that were represented by the words 'gross indecency' ..."[193]

Ten years after the release of the *Wolfenden Report* and after the British government had adopted its recommendations on homosexuality in England and Wales, the Supreme Court of Canada majority affirmed a judgement that virtually deemed all sexually active homosexuals "dangerous sexual offenders." A gay man convicted of "gross indecency" and likely to commit this act again was able to be incarcerated for life regardless of whether the act was committed with a consenting adult in private. The terms of this debate and such classifications as "adult" and "private" connected this debate to the conceptual framework of the *Wolfenden Report*. This set up a clash between the Wolfenden partial-decriminalization strategy and the more extensive criminalization strategy embodied in the workings of the dangerous-sexual-offender legislation. This set up a conflict between the general referencing of Canadian State formation — and in particular the Criminal Code — to legal developments in England and the institutionalization of homosexuality as a criminal sexual and social danger integrated into Canadian legislation from the U.S. These contradictory influences on Canadian sexual policing pulled Canadian sexual regulatory practices in different directions, creating an opening for reform discussions with the controversy produced in the media and Parliament over the Klippert decision.

The majority decision included the following:

> Whether the criminal law with respect to sexual misconduct of the sort in which appellant [Klippert] had indulged for nearly twenty-five years, should be changed to the extent to which it had been recently in England, by the Sexual Offenders Act, 1967 .... is obviously not for us to say; our jurisdiction is to interpret and apply laws validly enacted.[194]

This could be read as a call for the federal State to address the possibility of changing the law, since this was not the proper mandate of the courts — a debate that is still with us — and also to address the recently enacted recommendations of the *Wolfenden Report* in England.

The decision to reject the appeal was very controversial. It fit into a framework of speeding up law reform. This ensuing process of governmental reform was basically framed and organized by the very active text of the *Wolfenden Report*, which provided the strategic framework for reorganizing relations and organizing for Criminal Code reform in the Canadian context.

The media and politicians were quick to respond to the Supreme Court rejection of Klippert's appeal. This response created a particular conjuncture of relations pushing toward reform organized through the Wolfenden strategic framework. T.C. Douglas, leader of the New Democratic Party, asked a series of questions in the House of Commons and proposed a committee similar to the Wolfenden committee for Canada. In response, Justice Minister Trudeau expressed approval for more liberalized laws and stated that the government would study the request for a special committee. The debate was not focused on reform of the dangerous-sexual-offender section itself but instead on the "gross indecency" and "buggery' sections of the Criminal Code that Wolfenden addressed.

Toronto Star headlines after the verdict screamed "Supreme Court Ruling Makes Homosexual Liable for Life" and "Law on Homosexuality Will Be Amended." A *Star* editorial entitled "a Return to the Middle Ages" agreed with the dissenting judges' position. A Toronto *Globe and Mail* editorial, "Not Parliament's Intention," referred to the recent English reform.[195] Sidney Katz, in two *Toronto Star* articles, details the shocked responses of lawyers, psychiatrists, and what he refers to as "spokesmen" for Metro Toronto's homosexuals. He quotes one gay men as saying: "The court decision scares me. It makes me feel like a criminal. The decision is an open invitation to the police ..." and "I want the right to live and be accepted as a homosexual. No law can make us conform, therefore the law must be changed." In his second article, "Gentle George Klippert — Must He Serve Life?" Katz focused on Klippert himself.[196]

There was an important framing of this as a key "issue" and a mobilization of support for law reform. This helped to construct a public consensus leading toward reform. The *Edmonton Journal* was one of the few mainstream media to editorialize against reform arguing that there was a tendency for homosexuals to prey upon the young.[197]

"The State has no place in the bedrooms of the nation," said Pierre Trudeau in the context of his proposed reform legislation. He said he would also amend the dangerous offenders section in response to the Klippert case. Not until 1969, however, would the Commons Justice Committee propose exempting homosexuals who were not likely to cause "injury, pain or other evil." There would then have to be clearer evidence not only of a sexual offence but also of a "danger" to others.[198]

In the specific context created following the Klippert decision, the Wolfenden perspective provided a cogent and available way to respond. A number of very significant organizations, especially in the legal profession, came out in support of reform. The Canadian Bar Association, at its 1968 conference, supported the decriminalization of homosexual acts in private and also suggested lowering the age of consent for such acts to sixteen.[199]

The police, as the enforcers of heterosexual "law and order" and as an organization with a particular heterosexist character, vigorously and consistently opposed reform. The Toronto police opposed the 1967 reform in England, stating that "much crime can be traced to homosexuality."[200] A senior officer claimed that Canadian reforms would "encourage homosexuality, lead to an increase in violence, and probably corrupt young people."[201] The Canadian Association of Police Chiefs voted at their 1968 annual conference to oppose the reform legislation because it would lead to depravity, robbery, and murder.[202] This association of homosexuality and criminality had become an integral part of police operational policy: gay men became criminal suspects.[203] Police attitudes were also shaped by a determination to preserve their turf against encroachments from the psychiatric and medical professions. They wanted to keep all "deviant" sexual behaviour under police jurisdiction, which put them in conflict with major aspects of the increasingly hegemonic view of homosexuality as an illness or "condition."

The 1969 Criminal Code Reform: From Homophile Reform to Sexual Regulation

It was in this context that the 1969 Criminal Code reform took place. While grass-roots gay and lesbian activists helped get the discussion going, the reform itself was part of a broad political project of the dominant sectors of the Liberal Party and Canadian ruling agencies. Unlike grass-roots homophile activists who stressed the need for public education, State agencies did not take up these concerns from a gay/lesbian standpoint. Again, we can see the transformation from local grass-roots activism, even if organized through a historically specific homophile framework, to official discourse and practice. As homosexual-law reform was made into an official "issue," these more local community-based concerns were left behind. Doug Sanders' comments on the 1969 reform are very instructive here. Trudeau's remark about getting the State out of the bedrooms of the nation, says Sanders,

> takes the gay issue and describes it in non-homosexual terms ... Unfortunately, legalization occurs in a way in which the issue is never joined. The debate never occurs. And so homosexuals are no more real after the reform than before ... I felt that an issue had been stolen from us. That we had forgotten that the reform issue was an issue that could have been used for public debate and it had been handled in such a way that there had been none. The only thing that had a promise of helping people was a public debate. It didn't happen.

Lesbian and gay concerns, and our sexualities, were separated from our local everyday experiences and became questions instead of the regulation of sex in public or private along with whether it involved adults or youths. Clearly, aspects of homophile agitation such as claims to legitimacy and respectability through using the Wolfenden approach, and an earlier reliance on heterosexual "experts," facilitated the government in so interpreting homophile concerns. Still an important transformation took place in the late 1960s as homophile and lesbian and gay concerns were reduced to narrow issues of criminal-law reform.

While gay and homophile activists were moving far beyond the sickness model of homosexuality (the North American Conference of Homophile Organizations adopted the slogan "gay is good" in 1968, in the context of the social-protest movements of the 1960s),[204] the government continued to use this sickness discourse to confine and limit the debate. Says Sanders, "Those arguments were over as far as gays were concerned, but they weren't over in any public debate because there never had been a public debate on these issues."

In a February 1968 editorial, *ASK Newsletter* challenged the age restrictions of the proposed legislation:

> We congratulate the Justice Minister on his far-sighted Bill, however we deem to call it not enough. Why can a person of eighteen be old enough to enlist and fight for his country; yet not be considered old enough to choose the nature of his or her sexual habits ... It is though, our sincere hope that unless sex with those over eighteen and under twenty-one is contracted by financial arrangement, the law enforcement of Canada will turn a blind eye to those who choose the path they rightly consider their own.[205]

As secretary of NACHO, Sanders sent Pierre Trudeau a resolution from the NACHO conference in 1968. It read:

> The North American Conference of Homophile Organizations expresses sharp disappointment that Mr. Pierre Elliot Trudeau ... has seen fit to introduce the limited and inadequate provisions of the English homosexual law reform bill ... which makes 21 the age of consent for homosexual acts. Believing it to be offensive and unjustifiable for homosexual acts to be singled out for special treatment, the Conference encourages the Canadian government to ... enact provisions for age of consent which are identical for homosexual and heterosexual acts.[206]

They were able to criticize adult/youth lines of implementation of the Wolfenden strategy while basically accepting the public/private regulatory strategy. Unfortunately, the Canadian homophile movement was too scattered and weak (with ASK in the process of collapsing) to take advantage of the law-reform discussions to develop and impose its own agenda. It was unable to oppose or shift this transformation of the concerns that it had initially raised, partially because of the difficulties of organizing across the vast expanse of the Canadian State. This also produced a rupture between homophile activism prior to the 1969 reform and the gay and lesbian liberation movements that would come after it.

As mentioned earlier, this law-reform process took place as part of a wider series of social changes. The development of the post-war "Welfare State" and the hegemony of Keynesian economic and social interventionism created a space for the incorporation of medical and psychiatric practices within State agencies. This led to new combinations of

policies of sexual regulation linking psychiatric work with the criminal justice system
and sexual policing. It also led to the incorporation of aspects of sexual regulation into
State agencies increasingly outside the direct realm of the Criminal Code; for instance,
into family and social support policies. Eventually this led some State and professional
agencies to lessen their reliance on the police, courts, and Criminal Code in areas of
sexual and moral regulation; e.g., for acts involving two adults in private. At the same
time, given differences within ruling relations, especially over the necessity of heterosexual masculinity as an organizing ideology, the police, the military, and other powerful
State agencies remained firmly committed to the criminalization of homosexuality.

This social process was full of contradictions. Shifts in class and gender relations
gradually undermined the previous social organization of family and erotic life allowing
lesbians and gay men to exist at the lower levels of class and professional organization
where heterosexual ties were not a prerequisite. The development of corporate capitalism and increasingly national and extra-local forms of class and State organization
meant that the heterosexual family was no longer that integral to the social organization
of class and State relations. Rapid changes and developments in the markets for household goods, and a weakening and shifting of the previous gender specializations of
work, meant that all men no longer needed to have wives for domestic labour or sexual
services.[207] This led to some profound changes in the organization of heterosexual masculinities, but also opened up new possibilities for gay men and, in a different way, for
lesbians. The State and various professional agencies tried to organize and contain the
social spaces seized by gay men and lesbians as "private" where queer sex would not be
allowed to subvert "normal" sexual, gender, and social relations.

At the same time, professional and corporate executive men throughout the 1960s
and 1970s still most often needed a wife, a home, and kids doing well in school. A heterosexual social practice was still in many ways crucial in the worlds of business and the
professions. This led to a series of contradictions and social tensions. The public/private
means of sexual regulation was a way of managing these contradictions, allowing queers
to be tolerated in a limited and highly patrolled social space, while preserving heterosexual hegemony. The Wolfenden strategy and the 1969 criminal-law reform was not so
much a break in hegemony as a recognition that earlier strategies of regulation were no
longer effective.

The 1960s were a period of "liberal" reform and restructuring in a climate of general economic and social expansion and social struggle. The Liberals declared "war" on
poverty and established medicare. Social services were increased, schools and universities were expanded and liberalized, and divorce laws were broadened at the same time
as a series of sex-linked discussions opened up in the media and in popular culture.

Trudeau's accession to the leadership of the Liberal Party in 1968 highlighted the
shift toward a "new morality," although reform policies on abortion and sexuality had
their roots in the 1967 Pearson reforms regarding capital punishment and divorce.
Trudeau and the Liberal government, in the early years of his reign, attempted to bring
together a social bloc of diverse groups and classes through the use of the rhetoric of

the "Just Society," one aspect of which was liberalization of social policies in the moral and sexual spheres. The reforms surrounding abortion and sexual offences were an integral part of this shift.

The reform of the abortion law called for the establishment of a private moral realm — where in this case control was placed in the hands of the medical profession through hospitals and therapeutic abortion committees, on which sat at least three doctors. Abortions could now be approved for "health" reasons, but only in those hospitals that had established such a committee.[208] All others remained criminal offences. This legislation followed the lines of the English reform, which required that each abortion have the consent of two physicians. These changes were part of a broader process of reclassifying homosexuals, prostitutes, juvenile "sex offenders," and women seeking abortions as "sick" or "inadequate," but no longer as always criminal.[209] It has been argued that the 1969 abortion reform merely legalized and regularized existing hospital practice.[210] Similarly, it has been argued that, although it was sparked by the Klippert case, the sexual-offences reform merely codified the existing police practice of arresting gays only for acts in "public."

On December 21, 1967, Pierre Trudeau, minister of justice, introduced the first version of the sex-offences reform bill. The bill called for the lifting of sanctions against "buggery" and "gross indecency" for private acts between consenting adults of twenty-one or older. The sanctions would be retained for acts committed in public "or if two or more persons take part or are present" or if consent has been extorted, forced, or if a person "is feeble-minded, insane, or an idiot or imbecile."

The debates on the 1969 Criminal Code reform in the House of Commons and in the justice and legal affairs committee, to which it was referred for study, provide insights into the shifting policies of sexual regulation within Canadian State formation.[211] This also shows how textually mediated this debate was — including the extensive organizing capacities of the Wolfenden perspective and the sickness framework. As George Smith suggested, the record of this debate may be the most heterosexist document in Canadian governmental history,[212] although this is now rivalled by some of the debates in provincial legislatures over sexual orientation protection,[213] family recognition rights and spousal benefits,[214] and at the federal level over hate-crimes sentencing legislation.

For the purposes of analysis, the participants can be divided into two general camps. The first pro-reform camp was made up of the Liberals, the New Democrats, and some Conservatives whose discourse was basically organized through the conceptual framework of the *Wolfenden Report* with a particular interpretation tying it into the sickness framework. In the second anti-reform camp, were the Créditistes (a rural Catholic-based Social Credit party in Québec) and other Conservatives. The Créditistes conducted a filibuster to hold off adoption of those sections of the bill dealing with abortion, gross indecency, and buggery.

The speakers were all male with the sole exception of the only woman MP at the time, New Democrat Grace MacInnes. The discursive frameworks of both camps were organized by variants of the sickness model of homosexuality. These arguments developed in relation to each other in the debate as each side tried to link the concept of homosexuality as illness to their position. The Créditistes and some Conservatives used religious and other arguments as well, particularly as the sickness argument came to be hegemonized by the reform supporters as the debate went on.

The debate can be seen as a layering of different discourses organized through the text of the *Wolfenden Report* and earlier discourses of sexual regulation. In reading the transcripts of the debates, the discourse of the *Wolfenden Report* and the discourses of homosexual social danger, and degeneration come to life. Voices and texts from the past continue to have an active impact in shaping this debate.

As then Justice Minister John Turner explained, this proposal had been formulated with the input of the attorneys-general of the provinces, the legal profession, including the Canadian Bar Association, and the medical profession, as well as Crown prosecutors. Many social agencies participated in articulating this legal perspective. In particular, Turner stressed the significance of the input that had been received from legal "experts." In contrast, lesbians and gay men were not consulted, and while various professional and government bodies were involved, there was no broad discussion through a public commission or public hearings. This was a much more contained and rapid process of official change than that of the previously analysed Royal Commission on Criminal Sexual Psychopaths since the Wolfenden strategy was already available to be taken up in the law-reform process.

Professor Mewett, whom we met earlier, appeared before the Justice and Legal Affairs Committee at the urging of Mr. Wooliams of the Tories. He reported that the reform would make the Criminal Code conform to actual practice; that private clubs would be covered as "public" places; and that in his view, homosexuality among consenting adults "is a health matter rather than a matter for criminal law."

Turner introduced the bill with great fanfare. Bill C-150, the omnibus bill that included abortion, contraception, gambling, lotteries, and gun-control measures as well as reform of the sexual-offences laws, was, according to Turner, the "most important and all-embracing reform of the criminal and penal law ever attempted at one time in one country." It contained "matters of deep social significance" and took a stand on "some of the controversial questions of our time." He felt the bill reflected "the delicate balance between law and morals and the historic ideal of the rule of law in a free society." No other review of the criminal law had aroused as much interest, according to Turner, because this was the first attempt to reform the criminal law in an "orderly and understandable pattern," repealing those "provisions which had become obsolete." Its ideas, he argued, had already been accepted by public opinion in the last general election, and he explained that the government was dealing with the bill as an indivisible one, not as several individual items of legislation. The Standing Committee on Justice and Legal Affairs would deal with a clause-by-clause review:

> The government is of the opinion that this bill stands for the general principle of criminal and penal law reform and should be dealt with by the house on that basis ... We feel bound to the bill as the principal item of social re-

form in this session of Parliament. It is identified with our Prime Minister and our party.

The Créditistes and the Conservatives opposed this manner of dealing with the bill. They demanded separate reports, especially on homosexuality and abortion, so that they could vote on parts of the bill separately. The Liberals and the New Democrats defeated the opposition on this point, establishing the tactical terrain for the debate. Those opposed to either or both the "homosexual" and abortion provisions had to vote against the bill as a whole if they could not amend the bill to their liking.

In defending the sections of the bill dealing with "homosexuality" (actually the sections referred to "buggery" and "gross indecency") and abortion, the Liberals and the NDP relied on the public/private distinction and on differences between the realm of law and morality. This allowed them to bridge the gaps between these different sex-related practices through an administrative framework that tied together the regulation of these different practices. The Wolfenden strategy had a great deal of cogency in this context because it did this kind of work for supporters of the bill. Many of their arguments were lifted almost word for word from the *Wolfenden Report*. Said Turner:

> All that is immoral has not been and is not now criminal. I agree with and support the view that in the field of sexual behaviour the basic function of the criminal law is to preserve public order and decency ... In those certain areas of private behaviour which are more properly left to the conscience, which are in private and do not involve public order or corruption of others, particularly the young, we are of the view that this is no place for the criminal law.[215]

Within the justice and legal affairs committee he spelled this out even more clearly:

> We believe that the law and morals are two separate philosophical propositions ... that there are aspects of human life and relationships between people, which ... ought better be left to private morality than subject to public order within the strictures of the criminal law ... As between two consenting adults in private ... homosexual acts particularly — ought not to be within the purview of the criminal law ... This does not mean that the government is necessarily condoning, or promoting, or encouraging, this type of act between adults. It is merely saying that it is a matter of private morality and not a question of public law ... The fact that we are removing the public law in its criminal aspects from some types of conduct such as homosexuality between consenting adults in private and therapeutic abortion within the conditions specified in the bill ... has surely never been interpreted as... promotion or encouragement by the State, of this type of conduct.[216]

The government had more reaction from individuals on abortion than any other provision, said Turner. The bill was intended to clarify the law so that abortions approved by a committee of physicians in accredited hospitals would no longer be illegal, he stressed: "It does not promote abortion. It simply removes certain categories of abortion from the present place they have on the list of indictable offences." The limitations of the abortion reform that did not guarantee a woman's right to an abortion if that was her choice will be examined in the conclusion. It still has a lot to do with shaping the continuing controversies over abortion clinics and women's reproductive rights following the Supreme Court decision of January 28, 1988 decriminalizing abortion.[217]

The Conservatives pushed for clarification of the word "health" in this context, while Wooliams, Tory spokesman for the debate, and others used "right-to-life," anti-choice arguments. Opposition to abortion and opposition to homosexuality were linked in this debate. Some Conservatives, however, supported the government on the issue of abortion. The NDP supported the government's position but also suggested that it go further and remove all references to abortion in the Criminal Code, as Grace MacInnes had suggested in her private-member's bill, leaving the decision up to a woman and her doctor. The NDP went further in this area then in relation to the reform of homosexual-related offences. The Créditistes as a bloc opposed this section with a series of Catholic and moral conservative arguments, many of which also surfaced in the debate over homosexuality.

In motivating the sections of the bill dealing with gross indecency, Turner stated that these would

> not apply to any act committed in private between a husband or his wife or any two persons each of whom consents to the commission ... the bill strives to ... exempt from the criminal law acts of gross indecency between consenting adults in private ... it changes the substance of one particular offence under the criminal law.

In Turner's words, this section did not "legalize homosexuality," it merely exempted certain private adult conduct from prosecution. Similarly, he argued that liberalization of divorce laws did not mean that Parliament condoned divorce: "We are not for a moment conceding that homosexual acts are in any way to be equated to ordinary, normal acts of intercourse."

Turner quoted extensively from the *Wolfenden Report*. It was used as an authoritative way of dealing with and attempting to silence critics. He also pointed out, in one of the few specific references to lesbianism in the debate, that unlike the case in England, gross indecency in Canada since the 1953 reform covered "acts between women."[218] Under questioning, Turner agreed that setting the age of consent at twenty-one was arbitrary, but necessary: "To make it perfectly clear that we are not involving minors in the situation ... it was felt that the amendment should apply only to consenting adults."

Steven Otto disputed the opposition's contention that morality must be enforced by

law: "By and large, the defining of morality and immorality is being assumed by techno-
crats and psychiatrists rather than by the state." Like most of those supporting reform, Otto
relied on the opinions of medical and psychiatric experts building the sickness model as a
central organizing concept into arguments for public/private regulation: "… members of
the medical profession tell us that homosexuality is a sickness and that with present day
knowledge there is no remedy for it … These people should not be treated as criminal.
This definition has nothing to do with the old concept of morality."

Said Robert Kaplan, MP for Don Valley:

> There are few Canadians who would believe that laws exist governing volun-
> tary private conduct between a husband and wife or between unmarried
> couples of the opposite sex … Surely conduct given this context is a matter
> of taste and not of morality, and any element of gross indecency is in the eye
> of the beholder.

On homosexuality, Kaplan stated:

> This is a form of sexual perversion which arouses a sense of horror in most
> people. But many Canadians feel an equal sense of horror about the pre-
> sent treatment of homosexuals in this country. For example, our govern-
> ment has been holding in prison under an indeterminate or life sentence,
> confirmed by the Supreme Court … one Everett George Klippert.

He concluded, "… in any event the problem does not threaten social order and should
be taken away from judges and given to doctors and psychologists."

The Conservatives were divided, especially on abortion and homosexuality.
Wooliams called for a thorough review of the Criminal Code. He wanted a separate report on the sections dealing with homosexuality, but supported the bill's proposals in
this area while arguing for specific amendments to "clarify" it.

> Our standing committee must reach the conclusion in the light of scientific,
> psychiatric research and knowledge that imprisonment is largely ineffectual
> to reorient those with homosexual tendencies … if the law is ignored, if a
> law is unenforceable, if it is indeed unjust, is that not grounds to make the
> change even though we may abhor legal permissiveness.

He later outlined the dominant approach in the debate, although he is referring here
only to adult acts in private.

> I have always taken the position that we should not deal with homosexuality
> in the Criminal Code. This should be dealt with as a sickness or an ailment.
> It should be treated from a psychological or physical point of view by psy-

chiatrists or doctors ... I suggest that what we are attempting to do here is
legalize acts between two consenting adults over 21 years of age, a man and
a wife, indecent or homosexual, providing they are carried out in private.

Conservative leader Robert Stanfield wanted to see the bill split for voting and was
critical of the view that the government should not be concerned about morality in the
private sphere; yet he supported the reform because he felt that the existing section was
unenforceable.

The NDP supported the amendment. David Lewis, MP for York-South, suggested,
however, that Turner was exaggerating his claims; that the reform on homosexuality, like
that on abortion, did not legalize anything. Said Lewis:

I know that to normal people this practice is an odious one ...; but to make
it a crime in all cases is to be insensitive and cruel because this deviationism
obviously is due to certain psychological factors. This behaviour requires
charity and treatment rather than criminal prosecution.[219]

And:

Those of us who are supporting the amendment in respect of homosexuality are just as repelled as they are by that act. We are just as anxious to make
clear that it is an immoral and undesirable act, but we think the time has
come to modernize the law.

The NDP generally had a party line that homosexuals were ill and should be under a
doctor's care and not in jail. Another New Democrat, John Gilbert, discussed homosexual acts in washrooms:

One of the problems with which many Torontonians have been confronted
in respect to homosexuality is the frequency with which homosexuals hang
around public washrooms and lavatories. In fact, members of the morality
squad in Toronto take up positions in washrooms. They bore a hole in the
wall and by that method of detection have brought some homosexuals to
court. This seems to me to be a rather nauseating approach to criminal detection ... There must be protection for young persons who use the public
parks and public lavatories. It has been suggested in the *Wolfenden Report*
that municipalities pass by-laws to prevent loitering by homosexuals around
public washrooms ... They also indicate there is a place for the psychiatrist,
the clergyman, the social worker and the probation officer in helping to
deal with this problem.

Gilbert, however, expressed some scepticism about the sickness argument, noting that the *Wolfenden Report* had concluded that homosexuality was not a disease but a state or condition. NDPer Ralph Stewart (Cochrane) also noted that homosexuals did not consider themselves to be abnormal: "Homosexuality is considered by some people to be abnormal, but among those who are homosexuals it is considered normal for them."[220]

Arnold Peters, whom we met before, pointed out that this kind of amendment had been kicking around for a long time, at least partially referring to his own efforts. Most homosexuals and lesbians with whom he was acquainted, he said, were opposed to prostitution and were not interested in "spreading their addiction to the young," but wished to live "as near a normal life as possible." He used the argument that most homosexuals were "respectable" and tried to be "normal" to lessen the effect of arguments by the right wing. This also reflected some of the arguments for respectability put forward by the Council on Religion and the Homosexual with which he had been involved. He also pointed out that church attitudes toward homosexuality were changing.

This is the closest anyone came to defending the civil and human rights of lesbians and gay men, let alone our sexualities. Only G.W. Baldwin (Peace River) who referred to the *Wolfenden Report,* the Gigeroff study, and the Klippert case suggested, "I think these sections should be out of the Criminal Code altogether," as part of an argument for a broader study of this section.[221] And as Tory Pat Nowlan (Annapolis Valley) stressed "I remind the house that no one [who] has spoken in the debate has approved of these practices. They have all expressed repugnance of them."[222]

The reform camp managed to link the sickness model to their distinction between the public and private spheres. Adult "private" homosexuality was no longer to be criminal, but was to be an illness and these individuals should instead be under a doctor's or a psychiatrist's care. A number of speakers struggled to try to separate this notion of "illness" from moral notions. Privacy was narrowly defined, public broadly. When pressed, Turner said the presence of a third person, and activities in homosexual clubs, would be public in character.

In this narrow, "private" sphere, homosexual acts were to be decriminalized. In the broader public realm, same-gender sex would continue to be prohibited, and the debates and the reform itself contained clear instructions to the legal system and the police for sanctions to be retained and extended.

Opponents of Reform

The opponents of reform generally accepted a rather different sickness model of homosexuality, which was not tied to a public/private distinction. While they would have agreed more with the "moral conservative" position of Devlin in the Hart/Devlin debate on the need for a common (heterosexual/family) morality, they did not raise the debate on this level. Instead, they attempted to construct a course of action in opposition to that of the reform camp in which homosexuals were ill, but this would lead to detention and/or hospitalization rather than partial decriminalization. This continued aspects of the "homosexuals as a social danger" notion of the dangerous-sexual-offender/criminal-sexual-psychopath course of action. It also continued those aspects of the broader criminalization strategy in which concerns over illness and "treatment" were mobilized to secure a course of action of criminal detention.

They referred to the legal reform as the "permissive clauses relating to homosexuality." They instead argued that if homosexuals were really ill, then hospitals should be built for them where they could be treated. At times it seemed as though some of them felt that a determined "public health" campaign could wipe out homosexuality. They attempted to meld this perspective with strands of heterosexist discourse formed in previous periods, including religious-based arguments. This became more pronounced toward the end of the debate when they realized that the sickness argument had been effectively seized and used by the other side. They then generally shifted to the argument that there was insufficient evidence to determine whether homosexuality was criminal or an illness. As a result, this second camp was far more heterogeneous than the pro-reform group.

The Créditiste MP Laprise accepted a version of the sickness thesis.

> The duty of the government should be to protect these individuals by treating their sickness like that of any person ... With the appropriate means we can control homosexuality since we recognize and admit that it is a sickness.

Laprise criticized the Canadian Broadcasting Corporation for giving too much coverage to homosexuality, allowing "sexual perverts to express themselves freely and sometimes in an arrogant manner on the air." Laprise referred to "sexual perverts" who seduce boys and engage in murder to satisfy their lust. He equated opposition to homosexuality with defence of proper gender roles.

Créditiste leader Réal Caouette also initially held to the sickness model.

> Practically everyone agrees that homosexuality is a disease. Therefore instead of making it legal why not bring forward a bill aiming to build hospitals ... instead of allowing adults to commit such acts together.

Later he shifted to a different rhetoric.

> Are we stupid enough to believe that man has been made for man? The Good Lord created woman for man. God created man and woman, that is normal, natural and proper.

Other anti-reformers linked homosexuality with child molestation, "proselytization," "compulsive conversion," talked of it as an "evil," as a "contagion," as the "sin of sodom," as social decay, and as bringing about a falling birth rate. It was even claimed that "pernicious" perversions "will lead the nation to its destruction." Créditiste Bernard Dumont (Frontenac) argued that homosexuality led to national decline:

> Society is strongly opposed to Sodomy as it punishes murder and theft, be-
> cause it strikes at its roots, namely the family ... A resurgence of homosexu-
> ality and an increasing tolerance of its practices are inseparable from a
> declining civilization, are the stigmas of a decaying civilization.

Lambert, a Conservative, developed this further:

> We are basing our law on certain legislative amendments which have been
> introduced into the law of the United Kingdom ... But show me a country
> that is sicker at heart and sicker at soul than is Britain today ... if you go
> back in history you will see that the same line of conduct has brought down
> nations.

Said the Créditiste René Matte:

> If you read the history of certain countries, you realize that those who have
> accepted such depravity have been brought down as if by mere coincidence.
> This is what happened to Ancient Greece and Rome.

Matte called for a delay until further research into homosexuality — "that dreadful
plague" as he called it — had been carried out. Some of the contradictions of attempting to use the sickness argument to argue for continuing criminalization became
evident when he stated that "Once you legalize a disease you must legalize all others."
He later declared that only one percent of homosexuals were "truly sick" and that the
rest were just vicious. Homosexuality, he claimed, "leads youth astray, relaxes morals,
brings about decadence, causes disorders, and paves the way for anarchy." Contradictions became even clearer when, after a long speech by Créditiste André Fortin (Lot-
binière), the Parliamentary Secretary to the Minister of Justice, Jean-Charles Cantin
asked:

> Does the honourable member finally admit that homosexuals are not
> criminals ...
>
> *Mr. Fortin:* Exactly. They are not criminals, they are ill.
>
> *Mr. Cantin:* Then is it not precisely the intent of the proposed amendment
> that they no longer be regarded as criminals except when the protection of
> a youth is involved.

Other opponents brought up more clearly religious-based objections, even going so
far as to quote the Pope himself. Legal reform undermined Western society's roots in
the Bible, they said. The Créditistes claimed to have gathered a petition against homo-

sexuality and abortion and collected many letters from Québec residents in support of their opposition to reform on religious grounds.

Former Conservative prime minister John Diefenbaker continued to view homosexuals as a "security risk." He also associated abortion and homosexual reform with the growing "permissiveness," which was undermining the Judeo-Christian roots of society. Diefenbaker called for defence of family life, which was presumably assumed to be entirely heterosexual. Other opponents of reform advocated free psychiatric hospitals for homosexuals as well as education against homosexuality. Argued Downey:

> Surely our young people also deserve protection. The urge of these people to convert young persons to their ways is established ... the law should remain as a deterrent ... to protect average citizens, those who believe in the natural processes.

This same MP said that he had doubts about whether "homosexuals are in reality sick to the extent that is often presented in their favour." The sickness model continued to prevail in its different articulations on both sides of the debate, however.

The supporters of partial decriminalization managed to associate the sickness model with their position. After all, if a person is sick, he or she should be under the "care" of a doctor or psychiatrist, not locked up in prison. Some of the opposing speakers did question the sickness thesis and argued for other heterosexist discourses formed as part of earlier Social Darwinist, eugenic, moral conservative, and religious, especially Roman Catholic discourses. These discourses were not dead or simply archaic, but continued to play an active part in organizing debates and shaping social consciousness. They were shifted around and combined in new ways in this debate, especially in relation to sickness arguments.

The omnibus bill was passed on May 14, 1969 by a vote of 149 to 55, and became law in August of that year.[223]

The State, however, was not removed from the bedrooms of the nation. As Conservative Pat Nowlan, who also criticized the notion of a pluralistic society, put it in a comment that potentially deconstructed the crucial assumptions of the reform bloc: "The State does enter the bedroom every time we turn on the television set in the bedroom. Programs are under State regulation." State and social regulation continued to be very much present in the private realm after the reform. It is important to remember that even these partial decriminalization proposals were not extended to the military and the RCMP given the particular character of these institutions and the lack of a clearly defined "private" place in these institutions.

Strategies of sexual regulation were shifted, however. Lesbianism and homosexuality were not legalized, and there was nothing done to establish the human rights of lesbians and gays, a social right to be lesbian or gay, or to uproot the heterosexist assumptions at the heart of social and family policies. Rather a distinction was established between public and private sex, and, for the first time in Canadian law, between homosexual acts involving two consenting adults and those involving people below an age of consent set at twenty-one. These reforms helped demarcate a distinct sphere of private, adult homosexuality, the regulation of which was transferred from the police, courts and penal system to psychiatrists, doctors and other social agencies. In a broadly defined "public" realm, homosexual activities would be dealt with by the police and the law.

There is, as I have suggested, a major difference between the ways in which people in our everyday lives go about socially producing privacy and intimacy for ourselves and the ways in which "public/private" distinctions are deployed in the Wolfenden strategy and the 1969 Criminal Code reform as administrative classifications. As George Smith explains, referring to the situations established following the 1969 reform:

> The Criminal Code defines "public" first in terms of a "public place." According to Section 138, a public place is "any place to which the public has access by right or invitation, expressed or implied." Secondly, section 158 of the Code ... goes on to say that not only is a sexual act public and therefore illegal if it is committed in a public place, but it is also a public act if more than two persons take part or are present. What this means is that what is "public," and again illegal as far as sex is concerned, is very broadly defined. It covers all possible situations but one — two individuals behind a locked door. This essentially relegates all sexual activity to the bedroom.

And he goes on:

> Another important feature of the government's definition of "public" is that it treats the relation between "public" and "private" as proportional, like pieces of a pie. Thus these two terms are thought to be mutually exclusive. What is public is public: what is private, private. The two do not overlap in any way. Thus the larger the slice given to the public, the smaller the piece left over for private.[224]

In the broader public realm, queer sex was to continue to be prohibited.

The reform clearly led to public discussion. The extending criminalization of homosexual sex strategy was displaced, although this did not do away with associations between gay sex and sexual and social danger as we will see. At the same time that the "sickness" model became firmly established as the official explanation of homosexuality, the reform also acknowledged the existence of adult homosexual networks and accorded them a limited and contained private space. Lesbians and gays would take advantage of this opening to seize more social space and to become more visible. Yet the broad definition of "in public" and the character of such legal terms as "gross indecency" and "indecent act" sent a message to the police to step up their harassment and entrapment campaigns as queer networks became more visible. A perceptive critique of the reform in *Saturday Night* by a gay man points out that the police would continue to arrest gays and men engaging in homosexual sex in washrooms, baths, and parks.[225] In the longer term, the strategy mandated more specific surveillance and policing of gay sex in "public." The definition of "public," which this strategy produced, stands over and against gays as another instrument in the regulation of our lives.[226]

In 1971 a Canadian coalition of gay and lesbian liberation groups produced a statement, which reads in part:

> In 1969 the Criminal Code was amended so as to make certain sexual acts between consenting adults, in private, legal. This was widely misunderstood as "legalizing" homosexuality and thus homosexuals on an equal basis with other Canadians. In fact, this amendment was merely a recognition of the non-enforceable nature of the Criminal Code as it existed. Consequently, its effects have done but little to alleviate the oppression of homosexual men and women in Canada. In our daily lives we are still confronted with discrimination, police harassment, exploitation and pressures to conform which deny our sexuality.[227]

Nonetheless, the reform set the stage for the emergence of gay and lesbian liberation movements and for the expansion of gay and lesbian networks and communities. However, it also set the stage for many of the practices of sexual regulation that we still face today.

Notes

1. Jeffrey Weeks, *Sex, Politics and Society* (London and New York: Longman, 1981), pp. 240-241; Alex K. Gigeroff, *Sexual Deviations in the Criminal Law* (Toronto: Published for the Clarke Institute of Psychiatry by the University of Toronto Press, 1968), p. 83. The reference to the "nauseating subject" is from Gigeroff referring to Lord Vansittart introducing a debate in the House of Lords calling for the appointment of a committee on homosexuality, p. 83.
2. See Carol Smart, "Law and the Control of Women's Sexuality: The case of the 1950s" in Hunter and Williams, eds., *Controlling Women* (London: Croom Helm, 1981), p. 48. Also see Bland, McCabe and Mort, "Sexuality and Reproduction: Three Official Instances" in Barrett, *et al.*, eds., *Ideology and Cultural Production* (London: Croom Helm, 1979).
3. See Smart, *op. cit.*, pp. 49-50.
4. For more elaboration on this, see Gary Kinsman, Ph.D. thesis, "Official Discourse as Sexual Regulation," Department of Educational Theory, University of Toronto, 1989.
5. The report based its findings on documentary information provided by medical and criminal records. *The Wolfenden Report* (New York: Lancer, 1964), p. 20. The Wolfenden committee received submissions from many groups, including the Association of Chief Officers of Police for England and Wales, the Association of Headmasters, Headmistresses and Matrons of Approved Schools, the Association of Social and Moral Hygiene, the Association of Municipal Corporations, the Boy Scout Association, the British Medical Association, the British Psychological Society, the Church of England Moral Welfare Council, the General Council of the Bar, the Institute for the Study and Treatment of Delinquency, the Metropolitan Police, the

National Association of Probation Officers, the Public Morality Council, the Admiralty and the Air Ministry, the Home Office Prison Commission, and the War Office. *The Wolfenden Report*, Ibid., pp. 233-239.

6. See *The Wolfenden Report* (New York: Lancer, 1964) or other versions. Unless otherwise noted, these references refer to the Lancer, 1964 edition.

7. *Wolfenden Report* (London: Her Majesty's Stationery Office, 1962), p. 7.

8. *The Wolfenden Report*, Lancer, *op. cit.*, section 61.

9. *Ibid.*, pp. 23-24.

10. Stuart Hall, "Reformism and the Legislation of Consent" in National Deviancy Conference, ed., *Permissiveness and Control: The Fate of the Sixties Legislation* (London: MacMillan Press, 1980), p. 13.

11. *Ibid.*, p. 14. Also see John Stuart Mill, *On Liberty*.

12. *The Wolfenden Report, op. cit.*, pp. 39, 40-41. The following account is based on my reading of the report unless otherwise cited, particularly pp. 10-15, 43-48, 88-89, 108-143.

13. *Wolfenden Report, Ibid.*, pp. 13-14.

14. *Ibid.*, p. 20.

15. Bland, McCabe and Mort, "Sexuality and Reproduction: Three 'Official' Instances," *op. cit.*, pp. 103-104.

16. *The Wolfenden Report, op. cit.*, p. 53.

17. *Ibid.*, p. 22. This is one of the few references to lesbianism in the report.

18. *The Wolfenden Report, Ibid.*, p. 22.

19. *Ibid.*, p. 26. Note the assumption of the normality of heterosexual life and the heterosexual standpoint taken up here.

20. Paul Crane, *Gays and the Law* (London: Pluto, 1982), p. 68.

21. Quoted from the *Wolfenden Report* in Bland, McCabe and Mort, "Sexuality and Reproduction: Three 'Official' Instances" in Barrett, et al., eds., *Ideology and Cultural Production* (London: Croom Helm, 1979), p. 102. This long legal history of viewing "buggery" as a particularly horrific crime can even be seen in the Hughes Commission Report into what went on at the Mount Cashel Orphanage in St. John's in the 1970s and 1980s. Samuel Hughes writes of "buggery long known to the law as the 'abominable crime.'" See the Hughes Report, *The Royal Commission of Inquiry into the Response of the Newfoundland Criminal Justice System to Complaints, Volume One* (St. John's: The Queen's Printer, 1992), p. 200.

22. *The Wolfenden Report, op. cit.*, p. 67.

23. *Ibid.*, p. 78.

24. On prostitution and the *Wolfenden Report*, also see Carol Smart, "Law and the Control of Women's Sexuality: The case of the 1950s" in Hunter and Williams, eds., *Controlling Women* (London: Croom Helm, 1981), pp. 40-59, for an excellent analysis of prostitution legislation in England in the 1950s.

25. *The Wolfenden Report, op. cit.*, p. 87.

26. *Ibid.*, p. 85.

27. See Hall, op. cit., p. 10.

28. Bland, McCabe, and Mort, *op. cit.*, p. 84.

29. *United Church of Canada Annual Report No. 34*, 1959, p. 57.

30. Bland, McCabe, and Mort, *op. cit.*, p. 104.

31. Frank Mort, "Sexuality, Regulation and Contestation" in Gay Left Collective, ed., *Homosexuality: Power and Politics* (London: Allison and Busby, 1980), p. 39.

32. On Wolfenden's influence on English obscenity and anti-porn legislation, see Annette Kuhn, "Public versus Private: The Case of Indecency and Obscenity" in *Leisure Studies*, No. 3, 1984, pp. 53-65; Kuhn, "Covering Up Sex" in *New Statesman*, Feb. 24, 1984; and Beverly Brown, "Private Faces in Public Places" in *Ideology and Consciousness*, No. 7, 1980, pp. 3-16. On Canada, see Gary Kinsman, "Porn/Censor Wars and the Battlefields of Sex" in *Issues of Censorship* (Toronto: A Space, 1985), pp. 31-39. The Wolfenden approach influenced Canadian sexual

legislation on these matters at least up to the publication of the *Fraser Committee Report on Pornography and Prostitution* (Ottawa: Ministry of Supply and Services, 1985), 2 volumes.

33. Hall, *op. cit.*, p. 2.
34. Bland, McCabe, and Mort, *op. cit.*, p. 107.
35. Mort, *Ibid.*, p. 42.
36. See Kuhn, *op. cit.*, both articles, and Brown, *op. cit.*
37. See Victoria Greenwood and Jock Young, "Ghettoes of Freedom: An Examination of Permissiveness" in National Deviancy Conference, *Permissiveness and Control, op. cit.*, p. 166; and Jeffrey Weeks, *Coming Out* (London, Melbourne, and New York: Quartet, 1977), p. 11.
38. Charles Kerrigan, interview, "Gay Liberation and National Liberation" in *Rites*, V. 3, No. 2, June 1984, p. 15.
39. See Patrick Devlin, *The Enforcement of Morals* (New York: Oxford University Press, 1965); and R.M. Dworkin, *The Philosophy of Law* (Oxford: Oxford University Press, 1977).
40. See H.L.A. Hart, "Punishment and the Elimination of Responsibility," *Hobhouse Memorial Trust Lecture No. 31* (London: The Athlone Press, 1962); Hart, "Law, Liberty and Morality" in *The Harry Camp Lectures at Stanford University* (Toronto: Oxford University Press, 1963); and Yves Caron, "The Legal Enforcement of Morals and the So-Called Hart-Devlin Controversy" in *McGill Law Journal*, V. 15, No. 1, Feb. 1969, pp. 9-47.
41. "License and Liberty," from *Church Times*, London, Sept. 1957, reprinted in *United Church of Canada Annual Report of the Board of Evangelism and Social Services*, 1958, p. 115.
42. *Wolfenden Report* (New York: Stein and Day, 1963), p. 6, which was "published in the United States of America and Canada with the permission of Her Majesty's Stationary Office."
43. Esther Newton, *Mother Camp* (Chicago and London: The University of Chicago Press, 1979), p. 59.
44. See *The Body Politic*, No. 89, Dec. 1982, p. 28; and Bert Sutcliffe, Herbert Frederick Sutcliffe, "MBE, CD: An Autobiography," Toronto, 1981, unpublished manuscript, p. 156.
45. Ross Higgins, "Notes for a Gay History of Montreal" in *Pink Ink*, No. 2, Aug. 1983, p. 24; and his article "Montreal 1953" in *Pink Ink*, V. 1, No.5, Dec./Jan. 1984. Also see Leznoff, "Homosexual In Urban Society," M.A. Thesis, McGill University, Sociology Department, Montréal, 1954.
46. Grube, "Queens and Flaming Virgins: Towards a Sense of Gay Community" in *Rites*, V. 2, No. 9, p. 16.
47. The Municipal Hotel (67 Queen Street West) was frequented in the 1950s and early 1960s, Mulloney's Studio Tavern (66 Grenville Street) in the 1950s, the Hotel Metropole (141 King Street West) by the early 1960s, and the Red Lion bar of the Westbury Hotel in the early 1960s. Letro's (50 King Street East) was completely gay by 1965. By the 1960s, the St. Charles Tavern and the Parkside were predominantly gay. See Canadian Gay Archives, *Lesbian and Gay Heritage of Toronto* (Toronto: Canadian Gay Archives Publication No. 5, 1982). Also see Grube, *op. cit.*
48. See Becki Ross, "The House that Jill Built," University of Toronto, Ph.D. thesis, 1992, pp. 86-87; also see Lynne Fernie and Aerlyn Weissman, *"Forbidden Love"* (National Film Board) 1993.
49. The Regency Club on Prince Arthur Street was the first private gay club in Toronto. The Melody Room, 457 Church Street, was gay-owned; it was destroyed by fire in 1966. The Maison de Lys/The Music Room, 575 Yonge Street, was run from 1962 to 1966 by the previously mentioned Sara Ellen Dunlop and Richard Kerr. See Mary Axten, interview, *The Body Politic*, Dec. 1982, p. 27, for a description. See *Lesbian and Gay Heritage of Toronto, op. cit.*
50. See Robert Champagne, compiled and introduced, *Jim Egan: Canada's Pioneer Gay Activist* (Toronto: Canadian Lesbian and Gay History Network, 1988).
51. This is where Mama Quilla II, a Toronto lesbian feminist band in the late 1970s and early 1980s took its name from. See Becki Ross, *The House That Jill Built* (Toronto: University of Toronto Press, 1995), p. 68, and "The House That Jill Built," Ph.D thesis, *op. cit.*, p. 98.
52. The Oak Leaf is the oldest homosexual-identified institution still operating in Toronto. See *Lesbian and Gay Heritage of Toronto, op. cit.*

53. Grube, *op. cit.*, p. 16.
54. *Ibid.*; *Lesbian and Gay Heritage of Toronto*, *op. cit.*; and William Johnson, "The Gay World" in *Globe Magazine*, Jan. 13, 1968, pp. 5-8, reprinted in Mann, ed., *Social Deviance in Canada* (Toronto: Copp Clark, 1971), p. 386.
55. See Grube, *op. cit.*, p. 16. Also see David Churchill, "Coming Out in a Cold Climate: A History of Gay Men in Toronto During the 1950s," M.A. thesis, History (OISE), University of Toronto, 1993 and on the installing of morality lights on Philosopher's Walk, and on the bushes being cut down at Queen's Park and Hanlan's Point beach see, Mary Louise Adams, "Almost anything can happen: A search for sexual discourse in the urban spaces of 1940s Toronto" in *The Canadian Journal of Sociology*, V. 19, No. 2, 1994, p. 229.
56. See Newton, *Mother Camp, op. cit.*, p. 100.
57. See Mary Axten, *The Body Politic, op. cit.*; *Lesbian and Gay Heritage of Toronto*, *op. cit.*; and Johnson, *op. cit.*, p. 300, who reports that in 1968 a coffee shop near Avenue Road had regular drag shows for straight and gay audiences.
58. Newton, *op. cit.*, p. 37. Newton's book is a wonderful account of drag queens, female impersonators, and the formation of gay cultures in the 1960s in the U.S.
59. *Ibid.*, see p. 8.
60. See Jack Babuscio, "Camp and the Gay Sensibility" in Richard Dyer, ed., *Gays and Film* (London: British Film Institute, 1977), pp. 40-57; the critique of it by Andrew Britton, "For Interpretation: Notes Against Camp" in *Gay Left*, No. 7, Winter 78/79, pp. 11-14; and Richard Dyer, "It's Being So Camp as Keeps Us Going" in *The Body Politic*, Sept. 1977, pp. 11-13.
61. The following account of camp is based on Newton, *op. cit.*, pp. 105-111, and Cohen and Dyer, "The Politics of Gay Culture" in Gay Left Collective, eds., *Homosexuality, Power and Politics, op. cit.*, p. 178.
62. Newton, *op. cit.*, p. 110.
63. Jenny Livingston, *Paris is Burning*, 1990.
64. See Jackie Golsby, "Queens of Language: Paris is Burning" in Martha Grever, John Greyson, Pratibha Parmar, eds., *Queer Looks: Perspectives on Lesbian and Gay Film and Video* (Toronto: Between the Lines, 1993), pp. 108-115; and for a critical approach, Bell Hooks, "Is Paris Burning?" in Hooks, *Black Looks: Race and Representation* (Toronto: Between the Lines, 1992), pp. 145-156.
65. See Alan Miller, "The Way We Were" in *Action!*, V. 1, No.4, 1981; Miller, "Beefcake with Which No Labels Attached" in *The Body Politic*, No. 90, Jan. 1983, p. 33; Tom Waugh, "A Heritage of Pornography" in *The Body Politic*, No. 90, Jan. 1983, pp. 29-33; Waugh, "Photography, Passion and Power" in *The Body Politic*, No. 101, March 1984, pp. 29-33; Waugh, "Gay Male Visual Culture in North America During the Fifties: Emerging from the Underground" in *Parallelogramme*, V. 12, No. 1, Fall 1986; and Michael Bronski, *Culture Clash: The Making of Gay Sensibility* (Boston: South End Press, 1984), pp. 160-174.
66. See Michael Bronski, *Culture Clash, op. cit.*, p. 163. For an instance of censorship hitting lesbian-related material in Canada, see Mary Louise Adams, "Precedent-Setting Pulp: Women's Barracks was Deemed 'Exceedingly Frank'" in *Xtra!* No. 231, Sept. 3, 1993, p. 21.
67. Joan Nestle, "Butch-Femme Relationships: Sexual Courage in the 1950s" in *A Restricted Country* (Ithaca, New York: Firebrand, 1987), p. 100.
68. See Elizabeth Lapovsky Kennedy and Madeline D. Davis, *Boots of Leather, Slippers of Gold: The History of a Lesbian Community* (New York and London: Routledge, 1993). On the emergence of lesbian cultures in Canada, see the work of "Lesbians Making History" in Toronto including, their "People Think This Didn't Happen in Canada — But it Did" in *Fireweed*; "Lesbiantics 2," No. 28, Spring 1989, especially pp. 81-86.; Aerlyn Weissman and Lynne Fernie, directors, *Forbidden Love*, NFB, 1993; Becki Ross's edited collection *Forbidden Love: The Unashamed Lives of Post-War Canadian Lesbians*, forthcoming; Line Chamberland, "Remembering Lesbian Bars, 1955-1975" in *Journal of Homosexuality*, V. 25, No. 3, 1993, pp. 231-269; Elise Chenier, "Risks, Roles and Rounders: Lesbian Bar Culture in Toronto, 1950-65," paper pre-

sented at the "Out of the Archives" conference on bisexual, lesbian and gay history in Canada, at York University, January 1994 and her M.A. thesis, "Tough Ladies and Troublemakers: Toronto's Public Lesbian Community, 1955-1965." History Dept., Queen's University, Kingston, 1995; and Becki Ross, "The House That Jill Built: Reconstructing the Lesbian Organization of Toronto, 1976-1980," Ph.D. thesis, University of Toronto, 1992, pp. 86-87, p. 99.

69. See Joan Nestle, "Lesbians and Prostitutes: An Historical Sisterhood" in Nestle, *A Restricted Country, op. cit.*, pp. 157-177.

70. Newton, *op. cit.*, p. 111.

71. See articles in *Justice Weekly*, Nov. 3 and 24, 1956.

72. The Lesbian and Gay History Group of Toronto, "A History of the Relationship Between the Gay Community and the Metropolitan Police," submission to the Bruner Study, 1981, p. 2. The attribution of an organized community in the early 1960s is somewhat premature.

73. *Ibid.*

74. *Ibid.*, p. 3.

75. *Ibid.*; also see *Lesbian and Gay Heritage of Toronto, op. cit.*

76. A news item in *Gay* referred to a 1964 raid on a steam bath in Windsor. Also see Jack Batten, "The Homosexual Life in Canada: Will Trudeau's Change in the Law Make Any Difference?" *Saturday Night*, V. 84, No. 9, Sept. 1969.

77. See the work of "Lesbians Making History," and Elise Chenier, "Risks, Roles and Rounders: Lesbian Bar Culture in Toronto, 1950-65," paper presented at the "Out of the Archives" conference on bisexual, lesbian and gay history in Canada, York University, January 1994, and her M.A. thesis, "Tough Ladies and Troublemakers: Toronto's Public Lesbian Community, 1955-1965." *op. cit.*

78. Higgins, "Notes for a Gay History of Montreal," *op. cit.*, p. 24.

79. See George Smith, "Policing the Gay Community: An Inquiry into Textually-mediated Social Relations" in *International Journal of Sociology of the Law*, No. 16, 1988, pp. 163-183.

80. D.E. Sanders, "Sentencing of Homosexual Offenders" in *Criminal Law Quarterly*, No. 10, Nov. 1967, p. 27. (His name is misspelled as Saunders in this article.)

81. On the ideological work of "complaints" in mandating/justifying police action, see "Guelph Sex Video Policing: Internal Cop Documents" in *Rites* V. 3, No. 2, June 1986, p. 7.

82. *ASK Newsletter*, V. 1, No. 5, 1964.

83. Unless otherwise cited, all references to Bruce Somers and Doug Sanders refer to interviews with them in 1986. I talked with Somers on May 24 in Toronto and Rob Champagne and I talked with Sanders on June 14 in Vancouver. Sanders was involved in support for the Native rights movement in the 1970s and 1980s and won the Bora Laskin Award in 1985. Excerpts from these interviews are published in *Angles* (Vancouver), V. 3, No. 10, Oct. 1986, pp. 14-15, and *Rites* (Toronto), V. 3, No. 5, Oct. 1986, pp. 10-11, 15.

84. This is a reference to the Lupien/Boisvert case to which I refer later in this chapter. See Sanders, article in *Georgia Straight* (Vancouver), Sept. 27-Oct. 3, 1968, p. 10. This lack of police attention may in part have been due to the apparent absence of yellow press/police scandal sheets in Vancouver.

85. See D'Emilio, *Sexual Politics, Sexual Communities* (Chicago and London: The University of Chicago Press, 1983), pp. 57-91.

86. For instance, Doug Sanders was also involved in support for draft resisters to the American war in Vietnam and later in support work for the rights of aboriginal peoples.

87. From Rob Champagne interview cited earlier. Excerpts from this interview are published in *Rites*, V. 3, No. 6, Dec./Jan. 1986/1987.

88. See Neil Whaley, "His/Herstory, Gay Groundbreaker" in *Vancouver Gay Community Centre News*, Feb. 1983, pp. 39-41. Also, *The Body Politic*, No. 55, Aug. 1979, p. 26. Other references upon which this section is based are the *ASK Newsletter* and the previously cited interviews with Bruce Somers and Doug Sanders. See previously cited references to *Angles* and *Rites* interviews.

89. Whaley, *op. cit.*

90. See Alec Fadel, "Homosexual Offences in Ottawa 1950-1967: The Medicalization of the Legal Process," M.A. thesis, Concordia University, 1994.

91. This list of initial objectives may have been based on those of the Mattachine Society.

92. *ASK Newsletter*, V. 2, No. 6, June 1965.

93. *ASK Newsletter*, V. 1, No. 1, April 1964, p. 2. On Evelyn Hooker, see references in D'Emilio, *op. cit.*

94. For information on NACHO, see D'Emilio, *op. cit.*, pp. 197-199. NACHO was founded in August 1966.

95. Whaley, *op. cit.*

96. I have only seen the editorial for this issue.

97. Sanders letter to Larry Dewers, 1968, undated. In Sanders' files.

98. On Jane Rule, see Lynne Fernie and Aerlyn Weissman, directors, *Fiction and Other Truths: A Film about Jane Rule* (Great Jane Productions, 1995).

99. Whaley, *op. cit.*

100. *ASK Newsletter*, V. 2, No. 6, June 1965.

101. Whaley, *op. cit.*, p. 40. This periodization of ASK's first and second phase was suggested by Sanders in the June 1986 interview.

102. Whaley, *op. cit.*

103. *Ibid.*

104. *ASK Newsletter*, V. 1, No. 4, July 1964, p. 4.

105. On this see Becki Ross, "The House that Jill Built," Ph.D. thesis, *op. cit.*, p. 97, note 27. There are some similarities with the perspective held by the leaders of the Daughters of Bilitis in the U.S. in generally down working-class bar dykes and butch/femme cultures; see D'Emilio, *op. cit.*, pp. 92-125.

106. In June 1967, the newsletter reported that ASK members visiting Seattle met not only with the Dorion (homophile) group but also with the Female Educational Movement (FEM). ASK also reprinted an article by Lynda E.D. Turner on "Women in Canadian Society" and referred to Renate Wilson's article "What Turns Women to Lesbianism" in *Chatelaine*, Oct. 1966. Also see Bob Cummings, "The Lesbians" in *Georgia Straight*, Sept. 13-19, 1968, pp. 9-12; Oct. 4-10, 1968, pp. 9-12; and Nov. 1-7, 1968, pp. 9-12.

107. Bob Cummings, "The Lesbians" in *Georgia Strait, op. cit.*. Norma Mitchell is interviewed in the November issue.

108. Alastair Heron, ed., *Toward a Quaker View of Sex: An essay by a group of friends* (Friends Home Services Committee, London, 1963).

109. *ASK Newsletter*, V. 1, No. 2, May 1964.

110. *Ibid.*, p. 9.

111. United Church of Canada, Commission of Christian Marriage and Divorce, Toronto, 1960, pp. 14-16.

112. Dr. Tibor Chibes, professor of Pastoral Care, Wesley Theological Seminary, Washington, D.C., "Christian Attitudes Towards Homosexuality" in *United Church of Canada: Evangelism and Social Service Annual Report*, 1964, pp. 142-147.

113. Jack Cahill, "Homosexuals Cannot Be Christians, Montréal Church Leader Insists" in *Toronto Star*, June 1, 1966.

114. "Church Council Aims to Aid Homosexuals" in *The Globe and Mail*, June 2, 1965. This section is also based on the interview with Bruce Somers referred to earlier and one conducted in June 1994.

115. *Hansard*, p. 5413, 1969.

116. A Brief to be presented to the Ontario Select Committee on Youth by the Canadian Council on Religion and the Homosexual, 1966-1967, Doug Sanders' files.

117. From the interview with Somers, June 1994.

118. In England, both the church assembly of the Church of England and the Roman Catholic Advisory Committee supported the recommendations of the *Wolfenden Report*. On the impor-

tance of shifts within the churches in England in bringing about law reform, see Weeks, *Sexuality and Its Discontents* (London: Routledge and Kegan Paul, 1985), p. 35. In the U.S., a Council on Religion and the Homosexual was established in 1964 following a conference involving gay and lesbian activists and Protestant ministers. See D'Emilio, *op. cit.*, p. 193.

119. *ASK Newsletter,* V. 2, No. 4, July 1964.

120. On this see Alan Horsfall, "Battling for Wolfenden" in Bob Cant and Susan Hemmings, eds., *Radical Records: Thirty years of Lesbian and Gay history, 1957-1987* (London and New York: Routledge, 1988), pp. 15-33.

121. *ASK Newsletter,* V. 1, No. 8, Nov. 1964.

122. *Ibid.,* V. 1, No. 6, Sept. 1964, p. 3-5.

123. *Ibid.,* V. 1, No. 1, Apr. 1964, p. 3.

124. *The Globe and Mail,* July 25, 1964.

125. *Hansard,* 1969, p. 5413.

126. *ASK Newsletter,* V. 1, No. 6, Sept. 1964, p. 4; and *The Globe and Mail,* July 25, 1964, p. 4.

127. *Two,* Toronto, No. 5.

128. See interview with Sanders in *Angles* and *Rites, op. cit.*, and Nate Cole, "Lawyers Support Homosexuality Ban: Bar Association Defeats Bid to Follow British Proposal" in *Vancouver Sun,* June 16, 1966.

129. D.E. Sanders, "Sentencing of Homosexual Offenders" in *Criminal Law Quarterly, op. cit.*, pp. 25-29.

130. Sanders, "The Sentencing of Homosexual Offenders" in ASK version, June 1967, p. 3. The following two paragraphs are also based on this article.

131. From the interview with Sanders cited earlier. Also see Weisstaub, ed., *Law and Psychiatry in the Canadian Context* (Toronto: Pergamon Press, 1980), "The Queen v. Lupien," pp. 300-303.

132. Transcript of the Lupien/Boisvert case, pp. 8-10. The following quotes are also from this transcript.

133. *Ibid.,* p. 13.

134. Letter in holdings of Canadian Lesbian and Gay Archives, Toronto.

135. Letter from Doug Sanders to Paul Bédard, August 24, 1968; in Sanders' files.

136. Douglas E. Sanders, Submission to the Royal Commission on Security by ASK, 1968. Copy in holdings of the Canadian Lesbian and Gay Archives.

137. Interview with Doug Sanders, Calgary, June 1994.

138. Whaley, *op. cit.*, p. 41. A part of recovering Canadian lesbian and gay histories for the 1960s will be further examination and rediscovery of ASK's activities and its connections across the country.

139. Miller, "The Way We Were," *op. cit.*

140. See D'Emilio, *op. cit.*, p. 202.

141. *Gay,* V. 1, No. 8, July 30, 1964, p. 9.

142. This may have been related to Jim Egan's suggestion to set up a chapter of One in Toronto.

143. *Two,* V. 1, No. 1.

144. *Toronto Star,* Feb. 6, 1966; *Lesbian and Gay Heritage of Toronto, op. cit.*; and Miller, "The Way We Were," *op. cit.*

145. These columns were published in the Toronto *Telegram,* Apr. 11, 14, 15, 1964.

146. Jim Egan, "Guest Editorial" in *Two,* 1964, p. 19.

147. On this see D'Emilio, *op. cit.*, p. 202.

148. See Becki Ross, "The House That Jill Built," Ph.D. thesis, *op. cit.*, pp. 99, note 50. See Anonymous, "What is a Downtown Butch?" *Two,* July/Aug. 1966, p. 11.

149. *ASK Newsletter,* May 1967.

150. From Doug Sanders' files and from discussions with him.

151. *Hansard,* 1969, p. 8598.

152. Letter from Bédard to Doug Sanders, May 26, 1969, Sanders' files.

153. These remarks on Bédard are based on William Spencer, "Canada's Leading Homosexual Speaks Out" in *Weekend Magazine*, Sept. 13, 1969.

154. On Bédard see Ross Higgins', "Lives, Oral Narratives, and Writing the Past," presentation at the Out of the Archives conference, York University, Jan. 1994. A version of this will be in Sara Stratton and David Kimmel, eds., *Not Going Away: Essays on the History of Bisexuals, Lesbians and Gay Men in Canada*, forthcoming.

155. Sidney Katz, "The Homosexual Next Door" in *Maclean's*, Feb., 1964, No. 22, p. 11.

156. Sidney Katz, "The Truth About Sex Criminals" in *Maclean's*, July 1, 1947, pp. 12, 46-48.

157. This account is based on Rob Champagne's interview with Jim Egan, *op. cit.*; Sidney Katz, "The Homosexual Next Door" in *Maclean's*, Feb. 22, 1964, pp. 10-11, 28-30; Katz, "The Harsh Facts of Life in the 'Gay' World" in *Maclean's*, Mar. 7, 1964, pp. 18, 34-38; and *ASK Newsletter*, Dec. 1964, V. 1, No. 9. Also see the previously mentioned articles in the *Telegram* in 1964 and a 1966 CBC broadcast on the U.S. homophile movement. In 1967, John Hubert's play *Fortune in Men's Eyes*, which addressed homosexuality in the Canadian prison system, was published.

158. See "The Homosexual Next Door," *op. cit.*

159. See Katz, "The Harsh Facts of Life in the 'Gay' World," *op. cit.*

160. William Nichols, "Homosexuality: Changing the Law Could Raise Morality" in *The Vancouver Sun*, July 6, 1965.

161. Many of these supported the reform effort, including one by William Johnson, *op. cit.*

162. *The Vancouver Sun*, July 10, 1966.

163. Renate Wilson, "What Turns Women to Lesbianism" in *Chatelaine*, Oct. 1966, pp. 33, 130-134.

164. Réjeanne Rancourt and Thérèse Limages, "Homosexuality among Women" in *Canadian Nurse*, Dec. 1967, pp. 42-44. Also referred to in Becki Ross, "The House That Jill Built," Ph.D. thesis, *op. cit.*, p. 84.

165. See, for instance, articles by P. G. Thomson, "Sexual Deviation" in *Canadian Medical Association Journal*, No. 80, Mar. 1959, and Hubert Pascoe, "Deviant Sexual Behaviour and the Sex Criminal" in *Canadian Medical Association Journal*, V. 84, Jan. 28, 1961.

166. Anonymous, "Living with Homosexuality" in *Canadian Medical Association Journal*, V. 86, May 12, 1962. Also see Martin Bauml Duberman, "Gay in the Fifties," reprinted from *Gay Sunshine*, Spring 1977, in *Salmagundi*, No. 58-59, Fall 1982/Winter 1983, pp. 42-75; and also see Duberman's *Cures* (New York: Dutton, 1991).

167. Alan W. Mewett, "Sexual Offences in Canada" in *The Criminal Law Quarterly*, No. 2, May 1959, p. 29; also see Mewett's "Morality and the Criminal Law" in *University of Toronto Law Journal*, V. 14, 1962, in which he accepts the Wolfenden approach, arguing that where there is no social harm there can be no crime.

168. Raymond Spencer Rodgers, *Sex and the Law in Canada* (Ottawa: Policy Press, 1962).

169. *Ibid.*, p. 6.

170. Gigeroff's main work was *Sexual Deviation in the Criminal Law: Homosexual, Exhibitionistic and Pedophilic Offences in Canada* (Toronto: University of Toronto Press, 1968) and it is his main work referenced and used in this book. Other work includes "The Evolution of Canadian Legislation with Respect to Homosexuality, Pedophilia, and Exhibitionism" in *Criminal Law Quarterly*, No. 8 (1965/1966), pp. 445-454; "Phenomenological Investigation of Criminal Offences: Its Relevance to the Legislator," memo; "Sexual Offences in Relation to Homosexual, Exhibitionistic and Pedophilic Sexual Offences with Particular Reference to Canadian Legislation and Case Law," L.L.M. thesis, University of Toronto, 1966. Also, in collaboration with Mohr and Turner, "Sex Offenders on Probation: Homosexuality" in *Federal Probation*, No. 33, 1969, pp. 36-39.

171. K.G. Gray, foreword to *Sexual Deviation in the Criminal Law, op. cit.*, p. vi.

172. Gigeroff, *Sexual Deviation in the Criminal Law, op. cit.*, pp. 186-187.

173. *Ibid.*, p. 189.

174. *Ibid.*, p. 195.

175. *Ibid.*, p. 195.

176. The 37-percent figure is actually not from the *Wolfenden Report* but from the Kinsey Report on male sexual activity. At the same time, this is a very interesting entry of Wolfenden and Kinsey into a legal defence argument.
177. *Ibid.*, p. 196.
178. *Ibid.*, p. 199. The next quote is also from this page.
179. *Ibid.*, p. 201. The next quote is also from this page.
180. This is not actually the case. In a literal reading of the *Wolfenden Report*, this activity in a car in a parking lot would still be in "public."
181. Gigeroff, *Sexual Deviation in the Criminal Law, op. cit.*, pp. 211-212.
182. *Ibid.*, p. 204.
183. *Ibid.*, p. 207.
184. On this also see Alec Fadel, "Homosexual Offences in Ottawa 1950 to 1967: The Medicalization of the Legal Process," M.A. Thesis, Concordia University, History Department, 1994.
185. This account comes from an interview conducted by Doug Sanders with Klippert following his sentencing as a "dangerous sexual offender" at the Prince Albert Penitentiary. It was published as "An Exclusive Interview ..." *ASK Newsletter*, Vancouver, Feb. 1968, p. 16. Also see Sanders, "Homosexuality and the Law: The Mysterious Case of Everett George Klippert" in *Georgia Straight* (Vancouver), Sept. 27-Oct. 3, 1968, pp. 10-11, 17.
186. See the *Georgia Straight* article, *op. cit.*, p. 10.
187. *Ibid.*, p. 10.
188. See Memorandum of Argument in the Supreme Court of Canada, application for appeal, *Canada Law Reports*, Supreme Court of Canada, 1967 (Nov. 18, 1966); also see Yves Caron, "The Legal Enforcement of Morals and the So-called Hart-Devlin Controversy," *op. cit.* Also see Doug Sanders, "Homosexuality and the Law: The Mysterious Case of Everett Klippert" in *Georgia Straight, op. cit.*
189. See Memorandum of Argument in the Supreme Court of Canada: Application for appeal, *Canada Law Reports*, Supreme Court of Canada, 1967, *op. cit.*
190. See Gary Kinsman, Ph.D. thesis, "Official Discourse as Sexual Regulation," *op. cit.*, for more elaboration.
191. *ASK Newsletter*, No. 7, June 1967.
192. From the interview with Sanders cited earlier.
193. Gigeroff, *op. cit.*, p. 121.
194. *Canada Law Reports*, 1967, p. 836. This also demonstrates the tradition of legal reform in Canada flowing through Parliament and not the courts. This tendency has now been modified with the Charter and its conception of State formation, which allows the courts a greater role.
195. *The Star* headlines appeared on Nov. 7, 8, 1967. *The Globe and Mail* editorial is from Nov. 11, 1967.
196. See Sidney Katz, "Homosexuals Shocked by Life Term Ruling" in *Toronto Star*, Nov. 11, 1967. His second article appeared in the *Toronto Star* on Nov. 18, 1967.
197. Reported in Sanders, *Georgia Straight, op. cit.*, p. 10.
198. Klippert was released following the 1969 changes in the interpretation of this section. Attempts to contact him in the 1970s and 1980s were unsuccessful.
199. Lesbian and Gay History Group, "A History of the Relationship between the Gay Community and the Metropolitan Toronto Police," *op. cit.*, p. 3
200. *Telegram*, July 19, 1967.
201. *The Globe and Mail*, July 7, 1967.
202. *Toronto Star*, Sept. 7, 1968.
203. *Crane, op. cit.*, p. 41.
204. D'Emilio, *op. cit.*, p. 199.
205. *ASK Newsletter*, V. 5, No. 2, Feb. 1968.
206. Resolution adopted by the NACHO conference in Chicago, Aug. 13-17, 1968. It was forwarded to Trudeau in a letter dated Aug. 24, 1968, by Doug Sanders.

207. On some of this, see Barbara Ehrenreich, *The Hearts of Men* (Garden City: Double-Day/Anchor, 1983)
208. See Kathleen McDonnell, "Claim No Easy Victories: The Fight for Reproductive Rights" in Fitzgerald, Guberman, and Wolfe, *Still Ain't Satisfied: Canadian Feminism Today* (Toronto: The Women's Press, 1982), pp. 32-42; and her *Not an Easy Choice: A Feminist Re-Examines Abortion* (Toronto: The Women's Press, 1984), pp. 17-19. Also see Janine Brodie, Shelley Gavigan, and Jane Jenson, *The Politics of Abortion* (Toronto: Oxford University Press, 1992).
209. Victoria Greenwood and Jock Young, *Abortion in Demand* (London: Pluto, 1976), p. 17.
210. Eleanor Wright Pelrine, *Abortion in Canada* (Toronto: New Press, 1972), pp. 31-45.
211. The following references to the parliamentary debate come from *Hansard*, 1969, pp. 4717-8669, with breaks in between; and from the minutes of the proceedings of the Justice and Legal Affairs Committee, 1969, pp. 171-668, again with breaks.
212. George Smith, "In Defence of Privacy: Or Bluntly Put, No More Shit" in *Action!* publication of the Right to Privacy Committee, V. 3, No. 1.
213. On the Bill 7 debate in Ontario in 1986, see Becki Ross, "Sexual Dis/Orientation or Playing House: To Be or Not Be Coded Human" in Sharon Dale Stone, ed., *Lesbians in Canada* (Toronto: Between the Lines, 1990), pp. 133-145
214. On the Bill 167 debate in Ontario in 1994, see Nancy Nicol's video *Gay Pride and Prejudice* (1994).
215. *Hansard*, pp. 8576-8577.
216. Justice and Legal Affairs procedings, p. 659.
217. See Janine Brodie, Shelley Gavigan, and Jane Jenson, *The Politics of Abortion, op. cit.*
218. There was also a later reference by J.P. Nowlan (Annapolis Valley): "We have not yet heard a member speak in support of any form of homosexuality or lesbian conduct. Let us not forget that women are involved in this matter ... The only thing the chamber has heard about for the last four days is homosexuality, but let us not forget that there are lesbians in this country." (*Hansard*, p. 7757). Marcel Lambert also argued that adolescents of high-school years needed protection from "incipient" homosexuality. "You become aware of a ring of persons engaged in unnatural conduct. It may take place among girls, and I have known of that, or among boys. You tell them that not only is it morally wrong, but it is against the law." (*Hansard*, p. 7512).
219. I heard Mr. Lewis make the following remark in the mid-1970s in response to a question about gay rights: "My wife and I do not believe people should be discriminated against on the basis of how they were born."
220. *Hansard*, p. 7610
221. *Hansard*, p. 7767-68.
222. *Hansard*, p. 7759.
223. This included 11 Conservatives in favour and 44 against the law reform.
224. George Smith, "In Defence of Privacy" in *Action!*, *op. cit.*
225. Jack Batten, "The Homosexual Life in Canada: Will Trudeau's Change in the Law Make Any Difference?" *Saturday Night*, V. 84, No. 9, Sept., 1969, pp. 28-32.
226. George Smith, "In Defence of Privacy" in *Action!*, V. 3, No. 1, p. 1.
227. The Aug. 28 Gay Day Committee, "We Demand," in Jackson and Persky, ed., *Flaunting It!* (Vancouver and Toronto: New Star Books and Pink Triangle Press, 1982), p. 217.

9.
Gay/Lesbian Liberation and Communities

Gay/Lesbian Liberation

In the late 1960s there emerged new social movements focusing on gender and sexuality.[1] In "advanced" Western countries, patriarchal capitalism was transformed through the expansion of social services, increasing State responsibility for social reproduction, changes in social and family policies, growing numbers of married women joining the paid-labour force, a declining birthrate, the development of birth control and abortion technology, and the expansion of consumer markets into new areas of social life. All this eroded previous forms of family and sexual regulation, and led to the production of more visible sexual imagery and the emergence of visible gay and lesbian cultures. Sexuality was becoming more of a public issue in the media and advertising, aided by State adoption of more "liberal" sexual legislation.

"Sexual orientation" separated the questions of lesbianism and male homosexuality from gender inversion — as notions of sickness and deviancy — gained hegemony with the growth of medicine and psychiatry.[2] While we were still oppressed, these changes did allow more women and men to come out of "the closet" and begin to seize some social spaces from which we could more directly challenge the oppression we faced.

Heterosexual reproductive sexuality was now the absolute rule only among moral-conservative and new-right fundamentalists, and ties between sexuality and procreation became tenuous as sexuality as a more autonomous locus of pleasure, identity, and meaning gained in importance. Capital and State agencies now depended less on the heterosexual family form than in previous periods. It was in the context of revolts by blacks, First Nations people, young people, women and the Québécois that lesbians and gay men also rebelled. The growing numbers of lesbians and gay men living at least partly outside of or on the margins of heterosexual family relations — organizing their lives through their own cultural networks — created the basis for the gay and lesbian liberation movements.[3]

In June 1969 lesbian and gay street people, Puerto Rican drag queens, and bar fags and dykes fought back against a routine police raid at the Stonewall Tavern in New York City.[4] Street and bar people came together with new left activists to produce this movement. Thus was born the modern gay liberation movement. The Gay Liberation Front (GLF) and similar organizations were formed across the United States and throughout the Western world.[5] The GLF took its name from the National Liberation Front in Vietnam, which was then fighting against the U.S.-government attempt to deny the people of Vietnam their right to self-determination. The social ferment of the late 1960s social-justice and countercultural movements, earlier forms of homosexual activism, experi-

ences in the closets of the left, and the expansion of lesbian and gay networks and commercial ventures combined to create the conditions for this social movement.[6]

These movements turned the stigmatized category of homosexuality back on our
oppressors by articulating new, more positive lesbian and gay identities. The struggle
over homosexual/lesbian definitions is the terrain upon which this identification and
consciousness was built. These movements challenged the "internalization" of hatred
for homosexuality by lesbians and gay men as a form of "self-oppression."[7] Inspired by
the Black Power movements assertion that "Black Is Beautiful" we produced a parallel
affirmation that "Lesbian/Gay is Good." We challenged the privatization and invisibility
of homosexualities; we affirmed the need for lesbians and gay men to come out and
help build public communities. Through a process of contestation we affirmed, celebrated, and transformed our consciousness, laying the basis for the gay communities
and cultures of the 1970s, 1980s and 1990s. Taking advantage of the openings provided
by the contradictions in the "liberalization" of sexual regulations put in place in the
1960s, we attempted to smash through the boundaries of oppressive sexual regulation.

The early Gay Liberation Front groups viewed our struggle as linked to those of
other subordinated groups and attempted in the U.S. to form alliances with the Black
Panther Party and other groups. Unfortunately, there was often inadequate theorization
of the basis for these connections and attempts at unity often broke up on the rocky
shores of heterosexism.

The early movement tried to unite lesbians and gay men and to ally itself with a
feminist critique of sex and gender relations, but this initial unity was shattered as differences between lesbians and gay men exploded. Gay liberation remained a largely male-
dominated and white movement. Sexism among gay men did not disappear, and
feminism in and of itself began to show its limitations as an organizing strategy for gay
men. Many lesbians, who also experienced oppression as women, were very inspired by
and very involved in feminist organizing although they often faced hostility and even
purges in feminist groups in the U.S. and Canada.[8] Many lesbians experienced a pull toward both feminist and gay organizing. For lesbian organizing, feminism remained a key
reference point.[9] Movement efforts were also hampered by underlying assumptions of a
"natural" or essential gay or lesbian sexuality. The limits of this approach would not become fully visible until later.

The gay liberation movement emerged in an altogether different social context
from that of the early German homosexual rights movement of the late nineteenth and
early twentieth centuries and that of the 1950s and 1960s homophile organizations. Social changes in the intervening years put into question patriarchal relations and ruling
strategies of sexual regulation, allowing these new movements to go much farther. Influenced by the ideas of the new left and feminism, we no longer relied on the advice of
"experts" as had the early homophile groups. Gay Liberation challenged the power of
the psychiatrists, psychologists, and doctors. We were creating new social needs, capacities, and pleasures.

One of the first fronts of struggle was against the psychiatric and psychological practices constructing us as "mentally ill." After a series of "zaps" and confrontations with the psychiatrists and medical professionals the American gay liberation movement forced the American Psychiatric Association in 1973 to drop its classification of homosexuality as a mental disorder.[10] This had a major impact in Canada as well. The Association's new position read:

> A significant proportion of homosexuals are apparently satisfied with their sexual orientation, show no significant signs of manifest psychopathology, and are able to function as effectively as heterosexuals. Homosexuality, per se, therefore cannot be considered a mental disorder.[11]

American psychiatry recategorized homosexuality as a "sexual disturbance" — retaining the classification "sexual orientation disturbance (homosexuality)" in the case of people who were dissatisfied with their condition.[12] Despite its significant limitations, this decision did serve to challenge a central strategy of heterosexual hegemony. In 1980 "sexual orientation disturbance (homosexuality)" was changed to "homosexual conflict disorder," and in 1987 was included under "Other Sexual Disorders."[13] This has allowed for the continuing psychiatrization of some lesbians and gay men, including the use of aversion and "shock" therapy until relatively recently.

It was only after years of campaigning by the International Lesbian and Gay Association (ILGA) that the World Health Organization (WHO) — the United Nations agency responsible for international public health matters — changed its policy defining homosexuality as a sexual deviation and a mental disorder in 1991 by removing it from the International Kodex of Diseases. This definition continued to have some jurisdiction in Canada. Statistics Canada's *Manual for the Classification of Psychiatric Diagnoses*, which was published until the late 1970s, listed homosexuality as a mental disorder.[14] The Canadian Public Health Association, which distributes WHO information in Canada in its Mental Disorders Glossary and Guide, used to list sexual deviation under "neurotic disorders" — including homosexuality, bestiality, pedophilia, transvestism, exhibitionism, and transsexualism.[15] Homosexuality was defined as "exclusive or predominant sexual attraction for persons of the same sex with or without physical relationship."[16] These designations were offered as instructions for diagnosis. These practices continued to medicalize and psychiatrize some lesbians and gay men.[17]

There existed a degree of homophile organizing in Canada in the 1960s as we have seen, but it was of a fragmented character that did not endure. Many of the Canadian groups calling themselves homophile were not formed until after the 1969 law reform and the Stonewall riots, rendering the political composition and history of the Canadian movement different from the American. It may have been that the somewhat weaker development of gay and lesbian networks did not provide the basis for gay liberation and lesbian feminism in Canada until a few years later than in the U.S. What I present here is not intended to be anything like a history of the Canadian lesbian and gay liberation movements in the 1970s and 1980s. I will suggest, however, a number of them— that may help in its recovery.[18]

The University of Toronto Homophile Association was formed on October 24, 1969, more than two months after the criminal reform came into effect, and four months after the Stonewall riot. Other groups using the term "homophile" were formed across the country in 1970-1974.[19] The Community Homophile Association of Toronto (CHAT), which grew out of the University of Toronto group, was formed in February 1971 and for a number of years it was the largest and most influential homophile group in the country.

The first Canadian gay liberation group, the Vancouver Gay Liberation Front, was formed in November 1970. In Montréal, francophones formed the Front de Libération Homosexuelle (FLH) in 1971, modelled after the Front de Libération du Québec (FLQ) and the Gay Liberation Front in an attempt to combine gay liberation and Québécois nationalist consciousness.[20] Toronto Gay Action, which grew out of the political-action committee of CHAT, shared a number of characteristics with GLF groups; it coordinated the protest of 200 lesbians and gay men on August 28, 1971 in Ottawa, which criticized the limitations of the 1969 reform. More than a dozen groups came together for this first ever Canadian protest demanding many reforms that we still badly need today, including full human rights for lesbians and gay men, spousal and family benefits, the right to adopt children as lesbian and gay couples, age-of-consent-law reform, and a number we have only recently won including the repeal of the offence of "gross indecency," and the right to be gay or lesbian and serve in the Armed Forces.[21]

In the fall of 1971 the first issue of the Canadian gay liberation magazine *The Body Politic* was published by people associated with the Toronto Gay Action network. Most of the GLF- inspired groups became fragmented and disintegrated within a few years, in both English Canada and Québec.

Gays of Ottawa was founded in September 1971, the Gay Alliance for Equality in Halifax in 1972, the Gay Community Centre of Saskatoon in 1973, and the Community Homophile Association of Newfoundland (CHAN) was formed in St. John's in 1974.[22] These early groups spawned social service, self-help, and political organizations.

Tension between lesbians and gay men, which was largely caused by sexism on the part of the men, led to the formation of lesbian caucuses in mixed-gendered groups and to independent lesbian groups. In 1972 a number of lesbian members of CHAT — fed up with the sexism in the group — named themselves the CUNTS and stormed out of the group. Their declaration included:

> As lesbians we are oppressed both as cunts and dykes. Until the gays of
> CHAT see the necessity of struggling against sexism, until the structure of
> CHAT is revolutionized, then CHAT will reflect the status quo through le-
> galization and acceptance. Our energies will not be wasted on raising the
> consciousness of members of CHAT who should be raising their own. An in-

dependent lesbian group has been started. It is imperative that CHAT confront its own sexism.[23]

A series of often short-lived lesbian feminist groups were formed across the country including the Lesbian Organization of Ottawa Now (LOON), the Atlantic Provinces Political Lesbians for Equality (APPLE) based in Halifax, and the Lesbian Organization of Toronto (LOOT).[24] Many lesbians went on to play a leading role in the feminist movement or were already involved in feminist organizing. In British Columbia, lesbian feminists formed themselves into the Lesbian Caucus of the British Columbia Federation of Women.[25]

In many smaller centres that had no commercial facilities, lesbians and gays together built support networks and community centres, in some cases establishing self-help services ranging from phone lines to counselling centres. Others moved in the direction of fighting for gay civil and human rights. *The Body Politic* in Toronto, *Gay Tide* in Vancouver and many newsletters kept gay activists informed and in touch. Many lesbians read the gay media but also relied on feminist publications like *The Other Woman* (Toronto), *Pedestal* (Vancouver) and lesbian publications like *Long Time Coming* (Montréal).

From the mid-to late 1970s and in many ways throughout most of the 1980s, aside from when there were major periods of police repression, the main political current in the Canadian movement (generally stronger among male activists than among lesbians) was what was called the "human-rights strategy,"[26] which linked the fight for repeal of anti-gay legislation with the securing of human-rights protection for lesbians and gay men. The central focus of this perspective was the inclusion of sexual-orientation protection in human-rights legislation. This view was developed by such groups as the Gay Alliance Toward Equality (GATE) in Toronto and Vancouver and Gays of Ottawa. These groups established several Canadian gay and lesbian rights coalitions that eventually broke down in the late 1970s under the pressure of their own internal contradictions, political differences, opposition from many of the men to parity decision making with the women involved,[27] and the difficulties of organizing across the vast expanse of the Canadian State. These groups and their strategy helped maintain the public and political visibility that would open up social spaces and gain broader support for our rights. These campaigns for sexual-orientation protection laid the basis for important legislative and legal victories over the next two decades. Beyond Québec, major successes on the human-rights front would have to wait until the mid to late 1980s and 1990s.

The early wave of gay and lesbian liberation criticized the homosexual and lesbian commercial scene for its closetry, commercialization, and alienation. This critique was valid to a degree, but it tended to cut gay and lesbian liberationists off from their potential bases of support in the bars and commercial ghettoes. Among some lesbian feminists there was a rejection of "apolitical" and "nonfeminist" bar dykes and lesbians involved in butch/femme relationships.[28] There tended to be a wholesale dismissal of earlier forms of lesbian and gay life that prevented our movements from learning from past resistance and community formation. Paradoxically, however, perhaps the greatest gain of gay and lesbian liberation was the creation of the social conditions through which more lesbians, gays, and later bisexuals, could come out and create a more positive and public character for gay commercial ghettoes. In smaller centres and rural areas these movements helped foster important support networks, and important rural organizing was carried out by the Saskatchewan Gay Coalition across that province in the late 1970s.

White middle-class gay men in the cities could now benefit from consumer capitalist culture as gay men. The early GLF-type groups had sometimes disputed the limiting and artificial social categories of "heterosexual" and "homosexual." Paradoxically again, gay liberation and rights organizing tended to reinforce an exclusive gay identity and consciousness that often coded "gay" as white and middle class as well. Nevertheless, the early wave of activism sparked many lesbians and gay men into public and political activity. Heterosexual hegemony was challenged in very significant ways.

Toward Gay/Lesbian Communities

The 1970s witnessed the opening of more gay commercial facilities, ranging from bars and clubs to baths, from restaurants to bookstores. It was the period when the "ghetto has come out."[29] In Toronto, this visibility was intensified by the peculiarities of the emergence of gay space there and the city's geographical development. Toronto's gay commercial ghetto lies astride the Yonge Street strip and beside one of the city's most important commercial streets. The history of the gay scene in this area goes back at least to gay patronage of straight-owned bars along Yonge Street in the middle and late 1950s and the opening of the gay-owned Music Room in the 1960s.

Openly gay businesses emerged in the 1970s. These included bars, baths, clubs, law practices, and restaurants, and their patrons helped define and consolidate a sense of gay identity and community. In March 1978, the Toronto Lambda Business Council was incorporated as the first Canadian association of gay business owners. Its 1986 directory listed close to ninety member businesses, ranging from bars and baths to architects, florists, travel agents, real estate agents, and lawyers.[30] The Council includes only those businesses and professionals willing to be identified as gay. It does not represent large corporations in which public gay/lesbian identification is still largely an impediment to career advancement. Its main theme has been "Buy Gay."

Similar developments have taken place in West End Vancouver and in the "Village Gai" in Montréal. Generally there have been far fewer establishments opened that cater specifically to lesbians. In part this is because many women do not earn the same salaries/wages as men and therefore have less of a disposable consumer income. It is more difficult for lesbian entrepreneurs to amass the start-up funds for business ventures, and often credit and loans are not as forthcoming from banks for independent women; and more lesbians are caring for children, which cuts into their disposable consumer income. At the same time, some major lesbian businesses have been opened up in the larger centres. In the 1980s and 1990s more mainstream business interests have begun to market their commodities or services to the "gay market."

There has been what has been referred to as a mass "sexual migration" of gays and lesbians from rural areas to the larger cities,[31] where our sexualities are seen to be more acceptable, where heterosexual family connections are weaker, and where more anonymity is assumed. There is also a regional dimension to this process with many lesbians and gay men leaving Newfoundland and the Maritime provinces to move to the larger centres in central Canada, which are often seen to have more to offer to younger lesbians and gay men. This parallels the process of regional economic and social underdevelopment taking place within Canadian State and social formation. At the same time, many lesbians and gay men do make lives for themselves in rural areas and stay in the Atlantic provinces.[32]

This has led to concentrations of overtly gay men in certain urban neighbourhoods. Along with the commercial ghettoes, there have also emerged gay residential "ghettoes" in downtown Toronto and West End Vancouver, in close proximity to gay commercial areas. Lesbians are often perceived to be concentrated in different parts of these cities than gay men. Many open lesbians live along Commercial Drive in east-end Vancouver. It must be remembered, though, that most gays and lesbians do not live in these "ghettoes."

These residential concentrations have come to be considered gay electoral constituencies at all levels, with the most success being achieved at municipal levels.[33] In the 1993 federal elections ridings, in the West End of Vancouver, in downtown Toronto, and in the "Village Gai" area of Montréal were seen as having large gay voting blocs. Unfortunately, given class and other social divisions, many gays do not vote for progressive candidates and many non-gay voters live in these ridings. Gays who have become a media and often official politically identified "special interest group"[34] have created the social basis for openly gay or pro-gay politicians and have begun to exert some influence at the lower levels of State relations.

The unsuccessful Toronto aldermanic campaign of gay candidate George Hislop in 1980 was organized around these assumptions and was covered by the media within this framework.[35] This early effort prefigured the later successful efforts of NDPer Kyle Rae in Toronto, Raymond Blain in Montréal, and Glenn Murray in Winnipeg. At the end of 1993, there were openly gay men or lesbians on city councils in Vancouver, Edmonton, Winnipeg, Toronto, Kanata, and Montréal. Federally, NDPer Svend Robinson enjoyed significant support from the gay and lesbian communities long before he came out in 1988 as the first gay MP, which was a significant event in official Canadian politics. Robinson had already built up a broad-ranging reputation in support of social-justice struggles as a left NDPer before he came out. He and his office have been very helpful in a number of lesbian and gay rights and other social-justice struggles. Hostility to lesbian and gay rights from the Reform Party and Liberal backbenchers provoked Réal Ménard of the Bloc Québécois to publicly come out in 1994.[36]

This concentration of some gays and lesbians in specific urban zones has provided a solid base for resistance, first at Stonewall, but also against the light sentence given Dan White — the murderer of San Francisco Mayor George Moscone and gay city supervisor Harvey Milk, and against police raids on baths and bars in Montréal and Toronto as well.[37] Says John D'Emilio, "the bars proved themselves to be repositories of political consciousness and a place from which gay anger erupts."[38]

The "Gay Market"

The 1970s witnessed the opening of the "gay market" that has developed in the 1980s and 1990s. Straight business interests began to target gay men as a particular market in response to the emergence of openly gay establishments, the increasing visibility of the gay community, and gay entrepreneurs' and the gay media's attempts to sell it as a good business prospect. Reads a 1975 *Wall Street Journal* headline: "Campaigns to Sell to Homosexual Market Are Being Launched by More Big Firms."[39] These types of headlines can be found repeated in the mainstream media, including the business sections, over the next two decades. For instance, in 1992 the Toronto *Globe and Mail* reported that "Gay Marketing Is in The Pink."[40]

A major assumption of the gay market is that gay men have a higher-than-average disposable income, however, this premise is unsound and is a construction which gay business and the media have helped create. This image gives the impression that the gay community has a particular class — and by implication racial character — and no children or other dependents to support, even though there are gay men raising children and others involved in co-parenting. At the same time, as some are included in this construct of the "gay community" and "gay market," others are excluded.

Peter G. Frish, when he was publisher of *The Advocate*, claimed "We're the most influential of any minority."[41] This claim was based on a survey of 73,000 readers, which found that the income of the average gay household (of 1.4 persons) was about fifty percent above the U.S. national average.[42] This study and others like it deserve critical analysis. *The Advocate* is directed largely, but not entirely, at white professional, middle-class gays,[43] and while its readership is significant, it certainly does not reach all gay men. It is likely that it is the men who most mirror the ideals of publications like *The Advocate* who are most likely to respond to these surveys. Publishers of *The Advocate* themselves advertise that one of their readership's key features is this high disposable income and consumer lifestyle. In a full-page ad in the *New York Times* in 1981, *The Advocate* claimed, "There's an enormous amount of money in the gay market and it's available to smart advertisers in *The Advocate*."[44]

The Angus-Reid Group conducted a somewhat similar survey for Toronto's *Xtra!* magazine in 1993. *Xtra!* summed up the survey by declaring that its readers are "educated and affluent, cultured and well travelled."[45] As Steven Maynard writes in his critique of the construction of the gay market, "Using data generated by such marketing surveys, the media plays a key role in producing the gay market."[46]

The emergence of "gay capitalism" can be traced in Canada. A 1976 article in

Toronto Life discussed the "rise of gay capitalism"[47] and quotes Peter Maloney, then a gay businessman: "[gays are] people with a high disposable income, no children to spend it on and the urge to socialize." After using Maloney to set the frame, the article recounts how bars, magazines, and other business ventures have achieved success. "A buck is a buck," it concludes. "Who the hell cares if the wrist holding it is limp?" At the same time the article criticizes gay "militants" like *The Body Politic* crowd.[48]

This image of the gay market excludes lesbians, who generally do not have the same economic resources as men in this society, as well as lesbian and gay parents, workers, youth, and people of colour, and serves to drive a wedge between groups within gay/lesbian community formation. Treatment by the mass media, and by much of the gay media, of gay men as a white, middle-class, consumer market, is in part a process of class and racial differentiation within queer populations, which excludes working-class gays and people of colour from positions of power and influence.

Because heterosexual business interests accept gays as a consumer market, however, does not mean they support our rights, relationships, and sexualities. We are only accepted because we have money, and because we are consumers who can buy their commodities and services, not because we deserve human rights. While access to consumer goods and services for queers opens up new social spaces for us, and social contradictions we can exacerbate, the "gay market" provides little protection against police repression, nor does it ensure us spousal and family-recognition rights.[49] Capital may invest in the very same markets that the agencies of sexual and moral policing target for containment and regulation. As Steven Maynard asks,

> I think we need to ask ourselves if we are satisfied with the displacement of politics from the streets to the marketplace. How does a politics rooted in consumption speak to the many lesbians and gays who are excluded from the world of queer consumption in the first place? Or, how does a politics of the marketplace tackle such institutions as the police or the legal system?[50]

Both straight and gay commercial interests have shaped gay practices and communities. Gay and lesbian business people, however, have generally been more sensitive than straight owners to their clientele and are more likely to be associated with or at least tolerant of the movement. The owners of the Melody Room and the Music Room in Toronto in the 1960s are remarkable examples of people involved both commercially, socially, and politically. But most openly gay businesses are generally small, and, given their narrow profit margins, usually rather hostile to unions.[51] They tend to take up a rather anti-working-class orientation in relation to their employees.

These gay businesses, and much of the gay media, would have us believe that "liberation" consists of adopting a gay sexual orientation, "buying gay," being "out" in the ghetto, and frequenting gay establishments. In part this defines us by what we buy, as consumers, and the services we access. In a wonderfully subversive way the Queer Nation slogan "we're here, we're queer and we're not going shopping" can be read as a critique of this approach.

Lesbians have a much smaller commercial scene. This discrepancy has continued throughout the 1970s, 1980s, and into the 1990s leading to important inequalities and differences in the social spaces available to lesbians and gay men.

The concentration of gays in some urban zones, while it has had the positive aspect of creating possibly gay-friendly neighbourhoods — although often queerbashings take place in these areas as well — has sometimes also been tied up with middle-class processes of "gentrification" and the displacement of poor and working-class people from certain urban areas. This can also produce attitudes among some gay men that wish to preserve their real estate values and the quality of "their" neighbourhoods that can be mobilized against street people and street prostitutes.

Gay advertising and many media articles project a consumer- oriented, white, urban middle-class lifestyle. This gay life becomes associated with "leisure time." Readers enter into a world of images of what gay men are supposed to be like. This imagery generates new class and race stereotypes and norms, but it can also provide men just coming out with valuable information on how to meet other gay men as well as positive reinforcement for their queer practices.

New norms of sexual and social regulation are generated within gay community formation itself. We have to look at the forms of sexuality, which have

> emerged as central to its capitalist organization, the "sexually alluring," "liberated" woman who graces *Cosmopolitan*, the swinging self-confident affluent homosexual male who lives in the pages of *the Advocate*. What we are witnessing is the creation of new sexual stereotypes which are potentially as limiting as the old stereotypes (the sexless "lady" of some nineteenth-century textbooks, the degenerate pervert of twentieth-century psychiatrists).[52]

The expansion of the gay-male ghetto was built on previous cultural resistance and has been transformed by the gay liberation movement itself, business interests, the media, and the cultural production of gays within the constraints imposed by the hegemonic social order.[53]

Gay and lesbian cultures can be seen as attempts to deal with the contradictions presented to us by heterosexual hegemony.[54] Gay networks were transformed in the 1970s, through a process of social organization, into the "gay community" — bars, clubs, baths, restaurants, social networks, and

> a set of institutions, including political and social clubs, publications and bookstores, church groups, community centres, radio collectives, theatre groups and so on, that represent a sense of shared values and a willingness to assert one's homosexuality as an important part of one's whole life ...[55]

This community is organized not only by gays and lesbians: it is also organized by the police, the mass media, and class and State organization. The gay community is not a natural phenomenon but is historically produced through constantly shifting struggles and relationships.

Gay and lesbian cultures and communities are defined by our sexualities. "Sex ... is a primary means by which we can express ourselves as it confirms our distinct identity."[56] Our particularity, our social and "material" difference, is defined in relation to our sexualities — who we have it with, how we do it and all that gets built around this in our lives. Erotic cultures are produced not only by bodies at play in parks, cruising areas, private parties, houses, washrooms, but also in writings, photography, film and video, and in commercial establishments — bars, baths, clubs, bookstores, and gay and lesbian commercial pornographies.[57] These commercial settings, along with the discourses and practices of masculinities and femininities[58], and hegemonic sexual and cultural imagery, set limits on gay and lesbian eroticisms. In this sense bars, clubs and baths are not only businesses; as cultural and erotic institutions they are also moulded by their patrons. The bars have been and continue to be a major

> [focal] point of the gay and lesbian community. They are the most stable institution in a frequently unstable world. As such they shape the culture of gay life, even as they are shaped and change themselves. They contain within them all the contradictions and weaknesses of gay life. They, nonetheless, are our territory, even with all the control that the outside world exerts. They are the main places where gay people can be gay.[59]

The sense of gay community has been strengthened by our defence of our social and sexual gathering places. The gay men's baths in Toronto in 1981 were clearly viewed as our institutions, and an attack on them was an assault on the entire community. This was the case regardless of whether men went to the baths or not, just as defence of the bars has often involved people who do not frequent them. In the months following the bath raids and large demonstrations, there was a heightened sense of community. This production of a sense of shared community can also occur through public and visible battles over lesbian and gay rights. The mobilizations prior to and following the defeat of Bill 167 in Ontario in 1994 led to a higher level of organization and stronger sense of lesbian and gay networks across the province including in smaller centres where there had been little lesbian/gay organizing previously.[60]

Class, Race and Community

The gay and, to a lesser extent, lesbian communities that emerged in the 1970s, 1980s and into the 1990s created the social conditions for a new stratum of largely white doctors, lawyers, academics, church leaders, and business managers to form as the "expert" spokespeople for our communities.

This shifting class organization also reflects the problems gay and lesbian professionals have faced in advancement within the heterosexual-dominated professions, forcing them to organize to define and defend their own interests. This stratum represents itself as the respectable and legitimate representatives of the gay community since only they have the "proper" professional or managerial qualifications and credentials to do so. They stand in an administrative relation to community networks, mediating our concerns to State and professional bodies.

This has been most obvious in the fight against AIDS. In the Canadian gay and lesbian communities, people who do not have medical or professional qualifications have sometimes been excluded from or "organized out" of decision making in community-based AIDS groups.[61] Only broadly based grass-roots community organizations have been able to cut across this formation of an autonomous gay managerial and professional stratum with its own distinct social interests. In the response to the Toronto bath raids in 1981, for instance, the Right to Privacy Committee was able to draw on the valuable skills of professionals, but in such a way that these professionals were held accountable to a broad-based community organization made up of mostly working-class and street gays.[62] Unfortunately, when resistance died down, the professional/managerial stratum gained hegemony in many organizations.

In the organizing of the Campaign for Equal Families in Toronto in 1994-1995 in support of Bill 167 and then to attempt to keep spousal and family-recognition rights on the agenda, it was often difficult for those without official political connections, legal credentials, media experience, or leading positions in existing lesbian/gay organizations to get involved at the centre of decision making. Some who were able to present themselves as involved in families or spousal relations were able to get involved, but those who were not seen as being in the "family way," or as raising other lesbian/gay struggles — especially those more directly related to sexuality or that stressed the need to also address racism, or as being too "radical" — tended to be excluded or marginalized as well.

Within lesbian and gay communities there are major class divisions, and the growth of a distinct professional managerial strata is an important part of the class relations that have developed within our communities since the Stonewall riots. The emergence of this professional/managerial stratum has produced a social basis for a certain strategy of "assimilation" with heterosexual social relations through emphasizing that lesbians and gays are almost the same as heterosexuals — emphasizing sameness rather than difference — an association of lesbian and gay progress with the continuation of capitalist social relations, and for limiting lesbian and gay struggles to relatively narrow terrains. It is this layer within our communities who provide the main social basis for the hegemony of assimilationist and incorporatist perspectives — who want to achieve social "respectability" in a social order still based on oppression and exploitation.

While the queer nationalist activism of the early 1990s attempted to challenge this strategy of assimilation through emphasizing queers as markedly different from heterosexuals and an "in your face" response to homophobia, this activism was never able to fully locate the class and social basis of this assimilationist strategy. It was therefore unable to see the connections between queer struggles against heterosexist violence, homophobia, and social invisibility and other fronts of class struggle.

Queer nationalist activism was a rejection of assimilationist and simple civil rights approaches that had previously defined many organizing efforts within gay communities. This also ties into the need for a critique of "community" politics where the "community" often gets defined by this professional/managerial elite. In this sense, this activism was a response to the perspectives of the new professional/managerial elites that have gained hegemony in our communities, and in this context Queer Nation was a more youthful, less incorporated wave of activism. At the same time its implicit class politics were not clearly developed and at times could be dismissive of working-class concerns and struggles. This implicit class critique needs to be developed much more clearly in relation to the class struggles within lesbian/gay communities, which are interlinked with class struggles outside our communities. This would help to clarify the progressive basis of activism while at the same time clarifying challenges to the hegemony of the assimilationist professional/managerial strata over our communities. But instead of this, in Queer nationalism there has been an ideological linkage of anti-assimilationist politics with a militant anti-homophobic politics that locates the problems as backward homophobic ideas in the heads of straight people and some "self-oppressed" gays as well. This gets in the way of clarifying the progressive class and social character of this activism.[63]

Oppression and Difference within the "Gay and Lesbian Community"

Gay and lesbian political organizing has been hegemonized by a kind of "identity politics." This constructs a unitary identity for gays and lesbians that obscures the many social differences among and between us to privilege our common "sexual orientation." It prevents us from seeing some of the links between our various experienced oppressions and other forms of oppression and exploitation. The universal identity that has been constructed tends to be coded as white, adult and middle class.[64] This assumption of a common lesbian or gay identity — which emphasizes the unitary character of this identity — has stood in the way of recognizing and dealing with the many differences and lines of oppression within lesbian and gay community formation.

One of the first challenges to a unitary lesbian, gay, and even queer identity came from the growing self-organization of lesbians and gays of colour that began to occur in the mid-to late 1980s. Lesbians and gays of colour got together to support each other, to address their own needs, and began to challenge racism in the lesbian/gay communities and heterosexism in the black, Asian, First Nation and other communities. Black lesbians and gay men, and other lesbians and gays of colour, were generally excluded from gay images and often experienced racism within the gay and lesbian communities.[65] Within the First Nations, "two-spirited" peoples began to organize. These groups produced powerful challenges to the coding of gay and lesbian as "white" and began to challenge and transform white hegemony. This redefines and broadens lesbian and gay to include the experiences of lesbians and gays of colour and First Nations lesbians and gay men. In turn, some white lesbians and gay men attempting to develop an anti-racist practice have challenged white hegemony within lesbian/gay community formation by deconstructing the associations of lesbian and gay with "whiteness." While focusing on oppressive sexual regulation and the transformation of heterosexual hegemony, this emerging lesbian/gay liberation perspective is making racism, sexism and class relations central to queer concerns.

Lesbian and gay youth, given age laws (sexual age of consent and liquor laws regarding access to bars), are excluded from gay social and cultural institutions such as bars, and face ageism in broader social relations and lesbian/gay communities.[66] Despite the fact that they are being challenged in the courts, existing age-of-consent laws deny young gay men the right to legally engage in anal sex until they are eighteen — and then, of course, only with one other person in private.[67]

In response, lesbian, gay, and bisexual youth support groups have been formed across the country.[68] Many young lesbians and gay men face homophobia and heterosexism in the schools, are forced out of their homes by hostile parents, and must confront heterosexist social agencies and the police. As George Smith points out, the ideology of the "fag" is used in the schools to cut some young men out of regular social interaction and to mandate abuse and even violence against them.[69] I remember in my high school days when I was a socialist activist that simply refusing to laugh at anti-queer jokes was enough to get "commie, pinko, fag" scrawled across my locker.

Some adolescent males engage in hustling and male prostitution to survive, and some young women are forced onto the streets by their families. They often receive hostile treatment from the criminal "justice" system as well as social-service and welfare agencies that are supposed to assist them.[70] Most recently, the provisions of the youth-pornography law, which will be mentioned in more detail in the next chapter, have been used to criminalize the lives of some young gay men and hustlers in southern Ontario.[71]

Gay ghettoization can lead to the acceptance of social regulations defining a certain "private," "adult" homosexual space, which cuts us off from the work world as well as the nurturing of young people. The removal of the gay-male world from child-rearing, the school system, and youth, places gay fathers, gay child-care workers, and gay youth themselves in precarious positions.

Lesbians and gay men find themselves excluded from, on the fringes of, and within family relations.[72] The specific experiences of gay fathers and lesbian mothers, and their child custody struggles is sometimes neglected in the gay scene, frequently causing gay fathers to feel rather alienated from the ghetto and "community."[73] The lesbian and feminist communities have been much more supportive and understanding toward lesbian mothers and lesbians who want to become mothers and of the need to secure adoption rights so that the non-biological lesbian parent also has custody over the lesbian couple's child.[74]

Lesbians and gays living with disabilities face problems of access to social institutions not only in society at large but also within the lesbian/gay communities.[75] Particular problems are produced for those living with HIV/AIDS, many of whom are living with disabilities, despite the important social supports that exist in community-based AIDS groups.

The development of the gay ghetto has favoured gay men over lesbians, and some gay men over others. It has favoured the white and the middle class over the old, the young, the non-white, the disabled, the working class and the poor. It also encompasses divisions over HIV status and sexual and gender practices and identifications.

The production of queer cultures through the simple assertion of gay or lesbian identities tends to separate this community formation from that of other oppressed groups, and indeed from the many within queer communities who live multiple, shifting, and intersecting forms of oppression.

Cultural Productions: Resistance and Accommodations

Gregg Blachford's[76] perspective understands the contradictory features of gay-male cultural production that reproduces, resists, and is limited in its opposition to hegemonic heterosexual culture. He examines areas of gay cultural production, such as slang, to discern moments of opposition and concession. "The homosexual subculture … has its own slang which reflects the manner in which homosexuals perceive and structure the world in which they live." Gay-male language, he says, reflects both "traditional" patriarchal attitudes toward women and a particular stigmatization of effeminate homosexuals, as well as a ridiculing of masculinity, femininity, and heterosexuality. These contradictory moments affirm the place of gay men in the dominant patriarchal order, yet they are also potentially subversive of the institutionalization of hegemonic masculinity.

Blachford also examines gay-male cruising and sexual codes. He demonstrates that these contain moments of "sexual objectification" and sexual "promiscuity" — characteristics that are acceptable only in men in this society; but they also contain elements for the subversion of "legitimate" sexual norms, a vision of sex as recreation and play.

> There is then the possibility of re-reading the practice of casual sex as an example of creative transformation of and opposition to the dominant culture's view of what constitutes legitimate behaviour.

Blachford describes how the "expressive artifacts and concrete objects" of gay-male cultures in the 1970s, with their shift to a more "masculine" image, borrowed and transformed images from heterosexual masculinity, thus challenging the association of "effeminacy" with homosexuality. Blachford describes this phenomenon:

> First of all, the clothes are worn differently in the gay subculture from the way they are worn by "real men." They are much tighter fitting, especially

tailored to be as erotic and sensual as possible. Parts of the body will be purposely left exposed in an attempt to attract others ... These subtle changes and transformations of objects infuse the style with a new meaning of eroticism and overt sexuality — that is, they are used explicitly to make one appear sexy and attractive to other men. This can be seen as distinct from any celebration of masculinity as such. Instead, it may be an attempt to show that masculine or "ordinary" men can be homosexual too ... It forces the wider culture to question its stereotypes and question the legitimacy of linking femininity and homosexuality.

Blachford claims that this cultural production built on earlier gay cultures, but that the "masculinization" of the culture has shifted the context in which such cultural forms as "camp" operate.

Some connections can be made here with the rather different cultural production among lesbians of butch/femme cultures mentioned previously. However, given the different social location of lesbians as women, their transformation — shifting and playing around with social constructs of masculinities and femininities to create distinct erotic lesbian cultures — does not participate in possibly reinforcing hegemonic forms of masculinity in the same way.[77] At the same time, these constructs, no matter how transformed, can still limit the erotic and gender possibilities of sex and relationships between women.

Homosexual oppositional styles, Blachford argues, embody cultural assertion and resistance, but it is not in itself a means for ending oppression. Language may mock dominant values and provide a sense of solidarity for gays, but it will not in itself transform the relations that organize our oppression. Only political organizing will do so, although it can be enriched by cultural forms of resistance.

Oppositional cultures exist within a context defined by a hegemonic heterosexual culture that channels subordinate cultural production so that it accommodates the dominant culture. Gay cultural production like fashion trends, for example, can come to be dissociated from gay slang, social life, and sex, and is made available for commercialization on a broader scale. This process neutralizes and makes invisible their previous gay association.[78] It is possible for some heterosexual-identified men to take up, wear, and perform some of these cultural artifacts and to still hate queers.[79]

In the 1990s some similar developments have taken place in relationship to lesbians. Lesbians began to appear more in the mainstream media and popular culture and not always in extremely negative ways. There was the emergence of what some have referred to as "lesbian chic," which focused on the styles of usually white, middle-class and classically femininely "attractive" lesbians. Without addressing the actual lives and oppression experienced by lesbians, this coverage and marketing has focused on some of the styles but not the substance of lesbian experience.[80]

While acceptance of aspects of queer-originating cultural forms demonstrates a certain liberal tolerance, this is a very contradictory process. Forms of resistance and mo-

ments of transformation can be blunted, and moments of conciliation toward a con-
sumer-oriented patriarchal, racist, capitalism strengthened. Gay and lesbian communities, through our own cultural productions, cannot alleviate the conditions that have led
to our oppression. Other forms of dominant cultural production, such as sexism, racism, ageism, and class relations, also enter into the organization of gay and lesbian
ghettoes and communities.

Sexualities and Genders — Or the Strange Case of the Disappearance of Gender from Gay Men's Politics

One of the most significant features of contemporary gay-male imagery is the attempt to separate homosexuality from gender inversion. As we have seen, in the late
nineteenth and early twentieth centuries sex-scientific discourse associated homosexuality with effeminacy and gender inversion. However, this association was not only constructed "from above;" the cultural production and resistance of "fairies," "queers,"
and cross-dressers also produced aspects of this association "from below."[81] In turn lesbianism was associated with "masculine" women. These definitions have served to shape
the emergence of gay and lesbian cultures.

The separation of transvestism and transsexualism from homosexuality in the 1950s
and 1960s started to remove some of the symptoms of gender inversion from homosexual definitions. The concept of "sexual orientation" now emerged, as distinct from gender inversion. This created part of the basis for a masculine gay image to come to be the
hegemonic one in the gay-male ghetto in the late 1970s and 1980s. Cultural production
within the gay ghetto has moved in the same direction as the dominant currents of
sexological and sociological discourse. Social regulation of sexual deviance no longer focuses on gays as gender nonconformists, even though this remains one of the popular
discourses able to be remobilized against lesbians and gay men.

For gay men this is also related to the new commercialization of "masculine" men's
bodies in advertising and within consumer capitalism. Men's bodies are now also being
used to sell commodities and social images at the same time. Of course these displays of
men's bodies are most often coded with social power as opposed to women's displayed
bodies that are not. At the same time, this opening up of new consumer markets for
men does open up possibilities for homoerotic viewings of this imagery[82] while creating
cross-over markets that include both straight and gay men.

In this new context, images of "effeminate" homosexuals, "screaming queens," and
cross-dressers were and in many ways continue to be marginalized except as entertainment. While there has recently been more acceptance for cross-dressing within sectors
of the gay community this does not always carry over into less exclusionary practices for
those who live their lives as cross-dressers or as the other gender. The new "mascu-
linized" gay image has been universalized through social practices as *the* gay identity,
and this has hampered the expression of diversity within queer populations. This has
produced particular forms of exclusion and oppression for transsexuals, transvestites,

and transgendered people within gay and lesbian community formation. Despite a certain focus on drag and gender performances in "queer theory,"[83] this often looks "at transgendered individuals from a perspective containing very little understanding of the everyday lives and realities of transgendered people."[84]

The new macho look is merely a new form of "drag," revealing no more "natural" a gay lifestyle or "essence" than its predecessors. Some gay activists and theorists suggest that this process of cultural production has finally separated the social organization of sexual orientation from that of gender. Homosexuals have, in this view, through a process of evolution, been freed from the oppression of the past to live a more "natural" gay lifestyle. This shift is unfortunately paralleled in much "queer theory" that argues for a separation of the analysis of sexuality from gender that are viewed as autonomous discourses. This leads to a focus on sexuality abstracted away from gender relations separating the intersections of gender and sexuality that we continue to experience in our lives. At times, this suggests that analysis focusing on gender is not relevant for sexual analysis, or for analysis of homophobia. Gender is then no longer seen as crucial for gay men or even for lesbians in some queer theory.[85] It is almost as if gender disappears as a crucial question for gay men in much gay theorizing and analysis by the late 1980s.[86]

What has actually occurred, however, is that homosexuality as gender inversion has been transformed through a social process that has included the participation of gay men into a new definition using the concept of sexual orientation, which can include "normal" masculine gender identifications. This new categorization allows for greater visibility for gay men no longer automatically associated with deviant gender categories. But instead of freeing homosexuality from gender, the process has merely transformed one gender association for another. The current reconstruction and reorganization of gender relations does not mean the end of gender but that gender relations take on new forms. "Macho" homosexuality is still part of the spectrum of contemporary gender organization. Says John Marshall:

> The emergence of "macho men" within the contemporary gay world illustrates in an ironic way the extent to which definitions of male homosexuality continue to be pervaded by the tyranny of gender divisions.[87]

Within some currents of lesbian feminism there has been a parallel "naturalization" of lesbianism as *the* female sexuality and a rejection of gender-inversion practices and associations. Lesbianism is seen as the most "natural" sexuality for women based on the early mother/daughter relationship.[88] This theory represents a de-sexualization of lesbianism from genital sex to simply women loving women, along with a rejection of earlier butch/femme lesbian cultures.[89] This view obscures — if not denies — the important resistance of those women who asserted their own erotic lesbian identities and seized lesbian space by wearing male dress and affecting "masculine" lesbian practices, and of those women who adopted "femme" identifications in relation to these "butch" women establishing visible lesbian cultures.[90] This new "universal" lesbian identity does not deal with sexual- and gender-identification diversity among lesbians, nor adequately with class and race differences.[91] At the same time, within queer nationalist activism and queer theory that suggests it can overcome at least some of these problems, many lesbians find that they are once again subsumed under men's experiences that also tend to hegemonize queer definitions. Queer also gets coded as male and masculine.[92]

There is a tendency within patriarchal capitalism for sexuality to become more autonomous from the social organization of gender relations, particularly for men. The impact of this has been markedly different for women and men, given our different relationships to reproductive and nurturing labour, and the social division of labour more generally.

Separation of gender and sexuality cannot be complete, however, without overcoming sexism and heterosexism and totally transforming sex/gender relations. Forms of class and State organization, even if they depend less on the heterosexual family form than in the past, still rely on a social organization of gender that keeps women and gays subordinate, in the sexual realm as well as others.

A Parade of Sexualities!

A feature of gay/lesbian cultural formation and gay ghettoes in the larger urban centres is the development of diverse business establishments — various bars and baths for people from different class backgrounds and with diverse erotic preferences. These establishments are organized around particular sexual practices that can be traced back to the 1940s or earlier.

Various sub-categories of homosexuality and sexuality have resulted from the work of sexologists (the differentiation of pedophilia, transvestism, and transsexuality) and the diverse erotic cultures produced by those engaging in same-gender sex. There have consequently emerged new terrains of definition and resistance. Declares Gayle Rubin:

> Recently, a veritable parade out of Krafft-Ebing has begun to lay claim to legitimacy, rights and recognitions. There are now political organizations for prostitutes, pedophiles and sadomasochists.[93]

Individual and social identities are now not only being created around sexual "orientation," but also around diverse sexual practices. For instance, with gay and lesbian "sadomasochism" we are not seeing what was defined by Krafft-Ebing and the sexologists; we are seeing instead, as Foucault suggests, the production of new forms of sexuality, new ways of getting pleasure from the body that focus on the eroticization of consensual interpersonal power relations.[94] We are not seeing the liberation of some "natural" SM desire, as some of its practitioners would suggest, but the making of a new eroticism expressed through existing sexological categories. While needing to clearly defend consensual SM practices from State and right-wing attack, we have to recognize how SM practices play around with, subvert, and mimic hegemonic forms of social power. But as erotic practices, they can never fully transcend or subvert these power relations.[95]

Most significantly, perhaps, this affirmation of SM gay or lesbian identities and practices, and other erotically defined differences — along with assertions of lesbian and gay, black, people of colour, working-class, and other experiences — challenges unitary notions of homosexuality or lesbianism.

> The very extension and broadening of the available sexual categories as a result of the women's and gay movements points to their disintegration as unitary categories ... there are homosexualities, and the vast expansion of the gay subcultures in recent years has led to a proliferation of styles, specializations, and a burgeoning of new identities.[96]

Some people begin to identify more with a sexual practice (say sadomasochism) than with homosexuality. This represents a breakdown of older forms of sexual definition and regulation, along with a continuing incitement of sexuality as the truth of our beings with more and more complex differentiations.[97]

The emergence of gay communities has developed the new social and erotic needs of communities of men existing at least partially outside institutionalized heterosexuality. Lesbian communities, and the lesbian components of the feminist movement, have asserted the needs and desires of many women living outside institutionalized heterosexuality as well. I focus on gay men here, drawing in part on my own experiences.

These new social needs have challenged heterosexuality, masculinity, and oppressive sexual regulation. Yet the gay community both resists and accommodates oppression. Gay men can be led to fetishize our sexual identities, assuming the existence of some ahistorical and "natural" gay minority and forgetting the social and historical processes through which our sexualities and cultures have been made. This leads to a deflection of the profound challenge we can pose to heterosexual hegemony.

This is the context in which current debates over lesbian and gay history and politics are taking place. Some see the social-constructionist thesis, which has been argued for here, as questioning the "naturalness" of gay historical identity and ancestry.[98] Indeed, some do use the work of Foucault and other social constructionists to argue for the deconstruction of homosexuality, or gay, or lesbian in the immediate present rather than for its transformation as part of a broader social and historical process. In so doing, they confuse social categories and people's experiences. While a category can be deconstructed in discourse, our experiences can only be transformed through practical social and political activity. These people would have us abandon the only actual basis from which to struggle against heterosexual hegemony.

These critical historical perspectives provide us with a sense of our histories and an ability to see the social forces regulating our sexualities. Rather than deconstructing homosexuality, we must recognize the historical and very real social character of lesbian and gay cultures, their potential to transform sexualities and sexual rule, and what this suggests about the social construction of hegemonic heterosexuality as well. While the most far-reaching currents to emerge out of queer social constructionist work involved questioning the social construction of heterosexuality there seems to have been a short circuiting of these radical tendencies and a collapse of social constructionism into a more narrowly-defined focus on gays and lesbians. This led to the emergence of a series of intermediate positions between essentialism and social constructionism[99] and claims by some queer theorists that this debate had now been superseded.[100] While queer theory in some of its best contributions points to the need to contest and destabilize the hetero/homo duality, this is largely done in cultural terms and needs to be extended in more social, historical, and materialist directions.

Of Minorities, Communities and Ethnic Groups

In transforming homosexuality into a gay identity, we may not be merely resisting oppressive classifications, we may also be locking ourselves into another minority group. This could limit our critique of sex and gender relations and paralyze our struggles over sexual definition and regulation by implicitly assuming the "naturalness" of heterosexuality for the majority. Corresponding to this, a "natural" lesbian or gay community is postulated. According to Dennis Altman, the "ethnic homosexual" has emerged with

> the widespread recognition of a distinct cultural category which appears to
> be pressing for the same sort of "equality" in Western society as do ethnic
> minorities.[101]

The notion of an ethnic or quasi-ethnic community has been taken up by some gays and lesbians for various reasons, chief among which is that it already exists as a model of how communities are formed and their legitimacy established. It therefore provides a basis for gays to appeal for social rights to State agencies and professional groups by claiming we are like these other "legitimate" groups. This is how we can claim to be "respectable."

Some gay sociologists have tried to legitimize homosexuality by stretching existing sociological categories of "minority" group and community to cover our experiences. Some used "institutional completeness" in the 1970s to describe gay community formation in large cities. They contrast this "completeness" with Leznoff and Westley's account of Montréal homosexual networks in the early 1950s, which were described as having little formal organization and therefore were not "institutionally complete."[102] These gay sociologists imply that these earlier forms were underdeveloped. The same has been written about same-gender erotic cultures in "Third World" countries.

"Institutional completeness" was a term originally applied to the adaptation of ethnic immigrants to urban life.[103] Stephen O. Murray compares the emergence of the Toronto gay community in the 1970s to that of the city's ethnic communities; according to his criteria, "only in terms of familistic orientation is there a difference between the urban gay community and urban ethnic communities."[104] This is, of course, a significant difference. Murray concludes, however, that "the Toronto gay community fits the criteria of community as an entity at least as well as Toronto ethnic communities."[105] Such accounts not only misunderstand the social process of gay and lesbian community organization, but also the social relations through which ethnicity is itself organized, which include State immigration, employment, labour, and multicultural policies.[106]

The gay and lesbian communities must be seen differently. Here I use the word "community" in the everyday sense of people in society. The notion of community is internally defined by the resistance of gays and lesbians to oppression, and externally defined by the police, the mass media, and State policies. Community is, then, a social relationship between gay and lesbian resistance and heterosexual hegemony — not something that can be abstracted from this relation. It cannot be seen as a natural "thing" existing on its own outside this social and historical context.

This category of community is yet another instance of the opposition/accommodation combination that is the basis of our interaction with State agencies, as a basis for articulating ourselves with State relations, and for struggling for our civil and human rights as a legitimate group.[107] The notion of the gay community as a legitimate minority is clearly opposed by the forces of moral conservatism, conservative politicians, and until very recently by the police.[108] In response we must argue for our legitimacy, but we must also beware of getting trapped by "legitimacy" and "respectability."

Gays and lesbians are not an ethnic group and are not regulated as such by State agencies, nor are they born into a minority group. They are regulated by a system of sexual and gender relations, not by a system of ethnic regulations and relations. At the same time, for many, their lives are additionally defined by racial and ethnic regulations and this cannot be isolated from their experiences as queers. White gay men and lesbians often occupy positions of socially constructed "privilege" within these relations of racial and ethnic regulation, although this varies in the Canadian context in relation to language and different socially constructed ethnicities.

Lesbians and gays come to assume their sexual consciousness through a different social and psychological process that requires that they "come out" in order to join gay or lesbian communities. The contradiction between heterosexuality as a "universally" proclaimed sexuality and homosexuality as a "particular" subordinated sexuality cannot be understood by simply equating the gay struggle with that of ethnic minorities. At the same time, we must beware of tendencies that attempt to define what is "universally" queer, thereby ignoring the connections that directly link queers with other bases of oppression; many lesbians and gays are also oppressed on the basis of race, anti-semitism and ethnicity, and their experiences and oppression must be a defining aspect of lesbian and gay liberation.

The minority-community perspective obscures class, gender, and race differences.[109] This ignores the very real social differences lived by queers and favours "sexual orientation" over other dimensions of our experience,[110] which helps to create the basis for a professional, managerial, white, middle-class, gay stratum to speak for our community.

But it is not enough to simply recognize and celebrate differences, although this is far more desirable than denying them outright. As Himani Bannerji suggests, we need to problematize the very concept of "difference" and ask from whose standpoint it is defined.[111] This emphasis on "difference" can end up leaving white hegemony undisturbed since it is never defined as "different." People can be allowed their differences but white middle-class hegemony stays in place. This perspective can fail to move beyond a type of liberal pluralism that tolerates differences. Instead we must also address the underlying social relations of inequality and oppression within our communities. We must recognize and celebrate our differences but also act to challenge racism, sexism, and class relations in our communities and in social relations more generally.

The minority group perspective, which does not address how people make their way into this community, also tends to neglect the needs of those "coming out," particularly young people, and generally ignores sexuality. Focusing only on those who are already involved in the ghetto and the community ignores those people who engage in same-gender sex occasionally, and those who have not yet come out. It reinforces the absolute distinction between heterosexuality and homosexuality, denying the flux and fluidity of desires, and does not allow for the incorporation of bisexual concerns and politics. One of the political problems encountered in organizing defence for men accused of homosexual sex in washrooms and parks is that they do not always consider themselves gay and are not necessarily part of the narrowly defined gay community.[112] Sexuality must therefore be taken up in a broader context, going beyond self-defined gays to include people who engage in occasional same-gender sex.

Particularly disturbing in this context is the recent trend toward legitimizing this "natural" minority view through biological and sociobiological knowledge. A 1981 Kinsey Institute study opted for a biological explanation for homosexuality because they could find no adequate social explanation, and this perspective has set the framework for a number of other studies.[113] Some gay men who are research scientists have also begun to argue this position as have some gay rights activists.[114] Support for this position is usually stronger among gay men than among lesbians. It is understandable, in the face of right-wing accusations of "conversion" and "seduction," that some gay/lesbian activists take up naturalistic and biological determinist arguments. Such a position, however, will lock us into a framework, just as it did the early German homosexual-rights movement, that does not challenge heterosexual hegemony.

The new gay-minority approach directs us away from challenging the dominant forms of social life. By accepting the boundaries of an adult-defined community, we are accepting a strategy of regulation that would let us have a commercial ghetto but would keep us firmly out of areas that involve young people, schooling, and family policies. Attempts to raise the need to address the specific concerns of lesbian, gay, and bisexual youth in the schools have and continued to be a major focus for moral-conservative and right-wing opposition to lesbian and gay rights.[115]

Lesbians and gay men are not only members of minority communities: "It is not so much an oppressed minority that the gay movement is about as an oppressed sexuality."[116] In order to understand the dialectic between gay movements and communities, a number of distinctions must be made. The gay ghetto can be seen as commercial and residential concentrations of gays and lesbians. The community, on the other hand, can be seen as comprising those people who have a sense of belonging to such a community — patrons of bars and baths, ghetto residents, those involved in self-help organizations and social networks. This consciousness is the product of the conflict between gay and lesbian resistance and heterosexual hegemony. Our liberation movements are the social and political groups that defend these ghettoes and communities, but that also go beyond this to fight for an end to lesbian, gay, and bisexual oppression.[117] It is these movements that need to be nurtured and expanded in the 1990s.

Responsibility/Irresponsibility Distinctions

This minority-community position directs attention away from our sexual practices and lives — precisely the main concern of the right wing and the police. Gays and lesbians are treated as being not very different from the mainstream except for the genders of their sexual partners. This allows for distinguishing between "good" and "responsible" gays who strive for respectability and "bad" and "irresponsible" gays who are sexually and socially deviant. Vis-à-vis the AIDS crisis, the mass media have attempted to divide us into those who live "respectable" and "responsible" monogamous lifestyles, and those who engage in "irresponsible" and "anonymous, public and/or promiscuous sex." These terms are themselves defined by State and professional groups. During the AIDS crisis, "perverse" has come to mean "public" or "promiscuous" gay sex rather than homosexuality in general. Gay sexual practices have been "re-medicalized," and homosexual sex is again associated with sickness. All this has caused divisions within the gay community and has allowed State agencies to intervene in our social and community life under cover of "public health" measures.[118] Chapter 10 will look in more detail at the work of the mainstream media and social agencies in the social organizing of a "backlash" against gays.

In the context of AIDS, the spread of HIV, as in the infamous 1988 "AIDS Fiend Strikes Again" headline from Halifax's *The Chronicle Herald*,[119] has been blamed on "deviant" and "irresponsible" people living with AIDS/HIV (PLWA/HIVs) often visualized as gay or bisexual men. Conveniently, this framing does not address everyone's responsibilities for engaging in safer sex and needle-use practices in the context of AIDS or the responsibility of governments to provide explicit and culturally specific AIDS education to all people and communities.[120] At the same time, "responsible" PLWA/HIVs are portrayed as those who follow medical and other forms of professional advice and regulation despite the many problems with these medical and professional guidelines and relations.[121]

The evolution of lesbian and gay rights struggles in the context of the spaces opened up by the Charter has produced a new context for the deployment of responsibility/irresponsibility distinctions in relation to lesbians and gay men. Following the winning of basic human-rights protection in a number of province's human-rights legislation, struggles began to shift from basic human-rights protection to legal struggles for spousal benefits often backed by the union movement as it was quickly realized that sexual-orientation protection on its own would not lead to changes in the statutes that were standing in the way of such benefits. One of the first struggles was that of Karen Andrews, who was at the time a library worker and member of the Canadian Union of Public Employees. The Union supported her fight for family medicare coverage for her lesbian partner and the child the couple was raising, although this legal battle was lost in 1988. Subsequently, the Ontario government abolished health-insurance premiums and moved to individual coverage.[122]

Brian Mossop went to court when he was denied bereavement leave for the father of his partner because his partner was male. While he won before the human-rights tribunal in 1989 — where it was recognized that families had changed in character to include homosexual relationships — he lost at the Federal Court of Appeal in 1990, and at the Supreme Court of Canada in 1993.[123] In the previously mentioned Egan case for same-gender pension benefits under the Old Age Security Act, the federal Court of Appeal in 1993 decided against a spousal pension for Egan's partner Jack Nesbitt on the grounds he was not a "spouse."[124] In 1995, in a Supreme Court decision that finally recognized that Section 15 of the Charter must be read as including sexual-orientation protection, Nesbitt's right to a pension was nonetheless rejected. Other important spousal legal battles have been fought and some have been quite successful.[125]

The legal struggles involving the equality-rights section of the Charter have largely been defined by the lesbian or gay individuals involved and their lawyers. For a period, they were the ones who developed the lesbian and gay perspectives on these issues.[126] During the late 1980s, there were no major discussions in gay and lesbian organizations on which perspectives should be adopted in the fight for spousal benefits and for the recognition of queer families. No consensus was reached, and a number of quite different approaches were put forward among gay, lesbian, and feminist activists, and lawyers and legal theorists.

In 1989 the Coalition for Lesbian and Gay Rights in Ontario (CLGRO) held a conference to try to develop a common position on the struggle for spousal benefits and relationship recognition, and later established a working group of lawyers to determine the necessary changes in the provincial legislation.[127] CLGRO began to call for the provincial government to change provincial legislation that defined the "family" and "spouse" as exclusively heterosexual in character. While reinforcing many aspects of the minority-community perspective this new approach began to break away from certain aspects of this conceptualization by raising questions regarding lesbian and gay familial relations and lesbian/gay parenting. This further encouraged the rather abstract character of human-rights protection to address the particularities of our actual relationships and lives.

Bill 167: Spousal and Family Normalization Struggles

In this section, I briefly examine the 1994 Ontario struggle over spousal rights and family recognition for lesbian and gay couples and our children. Bill 167, drawn up by the provincial New Democratic Party government of Ontario after years of lobbying, pressure, and activism from lesbian and gay groups — especially CLGRO — would have changed fifty-six pieces of provincial legislation, granting lesbian and gay spousal and family relationships formal equality with common-law heterosexual relationships.[128] Every Tory voted against it; as did all but three Liberals and twelve NDPers, ensuring its defeat. Its defeat was an important setback for lesbian and gay organizing and for struggles for family recognition rights in particular. Similar legislative initiatives in other provinces and by the federal government will most likely be put on the back burner and will require heightened activism and coalition building to again be placed on the legislative agenda.

While the NDP government was forced to address this question because of pressure from CLGRO, lesbian and gay activists in the NDP, and other party members including union activists, its political strategy could only result in defeat. By deciding on a "free-vote" on this legislation, the government was clearly not committed to ensuring its passage, which means that caucus members were not bound by the party position on this question. The NDP government did not hold a free vote on its very controversial social-contract legislation, and in the case of Bill 167 the free vote was justified by suggesting that this legislation was a "moral issue" that raised "troubling questions" for some people. Rather than defining this as an important human-rights question, the NDP leading bloc instead ceded this terrain of argument to those opposed to the bill.

The NDP government appeared to push this legislation forward for a number of reasons which failed to ensure its passage. First, they wished to embarrass the Liberals who in their vast majority came to oppose this legislation and appeal to the Liberal Party constituency that often supports human rights. Second, they wished to shore up some of their support in the public-sector unions who took on the fight for lesbian and gay spousal benefits as their own struggle. Support for the NDP government had been plummeting in these unions given the social-contract legislation that denied union rights and has lead to layoffs and cutbacks in social services. Finally, they would strengthen their support among the lesbian and gay communities. They also knew that big business was not opposed to this kind of legislation and may have been prepared to go up against the moral-conservative right wing on this question. As Lyn Andrews and Sandra Whitworth expressed it:

The hatred of lesbians and gay men is so prevalent and acceptable that it seemed "natural" for the New Democratic Party to put the "troubling" issue of same-sex spousal benefits to a free vote. Likewise, as opposition mounted, the bill was watered down, with a promise to exclude adoption rights and spousal status, considered the most controversial features of the legislation. In other words, the NDP reaffirmed the hatred of gay men and lesbians even as they sought to alleviate it, and thus the defeat of the legislation was ensured.[129]

Moral-conservative forces across the province mobilized in opposition to Bill 167, which they portrayed as a threat to the family and to children. Roman Catholic priests across the province read letters to their congregations calling on church members to write letters opposing the legislation.

Given this situation, only an active organization of lesbians, gay men, union supporters, feminists, and others, and the building of a broad-ranging coalition in support of Bill-167 could have brought about a victory. This required mobilizing the maximum amount of pressure as quickly as possible through letter writing/faxing, but also through organizing people in the streets and promoting popular grass-roots education — which were the areas in which the right wing and even Liberal opposition made the most headway. The right wing's arguments needed to be confronted and undermined explicitly and publicly. Unfortunately, not enough of this was done.[130] And it was precisely the rights of adoption by the non-biological partner in relationships where the child was already being raised that were abandoned by the NDP at the last minute. It should be pointed out that support for adoption rights was much stronger among lesbians who supported Bill 167 than among many of the gay men whose main concerns focused on spousal benefits.

Despite unprecedented organization across the province, including many areas where there had never been any lesbian/gay organizing before, there were no major public displays of support for Bill 167 until after the defeat in the legislature when 8,000 gathered in angry protest outside Queen's Park and hundreds gathered in protests across the province. The potential for activity was no doubt there at an earlier point since a demonstration organized by left, feminist, and union groups to support Bill 167 and to oppose the free vote attracted 2,000 people on the Friday before the bill was defeated. But the Campaign for Equal Families did not stand behind this action; some leaders of the campaign seemed to have drawn the wrong lesson from the Bill 7 sexual-orientation campaign in 1986. Mobilizations were discouraged while the bill was being debated in the legislature but it was still passed. However, the balance of power was dramatically different in 1994, when only such mobilizations could have secured a victory.

Following the defeat, organizing across the province by the Campaign for Equal Families and the Coalition for Lesbian and Gay Rights in Ontario, involving people from close to thirty different cities and towns, continued for a number of months. Unfortunately, by 1995 activities had died down except for a series of public actions in Toronto in May and June of 1995. Following the legislative defeat, organizing on the legal front went forward. A series of Toronto lesbian families pushed for the legal rights of non-biological mothers, and a number of second-parent adoption cases proceeded through the courts. As a result, that May, Justice James Paul Nevins of the Ontario Provincial Court (Family Division), in a significant legal victory, decided the lesbian partners of four women could adopt their partner's biological children. The adoption orders were final, but Nevins' decision that the provincial Child and Family Services Act is unconstitutional because it restricts "spouse" to someone of the "opposite sex," could be challenged.[131] Meanwhile, the B.C. government changed the provincial Adoption Act in 1995 to allow lesbians and gay men to adopt children.[132]

Bill 167 was a very significant challenge to heterosexual hegemony, especially to the social institutionalization of the family and spouse as exclusively heterosexual in State and social policy. Some important legal victories have been won through the courts on this front in the context of Canada's Charter of Rights. But there are also very real and potential dangers in struggles for spousal and family recognition and in how they can become institutionalized. This is one of the reasons why a series of debates and controversies have been generated within the lesbian/gay and feminist movements over struggles for spousal and family status.

"Family" and "spousal" get used in these struggles and legal cases not only in the transformative sense of challenging heterosexual hegemony but also as part of "responsibilizing" and "normalizing" strategies. In part this is bound up with the conceptualization that spousal and family recognition brings with it *responsibilities* as well as rights.[133] This perspective also accepts the individualization of benefits in family/spousal contexts rather than providing social supports in non-familial or non-spousal forms, including social support for children. This is a practice of "normalization" since these spousal, family regulations are part of a web of historically established relations between families, places of employment, State regulations, and insurance corporations. It also develops an investment in ensuring that these familial/spousal defined benefits and conceptualizations continue. This strategy would incorporate some "queers" into familial/spousal relations as sites for regulation. These lesbians and gay men would no longer be constructed as "deviant," but instead would be defined as a variant of the norm. As a result, a new albeit limited social legitimacy would be granted to some lesbians and gay men.

This can be seen as an attempt to extend the Wolfenden approach of the establishment of the self-regulating adult homosexual in the "private" realm.[134] The realm of self-regulation would now be extended through this strategy to include certain spousal and familial associations and benefits in relation to employment and State agencies. It would "empower" lesbians and gay men, but only within these responsibilizing and normalizing relations.

The Wolfenden perspective also called for an intensification of criminalization practices against homosexual activities in the "public" realm and against those involving people under the age of twenty-one as we saw in chapter 8. In this newer variant, the contrast is between "responsibilizing" those involved in family/spousal relations and "irresponsibilizing" those who are not, and especially those who are defined as engaged in queer sexual activities outside spousal confines and who raise sexual questions involving young people.

There is a complementary trend toward the privatization of financial responsibility. For instance, same-gender spouses who obtain State recognition will be liable for each other's support.[135] Already in British Columbia a lesbian who applied for social assistance after her unemployment insurance ran out was told that she is not eligible for such assistance since her lover earns too much money. And this is in a province where she cannot receive same-sex benefits through her lover's work place plan.[136] Gay people living with AIDS/HIV could have lost the use of their Ontario drug card (allowing them to freely access some of the treatments they need) under Bill 167, since financial responsibility for them (including expensive AIDS/HIV drugs) would have to be assumed by their gay spouse, if they had such a relationship and their partner had a high enough income.[137] This again individualizes and privatizes economic responsibility within the spousal relationship, and would make it even harder to qualify for a drug card if you have a spouse, and would further restrict access by PLWA/HIVs to the treatments they need.

But many in the Ontario legislature were not willing to accept this "responsibilizing" strategy. The majority could not accept this claim for family and spousal status since it displaces the "normality" of only the heterosexual family. This tendency toward family/spousal normalization remains, therefore, only one tendency of development in current circumstances.[138] The 1994 defeat of this "responsibilizing" strategy demonstrates the continuing activity and resiliency of moral-conservative strategies of regulation that would deny lesbians and gay men any claim to be "responsible" or "respectable." This tendency toward respectability and responsibility is being produced both through currents within lesbian/gay organizing and also State and professional regulatory responses.

While pushing for the recognition that "we are family!" — if we so choose to define ourselves — and through the formulation of alternative social-support policies, we must avoid the traps of the "responsibilizing" strategy by also challenging the practices that simultaneously "irresponsibilize" some lesbians and gay men through sexual censorship and the continuing criminalization of consensual queer sex. Our proposals for transformation must address sexuality and challenge heterosexist hegemony. The affirmation of gay and lesbian identities and the formation of gay and lesbian communities has altered the terrain of sexual categorization and regulation, but it has not fundamentally disengaged us from this framework. Asserting our identities and communities is partially acceptable in patriarchal capitalist society as long as we remain ghettoized in a narrow, clearly demarcated social space, or for some, as long as we stay regulated within normalized spousal and family relations.

Private adult sexuality can be regulated more effectively by medical doctors and psychiatrists than by the coercive apparatus of the State. Although gay liberation has significantly challenged and displaced notions of illness, the AIDS crisis has been used to reconstruct them. As well, the policy of sexual regulation put in place in the 1960s contains internal contradictions that have emerged in the 1980s and 1990s.

State agencies firmly patrol the boundaries of our limited social spaces. Too much public visibility calls the police into action. As the public sphere becomes more heavily patrolled, social taboos tend to shift from homosexuality and lesbianism in general to the "recruitment" of youth,[139] lesbian parents raising children in a manless "horror world,"[140] "pedophilia," "public sex," "pornography" especially that relating to young people, "sadomasochism," and, AIDS.

> Homosexuality ... has not been accepted in society at large; rather the target for its control has switched. New techniques of surveillance and/or regulation are developing all the time, and they are a product not simply of a capitalistic mode of production nor of a simple evolution of attitudes, but of the complex interaction of social needs, historical practices, and the self-activity of those defined.[141]

Notes

1. These were not, however, the first movements to focus on gay and lesbian concerns — see chapter 2. There is a long history of organizing regarding sexual and gender relations going back to the last century.
2. See John Marshall, "Pansies, Perverts and Macho Men," and Dave King, "Gender Confusions: Psychological and Psychiatric Conceptualizations of Transvestism and Transsexualism" in Kenneth Plummer, ed., *The Making of the Modern Homosexual* (London: Hutchinson, 1981), pp. 133-154, 155-183.
3. See John D'Emilio, *Sexual Politics, Sexual Communities* (Chicago and London: The University of Chicago Press, 1983), pp. 176-239.
4. On the Stonewall riots, see Martin Duberman, *Stonewall* (New York: Dutton, 1993).
5. Later this would be extended to many countries in the "Third World."
6. For commentaries on and analysis of this early period, see Jay and Young, *Out of the Closets: Voices of Gay Liberation* (New York: Pyramid, 1974); and D. Teal, *The Gay Militants* (New York: Stein and Day, 1971), for the United States. See Aubrey Walter, ed., *Come Together: The Years of Gay Liberation, 1970-1973* (London: Gay Men's Press, 1980), and Jeffrey Weeks, *Coming Out* (London: Quartet, 1977), pp. 185-206, for England. For Canada, see Ed Jackson and Stan Persky, eds., *Flaunting It!* (Vancouver and Toronto: New Star Books/Pink Triangle Press, 1982); Paul-François Sylvestre *Les homosexuels s'organisent* (Montréal: Éditions Homeureux, 1979); and Becki Ross, *The House That Jill Built: A Lesbian Nation in Formation* (Toronto: University of Toronto Press, 1995), especially pp. 24-40.
7. See Andrew Hodges and David Hutter, *With Downcast Gays: Aspects of Homosexual Self-Oppression* (Toronto: Pink Triangle Press, 1977). This notion of self-oppression can be criticized just as can the notion of "false consciousness" because it does not adequately address the social context wherein people might, in this case, remain closeted (fear that they will be fired, etc.). These very real social pressures cannot simply be gotten rid of with moral pronouncements about "self-oppression." The social world and people's consciousness must both be trans-

formed. However, given the specific character of lesbian/gay oppression and the importance of psychological discourse in its organization, this understanding of "self-oppression" has been rather useful. At the same time, a certain overinvestment of gay and lesbian liberation politics in the necessity of "coming out" as a central strategy for liberation has led to continuing tendencies to blame those who will not or have not yet come out. This has informed the politics of "outing" in the 1990s, which views those who have not come out as not only "self-oppressed" but also as damaging to the gay and lesbian (and sometimes the AIDS) struggles. On this, see Larry Gross, *Contested Closets: The Politics and Ethics of Outing* (Minneapolis and London: University of Minnesota Press, 1993) and my review of it "Outing and the Dismantling of the Closet" in *Lesbian and Gay Studies Newsletter* V. 21, No. 2, July 1994, pp. 37-38.

8. See Becki Ross, *The House That Jill Built, op. cit.,* pp. 24-30.
9. For an account of feminist organizing in Canada that does not adequately address lesbian involvement, see Nancy Adamson, Linda Briskin, and Margaret McPhail, *Feminist Organizing for Change: The Contemporary Women's Movement in Canada* (Toronto: Oxford University Press, 1988) and also see Ruth Roach Pierson, Marjorie Griffin Cohen, Paula Bourne and Philinda Masters, *Canadian Women's Issues, Volume I. Strong Voices: Twenty-five Years of Women's Activism in English Canada,* (Toronto: James Lorimer, 1993).
10. R. Bayer, *Homosexuality and American Psychiatry* (New York: Basic Books, 1981). Also see Gay Flames's pamphlet No. 6, "Gay Liberation Meets the Shrinks," New York City, early 1970s.
11. David W. Weisstraub, *Law and Psychiatry in the Canadian Context* (New York and Toronto: Pergamon Press, 1980), p. 113.
12. See Harry and DeVall, *The Social Organization of Gay Males* (New York: Praeger, 1978), p. 2, and Thomas Szasz, *Sex by Prescription* (Hammondsworth: Penguin, 1981). It was only in 1995 that the American Medical Association reversed a thirteen-year-old policy of recommending "treatment" for gay men and lesbians who were unhappy with their homosexuality. See *Wayves* (Halifax) February 1995, p. 20.
13. See Bonnie Burstow, "A History of Psychiatric Homophobia" in *Phoenix Rising,* V. 8, No. 3/4, July 1990, p. S39.
14. Weisstraub, *op. cit.,* p. 113.
15. World Health Organization, *Mental Disorders: Glossary and Guide to Their Classification in Accordance with the Ninth Revision of the International Classification of Diseases* (Geneva: World Health Organization, 1978), pp. 40-41. Distributed in Canada by the Canadian Public Health Association. Sexual deviation and disorders are defined thus in this text: "The sexual activity of affected persons is directed primarily either toward people not of the opposite sex or toward sexual acts not associated with coitus normally, or toward coitus performed under abnormal circumstances." p. 40.
16. *Ibid.*
17. See Sheila Gilhooly and Persimmon Blackbridge, *Still Sane* (Vancouver: Press Gang, 1985) and *Phoenix Rising,* V. 8, No. 3/4, July 1990.
18. This history has yet to be pulled together, although valuable resources exist in publications, archives, in Jackson and Persky, eds., *Flaunting It!, op. cit.,* in Becki Ross's, *The House That Jill Built, op. cit.,* in some of the other references mentioned in this chapter, and in the memories and papers of people still actively involved in activism. On one small aspect of this history — the controversy over *The Body Politic's* publication of the "Men Loving Boys Loving Men" article in 1977 — it can be traced in part through Becki Ross's, "Like Apples and Oranges: Lesbian Feminist Responses to the Politics of *The Body Politic*" in *Fuse,* May/June 1993, V. 16, No. 4, pp. 19-28 and her book, *op. cit.,* pp. 165-175, although I feel that her account — while correctly pointing to the need to defend *The Body Politic* — does not adequately take into account the limitations of the paper's sexual-libertarian position during this period. Also see Chris Bearchell, Rick Bebout, and Alexander Wilson, "Another Look," in *Flaunting It!, op. cit.,* pp. 166-174. The last issue of *The Body Politic* appeared in Feb. 1987 (No. 135).
19. Paul-François Sylvestre, *Les homosexuels s'organisent* (Montréal: Éditions Homeureux, 1979),

pp. 40-42. Also see Marion Foster and Kent Murray, *A Not So Gay World: Homosexuality in Canada* (Toronto: McClelland and Stewart, 1972).

20. Ross Higgins, "The Linguistic Impasse: Gay Organizing in Montreal" in *Rites*, V. 2, No. 5, Oct. 1985, p. 8. Higgins also gave a presentation on the Front de Libération Homosexuelle at a conference on the History of Gay and Lesbian Militancy in Québec at the Université du Québec à Montréal sponsored by the Groupe Interdisciplinaire de Recherches et Études: Homosexualité et Société (GIREHS) on Mar. 31, 1995.

21. August 28 Committee, "We Demand" in Jackson and Persky, eds., *Flaunting It! op. cit.*, pp. 217-220. The offence of gross indecency was abolished on Jan. 1, 1988 but can still be used for offences alleged to have occurred prior to that date.

22. See Gays and Lesbians Together, *"Here To Stay" — Lesbians and Gays in Newfoundland: Fighting for Our Rights* (Gays and Lesbians Together, St. John's), 1991, p. 14.

23. Quoted in Becki Ross, *The House That Jill Built: A Lesbian Nation in Formation* (Toronto: University of Toronto Press, 1995), pp. 34-35.

24. On LOOT see Becki Ross, *The House That Jill Built: A Lesbian Nation In Formation, op. cit.* On lesbian organizing in Canada, also see Sharon Stone's "Lesbian Mothers Organizing" in *Lesbians in Canada*, pp. 198-208; and her "Lesbians Against the Right" in Jeri Wine and Janice Ristock, eds., *Feminist Activism in Canada* (Toronto: James Lorimer, 1991), pp. 236-253. On lesbian feminist organizing in the U.S. in relation to social movement-theory, see "Collective Identity in Social Movement Communities: Lesbian Feminist Mobilization" in Aldon D. Morris and Carol McClung Mueller, eds., *Frontiers in Social Movement Theory,* (New Haven and London: Yale University Press, 1992), pp. 104-129.

25. See Julia Creet, "A Test of Unity: Lesbian Visibility in the British Columbia Federation of Women" in Sharon Dale Stone, *Lesbians In Canada* (Toronto: Between The Lines, 1990), pp. 183-197.

26. See Brian Waite, "A Strategy for Gay Liberation" in Jackson and Persky, eds., *Flaunting It!, op. cit.*, pp. 221-223. Also see "Fifteen Years of Struggle," John Wilson interviews Tom Warner in *Rites*, V. 3, No. 9, Mar. 1987, p. 12.

27. On this see Bill Fields, "The Rise and Fall of the Fifty Per Cent Solution: Lesbians in the Canadian Gay Rights Movement," Paper, Faculty of Social Work, University of Regina, 1983. On file at the Canadian Lesbian and Gay Archives (Toronto).

28. See Becki Ross, *The House That Jill Built, op. cit.*

29. Editorial, "Within These Walls" in *Gay Left*, No. 2, Spring 1976, p. 4.

30. Lambda Business Council Membership Directory, 1986.

31. Gayle Rubin, quoted in John D'Emilio, "Gay Politics, Gay Community ..." in *Socialist Review*, No. 55, Jan./Feb. 1981, p. 93.

32. See Michael Riordan's forthcoming book, *Out Our Way* (Toronto: Between the Lines, 1996) on rural lesbians and gay men. Also see Patrick Barnholden, "A Different Drummer, Lesbians and Gays in the Region: An Activist's Overview" in *New Maritimes*, V. 11, No. 3, Jan./Feb., 1993, pp. 6-15.

33. For the San Francisco experience, see D'Emilio, "Gay Politics, Gay Community ..." *op. cit.*, particularly pp. 94-95. Also Randy Shilts, *The Mayor of Castro Street: The Life and Times of Harvey Milk* (New York: St. Martin's Press, 1982). On Vancouver, see Terence John Fairclough, "The Gay Community of Vancouver's West End: The Geography of a Modern Urban Phenomenon," M.A. paper, Dept. of Geography, University of British Columbia, Aug. 1985. Also see the new work on queer space and geography, such as in David Bell and Gill Valentine, eds., *Mapping Desire: Geographies of Sexualities,* (London and New York: Routledge, 1995).

34. The media construction of "special interest group" has been taken up by right-wing politicians to discount the concerns of the poor, trade unions, feminists, people of colour, and lesbians and gay men. The only group that it seems is never defined as a "special interest group" is big business. The term operates by constructing the group as having "special interests" that

are somehow counterposed to the "general interest." This has become an important discursive device for undercutting the legitimacy of a number of social-justice-seeking movements.

35. See Ed Jackson, "Close But Not Enough: The Toronto Municipal Elections" in Jackson and Persky, *Flaunting It!*, *op. cit.*, pp. 100-101.
36. See Douglas Sanders, "Constructing Lesbian and Gay Rights" in *Canadian Journal of Law and Society*, V. 9, No. 2, Fall 1994, pp. 137,143.
37. See Amber Hollibaugh, "Right to Rebel" in Gay Left Collective, eds., *Homosexuality: Power and Politics* (London: Allison and Busby, 1980), pp. 205-215. Also D'Emilio, "Gay Politics, Gay Community ..." *op. cit.*, pp. 100-101. In Toronto, 4,000 leaflets were distributed in bars on the evening of February 6, 1981 calling for a demonstration at midnight. See Gerald Hannon, "Raids, Rage and Bawdy Houses" in Jackson and Persky, *op. cit.*, pp. 273-276. Also see the film *Track Two* (Toronto: KLS Productions, 1982). The importance of bars was not as clear in the response to the defeat of Bill 167 in 1994 in Toronto, which was organized rather differently and focused around "familial" and spousal identifications.
38. D'Emilio, "Gay Politics, Gay Community ..." *op. cit.*, p. 101.
39. Wall Street Journal, May 12, 1975. Also see "Gays: A Major Force in the Marketplace" in *Business Week*, Sept. 3, 1979, p. 118.
40. "Gay Marketing Is in the Pink" in *The Globe and Mail*, Aug. 15, 1992, Section D4.
41. Quoted in *Business Week, op.cit.*
42. *Ibid.*, p. 118
43. See Dennis Altman, *The Homosexualization of America, The Americanization of the Homosexual* (New York: St. Martin's Press, 1982) p. 165.
44. The ad was reprinted in *Gay Community News*, Boston, Apr. 18, 1981, p. 2. Also see an advertising report for *Esprit*, an unsuccessful slick, commercial gay magazine in Toronto in 1975: "... more and more firms are turning their advertisements towards the gay marketplace ... today advertisers are realizing the vast market potential that has yet to be untapped ... the average homosexual wage earner brings home between $10,000 and $18,000 annually and they tend to spend more of their disposable income on clothes, records, movies, liquor, furniture, etc. than their counterpart in the straight world. Gay people are more image conscious and therefore tend to spend more of their disposable income to keep this up." "A Report on Advertising Possibilities and Potential in Canada: New Sales Views" in *Esprit*, 1975.
45. *Xtra!*, June 25, p. 25.
46. Steven Maynard, "What Color Is Your Underwear?: Class, Whiteness and Advertising" in *Border/Lines*, "Queer Licks Issue," No. 32, 1994, p. 6.
47. Ken Waxman, "The Rise of Gay Capitalism" in *Toronto Life*, Sept. 1976.
48. See Michael Lynch's review of the Waxman article in *The Body Politic*, Oct. 1976, "Our Image," p. 3.
49. At the same time, in response to our struggles for spousal benefits many large corporations have agreed to provide many of them. They often do not see any compelling financial reasons to oppose them and also may feel they can make for more committed and responsible employees.
50. Steven Maynard, "What Color Is Your Underwear?: Class, Whiteness and Advertising," *op. cit.*, p. 9.
51. See, for example, an article by Paul Trollope, "Bath Workers Vote Down Union: Organizer to Make Second Try" in *The Body Politic*, May 1979, No. 52, p. 14.
52. Jeffrey Weeks, "Capitalism and the Organization of Sex" in *Homosexuality, Power and Politics*, *op. cit.*, p. 11.
53. These constraints include the entry of dominant social relations into the organization of gay communities through police activity, licensing practices, media images, the limits of capital expansion for small businesses like bars and baths, the socially dominant patterns of eroticization that limits our imagination of sexual possibilities, and historically and socially defined forms of masculinity and femininity.

54. See Gregg Blachford, "Male Dominance and the Gay World" in Plummer, ed., *The Making of the Modern Homosexual* (London: Hutchinson, 1981), p. 184.

55. Altman, *The Homosexualization …, op. cit.*, p. 8.

56. See Gay Left Collective statement, "Self and Self-Image" in *Gay Left*, No. 9, p. 5.

57. I use pornography to cover sexually explicit materials per se. There are many types of pornography with different social characteristics and relations to social power. Since the mid-1980s in North America, a new lesbian porn made for lesbians has emerged and become the target for censorship in Canada.

58. On the social construction of femininities, see Dorothy E. Smith, "Femininity As Discourse" in *Texts, Facts, and Femininity: Exploring the Relations of Ruling* (London and New York: Routledge, 1990), pp. 159-208. We need more work on the discourses and practices of masculinities and femininities.

59. Christine R. Riddiough, "Culture and Politics" in *New American Movement: Working Papers on Gay/Lesbian Liberation and Socialism*, 1979, p. 14.

60. On this see Nancy Nicol, *Gay Pride and Prejudice* (video, 1994), and David M. Rayside, "Inside the Fringe: Mobilizing for Same-Sex Benefits in Ontario," unpublished paper presented at the Second Annual Meeting of The Canadian Lesbian and Gay Studies Association, Montréal, June 3-4, 1995.

61. See Gary Kinsman, "Managing AIDS Organizing: 'Consultation,' 'Partnership,' and the National AIDS Strategy" in William K. Carroll, ed., *Organizing Dissent: Contemporary Social Movements in Theory and Practice* (Toronto: Garamond, 1992), pp. 215-231.

62. Also see Tim McCaskell, "The Bath Raids and Gay Politics" in Frank Cunningham, Sue Findlay, Marlene Kadar, Alan Lennon, and Ed Silva, eds., *Social Movements/Social Change: The Politics and Practice of Organizing* (Toronto: Between The Lines, 1988), pp. 169-188.

63. See Steven Maynard, "When Queer is Not Enough" in *Fuse*, Fall 1991, pp. 14-18 and my unpublished paper "Queer 'Nations,' Queer Spaces: Academic Institutionalization and Queer Activism" in Canadian Sociology and Anthropology Association meetings, Charlottetown, 1992.

64. On the limitations of identity politics, see among others Mary Louise Adams, "There's No Place Like Home: On the Place of Identity in Feminist Politics" in *Feminist Review*, No. 31 (Spring, 1989), pp. 22-33. For a more poststructuralist critique, see Judith Butler, *Gender Trouble: Feminism and the Subversion of Identity* (New York: Routledge, 1990).

65. On racism and gay men of colour, see Anton, "Racism in the Gay Community: A Closer Look" in *Pink Ink*, V. 1, No. 2, Aug. 1983; Gerald Chan, "Out of the Shadows" in *Asianadian*, 1979; Richard Fung, "Gay Asians of Toronto" in *Asianadian*, V. 5, No. 4; and Richard Fung's videos, *Orientations* (1984), on gay Asians, and *Chinese Characters* (1986), on gay Asian men and white gay porn; Fung, "Looking for My Penis: The Eroticized Asian in Gay Video Porn" in Bad Object Choices, ed., *How Do I Look? Queer Film and Video* (Seattle: Bay Press, 1991), pp. 145-168; and Fung, "The Trouble with 'Asians'," in Monica Dorenkamp and Richard Henke, eds., *Negotiating Lesbian and Gay Subjects* (New York and London: Routledge, 1995), pp. 123-130; Kobena Mercer and Isaac Julien, "Race, Sexual Politics, and Black Masculinity: A Dossier" in Rowena Chapman and Jonathan Rutherford, *Male Order: Unwrapping Masculinity* (London: Lawrence and Wishart, 1988), pp. 97-164; Kobena Mercer, "Skin Head Sex Thing: Racial Difference and the Homoerotic Imaginary" in *How Do I Look? op. cit.*, pp. 169-222; and Tomas Almaguer, "Chicano Men: A Cartography of Homosexual Identity and Behavior" in *differences*, V. 3, No. 2, Summer 1991, special "Queer Theory, Lesbian and Gay Sexualities" issue, pp. 75-100; "Racism and Gay Male Porn: Taking Control of the Images," Gary Kinsman talks with Pei Lim, *Rites*, V. 3, No. 8, Feb. 1987, pp. 14-15. On lesbians of colour, see Audre Lorde, *Zami: A New Spelling for My Name* (New York: Crossing Press, 1982) and her *Sister Outsider* (New York: Crossing Press, 1984); "Lesbians of Colour, Loving and Struggling: A Conversation between Three Lesbians of Color" in *Fireweed*, Women of Color issue, Spring 1983, pp. 66-72; Makeda Silvera, "Sister Outsider: Rage and Vision," review of Audre Lorde, *Sister Outsider*, in *Rites*,

Sept. 1984, No. 4, p. 22; see *Rites*, Lesbians and Gays of Color issue, V. 2, No. 6, Nov. 1985; Makeda Silvera, "Man Royals and Sodomites: Some Thoughts on the Invisibility of Afro-Caribbean Lesbians," *Lesbians in Canada, op. cit.*, pp. 48-60 and many other anthologies; Makeda Silvera, ed., *Piece of My Heart: A Lesbian of Colour Anthology* (Toronto: Sister Vision, 1991); Jackie Goldsby, "What It Means To Be Coloured Me" in *Out/Look*, No. 9 (Summer 1990), pp. 8-17; Ekua Omosupe, "Black/Lesbian/Bulldagger" in *differences*, V. 3, No. 2, Special "Queer Theory: Lesbian and Gay Sexualities" issue, Summer 1991, pp. 101-111; Helen (charles), "'Queer Nigger': Theorizing 'White' Activism" in Joseph Bristow and Angelia R. Wilson, eds., *Activating Theory: Lesbian, Gay Bisexual Politics* (London: Lawrence and Wishart, 1993), pp. 97-106; karen/miranda augustine, "bizarre women, exotic bodies and outrageous sex: or if annie sprinkle was a black ho she wouldn't be *all* that" in *Border/Lines*, No. 32, 1994, "Queer Licks" issue, pp. 22-24; Dionne Brand, *Bread Out of Stone,* (Toronto: Coach House, 1994); also see Beth Brant, "The Good Red Road: Journeys of Homecoming in Native Women's Writing" in Linda Carty, ed., *And Still We Rise: Feminist Political Mobilizing in Contemporary Canada* (Toronto: Women's Press, 1993, pp. 355-369; and many of the essays in Mona Oikawa, Dionne Falconer and Ann Dector, *Resist: Essays against a Homophobic Culture* (Toronto: Women's Press, 1994). Also see the controversy over the publication of a racist ad in *The Body Politic*, No. 113, Apr. 1985, p. 30.

66. See Michael Alhonte, "The Politics of Ageism" in *Gay Insurgent*, No. 7, 1981, pp. 6-7, and his "Confronting Ageism" in Tsang, ed., *The Age Taboo* (Boston: Alyson, 1981), pp. 156-159; and *Young, Gay and Proud* (Boston: Alyson, 1980).

67. For the earlier period, see Mark Whitehead, "Gay Youth and Sexual Laws," for Gay Youth Group, 1976. In 1988 the age of consent for "anal intercourse" which replaced "buggery" was lowered to eighteen in "private" but was still criminalized if it involved more than two people or was in "public." There have recently been successful lower-level court challenges to the constitutionality of this section. In 1988 the offence of "gross indecency" was abolished and the basic age of sexual consent was set at fourteen. For sexual activity with those in positions of trust or authority or in a relation of dependence, the age of consent was set at eighteen. It is illegal to buy the sexual service of anyone under the age of eighteen. See "Young People and Sex" in *Forum 128* (Toronto), 1993.

68. See David Adkin's, *Out: Stories of Lesbian and Gay Youth* (National Film Board, 1993) and also the Central Toronto Youth Services video, *Pride and Prejudice.*

69. See George W. Smith, "The Ideology of 'Fag': The School Experience of Gay Students," unpublished manuscript, Ontario Institute for Studies in Education. Also see Didi Khayatt, "Compulsory Heterosexuality: Schools and Lesbian Students" in Marie Campbell and Ann Manicom, eds., *Knowledge, Experience, and Ruling Relations: Studies in the Social Organization of Knowledge,* (Toronto: University of Toronto Press, 1995), pp. 149-163.

70. See George Smith, "Fraser Committee Anti-sexual and Simplistic," an edited version of the Right to Privacy Committee submission to the Special Committee on Pornography and Prostitution, in *Action!*, V. 4, No. 1, 1984. For the problems lesbian, gay and bisexual youth encounter in residential services, see Carol-Anne O'Brien, Robb Travers and Laurie Bell, *No Safe Bed: Lesbian, Gay and Bisexual Youth in Residential Services,* (Toronto: Central Toronto Youth Services, 1993) and Carol-Anne O'Brien, "The Social Organization of the Treatment of Lesbian, Gay and Bisexual Youth in Group Homes and Youth Shelters" in *Canadian Review of Social Policies,* No. 34, 1994, pp. 37-57.

71. See Andrew Sorfleet and Chris Bearchell, "The sex police in a moral panic: How the 'youth porn' law is being used to censor artists and persecute youth sexuality" in *Parallelograme*, V. 20, No. 1, 1994, pp. 8-21; "Young People and Sex," *Forum 125* (Toronto), 1993; and John Greyson, *After the Bath*, broadcast on CBC Newsworld's *Rough Cuts*, May 5, 1995.

72. See Carol-Anne O'Brien and Lorna Weir, "Lesbians and Gay Men Inside and Outside Families" in Nancy Mandell and Ann Duffy, eds., *Canadian Families: Diversity, Conflict and Change* (Toronto: Harcourt Bruce Canada, 1995), pp. 111-140.

73. See Gay Fathers of Toronto, *Gay Fathers: Some of Their Stories, Experience and Advice* (Toronto: Gay Fathers, 1981). This book, however, does not adequately investigate the isolation that gay fathers experience and why they need support groups not only to deal with the problems in their families but also to make up for the lack of support from within the gay community.

74. On lesbian mothers, see Francie Wyland, *Motherhood, Lesbianism and Child Custody* (Falling Wall Press, 1977); Gillian E. Hanscombe and Jackie Foster, *Rocking the Cradle, Lesbian Mothers: A Challenge in Family Living* (Boston: Alyson, 1982); and Kathy Arnup, "Lesbian Mothers and Child Custody" in Ian Lumsden, ed., "Sexuality and the State" issue of the *Atkinson Review of Canadian Studies*, V. 1, No. 2, Spring 1984; Wendy Gross, "Judging the Best Interests of the Child: Child Custody and the Homosexual Parent" in *Canadian Journal of Women and the Law*, V. 1, No. 2, 1986, pp. 505-531; Sharon Dale Stone, "Lesbian Mothers Organizing" in her *Lesbians in Canada, op. cit.*, pp. 198-208; Dian Day, "Lesbian/Mother" in *Lesbians in Canada*, pp. 35-47; Katherine Arnup, "'Mothers Just Like Others': Lesbians, Divorce and Child Custody in Canada" in *Canadian Journal of Women and the Law*, V. 3, No. 1, 1989, pp. 18-32; Arnup, "'We Are Family!': Lesbian Mothers in Canada" in *Resources for Feminist Research*, V. 20, No. 3/4, Fall/Winter 1991, pp. 101-107; Katherine Arnup, "Finding Fathers: Artificial Insemination, Lesbians and the Law" in *Canadian Journal of Women and the Law*, V. 7, No. 1, 1994, pp. 97-115; and Arnup, ed., *Lesbian Parenting, Living With Pride and Prejudice* (Charlottetown: gynergy, 1995).

75. Gerald Hannon, "No Sorrow, No Pity," Jackson and Persky, *op. cit.*, pp. 64-72; and Joanne Doucette, "Being Disabled in the Lesbian Community: A Lot of Places are Out of Bounds" in *Rites*, V. 1, No. 9, Mar. 1985, p. 9; "Access For Disabled Women," Disabled Lesbian Caucus of the Disabled Women's Network, *Rites*, V. 3, No. 8, Feb. 1987, p. 4; and Joanne Doucette, "Redefining Difference: Disabled Lesbians Resist" in *Lesbians in Canada, op. cit.*, pp. 61-72.

76. Gregg Blachford, *op. cit.*, pp. 184-210. Blachford builds on the work of the Birmingham School of Cultural Studies in applying notions of resistance and accommodation to the experiences of gay men. The following references are to this article.

77. On this see Joan Nestle, "Butch-Femme Relationships: Sexual Courage in the 1950s" in Joan Nestle, *A Restricted Country* (Ithaca, NY: Firebrand, 1987), pp. 100-109; Joan Nestle, ed., *The Persistent Desire: A Femme/Butch Reader*, (Boston: Alyson, 1992); Elizabeth Lapovsky Kennedy and Madeline Davis, "The Reproduction of Butch-Fem Roles: A Social Constructionist Approach" in Kathy Peiss and Christina Simmons, eds., *Passion and Power, Sexuality in History* (Philadelphia: Temple University, 1989), pp. 241-256 and their *Boots of Leather, Slippers of Gold: The History of a Lesbian Community*, (New York: Routledge, 1993), especially pp. 323-371; and also see Lynne Fernie and Arelyn Weissman, *Forbidden Love* (National Film Board, 1993).

78. Dennis Altman does not seem to understand this with his notion of the "homosexualization" of America. He does not make an adequate distinction between the cultural production of oppressed groups like gays and the cultural production and reproduction of the dominant social order. This lets him place on equivalent levels the "Americanization" of gay culture — the effect of the hegemonic culture on gay cultures — and the homosexualization of America — the subordinate culture's impact on the dominant culture. His analysis misses how hegemonic cultural production systematically works to separate gay cultural production from its gay cultural, social, and erotic contexts, thereby repackaging it in a "neutral" straight fashion for the mass market. Altman, *op. cit.*

79. On some of this, see Stephen Madison, "A queered pitch" in *Red Pepper* (London), No. 9, Feb. 1995, p. 27.

80. See Rachel Giese, "Lesbian Chic: I Feel Pretty and Witty and Gay" in *Border/Lines*, "Queer Licks" issue, No. 32, 1994, pp. 27-29.

81. On this see Chauncey, *Gay New York* (New York: Basic, 1994) and Esther Newton, *Mother Camp* (Chicago and London: The University of Chicago Press, 1979).

82. See Steven Maynard, "What Color Is Your Underwear?: Class, Whiteness and Advertising" in *Border/Lines, op. cit.*

83. For instance, see Judith Butler's *Gender Trouble, op. cit.*, although she focuses more on gender "performativity" in social discourse than the actual social performance of gender. Also see the problems in Marjorie Garber, *Vested Interests: Cross-Dressing and Cultural Anxiety* (New York: HarperCollins, 1992).

84. Ki Namaste, "Too Queer for Middle America" in *Fuse*, V. 18, No. 4, Summer 1995, p. 27-28. Also see Kate Bornstein, *Gender Outlaw: On Men, Women and the Rest of Us* (London and New York: Routledge, 1994).

85. Gayle Rubin's, "Thinking Sex: Notes For a Radical Theory of the Politics of Sexuality" in Carole Vance, ed., *Pleasure and Danger: Exploring Female Sexuality* (Boston and London: Routledge and Kegan Paul, 1984), pp. 267-319, which argues for a separation of sexual and gender analysis, has had a major influence on the development of queer theory, including the very influential work on Eve Kosofsky Sedgwick in *The Epistemology of the Closet* (Berkeley: University of California Press, 1990). See my unpublished paper "'Queer Theory' Versus Heterosexual Hegemony: Towards a Historical Materialism for Gay Men and Lesbians," originally presented at the "Queer Sites" lesbian and gay studies conference in Toronto, May 14, 1993.

86. This observation comes from Didi Khayatt, personal conversation. An important exception who continues an important focus on gender in his work is George Chauncey including in *Gay New York* (New York: Basic Books, 1994).

87. Marshall, *op. cit.*, p. 154.

88. This is suggested in Adrienne Rich, "Compulsory Heterosexuality ..." in Stimpson and Persons, eds., *Women, Sex and Sexuality* (Chicago and London: The University of Chicago Press, 1980), pp. 62-91 and many other collections and in some interpretations built upon Rich's work.

89. See Esther Newton, "The Mythic Mannish Lesbian: Radclyffe Hall and the New Woman" in *Signs*, V. 9, No. 4, Summer 1984, pp. 557-575.

90. See Joan Nestle, "Butch-Fem Relationships: Sexual Courage in the 1950's" in *Heresies*, No. 12, pp. 21-24; Nestle, "The Fem Question" in Vance, ed., *Pleasure and Danger* (Boston, London, Melbourne and Henley: Routledge and Kegan Paul, 1984), pp. 232-241.

91. Mariana Valverde, "The Religion of the 'Race' of Women: A Critique of Mary Daly" in *Rites*, V. 2, No. 5, Oct. 1985, pp. 14-15; and her *Sex, Power and Pleasure* (Toronto: The Women's Press, 1985), pp. 192-198.

92. See Mary McIntosh, "Queer Theory and the War of the Sexes" in Joseph Bristow and Angelia R. Wilson, eds., *Activating Theory: Lesbian, Gay and Bisexual Politics* (London: Lawrence and Wishart, 1993), pp. 30-52.

93. Rubin, "Sexual Politics, the New Right and the Sexual Fringe" in Tsang, ed., *The Age Taboo, op. cit.*, p. 109.

94. See the interview with Foucault by Alexander Wilson and Bob Gallagher, "Sex, Power and the Politics of Identity" in *The Advocate*, No. 400, Aug. 7, 1984, pp. 27-30.

95. Didi Herman in her paper "Law and Morality Revisited: The Politics of Regulating Sado-Masochistic Porn and Practice," presented at the Canadian and American Law and Society Association conferences in June, 1994 raises some similar concerns, although in a far more alarmist and moralistic fashion. By suggesting that these practices need to be regulated and then not suggesting any non-criminal forms of regulation, Herman, by implication, lends support to criminalization perspectives. On SM, also see Mike Macnair, "The contradictory politics of SM" in Simon Sheperd and Mick Wallis, eds., *Coming On Strong: Gay Politics and Culture* (London: Unwin Hyman, 1989), pp. 147-162; Tim Edwards, *Erotics and Politics: Gay Male Sexuality, Masculinity and Feminism*, (London and New York: Routledge, 1994), especially pp. 74-89; Samois, *What Color is Your Handkerchief? A Lesbian S/M Reader* (Boston: Alyson, 1979) and *Coming to Power: Writings and Graphics on Lesbian S/M* (Boston: Alyson, 1981); and Robin Ruth Linden, Darlene R. Pagano, *et al.*, *Against Sadomasochism: A Radical Feminist Analysis* (East Palo Alto, CA: Frog in the Well, 1982) — which generally takes up a sexual pessimist and feminist

anti-pornography perspective — but a number of the contributions by feminists of colour make visible some important insights.

96. Jeffrey Weeks, "The Development of Sexual Theory and Sexual Politics" in Brake, ed., *Human Sexual Relations* (New York: Pantheon, 1982), p. 306.

97. For an elaboration of this position, see Mariana Valverde, "Feminism Meets Fist-Fucking: Getting Lost in Lesbian S and M" in *The Body Politic*, Feb./Mar. 1980. Also see her *Sex, Power and Pleasure, op. cit.*

98. See, for example, Ed Jackson, "History: Doing It in the Archives" in *The Body Politic*, No. 86, Sept. 1982, pp. 33-34, which records some of the discussion at the Wilde 1982 history conference. Also see Boswell's "Revolutions, Universals, Categories" in *Salmagundi*, No. 58/59, Fall 1982/ Winter 1983, pp. 89-113, wherein he makes a distinction between the "nominalist" (i.e., in his view the "emergence thesis") and what he calls the "realist" approach. Also, see the controversies surrounding the "Sex and the State" lesbian/gay history conference held in Toronto, July 1985. On this see Rick Bebout, "Sex and the State: Finding History, Making History" in *The Body Politic*, No. 118, Sept. 1985, pp. 30-33; Gary Kinsman, Pamela Walker, and Kerry Burke, "Sex and the State: Conference Notes" in *Rites*, V. 2, No. 4, Sept. 1985, pp. 8-9; the controversies include contributions by Wayne Dynes, Barry Adam, Gary Kinsman, and Stephen Murray in the *Sociologists' Gay Caucus Newsletter*, No. 45, Oct. 1985, and No. 46, Jan. 1986; and Jeffrey Weeks, "Sex and the State: Their Laws, Our Lives" in *History Workshop Journal*, No. 21, Spring 1986.

99. For instance, see Steven Epstein, "Gay Politics and Ethnic Identity: The Limits of Social Constructionism" in *Socialist Review*, No. 93/94 (May-Aug. 1987), pp. 9-56 and David F. Greenberg, *The Construction of Homosexuality* (Chicago: The University of Chicago Press, 1988), and my review of it in *The Canadian Journal of Sociology*, V. 15, No. 1, Winter 1990, pp. 112-115.

100. See Eve Sedgwick, *The Epistemology of the Closet, op. cit.*, p. 40.

101. Altman, "What Changed in the Seventies?" Gay Left Collective, ed., *Homosexuality, Power and Politics, op. cit.*, p. 61.

102. Joseph Harry and Devall, *op. cit.*, p. 135.

103. See Raymond Breton, "Institutional Completeness of Ethnic Communities" in *American Journal of Sociology*, V. 70, 1964, pp. 195-205.

104. Stephen O. Murray, "The Institutional Elaboration of a Quasi-Ethnic Community in Canada," Harry and Mon Singh Das, eds., *Homosexuality International Perspective* (New Delhi: Vikas Publishing House, 1980), p. 39.

105. *Ibid.*, p. 41.

106. See Roxana Ng, "Sex, Ethnicity or Class: Some Methodological Considerations," unpublished paper prepared for the British Sociological Society meeting, Apr. 1982; Ng, "Constructing Ethnic Phenomena: An Account from the Perspective of Immigrant Women" in *Canadian Ethnic Studies*, V. 8, No. 1, 1981, pp. 97-108; Ng, "Immigrant Women and the State: A Study in the Social Organization of Knowledge," Ph.D. dissertation, Sociology, Ontario Institute for Studies in Education; and Ng, "Immigrant Women in Canada: A Socially Constructed Category" in *Resources for Feminist Research*, V. 15, No. 1 (Mar. 1986), pp. 13-15. On the development of the Canadian State policy of multiculturalism, see Roxana Ng, "Multiculturalism as ideology: A textual analysis" in Marie Campbell and Ann Manicom, eds., *Knowledge, Experience, and Ruling Relations: Studies in the Social Organization of Knowledge* (Toronto: University of Toronto Press, 1995) pp. 35-48.

107. See, for example, the Toronto Right to Privacy Committee's brief presented by Bob Gallagher, Paul Rapsey, and John Burt to the Ontario Provincial Legislature's Standing Committee on Resource Development, Sept. 25, 1981, and the RTPC's "We Are a Community!" submitted to the Council of the City of Toronto's Neighbourhoods Committee concerning the Bruner report on relations between the Homosexual Community and the Police, on Nov. 3, 1981.

108. Paul Walter, president of the Metro Toronto Police Association, declared in 1981 that the Toronto police "have grave concerns about recognizing homosexuals as a legitimate minority

with status under human rights legislation." Quoted in Alden Baker's article "Gays No Minority Group, Police Association Says" in *The Globe and Mail*, Aug. 30, 1981. Renaissance, a right-wing moral conservative group, has also tried to separate gays from "legitimate" minorities as has Citizen's United for Responsible Education in Ontario. This has also become one of the main lines of attack used by right-wing groups in the U.S. The most recent federal politicians to reject lesbians and gay men as being part of a minority group are from the Reform party and Liberal backbenchers Roseanne Skoke and Tom Wappel.

109. See Joyn Cozijn, "Sydney 1981: A Community Taking Shape" in *Gay Information*, No. 9/10, Autumn/Winter 1982, pp. 4-10, for an interesting critique of "community" as a mirage of gay politics in the 1980s.

110. For a similar approach in relation to feminism, see Himani Bannerji, "Introducing Racism: Notes towards an Anti-Racist Feminism," and "But Who Speaks for Us? Experience and Agency in Conventional Feminist Paradigms" in her *Thinking Through: Essays on Feminism, Marxism, and Anti-Racism* (Toronto: Women's Press, 1995), pp. 41-95. Also see Elizabeth V. Spelman, *Inessential Woman: Problems of Exclusion in Feminist Thought* (Boston: Beacon Press, 1988).

111. See Bannerji, "But Who Speaks for Us?" *op. cit.*

112. See Gary Kinsman, "1984: The Police are Still With Us" in *Rites*, No. 1, May 1984; Gary Kinsman and Doug Wilson interview with Dennis Findlay and Philip McLeod, "Police Entrapment: Fighting Back with Courtwatch" in *Rites*, V. 1, No. 6, Nov. 1984, pp. 9-11.

113. See Bell, Weinberg, and Hammersmith, *Sexual Preference* (Bloomington: Indiana University Press, 1981). For a critique of this, see George Smith's review in *The Body Politic*, No. 79, Dec. 1981, pp. 29-30.

114. See Simon Levay, *The Sexual Brain* (Cambridge, M.A.: The MIT Press, 1994). For more critical commentary, see Kay Diaz, "Are Gay Men Born That Way?" in *Z Magazine* V. 5, No. 12, Dec. 1992, pp. 42-46; Gail Vines, *Raging Hormones: Do They Rule Our Lives?* (Berkeley, Los Angeles: University of California Press, 1993), especially pp. 85-123; and also see Gary Kinsman, "Not In Our Genes: Against Biological and Genetic Determinism" in *Sociologists' Lesbian and Gay Caucus Newsletter* No. 76, Fall 1993 Newsletter, pp. 4-6; and my "Queerness Is Not in Our Genes: Against Biological Determinism — For Social Liberation" in *Border/Lines*, No. 33, 1994, pp. 27-30.

115. An example of gay organizing that relied on this minority community approach in relation to schooling might help clarify its limitations as well as the persistence of the right-wing on these questions. In 1980, lesbian and gay groups approached the Toronto Board of Education to ask for a formal liaison committee between the board and the gay and lesbian community. Their main line of approach was that gays were a legitimate minority group just like the other communities that had liaison committees. This simple request provoked a beehive of opposition. Moral conservative groups like Renaissance and "Positive Parents" sprang into action, arguing that this proposal challenged the "traditional" family as well as "parents' rights" to control the moral upbringing of their children. They campaigned against the "recruiting" of young people by homosexuals. The media focused on this mobilization of bigotry, which they portrayed as "parental opposition" to the proposal; as a result, it was dropped like a hot potato. The board did, however, adopt a sexual-orientation protection clause, which applied to its own employees. Unfortunately, the needs and concerns of lesbian and gay students were ignored and the following clause was included in the resolution: "That the Board will not countenance the proselytization of homosexuality within its jurisdiction." No similar policy existed in relation to heterosexuality. Discussion of homosexuality was allowed only "when it arises out of the curriculum" and, of course, homosexuality was not a regular and legitimate part of the school curriculum. In adopting this anti-proselytization clause and in limiting discussion of homosexuality, the board gave ground to the heterosexist ideology that lesbians and gay men are a special threat to young people. In retrospect, it is clear that the Board did not view gays and lesbians as a minority community just like the others. The response elicited by the

simple request for a liaison committee posed fundamental questions about sexuality, schooling, and family. See Leo Casey, "Gay Rights, the Election and the Toronto Board" in *Mudpie*, V. 1, No. 6, Nov. 1980, p. 13; and Bob Davis, "Toronto's Right-Wing Hate Campaign: Some Thoughts" in *Mudpie*, V. 2, No. 4, Apr. 1981. Later in the 1980s the Board discussed a policy on sex education that included more progressive proposals for the teaching of issues regarding lesbianism and homosexuality. In 1986 there was a struggle again to have the Board address lesbian and gay concerns. This occurred after the federal government had made announcements regarding equality rights and the murder of a gay man by Toronto Board of Education students (on some of this see the fictionalized John Greyson video — *The Making of Monsters*), and it focused on the needs and concerns of lesbian and gay students themselves, many of whom spoke out quite strongly and forcefully at board meetings. In the end, there was only a partial victory. See John Campey, "School Board Votes to Fight Discrimination with One Hand Tied behind Its Back" in *Rites*, V. 3, No. 1, May 1986, p. 4. In 1991 the Toronto Board of Education majority supported efforts to integrate some lesbian and gay concerns into aspects of the school curriculum. A draft resource document was prepared by an advisory committee that did not include a single open lesbian or gay member, although it did include Joseph Berger — a psychiatrist notorious for his efforts to "cure" homosexuals. The first draft was critiqued by the Lesbian and Gay Employees Group of the Board for its heterosexist and homophobic content and a second draft was then produced, which was substantially rewritten with the inclusion of edited excerpts from the work of lesbian academic Helen Lenskyj. See Toronto Board of Education, "Sexual Orientation: Homosexuality, Lesbianism and Homophobia" in *A Resource Guide for Teachers of Health Education in Secondary Schools: Draft for Review* February 1992. The right wing responded that the new draft was "anti-family" and "anti-heterosexual," and Citizen's United for Responsible Education (CURE) began to mobilize "parental" opposition to the new Board policy. See John Campey, Tim McCaskell, John Miller, and Vanessa Russell, "Opening the Classroom Closet: Dealing with Sexual Orientation at the Toronto Board of Education" in Susan Prentice, ed., *Sex in Schools: Canadian Education and Sexual Regulation* (Toronto: Our Schools/Our Selves, 1994), pp. 82-100. For a similar controversy in Kingston, see "Kingston Board Controversy: Homophobia Got to Go!" *Rites*, V. 3, No. 9, Mar. 1987, p. 5. In New York City, the right wing was able to organize a furore over the Rainbow "multicultural" curriculum because it would have mentioned gay and lesbian families to grade-school children, which led to the proposed language being changed. See Margaret Cerullo, "Hope and Terror: The Paradox of Gay and Lesbian Politics in the '90s" in *Radical America*, V. 24, No. 3, p. 16.

116. Gay Left Collective, "Happy Families? Pedophilia Examined" in *Gay Left*, No. 7, Winter 1978/1979, p. 3.

117. For a similar discussion of the relationship between movement and community regarding lesbians and feminism, see Nym Hughes, Yvonne Johnson, and Yvette Perreault, *Stepping out of Line: A Workbook on Lesbianism and Feminism* (Vancouver: Press Gang, 1984).

118. See Gary Kinsman, "Whitewash: The Moral Panic" in *Pink Ink*, V. 1, No. 4, Oct. 1983, pp. 12-13; Dennis Altman, "AIDS: The Politicization of an Epidemic" in *Socialist Review*, No. 78, pp. 93-109; Evan Collins and Gary Kinsman, "The Politics of AIDS" in *Rites*, V. 1, No. 8, Feb. 1985, pp. 12-13, 17; Cindy Patton, *Sex and Germs* (Montréal: Black Rose Books, 1986) and her *Inventing AIDS* (London and New York: Routledge, 1990); Dennis Altman, *AIDS in The Mind of America* (Garden City, NJ: Anchor Press/Doubleday, 1986) and his *Power and Community, Organizational and Cultural Responses to AIDS* (London: Taylor and Francis, 1994); Gary Kinsman, "Their Silence, Our Deaths: What Can the Social Sciences Offer to AIDS Research?" in Diane E. Goldstein, ed., *Talking AIDS: Interdisciplinary Perspectives on Acquired Immune Deficiency Syndrome* (St. John's: Institute for Social and Economic Research (ISER), 1991), ISER Policy Papers No. 12, and my "Managing AIDS Organizing: 'Consultation,' 'Partnership,' and the National AIDS Strategy" in William K. Carroll, ed., *Organizing Dissent, Contemporary Social Movements in Theory and Practice* (Toronto: Garamond, 1992), pp. 215-231.

119. See Kinsman, "Constructing Sexual Problems: 'These Things Could Lead to the Tragedy of Our Species'," in Les Samuelson, ed., *Power and Resistance: Critical Thinking about Canadian Social Issues* (Halifax: Fernwood, 1994), p. 179 and p. 188 note 21. The headline comes from *The Chronicle Herald*, Sept. 19, 1988, p. 1.

120. Kinsman, "Their Silence, Our Deaths," *op. cit.*; "Managing AIDS Organizing," *op. cit.*; "Constructing Sexual Problems," *op. cit.*, pp. 179-181; and "'Responsibility' as a strategy of governance: Regulating people living with AIDS and lesbians and gay men in Ontario," forthcoming in *Economy and Society*, August 1996.

121. See "'Responsibility' as a strategy of governance: Regulating people living with AIDS and lesbians and gay men in Ontario," *op. cit.*

122. See Sanders, "Constructing Lesbian and Gay Rights," op. cit., especially p. 128; Didi Herman, Rights of Passage: Struggles for Lesbian and Gay Legal Equality (Toronto: University of Toronto Press, 1994), especially pp. 27-28, 59-61, 132-133; and Karen Andrews, "Ancient Affections: Gays, Lesbians and Family Status" in Katherine Arnup, ed., *Lesbian Parenting, Living with Pride and Prejudice* (Chalottetown: gynergy, 1995), pp. 358-377.

123. See Sanders, "Constructing Lesbian and Gay Rights," *op. cit.*, including p. 123; and Herman, *Rights of Passage, op. cit.*, pp. 25-26, 133-139.

124. See Sanders, "Constructing Lesbian and Gay Rights," *op. cit.*, pp. 103, 108, 123, 127; and Herman, *Rights of Passage, op. cit.*, p. 28.

125. See Sanders, "Constructing Lesbian and Gay Rights," *op. cit.*; and Herman, *Rights of Passage, op. cit.*

126. Also see Carol Allen, "Who Gets To Be Family: Some Thoughts on the Lesbian and Gay Fight for Equality" in Linda Carty, ed., *And Still We Rise: Feminist Political Mobilizing in Contemporary Canada* (Toronto: Women's Press, 1993), pp. 101-107.

127. See John Wilson, "Spousal Benefits Conference: On Our Own Terms?" *Rites*, V. 6, No. 4, Sept. 1989, pp. 4,18,; David Rayside, "Inside the Fringe: Mobilizing for Same-Sex Benefits in Ontario," unpublished paper presented at the Second Annual Meeting of the Canadian Lesbian and Gay Studies Association, Montréal, June 3-4, 1995, p. 4; and Susan Ursel, "Bill 167 and Full Human Rights" in Katherine Arnup, ed., *Lesbian Parenting: Living with Pride and Prejudice, op. cit.*, pp. 341-343.

128. See Sanders, "Constructing Lesbian and Gay Rights," *op. cit.*, pp. 122-123; David Rayside, "Inside the Fringe ..." *op. cit.*; Susan Ursel, "Bill 167 and Full Human Rights" in Katherine Arnup, ed., *Lesbian Parenting: Living with Pride and Prejudice, op. cit.*, pp. 341-351; and Nancy Nicol's video, *Gay Pride and Prejudice* (1994).

129. *The Globe and Mail*, June 23, 1994.

130. Some of these concerns are raised by Susan Ursel in "Bill 167 and Full Human Rights," *op. cit.*, p. 346-351.

131. See Jeff Lindstrom, "Limited Adoption Rights Granted, But Appeal Could Still Be Filed after Election" in *Xtra!* No. 276, May 26, 1995, p. 12.

132. See Cindy Filipenko, "BC Grits Slam Adoption" in *Xtra!* No. 276, May 26, 1995, p. 12

133. For more elaboration, see "'Responsibility' as a strategy of governance: Regulating people living with AIDS and lesbians and gay men in Ontario," forthcoming in *Economy and Society*, August 1996.

134. See Frank Mort, "Sexuality, Regulation and Contestation," Gay Left Collective, eds., *Homosexuality, Power and Politics* (London: Allison and Busby, 1980), and see chapter 8.

135. See Brettel Dawson, in Mariana Valverde, compiled, *Radically Rethinking Regulation Workshop Report*, Centre of Criminology, University of Toronto, 1994, pp. 20-22.

136. Barbara Findlay, "A lesbian's relationship is finally recognized, but only so the government can deny her a welfare cheque" in *Xtra!*, No. 257, Sept. 2, 1994, p. 15.

137. "Drug Cards and Welfare" in *Capital Xtra!* (Bill 167 Supplement), June 17, 1994, p. iii.

138. Brenda Cossman, in Mariana Valverde, ed., *Radically Rethinking Regulation Workshop Report, op. cit.*, pp. 23-24.

139. This shift to issues of youth sexuality can be seen, for instance, in the federal government's policy reports on sex-related questions: *The Badgley Report: The Report of the Committee on Sexual Offences against Children and Youths* (Ottawa: Dept. of Supply and Services, 1984), two volumes; the *Fraser Report: Report of the Special Committee on Pornography and Prostitution* (Ottawa: Dept. of Supply and Services, 1985), which shift a good deal of attention to sexual legislation focusing on distinctions between adult and youth. On this, see Deborah R. Brock and Gary Kinsman, "Patriarchal Relations Ignored: An Analysis and Critique of the Badgley Report on Sexual Offences against Children and Youths" in *Regulating Sex: An Anthology of Commentaries on the Badgley and Fraser Reports* (Burnaby: Simon Fraser University, 1986). On the youth-pornography law, see next chapter.

140. On this see Susan Hemmings, "Horrific Practices: How Lesbians Were Presented in the Newspapers of 1978" in Gay Left Collective, ed., *Homosexuality: Power and Politics* (London and New York: Allison and Busby, 1980), pp. 162-167.

141. Weeks, "Capitalism and the Organization of Sex," *op. cit.*, p. 18.

10.

Danger Signals: Moral Conservatism, the Straight Media, the Sex Police, and AIDS

Accommodation, "responsibilization" and "normalization," as outlined in chapter 9, are only several of the possible lines of development in the present period. There is also a right-wing, moral-conservative response to lesbian and gay liberation and feminism. The post-war years have seen the undermining of previous relations of social, sexual, and gender regulation, the emergence of new forms of sexual regulation, and the initiation of a profound crisis of the regulation of sexuality. Different groups are offering different solutions to this crisis. The feminist, lesbian, and gay movements, however hesitantly and implicitly, have posed significant challenges to dominant sexual and gender organization and have begun to create new forms of social and erotic life.

These social changes and struggles are occurring in the context of a profound shift in the organization of official politics and social policy in the 1980s and 1990s toward a focus on deficit reduction and "fiscal responsibility," and away from Keynesian social interventionism.[1] This leads toward the dismantling of many of the gains working class and poor people had won — often in a distorted form — within the "Welfare State," and has often, but not always, been coupled with a trend toward a more authoritarian strategy of State formation in the face of economic and social troubles in the "advanced" capitalist patriarchal countries.[2] In part this is motivated by a response to the excesses of "liberal" or "permissive" social- and moral-reform legislation identified with the 1960s, and more recently to the affirmative-action and social-equality programs that were won by black and feminist movements. This context has made the progress of queer-liberation struggles more difficult on a number of fronts. While there is now a more widespread liberal tolerance for lesbians and gay men than before there is also a vociferous anti-lesbian, anti-gay minority that has connections in very high places.

Moral Conservatism

Moral conservatives combat the gains of feminism and gay liberation by attempting to reestablish what they see as the basic features of previous sex/gender relations, patriarchal relations, and heterosexual hegemony. In the U.S., the moral-conservative new right has had the most success and has focused on opposition to women's reproductive rights, lesbian and gay rights, and increasingly the rights of immigrants and people on social assistance as well. The new-right "Moral Majority" would make abortion the equivalent of murder and cut off federal funding to any agency prohibiting discrimination against lesbians and gay men and to any group or individual suggesting that homosexuality is an "acceptable lifestyle." The Moral Majority would also cut funding for school programs that "tend to denigrate, diminish, or deny the role differences between the sexes as it has been historically understood."[3] In 1986, Reagan-appointed Supreme Court judges upheld the constitutionality of sodomy laws against homosexual acts that continue to exist in many States. In the U.S., the right wing is increasingly focusing on opposition to lesbians and gays, and is arguing that lesbians and gays are not a legitimate minority group and that they are demanding "special rights."[4] This new-right organizing achieved some success in influencing the Reagan and Bush regimes and in having some impact on the new Republican majority in the U.S. Congress.

In Britain, the Thatcher government's anti-union and "neo-liberal" economic policies also provided the context in 1988 for Section 28, which stated that a local authority shall not "promote the teaching ... of the acceptability of homosexuality as a pretended family relationship." This provided for the cutting off of State funding for any local government body that "promoted" lesbianism and male homosexuality.[5]

Some middle-class, and even working-class, strata experienced the social changes of the 1960s and 1970s and more recent changes as the breaking down of "social and moral order." Their anxieties were shaped by media portrayals of the "generation gap," the "youth revolt," the "crisis of the family," and common-sense conservative and traditionalist ideologies. Social disturbances were blamed on "permissive" legislation, the liberal bureaucratic State's intrusion into people's "private lives," and social movements such as feminism and gay liberation, which were portrayed as going beyond legitimate thresholds to question the family and moral order itself.

This moral-conservative "backlash" was fostered by both the contradictions and inadequacies of the 1960s "liberal" legislation and the social changes of post-war patriarchal capitalism. Middle-class elements are unable to see that it is social transformations within capitalism itself that has undermined the stability of their "family." Some of these members of the "silent majority" have called for an end to permissiveness, a return to law and order, and a return to a mythical security and stability of a past that never existed.

This anti-permissiveness, or moral authoritarianism, is shaped and organized by various religious and secular right-wing groups, conservative parties, elements of the mass media, and State agencies such as the police. These right-wing forces appear to provide real, workable solutions by feeding on the conservative attachment to "law and order" and racist, sexist, and heterosexist "common-sense" ideas that exist in popular culture and are recreated every day through the media and hegemonic social relations.[6]

The way in which people live is often bound up with certain gender and sexual "truths" — "the natural attitude" — for example, that only heterosexuality is natural and normal and that women and men have separate and distinct natural roles. Any challenge to this order is perceived as a threat to their existence. Open lesbians, gay men, and even bisexuals challenge these notions of gender and sexual normality, violating social boundaries. The assertion that lesbianism and homosexuality are equally valid ways of life poses a challenge to their sense of security in the world. The resultant fears and anxieties can be organized and hegemonized by moral-conservative politics.

In the moral-conservative view, "sexual liberation," prostitutes on city streets, abortion, pornography, sexuality education in the schools, AIDS education that includes safer sex, and lesbians and gays symbolize all the changes that have supposedly undermined the moral order — they are manifestations of social decay itself. These groups are upset over the public visibility of sex that, according to them, belongs only in the private realm. They are particularly opposed to "deviant" sexualities.

"Pro-family" ideology has become central to the moral-conservative world view. The family in new-right discourse is an organizing focus for many single-issue campaigns (from "right-to-life," and anti-gay campaigns, to opposition to the Equal Rights Amendment and anti-bussing positions earlier in the U.S., and anti-childcare and anti-social welfare positions). It is also a highly emotional symbol. The idea of "proper" family life embodies the racist, sexist, heterosexist, and anti-working-class politics of many moral conservatives. The image of this "proper" family does not include Native people, blacks, Asians, Latinos, the poor, single mothers and lesbians and gay men.[7] It is no wonder than that these people respond vehemently when queers affirm "We are Family, get used to it!"

This new-right family, however, does not exist. It is an abstract idea — a heavenly family, removed from all the contradictions and problems that actual family networks face in the real world. It does not include all family forms and social-support networks but only one particular form of heterosexual, middle-class, and largely white family. This ideological universal family has been placed at the centre of new-right moral discourse, unifying diverse political positions. The symbol appeals to the pro-family sentiments that exist within various classes and social groupings, making it possible to organize a social bloc of different social forces against liberal bureaucrats, moral "degenerates," and "anti-family" militants to move society and State policy in a moral-conservative direction.

In Canada, this reaction to gay liberation and feminism has been organized through right-wing groups such as Right-to-Life, Campaign Life, Renaissance International, Positive Parents, REAL Women of Canada, Citizen's United for Responsible Education (CURE), The Coalition for Family Values, and, more subtly, through the media and police actions criminalizing queer sex. On the official political front, the Reform Party is very hostile to lesbian and gay rights, as are federal Liberal Party backbenchers like Roseanne Skoke and Tom Wappel. Provincially, the Ralph Klein Conservative government in Alberta, which has been busy slashing social programs, has also been acting to oppose any advance toward human rights for lesbians and gay men, and has gone so far as to threaten the independent existence of the Alberta Human Rights Commission.[8] The 1995 election of a right-wing Conservative government in Ontario also makes the progress of lesbian and gay struggles in that province more difficult.

There are, however, many divisions and distinctions between many on the economic and political right wing in Canada and moral conservatives. Some political and economic right-wing groups do not support the moral and sexual agenda of the moral-conservative right, even though in general these currents are far more supportive of these campaigns than are liberal or social-democratic currents. The potential for moral-conservative organizing in Canada is not yet entirely clear, but what is clear is that they have been able to have an impact on the official political terrain in moving it to the right,[9] on media framing of "social problems" and even in constitutional legal challenges as intervenors.[10] There have been various attempts to bring together groups such as Campaign Life, Renaissance, and REAL Women of Canada with the right wing of the federal Conservative Party, and also with Liberal Party and Reform Party networks, and some of these efforts at different points have achieved some success. Several "pro-family" conservatives played a key role in the successful Dump Joe Clark (as leader of the federal Conservative Party) movement, and later a "Family Caucus" was formed within the Tory caucus. More recently, a "pro-family" grouping has formed in the federal Liberal caucus.

Given the different religious and political-party composition and history in Canada, it is unlikely that the contradictory strands of the traditional economic right wing and the "pro-family" moral right can be brought together into as coherent a political project as they have south of the border. The term "moral conservatism" is therefore more appropriate, I suggest, than "new right" in the Canadian context. Moral conservatives had some influence with the Mulroney government and played an important role in the passage of Bill C-49, which criminalizes "communication" for the purposes of prostitution, and in pushing the federal Tories to put forward broad-ranging anti-porn proposals and, in 1993, the new youth-pornography law.[11] At present, the main danger does not come directly from these moral-conservative groups themselves but from how their organizing has helped shift the terms of public debate and influenced State policy. Moral conservatives cannot be ignored and their arguments must be addressed explicitly and undermined in a popular fashion. In the current federal context, the active and mobilized moral-conservative opposition to the inclusion of sexual-orientation protection in the recently passed hate-crimes legislation makes it more difficult to quickly proceed with sexual-orientation protection.

The Straight Media: Organizing the Social Relations of "Backlash"

The mass media have played a key role in organizing the social relations of "backlash"[12] to lesbian and gay organizing. With the emergence of gay liberation, the gay community, the new conditions of gay life, and the urban gay ghettoes, new media framings were produced to deal with gays. Lesbians have been excluded from much of this media coverage perpetuating lesbian invisibility, and it has been harder for the mainstream media to portray lesbians as a sexual danger. In some media coverage, however, lesbians raising children without men have been portrayed as a social danger.[13] The media are not monolithic and can present contradictory narratives regarding queers. In relation to gay/lesbian struggles, some coverage adopts more liberal framings while others are more defined by moral conservatism. One of the available media framings that constructs gay men as a sexual danger and came to influence the media coverage of gay men in relation to AIDS is explored below.

This framing has been most clearly presented in the CBS TV network's *Gay Power, Gay Politics*,[14] which articulated a major pre-AIDS image of gay men, although the early AIDS coverage associating gay men with "promiscuous" sex and sexual "excess" and the spread of AIDS built upon this kind of framing. In this program, which was seen in Canada and which has influenced the media in this country, gay men are no longer portrayed as weak, effeminate, or pitiful. They are instead presented as the latest minority group to become politically powerful — a social menace, potentially dangerous and violent. Gay men in San Francisco are presented as using their political weight to push for "absolute sexual freedom,"[15] and the gay movement as going beyond "legitimate" demands. Let us look at how this program is itself part of the social relations of "backlash" against gays and, by association, lesbians.

Gay Power, Gay Politics was the subject of sharp protests from the U.S. gay movement.[16] Unfortunately, these challenges were largely confined to the discourse of professional "objective" journalism itself, which is an important terrain on which to challenge the media. We cannot limit ourselves, however, to this terrain. This program is not simply an unprofessional or biased account of the gay community in San Francisco. We must explore how *Gay Power, Gay Politics* was produced, how its "objective" and "factual" character was established through the routine procedures of mainstream journalism. These typical "objective" news-making procedures take up the standpoints of ruling institutions and are involved in the making of heterosexual hegemony. News making is an ideological practice.[17]

First, the various "facts" of a story are given order and meaning through the editing process by a story line;[18] in this case the emergence of the gay movement as a "social menace." The influence of various social institutions and relations are embodied in a story. In this case, these range from the editorial policies of CBS to the reliance on expert sources of information like politicians, coroners, the police, and other journalists. The claim of objectivity serves to obscure how these social relations have entered into the account. *Gay Power, Gay Politics* leaves viewers with the impression they are seeing the real world. The program does not seem to be the product of activity in specific social relations. The work of developing the story line, ordering the segments, and the editing process have all dropped out of view.

> Much if not every trace of what has gone into the making of the account is
> obliterated and what remains is only the text [or program in this case]
> which aims at being read as "what actually happened."[19]

Gay Power, Gay Politics uses routine methods of establishing its objectivity. These range from the documentary format and the validity inherent in the medium of film,[20] to the confirmation of statements by "native informants" in the gay community, to the citing of actual historical events like the City Hall riots, the murder of Harvey Milk and Mayor Moscone, a reliance on "expert witnesses" from official agencies,[21] and the editing process itself. This makes it appear as though gays are, to an extent, the authors of the program, and obscures how the interviewing and editing process are under the control of the producers.

The gay community is represented as white and male, and is portrayed from the vantage point of a gay elite of professionals and businessmen. The gay movement is associated with "public sex" through scenes of "open cruising" in Buena Vista Park, and with sadomasochism through a visit to an SM "parlour." Gays in San Francisco, who have supposedly "achieved full civil rights and economic power," are going beyond these legitimate demands and moving "provocatively into the political arena."[22] They are corrupting the political process by pushing for "absolute sexual freedom" (which has been given content by previous associations with "public sex" and SM). If gays can't get what they want through the established channels, then Cleve Jones, who is worked up as a militant, demagogic character, will lead the gay mob into the streets.

None of this has much to do with the actualities of gay life in San Francisco during these years. Scenes have been ripped from their context in the lives of gay men and placed in a mythical construction provided by the story line and the editing process. We cannot read through the final product — the program — to see the real world of gay men, nor the actual history of gay politics. In real life, San Francisco gays have not gained their full civil and human rights, lesbians do play an important role in the political movement, and the gay movement did not begin with Harvey Milk or the mayoralty elections. Those who have no specific knowledge of the gay community in San Francisco or elsewhere, however, will not be able to deconstruct the factual character of this account. This is why we need to develop critical media-literacy skills among broader groups of people so that the power of these media framings can be contested.

The program is created from a particular standpoint, which is not that of lesbians or gay men but that of a "public," which is assumed to be heterosexual and to embody traditional family values. The "public" and public opinion are constructed through typical media practices. The anchorman and reporter stand in for the public, asking the questions that the "public" would wish to have asked. *Gay Power, Gay Politics* embodies these social relations. It is part of organizing a social relation, a concerted course of action leading to a "backlash" against gay liberation.[23] The growth of the gay community and its organization as a political constituency poses a threat to sections of the ruling institutions and to right-wing and conservative groups. One of the responses is a negative portrayal of gay men. This is not the result of any simple conspiracy, but is "the logical outcome of the present organization of news gathering and processing and the assumptions upon which it rests."[24]

It is almost as though the "young toughs"[25] referred to in *Gay Power, Gay Politics,* are being called upon to keep gays in their proper place, out of public view. As Frank Pearce asks in describing the effect of the print media in England on queerbashers: "What were these boys if they were not agents of the 'public consensus' so artfully created by the papers?"[26]

During the 1980 Toronto municipal election, Art Eggleton, the victorious mayoralty candidate, hinted that "San Francisco-style gay-power politics" was entering Toronto's civic world.[27] Renaissance applied the CBS frame to the Toronto elections.

They wrote of the need to prevent "Toronto the Good" from becoming "San Francisco North" and spoke of "The Record of 'Gay Power Politics' in Toronto."[28] Much of the Toronto mass media used aspects of the CBS frame. They spoke of the spectre of gay-power politics taking over at City Hall. They speculated about the number and concentration of gays. Above all, the gay community began to be portrayed from the perspective of a "gay elite" of white, male businessmen, religious figures, professionals, and politicians.

We must also look at how this image of gay men affects the gay community, our political movements, and gay definitions. What are the implications of accepting the media's portrayal of the gay community? What are the implications for those of us in the movement who have been struggling for more democratic politics in the community? What are the implications of excluding racial minorities, working-class gays and lesbians from public presentations? What are the implications of associating gay political organizing with "public sex" and sadomasochism? Does this not once again open the door to attacks against the minority of "bad" or "irresponsible" gays who are involved in these sexual practices as opposed to "good," "responsible" gays and lead to an acceptance of State-defined distinctions between public and private? What are the implications of exaggerating our influence in and over established political structures? What does this mean for political organizing and other movement activity? This new image of gay men raises many intensely practical questions, as the right wing, the police, and the media continue to use these types of framings against us. They continue to draw on these types of images and narratives in constructing gay men as a sexual danger, including in the context of AIDS for engaging in "irresponsible" sex. But there also have been more liberal media framings in response to the growth of lesbian/gay communities and AIDS organizing.

We must challenge the mass media's right and ability to manufacture these stories about our lives. We must transform the media by placing it under greater community and democratic control.[29]

The Jacques Murder: Anatomy of a "Moral Panic"

The police and other agencies have also played a central part in organizing this "backlash." A new police policy regarding the Toronto gay community was signalled by the "clean up Yonge Street" campaign in the mid-1970s, and particularly by the "moral panic" organized through the media after the sex-related murder of Emanuel Jacques, a twelve-year-old boy, by a number of men in a Yonge Street establishment in the summer of 1977. Such groups as Renaissance, and Positive Parents have made continual use of the socially constructed images of gays as "child molesters" and "murderers" that were established as part of this moral campaign. A look at the media coverage of the Jacques murder should provide us with insight into the anatomy of "moral panic."

Yvonne Chi-Ying Ng contends that to fully understand what happened, this murder must be situated in its historical and social context.[30] A similar murder of a nine-year-old in 1973 had not set off a moral panic. What were the circumstances that prompted such a reaction to the Jacques murder, she asks? The answer lies in the particular alignment of social and political forces at the time of the murder.

> It is through the specific social context and historical conjuncture, not the incidents themselves, that we begin to understand why the social control apparatus chose to blame Yonge Street for the death of Jacques.

The key to the response to the Jacques murder is the "clean up Yonge Street" campaign.

Proposals to clean up the Yonge Street strip had first been advanced by politicians and "legitimate" business interests in 1972. Initially they received little support, and much opposition. It is important to examine the economic and social process behind these requests. With the large corporate investment in the Eaton Centre development on Yonge in the early 1970s, the Yonge Street strip became ripe for speculation. The price of land shot up, and many small businesses simply could not afford to stay. The sex industry, which was able to afford the higher rents, moved in. The Downtown Business Association (to become the Downtown Business Council in 1973), in an effort to reestablish the conditions for the return of "legitimate" small business to the area, submitted a brief to Mayor Crombie. He took up their cause, but without much success for a number of years.

This "clean up Yonge Street" campaign was defined by a number of social, moral, economic, and political interests. This included the business interests who wanted to reestablish themselves in the area, politicians like Crombie who felt it was best for the moral character of the city,[31] and plans for redevelopment, and the police who wanted the chance to clamp down on prostitutes and massage parlours. This intersected with a debate over the character of the city, particularly its downtown core. These forces came together in their desire to clear the main street of the sex trade, prostitutes, and visible homosexuals.

Then, in 1975, the provincial election campaign of Bill Davis's ruling Conservative Party focused on "law and order," which included support for cleaning up Yonge Street, the main street of Ontario's principal city. This campaign mobilized anti-permissive sentiments, the police having linked the Yonge Street strip to organized crime by associating the sex industry, prostitution, and homosexuality with the criminal underworld.

A special committee of Toronto City Council was established to prepare a report on the strip in February 1977. This report was released in June of the same year. The media was generally favourable to the proposals for a clean-up but there was still hesitation.

Then, on August 1, 1977, the horrible Jacques murder occurred, and was immediately framed by the media through the interpretive schema already established by the "clean up Yonge Street" campaign. The press treated the murder as a primary news story, playing up its most extraordinary features. The *Star* and the *Sun* juxtaposed articles on the murder with articles on the clean-up campaign. This particular association was established through statements by Premier Davis, Mayor Crombie, and others. Ng explains that this highlights "the crucial role played by ... government and State officials in defining what is the significant issue involved in the murder of Jacques." *The Globe and Mail* associated the murder with the strip and with the "sexual permissiveness" that had begun in the 1960s.

Through its selective representation of reality, the media play a clear ideological role.[32] The mass media rely on accredited sources, and thus the perspective of agencies of social regulation are part of the formulation of "objective" news accounts. Such media practices served to neutralize opposition and to create a public consensus for the clean-up campaign.

The sex industry, prostitutes, and particularly homosexuals were presented as "folk devils."[33] Coverage of the "homosexual murder" served to focus hostility against the whole gay community, and also against lesbians since they were often subsumed under the homosexual referent.[34] Demonstrations by members of the Portuguese community, of which Jacques had been a member, influenced by the media, called for cleaning up Yonge Street, for granting more power to the police, and for capital punishment for homosexuals. The media portrayed the child molester or child murderer as a homosexual stranger to be found lurking in seedy parts of the city, building on and re-mobilizing earlier framings from the 1950s and 1960s that I investigated earlier. According to Yvonne Chi-Ying Ng, "the relationship between homosexual behaviour, pedophilia, and murderous acts become a cluster of images that cemented in the public mind."

The "moral panic" thus created would have a lasting effect, defining the political terrain for discussions of the character of the city, Yonge Street, sexual permissiveness, prostitution and homosexuality for years to come.

By focusing on an unusually violent crime, the media obscured the common occurrence of sexual harassment and violence against children and young people in the family setting — which points to the application of the public/private distinction in social regulation, with the "public" coming to cover a non-domestic private establishment along Yonge Street. Sexual violence in the domestic private sphere does not attract the same police or media attention (although it may attract the attention of social workers) even though the violence may exceed that of the Jacques case. Sexual danger is constructed as being outside the familial, private realm.[35] The provincial government, for instance, prevented the release of a study of fifty-four child-abuse deaths in Ontario during the same year that Jacques was murdered.

The Jacques case and the "clean up Yonge Street" campaign signalled a further shift in the Toronto social climate for gay men and lesbians. The "clean up" campaign provided fertile ground for the growth of sentiments against the visibility of the gay ghetto, particularly in the Yonge Street area serving to mobilize the police with their practices of criminalization against this target. The Jacques murder has reappeared as ammunition in right-wing propaganda; it has also resurfaced in mass-media coverage of the 1981 bath raids and male prostitution on Yonge Street.

The Empire Strikes Back!

The mid-1970s were the beginning of more difficult times for many gay men all over Canada in relation to the sex police. Gay communities were becoming more public and visible. As mentioned before, the Criminal Code mandates the police to criminalize gay sex, although this had been modified in 1969 to direct the police more specifically against gay sex in "public" and that involving young people. The bawdy-house laws, however, allowed the police to go after men in bars and baths for engaging in "indecent" activities.

In 1975, thirty-five men were arrested as "found-ins" in a "common bawdy-house" (police language for a gay bath) in Montréal. In 1976, as part of the clean-up campaign preceding the Montréal Olympics, police raided the Club baths and the Sauna Neptune, charging more than 144 men. The same year twenty-eight men were charged in a raid on the Ottawa Club baths. In 1977, 146 men were charged as "found-ins" during a raid on the Truxx bar in Montréal, provoking a large demonstration of gay resistance in the downtown.[36] The police have been one of the central forces regulating the sexual and community life of gay men and to a different extent that of lesbians.

The Toronto police continued their policy of harassment and entrapment.[37] As an extension of the "clean up Yonge Street" campaign, the gay men's community became a more specific target. *The Body Politic* was raided in December 1977 and charges were laid in January 1978.[38] The next year the Barracks bath was raided, initiating the late 1970s-early 1980s wave of bath raids in the city.

In Montréal, Ottawa, Toronto, and later Edmonton, the police began to use the bawdy-house law more systematically against gay establishments. The raid on the Truxx bar in Montréal was one of the first contemporary uses of this law to mass arrest gay men. The Canadian bawdy-house legislation had originally been drafted to deal with houses of prostitution as part of the movement for sexual purity and defense of marriage. In 1917 the law was broadened to include any place existing "for the practice of acts of indecency," putting massage parlours on the same footing as bawdy-houses.[39] Section 179 of the Criminal Code currently defines a bawdy-house as "a place that is kept or occupied or resorted to by one or more persons for the purposes of prostitution or the practices of acts of indecency." This law is still in place even though there have been a number of attempts to challenge it in court. It was used in 1994 to round up 175 men as "found-ins" at the Katacombes bar in Montréal.

This section mandates the police to label gay baths, and even private residences, as places habitually resorted to for the performance of acts of indecency and, therefore, "common bawdy-houses." "Indecency" is currently defined as what the contemporary Canadian community is not prepared to tolerate — which, the police and Crown attorneys often argue, includes homosexual acts in private rooms in bath houses. To use the bawdy-house legislation the police must engage in prior surveillance work at a particular site to gather evidence to attempt to demonstrate that it is a place habitually resorted to for "acts of indecency" (gay sex). Once this evidence is accumulated, then the police can move in to arrest everyone in a particular establishment on the grounds that they were "found-ins" in a "common bawdy house."[40]

The assaults on the gay baths in Toronto broke with a policy of "grudging acceptance"[41] or negotiated deals between the police and the bath owners that had existed for decades with only occasional interruptions like the late-1960s raid on the International Steam Bath. The initial Barracks raid can be seen as the initiation of a new operational policy and, as Thomas Fleming suggests, as a way to gauge community reaction before proceeding with further police activity.[42] The police and the media attempted to associate the bath and its patrons with sadomasochistic practices and sexual paraphernalia, conjuring up images of sexual sleaziness, deviance, and violence.[43] In 1979 the Hot Tub Club was raided by fifty police officers.[44] Worse was to follow. The association of gay sex with dirt was also made clear in the code name "Operation Soap" given the 1981 police war on the gay community, incorporating an image of dirty gay sex being cleansed from the social body by police action.

The fall 1980 Toronto municipal elections witnessed the defeat of John Sewell, a supporter of gay civil rights and critic of police abuse, and aldermanic candidate George Hislop, a prominent gay figure, and the emergence of a vocal anti-gay right wing that had the tacit backing of the police. Police surveillance of the baths to be raided in 1981 likely preceded the election. The results, however, were interpreted by the police as a green light for attacks on gays.

On February 5, 1981, 150 police officers were deployed against the city's four major gay baths; 289 men were charged as "found-ins" and twenty as "keepers" of a common bawdy-house. On April 23, 1981, the police laid twenty-two new charges of conspiracy against George Hislop, gay activist Peter Maloney, and four other men. These charges once again associated gay leaders, and the gay community, with criminality.

The police consistently identified gay baths with organized crime. In testimony before the House of Commons Committee on Justice and Legal Affairs, Guy Lafrance of the Montréal police stated:

> Areas of this country are already blighted by the presence of homosexual bawdy houses, disguised as "bath" establishments, sex clubs, and operating from apartments and private homes ... such problems cannot be considered to be of a local or isolated nature; rather, they have international implications and many connections with organized crime.[45]

Donald Banks, then with the Intelligence Bureau of the Metro Toronto police force, and one of the key figures in organizing the 1981 raids, stated before the same committee:

> Evidence was brought back to me relating to these premises operating as common bawdy houses with an international flavour — directors and such of international finance — and monies leaving Canada into the United States from the operations of some places.[46]

Canadian money going to the U.S. How unusual, and how criminal!

In June 1981 the police raided two of the remaining baths in Toronto, arresting another twenty-one men on bawdy-house charges. And in 1983 the Back Door was raided again, in a smaller, more sanitized operation.

This police offensive was attempted moral regulation, an attempt to regulate the gay-male community, and our sexualities, by applying criminal categories — in this case, the bawdy-house legislation — to cover gay men's sex. As ideological justification for their crusade, the police made use of the media, political, and moral associations established during the "clean up Yonge Street" campaign. They promised to crack down on prostitution, the involvement of minors in "indecent" activity, and the alleged connection with organized crime. Says Thomas S. Fleming, "The charges of prostitution function as a moral key allowing the police entry to the baths."[47] No prostitution, involvement of minors, or evidence of organized crime, however, was documented by the police or demonstrated in court. Because of the organization of the Right to Privacy Committee (RTPC), nearly ninety percent of the men dragged through the courts were acquitted. Yet the police continued to justify their actions with the few guilty pleas entered and that their internal-police complaints' bureau received no complaints.[48] The police make use of a schema that divides the population between "the public" and "the scum"; in this situation mandated by the Criminal Code which continued to criminalize gay sex, they construct the "public" as heterosexual and the "scum" as gay.[49]

The reasons for the bath raids and the police campaign against the gay community has been the subject of some debate. A full analysis for this would require a much more detailed historical and sociological study than can be undertaken here; however, a few of the elements which would inform it can be sketched in. Most importantly police organization must be investigated in order to show how the Criminal Code has directed the police against gays including through the use of bawdy-house legislation. This section of the Criminal Code allows the police to inscribe instances of gay sex into "acts of indecency" in the bawdy-house section and therefore to attempt to produce it as crime.[50]

Two contextualizing social processes are also at work. First, Toronto is a city of growing racial, ethnic — and now — sexual minorities. The provincial and municipal establishment foresaw the need for a fairly militarized police force — which is not accountable to these minorities — to decrease the public visibility of these minorities and to keep them contained. Later struggles by the black community over police racism and violence, the gay communities, and others forced some modifications in policing organization, but the police still are a dominantly male, white, and heterosexual presence in the city.

Second, sectors of ruling agencies feared the visibility and concentration of gays in the downtown core. This is the social context in which the "clean up Yonge Street" campaign and the bath raids can be located. In the 1970s and early 1980s, the increasing visibility of the gay community interacted with plans for the redevelopment of the Yonge Street area and the downtown. Police policy sought to limit the visible and public growth of the gay community as the Criminal Code mandated them to do.

These police campaigns were not successful. The attempt to create a "moral panic" around the 1981 bath raids failed because of the widespread resistance by thousands of gays and our supporters. The police had clearly not expected such unprecedented an-

(mm) GLARE ✓

The Regulation of Desire

ger and rebellion. Indeed, the raids served to politicize, radicalize, and further define the gay community. Many lesbians were also involved in this process. Support came from feminists, unions, civil liberties and religious groups, and progressive members of city council.[51] It was in the context of the resistance to the bath raids that Gay Liberation Against the Right Everywhere, Lesbians Against the Right and the RTPC organized the first lesbian and gay pride day in Toronto to be held at the end of June.

The White and Sheppard Report documented the brutality of the bath raids,[52] and even the mainstream media adopted a critical attitude toward the police. City Council voted for a provincial independent inquiry into the bath raids, and established the city's own Bruner investigation into police/gay relations when the province refused to establish such an inquiry.

By documenting police harassment, the Bruner Report reflected the gains won by gay resistance[53] and it made many progressive recommendations, including sexual-orientation protection in human-rights legislation and the recognition of gays as a legitimate minority. Its central recommendation, however, was for the establishment of dialogue between the gay community and the police:

> It has been obvious throughout the study, and particularly in the complaints and counter-complaints between the police and the gay community and the attitude that each has toward the other, that the relationship suffers from an almost total lack of effective communication ... It is my view that a regular dialogue is key to improved relations between the police and gay community.[54]

This recommendation presented the main problem as a lack of communication. This assumption is not grounded in the experiences of gays and lesbians. The gay movement knew perfectly well what the police were up to, and the police, through their surveillance activities, had a profound understanding of the gay movement. The central problem was not lack of communication. The police still have the power to criminalize gay sex. As well, Bruner's approach tended to place the gay community and the police on the same level, whereas it is the police who have the power to arrest, raid, and to regulate erotic life.

A dialogue committee would manufacture gay consent for police activity. In a situation wherein no community has control over the police, wherein there is no police accountability to democratic bodies, and wherein anti-gay laws remain on the books, discussion of "problem areas"[55] like sexual activity in "public washrooms" or parks would only involve the gay community representatives in a process of policing ourselves. This could cause serious divisions in the community and make campaigns against police harassment very difficult given the apparently consensual relations established with them. Such a dialogue committee could also provide the police with detailed information which could later be used against us.

Perhaps a bit ahead of its time, the Bruner Report prefigured aspects of "community policing" that — although they had earlier beginnings — would be one policing strategy developed in England in response to black rebellions of the early 1980s to attempt to do more surveillance work of the black communities and to try to incorporate layers of the black community into the policing process.[56] These practices of "community policing" have been exported to police forces in many other countries, including in Canada. In Canada, some "liberal" forces within police departments and on city councils have taken up "community policing" as a more "democratic" form of policing. In a number of centres, dialogue committees between gay-community representatives and the police have been established with mixed results. In Toronto and elsewhere, such committees have been used to divide gay men and lesbians from others facing police harassment such as female, male, transvestite, and transsexual prostitutes. The most success appears to have been achieved in Ottawa with new training programs for police officers, but the Ottawa police continue to engage in racist practices against the local black community. These dialogue committees and forms of "community policing" can only work to the advantage of lesbian, gay, and other communities who have experienced police harassment if there are changes in the laws that continue to criminalize consensual sex, if there is a powerful form of autonomous independent review of police conduct, and if there is a profound democratization of control over the police.

While the Bruner Report contained many recommendations that legitimized our struggles, it also suggested a new means of regulation of the gay community and same-gender sex that had to be resisted. Gay movements can use the progressive demands of such reports to push forward our struggles while at the same time pushing beyond the boundaries of social regulation they suggest.

The 1980s battles between gay movements and the police are a manifestation of the social struggles over the State-defined distinction between "public" and "private." The police are trying to establish that sex in gay baths — and sometimes bars — and gay sex in parks and washrooms is "public" sex and therefore subject to their direct intervention. Central institutions and gathering places of gay-community formation would thus be rendered "public." This debate takes place in the context of the boundaries drawn by the 1969 reform and the contradictory developments to which it has led.

The gay movement in contrast has argued that gay institutions are part of the "private" sphere and therefore off-limits to the police. It has used the liberal notion of "right to privacy" not only as a defence in court; it has also turned the public/private distinction against State agencies by redefining and shifting the terms of the debate. This strategy not only includes the gay community and its institutions in the private realm; it also shifts the notion of privacy from the language of State discourse and places it in the social practices of everyday life. This notion of right to privacy builds upon the idea of privacy as a realm of individual choice, consent, and morality. But privacy is no longer only territorially defined: if you have sex in this place it is "public"; in that place "private." Instead, it focuses on the actual social practices people engage in to construct intimacy for themselves. "Right to privacy" is not used in a narrow, individualist sense, but in a collective sense — which requires that one looks at sex and social life from the standpoint of gays, and which moves beyond the boundaries of State-defined categories. It is quite possible to engage in a private act in a place defined by the State as public (for example, a washroom, with no one else present or a deserted or secluded part of a park).

> Privacy is something that is socially constructed in this society ... Indeed, in the middle of the night, when it is absolutely pitch black, a park might in fact be a very private place.[57]

The Toronto movement used right to privacy in a transformative fashion as a vehicle for defending gay men against the police. The dominant public/private strategies of regulation were thus put into question.

It should be pointed out, though, that there can also be grave dangers in accepting a narrow, State-defined notion of privacy.[58] Conservative gays in the U.S. have used the idea of privacy in this limited sense to win the support of anti-gay Republicans. This approach fundamentally accepts State definitions of public and private and the sexual policing that goes with them. It constructs gays who engage in sexual activities in "private" as "responsible," while others engaging in more "public" activities are "irresponsible" and police action may be justified against them. Claims to "right to privacy" are also no basis for queer claims to full social equality with heterosexuality and for dismantling the heterosexual hegemony at the heart of social and family policies.

The mass response to the bath raids in Toronto at least temporarily closed off options for the police. Their tactics had to change. The police began to regularly lay overcrowding charges against gay bars in 1981-1982. Surveillance, entrapment, and the arrest of men allegedly engaged in sexual acts in washrooms and parks increased significantly. In 1982-1983 more than 600 men were arrested in washrooms for homosexual "offences"; more than 600 "indecent act" arrests took place in Toronto in 1985.[59]

In 1983-1985 police action was extended across southern Ontario, with arrests in Orillia, Welland, Oakville, Oshawa, Peel region, Guelph, Kitchener/Waterloo, and St. Catharines. In most instances, the local police used video-surveillance equipment provided by the Ontario Provincial Police, including fibre-optic technology.[60] In many cases, the local media have published the arrested men's names; at least one man killed himself as a result.

Washroom arrests are hard to fight, particularly in small towns, because of the social stigma attached to the offence, the difficulty in mounting a legal defence, and that many of these men do not consider themselves to be gay or bisexual. Of the southern-Ontario centres, only in Guelph was there a protest against the video-surveillance arrests. A "Stop Policing Sexuality" demonstration was held, support activities for the men charged were organized, and legal challenges were launched.[61] Legal defence requires that our right to privacy be extended to include private sexual acts that take place in "public" places like washrooms. Two men having sex in a cubicle in a deserted washroom, for instance, having clearly taken measures to ensure their intimacy, are performing a private act.[62] This is, however, a difficult argument to make in court and in political organizing. There have been continuing washroom busts in the 1990s in St. John's, Newfoundland, and across southern Ontario.

Escalating Sexual Censorship: "Obscenity" and Canadian Customs

In Toronto, following the resistance to the bath raids, the police focused their attention more specifically against gay institutions. Obscenity charges were brought against Glad Day Bookshop, and new obscenity charges were laid against *The Body Politic* in May 1982. Obscenity legislation, which censors sexual presentations on the basis of "the undue exploitation of sex," does not treat all sexual images and texts equally. The law applies more harshly to same-gender presentations.[63]

In the Glad Day trial in 1983, presentations of lesbian and gay sexuality were seen as more "indecent" and "offensive" to community standards than similar heterosexual portrayals. In his judgement, Justice Vanek referred to the 1970 case of Regina versus Prairie Schooner in which the Manitoba Court of Appeal found that "lurid scenes of lesbianism" "went beyond what the community was prepared to tolerate." Vanek referred to the 1969 Criminal Code reform which decriminalized only homosexual acts between adults in private and which defined a public place as existing when "two or more persons are present or if it is a public place." Vanek stated that in the case of the two magazines, which Glad Day was charged with selling, the photographer must have been present, making the acts "public." Again referring to the 1969 reform, he stated that the acts depicted in the magazines "are made public by representing them graphically in a pictorial magazine, which sometimes depicts a third person."[64] Vanek was unable to determine any lowering of Canadian community standards since this earlier case had been heard.[65]

The 1969 reform therefore retained the idea that same-gender sex is more "indecent" and "obscene" than similar heterosexual acts. Obscenity legislation works to keep lesbian and gay sexuality in a subordinate position while buttressing heterosexual hegemony. This legislation lets the police regulate lesbian and gay communities and images of same-gender sex more generally. It helps establish "proper" images of sex, seriously limiting what lesbians and gays can view, read, discuss, and produce. It also limits what is available to heterosexuals about our lives. It is not only a denial of lesbian and gay freedom or speech and expression but also an important aspect of heterosexual hegemony and oppressive sexual regulation.

In the mid-1980s Canada Customs escalated its seizure of lesbian and gay materials. Using a new internal memorandum that labelled depictions of "buggery/sodomy" as "obscene,"[66] they routinely seized and refused entry to Canada to numerous materials destined for lesbian and gay bookstores across the country, especially Little Sister's in Vancouver and Glad Day in Toronto. Books and magazines seized at various times included hundreds of titles ranging from *The Joy of Gay Sex, Lesbian Sex, Macho Sluts, Prick Up Your Ears,* Jean Genet's *Querelle,* to bell hook's *Black Looks*[67] (as suspected "hate literature"), to the *Tom of Finland Retrospective*, to gay-male erotic writings and the lesbian sex magazines *Bad Attitude* and *On Our Backs*.[68] A number of sex videos (including safer-sex videos) made for lesbians and gay men have also been seized.

Federal anti-porn "obscenity" proposals announced in June 1986 would have banned all depictions of "anal intercourse" and many other sex acts as prohibited forms of "pornography" thereby further institutionalizing sanctions against presentations of lesbian and gay sex. I use "pornography" here to refer to sexually explicit materials that are usually, but not always, commercially produced; there are a number of different pornographies with different social characteristics. Fortunately, this bill died on the order paper. The main features of this legislation were continued in Bill C-54, which generated widespread opposition for its wide-ranging censorship proposals from librarians, civil libertarians, artists, and lesbians and gay men. The legislation was scrapped in the fall of 1988.[69]

In February 1992 the Supreme Court of Canada in the Butler decision both upheld the constitutionality of the obscenity section of the Criminal Code and also modified its interpretation.[70] The Women's Legal, Education and Action Fund (LEAF) intervened in this decision to argue for an anti-porn feminist position and to try to have the Supreme Court move from a "moral" definition of obscenity to one focused on "harm" to women and other groups. They hailed the decision as a victory for women.

As mentioned before, the key element of the "obscenity" section of the Criminal Code is "the undue exploitation of sex." This has usually been interpreted as meaning too much sexual explicitness for "community standards" to tolerate. The focus is on sexual explicitness, not on sexism or sexual violence. The Supreme Court in the Butler decision provided the police and courts with a new set of interpretations or tests of the meaning of this section, which focused on associations between sexuality and violence, "degradation," and "dehumanization."

The court said that sex coupled with violence is "obscene." How will the police and courts define sexual violence given they usually do not take context into account? Could this guideline be used against feminist films that are portraying depictions of sexual violence as part of organizing against such violence. We should remember that *Not a Love Story*, a feminist film against pornography was found unacceptable for public showing in Ontario by the provincial censor board in the mid-1980s because it used scenes from pornography as part of its critique of the porn industry.

The Supreme Court also found that representations of explicit sex that are "demeaning, degrading, and/or dehumanizing" are also obscene. A major problem comes with the interpretation of these words. These terms have multiple meanings and a great deal of vagueness carrying different meanings for different groups.[71] For many, gay and lesbian sex is per se "degrading," and there is a long history of criminalization and censorship lying behind this practice as the courts have found representations of lesbian and gay sexuality to be more obscene than similar heterosexual portrayals. For some, "degrading" refers to any sexual activities outside the confines of heterosexual marriage. "Degrading" is a sufficiently inclusive and expansive term to cover most acts of which a viewer disapproves. It becomes a collecting category that can include a number of unpopular and unorthodox sexual practices, some of which — like consensual queer sex — present no problems of lack of consent, coercion, or violence. As such, the term lacks any real precision to be able to defend materials such as gay and lesbian erotic materials, which are often treated differentially and unequally in present-day social practices.

How will the police interpret this? Past police practice suggests that the police would use this against depictions of lesbian and gay sex and also against other representations of consensual sex. Does this mean that the police could find a depiction of a man ejaculating onto another man's body "degrading" even though this is an activity encouraged in safer-sex practices for gay men? That is what the federal government's Bill C-54 attempted to do in 1987. Ontario Provincial Police Detective Sergeant Bob Matthews stated he would find such a representation of ejaculation "obscene" under the new guidelines. He is with project P, the joint Metro Toronto and Ontario Provincial Police's anti-porn squad. He stated on CBC radio (February 27, 1992) that the police will define "degrading" simply as too much explicit sex, suggesting that any implication that the characters participating in sex did not already know each other well would also make it obscene.

This police definition of "degrading" has nothing to do with feminist concerns over sexism and violence against women. This interpretation will strengthen the hand of the police in going after portrayals of consensual sex, especially images of lesbian and gay sexuality.

It was no surprise that one of the first obscenity charges laid following the Butler decision on April 30, 1992 was against Glad Day in Toronto for carrying the lesbian sex mag *Bad Attitude*. Glad Day was convicted in December 1992 in a decision that relied in part on the Butler decision.[72] And in July of 1992 Glad Day, whose proprietors had taken Canada Customs to court regarding twelve books and magazines that had been seized, lost its case with the judge, who based his judgement on the Butler decision and argued that depictions of casual gay sex with strangers are "obscene," and with suggestions that anonymous sex and anal sex are potentially harmful to the community.[73] Following the Butler decision, there seemed to be an intensification of Customs censorship directed at lesbian materials and on books and magazines destined for women's bookstores across the country.

AIDS: Making Us Sick Once Again

The AIDS crisis has been used to once again re-medicalize gay men and to associate gay men and sometimes bisexual men with sickness, disease, and death. This has helped to reconstruct relations of medicalization that the gay and lesbian movements had been rather successful in undermining in the 1970s and 1980s (see chapter 9). This has occurred even though AIDS is caused by a virus, and possible co-factors, and not by homosexuality or gay sex. As Dennis Altman put it, AIDS was homosexualized,[74] and the legacy of this homosexualization is still very much with us today. Out of government and professional neglect, community-based AIDS groups and AIDS activism emerged in the 1980s. AIDS organizing is one of the most profound social movements ever to emerge around health questions. Emerging as a social movement, it included the organization and politicization of People Living With AIDS/HIV (PLWA/HIVs) themselves.

It is worth reviewing the history of AIDS organizing and State and professional responses, since this is an important part of the context for queer organizing and sexual politics in the 1990s. In North America, AIDS groups first grew out of the largely — but not exclusively — white gay and lesbian movements of the early 1980s, and began to involve progressive health workers; often they were influenced by feminist health movements. Organizations developed in response to State inaction and indifference, major problems with the medical profession, and social discrimination against the communities most affected by AIDS. Community-based support and educational groups were first set up in the period 1982-1986 across the Canadian State. It is important to remember this history of activism, which is constantly in danger of being submerged and forgotten in the official texts of the AIDS crisis, such as in the 1990 National AIDS Strategy[75] documents and in much mainstream-media coverage.

In the early 1980s many State agencies basically ignored AIDS aside from the collection of epidemiological information, some job-creation funding for the first community-based groups, and some limited "public health" initiatives based on defence of the "general population" from those infected. The "general population" was coded as the "respectable" heterosexual population that excluded gays, injection-drug users, sex-trade workers, Haitians, and often other people of colour.

"Public health" is also not simply neutral or objective, despite it providing the basis for important gains in some areas. It is always important to ask which public and whose health is being defended. Historically, public-health practices were directed against the living conditions and ways of life of the poor and working class and against infectious diseases. It was part of the extension of social surveillance and regulation and the imposition of middle-class ways of life onto these groups.

The underpinnings of public-health practices regarding AIDS can be traced back to earlier campaigns against sexually transmitted diseases, tuberculosis, and infant mortality.[76] The campaigns against STDs, as mentioned earlier, were also rooted in sexist double-standards that blamed prostitutes and/or "loose" women for the spread of infection. These practices focused on contact tracing, partner notification, and quarantine. Public-health officials wanted people's names and identities in their work, and this has later on created major difficulties for the establishment of anonymous HIV testing where a person's name is not recorded to prevent possible discrimination. "Public health" is not for those who are already infected. Public-health practices have often make PLWA/HIVs into the problem, focusing on the irresponsible "deviants" who supposedly spread it,[77] even though the vast majority of people who spread HIV have no knowledge they are infected.

In the face of this inaction and the limitations of public-health practices, badly needed community-based support and education groups were set up in the larger centres across Canada. It was these groups that provided the first support for people living with AIDS — including support in dealing with discrimination and problems in hospitals and other medical institutions — and that undertook the first educational initiatives. They confronted the social process of AIDS stigmatization. These early community-based initiatives helped to turn back some of the social processes organizing AIDS-related discrimination and began to force State agencies and the medical profession to respond in a better fashion.

These community groups confronted the previously mentioned initial medical and social construction of knowledge regarding AIDS which was called Gay Related Immune Deficiency (GRID) in 1981. This was influenced by the medical discourse of immunology that focuses on the breakdown in internal dynamics of the immune system and by early epidemiological work conducted for the Centre for Disease Control in Atlanta, which focused on the homosexuality and gay lifestyle of some of those who were diagnosed early on.[78] These were mostly white gay men who had some regular interaction with the medical profession. Injection-drug users and others with less regular contact with the medical profession were coming down with these infections and dying at the same time, but they were not noticed by this early epidemiological gaze. GRID was picked up and amplified in the mass media as the "gay plague." We were informed in 1982, for instance, that the "Gay Plague Has Arrived in Canada" by a headline in the *Toronto Star*.[79]

Diseases are socially constructed, not simply biological or medical phenomena, and this early homosexualization has had a lasting impact on the social construction of AIDS. This re-medicalization of homosexuality built on pre-existing heterosexist practices, which organized discrimination against gay men and in a different way against lesbians and all people living with AIDS. Others were also designated as "high risk groups" — such as the Haitian communities — and discrimination was organized against them in a social context where they already experienced widespread racism.[80] While I was working at the AIDS Committee of Toronto in 1983, I received a number of calls from people asking if they should fire their Haitian housekeepers because of fears of AIDS. We can begin to see the kind of work that the concept of "high risk groups" can do. "High risk groups" — a concept used in epidemiology — was taken up in the media and used to organize discrimination against groups that were constructed as "threats." As AIDS activists began to stress in response, there are risk activities in which anyone can engage but no risk groups.

The media distinction between "guilty" and "innocent" people with AIDS built on notions of sexual and drug-use "deviance." If one were guilty, one was to be blamed. This organized social consciousness regarding AIDS. Through this social construction and the lack of official responses, years were lost in terms of needed social, health-care and medical action.

In 1983-1984 out of these community-based initiatives and especially from some gay men and some people living with AIDS came the practices of safe sex. These were a range of sexual practices people could engage in without fear of transmission of any causative agent — this was developed initially prior to HTLV-III (later called HIV) being identified. Safe-sex organizing among gay men made some very important gains in reducing rates of transmission. It was explicit, erotic, clear, in the language/culture of the community, did not put people down, and it empowered people through practical information and knowledge grounded in lived experiences. Viewed from a social construction of sexuality approach, it showed how sexual practices and sexualities can be socially and collectively transformed.[81] Unfortunately, these acquisitions have mostly been lost in official AIDS education.

In 1984 the "discovery" of a causative agent was announced — HTLV-III, later called HIV. This was tied to the medical discourse of virology, which became the hegemonic medical discourse regarding AIDS.[82] The theory assumed was that there was a single, viral, causative agent. This has had a major impact on research and research funding. Success for virology is viewed as an anti-viral agent that extends life leading it not to focus on the harms, side-effects, and impacts on quality of life that such drugs might have.

In the mid-1980s in Canada, the federal and other levels of government began to provide more than job-creation funding, and began to systematically fund community-based groups on the federal level through Health Promotions. Under Health Minister Jake Epp (1984-1988) there were major problems with the lack of action on treatment delivery for PLWA/HIVs and a lack of cooperation with community-based groups. State policies were almost completely defined by public health and later also by palliative care concerns, defending the "general public" from infection from PLWAs and affected communities and basically assuming all PLWAs were going to die relatively quickly. During these years, federal agencies began to do some educational work on prevention issues — but with major limitations.

Consistent State funding for community-based groups — which was an important victory — led to more State regulation of the work of these groups, and they increasingly became transformed from community groups with a participating and active membership with ties to gay and other communities into hierarchical, professionalized organizations in a similar process to that analyzed regarding other community-based groups.[83] More and more they came to be defined by State funding agencies and to define themselves as "service" organizations with "clients" and "volunteers." This is not to devalue the badly needed services these groups continued to provide, but to mark a shift in their social organization. Many of the groups initially set up to empower PLWA/HIVs and the communities affected by AIDS began to come to stand over these communities as part of a State-regulated process of mediation and management.

During these years, there was a transformation of safe sex into safer sex. Safe sex was shifted and sanitized, often placed in a medical or scientific language, and not in the languages and cultures of people who were being addressed. It became professionalized, medicalized, and also individualized, and was removed from its social and political roots. The focus on the "general population" was taken up in public-health education, and this population was assumed to be heterosexual. This was based on the hegemonic sexual ideology of there being two discrete and essential sexualities, which does not address men who see themselves as heterosexual but who occasionally have sex with other men. These men will also not be addressed by material addressed to gay men. Also, because heterosexism was not challenged in this education, it allows heterosexual men to continue to see gay men as "others" from whom they have nothing to learn in the context of AIDS and in other aspects of their lives.[84]

Profound misinformation was produced by focusing this official education against "promiscuity" and for monogamy. It is not the number of partners but the acts that are engaged in that is the problem, and serial monogamy with unsafe sex can be a risk. As Cindy Patton points out, women have largely been addressed in official AIDS discourse as either "vessels" of transmission (as mothers, and therefore a risk to the fetus) or as "vectors" of transmission (as prostitutes and "promiscuous" women — and therefore a risk to heterosexual men).[85] There has been little focus on the importance of women themselves.

There was also the hegemony of AIDS as universally fatal during these years, which led to no major focus on treatment. AZT, an anti-viral drug, began to be first publicized and was then released with great restrictions in 1986-1987 by Burroughs Wellcome. Research then being conducted continued to focus on HIV as the sole causative agent, and the search for a "magic bullet" anti-viral drug.

A major contradiction emerged in the later 1980s between the knowledge that there were various treatments that could extend people's lives and continuing State, professional and corporate practices standing in the way of this access. There was both a possibility of survival but also its denial. Out of this contradiction, a new treatment-based activism burst forth onto the streets (such as AIDS ACTION NOW! in Toronto and the AIDS Coalition to Unleash Power — ACT UP —in the U.S.). This activism gained widespread support from activists in community-based groups in the Canadian AIDS Society (CAS). This new AIDS activism engaged in actions such as burning an effigy of the Health Minister in Toronto in 1988 at an AIDS protest I helped organize. This meant that older strategies of the regulation of community-based groups and PLWA/HIVs were no longer working. This upsetting of the hegemony of earlier regulatory strategies set the stage for the development of the National AIDS Strategy under the new Minister of Health Perrin Beatty in 1990.

This treatment-based activism won some important — if limited — victories, like the use of the federal Emergency Drug Release Program (EDRP) to release some treatments on compassionate grounds (beginning in January 1989), the release and approval of aerosolized pentamidine (AP) as a preventative treatment for pneumocystis carinii pneumonia (PCP), the limited release of ddI (another anti-viral drug) and other drugs, and a commitment to a National Treatment Registry in the National AIDS strategy, which unfortunately — because of resistance from the medical elite and professional and academic disputes — is only now being established in 1995. These victories were very important to some people's survival and quality of life.[86]

For instance, PCP — which was the major cause of death among PLWAs in North America — could largely have been prevented during these years through the use of various prophylaxis or preventatives. By 1985 some primary care physicians were using septra and other drugs for PCP prophylaxis, but no major study was funded to determine the effectiveness of these and aerosolized pentamidine since there was no major profit motive, given that septra was an already-established inexpensive drug. Contrast this with the millions spent investigating AZT and the millions of dollars it made for Burroughs Wellcome. In the case of AP in Canada, they only undertook a placebo-controlled trial of this promising preventative. It was only through the efforts of PLWA/HIVs, AIDS activists, and some primary-care physicians that these preventative treatments have become a standard of care in much of North America where there is access to health and medical care, meaning that PCP is no longer the major cause of death.

This also led AIDS activists to challenge how clinical trials are organized, including the Canadian double-blind trial of AP I just mentioned. Double-blind placebo-controlled trials are those in which only some of those enroled in the trial actually receive the drug that might be of use to them. AIDS activists also raised ethical problems with the use of the "clinical endpoints" of death or opportunistic infection in the placebo arms of these trials as ways of determining whether a drug works. This had been put forward as good "clean" science, but the impact on people enroled was quite devastating, including leading to some deaths. These trials have been set up to provide product testing — not to provide treatment — and AIDS activists have pushed for open arms and the expansion of treatment delivery.[87]

Given the medical hegemony surrounding AIDS, it has been difficult for AIDS groups and PLWA/HIVs to claim and establish "expert" status while at the same time some gains have been made on this front. Some groups of PLWA/HIVs (usually gay, white, and middle class but not entirely) who were tied into PLWA networks in the U.S. and later Canada and other countries began to become more educated than their doctors about treatments, which led to a challenge to some of the powers of the medical profession. This also exposed major problems regarding treatment delivery in Canada. There is no State mandate to actually deliver treatments to the people who need it. This is a major problem with the health-care system for PLWA/HIVs and many others. Federal and provincial regulations focus on public health and, at the provincial level, on provincial health insurance and what is covered under it.

The Health Protection Branch on the federal level does not have a mandate for treatment delivery. Its public health mandate largely excludes and silences concerns regarding treatments. It only regulates product testing and approves products for release. The EDRP only relaxes these regulations on compassionate grounds in some situations, and it clearly recognizes the property rights of the drug companies. The EDRP allows the pharmaceutical companies to decide if and under what conditions a drug will be released. Treatment delivery is largely left up to medical professionals and the pharmaceutical corporations, and is almost a private contractual relationship entered into between doctor and patient. It is thus left up to the corporations and the profit motive and medical professionals to test drugs and provide people with treatments.

The major pharmaceutical corporations dominate applied research and they only develop drugs that are profitable for them. In the context of AIDS and many other conditions, this just does not work for treatment delivery. It creates major difficulties for PLWA/HIVs, and led AIDS activists to argue for catastrophic rights — the right of PLWAs and others in catastrophic life-threatening situations to have an unrestricted social right to access treatments they and their physicians believe to be beneficial.[88] AIDS activists also began to point to the possibility of AIDS/HIV becoming a "chronic manageable condition" through the use of treatments against the infections that actually kill people, treatments that slow down the progress of HIV replication, and through adequate social and financial support.

Treatment activism has also challenged priorities for research and the very social construction of medical knowledge. Although for too long treatment activists accepted the hegemony of anti-viral research that has produced the family of drugs — AZT, ddI, and ddC — which are highly toxic and of limited usefulness — they did begin to challenge the research agenda regarding the lack of priority given to treatments for the infections that kill people and to support research into alternative therapies. ACT UP produced research agendas, and Community Research Initiatives were set up by primary-care physicians and PLWA/HIVs in a number of centres, including Toronto, and these groups have done some groundbreaking research. Also, some AIDS activists began to challenge the theory that HIV was the sole cause of AIDS, supporting research into possible co-factors, and also into immune-system stimulation and rebuilding. Regarding the drug corporations and research-scientists' agendas, AIDS activists have faced a number of problems in confronting the power of drug corporations in the capitalist "medical industrial" complex.[89]

There are also problems created by the lack of funding for treatments, which means that some PLWA/HIVs are forced to make treatment decisions based on cost, and often there is no funding available for alternative therapies outside the Western medical model. Treatment is located largely in the sphere of personal consumption, which creates major problems for people who need access to treatments.

This treatment-based activism set the stage for a new federal strategy of regulation[90] of community-based AIDS groups defined by concepts of "consultation" and "partnership." In developing this strategy, the consultants for the federal government took up the term partnership from community-based groups (members of the Canadian AIDS Society) who used it to argue for State recognition of AIDS groups as leaders in the fight against AIDS and as equal and defining partners. They then shifted and uprooted this through the entry of discourses developed in business administration and labour management that deploy "partnership" from an administrative standpoint as a mechanism for integrating other groups under the hegemony of ruling agencies.

In this conceptualization of partnership, the community-based groups become just one of many partners with no special defining powers. "Partnership" then became a conceptual framework for hegemonic regulation. While there were some limited gains — like the commitment to a Treatment Registry and some recognition of the need on the part of PLWA/HIVs and doctors for treatment information — this AIDS strategy was still fundamentally defined by public health and palliative care. While some major tensions have developed over funding, this strategy has been far more effective in regulating AIDS groups than in meeting the needs of PLWA/HIVs or the communities most affected by AIDS.

There is a major dilemma facing AIDS organizing and other forms of progressive organizing around health concerns. These groups both need State funding and resources and medical knowledge, but must also avoid being regulated and defined by it. This requires organizing within and against State regulation and the medical profession.

Finally, since 1990 there has been a new focus on the relations of impoverishment and poverty that many PLWA/HIVs confront and are often thrown into after an AIDS/HIV diagnosis. Daily survival becomes an active process of work for PLWA/HIVs. There is a lack of access to and institutional problems with "hooking up" to social services and social supports, as Eric Mykhalovskiy and George Smith document,[91] and major inadequacies in these supports — in terms of funding for transportation needs, vitamins, adequate nutrition, adequate housing, along with the lack of funding for all needed treatments. This focus raises these social supports as necessary preconditions for health, and raises class questions as a central aspect of the social response to AIDS.

Initial organizing around AIDS was done mostly by white people — often white gay men — and this left its mark on AIDS organizations making it more difficult for questions of racism and sexism to be addressed within AIDS organizing. Relations of exclusion and alienation in community organizing and AIDS activism have meant that there were needs that were not being addressed. Over the last period, there has been a growing self-organization of people of colour regarding AIDS concerns, including the Black Outreach Project in Nova Scotia, various First Nations groups, and groups focusing on the needs of women, like Voices of Positive Women in Toronto. These efforts have challenged racism and sexism in AIDS organizing and also in the broader social response to AIDS. This organizing points us in the direction of realizing that to deal with AIDS we must also deal with how it is tied up with class, gender, and race oppression, which has allowed some activists who came out of organizing in the lesbian and gay communities to extend their political perspectives and to learn from the experiences of people oppressed and marginalized on bases other than sexuality. Finally, in this context, there is now an official State focus especially through the Krever Commission on problems with infections through the blood supply, which is partly because of intensified organizing by those who acquired HIV infection as hemophiliacs requiring blood products and also among those who received it from transfusions.

These efforts have broadened out AIDS organizing confronting other bases of oppression. The social organization of the AIDS crisis, which is a condensation of many social relations, means that AIDS activism must confront questions of sexuality, race, gender, class, ability, hemophilia, health care, the medical profession, research, the drug corporations, and many other questions. At the same time, gay and lesbian activists have been able to bring their important experiences to the development of a grass-roots response to AIDS, including the central necessity of challenging heterosexism in any effective response to AIDS. It has also meant that there have been struggles over the importance of recognizing the importance of gays in the social response to AIDS that some would wish to deny, and important struggles against heterosexism in State, professional, and even community practices. This poses profound and radical questions of social transformation that I return to in the conclusion.[92]

The AIDS crisis has forced gay activists to rely on former adversaries — the medical profession and State agencies — for badly needed information and resources. This reliance has at times hindered or contained our political response to AIDS as we have been wary of antagonizing government or medical bureaucrats. The dilemma is how to fight AIDS using badly needed medical and government resources while at the same time avoiding their strategies of containment of the gay community and other affected groups.

Re-mobilizing Homosexuality as a Danger to Young People

In the late 1980s and early 1990s, the narrative and imagery of male homosexuals as a special sexual danger to youth was re-mobilized in mass-media framing and in official government-commission-work processes building on the associations put in place in the 1950s and 1960s. Even though this conceptualization had its social roots in the past, it was still alive and possessed a certain resiliency in this new social context. In Newfoundland in 1989 and the early 1990s, the Hughes Royal Commission into why the police did not prosecute Christian Brothers for physical and sexual assaults on boys at the Mount Cashel Orphanage in the 1970s — along with associated media coverage — once again associated "child sexual abuse" with "deviant" homosexual sex. One of the central pieces of police evidence relied on in the commission work process was the 1975 police report *Child Abuse and Homosexual Acts at Mount Cashel Orphanage*, which was suppressed by authorities. This text embodied police attempts to criminalize homosexual activity, and brought this perspective with it into the commission work in 1989-1990. Rather than exploring the social and institutional power relations that led to the violence and harassment against these boys and young men, the commission often focused on homosexuality as the problem. This also served to obscure the actual gender character of the problem of sexual harassment and assaults against young people that often takes place in the private, familial realm against girls and young women as we have seen. It also shifts attention away from the pervasive physical assaults and corporal punishment that was part of the disciplinarian regime at Mount Cashel, and in the process "sexualizes" the abuse the boys and young men faced.[93] This framing was made available through media coverage to cover problems at other institutions across the country. In this framing, "child sexual abuse" becomes a problem that boys and young men faced in institutional contexts often from homosexual men.

The major federal-government investigations of sexual-related problems in the 1980s — the Badgley committee on Sexual Offences against Children and Youth and the Fraser Committee Report on Pornography and Prostitution — both focused on the need to re-deploy adult/youth distinctions in sexual regulation.[94] Even in the deliberations leading up to the 1988 legal change when the age of consent for anal intercourse was finally lowered to eighteen for acts in "private," the special vulnerability of young males to homosexual advances along with the supposed higher risk of HIV transmission through anal intercourse were cited in committee and by a Justice Department policy coordinator to justify a higher age of consent for this activity than for other sexual activities. Neville Avison, senior criminal-justice-policy coordinator in the Justice Department's policy program and research branch stated that the prohibition against anal intercourse involving those under eighteen would help stop the spread of AIDS and would curtail acts of anal intercourse that might confirm gayness in someone who was previously a latent homosexual. Part of this argument drew on the perspective embodied in the Wolfenden strategy that defined male homosexuality as a special danger to young men. As he put it:

> Homosexuality does not sustain what you would call the traditional Canadian values of family life and it's clear that the criminal law does have a role to play in maintaining traditional moral values as well as supporting medical ventures and psychological health of the population.[95]

Rather than calling for more and better safe-sex education — including on the proper usage of condoms for anal sex — they instead fell back on associating at least one central sexual practice they linked with homosexuality (although many heterosexuals engage in this act as we saw in the *Canada Youth and AIDS Study*, which reported that fifteen percent of "sexually active" youths reported engaging in this sexual activity[96]) with a sexual and a health threat. This was based in part on the unfounded assumption that HIV is more easily spread through anal than vaginal intercourse and runs contrary to the advise of AIDS groups who support the proper use of condoms for both vaginal and anal sex. Instead, this higher age of consent makes it more difficult to do safe-sex education by criminalizing these activities. Although there have now been successful lower court legal challenges to the constitutionality of eighteen as the age of consent for anal intercourse this remains the law. When challenged in court, the federal-government lawyers have relied on arguments similar to those that Avison put forward.[97] This historical, legal legacy continues to associate certain sexual practices with homosexual danger.

The Youth-Porn Law: Re-criminalizing Gay-Male Sex

In 1993 the Conservative government rushed Bill C-128 through the House of Commons and the Senate (it is now Section 163.1 of the Criminal Code). This law was supposed to protect young people by prohibiting "child pornography." For the first time it criminalized possession of "child pornography," which was in part defined as pictures depicting anyone who appears to be under eighteen in explicit sexual activities. This is based on the unfounded assumption that images of sexual acts involving young people incite sexual violence against young people. It also prohibits written materials or visual representations that advocate or counsel sexual activities involving people under the age of eighteen. This law makes it more difficult to undertake explicit safe-sex education or progressive sexuality education with young people, and many community-based AIDS groups have come out in opposition to it for this reason.

This law was used against Toronto artist Eli Langer for his line drawings that explored questions of adult/youth and youth/youth sexuality and child sexual abuse. (Langer later won in court in April 1995 and his work has been returned to him.) But this law is not only being used for sexual censorship but also as a way of criminalizing the lives of young male hustlers and consensual sex between men. It has been used against a number of male prostitutes in Toronto and London, Ontario, especially those who have made or participated in sex videos as part of their work or who made home movies. Almost all of these charges have been associated with male/male sexual activities, and the seizure provision of the law is being used to collect evidence that can be used to criminalize consensual homosexual sex, especially anal sex involving someone under the age of eighteen. Previously the police would have had little means to collect evidence against such consensual sex that occurs in "private."[98]

In London, police operations were launched after some sexually explicit videotapes were fished out of a river. The police created still pictures of the young, local male prostitutes in the videos and exhibited these pictures around the city to school officials, youth-agency workers, and to other young people. They were thus making these young men's private and work lives very public. As of April 1994, London police claimed to have interrogated more than two hundred young people and to have identified eighteen "victims." "Project Guardian" is now a joint project between the London, Ontario, and Toronto police forces.

Of the more than fifty men arrested so far, many are twenty-one years of age or younger. Of those convicted, very few are actually being convicted of youth-pornography offences. Instead, most are convicted for anal sex with someone under the age of eighteen and/or buying (or attempting to buy) the sexual services of someone under the age of eighteen. While no doubt there has been harassment and abuse involved in some of these interactions, the police are not differentiating between unconsensual and consensual activities. Most of the younger people who have been charged and those identified as "victims" are male prostitutes. Most of the young people charged are charged with making "obscene" material or with having anal intercourse with someone under eighteen years of age or both. At the same time, court decisions questioning the constitutionality of the age of consent of eighteen for anal sex is making it more difficult for the police to use this section of the Criminal Code in this way.

The arrests are often the result of police pressuring the young men to name their sexual contacts. One fifteen-year-old male prostitute says police threatened to charge him unless he cooperated by discussing one of his clients (who has since been arrested). "They said they wouldn't tell my parents" the fifteen-year-old says. "That's the only reason why I did it." But he says he later found the police talking to his parents. He is now afraid he will be thrown out of his house. "They think I'm a fag now [My parents told me] You're a queer, we don't like you any more."[99]

In April 1994 as part of this police operation a twenty-seven-year-old man pleaded guilty to anal sex with two men, aged twenty-seven and forty-two, since anal sex is a crime when there are more than two people present. All the participants were consenting but the event was recorded on video and retrieved by police from the bottom of a river. This demonstrated how the new youth-pornography legislation is being used to criminalize consensual homosexual sex the police would otherwise have no evidence to use against. Gay organizations like the Homophile Association of London Ontario and the Coalition for Lesbian and Gay Rights in Ontario have begun to protest against this targeting of sex between men and male prostitutes under this law.

In this instance, the very law designed to "protect" young people is actually being used against young people themselves and is being used against consensual gay sex and against male prostitutes. Needless to say, this legislation and the police action it mandates does nothing to get at the social roots of sexual violence and harassment against young people.

Criminalizing and Censoring the "Irresponsible" and Non-Familial

Last chapter I talked about the construction of the "familial-" and "spousal-" identified "responsible" gay and lesbian. At the same time, as we can see, other lesbians and gay men who make no claim to be involved in familial or spousal relations are constructed as "irresponsible"; these lesbians and gay men are consistently used by right-wing and moral-conservative groups to undermine the credibility of those constructed as being "responsible." This tendency coincides with continuing sexual policing of same-gender sexual practices and of State censorship of lesbian and gay erotic materials mentioned earlier in this chapter.

As Brenda Cossman suggests, for lesbians and gay men "it would seem that sexual, non-family subject positions are not legitimate."[100] "Responsibility" for lesbians and gay men is being constructed in terms of spousal and family relations that can lead to forms of self-regulation and self-management in these contexts. At the same time, for those who are not constructed as "familial" or "spousal," there is continued policing and oppressive regulation in areas regarding sexuality and social life outside spousal/familial contexts. These practices remain "deviant" and possibly "criminal," and are still constructed as some sort of "risk" or "threat" to others, especially to young people. As in *The Wolfenden Report*, those involved in sex with those under twenty-one (in the Canadian context now, anal sex with someone under eighteen), or engaged in sex-related activities that are too "public" and outside spousal realms, are still to be criminalized. The erotic practices of lesbians and gay men — the main social basis of our differences from institutionalized heterosexuality — remains a terrain of policing and criminalization.

This leads to an intensification of regulation in relation to sexual practices and sexualities which are a major aspect of our social *differences* from heterosexuals. By contrast, some *similarities* of family — and spousal classifications between heterosexual familial and some lesbian and gay relationships — are constructed as the route to "respectability." Some lesbians and gay men come to take up this strategy of "normalization" as their own, to govern their lives and in the process facilitate divisions between themselves and "irresponsible" queers. In organizing for Bill 167 in Toronto in 1994, there was an attempt to avoid dealing with the use of the youth-porn law against gay sex and other lesbian/gay struggles that could not be directly related to the struggle for "We are family!" This is why lesbian and gay organizing needs to avoid the polarities of this "responsible"/"irresponsible" strategy of regulation and to push beyond it, which requires addressing both our claims to spousal and familial status *and* the ending of the practices criminalizing and censoring our sexualities and lives.

The Military, the RCMP and Equality Rights

The institutions of Canadian State formation that had the most invested in defending the relations of heterosexual masculinity were also the most resistant to recognizing limited human-rights and anti-discrimination policies for lesbians and gay men. Until 1986, the RCMP Security Service regarded homosexuality as a "character weakness" and maintained a strict anti-gay and anti-lesbian hiring policy. They continued to pursue lesbians and gay men as a security risk after the 1969 Criminal Code reform, and strongly supported the federal refusal to amend the Canadian Human Rights Act to protect lesbians and gays from discrimination.[101]

In 1985, the RCMP released the document *RCMP Policy in Respect of Homosexual Conduct* amid the debate on the implementation of the equality rights section of the Charter of Rights. The document declared that homosexuality is "a bona fide operational impediment" because it undermines discipline, morale, public acceptance, and the RCMP's heterosexual "self-image"; because homosexuals are a "security risk"; because it undermines hierarchical rank and structure; because homosexuality is illegal under age twenty-one; because it conflicts with "majority rights"; and because it conflicts with RCMP policy to enforce "a strict compliance to the accepted moral standards." The document also argued that since communal living spaces like barracks and patrol cabins are "clearly not private places," "any homosexual acts committed in such places would in fact be criminal offences."[102] Once again, the limitations of the 1969 Code reform, which decriminalized only homosexual acts in private between two consenting adults, were used to argue against lesbian and gay rights. These policies were retained by the new civilian Canadian Security Intelligence Service which replaced the RCMP security service in 1984.[103]

In response to the federal government's declaration in 1986 that Section 15 of the

Charter, dealing with equality rights, would be interpreted to include sexual-orientation protection, the RCMP decided that lesbians and gays were free to join the force, but at first only if they were "out." In 1988, under pressure, official discrimination in hiring and promotion was ended. It remains to be seen what real effect these policy shifts have had on lesbian and gay applicants and current members and on more deeply rooted informal practices of discrimination.

In the military, the administrative order prohibiting lesbians and gay men from being in the military was modified slightly in 1976 to bring it more into line with contemporary discourse and to take into account the 1969 Criminal Code reform (although this meant very little real change). The new title was *Homosexuality: Sexual Abnormality, Investigation, Medical Examination and Disposal.* Key to this change was the use and definition of the term "homosexuality." The stages outlined for dealing with homosexuals were investigation, discipline, disposal, and release. It was now the Special Investigation Unit (SIU) that investigates cases.[104]

There have been many documented purges from the military.[105] Military defence of their anti-gay, anti-lesbian policies ranged from the potential for "blackmail" to concerns over proper military order, morale, and "operational efficiency."[106] Again, they argued that since there is no real "private" realm in the military, homosexuality just cannot be tolerated.

In 1989 a corporal who admitted to being gay had his security clearance revoked. He was then asked to submit a "voluntary release." He refused and took them to the Federal Court of Canada, which forced them to return his security clearance.[107] These policies continued in varying forms in the armed forces until 1992. In 1991 there was an attempt to end the ban on lesbians and gay men in the military, but this was scuttled due to a revolt by the "family caucus" in the Conservative caucus. Michelle Douglas took the government to court challenging the military ban. In October 1992, the case was settled very quickly. Federal lawyers conceded that "sexual orientation" was included in Section 15 of the Charter and that this discrimination could not be justified. The judge signed a consent order and the Department of National Defence announced the end of its discriminatory policy.[108] There remain continuing informal practices of discrimination, and gay/lesbian members of the military are not granted the same spousal financial support, as well as travel rights to be with their partners as are common-law heterosexual couples.

The Charter and Sexual Policing: The Contradictory Situation We Are In

The current situation in Canada is marked by two seemingly contradictory developments for lesbians and gay men and on the questions of human rights and sexuality more generally. These impact differently in our lives in relation to class, gender, race, age, and other social differences. On the one hand, the implementation of the equality rights section of the Canadian Charter of Rights and Freedoms and the Charter's outlining of at least a partially different pattern of State formation — in concert with our extra-parliamentary and legal struggles — has led to a situation of considerable pressure for sexual-orientation protection in human-rights legislation at the federal and provincial levels.[109] In some jurisdictions this has led to some progress on spousal benefits and even family-recognition fronts of struggle. (This trend was explored in more detail last chapter.) This is, however, only one side of the picture — the optimistic side, if you will.

At the same time, there also exists an extension and intensification of certain forms of sexual policing and censorship directed against us. This is evident in the video-surveillance arrests in southern Ontario, in the arrest of men on charges of "indecent acts," in the implementation of Bill C-49 against prostitutes and hustlers passed in late 1985 which has so far withstood a number of constitutional challenges, in the seizure by Canada Customs of lesbian and gay erotic materials, in the opposition mounted to explicit safe-sex education for gay men in the context of AIDS,[110] and in the ways the new federal youth-pornography law is being used in southern Ontario against hustlers and consensual gay sex. This escalation of sexual policing affects a number of our sex-related practices, from men who have sex in washrooms and parks, to gay hustlers, to young lesbians, gay men and bisexuals who need access to information about queer sexual practices, to community AIDS workers, to lesbians, gay men and bisexuals who read, view, write, and produce erotic materials.

While on an abstract and formal level, many State and social agencies and the federal government now recognize that we should enjoy equal rights with heterosexuals, they are still not willing to recognize our substantive rights to equality and freedom from oppression. They are unwilling to endorse the actual sexual activities or relationships in which we engage or to challenge the deeply rooted practices of heterosexual hegemony in Canadian State, legal, and social formation. Our rights as "private" individuals are recognized, while our real social and material differences — our erotic pleasures and the gender of those we love, are still not recognized as valid and equal. This situation continues some of the limitations of the 1969 reform. Doug Sanders' comments on then-Justice Minister Crosbie's remarks in response to the report of the equality-rights committee in 1986 is useful in clarifying this situation.

> Crosbie [the justice minister who introduced the equality rights position] has said that he is not condoning homosexuality in his present statements ... it is impressive to me how the current Crosbie attitude is constructed. It is put forward as it is the law anyway. There is no debate about "Oh God! we made a mistake." "Oops, we should have drafted Section 15 of the Charter more carefully."... The issue can be avoided on the one side by saying, "Well, we are not using a closed list of categories" so you avoid actually saying yes it's in ... This is all legitimated by law and law is beyond debate because it is so sanctified within the political system. So Crosbie can say, "Well, this is the law." And you don't come to grips with the issue.[111]

We therefore face a highly paradoxical situation: on the one hand we are closer than ever to winning sexual-orientation protection and in many areas spousal benefits, while on the other hand the police are still able to harass and arrest us for "queer" or "deviant" sex.

The ambiguity is perhaps highlighted in the recent decision in the Jim Egan spousal-benefits case mentioned in the introduction. On the one hand, the Supreme Court recognized that sexual orientation is included in the equality rights guaranteed in the Charter. On the other, for somewhat varying reasons, the majority decided that the different-sex definition of "spouse" in the Old Age Security Act did not constitute discrimination against pension benefits for same-sex couples or that this was a justified form of discrimination under the Charter.[112] While we have abstract rights when it comes to our lives and relationships, these rights in the substantive realm where they have real meaning in our lives don't really seem to exist. The practices of heterosexual hegemony have only been dislodged on the formal and abstract level of discrimination against "private" individuals on the basis of "sexual orientation" while the social practices of heterosexual hegemony relating to our sexualities and relationships have not been substantially challenged.

As Doug Sanders expressed it in relation to the limitations of recent legal decisions: "Homosexuals can have 'equality' so long as their lives are 'not condoned' and their presence is not forced into the consciousness of others."[113] In response we have to act to break through the boundaries of a limited individual formal equality to establish a social acceptance for our sexualities and relationships that must become part of the general social consciousness.

There have been two distinct reactions to the growth of lesbian and gay communities and our liberation movements. Most provincial Tories, the Reform Party, some federal Liberal backbenchers, the police establishment, and the moral conservatives would deny us recognition as legitimate communities, and — within the boundaries of what they can continue to get away with under the Charter — to continue to deny our civil and human rights in as many areas as they can. They want to retain, and indeed broaden, the definition of "public" and to extend public forms of regulation into the private realm. The boundary between public and private can be quite fuzzy indeed. Public/private categories, when they are found not to be working quite right, can be re-deployed and the boundaries between them shifted. These public/private categories are ones of rule, of social administration. These efforts may bring aspects of same-gender sex more directly under the jurisdiction of the police or other State agencies, re-criminalizing aspects of gay sex. When resistance to police practices like the bath raids is too strong, the sex police attack more vulnerable targets like the men who engage in washroom sex. They focus on those queers who can be portrayed as "irresponsible." This is part of a strategy of those groups who wish to see our visibility reduced. While the target is gay and lesbian visibility and defence of the relations of heterosexual hegemony, they focus on the supposed queer threat to young people, on washroom or "public" sex, lesbian or gay porn, queer SM, or that we supposedly "spread" HIV and AIDS.

As we saw in the Bill 167 debate in Ontario, they are adamantly opposed to family-recognition rights for lesbians and gays. These forces now have new ideological ammunition in a political and social climate defined by a fixation on deficit reduction and fiscal restraint, with attempts to construct and to discredit progressive social movements as "special interest" groups, and with the right-wing campaign against "political correctness" which is being used against a number of equality-seeking movements. The term "politically correct" originated in the feminist, gay, and left movements in the late 1970s and early 1980s as part of a critique of an overly moralistic and rigid form of politics. It was not intended as a weapon to be used against struggles against racism, sexism, and heterosexism. The term has now been taken over and colonized by the right wing, and has become a term used to mobilize opposition to anti-racist, feminist, and lesbian and gay movements.[114]

More liberal elements have adopted a different attitude, basically defending, modifying, and expanding the Wolfenden perspective of the 1969 reform and the right of two adults to practise homosexual acts in private. Most now believe, abstractly or generally, in civil and human rights for lesbians and gay men. This position, including interpretations of the Charter itself, is the result of years of campaigning by activists, who have won the support of other groups such as the federal, Ontario, Manitoba, Alberta, and Saskatchewan Human Rights Commissions, the trade unions, the United Church,[115] the feminist movement, and many other groups. Basic sexual-orientation protection has now been established in Québec, Ontario, Manitoba, Yukon, New Brunswick, Nova Scotia,[116] British Columbia, and Saskatchewan. The Alberta government is very hostile to human-rights protection for lesbians and gay men and the Liberal government in Newfoundland also remains adamantly opposed.[117] Following passage of the inclusion of sexual orientation as grounds for sentencing for hate crimes in June 1995 — which was opposed by some Liberal backbenchers — the Chrétien government seems prepared to postpone the introduction of such protection in federal human-rights legislation. While they state their general commitment to this goal, it seems to be placed on the back burner and only activist campaigns can alter this.

Sexual-orientation protection, while it is an important victory, is still a relatively limited tool for bringing about lesbian and gay liberation. It recognizes our right not to be discriminated against in a series of areas on the basis of our "orientation," but still permits our arrest under the Criminal Code if we engage in prohibited sexual acts, or if we engage in these acts in the "wrong" place. Sexual-orientation protection does nothing in and of itself to dislodge institutionalized heterosexuality in social, family, and other State policies nor to stop oppressive sexual policing. It does not stop criminalization of our sexualities or guarantee our spousal and family recognition rights.

In response to these limitations of basic human-rights reform, we have gone on to argue for recognition of our spousal benefits and recognition of our familial relationships as outlined in the last chapter. This has forced some liberal and social-democratic sectors to support these struggles and in response to develop a strategy supportive of normalizing and responsibilizing some lesbian and gay relationships.

This exists simultaneously with others of us being constructed as "irresponsible" through the strategy mobilized by criminalization and censorship practices.

These two basic trends are responding to a situation brought about by the contradictions of the 1969 reform legislation — and the ensuing social struggles — and the implementation of the equality-rights section of the Charter. While some homosexual acts were de-criminalized in the private realm, they have never been legalized or accepted as socially approved or equal activities. Major aspects of our oppression continue. Gay and lesbian sex remains fundamentally "indecent" and "obscene" under the law.

> There is a great measure of ambiguity inherent in a Criminal Code which legalizes sex between consenting adult males in private, while at the same time allowing their arrest on the grounds that such behaviour is indecent.[118]

Moral conservatives and the police have adopted a strategy of using the limitations and ambiguities of the practices coming out of the 1969 reform to criminalize and in some cases to re-criminalize aspects of gay sexual practice thereby decreasing its visibility. The strategy of more liberal sectors, while it reflects our gains, also includes re-deployment of the public/private and adult/youth categories of regulation in order to manage us as a social problem. In general, there has been a shift toward a greater focus on adult/youth distinctions which go far beyond the regulation of gay and lesbian sex. While sexual-orientation protection is supported by liberal sectors, it may only prevent discrimination on the basis of general "orientation" or on the basis of acts in private between two consenting adults, and not sex in other contexts. It may not be extended to cover our relationships and families. In response to a presentation I made to an Ontario hearing on human-rights legislation in 1981, James Renwick of the NDP stated:

> I have great difficulty in the relationship between adult homosexuals and young people, particularly in the school system, but elsewhere who have a trust responsibility in my view; the dominant cultural mores of the society, which is a heterosexual one, and the relationship of course to the parents in that system as well as the elected school boards in that system ... We are talking about an anxiety related to a cultural mores which is heterosexual. The problem is the question of advocacy or as the Board of Education for the City of Toronto said, proselytization.[119]

If these liberals and social democrats had their way, the public sphere would continue to be highly policed. Questions of family life, young people, and the school system would continue to be off-limits for lesbian and gay liberation. Attempts would be made to incorporate our movement into forms of self-policing and regulation. This strategy — while it could help legitimize adult gay ghettoes and communities, providing the conditions for more people to come out and for continuing liberation struggles — would not centrally address heterosexual hegemony. Some who advocate this approach are willing to accept lesbian/gay spousal/family relationship rights if they are incorporated into a strategy of "responsibilization" and "normalization."[120] This constructs major divisions in our communities.

Some of us — those who are not too "queer" — would be accepted into respectable straight society, but not on our own terms. Heterosexual hegemony would be retained, regulating our communities, our sexualities, and our cultures, and preventing any basic challenge to heterosexual hegemony and dominant sex/gender relations.

Our movements must form tactical blocs at times with liberal sectors against the forces of conservatism — in support of equality rights and sexual-orientation protection, for instance — while still keeping our own autonomy. We must continue to: demand repeal of all anti-gay and anti-lesbian laws; defend gays against entrapment in washrooms and parks; defend our community institutions; build alliances for democratic control of the police; push for the transformation of the laws continuing to criminalize queer sex; push for better human-rights protection and better human-rights commissions; push for a transformation of our portrayal in the mass media; demand health services for lesbians and gay men; demand adequate AIDS/HIV treatment and social supports; and demand fundamental changes in schooling and family and social policy including our spousal and family rights. All this means that we must go beyond the boundaries of the 1969 reform and the present strategy of sexual rule. A crucial part of this is opposing the polarization of "responsible"/"irresponsible" lines of regulation by bringing together our struggles against criminalization and censorship, and for our spousal and family rights as part of a socially transformative challenge to heterosexual hegemony. This also needs to be part of building broader coalitions with other oppressed and marginalized groups as part of building a revitalized socialist movement centrally defined by feminism, anti-racism, struggles for lesbian and gay liberation, and which clearly takes the side of working class and poor people.

Notes

1. On some of this, see Dorothy E. Smith and George W. Smith, "Re-organizing the Job Skills Training Relation: From 'Human Capital' to 'Human Resources'" in Jacob Muller, ed., *Education for Work, Education as Work: Canada's Changing Community Colleges* (Toronto: Garamond, 1990), pp. 171-176, 184-186.
2. For work on authoritarian statism, see Nicos Poulantzas, *State Power Socialism* (London: Verso, 1978), especially pp. 203-247; and Stuart Hall, *et al.*, *Policing the Crisis* (London: MacMillan Press, 1979), pp. 218-323. In my view these tendencies toward more authoritarian State formation are neither monolithic, inevitable nor free of contradiction.
3. See Gordon and Hunter, *Sex, Family and the New Right* (New England Free Press, Somerville, MA, 1979), reprinted from the Nov. 1977-Feb. 1978 issue of *Radical America*; Rosalind Pollack Petchesky, *Abortion and Women's Choice* (Boston: Northeastern University Press, 1985); and Allen Hunter, "In the Wings: New Right Organization and Ideology" in *Radical America*, V. 15, No. 1 and 2, Spring 1981, pp. 113-138.
4. See Margaret Cerullo, "Hope and Terror, The Paradox of Gay and Lesbian Politics in the '90s" in *Radical America*, V. 34, No. 3, pp. 10-16; An interview with Suzanne Pharr, "Commu-

nity organizing and the Religious Right: Lessons From the Measure 9 Campaign" in *Radical America*, V. 24, No. 4, pp. 67-75; and an interview with Suzanne Pharr, "Up against Hate: Lessons from Oregon's Measure Nine Campaign" in *Gay Community News*, Apr. 1993, pp. 3, 11; Cindy Patton, "Tremble, Hetero Swine!" in Michael Warner, ed., *Fear of a Queer Planet: Queer Politics and Social Theory* (Minneapolis and London: University of Minnesota Press, 1993), pp. 143-161; and Lisa Duggan, "Queering the State" in *Social Text*, No. 39, Summer 1994, pp. 1-14.

5. Quoted in Maggie French, "Loves, Sexualities, and Marriages: Strategies and Adjustments" in Ken Plummer, ed., *Modern Homosexualities, Fragments of Lesbian and Gay Experience* (London and New York: Routledge, 1992), p. 87; Vicki Carter, "Abseil Makes the Heart Grow Fonder: Lesbian and Gay Campaigning Tactics and Section 28" in Ken Plummer, ed., *Modern Homosexualities, op. cit.*, pp. 217-226; and see Davina Cooper, *Sexing The City: Lesbian and Gay Politics within the Activist State* (London: Rivers Oram Press, 1994).

6. Because of space limitations, I am unable to fully explore the emergence and organization of this "anti-permissive" sentiment. See the above sources for a fuller exposition of this process. Also see Hall, *et al.*, *Policing the Crisis, op. cit.*, for a wonderful analysis of the social organization of "moral panics" in England during the 1970s surrounding "mugging." They show how the media, the judiciary, and the police organized existing anti-permissive sentiments into a "moral panic" over racially-coded crime. Also Stuart Hall, "The Great Moving Right Show" in *Socialist Review*, No. 55 (V. 11, No. 1), Jan.-Feb. 1981.

7. See Hunter, *op. cit.*, pp. 129-133.

8. See Laurie E. Adkin, "Life in Kleinland: Democratic Resistance to Folksy Fascism" in *Canadian Dimension*, V. 29, No. 2, Apr.-May 1995, especially, p. 40. The right-wing Social Credit government in British Columbia in 1983-84 directly attacked the rights of lesbians and gay men, as well as those of many other groups. Under the banner of "restraint" and despite popular opposition, the government dismantled the province's Human Rights Commission and legislation and abolished rent controls, employment-standards legislation, and much more. Some of the cutbacks on women's services were justified by the Socreds because they allegedly served only "homosexual women." Women were told to take up the slack for abandoned government programs. The government's right-wing offensive not only restricted lesbians' and gay men's abilities to have our rights recognized and our grievances redressed, but also clearly limited the social space in which our communities could grow and organize. See Sara Diamond, "Lesbians against the BC Budget" in *Pink Ink*, No. 4, Oct. 1983, pp. 9-10; and Betty Baxter, "Building Solidarity" in *Pink Ink*, No. 5, Dec.-Jan. 1984, pp. 4,6-7.

9. Organizing by REAL Women, for instance, was partly responsible for the Secretary of State deciding to refuse to fund women's programs that supported women's right to choose on abortion or lesbian rights. See Becki Ross, "Heterosexuals Only Need Apply: The Secretary of State's Regulation of Lesbian Existence" in *Resources for Feminist Research*, V. 17, No. 3, Sept. 1988, pp. 35-39.

10. On the moral-conservative right wing in Canada, see Lorna Erwin, "REAL Women: Anti-Feminism and the Welfare State" in *Resources for Feminist Research*, No. 17, 1988, and her "What Feminists Should Know about the Pro-Family Movement in Canada: A Report on a Recent Survey of Rank-and-File Members" in Peta Tancred Sherif, ed., *Feminist Perspectives: Prospect and Retrospect* (Montréal and Kingston: McGill-Queen's University Press, 1988); and Didi Herman, *Rights of Passage: Struggles for Lesbian and Gay Legal Equality* (Toronto: University of Toronto Press, 1994), especially pp. 77-127.

11. Hudson Hilsden's moral-conservative Interchurch Committee on Pornography has been credited with helping the federal Tories formulate their anti-porn proposals. See editorial, "Sex Tory Style" in *Rites*, V. 3, No. 3, July/Aug. 1986, p. 3. The same Hilsden is also the chair of the "Coalition for Family Values" that fought against sexual-orientation protection in Ontario in 1986 and has been active in opposing Bill 167 in Ontario and the hate-crimes sentencing legislation on the federal level.

12. I try to not use "backlash" as an explanation for the opposition that feminists and lesbian/gay

activists confront. Rather I argue that the social relations of "backlash" that mobilize some people against these movements are socially organized in part through mass-media coverage. On some of this, see Janice Newson, "'Backlash' against Feminism: A Disempowering Metaphor" in *Resources for Feminist Research* V. 20, No. 3/4, Fall/Winter 1991, pp. 93-97.

13. For instance, see Susan Hemmings, "Horrific Practices: How Lesbians Were Presented in the Newspapers of 1978" in Gay Left Collective, ed., *Homsexuality: Power and Politics* (London and New York: Allison and Busby, 1980), especially pp. 162-167.

14. *CBS Reports: Gay Power, Gay Politics* (CBS News, 1980), broadcast over the CBS television network Sat., Apr. 26, 1980. Producers Grace Diekhous and George Crile. Also see Gary Kinsman, "To Whom is Homosexuality a Problem? The Social Construction of a New Media Frame for Gay Men: An Analysis of CBS Reports *Gay Power, Gay Politics*," unpublished paper, 1981; and the work of Jill Thomas and George Smith on the social construction of this production, including George Smith's "Telling Stories: CBS Woos Viewers with Sex, Violence, and Drama in Their Made-for-TV Special *Gay Power, Gay Politics*" in *Fuse*, Mar./Apr. 1981, pp. 62-64.

15. Harry Reasoner, the anchorman, uses this expression in the closing lines of the program.

16. See National Gay Task Force letter of complaint to the National News Council, and Randy Alfred's complaint to the National News Council, July 10, 1980.

17. Dorothy E. Smith, "The Ideological Practice of Sociology" in *Catalyst*, No. 8, 1974, pp. 39-54 and in *The Conceptual Practices of Power* (Toronto: University of Toronto Press, 1990), pp. 31-57.

18. See Edward Jay Epstein, *News from Nowhere* (New York: Random House, 1973), particularly chapter 5, "The Resurrection of Reality"; Mark Fishman, *The Manufacturing of News* (Austin, Texas: University of Texas Press, 1980); and George Smith, "Media Frames: How Accounts are Produced and Read" in *Fuse* Jan./Feb., 1983, pp. 279-283.

19. Dorothy E. Smith, "The Social Construction of Documentary Reality" in *Sociological Inquiry*, V. 44, No. 4, p. 260. Also in revised form in *The Conceptual Practices of Power, op. cit.*

20. See Gaye Tuchman, *Making News* (New York and London: The Free Press, 1978), p. 109.

21. Like the coroner, Mayor Feinstein, journalist Charles McCabe, and statistics from the Kinsey Institute.

22. George Crile in CBS Report's *Gay Power, Gay Politics, op. cit.*

23. For an elaboration of the active role of texts (including TV documentaries) in the organization of social relations, see Dorothy E. Smith, "The Active Text: A Textual Analysis of the Social Relations of Public Textual Discourse," unpublished paper prepared for the World Congress of Sociology in Mexico City, Aug. 1982. Also in *Texts, Facts and Femininity* (London and New York: Routledge, 1990), pp. 120-158.

24. Graham Murdock, "Political Deviance: The Press Presentation of a Militant Mass Demonstration" in *The Manufacture of News* (London: Constable, 1973), p. 173.

25. Used by Crile in CBS Report's *Gay Power, Gay Politics, op. cit.*

26. Frank Pearce, "How To Be Immoral and Ill, Pathetic and Dangerous All at the Same Time" in *The Manufacture of News, op. it.*, p. 300. On violence against lesbians and gay men also, see Gary David Comstock, *Violence against Lesbians and Gay Men* (New York: Columbia University Press, 1991); New Brunswick Coalition for Human Rights Reform, *Discrimination and Violence Encountered by Lesbian, Gay, and Bisexual New Brunswickers*, 1990; and Carolyn Gibson Smith, *"Proud but Cautious": Homophobic Abuse and Discrimination in Nova Scotia* (Halifax, Nova Scotia Public Interest Research Group, 1994).

27. Ed Jackson, "Close but Not Enough: The 1980 Toronto Municipal Election" in Jackson and Persky, eds., *Flaunting It!* (Vancouver and Toronto: New Star and Pink Triangle, 1982), pp. 265-266.

28. Renaissance, *Liberation*, Oct. 1980.

29. See Casey and Kinsman, "Whose Freedom and Whose Press?" in Jackson and Persky, *op. cit.*, p. 27. One front of struggle that has emerged out of queer and AIDS activism is what can be referred to as "media activism" or attempts to get more supportive framings adopted by the mass media by seizing the initiative and challenging and changing the language that is used.

One group that has emerged is Toronto's OUT!SPOKEN, an action and advocacy group to end media discrimination against lesbians, bisexuals, and Gays. See their *The* OUT!SPOKEN *Styleguide: A Guide for the Media on Lesbian, Bisexual, Gay and HIV/AIDS Issues* (Toronto) 1995.

30. Yvonne Chi-Ying Ng, "Ideology, Media and Moral Panics: An Analysis of the Jacques Murder," M.A. thesis, Centre for Criminology, University of Toronto, Nov. 1981. The quotes in this section, and this account, unless otherwise cited, are from this very insightful thesis.

31. On the moral character of the city and city streets and centres, see Mariana Valverde, "The City as Moral Problem" in *The Age of Light, Soap, and Water* (Toronto: McClelland and Stewart, 1991), pp. 129-154; and Carolyn Strange, *Toronto's Girl Problem: The Perils and Pleasures of the City, 1880-1930* (Toronto: University of Toronto Press, 1995).

32. On my use of ideological, see the work of Dorothy E. Smith including *The Conceptual Practices of Power, op. cit.,*; *Texts, Facts and Femininity, op. cit.*; and her "'Politically Correct': An Ideological Code" in Stephen Richer and Lorna Weir, eds., *Beyond Political Correctness: Toward the Inclusive University* (Toronto: University of Toronto Press, 1995), pp. 23-50.

33. Stan Cohen, *Folk Devils and Moral Panics* (London: MacGibbon and Kee, 1972).

34. See *The Body Politic*, Sept. 1977, pp. 1-2, 4.

35. On this see chapter 7 and my "Constructing 'Child Sexual Abuse': Mount Cashel, The Mass Media and Making Homosexuality a Social Problem," forthcoming, and "The Mount Cashel Orphanage Inquiry: The Inscription of Child Abuse," (talk by Gary Kinsman) in Chris McCormick, *Constructing Danger: The Mis/representation of Crime in the News* (Halifax: Fernwood, 1995), pp. 76-93.

36. See the Canadian Lesbian and Gay Rights Coalition, *Forum*, Winter 1979, V. 4, No. 1. The Truxx rebellion created the basis along with a behind the scenes lobbying campaign for sexual-orientation protection to be quietly adopted in Québec.

37. See Lesbian and Gay History Group of Toronto, "A History of the Relationship between the Gay Community and the Metropolitan Police," submission to the Bruner Study, 1981.

38. See Jackson and Persky, *Flaunting it!, op. cit.*, pp. 146-147. On the controversy over the publication of "Men Loving Boys Loving Men," see Becki Ross, "Like Apples and Oranges: Lesbian Feminist Responses to the Politics of *The Body Politic*" in *Fuse*, V. 16, No. 4, May/June 1993, pp. 19-28 and her *The House That Jill Built* (Toronto: University of Toronto Press, 1995), pp. 166-174.

39. See Stuart Russell, "The Offence of Keeping a Common Bawdy-House" in *Ottawa Law Review*, V. 14, No. 2, 1982, p. 275.

40. On the social organization of the police raids and how they were textually-mediated through the bawdy-house section of the Criminal Code, see George Smith, "Policing the Gay Community: An Inquiry into Textually-Mediated Social Relations" in *International Journal of the Sociology of Law*, V. 16, 1988, pp. 163-183.

41. Phil Scraton uses this expression in his work on the police to describe a negotiated tolerance between police and working-class "criminal" practices like street gambling. Also see Scraton, *The State of the Police* (London, Sydney: Pluto, 1985).

42. Thomas S. Fleming, "The Bawdy-House 'Boys': Some Notes on Media, Sporadic Moral Crusades, and Selective Law Enforcement" in *Canadian Criminology Forum*, V. 3, Spring 1981, p. 109.

43. See Gerald Hannon, "Making Gay Sex Dirty" in *The Body Politic*, May 1981, No. 73, pp. 6-10; and Fleming, *op. cit.*, p. 112.

44. See *Action!*, publication of the Right to Privacy Committee, V. 1, No. 3.

45. Mr. Lafrance, Justice and Legal Affairs Committee, Issue No. 81. Wed., May 5, 1982, p. 8.

46. *Ibid.*, p. 23.

47. Fleming, *op. cit.*, p. 105.

48. See Justice and Legal Affairs Committee, Issue No. 81, May 5, 1982, pp. 24, 26.

49. Schearing suggests that, "What distinguishes the scum from the public is that the scum are structurally in conflict with, and are enemies of, the public. The scum are ... 'in essence' trou-

blemakers, while the public are 'in essence' their victims. In distinguishing between the scum and the public as two classes who oppose each other as enemies, the police culture makes available to the police a social theory that they can use in the context of their work to define situations and to construct a course of action in response to them. This theory enables the police to transcend the situated features of encounters by relating them to a broader social context that identifies the 'real trouble-makers' and 'real victims.'" Clifford D. Shearing, "Subterranean Processes in the Maintenance of Power: An Examination of the Mechanisms Coordinating Police Action" in *Canadian Review of Sociology and Anthropology*, V. 18, No. 3, Aug. 1981, p. 288.

50. See George W. Smith, "Policing the Gay Community," *op. cit.* for an excellent analysis of the textually mediated character of police campaigns against the gay community. Also see Tim McCaskell, "The Bath Raids and Gay Politics" in Frank Cunningham, Sue Findlay, *et al.*, eds., *Social Movements/Social Change: The Politics and Practice of Organizing* (Toronto: Between the Lines/Socialist Studies, 1988), pp. 169-188.

51. See Tim McCaskell, "The Bath Raids and Gay Politics," *op. cit.*, pp. 169-188.

52. D. White and P. Sheppard, "Report on the Police Raids on Gay Steambaths," prepared by Alderman David White and Pat Sheppard, 1981.

53. Arnold Bruner, "Out of the Closet: Study of Relations between the Homosexual Community and the Police" in *Report to Mayor Arthur Eggleton and the Council of the City of Toronto*, Sept. 24, 1981. This report deals mostly with gay men. "Women in Gay Society" is a total of three pages, pp. 61-63.

54. *Ibid.*, pp. *159-160.*

55. *Ibid.*, p. 162.

56. See Stephen Hester and Peter Elgin, A Sociology of Crime (London and New York: Routledge, 1992), pp. 154-157; Phil Scraton, *The State of the Police* (London and Sydney: Pluto, 1985); Paul Gilroy, "Police and Thieves" in Centre for Contemporary Cultural Studies, *The Empire Strikes Back: Race and Racism in '70s Britain* (London: Hutchinson, 1982), pp. 143-182; Paul Gilroy, "The Myth of Black Criminality" in Martin Eve and David Musson, eds., *The Socialist Register 1982* (London: Merlin Press, 1982), pp. 47-56; and Paul Gilroy, "Lesser Breeds without the Law" in Paul Gilroy, ed., *'There Ain't No Black in the Union Jack: The Cultural Politics of Race and Nation* (Chicago: The University of Chicago Press, 1987), pp. 72-113.

57. George Smith, "In Defence of Privacy" in *Action!*, V. 3, No. 1.

58. See Scott Tucker, "Our Right to the World" in *The Body Politic*, July/Aug. 1982, No. 85, pp. 29-33; Leo Casey, "Sexual Politics and the Subversion of the Public Sphere: A Defense of Feminism and Gay Liberation" in Itala Rutter, ed., *Perspectives on Lesbian and Gay Liberation and Socialism* (New York: Democratic Socialists of America, early 1980s), pp. 8-16; and Scott P. Anderson, "Privacy: An Issue for the '80s?" *The Advocate*, No. 360, pp. 23-25.

59. These statistics are from the important work of Gay Court Watch in Toronto, which provided support for people arrested on gay-related charges.

60. On how local police request assistance from the Ontario Provincial Police and for an account of washroom sex in police language, see "Guelph Sex Video Policing: Internal Cop Documents" in *Rites*, V. 3, No. 2, June 1986, p. 7.

61. See Yanni Vassilas, "Guelph Fights Police Busts" in *Rites*, V. 2, No. 4, Sept. 1985, p. 4.

62. See Gary Kinsman, "1984—The Police Are Still with Us" in *Rites*, V. 1, No. 1, pp. 10-11; Gary Kinsman and Doug Wilson, "Police Entrapment Fighting Back with Court Watch" in *Rites* V. 1, No. 6, pp. 9-11; and George Smith, "In Defense of Privacy," *op cit.*

63. On the history of obscenity legislation in Canada, see Kirsten Johnson, "A History of Federal Obscenity Legislation in Canada" in her *Undressing the Canadian State: The Politics of Pornography from Hicklin to Butler* (Halifax: Fernwood, 1995), pp. 38-57; Gary Kinsman, "Porn/Censor Wars and the Battlefields of Sex" in *Issues of Censorship* (Toronto: A Space, 1985), p. 31-39; and Mariana Valverde and Lorna Weir, "Thrills, Chills and the 'Lesbian Threat,' or The Media,

the State and Women's Sexuality" in Varda Burstyn, ed., *Women against Censorship* (Vancouver and Toronto: Douglas and McIntyre, 1985), pp. 99-106.

64. Judge Vanek's judgement in the Glad Day trial, Mar. 4, 1983.

65. In 1984 the conviction against Kevin Orr, who worked at Glad Day, was overturned when the appeal judge agreed with the defence lawyer that Vanek had partially relied on the obsolete Hicklin obscenity test — which defined obscenity as anything that "depraves or corrupts."

66. Even though the prohibition on anal sex had been partially challenged in the *Joy of Gay Sex* case in 1987, Canada Customs memorandum D-911 was only changed to remove "anal pene-tration" as grounds for seizing materials in September 1994 just prior to Little Sister's chal-lenge to the constitutionality of Canada Custom's seizures in the B.C. Supreme Court finally being heard. See Cindy Filipenko, "Canada Customs Changes the Rules: Anal Sex Flip-flop Appears Timed to Influence Court Challenge" in *Xtra!* No. 260, Oct. 14, 1994, p. 1. Also see Chris Defoe, "Little Sister v. Big Brother" in *The Globe and Mail,* Oct. 8, 1994, C10. Also see Janine Fuller and Stuart Blackley, *Restricted Censorship on Trial* (Vancouver: Press Gang, 1995). On Jan. 19, 1996, the B.C. Supreme Court finally came down with its decision in the Little Sis-ter's case. The decision was only a partial victory and the basic constitutionality of Canada Customs censorship powers was upheld.

67. bell hooks, *Black Looks: Race and Representation* (Boston: South End Press, 1992). Also publish-ed by Between the Lines in Toronto.

68. There exists now not only the genre of "lesbian" porn made for the titillation of straight men, but also that made by and for lesbians. On *Bad Attitude,* one of the new lesbian sex magazines, see Ingrid MacDonald and Kate Lazier, "The Politics of Lesbian Sexual Imagination: Good Girls with Bad Attitudes" in *Rites,* V. 2, No. 4, Sept. 1985, pp. 14-15. On lesbian erotic images, also see Kiss and Tell, *Drawing the Line: Lesbian Sexual Politics on the Wall* (Vancouver: Press Gang, 1991) and their *Her Tongue on My Theory: Images, Essays and Fantasies* (Vancouver: Press Gang, 1994).

69. See Bill C-114 introduced in June 1986 and Bill C-54, tabled in May 1987. See Dany Lacombe, *Blue Politics: Pornography and the Law in the Age of Feminism* (Toronto: University of Toronto Press, 1994), pp. 99-136.

70. See Justice John Sopinka, Majority decision, Supreme Court of Canada, Donald Butler v. Her Majesty the Queen, 1992. I argue that the Butler decision was a partial shift in the definition and interpretation of the obscenity section that still focuses on the "undue exploitation of sex" clause. I argue this against both those who feel that the decision actually incorporated a feminist perspective and those who feel it is almost an entirely new and more dangerous piece of legislation. On interpretations of Butler, see Clare Barclay and Elaine Carol, "Obscenity Chill: Artists in a Post-Butler Era" in *Fuse,* V. 16, No. 2 (Winter 1992/1993), pp. 18-28; Thelma McCormack, "Keeping Our Sex 'Safe': Anti-Censorship Strategies vs. the Politics of Protec-tion" in *Fireweed,* Sex and Sexuality, V. 1. (Winter 1993), pp. 25-34; Kirsten Johnson, *Undressing the Canadian State: The Politics of Pornography from Hicklin to Butler* (Halifax: Fernwood, 1995), especially chapter 4, pp. 58-87; Dany Lacombe *Blue Politics: Pornography and the Law in the Age of Feminism* (Toronto: University of Toronto Press, 1994), pp. 133-136; and *Kiss and Tell: Her Tongue on My Theory, op. cit.,* pp. 75-92. Didi Herman in her account and analysis of the Butler decision seems to largely accept the Women's Legal Education and Action Fund's (LEAF) analysis of the decision and to not notice its implication for lesbians, gay men, and feminists involved in doing sexually explicit work. See her "Law and Morality Revisited: The Politics of Regulating Sado-Masochistic Porn and Practice," unpublished paper presented to the Cana-dian and American Law and Society Association Conferences, Calgary and Phoenix, June 1994.

71. On these questions, see Carole Vance, "Negotiating Sex and Gender in the Attorney Gen-eral's Commission on Pornography" in Lynne Segal and Mary McIntosh, eds., *Sex Exposed: Sexuality and the Pornography Debate* (New Brunswick, NJ: Rutger's University Press, 1993), pp. 29-49.

72. On the Bad Attitude trial following the Butler decision, see Becki Ross, "'Wunna His Fantasies': The State/d Indefensibility of Lesbian Smut" in *Fireweed*, Sex and Sexuality issue, V. 2, No. 38, Spring 1993, pp. 38-47.

73. Eleanor Brown, "Gay Sex Ruled Obscene: Court Rules Glad Days Porn is Degrading and Harmful" in *Xtra!* No. 202, July 24, 1992, p. 1, 21. See Glad Day Bookshop Inc. and Jearld Moldenhauer v. Deputy Minister of National Revenue for Customs and Excise, July 14, 1992, Ontario Court of Justice.

74. See Dennis Altman, "AIDS: The Politicization of an Epidemic" in *Socialist Review*, No. 78, V. 14, No. 6, Nov.-Dec. 1984, pp. 93-109; and Altman, *AIDS in the Mind of America* (Garden City, New York: Anchor Press/Doubleday, 1986). Also see the Canadian AIDS Society pamphlet, *Homophobia, Heterosexism and AIDS* (Ottawa, 1991); Gary Kinsman "'Their Silence, Our Deaths': What Can the Social Sciences Offer to AIDS Research?" in Diane E. Goldstein, ed., *Talking AIDS* (St. John's: Institute for Social and Economic Research (ISER) Press, ISER Policy Papers, No. 12, 1991), pp. 39-60; and Gary Kinsman, "Managing AIDS Organizing: 'Consultation,' 'Partnership,' and the National AIDS Strategy" in William K. Carrol, ed., *Organizing Dissent: Contemporary Social Movements in Theory and Practice* (Toronto: Garamond, 1992), pp. 215-231. The account presented in this section is based largely on these last three references.

75. See Health and Welfare Canada, *Building an Effective Partnership: The Federal Government's Commitment to Fighting AIDS* (Ministry of Supply and Services Canada, 1990), and *HIV and AIDS: Canada's Blueprint* (Ministry of Supply and Services Canada, 1990) and my critical analysis in "Managing AIDS Organizing," *op. cit.*

76. On the history of "public health," see Alan Sears, "'To Teach Them How To Live': The Politics of Public Health From Tuberculosis to AIDS" in *Journal of Historical Sociology*, V. 5, No. 1, 1992, pp. 61-83 and his "Before the Welfare State: Public Health and Social Policy" in *The Canadian Review of Sociology and Anthropology*, V. 32, No. 2, May 1995, pp. 169-188. Also see Cindy Patton, *Sex and Germs: The Politics of AIDS* (Montréal: Black Rose Books, 1985), pp. 58-61.

77. On this see Kinsman, "Constructing Sexual Problems: 'These Things May Lead to the Tragedy of Our Species,'" in Les Samuelson, ed., *Power and Resistance: Critical Thinking about Canadian Social Issues* (Halifax: Fernwood, 1994), pp. 179-181. This perspective is in contrast to the "Patient Zero" mythology partially produced in Randy Shilts, *And the Band Played On: Politics, People and the AIDS Epidemic* (New York: St. Martin's Press, 1987) and mass media coverage of it. For a critique, see Douglas Crimp, "How to Have Promiscuity in An Epidemic" in Crimp ed., *AIDS: Cultural Analysis, Cultural Activism* (Cambridge, MA: MIT Press, 1988), pp. 238-247. For a wonderful musical antidote to this perspective, see John Greyson's delightful *Zero Patience* (1993).

78. See Cindy Patton, *Inventing AIDS* (New York and London: Routledge, 1990).

79. Quoted in Canadian AIDS Society, *Homophobia, Heterosexism and AIDS, op. cit.* On Canadian media coverage, also see Ivan Emke, "Speaking of AIDS in Canada: The Texts and Contexts of Official, Counter-Cultural and Mass Media Discourses Surrounding AIDS," Ph.D. thesis, Sociology and Anthropology, Carleton University, 1991.

80. There was also widespread racism in the framing and construction of "African AIDS" through which colonial relations were reconstructed under the guise of scientific objectivity. See Cindy Patton, "Inventing 'African AIDS'" in her *Inventing AIDS, op. cit.*, pp. 77-97; and Simon Watney, "Missionary Positions: AIDS, 'Africa' and Race" in his *Practices of Freedom: Selected Writings on HIV/AIDS* (Durham: Duke University Press, 1994), pp. 103-120. Also see Renee Sabatier, *Blaming Others: Prejudice, Race and Worldwide AIDS* (Philadelphia: New Society, 1988); Paul Farmer, *AIDS and Accusation: Haiti and the Geography of Blame* (Berkeley: University of California Press, 1992); and Evelyn Hammonds, "Missing Persons, African American Women, AIDS and the History of Disease" in *Radical America*, V. 24, No. 2, pp. 7-23.

81. On this history see Cindy Patton, "Resistance and the Erotic: Reclaiming History, Setting Strategy as We Face AIDS" in Peter Aggleton, Graham Hart and Peter Davies, eds., *AIDS: So-*

cial Representations, Social Practices (London: Falmer Press, 1989), pp. 237-251. Also see Patton's *Inventing AIDS, op. cit.*

82. See Patton, *Inventing AIDS, op. cit.*, especially pp. 58-64.

83. See Roxana Ng, *The Politics of Community Services: Immigrant Women, Class and the State* (Toronto: Garamond, 1988) and Roxana Ng, Gillian Walker, and Jacob Muller, eds., *Community Organization and the Canadian State* (Toronto: Garamond, 1990).

84. In relation to heterosexual sex, penetrative vaginal intercourse is presented as the "real thing" and not the range of other sexual activities that some feminists had suggested in an attempt to expand safety and eroticism for women. Safer sex becomes simply the use of condoms in a form of condom reductionism — which is not to suggest that proper use of condoms is not crucial but that there are also other erotic activities that can be engaged in. There was also no focus on the re-negotiation of responsibility and power in heterosexual relations, even though it is much easier for a man to infect a woman through unprotected penis in vagina intercourse than the other way around. On some of this see the Women's Committee of ACT UP, *Women, AIDS and Activism* (Toronto: Between the Lines, 1991).

85. See Patton, *Inventing AIDS, op. cit.*

86. See Michael Callen, *Surviving AIDS* (New York: HarperPerennial, 1991).

87. See George Smith, "AIDS Treatment Deficits: An ethnographic inquiry into the management of the AIDS epidemic, the Ontario case," paper presented at the Fifth International AIDS Conference, Montréal, and his "Political Activist as Ethnographer" *in Social Problems*, V. 37, No. 4, Nov. 1990, pp. 629-648.

88. There was an important victory on this front in Ontario in December 1994 — after years of activist pressure — when the Ontario NDP government finally announced it would bring in a catastrophic drug-funding policy. Currently there are concerns that the new Conservative government may remove funding for some of the badly needed treatments from this program.

89. In research and clinical trials, there has been a focus on men and sometimes the exclusion of women from trials. This sexism has been linked to the lack of understanding of women's distinct experiences of HIV infection and AIDS — which has often led doctors to mis-diagnose women with HIV/AIDS. See ACT UP Women's Committee, *Women, AIDS and Activism op. cit.*

90. On federal AIDS policies, also see David Rayside and Evert Lindquist, "AIDS Activism and the State in Canada" in *Studies in Political Economy*, No. 39, Autumn 1992, pp. 37-76 and their "Canada: Community Activism, Federalism and the New Politics of Disease" in David L. Kirp and Ronald Bayer, eds., *AIDS in the Industrialized Democracies: Passions, Politics and Policies* (Montréal and Kingston: McGill-Queen's University Press, pp. 49-98. While these articles are very useful, I find that they tend to over-emphasize the impact of community-based groups on State policy and to underestimate the regulatory aspects of strategies adopted by State agencies.

91. See Eric Mykhalovskiy and George Smith, *Hooking Up to Social Services: A Report on the Barriers People with AIDS Face Accessing Social Services* (Toronto: Ontario Institute for Studies in Education/Community AIDS Treatment Information Exchange, 1994).

92. AIDS is also increasingly recognized as having a global character. It cannot simply be dealt with within the framework of the Nation-State. This international character is tied into global relations of racism and imperialism that must also be confronted. Dealing with AIDS on a global level requires the transfer of resources to affected parts of Africa and other parts of the "Third World," and ensuring that treatments are freely available in these countries.

93. See Gary Kinsman, "'Restoring Confidence in the Criminal Justice System': The Hughes Commission and Mass Media Coverage, Making Homosexuality a Problem" in *Violence and Social Control in the Home, Workplace, Community and Institutions: Papers Presented at the Twenty-sixth Annual Meeting of the Atlantic Association of Sociologists and Anthropologists* (St. John's: Institute for Social and Economic Research Conference Papers No. 3, 1992), pp. 211-269; my "The Hughes Commission: Making Homosexuality a Problem Once Again" in *New Maritimes*, V. 15, No. 3, Jan./Feb., 1993, pp. 17-19; and my forthcoming *"Constructing 'Child Sexual Abuse': Mount*

Cashel, The Mass Media and Making Homosexuality a Social Problem. "Also see "The Mount Cashel Orphanage Inquiry: The Inscription of Child Abuse," (talk by Gary Kinsman) in Chris McCormick, *Constructing Danger: The Mis/representation of Crime in the News* (Halifax: Fernwood, 1995), pp. 76-93.

94. See the *Report of the Committee on Sexual Offences Against Children and Youth* (1984), known as the Badgley Report, and the *Report of the Special Committee on Pornography and Prostitution* (1985), known as the Fraser Report. Also see Deborah R. Brock and Gary Kinsman, "Patriarchal Relations Ignored: An Analysis and Critique of the Badgley Report on Sexual Offences Against Children and Youths" in J. Lowman, M.A. Jackson, and S. Gavigan, eds., *Regulating Sex: An Anthology of Commentaries on the Findings and Recommendations of the Badgley and Fraser Reports* (Vancouver: School of Criminology, Simon Fraser University, 1986), pp. 107-125.

95. See Glenn Wheeler, "Tackling Abuse and Other Taboos" in *NOW*, Mar. 19-25, 1987, pp. 7-8.

96. See Alan King, Richard Beazley, Wendy Warren, *et al.*, *Canada Youth and AIDS Study* (Social Program Evaluation Group, Queen's University, Kingston, 1988), p. 86.

97. On May 24, 1995 the Ontario Court of Appeal released a decision agreeing with the constitutional challenge to the anal-intercourse age of consent being set at eighteen. Two of the judges found the law discriminatory on the basis of age while Rosalie Abella argued that it "disadvantages gay men by denying them until they are eighteen a choice available at the age of fourteen for those who are not gay ..." (Court of Appeal Justice Rosalie Abella quoted in *Northern Pride*, the publication of the Sudbury All Gay Alliance, Aug. 1995, p. 2-3). Also see Eleanor Brown, "Have Sex, Go To Jail; Court Ruling That Teens Can Have Anal Sex May Be Appealed" in *Capital XTRA!* No. 22, June 30, 1995, p. 21. In response, the London police and courts announced they would drop the twenty-two outstanding anal-intercourse charges against men rounded up through the use of the youth-pornography law. See the Coalition for Lesbian and Gay Rights in Ontario Aug. 1995 Newsletter, p. 6.

98. See Andrew Sorfleet and Chris Bearchell, "The sex police in a moral panic, how the 'youth porn' law is being used to censor artists and persecute youth sexuality" in *Parallelograme*, V. 20, No. 1, 1994, pp. 8-21; Forum 128, "Young People and Sex," (Toronto), 1993; Joseph Coutere researcher, "The Trials of London," on *Ideas* (CBC Radio), broadcast Oct. 7, 1994; and John Greyson, "After the Bath," broadcast on CBC Newsworld's *Rough Cuts*, May 5, 1995. Also see Gerald Hannon, "The Kiddie Porn Ring That Wasn't" in *The Globe and Mail*, Mar. 11, 1995; Joseph Coutere, "The London Kiddie Porn Ring That Isn't" in *Xtra!* No. 259, Sept. 23, 1994, p. 15; and Joseph Coutere, "Complaints Filed" in *Xtra!* No. 278, June 23, 1995, p. 35. The ability of the police to arrest and the courts to convict on anal-sex charges is now complicated by the recent Ontario Court of Appeal decision mentioned in note 97.

99. See "Youth Porn Campaign" in *Gazette* (Halifax), July/Aug., 1994, p. 17.

100. Brenda Cossman in Mariana Valverde compiled *Radically Rethinking Regulation Workshop Report* (Centre of Criminology, University of Toronto, 1994), p. 23.

101. Young, Wilson and Foster, "1984: James Bond Comes to Ottawa" in *Rites*, V. 1 No. 3, July/Aug. 1984, pp. 14-15.

102. "RCMP: No Queers Please" in *Rites*, V. 2, No. 3, July/Aug., 1985, p. 4.

103. Young, Wilson and Foster, *op. cit.*, pp. 14-15.

104. See *Rites*, V. 1, No. 10, Apr. 1985, pp. 3-5.

105. For instance, in 1974 a member of the armed forces in Petawawa, Ontario, was discharged for his homosexuality even though he had committed no crime nor been guilty of misconduct; information from the National Gay Rights Coalition, "The Homosexual Minority and the Canadian Human Rights Act," *op. cit.*, p. 14. In 1976 Jacques Gallant took the armed forces to court over discrimination. In 1977 Barbara Thornborrow and Gloria Cameron were expelled from the military when they were discovered to be lesbians. See Coalition for Gay Rights in Ontario, *The Ontario Human Rights Omission*, a brief to the members of the Ontario Legislature, 1981, p. 14. Darl Wood was expelled in 1978 and Stéphane Sirard in 1982. And in 1985 the Shelburne lesbian purge took place. The list could go on and on. The report of the fed-

eral committee on equality rights lists the numbers of discharges under CFAO-19-20: for 1981, 37; for 1982, 45; for 1983, 44; and in 1984, 38. See the Report of the Parliamentary Committee on Equality Rights, *Equality for All*, p. 30.

106. See Glenn Wheeler, "Unfit for Service" in *The Body Politic*, No. 91, Mar. 1983, p. 29. Many of these arguments are the same ones that have been used to prevent lesbians and gay men from openly serving in the U.S. military.

107. See Lawrence Braithwaite, "Armed and Dangerous: A Gay Soldier on Misogyny, Homophobia and Racism in the Canadian Armed Forces" in *Rites* Nov./Dec. 1991, pp. 13-14.

108. On this see Doug Sanders, "Constructing Lesbian and Gay Rights" in *Canadian Journal of Law and Society*, V. 9. No. 2, Fall 1994, p. 118.

109. On the impact of the Charter, see James E. Jefferson, "Gay Rights and the Charter" in *University of Toronto Law Review*, V. 43, No. 1, Spring 1985, pp. 71-89; and the *Report of the Parliamentary Committee on Equality Rights: Equality for All*, pp. 12-13. Also see Didi Herman, *Rights of Passage: Struggles for Lesbian and Gay Legal Equality* (Toronto: University of Toronto Press, 1994), although at times her account and analysis are rather far removed from extra-legal and extra-parliamentary struggles that have been an important part of this process; and Doug Sanders, "Constructing Lesbian and Gay Rights," *op. cit.*, p. 118.

110. For instance, there was an attempted "moral panic" organized against a safe-sex article for gay men that was part of the "Lesbian and Gay Supplement" of the *Muse* (The Memorial University Student paper) in St. John's and across the country in February 1991. See Patrick Barnholden, "A Gay Men's Guide to Erotic Safer Sex" in the "Lesbian and Gay Supplement" in *The Muse*, Feb. 15, 1991, p. 13.

111. From the interview with Doug Sanders cited earlier, June 1986.

112. On the Egan decision, see A. Lawyer, "Egan and Nesbitt: An Analysis" and "Supreme Court Rules" in *Wayves*, V. 1, No, 5, June 1995, p. 1; Philip Hannon, "Checkered Victory: No Pension for Spouse of 47 Years, Court Rules" in *Xtra!* No. 277, June 9, 1995, p. 1, 12.

113. See Doug Sanders, "Constructing Lesbian and Gay Rights," *op. cit.*, p. 120.

114. On the social organization of the campaign against political correctness, see Stephen Richer and Lorna Weir, eds., *Beyond Political Correctness: Toward the Inclusive University* (Toronto: University of Toronto Press, 1995), especially Dorothy E. Smith, "'Politically Correct': An Ideological Code," pp. 23-50 and Lorna Weir, "PC Then and Now: Resignifying Political Correctness," pp. 50-87.

115. On the various struggles within the United Church, see Michael Riordon, *The First Stone: Homosexuality and the United Church* (Toronto: McClelland and Stewart, 1990).

116. On the struggle in Nova Scotia, see my interview with Maureen Shebib, "The Long Lobby for Legal Protection" in *Rites*, Sept. 1989, pp. 8-9.

117. I was part of an unsuccessful lobbying campaign for sexual-orientation protection in Newfoundland and Labrador in 1991. See "'Here to Stay!' Lesbians and Gays in Newfoundland and Labrador: Fighting for our Rights" in *Gays and Lesbians Together* (Gays and Lesbians Together, St. John's, 1991). This struggle continues with the efforts of Newfoundland Gays and Lesbians for Equality. In late 1995 the Newfoundland Supreme Court ruled that sexual-orientation protection must be read into the provincial Human Rights code. *Wayves*, Nov. 1995, V.1, No.9.

118. Fleming, *op. cit.*, p. 109. I would use, however, the word "decriminalization" and not "legalization" to describe what took place in 1969.

119. Standing Committee on Resource Development Hearings on the Human Rights Code, Wed., Sept. 16, 1981, afternoon sitting, pp. 26-27. Renwick is now deceased. On the Board of Education, see note 115, chapter 9.

120. For more elaboration, see "'Responsibility' as a strategy of governance: Regulating people living with AIDS and lesbians and gay men in Ontario," forthcoming in *Economy and Society*, August 1996.

11.

From Resistance to Liberation

Lesbian/Gay Liberation: A Transformative Emancipatory Politics

In the 1990s lesbian and gay liberation — and challenges to heterosexual hegemony — must be situated within a broader context of sexual and social struggles; one characterized by struggles over the Charter of Rights and Freedoms and equality rights on the one hand, and intensified sexual policing and the continuing denial of our actual sexualities and relationships on the other. Heterosexual hegemony, as a key feature of oppressive sexual regulation, is being simultaneously eroded and reconstructed. To account for this situation it is important to survey the origins of lesbian and gay oppression and resistance. I have argued that lesbian and gay history has been one of resistance and survival in a hostile society; one of oppression and denial, but also one of desire, pleasure, community, and love.

The historical process in which we are engaged is far from over. The social forces organizing our oppression still predominate. We continue to be an embattled group that must continue to fight for liberation and to build alliances with other oppressed groups. If we do not continue our struggles we risk losing the social spaces and limited control over our bodies and our lives that we have established. At the same time, the victories that we have won, and the shifts we have forced in official sexual regulation through our struggles, also provide us with the knowledge that through our own movements we can transform the situations we are in.

Our oppression is rooted in the historical organization of class, State, gender, race, and sexual relations. A series of class and social struggles over the past 200 years in Canada led to the formation of heterosexual hegemony as an integral feature of ruling in this society. Our oppressions are also lived differently on the basis of our participation in relations of class, gender, and race. Our oppression, therefore, is not something separate from the class, gender, and racial organization of society.

From the standpoints of lesbians and gay men, heterosexuality, which is proclaimed to be normal and natural, can be seen as a recent historical creation.[1] It was constructed at the expense of other alternatives and possibilities, including the developing networks of same-gender lovers. There has always been resistance to this socially established norm, some of which I have reported on in this book, and we can learn much from it.

The forms of sexuality considered "natural," have been socially created and can therefore be socially transformed. Capitalist social relations and the system of sex-scientific classification created the potential for same-gender desire-based cultures and resistances to emerge. Naming the "abnormal" and "deviant" sexual practices allowed for the better policing and definition of the emerging heterosexual norm.

While some same-gender lovers had other names for themselves including fairy, queer, and dyke, others used homosexual and lesbian categories as a basis for resistance, redefining them to better express our own experiences, needs, and identities, as did Elsa Gidlow and Roswell George Mills in Montréal early this century. There has been a long struggle in which we are still very much engaged today over who will define and interpret queer experiences.

Past resistance has helped open up social spaces that we now often take for granted. We have built our own lesbian and gay cultures in the context of shifting sexual and social regulations. The contradiction between lesbian and gay experiences and heterosexual hegemony can be seen as a result of this historical and social process. This sense of "difference" that we experience is not natural: it has not been around for all time, nor will it last forever. The same can be said about the experiences of "normality" and "naturalness" that many heterosexuals express. These are historical and social creations.

At first glance, this appears to involve holding together two seemingly contradictory perspectives. We need to celebrate our experiences and legitimize our lives, cultures, and sexualities through the existing categories of lesbianism, gayness, or queerness. At the same time, these cultures and experiences have emerged fairly recently and are themselves historically and socially made. They are very real, however, in the present social and political contexts we face.

The categories through which we have named our experiences of the world are themselves socially organized. The process of coming out, which has been so central to gay liberation and the formation of gay and lesbian communities, is often described as the revelation of our "true" or "natural" sexuality and is therefore trapped in naturalist notions about sex.[2] For growing numbers of queer women and men in the 1990s, there is a growing contradiction in our lives between the possibilities of ending the regulation of "the closet" over our lives and the negative evaluations of queer sexualities it entails and the continued State and social defence of "the closet" and heterosexual hegemony.

In the context of a politics still largely defined by coming out and notions of "self-oppression," this led to some support for "outing" suspected gay men and lesbians in the U.S. in the early 1990s. At first, outing emerged from the anger developing in response to the devastation of the AIDS crisis in our communities. Confrontations developed with suspected closeted right-wing politicians who stood in the way of AIDS and gay-rights activism. This outing tactic was directed at exposing the hypocrisy of these politicians. But then outing was raised in relation to the suspected closeted rich and famous who, it was argued could, be good "role models" for younger lesbians and gay men. This approach targets how the mass media actively constructs people as heterosexual including "inning" people who might very well engage in same-gender passions.[3] At the same time I have major questions about whether liberation strategies can be advanced by relying on the "queer" identification of famous and wealthy individuals.

For these "outings" to work, the cooperation of the mainstream media is necessary. This is where major problems have been produced since queer activists quickly lost control over the definition of outing in the mass media. In outing people we are setting in motion media practices stigmatizing homosexuality and lesbianism. There is a long history of the media "outing" people in particularly vicious ways when those charged with homosexual-related offences have had their names appear in the media. This also suggests again that in relation to the mass media we need to transform not only the ways that homosexuality/lesbianism is portrayed but also the ways heterosexuality is constructed as "normal."

Most significantly for my purposes here, "outing" is also based on an essentialist approach to sexuality and sexual identification. It assumes that because someone has engaged in sex with a person of the same gender that this makes them gay or lesbian when this may not be how it works in these people's lives. It denies the historical and potentially fluid character of people's sexualities. Sometimes this approach can also lead to viewing closeted gays and lesbians as our worst enemies, further obscuring the relations of heterosexual hegemonic power. Instead we have to begin to deconstruct, destabilize, and transform the social relations constructing the relations of "the closet" so that the social basis for more people choosing to come out can be created and heterosexual hegemony can be more effectively challenged.[4]

Yet neither can the politics of coming out or the categories "lesbian" and "gay" be abandoned, as some social constructionists and "queer theorists" have suggested. They have a social reality to them that cannot be dismissed. There can be no liberal ("we're all just people"), idealist, or superficial abandonment of nor deconstruction of lesbianism and homosexuality. As Esther Newton exclaimed at the 1985 "Sex and the State" lesbian/gay history conference in Toronto, "We will deconstruct when heterosexuals deconstruct."[5] Abandonment of lesbian and gay identifications in the present situation would deny the specific features of our struggles, preventing us from engaging in the protracted process of transforming and deconstructing heterosexual hegemony and sexual rule. While lesbian and gay categorizations can be limiting, they must be both accepted and transformed as the basis for opposing oppression. There is no "pure" revolutionary subject lying somewhere outside these social experiences. There is no other basis from which resistance and transformation can be developed in the real world.

At the same time, we also have to recognize that there can be no prioritization of our queer identifications above our participation in gender, class, or race relations. As Duggan expresses it:

The production of a politics from a fixed identity position privileges those for whom that position is the primary or only marked identity. The result for lesbian and gay politics is a tendency to center prosperous white men as the representative homosexuals.[6]

Rather than viewing gender, race, class, and sexuality as separate designations, it is best to view them as combined with and shaping our queer practices and experiences.

In this sense, some of the criticism of identity classifications within queer theory

— despite their major insights — have gone a bit too far with their attempt to not
only deconstruct lesbian/gay conceptualizations but it seems lesbian and gay experiences as well.[7] The other way this problematic has been addressed within queer theory has been through the adoption of a form of what is described as "strategic
essentialism."[8] This involves a critique of identity categories and essentialism on the
theoretical level, *but* a practical political deployment of "essentialist categories and
identity politics in public debates because it is all anyone can understand."[9] I agree
with Duggan when she argues:

> I take the concerns that lead to the embrace of strategic essentialism seri-
> ously, but I think it is ultimately an unproductive solution. It allows sexual
> difference and queer desires to continue to be localized in homosexualized
> bodies. It consigns us, in the public imagination, to the realms of the par-
> ticular and the parochial, the defence team for a fixed minority, that most
> "special" of special interest groups — again, letting everyone else off the
> hook.[10]

Instead of adapting to essentialism for strategic or other purposes, I suggest that a
grounded historical materialist analysis of lesbian and gay oppression and the construction of heterosexual hegemony provides a non-essentialist historical basis for the social
making of lesbian and gay experiences. In this context, the construction of identity categories can be seen as a social accomplishment. When "identities" are seen not as natural
or as essential in character but rather as social practices, they can have a more contradictory character providing some basis for subversion and transformation. We need to
elaborate an analysis of the relation between our diverse experiences of oppression as
queers and how this gets transformed into conceptualizations of identity. Our multiple,
intertwined and relational experiences of oppression and identity classifications are not
the same. It is this gap we need to examine more fully to develop a politics that does not
rely on essentialist notions of identity but at the same time allows for the expression and
naming of our different social experiences and positions. We need to reject the limitations of identity politics while at the same time not dispensing entirely with "identities"
in present circumstances. But we do want to get at our experiences of oppression *and* affirmation in a different way providing a more expansive and grounded terrain for organizing against the various regulatory regimes we confront. In our critique of identity
politics, we cannot be dismissive of these underlying experiences of oppression and the
importance of naming experiences that have been silenced and denied.

Richard Fung addresses these complexities in relation to his experiences as a gay
Asian.

> During a conversation about the seventeenth-century invention of racial
> categories as we know them in the West, a friend of mine stated recently,
> "there is no race beyond racism." An antiracist politics, she suggested,

> could only develop through the negation of race; to celebrate racial identity
> entails the perpetuation of racism. I disagree. First, I do not experience my
> Asian identity only as racism; neither is my homosexuality only apparent to
> me in the face of heterosexism. Our identities are sources of pleasure as
> well as oppression. Second, "pride" in ourselves as Asian, gay or gay-Asian
> does not preclude a political awareness. It is often, in fact, an important fea-
> ture of political development.[11]

In order to undermine the relations of our oppression, we must accept the experiences and classifications of homosexuality, lesbianism, bisexuality, and/or queer as terrains of resistance and transform them to more fully conform to our diverse needs. We
have helped to make these definitions and have developed our needs and desires
through them. While rejecting the categories that ruling social agencies have imposed
on us, we have to maintain our ability to name our experiences of the world.[12] Our definitions of ourselves as a minority or distinct people needs to be built upon and transformed rather than abandoned. And we have to ensure that these notions of community
and minority are transformed and defined by working-class queers and lesbian and gay
people of colour. We must also not simply accept these categories as the end or the com-
pletion of our destinies, for this would serve only to limit our struggles to the small social spaces we already have.

Our "queer" identifications, communities, and movements are important weapons
in our battles against heterosexual hegemony. The assertion of social equality for lesbians and gay men in all its dimensions challenges the institutionalization of heterosexuality. We must move beyond affirmation and pride, however, to challenge the ruling
regime of sexual regulation. We must free ourselves from rigid sex and gender rules.
Gay and lesbian liberation cannot be reduced to a struggle for a new gay "ethnicity" or
for the liberation of some pre-existing gay, lesbian or bisexual desire. There is no need
to rely on the notion of a fixed or natural gay or lesbian minority. A historical-materialist
perspective, like the one developed here, sees an important social basis for our communities, cultures, and sexualities — a solid basis for fighting for our rights and needs in
the present. Seeing ourselves as a fixed minority, could, however, act as a strait-jacket,
preventing us from grasping the social and historical forces that have organized our oppression. This could prevent us from dealing with questions crucial to countering right-
wing and moral-conservative attacks and to transforming State sexual policies and the
social organization of pleasure. To accept minority status would be to fundamentally accept the existing hetero/homo polarity and a subordinate position within it. Informed
by a critical social-historical perspective, we can see the struggle we are engaged in as
one for sexual self-determination and control over the institutions defining and regulating sexualities — one to begin to remake desire and pleasure for ourselves.

> The strategic aim of the gay movement must not simply be the validation of
> the rights of a minority within a heterosexual majority, but the challenge to

all the rigid categorizations of sexuality ... which act to control people's behaviour in very rigid ways ... The struggle for sexual self-determination is a
struggle in the end for control over our bodies. To establish this control we
must escape from those ideologies and categorizations which imprison us
within the existing order.[13]

In turn this perspective is not only for queers, as it also opens up possibilities for heterosexual feminists and men against sexism who are willing to learn from queer experiences to also challenge the practices of heterosexual hegemony.

This process of social transformation for lesbian and gay liberation involves a defence of our communities, sexualities, and relationships, a challenge to the racial, class,
and gender organization of the gay and lesbian communities, and a change in lesbian-
gay-queer definitions to reflect our diverse needs. This social-historical dialectic of transformation was begun in the nineteenth-century and early twentieth-century struggles
between male and female same-gender lovers and ruling agencies over the meaning of
homosexuality; and continued with the gay liberation and lesbian feminist transformations from homosexual to gay and lesbian identities and cultures and now to queer identifications and movements. These struggles moved the categories of homosexuality and
lesbianism away from their anchorage in hegemonic forms of sex and gender regulation
and brought them closer to our own experiences of oppression and resistance. As the
Gay Left Collective has argued:

Freedom for gay people ... will develop as rigid cultural categories are broken down. It is a paradox that the only way for this to happen is through using these categories, organizing within them and bursting their bonds.[14]

There is a continual process of the construction and reconstruction of new regulatory
categories and classifications in response to our struggles and resistances and these
must be negotiated, shifted and transformed. Currently, as I outlined in the last two
chapters, strategies of dividing lesbians and gays between the "responsible" and the
"irresponsible" have to be addressed and challenged.

In the long-term historical sense, this kind of social-constructionist perspective
could lead to a breaking down of existing social categories through which we express
our sexuality and our identities — homosexual and lesbian as well as bisexual and
heterosexual. A world without the social classification of people on the basis of their
"inner" sexuality and gender is something we can only imagine.[15] We can also catch
glimpses of what this might be like in some of our struggles, relationships and experiences. For the present, however, this historical perspective guides us in the fight
against sexual rule and for democratic control over our erotic lives. It defines a strategic vision of the future.

Lesbian and gay-liberation struggles have challenged many of the practices that
regulate and define our sexualities for us, affirming new positive lesbian and gay prac-

tices by refusing to accept and also by transforming dominant sexual categories. We have refused the ways in which ruling agencies have defined our "difference" as disadvantage or sickness. We have challenged the ruling practices that define and regulate sexual deviance from psychiatric definitions of mental illness to police entrapment. We have struggled for a transformation of ruling categories to attempt to protect our sexual practices and communities from attack. We have challenged State definitions of public and private and took "privacy" out of the language of the State in the battles against the bath raids and used it as a means of defence of our communities. Lesbian and gay liberation, along with other social changes, created the basis for the expansion and visibility of gay commercial ghettoes and lesbian and gay communities.

Lesbian and gay communities exist within the confines of heterosexual hegemony. They are not simply playgrounds of pleasure. They both resist and accommodate oppression. Gay and lesbian liberation participates in the undermining of heterosexual hegemony, along with the feminist movement, men against sexism, and other groups. We challenge the dominant practices of sexual regulation allowing people to gain more control over their erotic lives through creating new contexts for erotic life, desires and pleasures.

Accommodation with heterosexual hegemony and oppressive sexual regulation exists within the gay community. The notion of gays and lesbians as simply a minority group, while providing a necessary basis for celebration and struggle, can also reconcile us with heterosexual hegemony.

The idea of a natural ahistorical gay or lesbian minority — along with the politics of coming out — has so far been the main basis for gay and lesbian politics, and has proved to be important to the affirmation of our identifications and struggles. Such naturalist notions, however, while they have allowed the gay and lesbian movements to move forward, cannot deal with the current social organization of "backlash" from the right wing, sections of the State, and the police, nor with the ambiguity of being partially accepted as "abstract" people yet open to legal charges for the sex in which we actually engage. These essentialist notions provide little basis for clarifying the complexities raised in our struggles for spousal and family recognition. Yet many of our campaigns continue to be predicated on the idea of a fixed lesbian or gay minority.

The idea of an essential gay-male sexual desire, which has marked gay-male sexual politics, can work to block challenges to how sexuality is socially organized and policed. This individualist perspective, which defines our struggle as one for liberation of some inherent, natural gay-male desire, has got in the way of gay men's response to AIDS since it can prevent us from seeing that gay sexuality can be transformed through our own social activities.[16] In the face of AIDS, many gay men are practising safe sex and have had to deal with transforming the sexual practices that have been associated with gay identities. For many of us, it is the first time we have had to deal with sexuality as a terrain of danger as well as pleasure.

Notions of a gay "community" can also hide the shifting class organization as well as other social differences within this community, as mentioned previously. The

existence of a gay "community" is also the basis for the emergence of a profes-
sional/managerial gay stratum as our respectable representatives. This, as mentioned
previously, provides a social basis for assimilationist strategies — and also to some extent the "responsibilization" — and "normalization" construction of struggles for
spousal and family recognition. As we have seen, the idea of social respectability and
responsibility has played a very dangerous role in the past.

Respectability and responsibility can be important social symbols, the terms of
which are defined by the ruling groups in society. The creation of respectable/responsi-
ble forms of sexuality may even at times — like at the end of the last century — be a crucial part of sexual and class rule, of reconstructing society, and managing social change.
Class is being organized and reorganized in the 1990s not only around economic questions but also around social, cultural, moral, and sexual issues. Part of how this is now
being done is in relation to divisions of social practices between the "responsible" and
the "irresponsible." The discourses of respectability/responsibility can still operate to
divide the gay and lesbian communities and to reconcile some of us with the relations of
oppression we face. The classifications of respectability and responsibility, for instance,
has been used to pit gay men against prostitutes and hustlers, as in West End Vancouver
and parts of downtown Toronto.

This has aligned parts of the community with strategies of sexual regulation that
harm our own ability to organise alliances for change. It can also be used against particular gay sexual practices such as washroom or park sex, or SM, or consensual sex between young people. It has been used in the midst of the AIDS crisis to criticize those
who are not involved in monogamous and "respectable" sex and to define other practices as "irresponsible," even if they involve safe sex. This can allow for State intervention and division of our communities.

By limiting our challenges to a tolerance of ourselves as an adult or "private" community, we can be accommodated with institutionalized heterosexuality; arguing that we
are just like straights except for what we do in bed can obscure the more radical aspects
of our struggle. This type of position has also informed aspects of struggles for spousal
and family recognition that would recognize our spousal and familial rights and responsibilities but within fairly narrow confines. While this would mark an important advance
it also subverts the transformative potential of our challenge to heterosexual hegemony
in family and social policies. These movements of accommodation — demands to be admitted as respectable, responsible law-abiding citizens on a heterosexist society's terms
— can lock us into major features of the present relations of sexual regulation and class
and gender organization.

Yet neither must our politics be confined to a simple libertarian knee-jerk anti-re-
spectability or "irresponsibility." Instead we must challenge this whole way of organizing
society and dividing up sexualities.

The affirmation of our differences from other groups — while vitally necessary for
the building of our communities and for building our own autonomous movements and
for the exploration of our sexual lives — also tends to cut us off from the experiences we

share with other oppressed groups and to ignore under the banner of "gay unity" or "gay/lesbian" unity the important differences of class, race, gender, age, and ability which criss-cross our communities.

A strategy toward the transformation of sexual rule depends not on some essential "difference" we share, but the common State and professional regulations we confront and on our political and social choices and the connections we make with other people. As John D'Emilio writes:

> Sexual orientation is not a sufficient basis of unity for our politics ... A politics of visibility is necessary but not sufficient. We now need a strategy that goes beyond coming out.[17]

The contradictory development of patriarchal capitalist society both facilitates and constrains social spaces for erotic same-gender cultures. Other forms of social and erotic life are denied and marginalized by heterosexual hegemony and sexual rule. The categorization of homosexuality and lesbianism, on the one hand, is inscribed within the field established by the current regime of sexual rule. Movements organized around homosexual and lesbian experiences, however, can move beyond the confines of this sexual regime.

Let me illustrate this point. The slogan that "gay/lesbian is just as good as straight" is an important starting point for our struggles. It still lies within the framework of sexual classification, separating gay or lesbian from straight, assigning value to sexuality, and perpetuating naturalist notions of sex. Yet by asserting equal value for deviant sexualities, it turns the ruling process of categorization on its head. "Gay is just as good as straight" can provide the beginning of a transformative social struggle, which would have to involve a protracted cultural revolution[18] on a number of fronts. Moving beyond the initial aim of the simple affirmation of gay/lesbian/queer identities, it becomes part of a struggle for control over the institutions and practices regulating our sexual lives. On the basis of sexual and social needs, pleasures, and experiences developed over the last several centuries, and on the basis of the growth of lesbian/gay, feminist, and men-against-sexism organizing, heterosexual hegemony can be challenged and transformed. This requires not only the elimination of the heterosexist apparatus of sexual policing and the establishment of full civil and human rights for lesbian and gays, but also the removal of social and family policies that have placed heterosexuality at the centre of State policy.

Our liberation politics therefore moves beyond its ghetto and community dimensions, which takes on a different character in smaller centres than in larger urban ones. A struggle based in our ghettoes, communities, and networks must be directed at the various institutions of oppressive sexual regulation — including the perspective laid down in the 1969 reform — and thus must challenge the power of the State and ruling relations on a number of fronts. The Criminal Code and the continuing criminalization of queer sex must be challenged as must the heterosexist assumptions upon which

State policy in so many areas is based. We must distinguish between lesbian and gay liberation as political and social movements and the various settings in which they operate. The emergence of gay ghettoes and gay, lesbian, and women's communities and
various lesbian and gay black, Asian, First Nation and other networks and communities
has led to increasing confusion between community and movement. This has had the
advantage of cutting across dismissals of lesbian and gay cultures by early Gay Liberation Front type groups and of establishing lesbian and gay movements in grass-roots
and community-based politics. On the other hand, it has tended to reduce our hori-
zons to the politics of the ghetto or the community, obscuring links with the broader
social settings in which our lives and communities are situated. The large Lesbian and
Gay Pride Day events and parades in Toronto in the 1990s involving hundreds of thousands of people are in many ways seen as a day for the ghetto and community to "come
out," and not as a day to also push forward our struggles to transform State and social
policies despite Pride Day's political beginnings in Toronto in 1981.

Ghettoes, communities, and networks, no matter how crucial, are not the same
thing as political liberation movements, although these two areas are intimately intertwined. Two intimately inter-related fronts for the struggle for lesbian/gay/queer liberation can be distinguished. First, the defence, and transformation of networks, ghettoes,
and communities, and second, struggles for the transformation of social norms and
State regulations. In Toronto, the resistance to the bath raids in 1981, which began as a
defence of the gay ghetto, quickly grew into a challenge to the legal and State policies
that organized the police operation. The struggle for Bill 167 and for defence of our
family and spousal benefits quickly grew over into a challenge to State family and social
policies even though the deployment of strategies of normalization and responsibilization somewhat limited this. Our struggles against continuing violence against us often
begin with the defence or support of individuals who have been attacked by queerbashers and grows into a challenge to policing practices that do not protect us, and the social
construction of heterosexual masculinity that leads some young heterosexual men to attack us. Our struggles for access to AIDS/HIV treatments, or for access to the social services we need, often begin with individuals but also grow over into challenges to State
and, in the case of treatments, pharmaceutical and medical regulations.

Community transformation must be based on grass-roots democracy in order to
prevent the emergence of an autonomous professional/managerial elite. In building
and defending our communities we are celebrating our differences. This process must
also involve questioning and challenging features of the social organization of gay/les-
bian communities. We must strengthen previously subordinated cultures within les-
bian/gay community formation: those of lesbians and gays of colour, youth,
transgendered people, older lesbians and gays, the physically challenged, and those oppressed on the basis of particular sexual practices. This transforms notions of gay/les-
bian communities through the incorporation of new needs and experiences. It requires
not only recognizing and celebrating our differences but also challenging and transforming relations of inequality and oppression. This will also involve questioning the

role of gay-business definition and control over the gay community and the establishing of more services and social spaces with democratic community control over them. Notions of community that are more democratic and pluralist would be the result of this process.

The second main front is the struggle outside the gay and lesbian communities narrowly defined: from the police and the legal system, to the media and popular culture, the schools, the medical profession and health care, and to social and family policies. A key aspect of this struggle is challenging State policies: legislation that organizes sexual policing, particularly Criminal Code offences like indecent acts, anal intercourse, bawdy-house legislation, and obscenity laws including Canada Customs regulations; and State policies that institutionalize heterosexuality as the social norm in social and family regulations. This latter area requires that we challenge legal discrimination against the unmarried, the notion that lesbians and gay men are not acceptable parents, and the lack of social recognition of lesbian and gay men's housing needs. Some of these struggles, like struggles for spousal benefits, have been located just as much in unions and workplaces as they have been in lesbian/gay communities. This begins to uproot the historical process whereby heterosexuality was, and continues to be, institutionalized as the social norm. Central to all these struggles is the affirmation of the full social equality of gay and lesbian ways of life including our sex lives and relationships with heterosexuality in all aspects of social life. All these struggles point to the need for popular control over social institutions, and point to the need for alliances with other oppressed peoples to fundamentally transform society.

The settings in which lesbian and gay liberation operate are also those of a more general sexual, gender, and social crisis. We are part of complex and shifting historical battlefields over sexual and gender relations. It is to this that I now turn.

The Battlefields of Sex

Variously defined and lived as danger and pleasure, sexuality is a contested terrain in the 1990s.[19] Major social and political struggles centre on who will define and control desire and pleasure in this a period of renegotiation and transition in sex and gender relations. Feminism and lesbian and gay liberation have transformed sexual regulation into an arena of social and political struggle as we have attempted to push for a major shift in the ways in which erotic and gender life is organized. In response to these same social changes, the forces of the right and some State agencies are battling to reassert and reconstruct heterosexual and patriarchal hegemonies. The stakes are high. We could move in the direction of more control over erotic life for lesbians, gays, bisexuals, women more generally, and anti-sexist men, or we could be forced to give in to pressure from moral-conservative mobilizations and move in a direction that closes off these possibilities for a considerable period of time. Past forms of sexual regulation are in crisis and new regulations are called for. Nothing is assured in these sex wars, as different groups attempt to develop their own solutions to the sexual crisis, and as major differences over sexual questions have emerged within and between the feminist, lesbian, gay, men-against-sexism, anti-racist and socialist movements.

In Canada in the 1980s and 1990s, major social struggles have focused on lesbian and gay sex, same-sex spousal and family rights, prostitution, abortion and women's reproductive rights, youth sexualities, sexual representation and pornography, AIDS and safe sex, the treatment and social support needs for PLWA/HIVs, and sexual violence against women and children. Battles over sexuality intersect with many other social struggles and conflicts.

Gays and cops have fought in the streets and in the courts over the distinction between public and private as the cops have raided baths, bars, washrooms, and even our homes to arrest men for having sex. The new youth-porn law has been used to criminalize the lives of some younger men who have sex with other men and to intend the re-criminalization of consensual anal gay sex. Canada Customs has continued and intensified its campaign of surveillance and seizures directed at lesbian and gay bookstores.

While governments ignored AIDS and the mass media participated in associating AIDS with homosexual sex, gay men and lesbians participated in building community-based groups to combat AIDS-related discrimination, to provide support for PLWA/HIVs, and pioneered practices of safe sex. We showed that sex did not have to be associated with the sexual dangers of sickness and death but could be practised safely and erotically. Meanwhile, moral-conservative groups fought against attempts to do the badly needed popular safe-sex education, especially that directed at young people. More recently, in the face of State, professional, and corporate obstacles, community-based groups and AIDS activists have pushed for greater attention to the treatment needs of PLWA/HIVs and their needs for financial and social support.

Pro-choice feminist groups are battling with "right-to-life" groups, the medical profession, and some governments over the abortion issue. The abortion reform was the other side of the homosexual-related reforms in 1969 and had much the same limitations since it allowed for only some abortions and established no social right for women to control their own bodies. Pro-choice feminists protested the lack of access by women to abortion services across the country on class, racial, linguistic and regional lines. They developed a strategy of setting up abortion clinics outside the law to dramatize the problems with the law and to begin to meet some women's need for access to abortions. This led up to the overturning of the abortion law by the Supreme Court of Canada in January 1988, which was an important victory. Despite the defeat of attempts to re-criminalize abortion, there are continuing problems of lack of access to abortion services in many parts of the Canadian State because the federal and most provincial governments are taking no responsibility for ensuring that women actually have access to these services. There are continuing problems with the obstruction of clinics and clinic staff by anti-choice forces, the shooting of Dr. Gary Ramolis, who performs abortions in Vancouver, fire-bombings, and other forms of harassment in many places in English Canada. There have also been problems securing health-insurance coverage for clinic abortions in a number of provinces.[20]

Pro-choice feminists are also reproductive-rights feminists who support not only a woman's right to gain access to birth control and abortion, if that is what she chooses, but also her right to bear the children she chooses to, including for lesbians. There has also been more focused concern generated on the regulation of what are referred to as "new reproductive technologies" in the late 1980s and 1990s. The controversial Royal Commission on New Reproductive Technologies was established in 1989 to investigate these technologies and to propose new forms of regulation for them.[21] The regulations that did exist were seen as being outdated and new technological developments were seen as requiring new regulations. The "reproductive technology" most used by lesbians is alternative insemination. Lesbians who are or get identified as lesbians have had difficulties accessing alternative insemination clinics that sometimes will only provide sperm to "proper" heterosexual couples. In 1993 two lesbians brought a human-rights complaint against a B.C. doctor for his refusal to provide insemination services to lesbians. In 1995 they won their case.[22]

While police and moral conservatives campaigned for clamping down on female prostitutes and hustlers, socialist and radical feminists and gay liberationists, as well as prostitutes themselves, were defending their rights.[23] The police and the moral conservatives were disturbed by the visibility of prostitutes on city streets, even though the police themselves, through their arrest patterns, had created street prostitution as a "public nuisance" in some urban zones.[24] Rather than deal with police practices and the legal, social, and economic realities that created prostitution in this form, the forces of the right took advantage of the legitimate concerns of residents — about noise and harassment — to call for more police powers to defend the respectability and status of these neighbourhoods. With the passage of Bill C-49, which criminalized "communication" for the purposes of prostitution in 1985, the police and moral-conservative groups basically got everything they were asking for. The powers of the police to regulate prostitutes in the "public" realm were extended. There have been a series of largely unsuccessful legal challenges to this section of the Criminal Code. But in the 1990s, the police want more powers to go after prostitutes. In 1995 City of Toronto proposals for the limited legal regulation of prostitutes were rejected by the police and did not get a favourable response from the federal government. At the same time, prostitutes'-rights activists are opposed to legal regulation since this makes the State their pimp and instead want the decriminalization of all prostitution-related activities. There has also been a focus on younger prostitutes working on the streets, but little investigation of the social roots of youth prostitution that often have to do with hostile families and the lack of social alternatives available to these young people.

Feminists have been demanding that State agencies recognize violence in a realm where patriarchal relations have allowed for relatively unregulated violence against women — the home. The Wolfenden perspective was built on public/private distinctions, which subordinate women in the "privacy" of the domestic realm. While there has been some limited progress on these fronts, the conceptualizations of "family violence" and "sexual assault," which mandate police and social-service work in this area, both obscure the gendered character of this problem and also define it as a problem that the police should and can deal with obscuring the broader social relations of patriarchal power that men's violence against women in the home is located in. This once again allows for the problem to be constructed as individual "deviant" or criminal men who may have come from a "dysfunctional family" thereby obscuring how "normal" patriarchal and familial relations foster the conditions for this violence. The setting up of transition houses for women needing to escape men's violence was an important victory for feminists. As these houses became institutionalized and more professionalized and State funded, however, they often became transformed into something close to new "poor houses" for some women as they participate in organizing women and their children into relations of poverty.[25]

Right-wing moral conservatives, State agencies, and many feminists, meanwhile, are challenging the existence of pornography — although for different reasons. While feminists object to the sexism and violence in much heterosexual pornography,[26] and in the media and culture more generally, for the right wing the problem is not only the public visibility of sexual representations but their sexually explicit character, particularly those dealing with "deviant" sex.[27] Unfortunately, State agencies have been able to use the anti-porn feminist point of view to create tighter State censorship of sexually explicit material, including queer images and texts.[28] Most feminist agitation against porn has made no distinction between different kinds of pornography so most often gay-male porn, which has a different social character, has been dealt with as if it had the same social meaning as straight-male porn. Some anti-porn feminists have therefore participated in efforts leading to a clampdown on gay-male porn and also erotic materials for lesbians. Anti-porn feminists have not only had their intentions transformed as their proposals have entered into State frameworks, they have also been complicit in producing some of these problems as in the Women's Legal, Education and Action Fund's intervention in the Supreme Court Butler decision that I wrote about last chapter. The federal State has also extended forms of sexual censorship in relation to young people with its youth-pornography law.

These struggles challenge and renegotiate in various ways the public/private strategy of sexual regulation undermining the central strategies of sexual rule and the sexual/reproductive aspects of gender regulation that were put in place in the post-war period in Canada. This strategy has coordinated and organized the social relations and courses of action of various State and professional agencies in relation to sexual and moral "problems." While it opened up certain possibilities for lesbian and gay community formation and for some women to have limited legal access to abortions, it has also constrained and policed the lives of gay men, lesbians, prostitutes, women more generally, as well as young people. In response to challenges to the public/private regulatory strategy there has also been a shift toward adult/youth lines of regulation, especially in relation to the youth-pornography legislation, the prohibition on the purchase of sexual services involving anyone under the age of eighteen, the setting of the age of consent for anal sex at eighteen, and in the controversies over and restrictions placed on sexuality and AIDS education for young people.[29]

It is in this context that State and various professional groups are spending a great deal of time and money in the study of sex-related questions. Once again, grass-roots concerns are being transformed into the categories of official discourse. Government reports in the 1980s like the *Badgley Report on Sexual Offences Against Children and Youth and the Fraser Committee Report on Pornography and Prostitution*, for instance, took up grass-roots feminist concerns about sexual violence against women and children and representations of violence and sexism in pornography, but transformed them in to a professional and administrative language.[30] It is useful to investigate how this worked in a bit more detail.

The Badgley Report did not seriously address the social relations behind the violence and harassment that young people face in society and in the domestic realm.[31] Instead, a series of legal and administrative measures were proposed: a new series of age-specific laws and the extension of sexual regulation along the lines of adult-youth regulation far beyond those originally outlined in the Wolfenden report regarding homosexuality. The recommendations would not empower young people to deal with sexual harassment and violence, but merely increase the protectionist powers of social agencies. The very right of young people to consent to any form of consensual sexual activity was put in question as new age-related offences against sexual activity, porn, and prostitution were outlined.[32]

The Fraser Report on pornography and prostitution, which has a more "liberal" flavour, also came up with a dangerous set of proposals. It dealt superficially with certain feminist concerns regarding porn while basically reapplying public/private and adult/youth categories of regulation. It found street prostitution to be a "social problem." The commission's mandate did not include an investigation of police practices and their effect on the social organization of prostitution. Sex-related questions were narrowed to the terrain of the legal system and in particular to the Criminal Code, to which a series of legal reforms were recommended.

In responding to these government reports, the federal Conservative government of the 1980s moved on some of the recommendations and not on others. First, they came up with Bill C-49 to be used against street prostitutes and hustlers; then the package of two bills presented to the House of Commons in June 1986 containing some of the Badgley Report's proposals on adult-youth sexual distinctions.[33] The anti-porn proposals mentioned last chapter, aside from designating anal intercourse and most other sexual acts as "pornography," would have denied people under the age of 18 access to sexually explicit material. These proposals would later influence the shaping of the youth-pornography law passed in 1993.

A central task of the movement to gain greater democratic control over our erotic lives is to challenge and displace these public/private and adult/youth regulatory strategies and the sexual policing and social policies they have mandated. In Canada, the social basis is there for a broad alliance of various progressive movements that could develop and fight for alternate sexual policies.

There exist many differences, however — gender, sexuality, class, race, language,

age, and ability — within and among the many groups that have been contained by these strategies of regulation. A number of debates and conflicts must be worked through before we can build the broad coalition for wide-ranging social and sexual transformation that we need. Beginning in the early 1980s, and continuing in somewhat different forms today, two main positions can be identified in the sex debates within feminism and lesbian and gay liberation, and more generally, in progressive circles. I will focus on the varying positions adopted on pornography to clarify some of the differences between these perspectives, but they also exist in relation to other sex-related controversies.

The first is what Mariana Valverde calls "sexual pessimism" which is most identified with anti-porn feminism but also informs the perspectives of other groups. This approach focuses on sex as a danger for women and for young people (especially girls) and has tended to produce a naturalist notion of men as sexually violent and predatory and women and young people as sexually passive and inactive. Women and young people are focused on only as "victims" and not as active agents in the construction of their sexual worlds. Women are often seen as completely defined by male or patriarchal power.[34] Anti-porn feminism, as we have seen, can be used by State agencies to increase its repressive and regulatory apparatus in order to "protect" women. The activities of some anti-porn feminists have also been incorporated into various strategies for cleaning up urban areas, strengthening the policing of consensual sexual practices, and stigmatizing "deviant" sex. Many proponents of this approach also see the need to "protect" young people from sexual activity and erotic materials. This has led them to not raise any significant opposition to the youth-porn law, nor have they raised many objections to Canada Custom's seizures of lesbian and gay porn.

The second position, the sexual libertarian perspective,[35] tends to view sex as a "natural" good in itself and often sees pornography as a form of sexual liberation. This approach has roots in some of the writings of earlier sex radicals like Wilhelm Reich[36] and some of the libertarian currents that came out of the "sexual revolution" of the 1960s and its interactions with sections of the male left. This position, which gained a significant following among gay men in the late 1970s and early 1980s, generalized from gay men's relatively positive experiences of sex and gay porn. This position has been used to align sections of progressive movements with the mainstream heterosexual porn industry itself and the mainstream media and cultural industries around abstract notions of "free speech." This position, while it opposes State censorship, also obscures the serious social problems of sexism, violence against women, racism and the oppression of young people in this society. Since this approach does not centrally address race and class it has faced significant criticism from gays and lesbians of colour.[37]

The hegemony of this approach was partially displaced in gay liberation circles with the impact of the AIDS crisis and the need for gay men to deal with the sexual dangers of unsafe sex. It remains as a kind of subtext, however, for many discussions of sexuality among gay men and other groups. It can be detected for instance when some minimize the possibilities that sex between an older man and a young man could be "abusive" or "exploitative." This displaces possible social-power imbalances and their impact on the sexual relationship by simply assuming that gay sex is everywhere and always "good." More recently, in response to anti-porn feminism, and in the context of an explosion of discussions about women's and especially lesbian sexualities that have included new explorations of sexual pleasures and the production of new erotic materials and pornographies, there has been an increase in support for a modified version of this perspective among some lesbians and feminists that does pay some attention to gender difference.

Contemporary sexual rule has defined two main polarities for our discussions of sexuality. These are united in viewing sexuality as natural. The first is the "moral conservative" position that sanctions only certain forms of sexuality and that would remove individual, collective and ethical or moral choices from the field of sexual possibilities. The second polarity ranges from the liberal position to the libertarian, and it asserts the right to do whatever one wants as long as it does not interfere with anyone else, or, sometimes (like in the Wolfenden strategy), as long as it is done in "private" and does not involve a young person. This approach usually assumes an individualist perspective and often abandons most political, ethical, or cultural criteria for evaluating sexual practices, once again obscuring the social dimensions of the organization and regulation of eroticism. Like libertarian approaches, these approaches generally neglect relations of gender, class, race, and age.

These polarities continue to confine the political direction of radical (radical in that they are trying to get to the social roots of the problem) sexual movements so that they can be hegemonized by various strategies of sexual rule — transforming movements of resistance into forms of accommodation with the existing order. This can perhaps be most clearly seen in some of the recent battles over sexual representation and pornography but has ramifications far beyond it. In the polarities established by the mass media and ruling discourse, the struggle is portrayed as one between censorship and free speech, or between puritanism and sexual liberation, reflecting the interests of the police and the moral conservatives on one side and the pornography industry, the mass media, and civil libertarians on the other.

In the last decade, liberal and one variant of radical feminist[38] concerns have been entered into the official debate, with the State censorship position often being argued on the basis of the need to "protect" women. These same agencies do little to bring about social and economic equality for women or to transform the social relations behind violence against women. The images of violence and sexism in much straight porn reflects and helps naturalize sexism and violence against women; as such this porn is part of a broad network of sexist relations that need to be challenged and transformed. To focus, however, on porn as a single issue or as the main cause of women's oppression is to focus on the sexually explicit as the problem and to feed into State censorship strategies that regulate on the basis of sexual explicitness and hit "deviant" sex the hardest.

Feminist and gay struggles on this terrain can be subsumed under one or the other of these dominant polarities. Anti-porn feminism has been used by the mass media and

State agencies to justify attempts to control queer sexual and other depictions. Anti-porn feminist rhetoric has even been taken up by some moral-conservative forces. Anti-porn feminism, through this process, is shifted in the direction of State protectionist strategies and away from building grass root movements for emancipation. On the other side, abstract free-speech arguments in defence of gay or lesbian porn can be used to align us with defence of the mainstream heterosexual porn industry and the monopolies that control this "free speech" in the mass media and the cultural industries. It can lead us to underestimate problems of racism, sexism and the oppression of young people. This "free speech" (which requires money to buy) has little to do with the free speech desperately needed by lesbians, gay men, feminists, working-class people, people of colour, and other oppressed people. At the same time as we fight, moves toward State censorship in the practices of Canada Customs, the "obscenity" section of the Criminal Code, or in the youth-porn law and for the defence and expansion of our freedom of speech, we need to do it on our own terms and not those defined for us by others who are defending a different set of social interests.

A third position — with which I identify — has developed that begins to address our different experiences of sexuality, gender, race, age, and class and that understands that gender relations still organize sexualities differently for men and for women in this society. This position, which opposes State censorship of sexual materials, also tries to deal with both the pleasures and dangers of sex[39] and to open up real sexual alternatives rather than merely defending what already exists. This is a more optimistic perspective which tries to minimize sexual danger while expanding the possibilities for sexual pleasure. Sex is addressed as neither "good" or "bad," instead its social context needs to be explored, and the sexualities of oppressed groups defended. This perspective first emerged in the early and mid-1980s in some of the feminist discussions coming out of the "sex wars" and in attempts to develop a feminist basis for anti-censorship practice. Since then many of these acquisitions have been forgotten as many of us have once again been forced into defensive anti-censorship struggles and these lessons have to be re-learned in the context of our current struggles.

Regarding pornography and censorship, this perspective moves us beyond the ideological distinctions of porn as a thing that is either "good" or "bad" and toward an investigation of how sexual representation has developed historically and of different types of pornographies, some of which — such as gay, lesbian, or feminist alternative porn — can have a positive and empowering effect on people's lives and sexualities. Moving beyond naturalist notions, this perspective investigates the historical roots of current sexual controversies in changing social relations and policies of sexual regulation. We must oppose all forms of State censorship of sexually explicit materials, which is a central part of sexual regulation — part of a State strategy to define for us what "proper" and "normal" images of sex are — which we know from historical experience will be used much more vigorously against lesbian, gay, feminist, and progressive oppositional sexual materials. But we must also address the very real concerns about sexism and sexist violence, racism, class, and age that are raised regarding pornography and sexuality more generally and struggle to challenge and transform these aspects along with cultural production more generally. Our approach to sexual censorship must be broadened to address social and marketplace forms of censorship as well and to begin to define what free speech for women, lesbians and gay men, people of colour, young people, and working-class people might look like.[40]

In the context of the struggle against the youth-porn law, this would involve avoiding the problems of State protectionist *and* sexual-libertarian responses. While calling for repeal of the legislation, this would entail prioritizing how this law is being used against young people themselves, including making it more difficult for young people to get the sexual knowledge and information they need in the context of AIDS and sexual health concerns, as well as to attempt to re-criminalize consensual gay sex. It would require putting forward clear alternate proposals for addressing the actual social roots of sexual harassment and violence against young people in relation to social inequalities between adults and younger people in this society, in the social-power imbalances in families and many social institutions in relation to young people, in the advertising and cultural practices "eroticizing" young people, and in the social construction of hegemonic forms of masculinity that associate masculinity with aggression and sexual power over others. This requires addressing problems of sexual harassment and violence against young people as a very real problem, but rather than accepting a State protectionist response that only makes things worse for young people, this approach attempts to develop a perspective that would facilitate the empowering of young people themselves and give them the resources and skills to be able to address both their right to say no to unwanted sex *but* also their right to say yes to the investigation and exploration of their own sexualities.[41] This develops a much more optimistic and socially transformative approach than either sexually pessimist perspectives that lean toward support for State protectionist responses or sexual-libertarian responses that would neglect the very real problems of sexual harassment and violence that young people experience.

The hegemonic strategies of sexual rule put in place early in the century and further defined and shifted with the application of the public/private, adult/youth regulatory strategy in the 1960s have been undermined. There is no longer a clear moral or political consensus about what is "normal" or "proper" or even "degrading" sex. Struggles have opened up from both progressive and reactionary directions against dominant State approaches to sex and gender regulation embodied in the 1969 Criminal Code reform and the Wolfenden perspective that lay behind it. Just as the Wolfenden Report and the 1969 Criminal Code reform were meant to manage historical changes while at the same time maintaining the rule of patriarchal and heterosexist social relations, various State agencies are presently attempting to do this in the context of the social struggles of the 1990s.

Unlike the reform period of the 1960s, the crisis in official sexual policy in the 1990s is occurring *after* the development of the contemporary gay, lesbian, and feminist movements. We could therefore be in a stronger position to define our own alternatives. The Charter can also be useful in pushing forward some of our legal struggles. At the same time, however, this is not a general period of "liberal" sexual and social reform on State levels; the official political agenda is dominated by a conservative focus on cutting social programs and the deficit, and there is a vociferous moral-conservative minority opposed to our rights. The present situation is therefore extremely complicated and it is very easy to lose our way as we navigate past the various strategies of sexual rule. The current situation is particularly dangerous because moral-conservative, liberal, and progressive sexual-political movements are all contesting for hegemony. It is easy for our movements to be divided and used by other forces to further their own projects — to end up furthering not our own liberation but another strategy of sexual rule. This is why it is important to avoid the limitations of sexually libertarian and sexually pessimistic positions and also the "normalization" and "responsibilization" strategies I outlined in the last two chapters.

There exists, as I have attempted to demonstrate throughout this book, a vast difference between how sexuality in all its complexity is experienced in everyday life and the categories officially developed to police and manage our erotic lives. Alternate sexual policies must deal not with sexual rule but with sexual experience and emancipation.

This takes us back to the some of the stories recounted in the preceding pages: Axel Otto Olson confronting the Royal Commission on Criminal Sexual Psychopaths in the 1950s, for instance, bringing into view the blackmail and harassment that gays faced as he was ruled to be outside the terms of reference of the committee. In recent government investigations, as well, many of the actual needs and concerns of prostitutes have been ruled outside the terms of reference of government reports on prostitution. Or we can look at the 1969 reform at which time the State took the homosexual issue away from homophile activists and redefined it in narrow legal terms; or to the clash following the bath raids in Toronto when gays disputed the ruling classification of our sexual lives by the police and argued for a radically different organization of sexual life from our own standpoint. In the Bill 167 struggle in Ontario, we began to challenge State definitions of the family as only heterosexual in character. We were defeated when the majority in the legislature defended the heterosexual character of "proper" and "normal" family relationships. These struggles and experiences give us ideas on very different starting places for developing an alternative approach to sexual regulation.

An alternative approach must develop social policies from the standpoints of oppressed peoples. In these areas, alternate sexual policies should embody and be defined by the experiences of lesbians and gays as well as other oppressed groups. These experiences are crucial resources to build on in challenging sexual rule. Out of the various progressive sexual-political movements have emerged alternative policy perspectives for non-oppressive sexual regulation.

Toward Erotic and Social Alternatives

The affirmation of diverse sexual practices could displace sexuality as the truth of our beings by moving away from the idea that particular sexual activities express an inner personal essence. There is no "true" sexuality, no single correct, moral sexuality. We must move away from the sexual classification of "types" toward the celebration and examination of our bodies, pleasures, and relationships.

In contrast to the moral-conservative position that focuses on a morality of acts and to naturalist notions of a single "natural" or "normal" sexuality, a "radical pluralist" perspective, as Jeffrey Weeks outlines it, dwells on relations rather than acts, and emphasises meaning and context rather than rules.[42] There would be no absolutes; instead, diversity, consent, and choice would be stressed. This approach would not abandon debate on ethical questions. Central to this perspective is the notion that sexual difference in and of itself is not a social problem and that there can be numerous consensual and ethical sexual choices. This is one of the approaches that has emerged out of the sex debates within and between progressive social movements and has emerged in the gay and lesbian movements.

Despite its insights, however, Weeks' approach is still tied too closely to a liberal pluralist perspective. While it tolerates and celebrates differences, it does not necessarily get at transforming the underlying relations of inequality and social power that shape forms of marginalization.[43] I suggest we need to combine the insights of "radical pluralism" with socialist-feminist and anti-racist perspectives of social transformation.

Pluralism in and of itself is not enough. In the wrong hands it can actually lead to new ways of marginalizing, ghettoizing, and containing unorthodox sexualities if the social relations organizing inequality and discrimination are not challenged and transformed. Pluralism is a necessary defence against moral conservatives, but in and of itself it does not get at the need to transform social relations and uproot oppression. It must be linked to the transformation of social relations from the standpoints of those who are oppressed by current sexual regulations.

As Mariana Valverde suggests,

> Weeks' concept of "radical pluralism" may be the necessary starting point for a nonabsolutist sexual ethics, and it may give us a defence against the rising tide of conservatism that one can detect in the AIDS panic. However, it has to be admitted (at least among feminists) that the notion of "pluralism" cannot provide any content for a feminist sexual ethic.[44]

In my view, "radical pluralism" transformed by combining it with the insights of socialist-feminism and anti-racism can point us toward the making of alternative perspectives for sexual regulation where people will have far more democratic control over their bodies, sexualities, and lives.

This requires a transformation of the law and social regulations in which the ruling moral/political perspectives that I have examined earlier are embodied. We can perhaps best think of this in relation to some of the "problems" that have been associated with female street prostitution such as noise and street harassment. To begin with, a shift is required to see these experiences from the standpoints of the prostitutes themselves.

These problems are not created by female prostitutes but through the ways in which this form of prostitution is policed and socially organized. A radical pluralist approach which would be supported by prostitutes'-rights activists and most feminists would lead to repealing the laws criminalizing prostitutes. This would itself get rid of a number of the "nuisance" problems associated with street prostitution that are created by policing and denying prostitutes access to working indoors.

But radical pluralism is limited in not addressing some of the underlying relations of economic, social, and sexual inequality shaping the way male/female prostitution is institutionalized in this society. A socialist-feminist approach — while fully supporting de-criminalization — would go further through posing the need for social and economic equality for women and the profound social changes that are needed to make this a reality. This would begin to undermine the sexist ways in which prostitution is currently organized in this society while empowering those who work as prostitutes to gain more control over their lives.

Once these kinds of social changes have begun, and outside the present framework of the criminal law, we could then begin to imagine the possibilities of getting different parts of local communities together to discuss, debate, and negotiate through how to deal with the common social space in their area. This would have to be based on the recognition that all people working and living in an area have needs and interests that must be addressed. In this new context, people would be able to come to some new consensus on their common use of this social space. This would not eliminate disputes or conflicts but would create a radically different context in which they could be resolved. It would lead to new non-oppressive policies of sexual regulation regarding this matter.

In our present social context with the criminal law, however, police policies, real estate interests, and moral and class prejudices against prostitutes (including the sexist double-standard), it is impossible to even begin to contemplate this radically different scenario. Elaborating a radical pluralist, socialist-feminist perspective requires thinking through how to create new social conditions where sexual disputes and problems could be resolved very differently, and where forms of sexual oppression could be undermined and eventually eliminated.

By proposing a shift in standpoint by starting from the experiences of the oppressed, the problem becomes oppressive strategies of sexual regulation. This directly engages us in the struggle to transform sexual regulation in an emancipatory direction. Beginning outside official discourse (in which gays, lesbians, prostitutes, and others are already pre-packaged as social problems), we start instead with the experiences of gay men, lesbians, prostitutes, and others to see instead how sexual policing and oppressive sexual regulation are the problems.

More generally, this opens up possibilities for the development of a radically different basis for sexual regulation. This would not be based on administrative categories standing over and against people's lives, but on the transformation of social relations, including policing, which would empower gays, lesbians, prostitutes, and other oppressed people. This requires a different kind of oppositional discourse organizing very different kinds of social and political relations between movements of sexual resistance and other movements for progressive social change. Dealing with progressive sexual change also involves us with class, gender and racializing relations since, as we have seen, sexual relations are bound up historically with these social relations. This involves us in moving beyond liberal strategies of sexual regulation and engaging in socialist, feminist, and anti-racist social transformation. Some ideas for this are being developed out of the practice of movements for sexual emancipation — they will become clearer through further struggles and discussions within and between our various movements.

One clear direction that comes out of these experiences is the need to focus on ending actual violence and transforming social-power relations and not on policing "deviant" or unorthodox sex. There is no need to code difference as disadvantage or deviance. We need to focus instead on social transformation and ending violence and the abuse of social power, not on dividing consensual sexualities into "deviant/normal" forms. The aim of this socialist-feminist radical pluralism would be to democratize sexuality by expanding the possibilities for non-exploitative sexual choices. This approach transforms the sexual agenda toward collectively clarifying the criteria on which to build our sexual communities and lives. An emphasis on choice, relationships, context, social equality, pleasure, and consent — taken together — could provide us with the initial basis for alternative sexual policies. One aim of such a perspective would be to expand the possibilities of choice and consent in people's erotic lives and to ensure that these words have a real social meaning. These could become part of a broader socialist-feminist transformation of social relations as against the present public/private, responsible/irresponsible, adult/youth, normal/deviant, monogamous/promiscuous, good girl/bad girl dichotomies, and act-specific categories that presently dominate and organize sexual rule. These alternate policies would focus not, on regulating acts themselves, or on location (whether it was in "public" or "private"), or on whether it was "deviant" sex or not but on questions of the character of the social relations involved.

Sexuality in the context of other social changes could become — as many of us have already begun to experience in partial ways in the present — a terrain for communication, play, desire, and pleasure. This would have to be part of a broader series of social changes that would create the social conditions for full equality for women, lesbians and gay men, young people, people of colour and working-class people.

Two men engaging in oral sex with each other would not be defined as "deviant" or "abnormal"; if one engaged in violence or harassment of the other — whether this occurred in a sexual context or not — then that would be grounds for social action. If a consensual sexual activity took place in a park where it disturbed no one it would not be considered a problem. If we are addressing a different-gender relationship in which coercive sex was forced on the women this would not be categorized as more "normal" sex since it was heterosexual in character. Instead the violence and coercion would be seen as the problem and various efforts would be mobilized to deal with this. These alternate policies could become a basis for social and sexual transformation.

In moving toward lesbian and gay liberation, we must challenge the dominant

polarities of sex regulation and develop alternative positions that are not hegemonized by other social groups, positions that are profoundly erotic, sex-positive, anti-sexist, and anti-racist, and that address our different experiences of sex as danger and
pleasure. This could develop an erotic-positive lesbian and gay-liberation perspective
that can defend all consensual same-gender sexual practices, providing space for their
affirmation and redefinition and for bursting the boundaries of the ruling sexual regime. Community discussion of sexual issues would be crucial, as would the development of new ways of settling sexual disputes that would not allow for openings for
State intervention into these vital community and movement debates. Rather than sti-
fling sexual discussions through forms of State and social censorship, we need more
sex-related discussions and debates and more sexual knowledge and literacy.

This process of sexual transformation would involve a critical tension between the
sexual practices and identities we live and love in the capitalist, patriarchal, and racist
present, and the social transformation to a very different context for erotic pleasure. A
transitional sexual politics would link the transformation of our present desires and
pleasures to a vision of a sexually transformed future.[45] This form of transitional politics
would be a pluralist perspective encompassing numerous forms of consensual sexualities; we would focus on opening up possibilities for more choice, consent, democracy,
and pleasure in sexual relationships. However, sexual practice itself would be only one
of many sources of pleasure and identification and would no longer be the main source
of identity formation. We would focus — not on the freeing of some inherent sexuality
— but on struggles over sexual norms and regulations.

One of the central aspects of this gay and lesbian liberation strategy would be the
building of alliances against institutionalized heterosexuality, which would bring together not only the gay, lesbian, and feminist movements, and anti-sexist men's groups,
but other groups as well. A key axis would be to move beyond the public/private,
adult/youth regulatory strategy to establish the complete social and sexual equality of
lesbian/gay/bisexual sexualities. Alternative policies would not focus on State-defined
administrative sexual categories, but rather on actual problems like sexual violence and
harassment and the relations in which these are embedded, as well as problems of police harassment, sexism, racism, and heterosexism rather than the "public" displays of
streetwalkers or sex in gay baths or bars. These new social policies would focus on the actual transformation of social relations and would be based on the empowering of lesbians, gay men, sex-trade workers, women more generally, young people, and people of
colour.

One crucial site for the oppression and regulation of lesbians and also gay men
has been in the regulation of family relations through State social and family policies.
This is also an important area where alliances with other groups that also face oppressive regulation in relation to their family and social support relations can be forged.
One of the weaknesses of the struggle for spousal benefits and family-recognition
rights is that it has not posed these questions or developed these kinds of alliances.
Instead, the main axis has been to argue that lesbian and gay couples and families

should have the same rights that heterosexual couples and families currently have. This has not led to any major challenge to the social form in which spousal benefits or families are legally and socially recognized beyond critiquing their heterosexual character. While this challenges the form through which these benefits and family rights are constructed in one major area, in other areas this social form is simply accepted and equality is demanded within it. This has been one the reasons why these struggles have been susceptible to at least partial incorporation into strategies of "normalization" and "responsibilization" of our relationships.

Questions about whether it is really the best social policy to allocate important benefits to people on the basis of where they work, and on the basis of the type of benefit package that their partners have at work, have rarely been raised. While some of these benefits have been gained as part of a social wage won by workers through union struggles, it is currently only a minority of the population in some unionized workplaces and professional, corporate, and administrative personnel who have access to these benefits. These benefit packages do nothing to help people living in poverty or the many who have no access to them. Of course, as long as heterosexuals are allocated benefits on these bases we must argue for them for same-gender couples as well. But we also must extend our struggles beyond simple equality claims to challenge the form these benefits take in a more transformative fashion. If we did this, important questions of the redistribution of social wealth and the benefits people deserve as social rights would become clearer. It would also become clearer that a claim to social resources would be justified on the part of people involved in doing the socially necessary and important work of rearing children, whether they are the biological parents of the child or not, or whether they have legal custody or not.

Seen in this light, discussions of alternate social support and family policies could create broader alliances — including anti-poverty groups — that queer activists could participate in along with feminists and other groups. These alternate social support and family policies would not only challenge heterosexism, they could also challenge other social inequalities and be a vehicle for addressing relations of poverty and class inequality. This poses important social-justice questions and begins to pose the need for a new form of democratic socialist society in which taking care of people's needs is at the centre of social policy.

These alliances would oppose dominant State family policies that group together a number of policies encompassing questions of social support, domestic labour, childrearing, sexuality, gender, and divisions of labour. In developing alternative social support policies, we would redefine the notion of social and community support to reflect how people actually live, which is often no longer within the "traditional" heterosexual family unit.[46] This would undermine ruling class and State organization of gender and familial relations and would allow people to live in socially supported settings outside institutionalized heterosexuality.

The family is also a key area in which to contest the influence of moral conservatism. The ideological heavenly family of moral conservatism must be brought down to earth so that its very real and painful contradictions can be addressed. Until recently, moral conservatives have been able to hegemonize much of the discussion around family policy beyond certain early liberal feminist initiatives regarding the division of property following divorce and questions of child support, while feminism and gay liberation — because we have often been immersed in our own defensive struggles — have not been able to respond adequately to people's needs, fears, hopes, and desires. This has changed somewhat in the 1990s as more feminists are grappling with how to create more gender equality in familial relations and as more lesbian and gay activism has focused on the theme of "We Are Family!"

Popular educational work could explain that only a minority of the population presently live in a "proper" heterosexual family: most people do not live in families with a wage-earning husband, a non-wage-earning wife, and several children. There are more households headed by single parents — mostly women — than ever before. We must therefore communicate the experiences and lessons of alternative support, family, and community networks that challenge State policies that still establish the nuclear heterosexual family as normative and which label all other relationships as "deviant." We must defend those family and support networks that are most under attack — lesbian mothers and gay couples, single parents, mothers on social assistance, immigrant families torn apart by discriminatory immigration laws, and battered women and children. We must expand people's possibilities to make choices about how they live their lives, and create the conditions for these choices to have real social meaning.

One of the reasons why questions of family relations can get quite heated is that they raise questions involving the rearing of children and the raising of young people. In the struggle for Bill 167 in Ontario in 1994, we needed a more radical and assertive approach to respond to this situation. We needed to more directly take up the arguments of the moral conservatives regarding children, and young people regarding adoption rights in particular. These arguments cannot be avoided. We needed to affirm that lesbians and gays are just as capable of raising children as are heterosexuals, and to specifically demolish all the right-wing arguments constructing us as bad parents and a threat to young people. We need to see more lesbian and gay parents speaking out about their experiences and also more children of lesbian and gay families speaking out as well.

These alternative social-support and family proposals could be based in important ways on the experiences of those of us surviving and loving outside institutionalized heterosexuality. This would involve gay men, lesbians, feminists, anti-sexist heterosexual men, and others willing to openly communicate their experiences,[47] and could be one of the best ways to undermine the influence of right-wing "pro-family" politics. We could demonstrate that people can and are living very fulfilling and pleasure-filled lives in a radically different context. To be socially equal, however, this requires that these forms of social support and family networks also receive State and social support, including financial support.

One of the major struggles gay and lesbian activists have been involved in for more than the last ten years has been AIDS organizing. As mentioned last chapter, AIDS activism has confronted problems with the social organization of treatment delivery and research, and the problems created by the pharmaceutical corporations and the medical profession for people living with AIDS/HIV. More recently, AIDS activists have been confronting the problems PLWA/HIVs face in accessing the social supports and services that they badly need. This has again broached questions of poverty and class relations of inequality and the need in responding to AIDS to put people's lives and health first. AIDS activism has therefore been forced to confront the problems created by the professional and capitalist social organization of health care, medicine, treatment, research, and social support in Canadian society.

As part of the relations of ruling, the practices of the State and professionals are largely oriented around notions of "health from above." One of the important outcomes of AIDS crisis has been the development of community-based AIDS groups, and a new way of addressing health concerns. We have begun to develop, however hesitantly and inconsistently, an approach based on the empowerment of people living with AIDS/HIV and the communities most affected by AIDS. This has sometimes been referred to as "health from below."[48] It entails a counter-hegemonic, transformative politics.

Community-based groups originally used the notion of partnership with government agencies as an attempt to shift State policies more in the direction of "health from below," especially with community-based groups playing a leading role in the social response to AIDS. In State strategies, however, this notion of partnership has been resituated as part of a hegemonic regulatory strategy based on "health from above," which creates problems for PLWA/HIVs and AIDS activists as we have seen.

We need to begin to define AIDS policies much more on our own terms. We have to resituate notions of "partnership" that recognize our leadership and define issues and policies from below. Key to this is a radical shift from reliance on public health and palliative care to qualitatively improved treatment access and the creation of the actual social conditions for HIV/AIDS to be a chronic manageable condition. This shift is tied into broader social transformations in health care, sexuality, the medical profession, research, the drug corporations, and in other areas — transformations that must put the needs and concerns of the people most affected by AIDS/HIV at the centre of social policy — and not profit rates or professional careers. AIDS can only be seriously addressed by dealing with fundamental features of the capitalist society we exist within. AIDS organizing must be a politics of social transformation, including building coalitions with other marginalized and oppressed groups around health care and other concerns. This holds out the possibility of fundamentally transforming the relations of health care allowing people to gain more control over their own health as individuals and groups.

There are especially important needs for coalitions and solidarity between groups, given current cutbacks on health care. We must not allow them to divide us like they have tried to do regarding funding for cancer versus AIDS, but instead we must argue,

The Regulation of Desire

as in the campaign for catastrophic drug funding in Ontario, for the best possible health care for everyone. In campaigning for social policies that meet the needs of PLWA/HIVs, we run up against current State policies attempting to cut back on health-care expenditures and social-support levels that will have a devastating impact of PLWA/HIVs and many other groups, and also with State defence of the profit rates of the big drug companies, which are prioritized over the needs and lives of the people most affected by AIDS.

In contesting sexual and social policies, gay and lesbian liberation, along with AIDS activism, confronts State and ruling relations. In the area of legal and social policy, the State and its institutions can become a contested terrain between different class and so-cial groups. We can open up some important social spaces and gain more access to so-cial resources through these struggles. In general, however, even in these contested terrains, ruling class — and social groupings — hold more power than marginalized and subordinated groups. State forms of organization attend to rule and administration over people's lives, which does not make them very useful vehicles for emancipation. This does not mean that we should not fight for reforms within State relations that will de-fend and extend the social spaces and resources we have been able to seize for ourselves. This is vital, but it means our major focus must be elsewhere.

While we must organize within State relations, including school boards and city councils, and while we must work with progressive left politicians like Svend Robinson at all levels, our main focus must remain outside these institutions in grass-roots cam-paigns, alliances with other oppressed people, and in building emancipatory and trans-formative political movements. It is these movements and their struggles that can gain certain footholds within State relations, can begin to transform them, and that are the main initiative behind progressive social changes. It is these movements that can reshape the ground on which official parliamentary and legal politics stand. For in-stance, without the existence of extra-parliamentary lesbian and gay movements, the preconditions for Svend Robinson to come out would not have existed, and the legal vic-tories we have won through the use of the equality-rights section of the Charter would also not have been possible.

Lesbian/Gay Liberation and a Socialist-Feminist Anti-Racist Future

Gay and lesbian liberation challenges the sexual policies of capitalist "civilization" and State formation. In so doing, it intersects with the historical process that has organ-ized class, gender, and race relations in capitalist patriarchal society. It is here that gay liberation meets up with socialist, socialist-feminist, and anti-racist projects of human emancipation and the making of a new society. Gay and lesbian liberation has chal-lenged heterosexism within the socialist tradition and has brought new terrains of social transformation into view. Yet a fundamental tension exists between autonomous sexual political movements like gay and lesbian liberation and the socialist tradition still hegemonized by forms of sexism and heterosexism, whether of the social-democratic

New Democratic Party variety[49] or that of the Leninist "revolutionary left." While the so-cialist movement in general is in crisis, there has been a rebirth of dynamic popular and social movements around a number of themes, including feminism and gay liberation, as well as continuing grass-roots union struggles. It is in the debates and struggles of these grass-roots movements for change, including within lesbian/gay movements, that the resources for new socialist movements are being created.[50]

There has been vibrant mass organizing around lesbian/gay concerns. While other sites of mobilization have often subsided, lesbian and gay struggles continue to be an im-portant site for people's radicalization. Queer struggles in the current social and politi-cal context are central and not peripheral to challenging oppressive social relations and to the process of social transformation. Queers need to play a central part of rebuilding a socialist movement that puts our concerns at the centre.

As I mentioned earlier in this chapter, lesbian and gay struggles for alternative so-cial support and family policies, and AIDS-activist struggles against the social organiza-tion of the medical and health-care systems and against the profit motive of the pharmaceutical corporations put the needs of people at the centre of social policy and not the careers of professionals or the profit rates of corporations. These pose crucial challenges to capitalist social relations and open the door to possible transitions toward a democratic socialist society. It is no accident that, historically, lesbian/gay struggles have achieved most of their political support from currents on the left, and that many lesbian and gay activists have also been socialist activists, and that we have received most of our opposition (but not all of it!) from the forces of the right. It is time for lesbian and gay activists to play a major part in rebuilding a vital socialist movement in this country. The progress of lesbian and gay liberation depends not only on building our autonomous movements — which are crucial — but also in having a socialist movement that can support us in our struggles and can more clearly develop an alternative to capi-talist social relations.

In this light, gay liberation can be seen as part of a broader social alliance for sex-positive, anti-sexist, and transformative social change. This alliance, in turn, would be an important part of a larger coalition struggling for popular democratic control and the transformation of the social relations organizing various forms of oppression. This poses important questions of autonomy *and* alliance for gay and lesbian liberation; we need an autonomous power base to challenge the specific features and character of our oppres-sion and to organize against the practices of heterosexual hegemony. No one else will do this for us. But if we are to succeed in our goal of fundamentally transforming social relations, we must build alliances with other groups. Clearly, since there are class differ-ences within gay and lesbian communities and movements just as there are in other movements, there will be different political tendencies within gay and lesbian liberation, not all of which will see building coalitions as a major objective. These alliances would have to respect the autonomy of movements and not subordinate the interests of one group or movement to another.

Gay and lesbian liberation enriches other struggles with our perspective of democratic control over the practices regulating sexualities and desires — and with our critique of heterosexism — and brings practices to other movements that often are subversive of hegemonic sexual categorizations, gender divisions, and heterosexual masculine hierarchies. Through this same process, progressive struggles within the lesbian and gay communities over sexist, racist, or class relations would also be enriched. Through involvement in transformative movements and coalitions we learn from people experiencing different forms of oppression, and we begin in response to transform ourselves and our movements. In turn, other movements also get transformed by what they learn from us.[51] This would be part of building socialist movements that could develop a vision of a socialism worth fighting for.

Gay and lesbian liberation through cultural and political resistance begins to contest and transform the common-sense acceptance of heterosexuality as normal and natural, organizing in its place a diversity of possible ethical sexualities and erotic practices. This would provide a way by which people could understand and organize their lives without heterosexual hegemony. This would involve a shift from a State organized heterosexual hegemony to a taking up of the social standpoints of gays, women, and other oppressed groups. The struggle to shift and transform sexual definitions, and regulations, opens up social spaces not only for those of us who presently define ourselves as lesbian, gay, or bisexual but also opens up alternatives for everyone. It opens up possibilities for those who would wish to explore the development of different gender desires outside the restrictions of institutionalized heterosexuality.

Sexuality is an aspect of social life that can be redefined and transformed by people themselves; it is not a "natural" instinctual force or "thing" that controls, defines, or drives our lives. This perspective moves us beyond sexual fetishism and reification to recover the social practices involved in the making of our sexualities. The politics of transforming sexual identifications and pleasures can lead to the subversive conclusion that sexuality is, in the end, a matter of social and political choice, not of destiny. Sexuality has no essential meaning other than that which is made of it socially. What sex "is" we must now decide and shape through our collective struggles. Gay and lesbian liberation, feminism, and men against sexism have begun to elaborate a vision and a practice of transformed sex/gender relationships. These movements are characterized by forms of prefigurative[52] change that can give people a sense of empowerment and a sense of the social and erotic pleasures of the future. We can begin to catch glimpses of a transformed world of love and desire in our everyday lives today, thereby envisioning an erotic-positive socialism. Gay liberation, in alliance with feminism and as part of a transformed socialist movement, can fundamentally transform the ruling regime of sexuality.

Lesbian and gay history provides some of the perspectives and inspirations for waging this transformative struggle for redefining sexuality and gender. Lesbian and gay history, like feminist, black, and working-class history, is as much about the future as it is about the past. It provides not only a view of the past from a very different place than the history of great white men they taught us in school, but also some of the resources for transforming the present and envisioning future possibilities.

In the end, this can only mean that we must gain control over the institutions that regulate and confine our sexualities and genders, so that we can remake for ourselves our pleasures, desires, and loves. This vision of the future is based in the struggles we are waging today to take our destinies into our own hands and away from the doctors, the sexologists, State agencies, the police, the legal system, and the mass media. The institutions that regulate our erotic lives have not been around for all time — they have developed as part of a historical process. We too are part of that history. These institutions can therefore be transformed. We can then begin to make the pleasures and desires of the future and build a world free of sexual danger.

Edward Carpenter, a homosexual socialist, used the term "Uranian" to describe what today we might call "homosexual" or "gay" (and I add in lesbian, bisexual and queer).

> It is possible that the Uranian spirit may lead to something like a general enthusiasm of humanity, and that the Uranian people may be destined to form the advance guard of that great movement which will one day transform the common life by substituting the bond of personal affection and compassion for the monetary, legal and other external ties which now control and confine society.[53]

Notes

1. See Jonathan Ned Katz, *The Invention of Heterosexuality* (New York: Dutton, 1995).
2. See earlier references in the first two chapters to sexual naturalism. Also see Jeff Minson, "The Assertion of Homosexuality" in *MF*, No. 5/6, 1981, pp. 17-39 for a critique of the politics of coming out as revealing the truth about one's personality. Nonetheless, Minson very dangerously tends to dismiss the relevance of any gay politics based on coming out or any politics based on homosexual identifications. The political problems of deconstructionist theory are very evident in this article. Some of these same problems are continued in deconstructionist currents within "queer theory." The focus on coming out and identity in gay politics was also shaped by the largely white middle-class gays who initially constructed this politics.
3. See Larry Gross, *Contested Closets: The Politics and Ethics of Outing* (Minneapolis and London: University of Minnesota Press, 1993).
4. *Ibid.*, and my review of it "Outing and Dismantling 'the Closet.'" Lesbian and Gay Studies Newsletter, V. 21, No. 2, July, 1994, pp. 37-38.
5. This conference was held in Toronto in July 1985. This comment was an important defining remark for the conference and was made in the closing session. It is remembered slightly differently by different people. See Ingrid MacDonald, "We'll Deconstruct When They Deconstruct" in *Resources for Feminist Research*, "Confronting Heterosexuality" Issue, V. 19, No. 3 and 4, Dec. 1990, p. 89. Lisa Duggan remembers it as "Deconstruct Heterosexuality First," in her very useful article "Queering the State" in *Social Text*, No. 39, Summer 1994, p. 6.
6. Lisa Duggan, "Queering the State," *op. cit.*, pp. 4-5.
7. This is sometimes the case in the work of Judith Butler and in many of the interpretations of her work. See Butler, *Gender Trouble, Feminism and the Subversion of Identity* (New York and London: Routledge, 1990).
8. See the work of Diana Fuss among others. See Diana Fuss, *Essentially Speaking: Feminism, Nature*

and Difference (New York and London: Routledge, 1989). On the limits of this strategy in relation to feminism, see Amanda Anderson, "Cryptonormativism and Double Gestures: the Politics of Poststructuralism," *Cultural Critique,* V. 21 1992. The conceptualization or "strategic essentialism" comes from the work of Gayatri Spivak.

9. Duggan, "Queering the State," *op. cit.*, p. 6.

10. *Ibid.*

11. Richard Fung, "The Trouble With 'Asians'" in Monica Dorenkamp and Richard Henke, eds., *Negotiating Lesbian and Gay Subjects* (New York and London: Routledge, 1995), p. 128.

12. For a similar position, see Jeffrey Weeks, "Exploring the Myths and Makings of a Sexual Minority" in *The Advocate*, No. 366, Apr. 28, 1983, pp. 35-36, 42-43.

13. Jeffrey Weeks, "Capitalism and the Organization of Sex" in Gay Left Collective, eds., *Homosexuality: Power and Politics* (London: Allison and Busby, 1980), pp. 19-20.

14. Gay Left Collective, "Happy Families? Paedophilia Examined" in *Gay Left*, No. 7, Winter 1978/1979, p. 4.

15. For some ideas we can look to utopian feminist fiction, including Marge Piercy's, *Woman on the Edge of Time* (New York; Fawcett Crest, 1976).

16. See Cindy Patton, *Sex and Germs* (Montréal: Black Rose Books, 1986); Patton, *Inventing AIDS* (New York and London: Routledge, 1990) and references in previous chapters.

17. John D'Emilio, "Gay Politics, Gay Community" in *Socialist Review*, No. 55, Jan./Feb. 1981, p. 103.

18. On this notion of cultural revolution, see Corrigan and Sayer, *The Great Arch* (Oxford: Basil Blackwell, 1985).

19. See Carole S.Vance, "Pleasure and Danger: Toward a Politics of Sexuality" in Vance, ed., *Pleasure and Danger: Exploring Female Sexuality* (London and Boston: Routledge and Kegan Paul, 1984), pp. 1-27.

20. See Janine Brodie, Shelley Gavigan and Jane Jenson, *The Politics of Abortion* (Toronto: Oxford University Press, 1992); and Patricia Antonyshyn, B. Lee and Alex Merrill, "Marching for Women's Lives: The Campaign for Free-Standing Abortion Clinics in Ontario" in Frank Cunningham *et al.*, eds., *Social Movements/Social Change* (Toronto: Between the Lines, 1988).

21. See Karen R. Grant, "The New Reproductive Technologies: Boon or Bane?" in Les Samuelson, ed., *Power and Resistance: Critical Thinking about Canadian Social Issues* (Halifax: Fernwood, 1994), pp. 151-164 and Rona Achilles "Assisted Reproduction: The Social Issues," in E.D. Nelson and B.W. Robinson, eds., *Gender in the 1990s* (Scarborough, Nelson, 1995), pp. 346-364. Also see Maria Mies, "New Reproductive Technologies: Sexist and Racist Implications," Mies and Vandana Shiva, *Ecofeminism* (Halifax: Fernwood/Zed, 1993), pp. 174-197..

22. See Richard Banner, "Lesbians Refused AI" in *Angles*, July 1993, p. 1. Also see Katherine Arnup, ed., *Lesbian Parenting* (Charlottetown, gynergy, 1995).

23. Valerie Scott, "Valerie Scott of CORP on Empowering Prostitutes: Whores Fight Back!" *Rites*, V. 3, No. 1, May 1986, pp. 8-9, 19.

24. In Vancouver, the police themselves drove hookers onto the streets even before the famous Hutt decision in 1978 said that street soliciting had to be "pressing and persistent" before the police could lay charges. See John Lowman, "Geography, Crime and Social Control," Ph.D. thesis, University of British Columbia, particularly chapter 8, "Proactive Law Enforcement and Displacement: The Problem of Street Prostitution in Vancouver, 1975-1979." Also see John Lowman, "You Can Do It, But Don't Do it Here: Some Comments on Proposals for the Reform of Canadian Prostitution Law" in Lowman, Jackson, Palys and Gavigan, eds., *Regulating Sex* (Burnaby: School of Criminology, Simon Fraser University, 1986), pp. 193-213. In Toronto, the "clean up Yonge Street campaign" had a similar impact and also drove women working in the sex trade onto the streets. With the late 1970s and early 1980s came the economic recession and more prostitutes and hustlers on the streets. Also see Debi Brock, "Regulating Prostitution, Regulating Prostitutes: Some Canadian Examples," Ph.D. thesis, Dept. Educational Theory, University of Toronto, 1989.

25. See among others Gillian Walker, *Family Violence and the Women's Movement: The Conceptual Politics of Struggle* (Toronto: University of Toronto Press, 1990).

26. On this see Gary Kinsman, "The Porn Debate" in *Fuse*, Summer 1984, pp. 37-84; and Gary Kinsman, "Porn/Censor Wars and the Battlefields of Sex" in *Issues of Censorship* (Toronto: A Space, 1985), pp. 31-39. Also see Tom Waugh, "A Heritage of Pornography" in *The Body Politic*, No. 90, Jan. 1983, pp. 29-33; and his "Photography, Passion and Power" in *The Body Politic*, No. 101, Mar. 1984, pp. 29-33; and his article, "Men's Pornography: Gay vs. Straight" in *Jump Cut*, No. 30, pp. 30-35.

27. For instance, proposed 1986 federal anti-pornography legislation focused on the sexually explicit character of material, and would have basically criminalized any visual depiction of sexual activity. Left alone would have been "soft-core" heterosexual porn like *Playboy*, which depicts women's naked bodies but which does not usually portray sexual activity itself, as well as sexism in advertising and the media. The concerns of feminists as they were originally articulated about sexism and violence in pornography are only superficially addressed, while the emphasis is on depiction of sexual activities. The bill would have also denied young people access to sexually explicit material; which would stand in the way of young people gaining more knowledge and control over their bodies and their sexuality. See Bill C-114 introduced in June 1986; a somewhat revised version of this bill was reintroduced in the spring of 1987. Neither of these bills was passed.

28. Anti-porn feminists have often focused against sexual depictions themselves. There have also been important perspectives put forward by anti-censorship feminists. See Varda Burstyn, ed., *Women Against Censorship* (Toronto: Douglas and McIntyre, 1985) and Lynne Segal and Mary McIntosh, *Sex Exposed: Sexuality and the Pornography Debate* (New Brunswick, NJ: Rutger's University Press, 1993.

29. See Susan Prentice, ed. *Sex in Schools: Canadian Education and Sexual Regulation* (Toronto: Our Schools/Our Selves, 1994).

30. Much of the work of the Badgley Committee relied on police work. See Deborah R. Brock and Gary Kinsman, "Patriarchal Relations Ignored: An Analysis and Critique of the Badgley Report on Sexual Offences against Children and Youths" in Lowman, Jackson, Palys and Gavigan, eds., *Regulating Sex: An Anthology of Commentaries on the Badgley and Fraser Reports* (Burnaby: School of Criminology, Simon Fraser University, 1986).

31. *Ibid.*; and see the Badgley Report itself, *Committee on Sexual Offences against Children and Youth: Sexual Offences against Children* (Ottawa: Dept. of Supply and Services, 1984).

32. *Ibid.*

33. Bill C-113 included a proposal hidden in the text to abolish the gross-indecency section of the Criminal Code. This was also recommended in the Badgley Report. It was done in January 1988, but this offence can still be used for offences committed prior to that date. This was very important in repealing an offence historically associated with the construction of the homosexual as a criminal category. This bill also lowered the age of consent for "buggery" in private to eighteen, which would still be above the age of consent for "normal" heterosexual activities to again provide some added protection against homosexuality.

34. On "sexual pessimism," see Mariana Valverde, *Sex, Power and Pleasure* (Toronto: Women's Press, 1985), pp. 14-15. For the anti-porn feminist view see the work of Catharine MacKinnon, a leading anti-porn feminist in the U.S. Mackinnon's work was used in the Women's Legal Education and Action Fund's intervention in the Butler case. See Kirsten Johnson, *Undressing the Canadian State: The Politics of Pornography from Hicklin to Butler* (Halifax: Fernwood, 1995), pp. 61-67.

35. On sexual libertarianism, see Weeks, *Sexuality and Its Discontents* (London: Routledge and Kegan Paul, 1985); Valverde, *Sex, Power and Pleasure, op. cit.*, pp. 16-17; and Kinsman, "The Porn Debate," *op. cit.*, and "Porn/Censor Wars," *op. cit.* Also see Kiss and Tell, "Questioning Censorship" in their *Her Tongue on My Theory* (Vancouver: Press Gang, 1994), pp. 93-110.

36. On Wilhelm Reich, see Paul A. Robinson, *The Freudian Left* (New York: Harper Colophon,

1969), pp. 9-73 and Wilhelm Reich, *The Sexual Revolution* (New York: Farrar, Strauss and Giroux, 1962).

37. On some of this see Courtnay McFarlane, "Censorship, Passion and Identity," and karen/miranda augustine, "bizarre women, exotic bodies and outrageous sex" in *Border/Lines*, No. 32, 1994, pp. 34-35, and 22-24. Also see the controversy over a racist ad published in *The Body Politic*, No. 113, Apr. 1985, p. 30.

38. Often in anti-censorship feminist and gay discussions, all currents within radical feminism are reduced to the anti-porn radical feminism of Andrea Dworkin and Catharine MacKinnon. There are, however, more grass roots and movement-oriented forms of radical feminism. It is only the current represented by Dworkin and MacKinnon that has gotten tangled up with some forms of liberal feminism that has influenced State discussions regarding the regulation of porn.

39. See Valverde, *Sex, Power and Pleasure, op. cit.*; some of the contributions in Vance, ed., *Pleasure and Danger, op. cit.*, although many of the contributions in this volume are clearly from a sexual libertarian direction; some of the contributions in Burstyn, ed., *Women against Censorship, op. cit.*; Ann Ferguson, "Sex War: The Debate between Radical and Libertarian Feminists" in *Signs*, V. 10, No. 1, Autumn 1984, pp. 106-112, although often her arguments are far too close to anti-porn feminism for me; Ilene Philipson, "The Repression of History and Gender: A Critical Perspective on the Feminist Sexuality Debate" in *Signs*, V. 10, No. 1, Autumn 1984, pp. 113-118. Also some of the comments in Weeks, *Sexuality and Its Discontents, op. cit.*, are useful here.

40. See Kinsman, "Porn/Censor Wars," *op. cit.*

41. This is what the Repeal the Youth Pornography Law Campaign attempted to do in 1994 and early 1995 in Toronto. See *Parallelogramme*, V. 20, No. 1, 1994, pp. 8-21.

42. See Weeks, *Sexuality and Its Discontents, op. cit.* Also see Lorna Weir and Leo Casey, "Subverting Power in Sexuality," *Socialist Review* No. 75/76, May-Aug. 1984, pp. 139-157.

43. I am being more critical here of "radical pluralism" than I was in the first edition of this book. I feel there are too many residues of a liberalism that does not transform social relations in Weeks' use of the term. There are also too many associations between his use of radical pluralism and the post-Marxist, postmodernist "radical democratic" politics of Ernesto Laclau and Chantal Mouffe and others who have abandoned notions of class struggle and the struggle for socialism. See Ernesto Laclau and Chantal Mouffe, *Hegemony and Socialist Strategy: Towards a Radical Democratic Politics* (London: Verso, 1985).

44. Mariana Valverde, "Beyond Gender Dangers and Private Pleasures" in *Feminist Studies*, V. 15, No. 2, 1989, pp. 247-248.

45. On a transitional sexual perspective, see Ferguson, "Sex War," *op. cit.*, although I disagree with her specific use of it.

46. Some ideas for a feminist "family policy" are developed in Jean Coussin and Anna Coote, *The Family in the Firing Line: Discussion Document On Family Policy*, a joint NCCL/CPAC publication, Poverty Pamphlet 51, Mar. 1981. Unfortunately, this useful pamphlet does not unearth the practices of institutionalized heterosexuality nor does it deal with lesbians and gay men in relation to the family. Also see Michelle Barrett and Mary McIntosh, *The Anti-Social Family* (London: Verso, 1982); and Lynne Segal, ed., *What is To Be Done about the Family?* (Harmondsworth: Penguin, 1983).

47. Amber Hollibaugh describes some of the experiences of lesbians and gay men talking about their lives and sexualities during the campaign against the Briggs Initiative in California. See Hollibaugh, "Sexuality and the State" in *Socialist Review*, No. 45, May/June 1979, pp. 55-72. This has also been the experience in some of the successful campaigns against right-wing anti-lesbian, anti-gay State referendums in the U.S.

48. Alan Sears, "AIDS and the Health of Nations: Public Health and the Politics of HIV Testing," unpublished paper given at the Canadian Sociology and Anthropology Association meetings, Victoria, 1990.

49. If any of us had any illusions, we saw — in the Bill 167 debate and defeat in Ontario — we cannot rely on the NDP for our liberation.

50. This point is also made in Hilary Wainwright's very useful book, *Arguments for a New Left: Answering the Free-Market Right* (Oxford: Blackwell, 1994) where she emphasizes the importance of social movements and the democratization of knowledge in the redefining and revitalizing of socialism. At the same time, her movement away from Marx's analysis of the exploitation of the working class means she becomes less critical of market relations than I feel is necessary.

51. See Carolyn Egan, Linda Lee Gardner, and Judy Vashti Persad, "The Politics of Transformation: Struggles with Race, Class, and Sexuality in the March 8th Coalition" in Frank Cunningham, *et. al.*, eds., *Social Movements/Social Change, op. cit.*, pp. 20-47.

52. See Sheila Rowbotham, "The Women's Movement and Organizing for Socialism" in Rowbotham, Segal and Wainwright, eds., *Beyond the Fragments* (London: Merlin, 1979), particularly pp. 132-144.

53. Edward Carpenter, "The Intermediate Sex" in Edward Carpenter, *Selected Writings. Volume 1, Sex* (London: Gay Men's Press, 1984), p. 238.

Index

117. *See also* eugenics; social purity.

fellatio, 30, 49.

female impersonator, 117, 229, 249.

feminism, feminist: 12, 115, 235, 330, 332, 385, 388, 403; backlash, 33; Bill 167 and, 314; films, 346; health movement, 348; heterosexual, 380; history, 404; in lesbian organizing, 289; liberal, 400; movements, 25, 33, 111, 307, 363, 381; publications, 292; organizing, 289; radical, 387, 391; rise of, 51; sexual ethic; sociological work, 312. *See also* men against sexism.

femininity, 13, 164-166. *See also* masculinity.

femme identifications, 305.

fetus, male, 32.

feudalism, 50, 55.

film industry, 136.

First Nations, 6, 288; and AIDS, 354; heterosexism in, communities, 300, lesbian and gay men, 300, 384.

Fleming, Thomas, 340-341. *See also* bath raids.

flogging, 102.

forensic clinics, 196-197. *See alo* Toronto Forensic Clinic.

forensic pychiatry, psychiatrists, 31, 58, 61, 122, 150-151. *See also* Toronto Forensic Clinic.

Fortin, Gerard, 101.

Foucault, Michel, 48n.7, 59, 306-307.

Fraser Committee Report on Pornography and Prostitution, 356, 389.

Freedman, Estelle, 150.

French-Canadian Catholics, 110.

Freud, Sigmund: 61, 250; writings on sexuality, 12;

Freudian, 237.

friendship(s): non-erotic, 118; passionate, between men, 59, 99; passionate, between women, 50, 59.

Frish, Peter G., 295. *See also The Advocate.*

Front de Liberation Homosexualle (FLH), 291. *See also* FLQ; GLF; Quebecois.

Front de Liberation du Quebec, 291.

fruit machine, 177-178, 181, 239. *See also* RCMP; security campaigns; Wake, F.R.

Fung, Richard: on experiences as gay Asian, 378-379.

Fulton, Ron, 249.

gay(s): activism/activists, 292, 305, 376; advertising, 297; American, liberation, liberationists, 290, 387; business, 292, 296, 385; child-care workers, 301; civil rights, 340; community, 295, 297-298, 304, 307, 309, 333, 335, 341, 381; cultures, 303; cultural production of, 297, 302-303; electoral constituencies, 294; elite, 5, 335-336; fathers, 301; as gender nonconformists, 304; ghetto, 11, 293-294, 297, 301-302, 304, 306, 310-311, 333, 338, 364, 381, 384; imagery, 304; liberation, 8, 12, 15, 25,180, 224, 289, 297, 317, 332-333, 400, 402-403; male cruising, 302; male language, 302; male porn, 388; male sexual desire, 381; men and class/race stereotypes, 297; men as sexual danger, 335; men as a consumer market, 296; movement, 334-335, 342; parents, 296; politics, 335; reformers, 223; scene, 293, 301, sex, 386; social subordination of, men, 33; sociologists, 308.

Gay, 181, 227, 233, 248, 250.

Gay Alliance for Equality in Halifax, 291.

Gay Alliance Toward Equality, 292.

"gay capitalism," 295.

Gay Community Centre of Saskatoon, 291.

Gay International, 248

Gay Left Collective, 380.

Gay Liberation Front (GLF), 288-289, 291, 384. *See also* FLH; National Liberation Front in Vietnam.

Gay Liberation Against the Right Everywhere, 342.

"gay market," 294-296. *See also* gay business; gay capitalism; gay ghetto; lesbian entrepreneurs.

gay-minority approach, 310.

"gay plague," 349. *See also* GRID; mass media.

Gay Power, Gay Politics, 334-335. *See also* CBC; media.

Gay Related Immune Deficiency (GRID), 349. *See also* "gay plague," mass media.

gay space, sites, 165-166, 293.

gay slang, 167, 303. *Also* homosexual slang.

Gay Tide, 292.

Gays of Ottawa, 291-292

"gayness", 376.

gender: 27, 305; boundaries, 171; dichotomies, 35; divisions, 404; division of labour, 157, 193; inequality, 33; inversion, 61, 122, 160-161, 174, 177, 304; normality, 331; performances, 305; regulation, 14, 25, 220, 388; relations, 219, 266, 305-306, 308, 377; segregation, 170; sexual conduct, 28.

Genet, Jean, 345.

gentrification, 297.

Georgia Straight (Vancouver), 236.

German homosexual-rights movement, 310.

Gide, Andre, 188. *See also Corydon.*

Gidlow, Elsa, 65, 124. *See also* Mills, George Roswell.

Gigeroff, Alex K., 129, 247, 253-254, 262.

Gilman, Charlotte Perkins, 123.

Girard, Philip, 174, 184. *See also* Canadian Immigration Act.

Glad Day Bookshop, 345, 347.

The Globe and Mail, 195; 228, 263, 295, 337.

Goldberg, Jonathan: on aboriginal cross-dressing, 92; on European accounts of sodomy, 92.

gonorrhoea, 117.

government: documents, 173; Royal Commissions, 185.

Gramsci, Antonio: on hegemony, 38.

Gray, Kenneth, 197-198; 253.

Greece, classical, 65.

grassroots: activism, 264; campaigns, 402; feminists, 389; gay/lesbian activists, 251; organizations, 299.

gross indecency, 64, 129, 169, 184, 192, 245, 254, 257; age of consent, 218; legal category of, 225; lesbianism and, 270; punishment for, 102; union struggles, 403.

Grossman, Allan, 195. *See also* Conservative Party; PAL.

Haitian(s), 348; communities, 349.

Hall, Radclyffe, 70, 137. *See also The Canadian Forum; The Well of Loneliness.*

Hall, Stuart, 221.

Hanlon, Michel, 228.

Also published by

SEX AND GERMS
The Politics of AIDS

Cindy Patton

Sex and Germs *is a valuable resource for increasing one's factual knowledge and political perspective about [this] alarming illness. Patton has carefully broadened the subject of dangerous germs and erotic impulses into a scholarly probe of AIDS' role in sexual oppression and the struggle for change.*
The Guardian

182 pages, index
Paperback ISBN: 0-920057-80-2   **$16.99**
Hardcover ISBN: 0-920057-82-9   **$45.99**

EMMA GOLDMAN
Sexuality and the Impurity of the State

Bonnie Haaland

This book focuses on the *ideas* of Emma Goldman as they relate to the centrality of sexuality and reproduction, and as such, are relevant to the current feminist debates.

A model for "integrative feminism" that focuses on individuality rather than on rights.
Common Knowledge

In its focus on Goldman's ideas...Haaland's work stands out among other literature.
Kinesis

201 pages, index
Paperback ISBN: 1-895431-64-6   **$19.99**
Hardcover ISBN: 1-895431-65-4   **$48.99**
L.C. No. 93-070392

SOCIAL AND SEXUAL REVOLUTION
Bertell Ollman

Ollman combines Marxist teachings with the revolutionary theories of Wilhelm Reich in formulating a socialist strategy that is appropriate to advanced capitalist societies.

228 pages
Paperback ISBN: 0-919618-84-7   **$12.99**
Hardcover ISBN: 0-919618-85-5   **$41.99**

CIVILIZATION AND ITS DISCONTENTED
John F. Laffey

1993 QSPELL Award Finalist

In the three extended essays of *Civilization and Its Discontented*, John Laffey explores various notions of civilization.

The craft of the historian is to study the past and analyze it for present and future generations. Laffey certainly does this.
The Montréal Gazette

180 pages, index
Paperback ISBN: 1-895431-70-0 $16.99
Hardcover ISBN: 1-895431-71-9 $45.99
L.C. No. 93-070388

THE IRRATIONAL IN POLITICS
Maurice Brinton

Brinton argues that our political perceptions have been conditioned by social and sexual patterns to reinforce the dominant ideology, which results in both a need for authority and an inhibition of autonomous thought.

A brilliant summary of the underlying causes of the irrational in public life.
Our Generation

72 pages
Paperback ISBN: 0-919618-24-3 $4.99
Hardcover ISBN: 0-919618-50-2 $33.99

WHEN FREEDOM WAS LOST
The Unemployed, the Agitator, and the State

Lorne Brown

Lorne Brown seeks to remedy the dearth of the 30s labour Canadiana with this study of little-known labour camps.
Books in Canada

208 pages, photographs
Paperback ISBN: 0-920057-77-2 $14.99
Hardcover ISBN: 0-920057-75-6 $43.99

BETWEEN LABOR AND CAPITAL
Pat Walker, ed.

Essays on the general topic of class divisions in the U.S., giving both traditional and novel definitions.

337 pages
Paperback ISBN: 0-919618-86-3 $9.99
Hardcover ISBN: 0-919618-87-1 $38.99

Black Rose Books

has also published the following books of related interests

Beyond O.J.: Sex, Race and Class Lessons for America, *by Earl Ofari Hutchinson*
Who Invented the Automobile: Skulduggery at the Crossroads, *by David Beasley*
Democracy's Oxygen: How the News Media Smother the Facts, *by James Winter*
Perspectives on Power: Reflections on Human Nature and the Social Order,
    by Noam Chomsky
Into the European Mirror: The Works of Julian Samuel, *edited by Aruna Handa and*
    John Kipphoff
Pirate Utopias, by Douglas Fetherling
Race, Gender and Work: A Multi-Cultural Economic History of Women in the
    United States, *by Teresa Amott and Julie Matthaei*
Frist Person Plural: A Community Development Approach to Social Change,
    by David Smith
The Oceans are Emptying: Fish Wars and Sustainability, *by Raymond A. Rogers*
The Trojan Horse: Alberta and the Future of Canada, *edited by Gordon Laxer and*
    Trevor Harrison
Free Trade: Neither Free Nor About Trade, *by Christopher D. Merrett*
Beyond Hypocrisy: Decoding the News in an Age of Propaganda, *by Edward S.*
    Herman
Communication: For and Against Democracy, *edited by Marc Raboy and Peter Bruck*
Common Cents: Media Portrayal of the Gulf War and Other Events, *by James Winter*
The Anarchist Collectives: Workers' Self-Management in Spain 1936-39, *edited by*
    Sam Dolgoff
Anarchist Organisation: The History of the F.A.I, *by Juan Gomez Casas*
Oscar Wilde: The Double Image, *by George Woodcock*
Aphra Behn: The English Sappho, *by George Woodcock*
The Anarchist Papers, *edited by Dimitrios Roussopoulos*
The Anarchist Papers II, *edited by Dimitrios Roussopoulos*
The Anarchist Papers III, *edited by Dimitrios Roussopoulos*

send for a free catalogue of all our titles
BLACK ROSE BOOKS
P.O. Box 1258
Succ. Place du Parc
Montréal, Québec
H3W 2R3 Canada
To order: (phone) 1-800-565-9523   (fax) 1-800-221-9985

Printed by the workers of
Les Éditions Marquis
Montmagny, Québec
for Black Rose Books Ltd.